Each volume of this series of companions to major philosophers contains specially commissioned essays by an international team of scholars, together with a substantial bibliography, and will serve as a reference work for students and nonspecialists. One aim of the series is to dispel the intimidation such readers often feel when faced with the work of a difficult and challenging thinker.

Ludwig Wittgenstein (1889–1951) is one of the most important, influential, and often-cited philosophers of the twentieth century, yet he remains one of its most elusive and least accessible. The essays in this volume address central themes in Wittgenstein's writings on the philosophy of mind, language, logic, and mathematics. They chart the development of his work and clarify the connections between its different stages. The authors illuminate the character of the whole body of work by keeping a tight focus on some key topics: the style of the philosophy, the conception of grammar contained in it, rule-following, convention, logical necessity, the self, and what Wittgenstein called in a famous phrase, "forms of life." A final essay offers a fundamental reassessment of the status of the many posthumously published texts.

THE CAMBRIDGE COMPANION TO
# WITTGENSTEIN

*The Cambridge Companion to*
# WITTGENSTEIN

Edited by Hans Sluga
*University of California, Berkeley*

David G. Stern
*University of California, Berkeley*

**CAMBRIDGE**
UNIVERSITY PRESS

Published by the Press Syndicate of the University of Cambridge
The Pitt Building, Trumpington Street, Cambridge CB2 1RP
40 West 20th Street, New York, NY 10011-4211, USA
10 Stamford Road, Oakleigh, Melbourne 3166, Australia

© Cambridge University Press 1996

First published 1996

Printed in the United States of America

Library of Congress Cataloging-in-Publication Data

The Cambridge companion to Wittgenstein / edited by Hans Sluga, David
G. Stern.
    p.     cm.
  Includes bibliographical references (p.        ).
  ISBN 0-521-46025-5 (hardcover). – ISBN 0-521-46591-5 (pbk.)
  1. Wittgenstein, Ludwig, 1889–1951.  I. Sluga, Hans D.
II. Stern, David G.
  B3376.W564C345   1996
  192 – dc20                                              96-5300
                                                              CIP

A catalog record for this book is available from the British Library.

ISBN 0-521-46025-5 hardback
     0-521-46591-5 paperback

# CONTENTS

v

vi      Contents

CONTRIBUTORS

DAVID BLOOR is Reader in Philosophy of Science at the University of Edinburgh and Director of the Science Studies Unit. He is the author of *Knowledge and Social Imagery* (1976), *Wittgenstein: A Social Theory of Knowledge* (1982), and *Scientific Knowledge, A Sociological Analysis* (1996).

STANLEY CAVELL is Professor of Philosophy at Harvard University. He is the author of numerous books including *Must We Mean What We Say?* (1969), *The Claim of Reason: Wittgenstein, Skepticism, Morality and Tragedy* (1979), *This New Yet Unapproachable America: Essays after Emerson after Wittgenstein* (1989), and *Philosophical Passages: Wittgenstein, Emerson, Austin, Derrida* (1994).

CORA DIAMOND is Professor of Philosophy at the University of Virginia. She is the author of *The Realistic Spirit: Wittgenstein, Philosophy and the Mind* (1991) and the editor of *Wittgenstein's Lectures on the Foundations of Mathematics, 1939* (1976) and of *Intention and Intentionality* (1979).

ROBERT J. FOGELIN is Professor of Philosophy at Dartmouth College. He is the author of numerous books including *Wittgenstein* (1976), *Hume's Skepticism* (1985), *Philosophical Interpretations* (1992), and *Pyrrhonian Reflections on Knowledge and Justification* (1994).

NEWTON GARVER is Professor of Philosophy at the State University of New York at Buffalo. He is the author of *This Complicated Form of Life: Essays on Wittgenstein* (1994) and (with S. Lee) *Derrida and Wittgenstein* (1994), and the editor of *Naturalism and Rationality* (1986) and *Justice, Law, and Violence* (1991).

vii

STEVE GERRARD is Assistant Professor of Philosophy at Williams College and the author of several articles on Wittgenstein, ethics, and the history of early analytic philosophy.

HANS-JOHANN GLOCK is Lecturer in Philosophy at the University of Reading and the author of *A Wittgenstein Dictionary* (1995) as well as of several articles on Wittgenstein, and the editor of *Wittgenstein's Philosophical Investigations: Text and Context* (1991).

MICHAEL KOBER is Assistant Professor of Philosophy at the University of Freiburg and the author of *Gewissheit als Norm. Wittgensteins erkenntnistheoretische Untersuchungen in "Über Gewissheit."*

THOMAS RICKETTS is Associate Professor of Philosophy at the University of Pennsylvania. He writes on Frege and Wittgenstein.

NAOMI SCHEMAN is Professor of Philosophy and Women's Studies at the University of Minnesota in Minneapolis. She is the author of *Engenderings: Constructions of Knowledge, Authority and Privilege* (1993) and the editor of *Feminist Interpretations of Ludwig Wittgenstein* (forthcoming).

HANS SLUGA is Professor of Philosophy at the University of California at Berkeley. He is the author of *Gottlob Frege* (1980) and of *Heidegger's Crisis: Philosophy and Politics in Nazi Germany* (1993) and the editor of *The Philosophy of Frege* (4 volumes 1993).

DAVID G. STERN is Assistant Professor of Rhetoric at the University of California at Berkeley. He is the author of *Wittgenstein on Mind and Language* (1995).

BARRY STROUD is Professor of Philosophy at the University of California at Berkeley. He is the author of *Hume* (1977) and *The Significance of Philosophical Scepticism* (1984).

DONNA M. SUMMERFIELD is Assistant Professor of Philosophy at Southern Illinois University, Carbondale. She is the author of several articles on Wittgenstein and of *Wittgenstein: Mental Representation and Covariance Theories of Content* (forthcoming).

# ABBREVIATIONS

AWL    *Wittgenstein's Lectures, Cambridge 1932–1935*, ed. A. Ambrose

BLBK    *The Blue Book*

BRBK    *The Brown Book*

BT    *Big Typescript*

CV    *Culture and Value*

LC    *Lectures and Conversations*

LFM    *Lectures on the Foundations of Mathematics*

LWI    *Last Writings on the Philosophy of Psychology*, vol. I

LWII    *Last Writings on the Philosophy of Psychology*, vol. II

LWL    *Wittgenstein's Lectures, Cambridge 1930–1932*, ed. D. Lee

NB    *Notebooks 1914–1916*

NL    *Notes on Logic*

OC    *On Certainty*

PG    *Philosophical Grammar*

PI    *Philosophical Investigations*

PO    *Philosophical Occasions, 1912–1951*

PR    *Philosophical Remarks*

PT    *Prototractatus*

RC    *Remarks on Color*

RFM    *Remarks on the Foundations of Mathematics*

RPPI    *Remarks on the Philosophy of Psychology*, vol. I

RPPII    *Remarks on the Philosophy of Psychology*, vol. II

TLP    *Tractatus Logico-Philosophicus*

WWK    *Wittgenstein and the Vienna Circle*

Z    *Zettel*

# THE CAMBRIDGE COMPANION TO
# WITTGENSTEIN

# Ludwig Wittgenstein:
# Life and work
# An introduction

## I

Ludwig Wittgenstein occupies a unique place in twentieth century philosophy and he is for that reason difficult to subsume under the usual philosophical categories.

What makes it difficult is first of all the unconventional cast of his mind, the radical nature of his philosophical proposals, and the experimental form he gave to their expression. The difficulty is magnified because he came to philosophy under complex conditions which make it plausible for some interpreters to connect him with Frege, Russell, and Moore, with the Vienna Circle, Oxford Language Philosophy, and the analytic tradition in philosophy as a whole, while others bring him together with Schopenhauer or Kierkegaard, with Derrida, Zen Buddhism, or avant-garde art. Add to this a culturally resonant background, an atypical life (at least for a modern philosopher), and a forceful yet troubled personality and the difficulty is complete. To some he may appear primarily as a technical philosopher, but to others he will be first and foremost an intriguing biographical subject, a cultural icon, or an exemplary figure in the intellectual life of the century.[1] Our fascination with Wittgenstein is, so it seems, a function of our bewilderment over who he really is and what his work stands for.

## II

Ludwig Wittgenstein was born in Vienna in 1889 as the youngest son of Karl Wittgenstein, a self-made entrepreneur and one of the richest men in the Austria of his time.[2] The family was on both sides largely

1

of Jewish extraction but had become Christianized a couple of generations earlier. Wittgenstein's great-grandfather, Moses Mayer, had adopted the family's new, distinguished name and had baptized his son under the name Hermann Christian. Though the Jewish heritage had, thus, apparently been left behind, it was to prove a lasting burden on Ludwig Wittgenstein's own mind. In the early 1930s he considered it necessary to "confess" his Jewishness to his closest associates.[3] And alluding to a thought from Otto Weininger's *Sex and Character* he wrote in his diary: "Even the greatest of Jewish thinkers is no more than talented (Myself for instance)" (CV, p. 18).

To his friend Drury he said at about the same time: "I am not a religious man but I cannot help seeing every problem from a religious point of view." And he added to this much later: "My thoughts are one hundred percent Hebraic."[4] If Wittgenstein's thinking was, indeed, one hundred percent Hebraic, his was a profoundly self-doubting Judaism which had always the possibility of collapsing into a destructive self-hatred (as it did in Weininger's case) but which also held an immense promise of innovation and genius. It was a state of mind that lay at the core of late Viennese culture and of the achievements of men like Freud, Mauthner, Kraus, and Schoenberg. It was also what made Wittgenstein's philosophical achievements possible. At the same time it remained for him a constant source of pain and of constant conflict with paternal authority.

Wittgenstein's father had made himself a leader in the Austro-Hungarian steel industry through the force of his domineering personality. But these qualities were also the source of persistent tensions in his relations with his five sons and three daughters. Karl Wittgenstein had precise expectations for each of them and insisted that his sons should follow him in business. Such pressures joined to a vulnerability inherited from the mother's side of the family eventually led to the suicide of three of Ludwig's older brothers. He, too, suffered from depressions and for long periods considered killing himself because he considered his life worthless, but the stubbornness inherited from his father may have helped him to survive. How problematic the relations between father and son were is illustrated by Ludwig's abandonment of the pursuit of engineering on which he had embarked at his father's insistence when the latter fell seriously ill and he was ensconced abroad at the University of Manchester. It is equally telling that, after his father's death, he gave part of his inheritance away to deserving artists and the rest to his siblings. Through the course of Wittgenstein's life we detect his need to reject paternal authority – not only that of his own father in the flesh, but subsequently also that of his spiritual father Bertrand Russell and eventually that of the entire "great stream of European and American civilization," as he wrote in the 1930s.

This spirit of rebellion was characteristic of the culture of *fin-de-siècle* Vienna in which he grew up. The Wittgenstein family belonged to that small social group from which the artistic, intellectual, and scientific achievements of that culture emerged.[5] Such illustrious figures of late Imperial Vienna as Johannes Brahms and Gustav Mahler, Karl Kraus, Sigmund Freud, and Adolf Loos, Gustav Klimt and Oskar Kokoschka are all, in some way or other, linked to the family's name. Though Wittgenstein spent his academic life in England, the effects of his early upbringing are clearly visible in his thinking. Among those who influenced his thought were such characteristically Viennese figures as the physicist Rudolf Boltzmann, the philosophers Ernst Mach and Moritz Schlick, Sigmund Freud and the philosopher of sexuality Otto Weininger, the critic and philosopher of language Fritz Mauthner, the political and cultural satirist Karl Kraus, and Adolf Loos, the architect.

Wittgenstein found in them an exhilarating sense of the new, linked in a characteristically Viennese fashion to a sweeping pessimism and skepticism. For Freud and Weininger, Kraus and Mauthner, as for many others, including Wittgenstein himself, the world was cast in the light of Schopenhauer's romantic pessimism. There emerged, thus, a paradoxical combination of conservatism and avant-gardism, a nostalgic commitment to the ideals of a dissolving past linked to a search for new forms and ideas. Adolf Loos's design of a skyscraper in the form of a gigantic Doric column is, perhaps, emblematic for this peculiar conjunction. In Wittgenstein's work it shows itself in a preoccupation with language and the mind, with mathematics and science, so characteristic for the new currents in Viennese thinking, coupled to an exceedingly somber view of life and a profoundly existential conception of the self. Wittgenstein's confidence that he had discovered a new kind of philosophizing is thus tied to his unvarying certainty that we live in dark times. In the preface to the *Philosophical Investigations* he wrote despondently in 1945: "It is not impossible that it should fall to the lot of this work, in its poverty and in the darkness of this time, to bring light into one brain or another – but, of course, it is not likely" (PI, p. vi). To his friend Drury he had said earlier: "The dark ages are coming again."[6] These were not just personal fears. The writings of Robert Musil and Hermann Broch, with whom Wittgenstein had much in common, give one a vivid sense of how pervasive this unease was in *fin-de-siècle* Vienna.[7]

The historical context of Wittgenstein's life is sharply illuminated by the fact that he was born only a few days apart from Adolf Hitler. It is one of the ironies of history that the future philosopher and the future dictator actually attended the same school for a year. There is, however, no evidence that the two got to know each other in that period. Nevertheless, it is intriguing to consider the ways in which their life paths were similar. Socially and economically they belonged, of course, to different worlds. While Wittgenstein was born into a Jewish bourgeoisie that had benefited from the Habsburg empire, Hitler was the illegitimate child of a minor customs official on the Austrian–German border and grew up without affinities for the empire. While Wittgenstein studied abroad in Berlin, Manchester, and Cambridge and thus became acquainted with the most avant-garde ideas, Hitler was living in Vienna as a homeless house painter, seeking admission to the local Academy of Art and imbibing a dark brew of racist and anti-Semitic doctrines. What united the two men despite these differences was the First World War which both of them experienced as low-level front line soldiers. It was an experience that proved traumatic for both of them. Like many other members of "the generation of 1914" they came out of the war alienated from the culture into which they had been born. In consequence, Hitler decided on a career as a political agitator and Wittgenstein abandoned his earlier lifestyle of luxury, adopted an austere, almost monkish existence, rethought his philosophical commitments, and turned away from what might otherwise have been a normal academic career. It is, perhaps, mere accident, yet it remains illuminating that both of them found philosophical inspiration in Schopenhauer.[8]

The fact that Wittgenstein is such a characteristic figure of the culture of his time assures that he will continue to draw the attention of scholars and the general public as long as *fin-de-siècle* Vienna and its philosophical, scientific, political, and cultural ideals continue to be objects of curiosity. Looked at in this wider historical context, he will be seen as the most distinctive philosophical voice of a cultural milieu that has profoundly shaped our century.

### III

But it would be entirely insufficient to think of him only in connection with this Viennese background. Wittgenstein's name is just as much connected with the Cambridge of the first decades of our century, a vital moment in the intellectual history of twentieth-century England. He had gone to England originally to continue a study of engineering which he had begun in Berlin, but while he was at the University of Manchester he became interested in the philosophical foundations of the mathematics on which his professional work relied. A friend brought him Bertrand Russell's 1903 book *The Principles of Mathematics* and that work was to launch him on his philosophical career. Its lengthy account of the logical and philosophical ideas of the German mathematician Gottlob Frege gave him the impulse to visit Frege in Jena. Frege, who was by then sixty-three years old and felt beyond his prime, in turn, advised him to go back to England and to work with Russell in Cambridge. Following Frege's advice Wittgenstein appeared one day in Russell's office and with that began a decisive period of collaboration between them.[9]

In Cambridge, Wittgenstein got to know some of the leading English intellectuals of the period, not only Russell, but also the mathematician Alfred North Whitehead, the philosopher G. E. Moore, the economist John Maynard Keynes, and the historian Lytton Strachey. But Russell was indubitably the most important figure as far as Wittgenstein was concerned. He and Frege were the two thinkers who initially influenced him most deeply. In them Wittgenstein had gotten to know the two leading figures in the emerging field of symbolic logic. They had invented a mathematically inspired logic no longer confined to the limitations of the traditional syllogistic which in essence went back more than two thousand years to Aristotle. Frege and Russell had set out to apply their new tool to the analysis of mathematical propositions with the goal of showing that mathematics as a whole (Russell) or, at least, arithmetic (Frege) could be treated as pure logic. In the course of their technical innovations the two had furthermore found it necessary to rethink a number of fundamental logical and philosophical concepts, in particular the notions of existence and universality, of meaning and representation; they had examined the functions of names, predicates, sentences, and logical connectives, the question how reality is mapped in language, and the distinction between the apparent and the real logical structure of propositions. Their work had thus produced a wholly new philosophical agenda and it was this new conception of the task of philosophy that Wittgenstein made his own once he appeared in Cambridge.

In the preface to the *Tractatus*, the first product of his endeavors, he generously acknowledged his debt "to Frege's magnificent works and to the writings of my friend Mr. Bertrand Russell" (TLP, p. 3). The book is indeed most profitably read with their thought in mind, though Wittgenstein does not slavishly follow either of them and does not hesitate to criticize them bluntly where he disagrees with them. Even in his later work, when his views had moved far beyond these beginnings, one can trace the continuing influence of Frege's and Russell's ideas on his thinking. One of the major tasks of recent Wittgenstein scholarship has been to follow the often subtle links between Wittgenstein's and Frege's ideas. Wittgenstein appears never to have abandoned his early admiration for Frege and it is, in fact, mainly through this connection that Frege is today recognized as a major philosopher. His comments on Russell, on the other hand, became more hostile as time went on. Late in life he could write in his notes:

Some philosophers (or whatever you like to call them) suffer from what may be called "loss of problems." Then everything seems quite simple to them, no deep problems seem to exist any more, the world becomes broad and flat and loses all depth, and what they write becomes immeasurably shallow and trivial. Russell and H. G. Wells suffer from this. (Z, 456)

This is hardly a fair comment, given all that Russell had done for him. Practically from the moment he had appeared in Cambridge, Russell had treated him as a very special person. In his autobiography Russell was later to speak of him as a "genius as traditionally conceived – passionate, profound, intense, and dominating."[10] Though Wittgenstein had no prior training in philosophy Russell looked at him as a collaborator rather than a student. He expressed his hope that Wittgenstein would continue his philosophical work where he himself had left off. Without Russell's generous support, Wittgenstein might not have had sufficient reassurance to continue with philosophy, the *Tractatus* might never have appeared in print, and Wittgenstein might never have resumed his career in the 1930s. Given the mutual suspicion they felt for each other later on, it is easy to overlook how crucial their collaboration was in the early period, how deeply Russell's concerns imprinted themselves in Wittgenstein's mind, and how even in later years Russell is never far from Wittgenstein's thinking.

In retrospect we see that the philosophical movement we now know under the name of "analytic philosophy" began its life in the interactions between Frege, Russell, and Wittgenstein. Frege's logical and philosophical writings between 1879 and 1903, Russell's work between 1899 and 1918, and Wittgenstein's *Tractatus* taken together define an agenda that has proved sufficiently rich to sustain philosophical debate for the rest of the century. They were united in their concern with the new logic and shared many assumptions about the philosophical significance of this logic. But each contributed also his own distinctive assumptions to the analytic tradition. While Frege brought epistemological concerns, Neo-Kantian ideas about the existence of different kinds of truth, and questions about the foundational structure of knowledge into the analytic debate, Russell added ontological considerations, questions about the structure and construction of reality, empiricist considerations about sense-data and their properties. Wittgenstein, finally, contributed elements of thought that relate back to his Viennese background: a positivistic conception of science and philosophy, a preoccupation with language, a skeptical attitude towards the world, a wariness of theoretical constructions, even a yearning for a simple, unmediated existence. The philosophical tradition that came out of their collaboration has developed far beyond these initial impulses, but it still shares many of Frege's, Russell's, and Wittgenstein's concerns. Above all it shares with them the sense of a new beginning in philosophy, a belief in a new kind of philosophizing which is no longer tied to the traditional and nationally bound forms of European thought, but that unites distinctive elements of the German, English, and Austrian traditions into a new synthesis, the first genuinely supranational tradition in European thought since the decline of the Middle Ages.

IV

Wittgenstein's collaboration with Russell in the period between 1911 and 1914 was intimate, stormy, and immensely productive. Russell had just finished his main work in logic, the gigantic *Principia Mathematica*, written in collaboration with Whitehead, and was eager to show that the new logic could be used effectively in philosophy. Ever since he had given up his early commitment to an idealist monism, he had been keen to show that reality consisted of a multiplicity of not further analyzable constituents. By 1911 he had come to think that the simple constituents of reality had to be primarily sense-data and their properties. His hope was now to establish an essentially empiricist picture of reality by means of an analysis effected with the tools of the new logic.

Wittgenstein's notes from that period make evident how much he identified with Russell's program. "Philosophy," he wrote at the time, "consists of logic and metaphysics: logic is its basis" (NB, p. 106). But even so he had little sympathy with Russell's empiricism and diverged from him in a number of specific ways, partly inspired by his reading of Frege and partly by his own philosophical intuitions.

The First World War was to bring this collaboration to an unexpected halt, since Wittgenstein, as an enemy alien, was now forced to return home. Back in Vienna he considered it his duty to enroll as a soldier in the army, but he remained determined to continue his philosophical studies. Two days after he had been assigned to a regiment in Krakow, he began a philosophical diary that starts with the anxious question: "Will I be able to work now?"[11] His notebooks from the period reveal that he could, in fact, work even under the most demanding conditions. Quite naturally, these notebooks began where his discussions with Russell had left off. They are filled, at first, with reflections on the question how propositions can depict facts and what the ultimate constituents of reality are. As the war dragged on, new themes appear, however, which seem far removed from the initial logical agenda. In June of 1916 we find him writing, all of a sudden: "What do I know about God and the purpose of life" (NB, p. 72). And soon later: "The I, the I is what is deeply mysterious" (p. 80). Wittgenstein is thinking now about ethics and esthetics, about good and bad consciousness, about the nature of happiness and about the question whether suicide is a sin. The experiences of the war have driven him to read Tolstoy and the Gospels, as we know from his letters. His notebooks also reflect a renewed interest in the ideas of Schopenhauer, Weininger, and Mauthner. Somewhat later he will write to his friend Paul Engelmann: "My relationship with my fellow men has strangely changed. What was all right when we met is now all wrong, and I am in complete despair."[12]

It was from these wartime notebooks that Wittgenstein extracted the *Tractatus Logico-Philosophicus* while he was in an Italian prisoner of war camp. The work reflected the whole course of his thinking from his earlier logical reflections to his later ethical and mystical musings. In large part it can certainly be read as an attempt to reconcile Russellian atomism with Fregean apriorism. When the work was finally published Russell could therefore praise it as a contribution to a theory of logic which no serious philosopher should neglect.[13] But the book does not restrict itself to the range of issues defined by Frege and Russell. It is equally moved by moral and metaphysical concerns. For this reason Wittgenstein accused Russell angrily of having misunderstood the meaning of his book. "Now I'm afraid you haven't really got hold of my main contention, to which the whole business of logical propositions is only a corollary," he wrote to his former mentor in August 1919: "The main point is the theory of what can be expressed [*gesagt*] by propositions – i.e. by language – (and, which comes to the same, what can be *thought*) and what cannot be expressed by propositions, but only shown [*gezeigt*]; which, I believe is the cardinal problem of philosophy."[14] In the same letter Wittgenstein complained that Frege, too, had failed to understand his book. Mournfully he concluded: "It is very hard not to be understood by a single soul." At about the same time he wrote to the Austrian publicist Ludwig von Ficker that the real intention of the book was an ethical one, that he wanted to delimit the nature of the ethical from within. "All of that which *many* are *babbling* today, I have defined in my book by remaining silent about it."[15]

It is not difficult to understand why so many readers have been both baffled and fascinated by the *Tractatus*. Composed in a dauntingly severe and compressed style, and organized by means of a numbering system borrowed from *Principia Mathematica*, the book meant to show that traditional philosophy rests on a radical misunderstanding of "the logic of our language." Following in Frege's and Russell's footsteps, Wittgenstein argued that every meaningful sentence must have a precise logical structure which, however, is generally hidden beneath the clothing of the grammatical appearance of the sentence and requires, therefore, an extensive logical analysis to be made evident. Such an analysis, Wittgenstein was convinced, would establish that every meaningful sentence is either a truth-functional composite of other simpler sentences or an atomic sentence consisting of a concatenation of simple names. He argued furthermore that every atomic sentence is a logical picture of a possible state of affairs which must have exactly the same formal structure as the atomic sentence that depicts it. Wittgenstein employed this "picture theory of meaning" – as it is usually called – to derive conclusions about the world from his observations about the structure of the atomic sentences. He postulated, in particular, that the world must itself have a definite logical structure, even though we may not be able to determine it completely. He also held that the world consists primarily of facts, corresponding to the true atomic sentences, rather than of things, and that those facts, in turn, are concatenations of simple objects, corresponding to the simple names of which the atomic sentences are composed. Because he derived these metaphysical conclusions from his view of the nature of language Wittgenstein did not consider it essential to describe what those simple objects, their concatenations, and the facts consisting of them are actually like, thus producing a great deal of uncertainty and disagreement among his interpreters.

The assertions of the *Tractatus* are for the most part concerned with spelling out Wittgenstein's account of the logical structure of language and the world and these parts of the book have understandably been of most immediate interest to philosophers concerned with questions of symbolic logic and its applications. But for Wittgenstein himself the most important part of the book lay in the negative conclusions about philosophy which he reached at the end of his text. He argued there, in particular, that all sentences which are not atomic pictures of concatenations of objects or truth-functional composites of such are strictly speaking meaningless. Among these he included all the propositions of ethics and esthetics, all propositions dealing with the meaning of life, all propositions of logic, indeed all philosophical propositions, and finally all the propositions of the *Tractatus* itself. While these were according to him strictly meaningless, he thought that they nevertheless aimed at saying something important, but that what they tried to express in words could really only be shown.

As a result, Wittgenstein concluded that anyone who understood the *Tractatus* would finally discard its propositions as senseless, that he would throw away the ladder after he had climbed up on it. Someone who had reached such a state would have no more temptation to utter philosophical propositions. He would see the world rightly and so would recognize that the only strictly meaningful propositions are those of natural science; but natural science could never touch what was really important in human life, the mystical. That would have to be contemplated in silence. For "whereof one cannot speak, thereof one must be silent," as the last proposition of the *Tractatus* declared.

V

Given such thoughts it was only natural that Wittgenstein should not afterward embark on an academic career. He did not return to Cambridge after the war but withdrew from philosophical engagement and set out to construct a new, postphilosophical life for himself in Austria. It was only ten years later that he felt once again the need for work in philosophy. The years between 1919 and 1929 were, thus, a period of dormancy for him as far as the active pursuit of philosophy is concerned.

Among the projects he took up in those years was the construction of a house for his sister which he carried out with the help of his friend Paul Engelmann, an architect by profession and a student of Adolf Loos. While the house clearly reveals the influence of Loos, whom Wittgenstein had known intimately before the First World War, it is just as much an architectural representation of the philosophical views of the *Tractatus* and an attempt to give visual expression to its logical, esthetic, and ethical ideals. As such it is revealing in respect to both the *Tractatus* and the early phase of the analytic tradition in philosophy to which the book belongs. For the house is indubitably a specimen of cultural modernism and, specifically, of the formalist modernism evident in Mondrian's paintings, in Bauhaus architecture, and in the assumptions of French structuralism.[16] Wittgenstein's later rejection of the Tractarian philosophy can be assimilated, for similar reasons, to the antiformalist tendencies within modernism, most notably the emergence of abstract expressionism, action painting, and informalism in postwar art whose later expression in architecture, literature, and philosophy has found recognition under the label of postmodernism. Wittgenstein's development from the *Tractatus* to the *Philosophical Investigations* parallels that of the culture at large. The same holds for the analytic tradition as a whole which has also progressed from the single-minded pursuit of an ideal of formal unity to the acceptance of informality, pluralism, and proliferation of forms. While there are those in the analytic tradition who hold fast to the original vision and therefore value Wittgenstein's *Tractatus* more than his later writings, the tradition as a whole has become inclusive of a manifold of philosophical endeavors. Analytic philosophy, initially an archetype of modernist sensibility, has thus come to acquiesce to the pliability of the postmodern. And in this process Wittgenstein's own development after 1918 has been of decisive importance.[17]

### VI

Though Wittgenstein was initially determined to withdraw altogether from philosophy after he had completed the *Tractatus*, he found himself inevitably drawn back to the subject along a number of different tracks. It may be useful to highlight three of them in this context: Wittgenstein's career as a school teacher, his growing interest in psychology and specifically in Freud, and his contacts with the Vienna Circle.

Having been released from the Italian prisoner of war camp and with no wish to pursue an academic career, Wittgenstein decided to enter a teachers' training college in 1919. After completing the course a year later he taught primary school for some six years in the mountains of lower Austria. The experience was to prove not altogether happy for him. His unsettled state of mind, his demanding intellect, and his impatience made him less than an ideal school teacher. His school experience was, nevertheless, to prove an important source of philosophical ideas in later life.

Where Frege, Russell, and he himself in the *Tractatus* had considered language in relation to logic, mathematics, and science, his attention was now drawn to the informal language of everyday life, to the fact that language is primarily a medium of communication, and that as such it does not follow strictly prescribed rules. And where he had previously taken language as given, his attention was now drawn to the way language is learned and more generally to the whole process of enculturation.[18]

His teaching experience forms the background to the turn his philosophical thought was going to take in the 1930s. The development was to bring him back to the ideas of Fritz Mauthner with whose writings he had been familiar since the time of the *Tractatus*. In that book he had dismissed Mauthner curtly by writing: "All philosophy is a 'critique of language' (though not in Mauthner's sense)" (TLP, 4.0031). At the time he had sided with Russell against Mauthner's antiformalist and skeptical view of language. In his voluminous work *Beiträge zu einer Kritik der Sprache* (1901–2) Mauthner had reworked Ernst Mach's skeptical ideas into a philosophy of language. He had argued that language cannot be understood on the model of formal, logical calculi, but that it must be considered an instrument designed to satisfy a multiplicity of human needs. As such it is inevitably an imperfect tool for exploring and depicting reality. Such ideas could appeal to the post-Tractarian Wittgenstein. But even in the earlier period he had harbored a secret sympathy for Mauthner's iconoclastic views. That is made evident by the fact that he borrowed the metaphor of language as a ladder which one must throw away after one has climbed it from Mauthner who, in turn, had taken it from Sextus Empiricus. Wittgenstein's affinity to Mauthner is, indeed, evident in all phases of his philosophical development, though it is most obvious in his later writing. His wariness of scientific theorizing, his skepticism towards psychology, his anti-Cartesian reflections on the self, and in particular his picture of language are all in agreement with Mauthner. When he later rejected the idea of language as a single, unified structure and instead wrote that "our language can be seen as an ancient city: a maze of little streets . . . surrounded by a multitude of new boroughs" he was, once again, employing a metaphor he had borrowed from Mauthner.

During his training as a teacher Wittgenstein had also been made to read a number of psychological writings. Among them was the work of Karl Bühler, an educational psychologist who, despite Wittgenstein's characterization of him as a charlatan, may have been important to him as a forerunner of Gestalt psychology, a topic

Wittgenstein was to concern himself with in later years. A comparison of section xi of part II of the *Philosophical Investigations* with Wolfgang Köhler's book *Gestaltpsychology* proves illuminating. The Wittgenstein of the *Tractatus* had been resistant to the issues of psychology and had expressed that sentiment vividly in his book. Even so, it appears that at this early point Wittgenstein was already attracted to some ideas in psychology given his fascination with Weininger's controversial *Sex and Character*. It is still unclear what drew him to Weininger's peculiar mix of gender-theoretical, antifeminist, self-laceratingly anti-Semitic ideas with elements of Kantian transcendental philosophy, but to Drury he explained that the work had been that of a "remarkable genius" because "Weininger at the age of twenty-one had recognized, before anyone else had taken much notice, the future importance of the ideas which Freud was putting forward."[19]

Freud himself became of interest to Wittgenstein when one of his sisters underwent analysis with him. Though he remained hostile to Freud's theoretical explanations of his psychoanalytic work, he was fascinated with the analytic practice itself and subsequently came to speak of his own work as therapeutic in character. According to Rush Rhees he even called himself "a disciple" and "a follower of Freud" in the 1940s (LC, p. 41). He still thought of Freud's influence as largely harmful and insisted that what Freud was offering as a theory had in reality the character of a "powerful mythology" (LC, p. 52).[20] Still, the influence of psychological questions on Wittgenstein's philosophical thought after 1930 is evident.

When the Vienna Circle, a group of positivist-minded philosophers and scientists, had come together in Wittgenstein's hometown in the mid-twenties their search for new philosophical inspiration had led them to the *Tractatus* and, having discovered that its author was actually living in Vienna, they sought to draw him into their deliberations. Wittgenstein resisted their approach but kept indirect contact with the group through some of its members, particularly Moritz Schlick and Ludwig Waismann. Though he later played down the significance of his association with the Vienna Circle, Waismann's notes on his conversations with Wittgenstein reveal that for a while he actually came to subscribe to the verificationist principle of meaning advanced by the group, that is, the assumption that the meaning of a sentence is fixed by its method of verification. However, Wittgenstein eventually transformed this principle into the more generous thesis that the meaning of a sentence is its use – one of the mainstays of his later philosophy.

Wittgenstein's contact with the Vienna Circle was significant, perhaps, also for another reason. In late 1928 his friends in the Circle took him to a lecture by the Dutch mathematician L. E. J. Brouwer from which he emerged galvanized, according to all reports.[21] In that lecture Brouwer had laid out his own program for an intuitionist foundation of mathematics. There is no reason to think that Wittgenstein ever subscribed to mathematical intuitionism. Unlike Brouwer he certainly never rejected the use of the principle of the excluded middle. But Brouwer must have struck a responsive chord in his thinking – possibly because he attacked formalism and the assumption of the reliability of logic and because he laid out a picture of mathematics as a human construction. What may also have struck a responsive chord in Wittgenstein was that Brouwer presented his thought in philosophical terms derived from Schopenhauer. There is, in any case, no doubt that Brouwer's talk contributed to Wittgenstein's decision to return to an active engagement in philosophy. It may also have stimulated his interest in the philosophy of mathematics, for in the decade and a half that followed he concerned himself more intensively with this topic than at any earlier moment in his life.

## VII

When Wittgenstein returned to Cambridge in 1929, he did so initially with the limited objective of fixing up certain remaining difficulties in the *Tractatus*. The problem that concerned him at this point stemmed from the central thesis of the book according to which all logical relations between propositions are explicable in terms of their truth-functional composition out of simpler ones. Wittgenstein had discussed a number of apparent counterexamples to that thesis in the *Tractatus*, but by 1929 he had concluded that he had failed to resolve the difficulty. How was one to account for the fact that the propositions "This surface is red" and "This surface is green" are incompatible when they are taken to refer to the same whole surface at a given moment? They certainly did not seem to be truth-functionally complex. The "color exclusion" problem thus presented a potentially damaging problem for a central element of the *Tractatus* philosophy and it was this problem that Wittgenstein was determined to solve when he returned to Cambridge.

What brought him back was then not a new philosophical outlook, but a sense that the original project of the *Tractatus* had not yet been completed. Two lectures from the time, the essay on logical form (PO, pp. 29–35) and the lecture on ethics (PO, pp. 37–44), reveal how deeply he was still attached to the assumptions of his earlier book. Of these essays the second is of particular interest because it shows how much Wittgenstein's thinking in the *Tractatus* was really motivated by ethical concerns.

Once he had begun to rethink certain elements of the *Tractatus*, Wittgenstein found himself forced to dismantle more and more of its philosophical assumptions. Within a few months the elaborate structure of the *Tractatus* collapsed like a house of cards. But that collapse did not leave him in despair; on the contrary, it opened up the floodgates of new thoughts. There is, perhaps, no other period in Wittgenstein's life in which ideas came to him so copiously. There is certainly no other period in which he wrote so much. As he abandoned the assumptions of the *Tractatus* he explored a number of different philosophical routes. In the *Philosophical Remarks*, which he composed early in this period, we find him struggling with a phenomenalism that assigns primacy to personal experience and the language of experience. But this position is soon left behind and his thinking turns to the critique of these assumptions. For a while he sees himself as a phenomenologist of language and boasts that he has found a new philosophical method that will allow systematic progress as in the sciences. That idea is also left behind quickly.

Wittgenstein's most decisive step in the middle period was to abandon the belief of the *Tractatus* that meaningful sentences must have a precise, though hidden logical structure and the accompanying belief that this structure corresponds to the logical structure of the facts depicted by the sentences. The *Tractatus* had, indeed, proceeded on the assumption that all the different symbolic devices which can be used to describe the world must be constructed according to the same underlying logic. In a sense, then, there was only one meaningful language and from it one was supposed to be able to read off the logical structure of the world. In the middle period Wittgenstein came to conclude that this doctrine constituted a piece of unwarranted metaphysics and that the *Tractatus* was itself flawed by what it had set out to combat, that is, a misunderstanding of the logic of our language. Where he had previously held it possible to ground metaphysics on logic, he now argued that metaphysics leads the philosopher into complete darkness. Turning his attention back to language, he concluded that almost everything he had said about it in the *Tractatus* had been in error. There were, in fact, many different languages with many different structures which could serve quite different needs. Language was not a unified structure, but consisted of a multiplicity of simpler substructures or language-games. And from this followed the momentous conclusion that sentences cannot be taken to be logical pictures of facts and that the ultimate components of sentences cannot be taken as names of simple objects.

These new reflections on the nature of language served Wittgenstein, in the first place, as an aid to thinking about the nature of the human mind, and specifically about the relation between private experience and the physical world. He argued against the existence of a Cartesian mental substance that the word "I" did not serve as a name of anything, but occurred in expressions meant to draw attention to a particular body. For a while, at least, he also thought he could explain the difference between private experience and the physical world in terms of the existence of two languages, a primary language of experience and a secondary language of physics. This dual-language view, which is evident both in *Philosophical Remarks* and in the *Blue Book*, Wittgenstein was later to give up in favor of the view that our grasp of inner phenomena is dependent on the existence of outer criteria.

From the mid-1930s onward Wittgenstein also worked hard on issues in the philosophy of mathematics. Renewing the *Tractatus* attack on Frege's and Russell's logicism, he argued now more vehemently that no part of mathematics could be reduced to logic. Instead, he set out to describe mathematics as part of our natural history and as consisting of a number of diverse language-games. He also insisted that the meaning of those mathematical language-games depended on the uses to which the formulae were put. Applying the principle of verification to mathematics he held that the meaning of a mathematical formula lies in its proof. These remarks on the philosophy of mathematics have remained among Wittgenstein's most controversial and least explored writings.

In Cambridge, Wittgenstein found himself all of a sudden to be part of a regular academic community. While his relations with Russell were now becoming strained, he found new contacts in G. E. Moore, the mathematician Frank Ramsey, and the economist Pierro Sraffa as well as a growing number of students. The new Wittgenstein who emerged in this period shared with Moore an interest in the working of ordinary language and the assumptions of common sense. For all that he never held Moore in the same respect in which he had once held Russell. He admired Moore's dedication and moral purity, but remained wary of his philosophical powers. In order to set himself off from Moore, he described himself as "the common-sense man, who is as far from realism as from idealism" in contrast to Moore's "common-sense philosopher" who believes himself justified in his realism (BLBK, p. 48). When Moore attended Wittgenstein's lectures in the period between 1930 and 1933, he found much that intrigued but also much that bewildered him. But, above all, he was impressed by "the intensity of conviction with which he said everything which he did say, . . . [and] the extreme interest which he excited in his hearers."[22]

Where Wittgenstein had singled out Frege and Russell for mention in the preface of the *Tractatus* he similarly singled out Ramsey and Sraffa for praise in the preface of the *Philosophical Investigations*. Ramsey, he says, helped him to see the mistakes in his earlier book "in innumerable conversations during the last two years of his life" (PI, p. vi). Ramsey, in turn, held Wittgenstein's work on the foundations of mathematics in highest esteem and called him "a philosophical genius of a different order from any one else I know" and praised him particularly for his work on the foundations of mathematics (PO, p. 48). Wittgenstein's extensive work on the philosophy of mathematics during the 1930s may very well have been sparked by those conversations with Ramsey. Sraffa, on the other hand, is thanked in the *Investigations* for his "always certain and forceful" criticism of Wittgenstein's new ideas. Wittgenstein writes: "I am indebted to *this* stimulus for the most consequential ideas of this book" (PI, p. vi).

When Wittgenstein came back to Cambridge he found himself suddenly, at the age of forty, at the start of a career as a university teacher. The man who had already gained some fame as the author of an important but difficult book became now a living presence at

Cambridge. His classes attracted a small but regular following of gifted students, among them philosophers such as Norman Malcolm, Rush Rhees, and Elizabeth Anscombe and mathematicians such as Alan Turing and Georg Kreisel. The lecture notes kept by some of these students and their later reminiscences give us a vivid picture of Wittgenstein's presence and work in this period.[23]

Of the greatest significance are two texts from this period which Wittgenstein dictated to his students between 1933 and 1935. They are respectively known as the *Blue Book* and the *Brown Book*. By this time Wittgenstein had begun to formulate the ideas that are identified as his later philosophy. In a concise form Wittgenstein develops many of these ideas for the first time in these two books. Nevertheless, it is misleading to characterize these texts simply as "preliminary studies for the 'Philosophical Investigations' " as the published edition calls them. The views Wittgenstein expresses at this point are clearly related to those of the *Philosophical Investigations*, but they are not the same. While he assumes now that language consists of a number of different substructures, individual language-games, he still thinks of these structures as circumscribed by strict rules. He has, in other words, not yet reached the conclusion that only some language-games are governed by precise rules while others are much looser structures. For this he will first have to develop a critical view of the function of rules, a topic that is not yet evident in the *Blue and Brown Books* but is of central significance in the *Philosophical Investigations*. Furthermore, while he allows now the possibility of both physical descriptions and psychological utterances, he also does as yet have no precise understanding of their relations to each other. For that he will have to work out his so-called private-language argument and his criterial account of the inner–outer relation, two themes as yet untouched in the early 1930s.

Wittgenstein's influence on his students was not always to the good. He overpowered them at times with the intensity of his mind and did not always allow them to develop along their own paths. We can gain a sense of this questionable effect from O. K. Bouwsma's description of the influence Wittgenstein had on him:

Wittgenstein is the nearest to a prophet I have ever known. He is a man who is like a tower, who stands high and unattached, leaning on no one. He has his own feet. He fears no man. . . . But other men fear him. . . . They fear his judgment. And so I feared Wittgenstein, felt responsible to him. . . . His words I cherished like jewels. . . . It is an awful thing to work under the gaze and questioning of such piercing eyes, and such discernment, knowing rubbish and gold! And one who speaks the word: "This is rubbish!"[24]

While the force of Wittgenstein's personality attracted some, it produced resistance in others. The result was that an aura of esotericism began to surround Wittgenstein's thinking which was intensified by the fact that Wittgenstein published nothing after 1929 so that his new work in philosophy came to be known only indirectly and by hearsay. The adulation and the resistance combined together did not always work in favor of a balanced and critical assessment of that philosophy.

### VIII

Wittgenstein's middle period is characterized by extensive work on a broad, but quickly changing front. By 1936, however, his thinking was settling down once again into a steadier pattern and he now began to elaborate the views for which he was to become most famous. Where he had constructed his earlier work around the logic devised by Frege and Russell, he now concerned himself mainly with the actual working of ordinary language. This brought him close to the tradition of British common-sense philosophy that G. E. Moore had revived. Wittgenstein thus became one of the godfathers of the ordinary language philosophy that was to flourish in England and, particularly, in Oxford in the 1950s. In the *Philosophical Investigations* he emphasized that there are countless different kinds of use of what we call "symbols," "words," and "sentences." The task of philosophy was to gain a perspicuous view of those multiple uses and thereby to dissolve philosophical and metaphysical puzzles. These puzzles were the result of insufficient attention to the working of language and could only be resolved by carefully retracing the steps by which they had been reached.

Wittgenstein thus came to think of philosophy as a descriptive, analytic, and ultimately therapeutic practice. In the writings that exemplified this new conception he abandoned the tight numbering scheme of the *Tractatus* and composed the text as a series of loosely organized and successively numbered remarks. In the preface to the

*Philosophical Investigations* he called his book "an album" consisting of "a number of sketches of landscapes which were made in the course of . . . long and involved journeyings" (PI, p. v). In place of the dogmatic style of assertion that had characterized the *Tractatus* he also now adopted a form of conversational writing in which ideas were developed in an interchange between an imaginary interlocutor and Wittgenstein speaking in his own voice. These stylistic changes corresponded, of course, to his new way of understanding both philosophy and language. The *Investigations* set out to show how common philosophical views about meaning (including the logical atomism of the *Tractatus*), about the nature of concepts, about logical necessity, about rule-following, and about the mind–body problem were all the product of an insufficient grasp of how language works. In one of the most influential passages of the book he argued that predicates do not denote sharply circumscribed concepts, but mark family resemblances between the things labeled with the predicate. He also held that logical necessity results from linguistic convention and that rules cannot determine their own applications, that rule-following presupposes the existence of regular practices. Wittgenstein went on to maintain that the words of our language have meaning only insofar as there exist public criteria for their correct use. As a consequence, he argued, there cannot be a completely private language, that is, a language which in principle can only be used to speak about one's own inner experience. This "private language argument" has been the cause of much debate. Interpreters have disagreed not only over the structure of the argument and where it is to be found in Wittgenstein's text, but also over the question whether Wittgenstein meant to say that language is necessarily social. Because he maintained that in order to speak of inner experiences there must be external and publicly available criteria, he has often been taken to be an advocate of a logical behaviorism, but nowhere does he deny the existence of inner states. What he says is merely that our understanding of someone's pain is connected to the existence of natural and linguistic expressions of pain.

The Second World War meant another disruption in Wittgenstein's philosophical work. Once again he felt called to serve in the war effort in a lowly capacity, working first as a hospital porter and then as a technical assistant in a medical laboratory. This new disruption signaled in effect the end of his academic career. In 1947 he gave his last lectures at Cambridge. His goal was now to bring the material he had worked out in the prewar period to completion. Even so, he never succeeded in producing a finished version of the *Philosophical Investigations*.

But these last years were not just a period of consolidation for him. Perception and knowledge now became topics of philosophical interest to him. In the *Philosophical Investigations* he had repeatedly drawn attention to the fact that language must be learned. This learning, he had said, is fundamentally a process of inculcation and drill. In learning a language the child is being initiated in a form of life. In the last stage of Wittgenstein's thinking the notion of form of life is taken up and serves to identify the complex of natural and cultural circumstances which are presupposed in language and in any particular understanding of the world. In notes written between 1948 and 1951 now published under the title *On Certainty* he insists that every particular belief must always be seen as part of a system of beliefs which together constitute a world-view. All confirmation and disconfirmation of a belief always already presupposes such a system and is internal to it. This does not mean that he was advocating a careless relativism. His view is rather a form of naturalism which assumes that forms of life, world-views, and language-games are ultimately constrained by the nature of the world. The world teaches us that certain games cannot be played.

Wittgenstein's final notes illustrate the continuity of his basic concerns throughout all the changes his thinking underwent. For they reveal once more how he remained skeptical about all philosophical theories and how he understood his own undertaking as the attempt to undermine the need for any such theorizing. The considerations of *On Certainty* are evidently directed against both philosophical skepticism and philosophical refutations of skepticism. Against the philosophical skeptics Wittgenstein insisted that there is real knowledge. But this knowledge is always dispersed and not necessarily reliable; it consists of things we have heard and read, of what has been drilled into us, and of our own modifications of this inheritance. We have no general reason to doubt this inherited body of knowledge, we do not generally doubt it, and we are, in fact, in no position to do so. *On Certainty* concludes therefore that it is impossible to refute skepticism by drawing on propositions which are considered absolutely certain such as Descartes's "I think, therefore

I am" or Moore's "I know for certain that this is a hand here." The fact that such propositions are considered certain, Wittgenstein argued, indicates only that they play an indispensable, normative role in our language-game; they are the riverbed through which the thought of our language-game flows. Such propositions cannot be taken to express metaphysical truths. Here, too, the conclusion is that all philosophical argumentation must come to an end, but that the end of such argumentation is not an absolute, self-evident truth, that it is rather a certain kind of natural human practice.

Wittgenstein remained philosophically active until the end of his life. The last entry into the notebooks from which the text of *On Certainty* is taken was written only days before his death of prostate cancer in April 1951. On his deathbed he told his friends that he had lived a wonderful life. Norman Malcolm, who was one of those friends, wrote afterward:

When I think of his profound pessimism, the intensity of his mental and moral suffering, the relentless way in which he drove his intellect, his need for love, together with the harshness that repelled love, I am inclined to believe that his life was fiercely unhappy. Yet at the end he himself exclaimed that it had been "wonderful"! To me this seems a mysterious and strangely moving utterance.[25]

## IX

Wittgenstein's thinking is characterized by an ambivalent and even paradoxical attitude toward philosophy. For he entertained, on the one hand, a profound skepticism with regard to philosophy – hence his quick and often harsh dismissals of the claims of traditional philosophy – but he tempered that attitude at the same time with a genuine appreciation for the depth of the philosophical problems. In the *Tractatus Logico-Philosophicus* he maintained, for instance, that the whole of philosophy is full of fundamental confusions, and that "most of the propositions and questions to be found in philosophical works are not false but nonsensical" (TLP, 3.324 and 4.003). But this critique is modified by his appreciation of the truth contained in these confusions and mistakes. "In a certain sense one cannot take too much care in handling philosophical mistakes," he wrote later, "they contain so much truth" (Z, 459). In consequence he was critical not only of traditional philosophy, but also of those who in his opinion failed to appreciate the complexity of the philosophical problems.

These observations result in a peculiarly ambivalent attitude towards philosophy which is, perhaps, best captured in the following statement from the *Philosophical Remarks*, repeated in *Zettel*:

> How does it come about that philosophy is so complicated a structure? It surely ought to be completely simple, if it is the ultimate thing, independent of all experience, that you make it out to be. – Philosophy unties knots in our thinking; hence its result must be simple, but philosophizing has to be as complicated as the knots it unties. (Z, 452)

Though Wittgenstein dismissed traditional philosophy, he did so always for philosophical reasons. He was certain that something important could be rescued from the traditional enterprise. In the *Blue Book* he spoke of his own work therefore as "one of the heirs of the subject that used to be called philosophy" (BLBK, p. 28). The characterization suggests that traditional philosophy is now dead, but that it has left an inheritance to be disposed of; it also suggests that there are a number of heirs to the philosophical heritage and that Wittgenstein's own work should be thought of as just one of them.

If one wants to identify historical antecedents to this view, one should probably look to Schopenhauer's famous denunciation of "University philosophy" and to his conception of a philosophy that transcends metaphysical theorizing and that sets itself the goal of a philosophical mode of life in which the endpoint is philosophical silence. Schopenhauer was certainly a crucial figure in Wittgenstein's philosophical development. Though he is acknowledged as an influence in 1931 when Wittgenstein wrote "Boltzmann, Hertz, Schopenhauer, Frege, Russell, Kraus, Loos, Weininger, Spengler, Sraffa have influenced me" (CV, p. 19), his real importance in shaping Wittgenstein's overall conception of philosophy is as yet insufficiently recognized.

What Wittgenstein rejected in traditional philosophy was, above all, its theorizing impulse. Both in his early and in his later writings, he is outspoken on this point. Already in the *Tractatus* he insists that "philosophy is not a body of doctrine but an activity" (TLP, 4.112). And in the *Philosophical Investigations* he adds that "it was true to say that our considerations could not be scientific ones. . . .

And we may not advance any kind of theory" (PI, 109). Wittgenstein motivated this antitheoretical attitude in philosophy at times by expressing a profoundly critical attitude toward modern civilization as a whole and, in particular, toward its constructive and "progressive" character. In 1930 he wrote: "Our civilization is characterized by the word 'progress.' . . . Typically it constructs. It is occupied with building an ever more complicated structure and even clarity is sought only as a means to this end, not as an end in itself. For me on the contrary clarity, perspicuity are valuable in themselves" (CV, p. 7). And to this he added that the spirit of the great stream of European and American civilization was "alien and uncongenial" to him. "I have no sympathy for the stream of European civilization and do not understand its goals, if it has any" (CV, p. 6).

There are two elements here that have made Wittgenstein's philosophical critics uncomfortable. For one thing, Wittgenstein insists generally on a sharp distinction between philosophy and science, in sharp contrast to those movements in the twentieth century that have sought to reconstruct philosophy in a scientific manner. Wittgenstein rejects any conception of philosophy that would make it into a quasi-scientific enterprise. Accordingly, he writes in the *Blue Book:* "Philosophers constantly see the method of science before their eye, and are irresistibly tempted to ask and answer questions in the way science does. This tendency is the real source of metaphysics and leads the philosopher into complete darkness" (BLBK, p. 18). It is also clear that he feels generally antipathetic to science or, at least, distanced from it. "I am not aiming at the same target as the scientists," he writes, "and my way of thinking is different from theirs" (CV, p. 7). And: "We cannot speak in science of a *great,* essential problem" (CV, p. 10). And finally: "I may find scientific questions interesting, but they never really grip me" (CV, p. 79). To philosophers steeped in the values of science such remarks must naturally sound offensive.

If Wittgenstein's goal is not the formulation of any philosophical theory, we may ask what he sees as the outcome of his undertakings. This he describes variously as showing what cannot be manifestly expressed in language or as describing the evident features of our practices. In either case he holds that "the work of the philosopher consists in assembling reminders for a particular purpose" (PI, 128). That purpose is at times described as therapeutic in character, as aiming for instance at the disappearance of the problem of life. "We feel that even when all *possible* scientific questions have been answered, the problem of life remains completely untouched. . . . The solution of the problem of life is seen in the vanishing of the problem" (TLP, 6.521–6.522). Elsewhere, he describes philosophy as "a battle against the bewitchment of our intelligence by means of language," and declares that "the real discovery" is "the one that gives philosophy peace" (PI, 109, 133). The use of therapeutic language is clearly connected with the critical interest in Freud which he developed in the 1930s.

It would probably not be wrong to think of Wittgenstein as being fundamentally a thinker inspired by moral and religious motivations rather than scientific ones. Nevertheless, he has been and remains of interest to philosophers whose conceptions of their own undertaking differs radically from his, for he addresses himself to philosophical issues they recognize and uses methods and tools with which they are familiar.

X

In describing Wittgenstein's life and work my purpose has been to provide readers with a general map for approaching the essays in this collection. I have certainly not tried to give a comprehensive account of Wittgenstein's life and work. Readers familiar with the current state of Wittgenstein scholarship will have found little that is new in my exposition. They will also be aware that there exists no consensus among the interpreters on how Wittgenstein's work should be approached and what is of lasting significance in it.

This collection of essays is meant to provide a picture of the diversity of philosophical views that exist in regard to Wittgenstein's work. There are, as I said at the beginning, very different ways in which one can approach Wittgenstein, his life and his work. This volume is concerned with the strictly philosophical side of Wittgenstein; it does not explore the biographical and historical context in which that philosophy emerged. But within these limitations, the volume seeks to show that the work can be explored from a number of different perspectives. Given the state of the philosophical discussion, it seems appropriate to acquaint readers with the disagreements between Wittgenstein's interpreters as well as with their agreements, to show them that various approaches are possible when reading Wittgenstein's work. The essays in this volume are therefore not meant to be pieces of a tightly constructed jigsaw puzzle that makes up a single picture. They are rather explorations, diverse in style, method, and outlook, of a diverse array of themes in Wittgenstein's work. None of the contributions to this volume aims at encyclopedic completeness; none of them seeks to attain the status of a survey article. Wittgenstein is still so close to us and the ore of his thought is as yet so unexplored that any attempt at a definitive exposition of his ideas would be doomed to failure. What is important to show is, thus, that his work continues to have a rich and invigorating influence on contemporary thinking in philosophy. It is, in any case, impossible to give as yet a definitive assessment of his philosophical significance. The essays that make up this volume are meant, therefore, to alert readers to some of the most important and most interesting issues raised in Wittgenstein's philosophical writings. All of them are, moreover, conceived with the idea of inspiring readers to go directly to Wittgenstein's own writings. No critical exposition, no exegesis, no commentary, no rational reconstruction can take the place of the study of the original texts.

It seems appropriate to begin this collection with an essay discussing Wittgenstein's conception of philosophy. Robert Fogelin undertakes this task in an admirably lucid account of Wittgenstein's critique of traditional philosophy. The pieces that follow Fogelin's exposition show in various ways how this critique inspires a wealth of other philosophical ideas in Wittgenstein's writings. The order of these essays is roughly that of Wittgenstein's own philosophical development. Both Tom Ricketts and Donna Summerfield focus on the Wittgenstein of the *Tractatus*, one relating him more to Frege, the other to views derived from Russell. Newton Garver examines Wittgenstein's shift from a concern with logic to a concern with grammar, a shift that took place in the early 1930s. Steve Gerrard's, Hans Johann Glock's, and Cora Diamond's contributions deal with Wittgenstein's thinking about logical necessity, mathematics, and ethics – themes that in one way or another preoccupied him after his return to Cambridge. Stanley Cavell's contribution offers us a thoughtful and reflective reading of the initial sections of the *Philosophical Investigations* and Barry Stroud one on aspects of Wittgenstein's account of meaning that are most clearly elaborated in that same text. Michael Kober, finally, provides a careful analysis of Wittgenstein's last notes, the material collected in the volume *On Certainty*.

Nevertheless no strictly historical arrangement of the material is aimed at in this volume. The reason is that some of the contributions deal with themes, ideas, or concepts in Wittgenstein's philosophy, and not with a particular text or a particular period in his development. While some contributions are concerned with specific texts, others explore themes and concepts that Wittgenstein pursued at different times. My own discussion of Wittgenstein's changing reflections on the self is an example of this genre. Moreover, while some essays are mainly exegetical or critical in character, others seek to apply or extend Wittgenstein's considerations in new ways. David Bloor's provocative discussion of Wittgenstein's supposed idealism and Naomi Scheman's imaginative essay on the concept of form of life provide two very different examples of this style of writing.

The volume closes with David Stern's discussion of the status and availability of Wittgenstein's writings. Given the uncertainties that surround even major texts like the *Philosophical Investigations* and the controversies about the editorial policies followed in the publication of Wittgenstein's manuscripts, Stern's essay should be an important help for the reader. Finally, a list of further readings is provided which may prove helpful for the beginning student of Wittgenstein's work. The volume closes with an extensive bibliography put together by John Holbo, my research assistant for this project, who deserves thanks also for a variety of other valuable tasks he carried out in connection with this volume.

## XI

Despite the indubitable influence Wittgenstein has had on the development of recent philosophy, his position within the philosophical discipline remains contested. His resistance to theorizing, the aphoristic style of his writing, his frequently stated antiphilosophical sentiments, and the highly personal, even existential tone of his thinking make it difficult to fit him into the framework of academic philosophy.

Though Wittgenstein's work is sometimes technical and often

exceedingly detailed and painstaking, and though the course of his thinking is often difficult to follow, it covers at the same time an exceptionally wide range of philosophical and quasi-philosophical topics and manages to speak about them with an unusual freshness, in a precise and stylish language, often with the help of surprising and illuminating images and metaphors. It is therefore not surprising to find that some interpreters call him "a philosopher of genius" or say that in his philosophical writings one enters "a new world."[26]

But others have maintained with equal seriousness that his importance for philosophy has been highly overrated. Hostile comments are not difficult to find, such as Bertrand Russell's bitter complaint that "the later Wittgenstein . . . seems to have grown tired of serious thinking and to have invented a doctrine which would make such an activity unnecessary."[27] That philosophical judgments about Wittgenstein should differ so much is perhaps not surprising in a thinker whose views are always highly personal and sometimes radically idiosyncratic. In this respect one might want to compare him to Nietzsche. Both have been acclaimed as new starting points in philosophy and both have been dismissed as not really being philosophers at all.

Yet a third group of interpreters has suggested a middle path. They have argued that it is best to ignore Wittgenstein's general remarks about philosophy and to concentrate on his discussion of concrete philosophical issues. They have said that, when one does so, it may be possible to discover a coherent and important series of arguments hidden in the apparently scattered series of remarks. Some have gone so far as to assume the existence of a whole philosophical system. Does Wittgenstein have philosophical doctrines despite his insistence that there are no philosophical propositions? There are certainly arguments to be found in his texts and propositions that seem to be making affirmative claims.

In trying to explain the fascination that Wittgenstein and his work exert, it may, finally, help to remind ourselves of the similarities between Wittgenstein's way of doing philosophy and the style of philosophy adopted by Socrates. Wittgenstein himself once acknowledged a similarity between his conception of philosophy and the Socratic doctrine of reminiscence.[28]

What strikes the reader of the *Philosophical Investigations* who keeps this idea in mind is the dialogical style adopted in it. Each section seems to involve an exchange between an imaginary interlocutor – who may represent a traditional philosophical view, the assumptions of a superficial common sense, or even Wittgenstein's own former opinions – and Wittgenstein, the author of the remark. The writing, thus, has the qualities of an inner dialogue, resembling the conversations between Socrates and his partners in the Platonic texts. Like the Socrates of the early dialogues Wittgenstein seems, moreover, to be generally engaged in an elenctic reasoning which does not seek to determine universally valid doctrines but wants to expose the assumptions inherent in the interlocutor's reasoning. Like Socrates, he sees himself as a healer as well as a thinker. We are also reminded of Socrates by Wittgenstein's disregard for offices and institutions. Though he taught at Cambridge for more than a decade, he never let himself be enveloped in the prevailing scholastic mist and the petty obsessions of academic philosophy. He is always someone determined to think his own thoughts, never just a professor of philosophy. He speaks for no one but himself. Far from assigning a superior status to his profession he understands it at all times as his own private "daimonion."

What reminds one, perhaps, most of Socrates in Wittgenstein are the patience and persistence with which he pursues his questions. Unhurried and yet relentless, both of them tease and harry the problems that concern them, hunting them down into their most hidden caves and corners. No turn of the question is too small for them, no trail too insignificant to pursue. Tirelessly they come back, again and again, to what preoccupies them. Profoundly concerned with the very words into which we have cast our philosophical predicaments, they still never lose sight of the great issues that lie behind them.

Wittgenstein once suggested that it should be possible to write a philosophical text that consists of nothing but questions. His writing is, indeed, anything but constative in character. He suggests, asks, admonishes, calls for experiments in thought, action, and imagination. He demands from his readers a constant active engagement in thinking. It is perhaps, in these characteristics that he reveals his true significance as a philosopher. We need not agree with the conclusions that his thinking leads him to, we need not be preoccupied with the particular questions that concern him, but like Socrates he stands before us as a model of what it means to be a philosopher.

NOTES

1 In Thomas Bernhard's bizarre yet hypnotic *Wittgenstein's Nephew* he appears as the invisible uncle who might easily have been the madman his nephew actually is, just as the mad nephew might have been the philosopher. The novel is written as a counter-*Tractatus* with *no* structure, *no* subdivisions in the text, concerned *entirely* with talk about death, the meaning of life, pain, and the inner states. At the same time it shares Wittgenstein's dark view of the age which Bernhard just like Wittgenstein sees in Schopenhauerean terms. Derek Jarman's stylish and highly stylized film – best seen as part of a trilogy together with *Caravaggio* and *Edward II* – depicts, on the other hand a paradigmatic gay life. For Jarman, Wittgenstein's story becomes part of his own search for gay liberation.

2 Wittgenstein's family background is described in Brian McGuinness, *Wittgenstein: A Life*, vol. 1, *Young Ludwig 1889–1921* (Berkeley and Los Angeles: University of California Press, 1988). There exist now a number of excellent biographical studies of Wittgenstein. A helpful, short account can be found in Norman Malcolm's *Ludwig Wittgenstein: A Memoir* with its biographical essay by G. H. von Wright. The most detailed and up-to-date biography is Ray Monk's highly readable *Ludwig Wittgenstein: The Duty of Genius* (New York: The Free Press, 1990).

3 A richly evocative account of this is given in Fania Pascal, "Wittgenstein: A Personal Memoir," in C. G. Luckhardt, ed., *Wittgenstein: Sources and Perspectives* (Ithaca: Cornell University Press, 1979), pp. 23–60.

4 M. O'C. Drury, "Some Notes on Conversations with Wittgenstein" and "Conversations with Wittgenstein," in Rush Rhees, ed., *Ludwig Wittgenstein: Personal Recollections* (Totowa, N.J.: Rowman and Littlefield, 1981), pp. 94, 175.

5 The best characterization of that milieu is to be found in Carl E. Schorske's *Fin-de-Siècle Vienna: Politics and Culture* (New York: Alfred A. Knopf, 1980). Alan Janik's and Stephen Toulmin's widely read book *Wittgenstein's Vienna* (New York: Simon and Schuster, 1973) is more anecdotal, less reliable, and more superficial in its analyses.

6 Drury, in Rhees, *Personal Recollections*, p. 152.

7 Of most interest in this connection are Musil's *The Man without Qualities*, trans. Sophie Wilkins (New York: Alfred A. Knopf, 1994) and Broch's *Hofmannsthal und seine Zeit* (Munich: Piper, 1964).

8 I describe Hitler's familiarity with Schopenhauer in my book *Heidegger's Crisis: Philosophy and Politics in Nazi Germany* (Cambridge, Mass.: Harvard University Press, 1993), pp. 179–81. For Wittgenstein's relation

to Schopenhauer see D. Weiner, *Genius and Talent: Schopenhauer's Influence on Wittgenstein's Early Philosophy* (London and Toronto: Association of University Presses, 1992).

9 Ronald W. Clark, *The Life of Bertrand Russell* (New York: Alfred A. Knopf, 1976), chs. 7 and 8, gives us a vivid description of their encounter.

10 Bertrand Russell, *The Autobiography of Bertrand Russell* (Boston: Little, Brown, and Company, 1968), vol. 2, p. 136.

11 L. Wittgenstein, *Geheime Tagebücher: 1914–1916*, ed. W. Baum (Vienna: Turia and Kant, 1991), p. 13. It is useful to consider this text in conjunction with Wittgenstein's *Notebooks 1914–1916* in order to gain a more complete picture of his thinking in that period.

12 Paul Engelmann, *Letters from Ludwig Wittgenstein with a Memoir* (Oxford: Blackwell, 1967), p. 25.

13 Even some recent interpreters have characterized the book without further qualification as "a work in philosophical logic." Cf. H. O. Mounce, *Wittgenstein's Tractatus: An Introduction* (Chicago: University of Chicago Press, 1981), p. 1.

14 L. Wittgenstein, *Letters to Russell, Keynes, and Moore*, ed. by G. H. von Wright (Ithaca: Cornell University Press, 1974), p. 71.

15 L. Wittgenstein, "Letters to Ludwig von Ficker," in C. G. Luckhardt, ed., *Wittgenstein: Sources and Perspectives* (Ithaca: Cornell University Press, 1979), p. 95.

16 Peter Galison has discussed the confluence of the philosophical ideas of Wittgenstein and the Vienna Circle and the stylistic conceptions of the Bauhaus in his essay "Aufbau/Bauhaus: Logical Positivism and Architectural Modernism," in *Critical Inquiry* 16 (1990), pp. 709–52.

17 Hans Sluga, "Zwischen Modernismus und Postmoderne: Wittgenstein und die Architektur," in J. Nautz and R. Vahrenkamp, eds., *Die Wiener Jahrhundertwende* (Vienna: Böhlau, 1993).

18 The significance of this episode of Wittgenstein's life for his subsequent philosophizing has as yet been insufficiently explored. An important start for such an examination is made in Konrad Wünsche, *Der Volksschullehrer Ludwig Wittgenstein* (Frankfurt: Suhrkamp, 1985).

19 Drury, in Rhees, *Personal Recollections*, p. 106.

20 Was there an element of overcompensation in Wittgenstein's combative references to Freud? He was certainly sexually repressed (Monk, *The Duty of Genius*, p. 585), uneasy about his homoerotic impulses, disturbed by his relations with his father and mother, full of anxieties, subject to depression and suicidal wishes. In other words, he was, in a sense, the typical client in Freud's practice. But he never underwent psychoanalysis and resisted the descriptions Freud offered of the mental scene. It is tempting to think of the therapy Wittgenstein envisaged in

his own writings as alternative to the Freudian variety and that he saw himself as the test case for the effectiveness of his own therapeutic method. That Wittgenstein's preoccupation with the self may have had one root in his own psychological condition, does, of course, not affect the question of the validity of his observations in this area.

21  L. E. J. Brouwer, "Mathematik, Wissenschaft und Sprache," *Monatshefte für Mathematik* 36 (1929), pp. 153–64.

22  G. E. Moore, "Wittgenstein's Lectures in 1930–33," in PO, pp. 50–1.

23  Ludwig Wittgenstein, *Lectures, Cambridge 1930–1932*, ed. Desmond Lee (Chicago: University of Chicago Press, 1980); *Lectures, Cambridge 1932–1935*, ed. Alice Ambrose (Chicago: University of Chicago Press, 1979); *Lectures on the Foundations of Mathematics*, ed. Cora Diamond (Ithaca: Cornell University Press, 1976).

24  O. K. Bouwsma, *Wittgenstein: Conversations 1949–1951* (Indianapolis: Hackett Publishing, 1986), pp. xv–xvi.

25  N. Malcolm, *Ludwig Wittgenstein: A Memoir*, 2nd ed. (Oxford: Oxford University Press, 1984), p. 81.

26  Peter Strawson, "Review of Wittgenstein's Philosophical Investigations," in G. Pitcher, ed., *Wittgenstein* (London: Macmillan, 1968), p. 22; David Pears, *The False Prison* (Oxford: Clarendon Press, 1987), vol. 1, p. 3.

27  Bertrand Russell, *My Philosophical Development* (London: Allen and Unwin, 1959), pp. 216–17.

28  Malcolm, *Ludwig Wittgenstein: A Memoir*, p. 51.

# 1    Wittgenstein's critique of philosophy

Philosophy is a battle against the bewitchment of our intelligence by means of language.

(PI, 109)

## I INTRODUCTION

In this essay I shall try to describe the central features of Wittgenstein's critique of traditional philosophy as they appear in their most mature form in the *Philosophical Investigations* and in the *Remarks on the Foundations of Mathematics*.[1] The leading idea can be stated quite simply: Philosophers are led into confusion because they are antecedently disposed to view various uses of language in ways inappropriate to them. This is not usually (or simply) a matter of reasoning from false premises about language but is, instead, a tendency to view language from a skewed or disoriented perspective. The proper task of philosophy—indeed, its whole task—is to *induce* us to abandon such improper perspectives.

Wittgenstein uses various similes and metaphors to indicate how we can be captured by an inappropriate orientation: "It is like a pair of glasses on our nose through which we see whatever we look at. It never occurs to us to take them off" (PI, 103). Notice that this passage does not suggest that we exchange our glasses for a better pair. We should simply take them off, for our "uncorrected" way of viewing the world was adequate to begin with.

Yet, as Wittgenstein saw, an incorrect way of viewing things can become deeply entrenched and hence difficult to dislodge. The parts of a philosophical perspective are intermeshed, so, even if one support

34

is dislodged, others remain to bear its burden. Worse yet, under pressure, philosophical positions can mutate into new positions embodying the same basic misapprehensions. Furthermore, in the grip of a philosophical commitment, criticisms that should count as decisive are treated as difficulties that can be resolved only after a very long, very difficult, and, of course, extremely subtle conceptual investigation. For these and other reasons, only a complete global reorientation can break the spell of a *picture that holds us captive* (PI, 115). Invoking a comparison with relativity theory, Wittgenstein puts it this way: "(One might say: the axis of reference of our examination must be rotated, but about the fixed point of our real need)" (PI, 108).

I think that the deep entrenchment of philosophical orientations – their resistance to direct refutation – helps explain the complexity of Wittgenstein's own writings. His attacks often lack the structure of direct arguments because their targets are often resistant to direct arguments. His writing is complex and shifting because its target is complex and shifting.

Employing another simile, Wittgenstein often compares his procedures with therapy – in particular, psychological therapy: "The philosopher's treatment of a question is like the treatment of an illness" (PI, 255). And, more famously:

The real discovery is the one that makes me capable of stopping doing philosophy when I want to. – The one that gives philosophy peace, so that it is no longer tormented by questions which bring *itself* in question. – Instead, we now demonstrate a method, by examples; and the series of examples can be broken off. – Problems are solved (difficulties eliminated), not a *single* problem.

There is not a philosophical method, though there are indeed methods, like different therapies. (PI, 133)

Taking him at his word, Wittgenstein is not attempting to replace earlier philosophical theories by one of his own. His aim is not to supply a new and better pair of glasses, but, instead, to convince us that none is needed. I take this to be the *core* idea of Wittgenstein's later philosophy as it appears in the *Philosophical Investigations* – and in the *Remarks on the Foundations of Mathematics* as well.

I realize, of course, that by concentrating on the therapeutic – purely negative – side of Wittgenstein's later philosophy, many will think that I am missing its most important aspect – the doctrine that relates meaning to use. "For a *large* class of cases – though not for all – in which we employ the word 'meaning' it can be defined thus: the meaning of a word is its use in the language" (PI, 43). There are those who think it possible to take passages of this kind and build upon them a substantive theory of meaning – a theory that can, in turn, be used to solve metaphysical problems. The leading representative of this program has been Michael Dummett. Concerning his relationship to Wittgenstein, he writes:

We all stand, or should stand, in the shadow of Wittgenstein, in the same way that much earlier generations once stood in the shadow of Kant; . . . Some things in his philosophy, however, I cannot see any reason for accepting: one is the belief that philosophy, as such, must never criticize but only describe. This belief was fundamental in the sense that it determined the whole manner in which, in his later writings, he discussed philosophical problems; not sharing it, I could not respect his work as I do if I regarded his arguments and insights as depending on the truth of that belief.[2]

It is because of his disagreement on this point that Dummett acknowledges that his own program is, in an important sense, "anti-Wittgensteinian."

Yet, as the closing sentence indicates, Dummett still takes his enterprise to be Wittgensteinian in some fundamental way. Starting from passages like §43, Dummett attempts to construct what he calls "a model of meaning" (Dummett 1991, 14–15) and then, with this in hand, he tries to use it to solve – or at least clarify – metaphysical controversies. I wish to suggest that this aspect of Dummett's position is as deeply anti-Wittgensteinian as his acknowledged rejection of Wittgenstein's descriptivism. Wittgenstein's later philosophy contains no theory of meaning, nor does the resolution of philosophical perplexities wait upon the construction of such a theory. My assumption is that Wittgenstein was in earnest when he made remarks of the following kind:

Philosophy simply puts everything before us, and neither explains nor deduces anything. – Since everything lies open to view there is nothing to explain. For what is hidden, for example, is of no interest to us. . . . (PI, 126)

The work of the philosopher consists in assembling reminders for a particular purpose. (PI, 127)

If one tried to advance *theses* in philosophy, it would never be possible to debate them, because everyone would agree to them. (PI, 128)[3]

Though Wittgenstein's criticisms of philosophy are multifaceted and complex, at least for convenience I shall divide them into two broad categories: the first is an attack on what I shall call *referentialism*, the second is an attack on what I shall call, for want of a better name, *logical perfectionism*.

(i) *Referentialism*, as I shall use this word, is the view that the *presumptive* role of words is to stand for or refer to things, and the *presumptive* role of sentences is to picture or represent how things stand to each other. I use the word "presumptive" because it is probably hard to find a philosopher worth taking seriously who held that *all* words stand for things or that *all* sentences represent how things stand to one another. Rather, philosophers have often uncritically adopted this perspective in areas where it does not apply, with the result that philosophical confusion ensues. Wittgenstein points to the writings of St. Augustine and to his own *Tractatus* as examples of this tendency.

(ii) As I shall use the expression, *logical perfectionism* refers to the view, often tacitly assumed, that the rules underlying and governing our language must have an ideal structure – they must, for example, be absolutely rigorous and cover all possible cases. Here Wittgenstein speaks of our "tendency to sublime the logic of our language" (PI, 38). Wittgenstein associates this view with Frege and, again, with his own *Tractatus*. As we shall see, Wittgenstein's attacks on referentialism and logical perfectionism are interwoven in complex and subtle ways, and thus their separation is somewhat arbitrary. Still, these categories provide a convenient scheme of organization.

## II AGAINST REFERENTIALISM

### Names and objects

The attack upon what I have called referentialism opens the *Philosophical Investigations*. After citing a passage from St. Augustine's *Confessions*, Wittgenstein remarks:

These words, it seems to me, give us a particular picture of the essence of human language. It is this: the individual words in language name objects – sentences are combinations of such names. – In this picture of language we find the roots of the following idea: Every word has a meaning. The meaning is correlated with the word. It is the object for which the word stands. (PI, 1)

Wittgenstein then adds: "Augustine does not speak of there being any differences between kinds of words."

To counter this tendency to think that all words work in the same (referential) way, Wittgenstein immediately introduces a language game where words function in transparently different ways.

I send someone shopping. I give him a slip marked "five red apples." He takes the slip to the shopkeeper, who opens a drawer marked "apples"; then he looks up the word "red" in a table and finds a colour sample opposite it; then he says the series of cardinal numbers – I assume that he knows them by heart – up to the word "five" and for each number he takes an apple of the same color as the sample out of the drawer. – It is in this and similar ways that one operates with words.[4]

In the next entry Wittgenstein tells us that the Augustinian picture of language can be viewed in two ways: as "a primitive idea of the way [our actual] language functions" or as "the idea of a language more primitive than ours." Illustrating the second point, he presents a new language game where, as he says, "the description [of language] given by St. Augustine is right." In this language game, a builder calls out such words as "slab" or "beam" and an assistant then brings the builder a slab or beam. Wittgenstein draws a modest conclusion from this comparison between these two language games: "Augustine, we might say, does describe a system of communication; only not everything that we call language is this system" (PI, 3). He then adds that this description of language might be appropriate, "but only for this narrowly circumscribed region" of language.

But Wittgenstein soon deepens his criticism of the Augustinian picture by challenging its conception of naming itself. In that picture, as we saw, the meaning of a name is the object it stands for. That, however, cannot be right, for ordinary names – say names of people, since a name can continue to have a meaning after its bearer ceases to exist.

It is important to note that the word "meaning" is being used illicitly if it is used to signify the thing that "corresponds" to the word. That is to confound the meaning of a name with the *bearer* of the name. When Mr. N. N.

dies, one says that the bearer of the name dies, not that the meaning dies. (PI, 40)

So there are at least two things wrong with the Augustinian picture of language: Naming does not provide an adequate model for *all* uses of language, and this picture does not give an adequate account even for *naming* itself. Now let us suppose that Wittgenstein is right in these claims – as he surely is. What relevance do they have for philosophy?

This may seem an odd question to ask at the end of a century in which philosophers have been obsessed with problems concerning the nature of language, but, still, it is worth asking explicitly. Wittgenstein himself answered it in fundamentally different ways in his earlier and later writings. In the *Tractatus* he held that the analysis of language could reveal both the underlying structure of thought and the underlying structure of reality concomitant with it. That the study of language – in particular, its analysis – can *further* philosophical activities is the fundamental assumption of classical analytic philosophy. A second, opposing, reason for philosophers to study language is not to further the philosophical enterprise, but to curb it. "Philosophy is a battle against the bewitchment of our intelligence by means of language" (PI, 109). Of course, a compromise might be struck between these two approaches. Pointing out misunderstandings of language can be used to block bad philosophizing; attaining a correct understanding can be used to promote good philosophy. Many philosophers writing today (Dummett, Wright, Peacock, and others – all of whom acknowledge Wittgenstein as an important influence) embrace this compromise. As far as I can see, Wittgenstein, in his later writings, showed no interest in this middle ground.

To return to the original question: What *philosophical* difference does it make if a philosopher supposes (falsely, as Wittgenstein thinks) that naming presents the fundamental paradigm of how words have meaning and, furthermore, that the meaning of a proper name is just the object it stands for? Wittgenstein traces a number of persistent philosophical errors to these related mistakes. The first concerns the perplexity that arises when we use proper names for things that no longer exist or, perhaps, never existed. Wittgenstein imagines someone under the spell of the referential picture of names reasoning as follows:

If "Excalibur" is the name of an object, this object no longer exists when Excalibur is broken in pieces; and as no object would then correspond to the name it would have no meaning. But then the sentence "Excalibur has a sharp blade" would contain a word that had no meaning, and hence the sentence would be nonsense. But it does make sense; so there must always be something corresponding to the words of which it consists. So the word "Excalibur" must disappear when the sense is analyzed and its place be taken by words which name simples. It will be reasonable to call these words the real names. (PI, 39)

Here one begins with the belief that the meaning of a proper name is its bearer – a belief based, perhaps, on the fact that proper names commonly do have bearers and are typically used to refer to them. We next note that some names lack bearers, but, for all that, sentences containing them can still be significant. This presents two choices: (i) We can abandon the claim that the meaning of a proper name is the object for which it stands and then try to give an alternative account of proper names that allows them to have meaning even in the absence of a bearer, or (ii) we can continue to accept the referential account of names and try to find a method of analysis that makes apparent bearerless names disappear. But a problem remains on the second approach. Even if the sentence so analyzed contains only names that *in fact* have bearers, one of these bearers might go out of existence and the original problem of meaning-loss would be posed anew. How could the meaning of the sentence "NN is the son of MM" go from being meaningful to being meaningless simply through MM's demise? This, together with other considerations, leads to the idea that, in a proper notation, all potentially bearerless proper names (i.e., virtually every word we commonly call a proper name) must be analyzed away, to be replaced by names (if any) which, in principle, can not suffer reference loss.[5]

This is not the end of the story, for the demand for bearer-guaranteed proper names can lead to the idea that the demonstratives "this" and "that" are genuine proper names – an idea mocked in §45.

The demonstrative "this" can never be without a bearer. It might be said: "so long as there is a *this*, the word 'this' has a meaning too, whether *this* is simple or complex." – But that does not make the word into a name. On the contrary: for a name is not used with, but only explained by means of, the gesture of pointing. (PI, 45)

As Wittgenstein remarks in the next section, this referential view of language can also lead to the introduction of entities possessing just those features that guarantee that they will not let their counterpart names down by going out of existence. Here Wittgenstein speaks of "both Russell's 'individuals' and my 'objects' " (PI, 46). Both do exactly the job that needs to be done. Tractarian objects, for example, being eternal, secure language against the threat of reference failure. With this, they secure language against the possibility of meaning failure that the possibility of reference failure supposedly carries with it. Being unchanging, they prevent arbitrary meaning shift. Being simple, they provide the stopping place for analysis. Et cetera.

There were, of course, other commitments beyond the reference theory of name-meaning and the picture theory of sentence-meaning that contributed to the philosophical construct presented in the *Tractatus*. Wittgenstein's commitment to the strictness of logical rules and, generally, to definiteness of sense played a crucial role as well. This will be a topic for close examination in the second part of this essay. Here we can note how the referential picture of language creates and continues to drive an illegitimate philosophical enterprise – an enterprise that can consume the intellectual energies of thinkers of the first order over many years.

What is Wittgenstein's alternative to the referential account of proper names? His answer, roughly, is that our use of proper names is governed by a loose set of descriptions, and just as a descriptive expression can be meaningful even though nothing falls under it, so too a proper name can be meaningful even if it lacks a bearer. The distinctive feature of this account, which sets it apart from similar views found in the writings of Frege and Russell, is that the set of descriptions can form a loose, shifting cluster and thus lack a definite or determinate sense. This rejection of definite sense for proper names is, however, part of a general critique of the dogma of definiteness of sense and is better discussed under the heading of *logical perfectionism*.

### Expressing the mental

Another area where, according to Wittgenstein, the referential view of language has generated philosophical confusion concerns our talk about the mental. When we ascribe a pain, a thought, an intention, et cetera, to ourselves, it seems, except in the most extraordinary circumstances, that we cannot be mistaken in this ascription. Things seem very different with the ascription of mental predicates to others. We are not, as philosophers commonly say, "directly aware" of their pains, thoughts, and intentions, and we ascribe such predicates to them only inferentially. Reflecting on these matters, we find ourselves inclined to say such things as "I can only *believe that* someone else is in pain, but I *know* it if I am" (PI, 303).[6] This further inclines us to suppose that we attribute mental predicates to others using some form of analogical reasoning. Unfortunately, under scrutiny, such analogical arguments appear too weak to give us good reason to suppose that another person has what I have when I attribute, say, pain to both of us. These considerations can lead one to skepticism concerning the contents (even existence) of other minds. To avoid skepticism, we might adopt a behavioristic analysis of ascription of mental predicates to others – a view which, in one of its forms, equates the possession of mental qualities in others with their dispositions to behave in certain ways. Yet behaviorism seems wrong. When I ascribe pain to another, it's a *feeling* I am ascribing to her – a feeling *I* have had and now, I suppose, *she* is having. Behavior may be my only evidence for such an ascription, but it is not what I am talking about. But the ascription of pain to another seems to depend upon some form of analogical reasoning, and the unsatisfactory character of this reasoning again leads us to a familiar form of skepticism.

Wittgenstein attempts to undercut these disputes concerning the mental by showing that they depend upon a faulty, referential view of language:

"But you will surely admit that there is a difference between pain-behavior accompanied by pain and pain-behavior without any pain?" – Admit it? What greater difference can there be? – "And yet you again and again reach the conclusion that the sensation itself is a *nothing*." – It is not a *something*, but not a *nothing* either! The conclusion was only that a nothing would serve just as well as a something about which nothing could be said. We have only rejected the grammar which tries to force itself on us here. (PI, 304)

The passage continues in a way that is of particular interest to our present concerns:

The paradox disappears only if we make a radical break with the idea that language always functions in one way, always serves the same purpose: to convey thoughts – which may be about houses, pains, good and evil, or anything else you please.

The clear implication of this passage is that philosophical problems about the mental have arisen through treating mental ascriptions on the model of talk concerning chairs, houses, and the like. Wittgenstein's point, then, is not to deny, for example, that people remember things; it is to reject the picture of remembering as an inner process.

"But you surely cannot deny that, for example, in remembering, an inner process takes place." – What gives the impression that we want to deny anything? When one says "Still, an inner process does take place here" – one wants to go on: "After all, you *see* it." And it is this inner process that one means by the word "remembering." – The impression that we wanted to deny something arises from our setting our faces against the picture of the 'inner process.' What we deny is that the picture of the inner process gives us the correct idea of the use of the word "to remember." We say that this picture with its ramifications stands in the way of our seeing the use of the word as it is. (PI, 305)

A few sections later he expands on this, saying:

How does the philosophical problem about mental processes and states and about behaviourism arise? – The first step is the one that altogether escapes notice. We talk of processes and states and leave their nature undecided. Sometime perhaps we shall know more about them – we think. But that is just what commits us to a particular way of looking at the matter. For we have a definite concept of what it means to learn to know a process better. (The decisive movement in the conjuring trick has been made, and it was the very one that we thought quite innocent.) (PI, 308)

This is as clear an instance as any of Wittgenstein citing what I have called the referential picture of language as the source of philosophical perplexity. As long as that picture holds us captive, we will be unable to give a correct account of the way in which our talk about the mental functions, and until that is done, the mysteries of the mental will remain.

What we expect next, of course, is for Wittgenstein to replace this false picture of how mental terms function with a correct one. Furthermore, to be true to his methods, this should consist in pointing to commonplaces that the false picture screens from us. Wittgenstein makes some gestures in this direction by suggesting that the utterance "I am in pain" is used to *express* pain rather than describe it.

How do words *refer* to sensations? – There doesn't seem to be any problem here; don't we talk about sensations every day, and give them names? But how is the connexion between the name and the thing named set up? This question is the same as: how does a human being learn the meaning of the names of sensations? – of the word "pain" for example. Here is one possibility: words are connected with the primitive, the natural, expressions of the sensation and used in their place. A child has hurt himself and he cries; and then adults talk to him and teach him exclamations and, later, sentences. They teach the child new pain-behaviour.

"So you are saying that the word 'pain' really means crying?" – On the contrary: the verbal expression of pain replaces crying and does not describe it. (PI, 244)

The interpretation of this and like passages is controversial, but the general idea seems to be this: Humans naturally respond to injuries in largely common ways. For example, they wince and cry out in a characteristic manner. These common (or primitive) responses provide the basis for training a child to use the word "pain" and related words. The key idea is that this training consists in shaping and articulating these primitive responses into a new form of "pain behavior." Saying I am in pain expresses my pain, it does not describe it. Similarly, saying "I expect him any minute" is an expression of my expectation – a part of my expectant behavior and does not describe it; et cetera.

In fact, PI, 221 admits of two different readings depending upon how much weight one places on the expression "Here is one possibility." On an austere reading, he is *merely* suggesting a possibility and is in no way committing himself to a substantive position. To use an expression he employs elsewhere, he is merely presenting us with an "object of comparison" (PI, 131) that is intended to help break the spell of a fixed way of looking at things. This reading conforms with the general line of interpretation presented in this essay.[7] On the other side, there are a great many passages in the *Philosophical Investigations* and in his other writings that suggest that Wittgenstein was committed – in outline at least – to something like an expressivist account of first person mental utterances.[8] Elsewhere I have attributed such a substantive view to Wittgenstein. I have also expressed reservations concerning it.[9] The question, then, is whether Wittgenstein, in this area at least, has transgressed his self-imposed restrictions against substantive philosophical theorizing. I am inclined to think that he has. Having said this, I do not think that the transgression, if it occurs, is seriously compromising. According to Wittgenstein, problems about the mental arise because of the uncritical assumption that mental terms get their meanings through referring to "hidden" mental processes. On that assumption, problems about the mental are intractable. Wittgenstein's comparison of statements about the mental with natural expressions of feeling is an attempt to break the spell of one way of viewing such discourse through noting similarities to certain nonreferential uses of language. A further commitment to the substantive truth of a theory based upon this comparison, though out of place, does not destroy the therapeutic role of the comparison.[10]

### Logic and mathematics

Since this topic will be treated in detail elsewhere in this volume, I shall not go deeply into Wittgenstein's complex views on logic and mathematics. I shall only make some general remarks about the way in which Wittgenstein's antireferentialism bears on these topics. Wittgenstein's antireferentialism with respect to logic and mathematics goes back to the *Tractatus*. There he remarked: "My fundamental idea is that the 'logical constants' are not representatives; that there can be no representatives of the *logic* of facts" (TLP, 4.0312). Later, at 4.441, he says, "There are no 'logical objects'" – a claim he repeats at 5.4. But if that is right, what are we to make of *propositions of logic*; if they are not about logical objects, what are they true of? Wittgenstein's answer is that they are not true of anything at all.

Tautology and contradiction are the limiting cases – indeed the disintegration – of the combination of signs. (TLP, 4.466)

But in fact all the propositions of logic say the same thing, to wit nothing. (TLP, 5.43)

The *Tractatus* contains a parallel line concerning the truth of mathematics:

Mathematics is a logical method.

The propositions of mathematics are equations, and therefore pseudo-propositions. (TLP, 6.2)

Then, quite remarkably, this passage:

Indeed in real life a mathematical proposition is never what we want. Rather, we make use of mathematical propositions *only* in inferences from propositions that do not belong to mathematics to others that likewise do not belong to mathematics.

(In philosophy the question, "What do we actually use this word or this proposition for?" repeatedly leads to valuable insights.) (TLP, 6.211)

Reading the opening sections of the *Philosophical Investigations*, it is easy to assume that the particular picture of language that Wittgenstein attributes to St. Augustine he also attributes to himself in his Tractarian period. That is right, of course, about various features of that system, including, for example, its treatment of proper names. Yet with respect to the propositions of logic and mathematics he began to free himself of this picture of language. He did this, as the closing parenthetical remark indicates, by examining what "we actually use this word or proposition for."

It seems, then, that in the *Tractatus* Wittgenstein had already won through to ideas about logic and mathematics characteristic of his later writings, and done so for similar reasons. That, however, is not right. Though he rejected the referential picture at one level, he restored it at another. This comes out in Wittgenstein's doctrine of showing:

The fact that the propositions of logic are tautologies *shows* the formal – logical – properties of language and the world. (TLP, 6.12)

The logic of the world, which is shown in tautologies by the propositions of logic, is shown in equations by mathematics. (TLP, 6.22)

Here a naive referentialism seems to be replaced by a sneaky, back-door referentialism. Propositions of logic and mathematics are still seen in the guise of propositions, but as failed propositions. Furthermore, it is through revealing themselves as failed propositions that they are able to do something no proper proposition is able to do: reveal to us the necessary structures of thought and reality. This, I think, is a striking example of a philosophical commitment being transformed under pressure, maintaining its grip even when nominally rejected.

The situation is altogether different in Wittgenstein's later reflections on these topics as they are found in their most fully developed form in the *Remarks on the Foundations of Mathematics*. Instead of viewing mathematical expressions as failed attempts to state or describe necessary connections, Wittgenstein treats them as perfectly successful attempts to do something else. Again, according to Wittgenstein, philosophers of mathematics (I suppose from Plato to the present) have been misled by grammatical analogies:

Might we not do arithmetic without having the idea of uttering arithmetical *propositions*, and without ever having been struck by the similarity between a multiplication and a proposition?

Should we not shake our heads, though, when someone shewed us a multiplication done wrong, as we do when someone tells us it is raining, if it is not raining? – Yes; and here is a point of connexion. But we also make gestures to stop our dog, e.g. when he behaves as we do not wish.

We are used to saying "2 times 2 is 4," and the verb "is" makes this into a proposition, and apparently establishes a close kinship with everything that we call a 'proposition.' Whereas it is a matter only of a very superficial relationship. (RFM I, appendix I, 4)

I have quoted this passage in full, because it is a model of Wittgenstein's method of noting similarities and marking differences. "2 times 2 is 4" is similar to "It is raining" in that both contain the word "is." He further notes that both multiplications and reports of the weather can be "done wrong" and, for this reason, call forth gestures of correction – perhaps a negative shake of the head. Similarities of this kind tempt us to assimilate both utterances under a single paradigm. Yet a dog can also be corrected using a negative gesture or a negative word, and, anyway, we all know the use of the utterance "2 times 2 is 4" – it expresses a multiplication rule. It's something that we *go by* when performing calculations. Its use is something that we have acquired through a particular training – a training different in fundamental ways from the training needed to speak accurately about the weather. Reflections of this kind are intended to cure us of the habit of assimilating mathematical expressions under a misleading paradigm of assertions about how things are. If Wittgenstein is right, this assimilation casts even the simplest mathematical expressions in the wrong light and thus makes them seem mysterious.

Here it might be useful to return to the opening section of the *Philosophical Investigations*, where Wittgenstein briefly alludes to numbers used in counting. There he tells us that the person sent to the shop "says the series of cardinal numbers – I assume that he knows them by heart – up to the word 'five' and for each number he takes an apple of the same colour as the same out of the drawer" (PI, 1). This example was intended to show that words do not all work in the same way, in particular, they do not all serve to stand for or represent objects. I think that Wittgenstein believed that this simple language game makes it evident that the word "five" does not function in this way. I also think that Wittgenstein thought that once our conceptual blinders are removed, we will see that mathematical expressions are better treated as rules (or better associated with rules) than treated as assertions (or associated with them), for taken as rules they are not mysterious – taken as assertions, they can be.

One brief note before closing this section. Throughout this discussion of Wittgenstein's antireferentialism, I have avoided the use of the expression "antirealism." I have done this because *antirealism* is now commonly associated with a specific research project, pursued most notably by Michael Dummett and Crispin Wright, of using intuitionistic logic as the basis for a theory of meaning. Both Dummett and Wright find at least pointers toward such a theory in Wittgenstein's later writings. They may be right in this. Still, it is important to note that antireferentialism, as I have described it, does not entail antirealism in the robust sense found in the writings of Dummett and Wright. A philosopher can hold that numerals are not referring terms and that arithmetic expressions, for example, function as rules without thereby placing any limitations on the form that mathematical rules, proofs, et cetera, are allowed to take. Nothing prevents an antireferentialist from accepting the rules and laws of classical logic and classical mathematics. That Wittgenstein was an antireferentialist with respect to mathematics strikes me as being quite beyond doubt. Whether he was also an antirealist, and, if so, in what way and to what extent he was an antirealist are much more difficult questions to answer. In any case, it is not part of my present charge to do so.[11]

## III  LOGICAL PERFECTIONISM

### Rules and meaning

If we try to understand the meaning of a word or expression by examining its use in the language, it seems natural to look for the rules that govern the use of such a word or expression. Wittgenstein explicitly makes this connection in *On Certainty:*

A meaning of a word is a kind of employment of it.
  For it is what we learn when the word is incorporated into our language. (OC, 61)

That is why there exists a correspondence between the concepts "rule" and "meaning." (OC, 62)

In a number of places in the *Philosophical Investigations*, Wittgenstein illustrates this correspondence between rules and meaning by comparing words with pieces in chess:

We are talking about the spatial and temporal phenomenon of language, not about some non-spatial, non-temporal phantasm. . . . But we talk about it as we do about the pieces in chess when we are stating the rules of the game, not describing their physical properties.
  The question "What is a word really?" is analogous to "What is a piece in chess?" (PI, 108)

At the same time, he recognizes a danger in treating our actual language on an analogy with "games and calculi which have fixed rules": "But if you say that our languages only *approximate* to such calculi you are standing on the very brink of a misunderstanding. For then it may look as if what we were talking about were an *ideal* language" (PI, 81). This misunderstanding can take a second form: instead of supposing that our actual language is only an approximation to an ideal language, we can suppose that it already embodies such a system of clear and strict rules, only in a manner deeply hidden from us: "The strict and clear rules of the logical structure of propositions appear to us as something in the background – hidden in the medium of the understanding. I already see them (even though through a medium): for I understand the propositional sign, I use it to say something" (PI, 102). Later, he speaks of the "crystalline purity of logic," remarking that, of course it was not "a *result of investigation:* it was a requirement" (PI, 107).

It seems to me that Wittgenstein's assault on the presumed purity, sublimity, or, as I have called it, perfection of logic cuts deeper than his attack on naive referentialism. While holding that language use is a rule-governed activity, he further holds that these rules need not be clear, need not be complete, and, perhaps, need not even be consistent. I shall discuss these topics under the headings of the *indeterminacy, underdetermination,* and *incoherence* of rules. I shall conclude by examining the way referentialism and logical perfectionism can combine to create the illusion of ideal entities as the *referential counterparts* of rules.

### The indeterminacy of rules

At §65 Wittgenstein has an interlocutor complain:

"You take the easy way out! You talk about all sorts of language-games, but have nowhere said what the essence of a language-game, and hence of language, is: what is common to all these activities, and what makes them into language or parts of language." (PI, 65)

He replies:

And this is true. – Instead of producing something common to all that we call language, I am saying that these phenomena have no one thing in common which makes us use the same word for all, – but that they are *related* to one another in many different ways. And it is because of this relationship, or these relationships, that we call them all "language."

In §66 he compares our use of the word "language" with our use of the word "game," claiming that an investigation shows that games lack any common feature running through them in virtue of which they are all called games. What an examination of the actual use of this term reveals instead is "a complicated network of similarities overlapping and crisscrossing: sometimes overall similarities, sometimes similarities in detail." In §67 he tells us that he "can think of no better expression to characterize these similarities than "family resemblance." In this section he further claims that "kinds of number form a family in the same way." Then, at §108 he makes this more general remark: "We see that what we call 'sentence' and 'language' has not the formal unity that I imagined, but is the family of structures more or less related to one another" (PI, 108).

These passages concerning family resemblance have attracted a great deal of attention, often with philosophers arguing whether Wittgenstein was right or not in applying this notion to particular instances.[12] It is important, however, to place this discussion in the broader context of his attack on what he calls the *"preconceived idea* of the crystalline purity" of logic. The continuation of the last cited passage explicitly makes this connection:

> But what becomes of logic now? Its rigour seems to be giving way here. – But in that case doesn't logic altogether disappear? – For how can it lose its rigour? Of course not by our bargaining any of its rigour out of it. – The *preconceived idea* of crystalline purity can only be removed by turning our whole examination round.

Wittgenstein's point is that our language actually does work – and work satisfactorily – without conforming to the logician's demand for rigor.

Wittgenstein's account of proper names touched on earlier should be seen as part of the same program of desublimating the logic of our language. On the contemporary scene, Wittgenstein's discussion of proper names is usually seen as an anticipation of John Searle's "cluster theory."[13] And Searle, as he acknowledges, drew inspiration from Wittgenstein's writings. It is worth noting, however, that Wittgenstein's concerns are fundamentally different from Searle's. For Searle, giving a correct account of the way proper names function is part of a general project of providing a theory of meaning for natural languages. Wittgenstein, I have suggested, has no such goal – indeed, he would reject it. The point of Wittgenstein's discussion is not to give a correct account of proper names, but to cite a striking instance of language being employed successfully in the absence of determinate rules. This becomes clear when we examine the general conclusion (or moral) that Wittgenstein draws from these reflections: "I use the name 'N' without a *fixed* meaning. (But that detracts as little from its usefulness, as it detracts from that of a table that it stands on four legs instead of three and so sometimes wobbles)" (PI, 79).

It is important to see the rhetorical force of the examples that Wittgenstein uses in discussing family resemblance. He begins, innocuously enough, with games. Our predisposition to essentialism may lead us to suppose that there must be something that all games have in common that makes them games. Yet if Wittgenstein convinces us that games form only a family, the loss may not seem great. We might be content to say that ordinary language is defective in this regard. But to be told "numbers form a family in the same way" and that names can be used "without a fixed meaning" is to discover indeterminacy of meaning where we would least expect it. That discovery should nullify the presumption that the search for determinate rules and definite sense should always be our starting place (or default mode, as it were), only to be abandoned as a last resort.

### The underdetermination of rules

Closely connected with the idea that we may sometimes use words without clear or definite rules is the thought that our rules may sometimes be underdetermined or incomplete in the sense of leaving gaps.

I say "There is a chair." What if I go up to it, meaning to fetch it, and it suddenly disappears from sight? – "So it wasn't a chair, but some kind of illusion." – But in a few moments we see it again and are able to touch it and so on. – "So the chair was there after all and its disappearance was some kind of illusion." – But suppose that after a time it disappears again – or seems to disappear. What are we to say now? Have you rules ready for such cases – rules saying whether one may use the word "chair" to include this kind of thing? But do we miss them when we use the word "chair"; and are we to say that we do not really attach any meaning to this word, because we are not equipped with rules for every possible application of it? (PI, 80)

The problem here is not one of vagueness – we are not inclined to treat this instance as a borderline case of being a chair. We are stumped as to what to say at all. We have a similar reaction when philosophers present us with science-fiction examples concerning personal identity. Suppose a machine can turn a single living human being into two living human beings, both indistinguishable from the first human being except that each has only half of the original person's matter – the other half being supplied by the machine. Are each of these new human beings the same person as the original human being? Here we are inclined to say various things. If we are struck by the fact that the original person died in the machine (with his constituent atoms completely reorganized), then we will be inclined to say that neither person is identical with the original person. If we are struck, however, by various continuities in the mental life of these creatures, we may be inclined to the opposite conclusion. Reflection on examples of this kind has led many philosophers to suppose that personal identity must be a deep and subtle notion that demands a deep and subtle analysis.[14] A Wittgensteinian alternative is that the rules governing our application of the concept of personal identity simply do not cover this case. In this sense, we can say that the rules governing the use of this concept are incomplete. Yet it is an innocent incompleteness that can be left standing until human duplicators present themselves as a practical problem. The rudimentary mistake is to suppose that the rules governing this concept must already cover all cases – something we would see if we understood these rules adequately. It is even a mistake to take the assumption of the completeness of rules as a regulative principle. If anything, a presumption should run in the opposite direction. Since it is easy to find examples where the rules governing the use of a concept do not cover all cases, and since it is clear that these supposed gaps do not affect the practical employment of these concepts, we should be cautious in supposing that the rules governing a concept possess greater completeness (and, we can add, greater determinacy) than the actual employment of that concept demands. I think that this is one of Wittgenstein's fundamental insights, but one whose implications have not been adequately appreciated – even by many who think of themselves as working in his shadow.

## The incoherence of rules

Wittgenstein sometimes seems to condone contradictions – or at least not to take their threat with the seriousness that others do. I think that this is right. Appreciating why exhibits the depth of his critique of traditional ways of doing philosophy.

It will be useful to begin with an example. Two people play a game with rules that are inconsistent in the following way: Situations can arise where the rules make incompatible demands – for example, a particular player is supposed to move, but also not allowed to move.

This need not happen in every game, but it is a possibility. We might say that such a system of rules is dilemma-prone.

Now let us suppose that by good fortune people playing this game do not encounter those instances where the rules yield incompatible demands. More interestingly, the point of the game might be such that there is no good reason for the players to bring about this situation. It could only arise if both players moved stupidly or pointlessly. Does the fact that this game is dilemma-prone show that it is not a real game? Most people would say no. We can next suppose that someone stumbles on the latent inconsistency and its existence becomes generally known. Would the game *then* cease to be a real game? Would it be restored to being a game only *after* the inconsistency in the rules was removed? The answer to both questions is no. People might simply note the inconsistency as a curiosity, then ignore it since, after all, it will make no difference in serious play.[15]

The question I wish to raise is this: Could our language, or at least some portions of it, be dilemma-prone in the way this game is? Beyond this, could the inconsistency be recognized yet ignored, just as the players of the game ignore the inconsistency in their rules? At various places Wittgenstein seems to suggest an affirmative answer to both these questions. The following passage from the *Remarks on the Foundations of Mathematics* provides a striking example of this:

Let us suppose that the Russellian contradiction had never been found. Now – is it quite clear that in that case we should have possessed a false calculus? For aren't there various possibilities here?

And suppose the contradiction had been discovered but we were not excited about it, and had settled e.g. that no conclusions were to be drawn from it. (As no one does draw conclusions from the "Liar.") Would this have been an obvious mistake?

"But in that case it isn't a proper calculus! It loses all *strictness!*" Well, not *all*. And it is only lacking in full strictness, if one has a particular ideal of rigour, wants a particular style in mathematics.[16] (RFM, V-12)

This passage is remarkable in a number of respects, but it is the closing sentence, with its reference to "a particular ideal of rigour," that interests me here. The thought that a formally defective system of rules is no system at all is not an empirical truth; in fact, on its face, it seems an empirical falsehood. I say that this *seems* to be an empirical falsehood because it could turn out that the actual rules governing our language do meet the logician's ideal of rigor. The error is to take the satisfaction of this ideal as a success condition on any proper account of the rules of our language – rejecting those that do not meet this standard, and giving high marks to those that approximate it, however exotic and arbitrary they may be in other respects.

### The referential counterparts of rules

In the previous section I have been concerned with Wittgenstein's attack on the philosopher's tendency to sublime the logic of our language – to treat the logical order as a "*super*-order between – so to speak – *super*-concepts" (PI, 97). I will conclude this discussion with a brief remark on a topic of first importance: our tendency to suppose that corresponding to our rules there exist ideal counterparts. What I have in mind appears in passages of the following kind:

You were inclined to use such expressions as: "The steps are *really* already taken, even before I take them in writing or orally or in thought." And it seemed as if they were in some *unique* way predetermined, anticipated – as only the act of meaning can anticipate reality. (PI, 188)

Later he speaks of "the idea that the beginning of a series is a visible section of rails invisibly laid to infinity," and he wonders where this idea comes from (PI, 218). His answer to this question is remarkably simple:

"All the steps are really already taken" means: I no longer have any choice. The rule, once stamped with a particular meaning, traces the lines along which it is to be followed through the whole of space. – But if something of this sort really were the case, how would it help?
    No; my description only made sense if it was to be understood symbolically. – I should have said: *This is how it strikes me.*
    When I obey a rule, I do not choose.
    I obey the rule *blindly.* (PI, 219)

The key passage here is the claim that the remark "only made sense if it was understood symbolically." An idea echoed two sections later: "My symbolical expression was really a mythological description of the use of a rule" (PI, 221). In employing a rule that I have mastered, I act as a matter of course. I write down a series of numbers. The actual sequence I produce, combined with the ability to produce more of the same, creates the picture of the members of the sequence already existing before I get to them. "This," as Wittgenstein says, "is how it strikes me." The crucial point is that this picture, however naturally it arises, *plays no role in the application of the rule.* In a manner of speaking, it is epiphenomenal. Even if we conjure up such a notion, it is the *result* of our ability to apply a rule, not its ground or support.

The notion of following a rule is central to Wittgenstein's later philosophy, but, as he saw, it is also a natural source of philosophical illusion. Pressures seem to come from every side to turn this notion into a super-concept. It is a central task of Wittgenstein's later philosophy to fight this tendency by showing that rules are neither sublime nor are they mysterious – though they may be complicated, as our life is.

NOTES

1 I shall, however, make occasional references to Wittgenstein's other works for the sake of comparison or elaboration. I have said almost nothing concerning the large secondary literature on this subject. Much that I say here has been said before by others and by myself. There is hardly a single point I make that at least some commentators might not challenge. It seems to me that extensive excursions into the secondary literature are ruled out by limitations of length, whereas selective comments would seem arbitrary. I have, therefore, concerned myself almost exclusively with primary texts.

2 Michael Dummett, *The Logical Basis of Metaphysics* (Cambridge, Mass.: Harvard University Press, 1991), p. xi.

3 In his *Wittgenstein on Mind and Language,* David G. Stern points out that such remarks about philosophy (indeed, some of these very remarks) were written as early as 1931. In this excellent study of Wittgenstein's philosophical development, Stern shows how these ideas were preserved and expanded as Wittgenstein's attempts to find a theory to replace the *Tractatus* gave way to the revolutionary idea that there is no task for such a theory to perform. All this, however, is Stern's story to tell. See David G. Stern, *Wittgenstein on Mind and Language* (New York: Oxford University Press, 1994).

4 The entry continues in the following remarkable way:

"But how does he know where and how he is to look up the word 'red' and what he is to do with the word 'five?' " – Well, I assume that he *acts* as I have described. Explanations come to an end somewhere. – But what is the meaning of the word 'five'? – no such thing was in question here, only how the word 'five' is used.

In these few sentences, Wittgenstein foreshadows three of his most fundamental ideas: the primacy of action over thought, the limits of explanation, and the identification of meaning with use. Much though not all of the *Philosophical Investigations* can be viewed as an extended elaboration on these themes introduced at the very start of his reflections.

5 The qualification "if any" is intended to leave open the possibility that sentences containing proper names could be analyzed into sentences containing no proper names at all, a possibility suggested by Wittgenstein in the TLP, 5.526.

6 In response, Wittgenstein presents the challenge "Just try – in a real case – to doubt someone else's fear or pain" (PI, 303).

7 It is also the reading favored by the editors of this volume.

8 Similar passages ranging over a wide variety of mental ascriptions occur throughout the *Philosophical Investigations* concerning, for example, fear and joy, 142; pain, 245, 288, 293, 302, 310, 317; sensations, 256; memory, 343; wishes, 441; expectation, 452–3; hope, 585; intention, 647; grief, p. 174; dreams, p. 184; mourning, p. 189; and recognition, p. 197. *Zettel* contains a large number of similar passages as well. Z, 488 is particularly interesting, since it gives a programmatic sketch of his general approach to mental predicates.

9 See Robert J. Fogelin, *Wittgenstein*, 2nd ed. (London: Routledge and Kegan Paul, 1987), ch. 13.

10 I am not entirely satisfied with this "compromise," but the text, as far as I can see, is genuinely perplexing. I discuss the question whether Wittgenstein, at times at least, violates his own strictures against substantive philosophizing in an appendix to *Pyrrhonian Reflections on Knowledge and Justification*. My conclusion is that he sometimes does – particularly in *On Certainty*, where I claim to detect considerable backsliding toward doing philosophy in the old way. See *Pyrrhonian Reflections on Knowledge and Justification* (New York: Oxford University Press, 1994), appendix II. In *Wittgenstein* (1976 and 1987) I make a similar claim about *certain aspects* of his so-called private language argument. But even if Wittgenstein is sometimes subject to his own strictures, this does not show that these strictures are unwarranted. What these lapses – if they occur – might show is that "battle against the bewitchment of our intelligence by means of language" is a serious engagement.

11 In Chapter 7 of this volume Cora Diamond argues for the stronger claim that Wittgenstein was not an antirealist (in the post-Dummett sense of the term).

12  For example, I have suggested that Wittgenstein's rather casual applica-
    tion of the notion of family resemblance to "our concepts in aesthetics or
    ethics" (PI, 77) is probably a mistake, since evaluative terms do not ex-
    press a loose cluster of descriptions but perform a different role in our
    language – roughly, to commend or prescribe. Though this still strikes
    me as being correct, I would put less weight on it now than I originally did,
    since the rules governing commending, assessing, evaluating, et cetera,
    often seem to be loose or indefinite in just the way Wittgenstein has in
    mind. If that is correct, then the right view of the function of evaluative
    terms would simply be a modulation of Wittgenstein's stated view. For
    my original reflections on these matters, see Fogelin, *Wittgenstein*, pp.
    136–8.

13  See John Searle, "Proper Names," *Mind* 67 (1958), pp. 166–73.

14  For two examples out of many, see Robert Nozick, *Philosophical Expla-
    nations* (Cambridge, Mass.: Harvard University Press, 1981), ch. 1, and
    Derek Parfit's book-length study *Reason and Persons* (Oxford: Claren-
    don Press, 1984).

15  This example was suggested to me by a passage in the RFM, III-77: "Let
    us suppose, however, that the game is such that whoever begins can
    always win by a particular simple trick, but this has not been realized; –
    so it is a game. Now someone draws our attention to it; – and it stops
    being a game." I remember discussing this passage and its extension to
    inconsistent games with Ruth Marcus in the early 1970s. She later cited
    it in her now-famous "Moral Dilemmas and Consistency" (*Journal of
    Philosophy* 77 [3], pp. 121–36). I was quite persuaded by her use of
    examples of this kind for dealing with moral dilemmas, but, as I recall,
    she was not persuaded by my use of them in dealing with logical para-
    doxes. I first ventured ideas along these lines – both as a reading of
    Wittgenstein and a position of independent interest – in an essay enti-
    tled "Hintikka's Game Theoretic Approach to Language," *Philosophy of
    Logic: Proceedings of the Third Bristol Conference on Critical Philoso-
    phy (1974)*, ed. Stephan Körner (Oxford: Basil Blackwell, 1976).

16  This is not an isolated passage expressing a view otherwise absent from
    Wittgenstein's writings. Just as strikingly, at RFM, V-28 he remarks:

    If a contradiction were now actually found in arithmetic – that would
    only prove that an arithmetic with *such* a contradiction in it could
    render very good service; and it will be better for us to modify our
    concept of the certainty required, than to say that it would really not yet
    have been a proper arithmetic.

# 2  Pictures, logic, and the limits of sense in Wittgenstein's *Tractatus*

Wittgenstein's enigmatic conception of sentences as pictures and his attempt to recast logic in essentially truth-functional terms have long fascinated readers of the *Tractatus*. I hope in this essay to clarify the content and motivation of Wittgenstein's view of sentences as pictures and to relate this conception to his views on logic. At the beginning of the foreword to the *Tractatus*, Wittgenstein tells his readers that the *Tractatus* is not a textbook, that perhaps only someone who has had the thoughts it expresses will understand it. The foreword also suggests that the *Tractatus* is in large measure a response to and critique of Frege's and Russell's views. My strategy then is to examine how aspects of the *Tractatus* emerge against the backdrop of problems that Frege's and Russell's views posed for Wittgenstein.

## I THE OLD LOGIC

Wittgenstein rejected Frege's and Russell's universalist conception of logic – what he disparaged as the old logic – while retaining their inchoate but guiding assumptions first that logic frames all thought, and second that it is possible to give a clear, completely explicit, and unambiguous expression to the contents judged true or false. To begin with, let us survey some of the leading features of the old logic and then consider briefly some of Wittgenstein's dissatisfactions with it.

On the universalist conception of logic, the logical laws that mediate demonstrative inference are maximally general truths.[1] That is, they are laws that generalize over all objects, properties, and relations; and their formulation requires only the topic-universal vocabulary needed to make statements on any topic whatsoever – for example, sign for conjunction and negation as well as quantifiers to express generality. This topic-universal vocabulary is the proprietary vocabulary of the science of logic and symbolizes the indefinably simple notions of logic, the logical constants. The quantifiers and variables in logical laws generalize without restriction over logical types. Thus, on a universalist view, there are no different universes of discourse for quantifiers; and no use is made of varying interpretations of a language. Indeed, Frege scorns talk of varying interpretations of sentences as a confused way of expressing what is properly said by the use of quantification, including quantification into predicate positions. As a result, contemporary semantic conceptions of logical truth and consequence are completely absent from the universalist view. On the universalist view, then, logic is thus a science in its own right, one that is directed at reality in the same way that physics is, but at reality's more general features.[2]

Laws of logic should mediate demonstrative inference in every science whatsoever. On the universalist conception, the maximal generality of logical laws secures their universal applicability. For example, to prove All cats are warm-blooded, from "All cats are mammals," and "All mammals are warm-blooded," the universalist logician first proves the generalization:

> For all F, G, and H, if all F are G, then if all G are H, all F are H.

Here Frege understands the letters "F," "G," and "H" to be quantified variables over concepts. Three applications of the logical inference of substitution to this generalization yield an instance of it that contains designations for the three specialized concepts that figure in the premises and desired conclusion. Two applications of modus ponens to this instance and the premises then yield the conclusion. The science of logic, by dint of the generality of its fundamental laws, thus provides a framework that encompasses all the sciences. And for Frege, truth is scientific truth – there are no truths outside of this framework, no truths not subject to logic.

Frege aimed to formulate logical principles in such a way that their application would force the fully explicit statement of the premises on which any logically inferred conclusion rests. He found that the irregularity and ambiguity in the colloquial expression of topic-universal logical notions to be an obstacle to this enterprise. He thus devised his logical notation, his *begriffsschrift*, as an alternative to everyday language. Having devised the begriffsschrift, Frege formulates logic along the lines of a formal system via axioms and inference rules. Frege's axioms are a selection of maximally general truths. The axioms should not themselves stand in need of proof: they should be self-evident in that anyone who understands them should simply recognize them to be true. The inference rules are self-evidently truth-preserving, notationally specified manipulations of begriffsschrift sentences. Although the begriffsschrift itself contains just the vocabulary required for the science of logic, it can, by the addition of the requisite specialized vocabulary, be expanded to incorporate any science and any line of demonstrative reasoning.[3] The begriffsschrift is thus a framework for a language in which to say everything that can be said. Its limits are the limits of sense.

Before proceeding to use logic to state proofs, Frege and Russell alike find themselves compelled to talk about logic, about their fundamental logical notions, and about the intended construal of their notations. In thus erecting logic, they face what Henry Sheffer, in his review of the second edition of *Principia Mathematica*, calls the logocentric predicament: *"In order to give an account of logic, we must presuppose and employ logic."*[4] Every statement setting forth an alleged fact must be subject to logic, including those that communicate the fundamental ideas required fully to understand logic. All of Frege's and Russell's instruction and foundational explanations, to the extent that they indeed communicate truths, must have a place in the framework that logic, on the universalist conception, provides for every statement.

Just here Frege and Russell encounter a difficulty or awkwardness that emerges most starkly in their discussions of type-theoretic distinctions. Both Frege and Russell adopt type-theoretic formulations of logic in which quantificational generality, while intrinsically unrestricted, is also intrinsically stratified. Loosely speaking, in a type-theoretic formulation of logic there is one vocabulary of variables for generalizing over individuals, another for properties of individuals, still another for properties of these properties, and so forth; but there are no variables that generalize over all entities, individuals and properties alike. As a consequence, it is impossible to describe this type-theoretic hierarchy within a type-theoretic formulation of logic. For the description of this hierarchy requires the use of variables ranging over entities of different types, as my brief description itself exhibits. Thus, there appear to be facts – facts about distinctions of type – that cannot be captured within a type-theoretic formulation of logic.[5]

Wittgenstein early on rejects a universalist conception of logic. In one of his first letters to Russell, he writes, "Logic must turn out to be of a TOTALLY different kind than another science."[6] In the *Tractatus*, Wittgenstein underlines his rejection of the universalist conception by calling the sentences of logic tautologies that say nothing (6.1; 6.11). For Frege, even if the basic axioms of logic are self-evident, the laws of this science are not trifling; nor do they lack content. Furthermore, both Frege and Russell, explicitly rejecting Kant's view, believe that logical proof is a source of new knowledge.[7] Let us consider some of Wittgenstein's dissatisfactions with Frege's and Russell's old logic.

Wittgenstein rejects generality as the mark of the logical: "The mark of logical propositions is not their general validity [*Allgemein-gültigkeit*]"[8] (6.1231). Frege has no overarching conception of logical truth or logical consequence. The closest he comes to the latter is to say that one truth is logically dependent on another, if it is provable from it and logical axioms by logical inferences.[9] Frege gives no general explanation of what makes an axiom or inference logical beyond generality. Indeed, Frege himself feels no need to provide a wholesale criterion of the logical. For his purposes, it is enough to display the logical on a retail basis via his particular axiomatic formulation of logic, a formulation he never claims to be exhaustive. The inadequacy of generality as a sufficient condition of the logical becomes salient after Russell's paradox. For consideration of logicism within the framework of *Principia Mathematica* highlights the existence of maximally general statements that are neither provable nor refutable from self-evident maximally general axioms. The axioms of choice, infinity, and reducibility are examples. Faced with the question unobvious, unprovable maximally general statements pose concerning the extent of logic, the universalist logician can draw a boundary only by supplementing generality with a brute appeal to self-evidence as a mark of a logical axiom, an appeal Wittgenstein finds lame (6.1271).

More is at stake here than the nominal demarcation of the subject of logic. For Frege, the ability to reason, to draw demonstrative inferences, plays a regulative role in thinking, inquiry, and communication.[10] Frege aims to make explicit in his axiomatization of logic the principles that are in some sense implicit in the exercise of this ability. As a consequence of this status, logical principles are rationally undeniable – their falsity cannot be coherently thought. In contrast, the falsity of other claims, even of evident truths, can be coherently thought. The universalist logician represents this by using logic to prove conditionals whose logically irrefutable antecedents contain as a conjunct the counterfactual assumption. This procedure is not applicable to whatever principles the universalist logician identifies as the principles of logic.[11] However, nothing intrinsic to these logical axioms, as the universalist logician construes them, explains their special status. Their generality cannot explain this status, especially once it is conceded that there are maximally general statements that are neither logically provable nor refutable. Nor can self-evidence explain this status, as the falsehood of evident nonlogical truths can be entertained. Indeed, when we reflect on the way the ability to draw inferences frames any inquiry and is a precondition for thinking itself, it begins to look as if there can be no *principles* of inference, no logical truths on a par with other truths as the universalist logician puts them.

Frege's problematic conception of logical inference points toward this conclusion as well. Frege is fully aware that his presentation of logic as a formal system requires, in addition to logical axioms stated in begriffsschrift, inference rules that are set forth extrasystematically. He believes that inference rules in a rigorous formulation of logic should be kept to a minimum and that basic modes of inference should be captured by logical axioms so far as possible. As illustrated above, typically inference from one nonlogical statement to another will be mediated by a general logical law. However, among Frege's inference rules is modus ponens, a rule that permits the inference of a singular statement from two singular statements. Wittgenstein believes that all logical inference has the immediate character of applications of modus ponens. He thinks that it is neither necessary nor desirable that logical inference be mediated by general truths. Indeed, he thinks there are no general laws that justify individual inferences. After all, if there were, then these justifications should be added to the premises for the inference, leading either back again to immediate inferences unjustified by general laws or to the vicious regress Lewis Carroll observed.[12]

Wittgenstein wants an understanding of the logical connectedness of sentences and the thoughts they express that makes this connectedness intrinsic to them. Sentences, and the thoughts they express, represent a reality outside of them either correctly or incorrectly. Moreover, sentences represent what they do independently of their truth or falsity. That a sentence implies some others, contradicts others, and is independent of still others, and so forth, must somehow be rooted in the nature of the sentence as a representation of reality. This approach to logical connectedness leads Wittgenstein to deny that there are logical principles like those Frege and Russell identify, to deny indeed that there is any body of theory that sets forth the logical connectedness of sentences (see 6.13). On his view, the task of the logician is rather to make perspicuous the logical connections intrinsic to statements via a clear rendition of those statements.

## II RUSSELL'S MULTIPLE RELATION THEORY OF JUDGMENT

In the *Tractatus*, Wittgenstein maintains that sentences represent reality by modeling it. This view of sentences as models or pictures can be motivated as a reaction to the inadequate conception of representation that lies at the heart of Russell's multiple relation theory of judgment. Wittgenstein's alternative to Russell's theory, nevertheless, shares with it a commitment to a correspondence conception of truth.

Russell did not hold to a correspondence view of truth before 1910. After his break with idealism in 1900, Russell espoused and elaborated G. E. Moore's metaphysics of propositions as a foundation for logic. Russell thus embraced an atomism in which independently subsisting ontological atoms are combined into nonlinguistic, nonmental complexes, Moore's and Russell's propositions. These propositions are either true or false. On this view, judgment is a dyadic relation between minds and propositions. For Iago to judge that Desdemona loves Othello is for Iago to bear the relation of judging to a proposition that, for this example, we may take to be a complex in which the relation of loving joins the individual Desdemona to the individual Othello. This proposition is true. Similarly, for Othello to judge that Desdemona loves Cassio is for Othello to bear the judging relation to the proposition that Desdemona loves Cassio, a complex in which the relation of loving joins Desdemona to Cassio. In this case, however, the proposition is false.

For our purposes, what is noteworthy about this view of judgment is the absence of any fundamental notion of representation.[13] There is no further realm of facts that inflicts truth or falsity on propositions. Instead, Moore and Russell take truth and falsity to be unanalyzably simple properties of propositions. True and false propositions thus subsist on an ontological par; a fact – if we wish to use the word – is just a proposition that is true.[14]

Russell became dissatisfied with this understanding of truth.[15] He wanted an explanation of the difference between the truth and falsity of judgment in terms of "the presence or absence of a 'corresponding entity' of some sort."[16] His leading idea was that Iago's judgment that Desdemona loves Othello is true, if there is a fact corresponding to it, and false in the absence of a corresponding fact. Such an account of truth promises to avoid the posit of false propositions on a par with true ones. For with it, Russell can identify the complex in which the relation of loving joins Desdemona to Othello with the fact that Desdemona loves Othello, while denying that there is any complex in which the relation of loving joins Desdemona to Cassio. Russell thus exchanged the metaphysics of propositions for one of facts.

This metaphysical shift obviously requires a new theory of judgment. The multiple relation theory is the alternative Russell proposed. There are two parts to the theory: the analysis of judgment and the characterization of the correspondence of judgments so analyzed with facts that inflicts truth on some of them. The characterization of correspondence provides Russell's account of representation: it explains what makes a given judgment the judgment that such and so is the case. Russell's theory changes considerably from 1910 through 1913. On the 1910 and 1912 versions of the multiple relation analysis, the relation of judging is a multiple (as opposed to dyadic) relation that holds among a mind and other ontological items. For example, for Iago to judge that Desdemona loves Othello is for a tetradic relation of judging to hold among Iago. Desdemona, the relation of loving, and Othello respectively. The sentence "Iago judges that Desdemona loves Othello" can thus be perspicuously rewritten as "Judges (Iago, Desdemona, Loving, Othello)." Judgments are thus facts formed by a relation of judging. Notoriously, Russell never extended the multiple relation analysis to nonatomic judgments.[17]

The multiple relation analysis must capture the difference between the judgment that aRb and the judgment that bRa. To this end, Russell must explain why a's bearing R to b, not b's bearing R to a, is the possibility whose obtaining would verify the judgment that aRb. In 1912, Russell proposed the following theory:

> It will be observed that the relation of judging has what is called a "sense" or "direction." We may say, metaphorically, that it puts its objects in a certain *order*, which we may indicate by means of the order of the words in the sentence. . . . Othello's judgment that Cassio loves Desdemona differs from his judgment that Desdemona loves Cassio, in spite of the fact that it consists of the same constituents, because the relation of judging places the constituents in a different order in the two cases. . . . This property of having a "sense" or "direction" is one which the relation of judging shares with all other relations.[18]

So, on this view, the difference between s's judging that aRb and s's judging that bRa is the difference between J(s,a,R,b) and J(s,b,R,a):[19] two arguments of the same logical type are permuted in these judgment-facts. What makes this difference the difference at issue must be the exploitation of the intrinsic ordering of argument positions in relations to characterize the correspondence that makes a judgment true: a judgment-fact of the form

$$J(x,y,\phi,z)$$

is true, if the relation occupying the third argument position relates the individual occupying the second argument position to the individual occupying the fourth argument position. That is, there is a fact in which y occupies the first argument place of $\phi$, and z the second.

A sweeping change in Russell's conception of relations forces him to give up this 1912 account of correspondence. In particular, in 1913, Russell became persuaded that the argument places in relations are not intrinsically ordered: one cannot speak generally of the first, the second, etc. argument position in a relation or in a complex formed by a relation. Let us consider the reasons for this shift and how Russell modifies his theory of judgment to attempt to accommodate it.

Russell holds that the central error of idealism is its denial of the reality of relations; and throughout his career, he maintains that among independently subsisting ontological atoms, there are asymmetric relations. Now given any relation R, there is a converse relation S such that ySx if and only if xRy. Thus, the relation *child of* is the converse of *parent of*. In *Principles of Mathematics*, Russell had asked whether the proposition

a is a child of b

is distinct from the proposition

b is a parent of a.

He concluded there that they are, appealing in effect to the ordering of the argument positions that is intrinsic to relations.[20] Russell thus became committed to the thesis that if an asymmetric relation R is among the ontological primitives, its converse is as well.[21]

In the 1913 *Theory of Knowledge* manuscript, Russell reversed himself, deciding that the sentences "a is a child of b" and "b is a parent of a" are synonymous after all, that they express the same judgment, that if true they correspond to the same fact.[22] He does not, however, maintain that one of these sentences should be analyzed as a definitional abbreviation of the other, thus selecting one of the relations *child of* or *parent of* as the genuine ontological primitive. There can be no basis for choice here. Instead, Russell maintains that there is only one relation here, not two: the relational predicates "is a child of" and "is a parent of" name the same asymmetric relation. However, the sentences "a is a child of b" and "a is a parent of b" express distinct judgments. Russell accommodates this fact by denying what he had affirmed in *Principles*, that the sense of a relation is intrinsic to it:

In a dual complex, there is no essential order as between the terms. The order is introduced by the words or symbols used in naming the complex, and does not exist in the complex itself. . . . We must therefore explain the sense of a relation without assuming that a relation and its converse are distinct entities.[23]

He continues on the next page:

Sense is not in the relation alone, or in the complex alone, but in the relations of the constituents to the complex which constitute "position" in the complex. But these relations do not essentially put one term before the other, as though the relation went from one term to another; this only appears to be the case owing to the misleading suggestions of the order of words in speech or writing.[24]

Russell's idea here is that there are two ways an asymmetric dyadic relation can combine individuals into a complex. These two ways can be symbolized linguistically by the order in which the relata are mentioned in a sentence. But in denying that sense is intrinsic to asymmetric relations, that asymmetric relations are essentially "from" one relatum "to" the other, Russell denies that there is a *general* distinction between the first and second argument position of an asymmetric relation. We cannot, for example, speak of the first argument positions in the relation named by "is a child of" and "envies," asking whether in two facts formed respectively by these two relations the first argument position is filled by the same individual.

This revised conception of relations blocks Russell's 1912 characterization of correspondence truth for judgments involving asymmetric relations. For this account had specified the corresponding complex by matching ordered argument places in judgment-facts and other facts, as illustrated a few paragraphs back.[25] Russell thus needs a new analysis of the judgments that aRb and bRa and a new account of how one of these judgments can be true and the other false. Very briefly, Russell proposes that, where R is asymmetric, the judgment that aRb is a complicated existential generalization asserting the existence of a complex with certain features. This existential generalization does not involve the relation R, but nevertheless is, Russell argues, true just in case it is a fact that aRb. There is then, on this analysis, no atomic judgment that aRb, only a molecular surrogate.[26] However Russell might extend the multiple relation theory to generalizations, one problem appears insuperable. The reasoning Russell uses to go from the premise that the existentially general surrogate for the judgment that aRb is true to the conclusion that a really bears R to b is, on the theory's own telling, inaccessible. For according to Russell's theory, there is no judgment-fact with which to identify Russell's conclusion, since there is no atomic judgment that aRb. Russell's revised conception of relations in the context of the multiple relation theory thus leads him to a desperate expedient that makes asymmetric relations inaccessible to cognizers as objects of judgment.

In the October 1913 "Notes on Logic," Wittgenstein repeatedly criticizes Russell's multiple relation theory of judgment.[27] Summarizing his critique in the opening section of NL, he says:

When we say A judges that etc., then we have to mention a whole proposition which A judges. It will not do either to mention only its constituents, or its constituents and form, but not in the proper order. This shows that a proposition itself must occur in the statement that it is judged. . . . (NL, p. 94 [1])

Wittgenstein does not mention the problem that asymmetric relations pose for the theory. However, on 20 May 1913, immediately before Russell drafted the chapter in *Theory of Knowledge* in which he identifies relations and their converses, Wittgenstein in conversation presented Russell with objections to a previous version of the multiple relation theory. This chronology combined with Russell's reversal of a position that had been stable since 1903 leads me to suspect that Wittgenstein was the source of the synonymy argument against the 1912 characterization of correspondence-truth.[28] My purposes here do not require examination of other features and difficulties with the 1913 version of the multiple relation theory. Early in 1913 Wittgenstein was moving in a very different direction.

### III  THE CONCEPTION OF SENTENCES AS PICTURES

Unlike Russell, Wittgenstein concentrated, not on a theory of judgment, but on a theory of symbolism, of the linguistic representations we use to express thoughts. The problem I have exposed for Russell's multiple relation theory infects a Russellian view of language as well. On this view, atomic sentences at the bottom level of analysis are combinations of names of ontological atoms of different types – individuals, properties of individuals, dyadic relations of individuals, et cetera. Names are merely labels for ontological atoms with which we are acquainted. Somehow combinations of names of the atoms into sentences (express judgments that) are rendered true or false by the subsistence of facts involving the named atoms. Asymmetric relations pose problems for this crude view of language parallel to those they pose for the multiple relation analysis. If predicates are nothing but labels for relations whose argument places are not ordered, then it is difficult to explain how "a is a child of b" and "b is a child of a" would correspond if true to different facts, while the formally parallel pair "a is a child of b" and "b is a parent of a" would correspond to the same fact.

In his January 1913 letter to Russell, Wittgenstein announced a new approach to a theory of symbolism, one in which "Qualities, Relations (like Love), etc. are all copulae!"[29] Here Wittgenstein breaks with the Russellian view of language by ceasing to treat unary and relational predicates as names of ontological atoms combined by a copula with names of individuals. This, I maintain, is the root of the conception of sentences as pictures. "Notes on Logic" presents Wittgenstein's new approach in some detail.

The crude Russellian view of language treats sentences as collections or mixtures of names. Wittgenstein rejects such a conception of sentences (3.141). In NL as in the *Tractatus*, Wittgenstein emphasizes the difference between sentences and names. Unlike names, sentences are true or false because they agree or disagree with the facts, because they have sense (see 3.144 and NL, p. 101 [8]). Sentences can agree or disagree with facts, because they are themselves facts. "In aRb it is not the complex that symbolizes but the fact that the symbol 'a' stands in a certain relation to the symbol 'b.' Thus facts are symbolised by facts, or more correctly: that a certain thing is the case in the symbol says that a certain thing is the case in the world" (NL, p. 96[4]). The basic indefinably simple elements of atomic sentences are names and forms, forms being the linguistic correlates of the copulae of the January 1913 letter. Wittgenstein says:

> The indefinables in "aRb" are introduced as follows:
>     "a" is indefinable;
>     "b" is indefinable;
> Whatever "x" and "y" may mean, "xRy" says something indefinable about their meaning. (NL, p. 99[5])

In NL, Wittgenstein continues to follow Russell in treating names as unproblematic labels for objects. Forms are not labels; they symbolize differently.

> But the form of a proposition symbolizes in the following way: Let us consider symbols of the form "xRy"; to these correspond primarily pairs of objects, of which one has the name "x," the other the name "y." The x's and y's stand in various relations to each other, among others the relation R

holds between some, but not between others. I now determine the sense of "xRy" by laying down: when the facts behave in regard to "xRy" so that the meaning of "x" stands in the relation R to the meaning of "y," then I say that the [facts] are "of like sense" [gleichsinnig] with the proposition "xRy"; otherwise, "of opposite sense" [entgegengesetzt]; I correlate the facts to the symbol "xRy" by thus dividing them into those of like sense and those of opposite sense. To this correlation corresponds the correlation of name and meaning. Both are psychological. Thus I understand the form "xRy" when I know that it discriminates the behaviour of x and y according as these stand in the relation R or not. In this way I extract from all possible relations the relation R, as, by a name, I extract its meaning from among all possible things. (NL, p.104[6]. See also NL, p. 95[3].)

Consider then the form "x envies y." Pairs of objects may or may not be related in various ways. One individual may envy a second or not, may esteem a second or not, may love a second or not. Our form symbolizes in that it is fixed when two individuals are so related as to agree with the form. We can think of this determination in terms of a general rule for comparing sentences of that form with the facts. A sentence itself is a fact, and a sentence of the form "x envies y" is a fact in which a name in the x-position ENVY-leftflanks a name in the y-position. Such a sentence agrees with the facts just in case the individual designated by the name in the x-position envies the individual designated by the name in the y-position. Otherwise, the sentence disagrees with the facts. That is: that "a" ENVY-leftflanks "b" says that a envies b. There is an arbitrariness in the use of names to designate objects: for example, "Iago" might have been used instead of "Othello" as a name for Othello. There is a similar arbitrariness in connection with forms: that one name ENVY-leftflanks another might have been used to say that one individual esteems another. That a name labels a particular individual and that one dyadic form symbolizes a particular dyadic relation over objects are both psychological contingencies in the establishment of a particular symbolism.

Not only may we use the holding of a dyadic relation over names to symbolize the holding of various dyadic relations over individuals; we can use a dyadic relation over individuals in different ways to symbolize the same facts. For example, that one name ENVY-leftflanks another might have been used to say that the second named individual envies the first named, rather than the other way around. The problems relations pose for the Russellian view of language now vanish. Consider the following two forms, xRy and xSy. Sloughing over use-mention niceties, suppose that we have the following two rules:

(1) that xR-leftflanks y says that x is a child of y.
(2) that xS-leftflanks y says that y is a child of x, i.e., says that x is a parent of y.

These are different rules of agreement for our two forms in that a sentence of the form "xRy" does not say what the corresponding sentence of the form "xSy" says. Nevertheless, both "aRb" and "bSa" say that "a is a child of b." Indeed any sentence of the form "xRy" says what the corresponding sentence of the form "ySx" says. There is then nothing that can be said using the one form that cannot be said using the other one. There is no more point to having sentences of both forms in the language than there is for having multiple names of the same object.[30]

The Russellian view of language assimilates the correlation of relational predicates to relations to the use of proper names to label individuals. On Wittgenstein's alternative view, forms of sentences symbolize via a general rule setting forth when sentences of that form agree and disagree with the facts. The general rule depends on a structural similarity between sentences and the facts that verify them if they are true. In my examples above, the rule depends on sentences of the form x envies y being themselves facts in which a name bears an asymmetric dyadic relation to another name.

So, do "child of" and "parent of" designate the same relation, or do they designate different relations? For Wittgenstein, the question is misconceived. Russell takes relations to be a type of thing – they are constituents of facts, objects of acquaintance, and the designata of names; they may themselves have properties and be the relata of still further relations. All this is what the reality of relations comes to for him. So conceived, Wittgenstein rejects the reality of relations, Russell's most cherished ontological thesis.[31] Relations are not things, are not entities; relations cannot be labeled or designated. Unlike "a" and "b," "R" is not a symbol in "aRb." Instead, roughly put, the holding of a relation over objects is symbolized by the holding of a relation over names of those objects. But this way of talking is itself misleading for its use of "object" and "relation" as a contrasting pair of common nouns.[32]

*Not.* "the complex sign 'aRb' says that a bears R to b," but *that* "a" bears a certain relation to "b" says *that* aRb (TLP, 3.1432, my translation repeated from NL, p. 106[5]).

The principle attraction of this conception of atomic sentences is its understanding of sense. The sense of an atomic sentence is fixed by rules that specify the object each name labels and by a general rule that specifies what sentences of that form say, that is, when sentences of that form agree with the facts. This view thus makes the possession of true–false poles intrinsic to atomic sentences in the context of a view of truth as agreement with the facts. Wittgenstein will exploit the essential bipolarity of atomic sentences to arrive at an understanding of logical connectedness. Before considering this understanding, we need to see how the NL account of the sense of atomic sentences in terms of names and forms metamorphoses into the Tractarian conception of sentences as pictures.

The *Tractatus* on its face presents a very different conception of atomic or elementary sentences than NL. Here Wittgenstein no longer describes elementary sentences in terms of names and forms. Instead he says: "The elementary proposition consists of names. It is a connexion, a concatenation of names" (4.22). And he maintains that sentences are pictures. These changes are, I shall argue, more terminological than substantive. The Tractarian conception of sentences as pictures is more a natural deepening than a revision of the NL conception of sentences and representation.[33]

At the very opening of the *Tractatus*, Wittgenstein says that the world is all that is the case, the totality of facts. Remark 2 states that what is the case is in turn fixed by the obtaining of atomic facts or states of affairs (*Sachverhalt*). Wittgenstein explains picturing in the 2.1's. A picture is a determinate arrangement of pictorial elements. In the case of elementary sentences, these pictorial elements are the names. At 2.15, Wittgenstein says: "That the elements of the picture are combined with one another in a definite way, represents that the things are so combined with one another"[34] (see also 4.0311). Wittgenstein calls the way the elements are arranged in a picture the structure of the picture, and the possibility of this arrangement of these elements the picture's form of depiction or modeling (*Abbildung*).

The 2.15's elaborate this idea of picturing. According to 2.1514, it is in virtue of the coordinations or correlations between names and objects that the configuration of names into elementary sentences represents a configuration of objects into a state of affairs. Just here Wittgenstein's conception of picturing becomes mysterious. How does a correlation of pictorial elements with objects insure a correspondence between the ways that the elements can be arranged in pictures and the ways that objects can be arranged in states of affairs? Applying the conception to language, we might suppose that somehow the names must have the very same possibilities of arrangement into sentences as the objects they designate have into states of affairs. However, on this interpretation, elementary sentences are very unlike ordinary sentences. For the ways in which words are related to each other in ordinary sentences are not the ways in which things are related in the facts described. Indeed the phrasing of 3.1432 recognizes as much: "*that* 'a' bears a certain relation to 'b' says *that* aRb." And Wittgenstein does conceive of ordinary sentences as pictures (see 4.011–012 and 4.016). In addition, Wittgenstein's contrast in the 2.16's between form of representation (pictorial form) and logical form suggests that strict identity between the ways that pictorial elements can combine into pictures and objects into states of affairs is not necessary for a picture to present a state of affairs. But if we abandon the supposition of identity between the ways that pictorial elements may be arranged in pictures and things arranged in reality, it seems that something more than a mere correlation of pictorial elements and objects is required to make an arrangement of names into a representation of a state of affairs.

The answer to this dilemma is that the correlations Wittgenstein speaks of in the 2.15's are not "mere correlations."[35] In NL, Wittgenstein explains how atomic sentences have sense in terms of the different ways in which names and forms symbolize, in terms of rules of designation for names and rules of agreement for forms. In NL, Wittgenstein says nothing about names and designation, following Russell in treating names as unproblematic labels for objects. Just here the *Tractatus* improves on the treatment of NL. Rules of designation and rules of agreement presuppose each other in the following fashion. Rules of agreement presuppose the possibility of correlating names with objects: that one name ENVY-leftflanks another says that *the bearer* of the first name envies *the bearer* of the second. A less obvious presupposition runs the other direction. It is only within sentences after the erection of rules of agreement that names symbolize, designate, or mean objects. There is no giving of *names*, no dubbing, apart from the erection of these rules.

In the *Tractatus*, then, Wittgenstein fully appreciates these points and rejects Russell's conception of names as simple labels for objects of acquaintance. This is indeed the significance of Wittgenstein's invocation of Frege's context principle at 3.3: "Only the proposition has sense; only in the context of a proposition has a name meaning." The *Tractatus* employs two intertwined notions of representation distinguished in German by the verbs "*vertreten*" and "*darstellen*." Names in sentences represent (*vertreten*) objects in that the names go proxy for objects in sentences (2.131; 3.203; 3.22). Sentences in which names go proxy for objects represent (*darstellen*) situations in logical space, the holding and not holding of atomic facts (2.201–202). In order for names to go proxy for objects in sentences, it must be fixed what possibilities of combinations of names into sentences present what possibilities of combinations of objects into states of affairs. No mere correlation of names with objects makes those names into representatives of the objects in sentences in the absence of such a coordination of possibilities of combination. In the *Tractatus*, then, there are not separate rules of designation and rules of agreement. There is for a language only the single rule that projects the sentences of that language onto reality, onto states of affairs (see 4.0141). The rule does this by coordinating names and the ways that names can form sentences with objects and the ways that objects can form states of affairs. The coordinations spoken of in the 2.15's are thus thick, nonextensional correlations made by the rule of projection for a language. It is these thick correlations that constitute sentences as models of reality, that give names feelers so that sentences composed of those names are laid like measuring sticks against reality.

On this interpretation, then, relations are not among the simple objects of the 2.0's. Elementary sentences represent (*darstellen*) atomic facts. An atomic fact is a combination of objects in which the objects are related in a definite way, in which the objects "hang together in each other like the links of a chain" (2.03). In the analogy between atomic facts and chains, Wittgenstein rejects Russell's view of relations as ontological atoms that have the role of joining other ontological atoms together into complexes. Nor is there any ontological glue linguistically symbolized by the copula that binds individuals and relations into atomic facts. Nothing joins objects together into states of affairs. Instead, they have their intrinsic possibilities of combination with each other into states of affairs. Pretending still that "a envies b" is an elementary sentence, this sentence represents one of the possibilities in which a and b can hang together. These possibilities are not "purely formal." Two objects a and b can also hang together in that the second envies the first, or the second esteems the first, or the first loves the second, etc. Nothing in a sentence goes proxy for or names a relation. This is the lesson which Wittgenstein extracts from the difficulties Russell lands in over asymmetric relations. Rather the atomic sentences in which names are representatives (*vertreten*) of objects represent (*darstellen*) those objects as related in a particular way. There is no *vertreten* of relations, but only the *darstellen* in atomic sentences of the holding of relations, the modeling of objects as combined in a particular way. Thus, the role played in NL by Wittgenstein's distinction between the way that names symbolize and the way that forms symbolize is taken up in the *Tractatus* by the distinction between *vertreten* and *darstellen*.

Can we think of elementary sentences on the model of "a envies b," as I have been urging? 4.22 states that an elementary sentence consists of names. I have insisted that "a envies b" has only two names. There thus are more than names in this putative elementary sentence. Is my interpretation consistent with 4.22? Here we must remember that sentences are facts: the sentence in question is "a" 's ENVY-leftflanking "b." This fact is a chaining together of names in a way entirely analogous to the way in which the state of affairs of a's envying b is a combination of objects.[36]

Examination of Wittgenstein's distinction between form of representation or modeling (*Form der Abbildung*) and logical form illuminates his conception of sentences as pictures. In NL, Wittgenstein assumes the correlations that give atomic sentences their sense. In the *Tractatus*, he inquires after the preconditions for these thick correlations. Pictures are themselves facts. Wittgenstein says that for a picture to model reality in the way it does, it must, as a fact, have something in common with the reality it models. Wittgenstein calls this common something the form of representation (*Form der*

*Abbildung*, of modeling) (2.17). He goes on to say that in order for a picture to model reality in any way at all, there is a shared minimum it must have in common with reality, what Wittgenstein calls logical form (2.18). I have already rejected the idea that shared representational form plus thin, extensional correlations of names and objects explain how pictures represent, an interpretive approach that makes representational form entirely mysterious. To understand Wittgenstein's view here, let us take the advice that 3.1431 proffers:

> The essential nature of the propositional sign becomes very clear when we imagine it made up of spatial objects (such as tables, chairs, books) instead of written signs.
>
> The mutual spatial position of these things then expresses the sense of the proposition.

3.1431 calls to mind the following sort of model or representation: the use of arrangements of blocks on a surface to represent the relative spatial positions of some group of things, say cars at the scene of an accident, to adapt an example from Wittgenstein's pre-*Tractatus* notebooks (NB, 29.9.14, p. 7). We can specify a general rule that projects arrangements of blocks onto the scene of the accident by assigning blocks to cars and stipulating that the relative spatial positions of the blocks are to represent that the cars they name at the time of the accident had the same relative spatial positions. For example, that block 2 is twice as far to the right of block 1 as block 3 is to the left along a straight line says that car 2 is twice as far to the right of car 1 as car 3 is to the left along a straight line. Although this rule of projection is salient, it is not the only one. We might use an arrangement of blocks to represent cars to stand in the mirror image of this arrangement. For example, that block 2 is twice as far to the right of block 1 as block 3 is to the left along a straight line says that car 2 is twice as far to the *left* of car 1 as car 3 is to the *right* along a straight line. Both of these two rules for projecting arrangements of blocks onto the scene of the accident exploit the same precondition: namely each block can stand to the other blocks in the same relative spatial positions that each car can stand to the other cars. Thus, any general rule that uniquely associates every relative spatial arrangement of blocks with a relative spatial arrangement of cars can be used to project arrangements of blocks onto the scene of the accident. The possibility of common relative spatial arrangements is the form of representation that enables arrangements of blocks, via either of our two projection rules, to model the relative spatial positions of the cars. Shared representational form does not then fix how a picture is to be compared with the depicted reality. Rather, it is the condition for the picture modeling the reality in the way it does – it is the condition for the erection of one of a family of rules of projection.

Modeling does not require that the pictorial elements and the represented objects share the very same possibilities of combination. It only requires a formal "isomorphism" between the possible configurations of pictorial elements into pictures and of objects into facts. For example, consider a twenty-note melody, each produced at one of eight given pitches. The melody can be (correctly or incorrectly) represented by a score that consists of a series of twenty dots, each placed on or below one of four parallel lines, a staff. Here the spatial order of the dots represents (*darstellen*) the temporal order of the notes; the position of the dots on the staff, the absolute pitch of the notes; the relative position on the staff, the relative pitch. There are eight pitches and eight positions on the staff. The temporal ordering of the notes is a discrete series, and so is the spatial ordering of the notes. These are the formal similarities between scores and melodies that are the shared form of representation, the "isomorphism-type," that enable scores to represent melodies. As in the previous case of the arrangements of blocks, there are alternative projection rules exploiting these formal similarities. For example, the left-to-right order of the dots might represent the earlier-to-later order of the notes; but the right-to-left order of the dots could represent this equally well.

The form of representation common to a picture and the reality it depicts thus guarantees that possible configurations of things can be modeled by possible configurations of pictorial elements. It thus secures that any projection rule that exploits it uniquely associates possibilities for pictorial elements with possibilities for the represented things. 2.172 states: "The picture, however, cannot represent [*abbilden*] its form of representation [*Abbildung*]; it shows it forth" (see 4.041). In the two examples of pictures I have presented, some relationships among the depicted objects are not separately represented but are built into pictures by the common form of representation exploited by the rule of projection by means of which the picture represents some reality in the particular way that it does. For example, if an arrangement of blocks represents car 1 to the right of car 3 and car 2 to the right of car 1, then it automatically represents car 2 to the right of car 3. This is so, regardless of which of our two sample rules is used to project the blocks. Any projection rule erected on the basis that the blocks and cars share the same possibilities of relative spatial position will use a transitive spatial relation among blocks to represent a transitive spatial relations among cars. This feature of the way arrangements of blocks represent arrangements of cars reveals that these arrangements of blocks do not represent, do not model, the transitivity of *to the right of*. For it is impossible to arrange the blocks, for example, to represent car 1 to the right of car 3, car 2 to the right of car 1, but car 2 not to the right of car 3. What a picture cannot incorrectly model, it does not model.

Shared representational form (typically) guarantees that there are several ways of projecting arrangements of pictorial elements over the reality depicted. Furthermore, a domain of facts may be represented in different ways by pictures whose form of representation differs. For, as we have seen, pictures may have more or less in common with what they represent. Logical form is that minimal formal similarity between the possibilities for pictorial elements and possibilities for things necessary to coordinate unambiguously the former with the latter: "What every picture, of whatever form, must have in common with reality in order to be able to represent it at all – rightly or falsely – is the logical form, that is, the form of reality" (2.18).

How does this conception of representational and logical form apply to familiar sentences? Here we encounter a problem. I noted how the transitivity of the relation *to the right of* is built into the representation of the accident scene by the spatial models. Here a transitive relation represents (*darstellen*) a transitive relation. However, the syntactic relation of *RIGHT-leftflanking* over words is not transitive. Suppose we were to project sentences onto the accident scene via the rule: the one name RIGHT-leftflanks another says that the car represented by the first name is to the right of the car named by the second. Then, using these sentences, it seems that we could represent car 1 to the right of car 3, car 2 to the right of car 1, but car 2 not to the right of car 3. But this is not a possible arrangement of the cars. Hence, our sentences don't share a form of representation with the reality they represent (2.151).

Wittgenstein's answer to this problem will draw on his conception of logic and analysis. Briefly, sentences can represent one car to the right of another without use of a transitive relation. However, the attempt to represent car 1 to the right of car 3, car 2 to the right of car 1, but car 2 not to the right of car 3 will be a sentence that represents nothing, a sentence that is a *sinnlos* contradiction (see the 4.46's). This in turn will require that the sentences that represent one car to the right of another be molecular sentences. These sentences do not model one car's being to the right of another. Instead, they represent this situation by modeling some underlying state of affairs, by analyzing *to the right of* in terms of some more basic way that things can be combined. It is a condition of this analysis that the sentence that, so to speak, asserts an instance of the transitivity of *to the right of* be a tautology.[37]

## IV  LOGICAL INTERCONNECTEDNESS

"A sentence is a sentential sign in its projective relation to the world" (3.12). We have seen what this projective relation comes to in the case of elementary sentences. Names together with their possibilities of combination into sentential signs are correlated with things and their possibilities of combination into states of affairs. The possibility of such a correlation is secured by the form of representation the sentential signs share with reality. This correlation projects the sentential signs onto reality, making them models of reality. Each sentence, like a tableau vivant (4.0311), presents a possible state of affairs. The sentence agrees with reality, if the state of affairs it presents actually obtains. It disagrees with reality, if the presented state of affairs does not actually obtain.

The conception of elementary sentences as pictures makes their agreement or disagreement with reality – their possession of true–false poles, of sense–intrinsic to them. These intrinsic true–false poles make it possible to form other sentences that are truth-functions of elementary sentences. A truth-function of elementary sentences arises from a truth-operation on the true–false poles of elementary sentences: the sense of the truth-function, its conditions for agreement with reality, are fixed by the truth-operation in terms of the obtaining or not of the states of affairs presented by the elementary sentences. So, for example, negation is a truth-operation that reverses the sense of a sentence: the negation of a sentence agrees with reality just in case the negated sentence disagrees. And the conjunction of several sentences agrees with reality just in case each of the conjoined sentences does. As these formulations make evident, truth-operations are not restricted in application to elementary sentences. Truth-operations can be iterated to obtain from truth-functions of elementary sentences further truth-functions of those elementary sentences (see 5.31). In this way, then, the conception of a sentence as a sentential sign in its projective relation to the world is extended from elementary sentences to truth-functions of these so that, as Wittgenstein puts it in NL, "Molecular propositions contain nothing beyond what is contained in their atoms; they add no material information above that contained in their atoms" (NL, p. 98 [11]).

Wittgenstein's use of the now familiar truth-table notation in the 4.4's is designed to bring out this conception of truth-functionally compound sentences. Wittgenstein does not introduce truth-tables as a metalinguistic device to calculate the logical properties of object language sentences. Wittgenstein's truth-tables are object language expressions – they are expressions of truth-functions of elementary sentences, an alternative to Russell's or Frege's notation. Wittgenstein believes that Russell's notation misleads, for it notationally tempts us to think of the sentential connectives "¬" and "v" as representing a property of or relation over items signified by sentences (see NL, p. 98[10]). The truth-table notation does not carry any such temptation with it (4.441). Letting "p" and "q" stand in for elementary sentences, Russell expresses the disjunction of p with the negation of q by "p v ¬q." Using the truth-table notation, Wittgenstein replaces this sentential sign with the sentential sign:

p q
T T T
T F T
F T F
F F T

A row of "T" 's and "F" 's underneath the elementary sentences indicates a truth-possibility of these sentences. For example, the second row indicates the possibility that the state of affairs presented by "p" obtains and that presented by "q" does not obtain. The four rows of "T" 's and "F" 's then exhaust the truth-possibilities of these sentences. Marking a row with "T" in the rightmost final column signifies that the truth-functionally compound sentence agrees with the indicated truth possibility. So, in the example, the truth-function agrees with reality if the second truth-possibility is realized, if "p" is true and "q" false. Marking a row with "F" indicates disagreement (see 4.43). Our example sentence is thus an expression of agreement and disagreement with the truth-possibilities of "p" and "q" (4.4; 4.431). The complex of "T" 's and "F" 's in one of Wittgenstein's tabular sentential signs – or Russell's sentential connectives with scope demarcating parentheses – are used to express a particular truth-function of the contained elementary sentences. Signs for logical operations do not then symbolize as the expressions in elementary sentences do. In particular, their use requires no coordinations of names and objects in addition to those that project elementary sentences onto reality. Signs for logical operations are thus a sort of punctuation (5.4611).

Suppose we have a body of elementary sentences and the sentences that are truth-functions of these.[38] We can characterize a notion of sense over all these sentences that provides an overarching notion of logical consequence. The truth-grounds or truth-conditions of a sentence are those truth-possibilities of elementary sentences that would verify the sentence. When all the truth-grounds of one sentence q are also truth-grounds of another sentence p, then (the truth) of p follows from (the truth) of q and we can say that the sense of p is contained in the sense of q (see 5.11–5.12's). Furthermore, if p and q have the same truth-grounds, they are the same truth-function of the same elementary sentences. They thus stand in the same projective relation to reality and so have the same sense. They are notational variants of the same sentence (5.141).

On this view of consequence, there is no call to appeal to general laws – to the universalist logician's maximally general, topic-universal truths – to justify the inference of one sentence from another. All inference has the immediate character that, for Frege, characterizes applications of modus ponens. Moreover, the justification for any inference is not stated by any generalization.[39] Rather, inference is grounded in the sentences themselves, in the structures of the sentences that ensure that the truth-grounds of all the premises are also truth-grounds of the conclusion.

If p follows from q, I can conclude from q to p; infer p from q.

The method of inference is to be understood from the two propositions alone.

Only they themselves can justify the inference.

Laws of inference, which – as in Frege and Russell – are to justify the conclusions, are senseless [*sinnlos*] and would be superfluous.

All inference takes place a priori. (5.132)

Among the truth-functions of a group of elementary sentences is the extreme case of a truth-function that is verified by all the truth-possibilities of the elementary sentences. Such a truth-function, being true under all conditions (unconditionally true), has no truth-*conditions* and represents no possibility of the obtaining or not of states of affairs. It thus lacks sense (*sinnlos*), without being nonsense (*unsinnig*) (4.461's). These truth-functions are Wittgenstein's tautologies. The iterated applicability of truth-operations to elementary sentences sufficient to yield all truth-functions of them insures the existence of sentential signs that are thus unconditionally true. Tautologies then are sentence-like formations, notational artifacts, in which, as Wittgenstein puts it, the conditions for agreement with the world of the component sentences cancel each other (4.462). Parallel remarks hold for contradictions, for a truth-function of elementary sentences that is falsified by all its truth-possibilities.

Tautologies are the sentences of logic, the truths of logic (6.1). The distinction in the old logic between the self-evident logical axioms and their deductive consequences disappears; all logical truths are on a par (6.127). On the universalist conception, logical laws are substantive generalizations that mediate inferences over the sentences of the various special sciences. In contrast, Wittgenstein's tautologies say (represent) nothing. Moreover, as we have seen, they play no essential role in proofs in mediating inferences among sentences with sense (6.122). There is, though, this connection between inference and logical sentences: if p follows from q, then the material conditional

> If q then p

is a tautology.

Wittgenstein's extension of the conception of sentences as pictures from elementary sentences to truth-functions of these thus

appears to contain at least a partial understanding logical connectedness. Intrinsic to elementary sentences are their true–false
poles; and with this comes the possibility of forming sentences that
are truth-functions of the elementary ones. Wittgenstein characterizes in truth-functional terms a notion of sense containment over
these truth-functions that is simultaneously a notion of consequence. Here then is a notion of consequence grounded in an understanding of how truth-functions of elementary sentences represent
reality. This notion of consequence does justice to the special status
of logic, for it avoids the posit of logical laws, of a subject matter for
logic.

Wittgenstein audaciously maintains that this understanding of logical connectedness is exhaustive: when one sentence follows from
another, they are truth-functions of elementary sentences, and the
sense of the second contains the sense of the first. To this end, Wittgenstein explains quantificational generality in truth-functional
terms. Briefly and roughly, a universal generalization is the result of
applying the truth-operation of conjunction to a class of sentences
given by a sentential variable. An example of a sentential variable is a
sentence in which an expression has been replaced by a blank, leaving
a sentential form or function. The sentential variable has as values
any sentence that would result from filling the blank with a syntactically admissible expression. So "$(\forall x)\phi x$" is the conjunction of all
sentences of the form "$\phi x$," all sentences that result from uniformly
filling the blank "x" with a syntactically admissible expression[40] (see
3.31's, 5.501's, 5.52's). Furthermore, Wittgenstein eliminates the
identity sign from sentences that represent reality, using instead identity and difference of names to express identity and difference of
objects (5.53). Wittgenstein thus construes the incontestable core of
Frege's and Russell's logic – quantificational logic plus identity – in
his truth-functional terms.

Although Wittgenstein's conception of elementary sentences as
pictures makes their true–false poles intrinsic to them, nothing in
this conception requires that elementary sentences be independent
of each other. Indeed the spatial models he uses to communicate his
conception are sentences that fail to be independent. For consider
again the representation of the relative positions of five cars in an
intersection by spatial arrangements of five blocks of wood: the
truth of any such representation precludes the truth of any other.

However, the conjunction of any two such representations fails to be a contradiction, as Wittgenstein characterizes contradiction. If such sentences count as elementary sentences, the truth-functional characterization of logical connectedness fails to be exhaustive. While sharply criticizing the universalist logician's account of the applicability of logic (see the 5.55's), Wittgenstein retains the idea that logical connectedness must be understood in "formal" terms, in terms that do not draw on the particular content that distinguishes various sentences. An exhaustive account of logical connectedness in Wittgenstein's truth-functional terms delivers just such an understanding. He accordingly imposes the requirement of logical independence on elementary sentences.

There is another pressure shaping Wittgenstein's conception of elementary sentences. On Wittgenstein's conception of truth as agreement with reality, the sense of a sentence is the possible situation in logical space it represents (2.202; 4.031). Wittgenstein's talk of logical space alludes to the logical connectedness of sentences. On the universalist conception of logic, the basic laws of the maximally general science embrace every science – there is just one logic. Again, while Wittgenstein rejects the universalist account of the way in which logic frames every claim, he adheres to the idea of a single framework embracing every sentence (see 6.124). There is just one logical space in which every sentence with sense determines a location. Each sentence with sense is related to every other, if only by the relation of independence.

This theme underlies the so-called argument for simple objects at 2.0201–2.0212. Every sentence with sense must have a fully determinate sense in order to determine a location in logical space. In particular, there can be no factual (statable) presuppositions for the truth or falsehood of a sentence, for the situation it represents to obtain or not. Any such alleged presupposition, being required for the truth of the sentence, is a part of the sense of the sentence. Once we count the presupposition as a part of the sense of the sentence, we are forced to recognize a scope ambiguity in what we had taken to be the negation of the original sentence.[41]

Sentences of everyday language do carry with them apparent existential presuppositions: they say something, and so have a truth-value, only if the names occurring in them designate items. Indeed, the spatial models Wittgenstein calls to our attention have such apparent existential presuppositions. For example, a formulation of the rule projecting my envisioned spatial models to the accident scene will contain designations of the five cars there. Thus projected, these models seem to presuppose the existence of these cars. As Wittgenstein views matters, the five blocks of wood function as designations of complexes. The existence of these complexes is a matter of other relatively simpler items being related in a certain way. These facts, whose obtaining constitutes the existence of the complex, can be set forth in sentences. The sense of these sentences is contained in the sense expressed by the original model. If one of the putatively designated complexes does not exist – if one of these sentences is false – then the original model is simply false, not nonsensical (without truth-value) (3.24). We can thus clarify what the original model says by use of a sentence that replaces designations of complexes by sentences describing their constitution.[42] This clarifying replacement for the original model may itself carry further apparent existential presuppositions. These can be handled similarly. As the original model does represent a situation in logical space, does have a determinate sense, it must be possible to express that sense in an entirely explicit way without using a designation of any complex.

The existence of the objects meant by the names that occur in such fully analyzed expressions of the original sense (3.201) is not then a matter of other objects being related in some way. But why can't there be sentences that assert the existence of these objects, sentences that would then express existential presuppositions of fully analyzed sentences? Such sentences would be like those Russell discusses in *Principles of Mathematics* that say that each term, each entity, has being. Russell notes the special status of such sentences:

If A be any term that can be counted as one, it is plain that A is something, and therefore that A is. A is not must always be either false or meaningless. For if A were nothing, it could not be said to be. A is not implies that there is a term A whose being is denied, and hence that A is. Thus unless A is not be an empty sound, it must be false – whatever A may be, it certainly is.[43]

So, where "A" is a name that occurs in a fully analyzed sentence, could there be a sentence "A is" that asserts the existence of A?

As Russell argues, such sentences would presuppose their own truth. But for this very reason, the admission of such sentences violates Wittgenstein's understanding of truth as agreement with facts. Sentences are pictures of reality that are true or false in virtue of their agreement or disagreement with reality. This view of representation underlies Wittgenstein's insistence on the bipolar character of any representation, his identification of the possession of sense (representing a possible situation) with the possession of a truth-value. The true-false poles of a picture cannot be pulled apart: a picture that in fact agrees with reality might have disagreed, and vice versa. As I noted in the discussion of representational form in §3, what cannot be incorrectly modeled by a picture is not modeled by it at all:

The picture represents what it represents, independently of its truth or falsehood, through the form of representation. (2.22)

Wittgenstein's view thus rules out representations that presuppose their own truth. For to admit a representation that presupposes its own truth is to admit a representation whose truth does not consist in its agreement with reality, a picture whose truth can be recognized without comparing it with reality (2.223–4; 3.04–5). No subject-predicate sentence, no representation with true-false poles can then represent that a simple object exists and thus state a presupposition of a fully analyzed sentence.

In sum, on Wittgenstein's view of sentences as logically interconnected pictures, a sentence – a sentential sign in its projective relation to the world – shows how things stand if it is true, and says that they do so stand (4.022). In thus determining a location in logical space, with each sentence the whole of logical space must be given (3.42). Logical space is given by what any sentence has in common with any other, by the general form of sentences. Wittgenstein announces with great fanfare at 4.5 that the general form shared by the sentences of any language, by sentences expressing any possible sense, is: such and such is the case (*Es verhält sich so und so*). The sense any sentence expresses can be expressed by a truth-function of independent elementary sentences; this truth-function will stand in the same projective relation to the world. Such fully explicit representations make patent the logical relationships that bind the situations represented into one logical space. A sentence is then a truth-function of elementary sentences (see 5 and 6). This is what any representation shares with any other; this is their essence (5.47–472). The iterated application of truth-

operations to the totality of logically independent elementary sentences thus fixes the limits of sense (4.51).

## V THROWING AWAY THE LADDER

Wittgenstein's thought in the *Tractatus* begins with the idea that
our sentences are logically interconnected representations that are
made true or false by what is the case. As I have presented it, the
*Tractatus* is an attempt to work out what this idea requires of language on the one side and the world on the other. But what sort of
understanding here does the *Tractatus* in the end deliver?

The *Tractatus* opens with a refinement of Russell's metaphysics
of facts. The 1's introduce a notion of fact: the world is all that is the
case, the totality of facts. The metaphysics of objects and atomic
facts sketched in the 2.0's develops this notion of fact: what is the
case is the obtaining of atomic facts, and atomic facts are combinations of objects. Let us consider briefly what Wittgenstein says by
way of characterizing this combination. At 2.011 Wittgenstein tells
us that it is essential to objects that they can be constituents of
atomic facts. 2.012 repeats much the same idea: "In logic nothing is
accidental; if a thing *can* occur in an atomic fact the possibility of
that atomic fact must already be prejudged in the thing." In contrast
to what is essential to objects, what is accidental is whatever happens to be the case, the facts; and any fact about an object is a matter
of its being combined with other objects into atomic facts. As 2.012
indicates, an object's possibilities of combination with others –
what Wittgenstein calls the form of the object (2.0141) – is not a
matter of the object's being combined with others. An object's form
is not a fact about it; rather "objects contain the possibility of all
states of affairs [*Sachlage*]" (2.014).

Wittgenstein's discussion of the simplicity of objects in the 2.02's
elaborates on this priority of objects to atomic facts. Wittgenstein
calls objects the substance of the world (2.021), and at 2.0271 he tells
us: "The object is the fixed, the existent [*Bestehende*]; the configuration is the changing, the variable [*Unbeständige*]." This talk of
change and instability, with its temporal connotations, should not be
taken literally. 2.024 makes this clear: "Substance is what exists
[*bestehen*] independently of what is the case." The alterations Wittgenstein has in mind in 2.0271 are the differences in configurations of

objects that distinguish various conceivable worlds (*gedachte Welt*) from the actual (*wirklich*) one (see 2.022). Traditionally, a substance is the subject of change, is what endures through change of properties. Behind various elaborations of this notion of substance lies the following idea: change can be intelligibly conceived only against a backdrop of something constant against which the change occurs. Wittgenstein's talk of substance in the 2.02's alludes to this philosophical theme. However, Wittgenstein's point is that any conception of fact, of what is the case, requires as a backdrop a conception of what might be, even if it is not, the case. So, in the metaphysics limned in the 2.0's we have necessities – the forms of objects – that determine the range of possibilities, possibilities of combination of objects into atomic facts. What is the case, the facts, the world, is then fixed by the atomic facts that obtain.

This discussion of the metaphysics of the 2.0's, a discussion that draws heavily on Wittgenstein's own rhetoric, is dangerously misleading. It ineluctably suggests by its very grammar that the determination of the range of possibilities by the forms of objects is itself some sort of fact. Furthermore, talk of atomic facts as obtaining or not obtaining – see 2, 2.04–2.06, and 4.21 – reifies possibilities and treats actualization as a property that some possibilities possess. We have already observed that, on the conception of fact presented in the 2.0's, an object's form is not any sort of fact about it. Moreover, it is clear that Wittgenstein does not countenance possibilia in his ontology. To do so would undermine the identification at 2.01 of atomic facts with combinations of objects: "In the atomic fact the objects are combined in a definite way" (2.031). Their being related in a determinate way, their being configured thus and so, constitutes the obtaining of the atomic fact. The obtaining is not a property that the combination of objects has or lacks. So, if an atomic fact does not obtain, there is nothing, no entity, that fails to obtain. This conclusion is reinforced from another textual direction. The reification of possible atomic facts would make them independent of what is the case. They would then play the role that the 2.02's unambiguously assign to objects. Indeed, Wittgenstein calls attention to the oddity of his talk of atomic facts obtaining by using the same word here, *bestehen*, as he uses in the 2.02's to contrast objects with atomic facts.

Wittgenstein's rhetoric in the 2.0's is carefully calculated both to limn a metaphysical picture and simultaneously to cancel the incompatible implicatures that any presentation of this metaphysics carries with it. What I have called careful calculation may, however, with equal justice, be labeled philosophical incoherence. True statements set forth facts. If there are no facts as to how objects, by virtue of their forms, contain the possibility of all situations, there is no description of the role that objects play in Wittgenstein's metaphysics. And no description means, after a fashion, no conception. We think that we have grasped the metaphysics Wittgenstein sketches in the 2.0's. When subsequently we reflect on Wittgenstein's words, on the view we take these words to convey, we realize that, on their own telling, they do not communicate a view at all. Wittgenstein's words pull themselves apart. We have then in the 2.0's a version of the difficulty I noted earlier in §1 in connection with Frege's and Russell's explanation of type-theoretic distinctions. Wittgenstein is acutely aware of this feature of his rhetoric. The rendition of the metaphysics of facts in the 2.0's is not intended to stand on its own as a piece of metaphysical theorizing.[44]

At the most general level, a view of truth as agreement with reality makes the notion of a sentence (representation) and of a fact interdependent: facts are what are representable in sentences and so are what make these sentences true or false. There is no conception of a fact, of something's being the case, that is not representable in sentences – this would be a fact that is not a truth. Our purchase on both these notions comes through the use of the logically connected sentences of language to make claims, to express thoughts. Thus in the *Tractatus* numbering scheme the first comment on 2 is 2.1, "We make to ourselves pictures of facts."

We have the ability to construct languages capable of expressing every sense, of representing every possibility (4.002). Each sentence with sense depicts a possible situation in logical space and says, correctly or incorrectly, that the represented situation obtains (4.022). To understand a sentence is to be acquainted with the situation it represents (4.021), to know what is the case, if the sentence is true (4.024). This understanding is not, however, itself a piece of knowledge, something that might be set forth in some further sentence. Rather, to understand a sentence is to be in a position to see what sentences follow from it and what ones are independent of it. To understand a sentence is thus to be able to discriminate the possibility it represents from other possibilities. To make these discriminations is not to discover anything to be the case. On the contrary, only against the backdrop of these discriminations is there such a thing as saying something, as identifying how things do stand.

Accordingly, there is no sentence that says that it is a possibility that Desdemona loves Othello. There is only the sentence that says that Desdemona loves Othello. But the sentence, "Desdemona loves Othello," in saying what it does, in making sense, displays the possibility of Desdemona's loving Othello. We have no purchase on the notion of possibility except that given in the discrimination of possible situations in logical space that constitutes the understanding of language. There is then no explanation for the possibility of Desdemona's loving Othello – for our sample sentence's making sense – that goes beyond translating this sentence by some other that perhaps gives more perspicuous expression to the same sense. 5.525 tells us:

> Certainty, possibility or impossibility of a state of affairs [*Sachlage*] are not expressed by a proposition but by the fact that an expression is a tautology, a significant proposition or a contradiction.
>
> That precedent to which one would always appeal, must be present in the symbol itself. (See also 3.4.)

The task of the logician is not to identify logical truths. Rather, it is to devise a perspicuous notation for the expression of the sentences of the sciences. When one sentence follows from another, then the sense of the former – the situation it represents – is contained in the sense of the latter. This relationship should be patent in the expression that each receives in a logical notation: ". . . we can get on without logical propositions, for we can recognize in an adequate notation the formal properties of the propositions by mere inspection" (6.22. See also 6.1233 and the 5.13's). We saw §4 how Wittgenstein's truth-functional understanding of logical connectedness articulates this theme. We find here, however, no theory of logical connectedness, no sentences that say one sentence follows from another. Beyond the development of the notation, there is merely what Wittgenstein takes to be the journeyman's labor of working out "mechanical expedient[s] to facilitate the recognition of tautology, where it is complicated" (6.1262).

The say–show distinction links the metaphysics of the 2.0's with

Wittgenstein's view of sense and logic. We saw how the 2.0's contrast what is essential to objects, their possibilities of combination, with what is accidental to them, their configuration into atomic facts. Wittgenstein calls what is essential to objects their internal properties, and what is accidental to them their external or material properties (2.01231). It is clear that in speaking of internal and external properties, Wittgenstein does not mean that there are two kinds of property possessed by objects, two sorts of facts concerning them. We have here another instance of Wittgenstein's unavoidably deceptive rhetoric. An object's possibilities of combination are not, properly speaking, properties possessed by objects. 2.0231 makes this point: "The substance of the world *can* only determine a form and not any material properties. For these are first presented [*darstellen*] by propositions – first formed by the configuration of objects." 2.0232 tersely restates this point in a way designed to offset the lingering insinuation that forms are another sort of property: "Roughly speaking: objects are colourless."

How then is the contrast between internal properties/form and external properties/fact to be understood? The mention of sentences in 2.0231 points toward the 4's, especially the 4.12's where Wittgenstein returns to this issue in his discussion of showing and saying. 4.1 states, "A proposition presents [*darstellen*] the existence and non-existence of atomic facts." In the 4.11's, Wittgenstein's emphasis is on what sentences represent, the possibilities whose obtaining is investigated by the sciences. In the 4.12's, the focus shifts to what sentences do not represent.

> Propositions cannot represent the logical form: this mirrors itself in the propositions.
> That which mirrors itself in language, language cannot represent [*darstellen*].
> That which expresses *itself* in language, *we* cannot express by language.
> The propositions *show* the logical form of reality.
> They exhibit it. (4.121)

I noted earlier how there are no sentences that represent the existence of simple objects. Just as there is no conception of a possible fact save as a situation in logical space representable by a sentence, there is no conception of a constituent of a possible atomic fact, of an object, save as what is meant by the names that can occur in fully analyzed sentences.[45] The existence of these objects is something that is shown: "Thus a proposition 'fa' shows that in its sense the object a occurs, two propositions 'fa' and 'ga' that they are both about the same object" (4.1211). Similarly there are no sentences that represent the internal properties of objects. These are mirrored in language by the possibilities of combination by names into sentences – this is how they are linguistically formulated.

The distinction between internal and external properties is the distinction between what is mirrored in language and what the sentences of language represent. The incoherence of the 2.0's is thus overcome by the say–show distinction elaborated in the 4.12's. We are led to the say–show distinction by the way that the earlier remarks pull themselves apart. At this point, we can throw away the earlier remarks: there is no theory of the constitution of the world, no ontological theory with the generality to which Russell's theory of types aspires. The pursuit of theory, of description, of representation at this level of generality is the pursuit of an illusion.

Of course, this talk of what is said and what is shown itself misleads, just like the earlier talk of internal and external properties. It suggests that there are two kinds of fact: the garden variety facts set forth in true sentences and extraordinary facts about the constitution of any possible world shown by sentences. 4.1212 counteracts this grammatical insinuation: "What *can* be shown, *cannot* be said." Cora Diamond has persuasively urged that it is a mistake to think of what is shown as deep, ineffable, necessary truths about reality. Such an understanding of what is shown, she says, makes Wittgenstein chicken out: on the chickening-out interpretation, what is shown is "this whatever-it-is, the logical form of reality, some essential feature of reality, which reality has all right, but which we cannot say or think it has."[46] She continues: "What counts as not chickening out is then this, roughly: ... to throw away in the end the attempt to take seriously the language of 'features of reality.' " As I have stressed, on a resolute, consistently applied conception of truth as agreement with reality, there are no facts about or features of reality that sentences cannot represent, no ineffable truths. Rather, the attempt to say what is shown leads to nonsense, to what we on reflection recognize to be plain gibberish –

" 'Twas brillig, and the slithy toves did gyre and gimble in the wabe" – sentence-like formations in which some signs have been given no significance (see 6.53).

There is no resolution of the incoherence of Wittgenstein's rhetoric of saying and showing parallel to the gloss that the say–show distinction offers of earlier talk of internal and external properties: the difference between what is said and what is shown is, as it were, neither sayable nor shown. In the context of the 4.1's, the incoherence in Wittgenstein's rhetoric here draws us away from the illusory goal of saying what can only be shown to the activity of saying clearly what can be said, the activity of philosophy (4.112). In saying clearly what can be said, we serve the interests that had led us to aspire to a general description of the constitution of the world. In particular, by saying clearly what can be said, philosophy

. . . should limit the unthinkable from within the thinkable. (4.114)

It will mean the unspeakable [*das Unsagbare*] by clearly displaying [*darstellen*] the speakable. (4.115)

The *Tractatus* imagines an attempt to think through at the most general level what a conception of sentences as logically interconnected representations of reality requires.[47] At its opening, it presents what appears to be an alternative theory to Russell's flawed one. We see through this appearance, when we realize that on the theory's own apparent telling, there can be no such theory. When we throw away the ladder, we give up the attempts to state what this conception of representation and truth demands of language and the world, give up trying to operate at an illusory level of generality, without however rejecting the conception of truth as agreement with reality. Rather, we understand what this conception comes to, when we appreciate how what can be said can be said clearly, when we appreciate the standard of clarity set by the general form of sentences.[48]

NOTES

1   I shall focus on Frege's version of the universalist conception, as it is clearer and better motivated than Russell's. Most of the features of Frege's views that I highlight have parallels in Russell.

2   For Frege's expression of this viewpoint see *Die Grundgesetze der Arithmetik* (Jena: H. Pohle, 1893), vol. 1, Vorwort, p. xv, and also

"Logik" (1897), *Nachgelassene Schriften*, ed. Hans Hermes, Friedrich Kambartel, and Friedrich Kaulbach (Hamburg: Felix Meiner, 2nd ed., 1983), p. 139. Russell encapsulates the universalist conception in *Introduction to Mathematical Philosophy* (London: George Allen and Unwin, 1919), p. 169.

3 See Gottlob Frege, *Begriffsschrift* (Halle: L. Nebert, 1879), Vorwort, p. vi.

4 Henry M. Sheffer, "Review of Whitehead, Alfred North, and Russell Bertrand, *Principia Mathematica*, vol. I, 2nd. ed., 1925," *Isis* 8 (1926), p. 228.

5 Benno Kerry raises a form of this objection against Frege. For a lucid discussion of the difficulty Frege faces here, see Michael Resnik, "Frege's Theory of Incomplete Entities," *Philosophy of Science* 32 (1965). For defenses of Frege's concept–object distinction against these objections, see Cora Diamond, "What Does a Concept-Script Do?" in *The Realistic Spirit* (Cambridge, Mass.: MIT Press, 1991) and my "Generality, Meaning, and Sense in Frege," *Pacific Philosophical Quarterly* 67 (1986).

6 Ludwig Wittgenstein, *Letters to Russell, Keynes and Moore*, ed. G. H. von Wright (Ithaca: Cornell University Press, 1974), letter of June 22, 1912, p. 10.

7 For a trenchant discussion of Wittgenstein's use of the word "tautology" see Burton Dreben and Juliet Floyd, " 'Tautology' – How not to use a Word," *Synthese* 87 (1991), pp. 23–49.

8 Quotations are from the C. K. Ogden translation of the *Tractatus*.

9 Gottlob Frege, "Über die Grundlagen der Geometrie" (1906 series), *Jahresbericht der Deutschen Mathematiker-Vereinigung* 15 (1906), p. 424.

10 Frege brings out the regulative status of logical principles in *Die Grundgesetze der Arithmetik*, Vorwort, esp. pp. xvi–xix.

11 Frege affirms the conceivable falsehood of the allegedly self-evident axioms of Euclidean geometry, contrasting them with logical laws, in *Die Grundlagen der Arithmetik* (Breslau: W. Koebner, 1884), §14. Russell's 1903 views on the inconceivability of the falsity of logical principles converge with Frege's. See *Principles of Mathematics* (London: George Allen and Unwin, 1937 [original publication 1903]), §17, p. 15. Russell cannot, I think, sustain this view when, faced with the difficulty of justifying the axiom of reducibility, he opines that a logical axiom may be justified by its consequences. See "The Regressive Method of Discovering the Premises of Mathematics" (1907) and "The Theory of Logical Types" (1910), §vii, both reprinted in Russell, *Essays in Analysis*, ed. Douglas Lackey (New York: George Braziller, 1973).

12 Lewis Carroll, "What the Tortoise Said to Achilles," *Mind* n.s., 4 (1895).

13 Russell's theory of denoting concepts in *Principles of Mathematics*, the theory rejected in the 1905 paper "On Denoting," does introduce a representation-theoretic element into Russell's theory of propositions.

14  See G. E. Moore, "The Nature of Judgment," *Mind* n.s., 8, esp. pp. 180–1
    and 192; and Moore, "Truth and Falsity," *Dictionary of Philosophy and
    Psychology*, ed. James Mark Baldwin (New York: Macmillan, 1901),
    vol. 2, p. 717. For Russell's statement of this point, see "Meinong's
    Theory of Complexes and Assumptions," in *Essays in Analysis*, esp. pp.
    75–6 (original publication in *Mind*, 1904). This paper reveals that Rus-
    sell is from the outset uneasy with Moore's treatment of truth as just
    another unanalyzably simple concept. See also Russell's discussion of
    truth in *Principles of Mathematics*, §52, pp. 48–9.

15  For a discussion of the philosophical shift that Russell's adoption of the
    multiple relation theory represents and of Russell's stated motivations
    for the theory, see Peter Hylton, *Russell, Idealism, and the Emergence
    of Analytic Philosophy* (Oxford: Oxford University Press, 1990), pp.
    333–42.

16  Bertrand Russell, "On the Nature of Truth and Falsehood," *Philosophi-
    cal Essays* (London: George Allen and Unwin, 1966 [original publication
    1910]), p. 152. Russell states objections to his earlier views in this paper,
    pp. 151–3, and in *Theory of Knowledge: The 1913 Manuscript*, ed. Eliza-
    beth Eames, *The Collected Papers of Bertrand Russell* (London: George
    Allen and Unwin, 1984), vol. 7, pp. 152–3. See also Bertrand Russell, *The
    Problems of Philosophy* (Oxford: Oxford University Press, 1959 [original
    publication 1912]), pp. 120–1.

17  Russell projected a third part to *Theory of Knowledge* that would extend
    the multiple relation theory to molecular judgments, including general-
    izations. Confronted with Wittgenstein's objections to the multiple rela-
    tion analysis, Russell abandoned the manuscript, never drafting the
    third section. I believe that it is problems with Russell's theory of
    atomic judgments that discredit it in Wittgenstein's eyes and lead Rus-
    sell to give up the approach.

18  Russell, *Problems of Philosophy*, pp. 126–7. Russell in *Philosophical
    Essays*, p. 158, had suggested that in x's judgment that aRb [J(x,a,R,b)] R
    can enter as an argument for the judgment-relation as having one of two
    "directions." This account in effect replaces relations as ontological
    atoms with relations with senses. Russell understandably abandons it.
    For further discussion of difficulties with the 1910 version of Russell's
    theory, see Nicholas Griffin, "Russell's Multiple Relation Theory of
    Judgment," *Philosophical Studies* 47 (1985), pp. 219–20.

19  Russell, *Problems of Philosophy*, pp. 128–9.

20  See Russell, *Principles of Mathematics*, §219, p. 228.

21  I take this thesis to be explicit in Russell, *Principles of Mathematics*,
    §219, p. 229: "Hence R and Ř[= the converse of R] must be distinct, and

'aRb implies bŘa' must be a genuine inference." That is, the sentence "bŘa" is not a definitional transcription of "aRb."

22  Hylton plausibly suggests that Russell's shift to a correspondence view of truth leads him to coarser standards for synonymy. See Hylton, *Russell, Idealism*, pp. 351–2.

23  Russell, *Theory of Knowledge*, p. 87.

24  Ibid., p. 88.

25  Griffin's account of the 1912 version of the multiple relation theory misses the use Russell makes of the ordering of the argument positions of relations in characterizing truth. Consequently, Griffin misunderstands Russell's reasons for rejecting the 1912 version in 1913. See Griffin, "Russell's Multiple Relation Theory," pp. 220–1.

26  Russell does not renounce asymmetric relations and facts formed by them. He cannot and does not in this setting treat signs for asymmetric relations as incomplete symbols to be eliminated by analysis. Russell thinks that the difference between a symmetric and an asymmetric relation is that a symmetric relation can combine its relata in only one way. There are thus atomic judgments involving symmetric relations like similarity, since J(x,a,similarity,b) is true just in case there is a complex whose only constituents are a, similarity, and b. I hope to discuss Russell's 1913 version of the multiple relation theory at greater length on another occasion.

27  Hereafter cited in the text as NL with references to pages and paragraphs of appendix I of Ludwig Wittgenstein, *Notebooks 1914–1916*, 2nd ed., ed. G. H. von Wright and G. E. M. Anscombe (Chicago: University of Chicago Press, 1979), hereafter cited in the text as NB. Brian McGuinness discusses the genesis of NL in *Wittgenstein: A Life. Young Ludwig, 1889–1921* (Berkeley and Los Angeles: University of California Press, 1988), pp. 184–7.

28  For a chronology and discussion of Wittgenstein's conversations with Russell in the spring of 1913, see McGuinness, *A Life*, 1988, pp. 172–4.

29  Ludwig Wittgenstein, *Letters to Russell*, p. 19.

30  I take it that if a form "xRy" is used to symbolize a symmetric relation, then "aRb" and "bRa" are orthographic variants – these are the same sentence. Here the relation between the names is not R-right standing, but R-standing. Wittgenstein's theory of symbolism can be viewed as a consistent thinking through of the idea that Russell broaches to deal at the linguistic level with asymmetric relations in Russell, *Theory of Knowledge*, pp. 87–8, quoted above, p. 67–8.

31  In saying that Wittgenstein rejects the reality of relations, I do not mean that he embraces the Idealist view Russell earlier abandoned, the view

that relations are somehow the product of the cognizing mind. Frege handles type-theoretic distinctions much more carefully than Russell; and clearly Frege's construction of a notation that automatically enforces type-theoretic distinctions influences Wittgenstein. However, Wittgenstein would equally reject Frege's understanding of these distinctions as making relations into things, as Frege allows both the designation of relations and allows relations to fall under higher-level concepts.

32  Wittgenstein discusses the difficulties in describing how relations in sentences, as opposed to names, symbolize in the 1914 "Notes dictated to Moore," appendix II in NB, pp. 109–10. Desmond Lee reports that in a conversation about 2.01 in 1930–1, Wittgenstein said: "Objects also include relations; a proposition is not two things connected by a relation. Thing and relation are on the same level. The objects hang as it were in a chain" (*Wittgenstein's Lectures, Cambridge 1930–1932*, ed. Desmond Lee [Totowa, N.J.: Rowman and Littlefield, 1982], p. 120). This is a peculiar remark. If an atomic fact is not two objects connected by a relation, then there seems to be no ground for calling any constituent thing in it a relation. Whatever Wittgenstein may have had in mind here, this view of relations is utterly unlike either Russell's or Frege's. I am grateful to Denis McManus for bringing this remark from Lee's lecture notes to my attention.

33  In this interpretation of Wittgenstein's development, I am indebted to Brian McGuinness's instructive discussion in "The *Grundgedanke* of the *Tractatus*," in *Understanding Wittgenstein*, ed. G. Vesey (Ithaca: Cornell University Press, 1974).

34  The German reads: "Dass sich die Elemente des Bildes in bestimmter Art und Weise zu einander verhalten, stellt vor, dass sich die Sachen so zu einander verhalten." I think that the Pears–McGuinness translation of 2.15 – "... represents that the things are related *in the same way,*" (italics mine) – is philosophically tendentious for being misleadingly definite.

35  Here I am indebted to Warren Goldfarb, who for years has urged the insufficiency of thin correlations or "dubbings" to constitute the representing relation between pictures and reality.

36  I take 4.24 to support this interpretation. It may help to ease textual qualms to observe here that while elementary sentences consist of names, not every expression in an elementary sentence is a name. Indeed, the notion of an expression introduced at 3.31 leads to an understanding of quantification that permits quantification into the position occupied by relational predicates.

37  It should be noted in this connection that Wittgenstein introduces an alternative to Frege's and Russell's technique for defining an ancestral of

a relation (4.1252 and 4.1273). Wittgenstein's technique secures that the statement that says that the ancestral of a particular relation is transitive will be tautologous.

38 For an instructive discussion of Wittgenstein's handling of the notion of *all* truth-functions of elementary sentences, see Göran Sundholm, "The General Form of an Operation in Wittgenstein's *Tractatus*," *Grazer Philosophische Studien* 42 (1992).

39 On Wittgenstein's view, these are just further truth-functions of elementary sentences.

40 In this connection, I should mention that a class of sentences may also be presented by a formal law that generates a series of sentences. In the *Tractatus*, this device replaces Frege's and Russell's technique for defining the ancestral of a relation. See 5.501 and 4.1273.

41 Following a suggestion of W. D. Hart in "The Whole Sense of the *Tractatus*," *The Journal of Philosophy* 68 (1971), p. 280, I believe this scope ambiguity is the indeterminateness in a sentence containing a designation of a complex mentioned in 3.24. I am also indebted to Hart's suggestive discussion in this paper of Wittgenstein's conception of clarity in the *Tractatus*.

42 Of course, the way the complexes are related, so to speak, may have to be modeled in a different way as well.

43 Russell, *Principles of Mathematics*, §427, p. 449. See also §47, p. 43. I am indebted to Warren Goldfarb for pointing out the relevance of these passages to the 2.02's.

44 I am indebted throughout this section to Brian McGuinness, who, noting the misleading character of Wittgenstein's rhetoric in the 2.0's, makes this point in his insightful paper "The So-called Realism of the *Tractatus*," in Irving Block, ed., *Perspectives on the Philosophy of Wittgenstein* (Cambridge, Mass.: MIT Press, 1981), p. 63.

45 Rush Rhees makes this point in " 'Ontology' and Identity in the *Tractatus* à propos of Black's *Companion*," in his collection *Discussions of Wittgenstein* (New York: Schocken Books, 1970), p. 25.

46 Cora Diamond, "Throwing Away the Ladder," in Diamond, *The Realistic Spirit*, p. 181.

47 In this paragraph I draw on ideas in Cora Diamond, "Ethics, Imagination and the Method of Wittgenstein's *Tractatus*," in Richard Heinrich and Helmuth Vetter, eds., *Bilder der Philosophie: Reflexionen über das Bildliche und die Phantasie* (Vienna: R. Oldenbourg Verlag, 1991), esp. §34.

48 I am indebted to Burton Dreben, Cora Diamond, Juliet Floyd, Peter Hylton, and especially Warren Goldfarb for assistance and encouragement in writing this paper.

# 3 Fitting versus tracking: Wittgenstein on representation

## I THE PROBLEM OF REPRESENTATION

*How is it possible for signs to point? How is it possible for signs to point to what is not there?* These questions are extremely general ones about *intentionality*, the property of "aboutness" or "ofness" whereby one part of the world (a sign such as the words "the stoplight" or "The stoplight is red") *represents* some other part of the world (e.g., an object such as a particular traffic signal or a state of affairs such as the traffic signal's being red).

(a) *How is it possible for signs to point?* The obvious fact that signs point to something other than themselves is puzzling because it is difficult to see how to avoid a threatened regress of interpretations: an ordinary sign, for example, the linguistic sign "plus" or "Playful," can be interpreted in various possible ways. Linguistic signs, after all, are arbitrary. The linguistic sign "Playful," as uttered by me on a particular occasion, may be interpreted by my hearer as the name of a particular gray cat or as an attribution of the quality of playfulness to the creature in front of me or even (nonstandardly) as a sign for the color gray. Once we notice this, we feel the need to find something that will single out just one of the possible alternative interpretations in order for signs to succeed in pointing to something beyond themselves. But how is this singling out to be accomplished? If, in response to a request to give an interpretation of the linguistic sign "Playful," I utter "my pet cat" or point toward a certain lounging feline, I apparently succeed only in producing more signs (words or gestures) that themselves admit of more than one interpretation. After all, "my pet cat" is itself just a set of arbitrary linguistic signs, and when I point toward a certain lounging feline, I am equally pointing to something exhibiting the quality of playfulness and to something gray. If that to which we appeal in the attempt to give the interpretation of one sign is itself a sign that can be interpreted in various possible ways, we risk launching an infinite regress of interpretations.

(b) *How is it possible for signs to point to what is not there?* The obvious fact that signs can point to what is not there is equally puzzling. Clearly, we can talk and think about objects that do not exist (e.g., unicorns) and we can say and think what is false (e.g., The president of the United States in 1996 is Ronald Reagan). And yet it is tempting to think that signs refer to objects or pick out states of affairs due to some special connection between signs and objects or states of affairs. For example, at one point in his career Bertrand Russell thought that it is our direct epistemological acquaintance with an actually existing object that gives the corresponding sign its power to refer to that object. But if an object must exist to enable a sign to refer to it, a sign for which there is no corresponding object should be meaningless, and we should not be able to talk or to think about objects that do not exist. And if we construe the relationship between a sentence and a state of affairs on the model of the relationship between a name and an object, a sentence for which there is no corresponding state of affairs should be meaningless, and we should not be able to say or to think what is false. In short, *misrepresentation* should be impossible.

## II FITTING VS. TRACKING THEORIES OF CONTENT DETERMINATION

Two sorts of theories may be proposed as explanations of how intentionality is possible: fitting theories (shared feature theories, iconic theories) of content determination and tracking theories (covariance theories, indexical theories) of content determination. Many attempts to explain how signs point fall into the class of fitting theories. Such theories, I argue, share features that make them particularly bad regress-stoppers – they inevitably leave room for alternative possible interpretations. By contrast, tracking theories appear to provide just the kind of alternative that can cut off the possibility of alternative interpretations and thus halt the regress. However, tracking theories are particularly susceptible to the problem of how signs can point to what is not there, a problem that may prove to be just as troubling and just as intractable.

A theory of content determination contrasts with a semantic theory and with a compositional theory in roughly the following way: a semantic theory specifies *what* the meaning/content (i.e., semantic value) of the basic expressions of a language are; a compositional theory explains how the semantic value of complex expressions depends upon the semantic value of basic expressions; a theory of content determination specifies what makes it the case that (what it is in virtue of which) the basic expressions have the semantic values that they do. A theorist interested in developing one of these types of theories would ask different questions from theorists developing another of these types of theories. A semantic theorist would ask: what semantic values do the expressions of the language have? For example, does every expression have both a sense and a reference? By contrast, a compositional theorist would ask: how are the semantic values of complex expressions of the language related to (e.g., composed out of) simpler expressions? Finally, a theorist of content determination would ask: in virtue of what does an expression have the semantic value that it has? A fair amount of confusion has resulted from regarding theories that answer any of these very different questions as "semantic theories."

By contrast with both semantic theories and compositional theories, theories of content determination attempt to specify what makes it the case that expressions have the semantic values that they do. Theories of content determination thus purport to explain not primarily what signs point to, but *how* they point to something other than themselves; they purport to offer a theory of how intentionality is possible by offering a theory of what determines the meaning/content.[1] Thus, they seem the right place to look for an answer to our questions about how signs point.

The basic insight of *fitting theories* is that signs point in virtue of resembling other things and they point to what they resemble. More generally, signs have semantic value in virtue of resemblance/similarity/shared structure: structural relationships among the elements of a representation may be said to "mirror" or to "model" structural relationships among the elements of what is represented. For example, according to one simple resemblance theory, what we might call the "image theory," signs point because they are associated with images and images point because they share features with other things and they point to that with which they share (the most) features.[2] For another example, according to a simple mapping theory, signs point because the elements of a representation or model can be placed in a one-to-one correspondence with elements of the represented world.[3]

Fitting theories of content determination contrast with tracking theories (covariance theories, indexical theories) of content determination. The basic insight of tracking theories is that signs point in virtue of tracking other things and they point to what they track. More generally, signs have semantic value in virtue of a nonaccidental connection between signs and what they "mean." Although there are significant differences between various versions of tracking theories, such theories share some central features: (a) a sign's having content is a matter of its covarying in a nonaccidental or nonarbitrary way with something other than itself; (b) a sign's content is determined by that with which it covaries; (c) signs point, in the first instance, to what is there.[4]

The differences between fitting theories and tracking theories, I suggest, stem from emphasizing one or the other of two features that each play a role in everyday concepts of representation, for example, in the concept of a picture. On the other hand, we notice, pictures (e.g., a painting, a photograph, a video, or even a cartoon of Bill Clinton) resemble or are in some way similar to what they are pictures of. There is often something in common between pictures and what they represent, some shared features or properties or set of relationships such that the former "fits" the latter. On the other hand, we notice, some pictures are related to their objects in a way other than mere resemblance – for example, a photograph or video of Bill Clinton is in some way produced by and/or under the control of the man Bill Clinton in a way that a drawing resembling Bill Clinton but produced by someone who has never seen or heard of him is not; the former, but not the latter, "tracks" certain features of the man Bill Clinton in virtue of some nonaccidental connection between the man and the photo.

Fitting theories contrast with tracking theories in at least three important ways. First, whereas in a fitting theory the occurrence of the sign is *independent* of the occurrence of what is represented, in a tracking theory the occurrence of the sign is *dependent* upon the occurrence of what is represented. Just as a picture may resemble an actual person completely unknown to the drawer, so, according to fitting theories, a sign may resemble, and so come to represent, something with which it has no connection other than mere resemblance. Thus, according to fitting theories, a sign may resemble an object, event, or situation that does not actually exist or has not actually taken place; it may represent "what is not" as well as "what is." By contrast, just as a photograph must be a photograph of something actual, so, according to tracking theories, a sign represents first and foremost only "what is," that is, what actually exists or has existed.

Second, whereas in a fitting theory the semantic value of an expression is determined by something *internal* to the system of representation, in a tracking theory the semantic value of an expression is determined by something *external* to the system of representation. Just as it may be the relationships among the elements of a cartoon, the lines and shapes and colors, that give it "life," rather than the fact that some particular person served as a model for the cartoonist's drawing, so, according to fitting theories, it is the relationship among signs, perhaps within a system of signs, that gives them "sense," rather than some external relationship to objects, events, or situations in the external world. Thus, according to fitting theories, whether a sign succeeds in representing something that exists external to the system of signs, and, if so, what, is a contingent matter which depends upon how the sign (or system of signs) "fits" onto what there is. But that a sign makes "sense" is not contingent. Rather, that a sign makes sense is internal to the sign or system of signs; it is guaranteed by the relationship of elements within the sign or the sign's relationship to other signs in the system. By contrast, just as it may be the fact that the beeps of a Geiger counter covary in a dependable way with radioactive elements in the environment, rather than any similarity between the beeps and the radioactive elements, that makes the Geiger counter a Geiger counter, so, according to tracking theories, it is the existence of a nonaccidental connection between signs and objects, events, or properties in the external world that confers "meaning." Thus, according to tracking theories, whether a sign succeeds in representing something that exists external to the system of signs, and, if so, what, is in no way a contingent matter – the semantic value a sign has is conferred only by that external relationship.[5]

There is a third difference between fitting and tracking theories. As we have just seen, fitting theories treat semantic value as something that arises within (something that is "internal" to) a sign or system of signs, whereas tracking theories treat semantic value as something that does not arise within (something that is "external" to) a sign or system of signs. Perhaps not surprisingly, fitting theorists also tend to suppose that the properties that confer semantic value on signs are epistemically accessible in some privileged or special way to the "meaner" (i.e., the person doing the meaning), whereas tracking theorists tend to suppose that the properties that confer semantic value on signs need not be epistemically accessible in any special way, and indeed, in any way at all, to the "meaner."[6] In fact, I suspect that the intuition that *of course* we have privileged access at least to the properties that confer semantic value on our words is in part what motivates many fitting theories: how could meaning have anything to do with external connections between my signs and the world, when I have no special access to such external connections?

### III  FITTING THEORIES

Before considering the central difficulty faced by fitting theories, it may further understanding to present an example of a fitting theory that is somewhat more sophisticated than the simple image theory sketched above. We'll look briefly at a theory proposed by Bertrand Russell in one phase of his philosophical development.

According to Russell in *The Analysis of Mind*, "speech is a means of producing in our hearers the images which are in us."[7] But images, according to Russell, are inherently vague, because they resemble so many different things. This vagueness can be overcome, to a certain extent, by appeal to certain causal relations into which the images enter. Vague images come to represent more determinately in virtue of the fact that the associative patterns into which they enter "fit" or "map onto" causal patterns displayed by what is represented.

If we find, in a given case, that our vague image, say, of a nondescript dog, has those associative affects which all dogs would have, but not those belonging to any special dog or kind of dog, we may say that our image means "dog" in general. If it has all the associations appropriate to spaniels but not others, we shall say it means "spaniel"; while if it has all the associations appropriate to one particular dog, it will mean that dog, however vague it may be as a picture. The meaning of an image, according to this analysis, is constituted by a combination of likeness and associations. It is not a sharp or definite conception, and in many cases it will be impossible to decide with any certainty what an image means. I think this lies in the nature of things, and not in defective analysis.[8]

This view is much closer to a fitting theory than to a tracking theory, even though causal regularities are involved. Note that the causal connections to which Russell appeals are not connections linking the thing represented (e.g., my dog Spot) to a sign/representation/image (e.g., "Spot" or a particular mental image). Rather, the causal connections link my image (a representation/sign) to other thought-signs, utterances, or behavior (e.g., my smiling in the way I smile when I actually see Spot and in a way that I do not smile when I see dogs in general). On Russell's proposal, an image does not mean everything it "resembles" – it resembles far too many things. Its resemblance, qua image, leaves the meaning of an image far too indeterminate. But if we take into account not only what an image "resembles" but also what its pattern of associations "fits," we can narrow down the range of possible meanings. In short, my mental image of a dog, taken together with its functional/causal role in my mental life and behavior, may "fit" onto my dog Spot, taken together with his causal efficacy, in a way that my mental image by itself does not.

According to Russell, this associationist version of a fitting theory can then be generalized to cover the meaning of words as well as of images:

We may give somewhat more precision to the above account of the meaning of images, and extend it to meaning in general. . . . The word "dog" bears no resemblance to a dog, but its effects, like those of an image of a dog, resemble the effects of an actual dog in certain respects . . . the relation which constitutes meaning is much the same in both cases. A word, like an image, has the same associations as its meaning has. The theoretical understanding of words involves only the power of associating them correctly with other words; the practical understanding involves associations with other bodily movements.[9]

Russell thus appears to have stumbled onto what contemporary philosophers of mind would call a "functional role" theory of content determination, a view that is a fitting rather than a tracking theory. Someone who adopts a functional role theory of this type hopes to extend or to generalize the notion of resemblance: whereas the simple resemblance theory exploits the fact that a picture or mental image may be said to be similar to what it represents, a functional role theory exploits the fact that whole sets of (actual and/or possible) relationships among elements in a system of representations may be said to "mirror" whole sets of (actual and/or possible) relationships among elements in a system of representeds. Unlike pure tracking theories, these functional role/use theories make essential use of the idea of resemblance; though a particular sign need not resemble that to which it points, the functional role of the former must "fit" or "agree with" or "resemble" the functional role of the latter. Functional relationships among the elements of representations may be said to "mirror" or to "model" functional relationships among the elements of what is represented. Insofar as what a representation represents is taken to be determined by these patterns of similarity, again we have a fitting (iconic, shared feature) theory of content determination.

### Alternative interpretations

The primary and most troubling problem of fitting theories is that, because they appeal only to features of signs and to relationships among signs, they fail to stop the regress of interpretations. According to fitting theories generally, representation is supposed to result from the possibility of a mapping of representations onto that which is represented: determinate representation results when there is a unique way of "fitting" signs onto the world. But there are always various possible ways of "fitting" signs onto that to which they point, various possible ways in which signs can be said to "map" onto that which they represent, so no determinate "interpretation" is fixed by any sign or set of signs. In short, fitting theories inevitably leave a "gap" between signs and that to which they point, in the following sense: signs succeed in pointing beyond themselves only to the extent that the relationships set up within a sign or system of signs "fit" onto relationships existing external to the sign or system of signs. This leaves room for various possible ways of fitting, various possible mappings, various possible "interpretations." Given the nature of fitting theories, any attempt to fill the gap, to determine a unique interpretation, will appeal to something that belongs to the side of representations rather than to the side of what is represented. As such, it is always possible to raise again the question of how that something itself "fits" onto the world. Fitting theories thus do not provide, but point to the need for, a way of stopping the regress that is "not a matter of interpretation" (PI, 201). Fitting theories try to stop the threatened regress of "interpretations" by finding something that will serve as a "last" interpretation (see BLBK, p. 34). But they can offer nothing other than more signs and all signs appear to admit of alternative possible interpretations.

To see in more detail how fitting theories run into difficulty, it may help to examine some of the simple "fitting theory" proposals for stopping the regress that Wittgenstein considers and rejects in his later work, the *Philosophical Investigations*. Faced with a threatened regress of the interpretation of one linguistic sign by another, it is natural to locate the difficulty in the nature of the signs. Of course, one may suppose, it is hopeless to stop a regress of interpretations by appeal to mere linguistic signs, since they are inevitably subject to various possible interpretations. But not all signs suffer from the deficiency of linguistic signs. This intuition was expressed clearly in 1923 by some of Wittgenstein's contemporaries: "An exceptional case occurs when the symbol used is more or less directly like the referent for which it is used, as for instance, it may be when it is an onomatopoeic word, or an image, or a gesture, or a drawing. In this case . . . a great simplification of the problem involved appears to result."[10] In short, the suggestion appears to be that some signs, unlike ordinary linguistic signs, do not admit of various possible interpretations, since they are "more or less directly like" that to which they point (i.e., they resemble that to which they point). Consider, in that vein, the following proposals discussed and dismissed by Wittgenstein in the *Philosophical Investigations*.

### Ostensive definition

Someone encountering for the first time this puzzle about how signs point might suppose that ostensive definition (i.e., the gesture of pointing to the object meant while uttering the appropriate linguistic sign) provides a simple solution to the puzzle. Rather than producing another linguistic sign that needs to be interpreted, one merely points to the object meant. Perhaps, so the suggestion goes, it would be difficult to point unambiguously to some sorts of objects (e.g., numbers rather than numerals), but others will be easy (e.g., ordinary middle-sized physical objects). According to this proposal, the gesture of pointing is itself a sign, but it is a sign that "fits" onto what it means in a way that ordinary linguistic signs do not.

Wittgenstein grants that we do ostensively define all sorts of things, but he gives short shrift to the idea that an appeal to ostensive definition will do the trick. To accompany a word by a gesture of pointing is merely to offer another sign which can, in turn, be interpreted in various possible ways: for example, if I point to a person and utter "Sally," the person to whom I am giving the ostensive definition may take me to be giving the name "of a colour, of a race, or even of a point of the compass" (PI, 28). As Wittgenstein insists: "an ostensive definition can be variously interpreted in *every* case" (PI, 28). To offer additional words designed to avert misunderstandings of the pointing is merely to offer yet more signs which can, in their turn, be interpreted in various possible ways. Suppose, for example, that I try to avert a misunderstanding by uttering " 'This *colour* is called so-and-so' " or by uttering " 'This *length* is called so-and-so' " (PI, 29). Clearly, more than one interpretation of the words "color" and "length" are possible. Wittgenstein's interlocutor objects: "Well, they just need defining." And Wittgenstein retorts: "Defining, then, by means of other words! And what about the last definition in this chain? (Do not say: 'There isn't a "last" definition.' That is just as if you chose to say: 'There isn't a last house in this road; one can always build an additional one')" (PI, 29). We end up no further along than when we began: we begin and we end in a situation in which various interpretations are possible, and we feel the need to find something which will exclude all but one of the possible interpretations.

It may seem that a picture or drawing, unlike an ordinary linguistic sign or even a bodily gesture, may "directly resemble" what it pictures in a way that may stop the regress of interpretations. And yet, any two things are similar in some respects and not in others, in a way that opens the door to various possible interpretations. As Wittgenstein puts the point: "I see a picture; it represents an old man walking up a steep path leaning on a stick. – How? Might it not have looked just the same if he had been sliding downhill in that position?" (PI, 139). Just as any gesture may be variously interpreted, so also any picture or drawing may be variously interpreted. Just as any gesture can be "fitted" onto that to which it points in more than one way, so also any picture or drawing can be "fitted" onto what it pictures in more than one way. Neither ostensive definitions nor ordinary pictures will stop the regress of interpretations; both are themselves merely signs that admit of various possible interpretations.

### Mental images

Some may suggest that we have so far ignored an obvious point. Of course we cannot hope to fix the interpretation of one linguistic sign by appeal to another that itself requires interpretation, since that leads to an infinite regress of interpretations. And of course we cannot hope to fix the interpretation of one linguistic sign by appeal to anything else that ends up functioning as a sign that requires interpretation, as ordinary gestures, drawings, and samples invariably do. What we need is something that is not itself a sign standing in need of interpretation, but that will serve to fix the interpretation of other signs. Perhaps, then, we should look, not outward toward gestures, drawings, and samples that themselves turn out to function as mere signs which can be variously interpreted, but inward toward our own *thoughts* or *mental images*. Our own thoughts and mental images surely cannot be said to stand in need of interpretation. In fact, we cannot interpret our own internal thoughts or mental images as we can interpret external signs; we have them, and no question arises or can arise as to what they mean.

But Wittgenstein refuses to allow that the question of whether a representation is mental and inner or physical and outer makes any difference at all to the problem he is after: "And can't it be clearly seen here that it is absolutely inessential for the picture to exist in his imagination rather than as a drawing or model in front of him; or again as something that he himself constructs as a model?" (PI, 141). I will suggest that there is an excellent reason for Wittgenstein to refuse to allow that the fact that a picture exists in the imagination rather than as a drawing or model will solve his problem.

According to the fitting theory on offer, we need to distinguish between linguistic signs on the one hand and mental signs (thoughts)

on the other: linguistic signs point, that is, language has intentionality, because thoughts have intentionality; the regress of interpretations is stopped because thoughts need no interpretation in order to represent.

So far, so good. However, there is an important distinction to be
made at this point, a distinction we may refer to as a distinction
between *original* and *brute* intentionality. If a state or event has
original intentionality, its capacity to represent something other
than itself cannot be explained by appeal to the *intentionality* of any
other states or events (its "aboutness" is "first" or "original"), but
its capacity to represent may nevertheless require explanation. By
contrast, if a state or event has *brute* intentionality, its capacity to
represent something other than itself cannot and need not be explained at all.[11]

According to the fitting theory on offer, thought, rather than
language, has original intentionality: we explain the "aboutness" of
linguistic signs by appeal to the "aboutness" of thoughts. But to
say this leaves the "aboutness" of thoughts themselves unexplained. The threatened regress of interpretations challenges the
very possibility of intentionality; fitting theories of content determination are designed to explain the possibility of intentionality.
An appeal to the intentionality of thoughts that stops here does not
halt the regress or explain how intentionality is possible. Rather, it
treats the intentionality of thought as an unexplained primitive,
saying, in effect, that the intentionality of thought is not only
*original*, but also *brute*. In short, such a response, if it goes no
further, presupposes precisely what it was supposed to explain, that
is, the possibility of intentionality.

By contrast, if thoughts are taken to have original but not brute
intentionality, then the question of how thoughts point will rear its
head: even if thoughts do not represent in virtue of the intentionality of any other states, so long as their intentionality is not
brute, we still need some explanation of how thoughts manage to
point to something other than themselves. Fitting theorists have
one general answer available to them: thoughts point in virtue of
resembling their objects. For example, mental images point in virtue
of resembling states of affairs. But now it is the appeal to *resemblance*, not the appeal to the mental character of that which bears
the resemblance, which has to do the work of providing the explana-

tion of the intentionality of the mental. And so, as Wittgenstein insists, "can't it be clearly seen here that it is absolutely inessential for the picture to exist in his imagination rather than as a drawing or model in front of him; or again as something that he himself constructs as a model?" (PI, 141). Since any two things, mental or not, are similar in some respects, and not in others, the door is open for various possible ways of "fitting" a mental image onto the world that is represented.[12]

### IV  TRACKING THEORIES

As we have seen, fitting theories try to stop the threatened regress by finding something that will serve as a "last" interpretation. But they offer only more signs and all signs appear to admit of alternative possible interpretations. Fitting theories thus do not provide, but point to the need for, a way of stopping the regress that is not a matter of interpretation. Immediately following Wittgenstein's famous statement of a paradox about rule-following at *Philosophical Investigations* 201, Wittgenstein expresses his dissatisfaction with any attempt to try to stop a regress in the way the fitting theorist tries to do:

> It can be seen that there is a misunderstanding here from the mere fact that in the course of our argument we give one interpretation after another; as if each one contented us at least for a moment, until we thought of yet another standing behind it. What this shows is that there is a way of grasping a rule which is *not* an *interpretation*, but which is exhibited in what we call "obeying the rule" and "going against it" in actual cases. (PI, 201)

At first glance, tracking theories appear to offer just the sort of solution Wittgenstein seeks. As we shall see, the problem of alternative interpretations simply disappears for tracking theories, since tracking theories forge a much more intimate connection than do fitting theories between signs and that to which they point. Whereas fitting theories have difficulty ruling out the possibility of alternative interpretations, pure tracking theories do not admit the need for, or possibility of, alternative interpretations, since an objective and external relation between signs and what they represent determines content. In sum, whereas fitting theories have difficulty with getting signs to point to what is actually there, tracking theories *guarantee* that signs will point to what is actually there, by building that feature into the basis of the theory.[13]

Unlike fitting theories, tracking theories deny that a sign's similarity to particular things determines that it represents those things; rather, a sign represents all and only what it "tracks." According to tracking theorists, what a sign tracks is not "up to us"; what a sign tracks is not a matter open to our "interpretation" and control. Let's look a bit more closely at the way in which tracking theories seek to exclude the possibility of alternative interpretations: if representation is a matter of the nonaccidental or nonarbitrary covariance of signs and that to which they point, then it is not a matter of interpretation at all; if there are sufficiently tight connections between signs and that to which they point, then content is completely determined by those connections. In short, content is objectively determinate and thus not subject to the variability of our interpretations; content is determined by that which is external and thus there is no possibility of various ways of "fitting" our representations onto that which is external.

Two points here are worth stressing. Tracking theories make content (a) independent of our interpretation and control and (b) objectively determinate. Consider, for example, causal versions of tracking theories, that is, versions according to which the connection between a sign and what it represents is a naturalistic causal relation. If it is the naturalistic causal relation between a sign and an object (or property) in virtue of which the sign is "about" the object (or property), then what the sign is "about" is not up to us. The world, not the thinker/speaker, determines the correct interpretation, which is to say that it is not a matter open to our interpretation at all. Causal connections, not interpretations, determine content.[14]

The second point, though related, is different: (b) pure tracking theories make content objectively determinate. Consider, for example, the crude causal/behaviorist theory that Russell introduces (but does not endorse) in "On Propositions: What They Are and How They Mean": "John" means John if and only if "John" is caused by John's appearance and in turn causes John to appear.[15] More generally, "X" means X if and only if "X" is caused all and only by the occurrence of Xs and in turn causes all and only Xs to occur. Like all pure tracking theories, this crude causal/behaviorist theory makes content objectively determinate. This theory says exactly what the extension of "John" is: the set of all the causes and effects of tokens of that symbol. Metaphysically speaking, content is perfectly determinate. The general point is this: pure tracking theories have what appears to be an extremely important advantage over fitting theories, that is, they make content objectively determinate by appeal to something external, to something that is not a matter of our interpretation. They promise both complete determinacy and utter independence of interpretation.

But now notice that a serious problem arises immediately: how is it possible for signs to point to what is *not* there? If a sign's content is determined by that with which it nonaccidentally covaries, how can any sign have content in the absence of that with which it covaries? This problem, relatively unobtrusive for fitting theories, looms large for tracking theories. With their focus on guaranteeing reference to what *is* there, the connection between signs and that to which they point becomes so tight that pointing to what is *not* there becomes the major challenge. The problem takes various forms:

> *Nonexistent objects:* How is it possible to think about objects that do not exist and never have (e.g., unicorns)?
>
> *Falsehood and other sorts of error:* How is it possible to think what is false (e.g., The president of the United States in 1996 is Ronald Reagan) or to misrepresent something as what it is not (e.g., to think of a horse on a dark night as a cow)?
>
> *The robustness of meaning:* How is it possible to think of something, correctly or incorrectly, in its absence? (e.g., I may think of Excalibur, a sword, when it no longer exists; I may think of milk when I look in a refrigerator that contains none; I may think of a cow when my child asks where milk comes from, though there are no cows anywhere nearby).

In our discussion of fitting theories, we saw that, at least by the time he wrote the *Philosophical Investigations*, Wittgenstein rejects resemblance theories and, more generally, fitting theories, because they fail to stop the regress of interpretations, offering only more signs that themselves may be "fitted" onto the world in more than one way. Tracking theories, because they appeal to external relations to link signs to their objects, appear to halt this regress of "interpretations." And yet, as we have seen, they face the troubling problem of how signs can point to what is not there. In what follows, we will see that the later Wittgenstein was aware of this central problem for tracking theories.

The later Wittgenstein acknowledges the prima facie appeal of something like a causal version of a tracking theory in some of the central *Philosophical Investigations* passages on rule-following. Whereas some signs (names) are supposed to point to objects and others (complete sentences) are supposed to point to the states of affairs that make them true, still others (the expressions of orders or commands or rules) are supposed to point to the actions that would constitute carrying them out. At *Philosophical Investigations* 198, Wittgenstein responds to a skeptical interlocutor's query about how rule-expressions can point to actions:

"But how can a rule shew me what I have to do at *this* point? Whatever I do is, on some interpretation, in accord with the rule." – That is not what we ought to say, but rather: any interpretation still hangs in the air along with what it interprets, and cannot give it any support. Interpretations by themselves do not determine meaning.

"Then can whatever I do be brought into accord with the rule?" – Let me ask this: what has the expression of a rule – say a sign-post – got to do with my actions? What sort of connexion is there here? – Well, perhaps this one: I have been trained to react to this sign in a particular way, and now I do so react to it.

Wittgenstein appears, at first glance, to reject the attempt to give "interpretations" in favor of a broadly causal account of the relation between the expressions of rules and the actions to which they are supposed to point. And yet, he stops short of doing so. The passage just cited continues: "But that is only to give a causal connexion; to tell how it has come about that we now go by the sign-post; not what this going-by-the-sign really consists in. On the contrary; I have further indicated that a person goes by a sign-post only in so far as there exists a regular use of sign-posts, a custom" (PI, 198). Wittgenstein seems to think that a causal account will not do, that it must at least be supplemented in some way, for example, by appeal to a custom or practice.[16]

What is the central problem, according to the later Wittgenstein, with a causal/tracking account of the relation between signs and that to which they point? At *Philosophical Investigations* 51, he discusses a language-game which "serves to describe combinations of coloured squares on a surface," squares which "form a complex like a chessboard" (PI, 48). The words of this language are "R," "G," "W," "B," sentences of this language consist of series of these words, and the sentences are supposed to describe particular arrangements of red, green, white, and black squares.[17]

In describing language-game (48) I said that the words "R," "B," etc. corresponded to the colours of the squares. But what does this correspondence consist in; in what sense can one say that certain colours of squares correspond to these signs? For the account in (48) merely set up a connexion between those signs and certain words of our language (the names of colours). – Well, it was presupposed that the use of the signs in the language-game would be taught in a different way, in particular by pointing to paradigms. Very well; but what does it mean to say that in the *technique of using the language* certain elements correspond to the signs? – Is it that the person who is describing the complexes of coloured squares always says "R" where there is a red square; "B" when there is a black one, and so on? But what if he goes wrong in the description and mistakenly says "R" where he sees a black square – what is the criterion by which this is a *mistake?* – Or does "R" 's standing for a red square consist in this, that when the people whose language it is use the sign "R" a red square always comes before their minds?

Wittgenstein asks what the correspondence between signs (e.g., "R") and that to which they are supposed to point (e.g., the red colored square) "consists in." He first points out that the initial description of the language-game at *Philosophical Investigations* 48 merely translates the words of the language-game under consideration into words with which we are already familiar, into words which already "point." When the interlocutor suggests that the connection is set up when the language is learned, for example, by pointing to paradigms, Wittgenstein seems to brush the suggestion aside. *However* the connection is set up, what does it consist in? What is it for a word of the language in question to correspond to a particular colored square?

Notice that Wittgenstein then alludes to the two main answers we have been considering. On the one hand, one might say that the connection consists in the fact that "the person who is describing the complexes of coloured squares always says 'R' where there is a red square." This is a tracking theory. On the other hand, one might say that the connection consists in the fact that "when the people whose language it is use the sign 'R' a red square always comes before their minds." This recalls an image version of a fitting theory. We've seen why Wittgenstein rejects fitting theories. But in this passage (PI, 48) he also rejects tracking theories: "what if he goes wrong in the description and mistakenly says 'R' where he sees a black square – what is the criterion by which this is a *mistake?*" Our discussion of the problems tracking theories have with getting signs to point to what is not there enables us to understand the difficulty to which Wittgenstein alludes. If the connection between "R" and that to which it points is constituted by covariance, then whatever "R" covaries with will constitute its content. If a person says "R" in the presence of a red square on one occasion and in the presence of a black square on another occasion, then "R" *means* red-or-black square, and there is *no* criterion by which her response is a *mistake.* Whatever the person says will be right! As Wittgenstein writes in a somewhat different context: "And that only means that here we can't talk about 'right' " (PI, 258).

Serious difficulties thus face both fitting and tracking attempts to explain intentionality. As the Wittgenstein of the *Philosophical Investigations* recognized, fitting theories apparently fail to explain how signs can point to what is; tracking theories apparently fail to explain how signs can point to what is not. Both fitting and tracking theories thus fail to explain something that seems obvious: we talk and think about things, both as they are and as they are not. In the face of these difficulties, it is tempting to think of the intentionality of thought as remarkable and mysterious. At various points in the *Investigations*, Wittgenstein gives voice to this temptation, even as he warns us against it.

"Thought must be something unique." When we say, and *mean,* that such-and-such is the case, we – and our meaning – do not stop anywhere short of the fact; but we mean – *this is so.* But this paradox (which has the form of a truism) can also be expressed in this way: *Thought* can be of what is *not* the case. (PI, 95)

A wish seems already to know what will or would satisfy it; a proposition, a thought, what makes it true – even when that thing is not there at all! Whence this *determining* of what is not yet there? This despotic demand? ("The hardness of the logical must.") (PI, 437)

## V   THE *TRACTATUS* SOLUTION: A TWO-LEVEL THEORY

Throughout his philosophical life, Wittgenstein wrestled with the problem of how signs point to what is not there. In the *Tractatus*, he raises it by asking how a proposition can be meaningful but false.[18] Even before the *Tractatus*, he had given graphic expression to the problem: "How can there be such a thing as the form of *p* if there is no situation of this form? And in that case, what does this form really consist in?" (NB, p. 21). In the *Philosophical Investigations*, Wittgenstein raises the same problem again, but this time, it takes various forms: How can names refer to objects that I may misidentify? How can rules direct actions that I may fail to carry out? How can expectations point to events that may not occur? Whatever the form, this is arguably *the* central problem of Wittgenstein's writings, a problem that stems from his concern with the nature of representation.

Wittgenstein is famous for having offered a "picture" theory of meaning or representation. That theory is often caricatured as something like a simple resemblance or mapping theory, a theory of the kind we have called "fitting theories." However, as we saw above, the ordinary notion of a "picture" or "model" contains both "fitting" and "tracking" elements. For example, a photograph of my son Anthony *resembles* him, but it also *tracks* certain features of his. In fact, we could say that the resemblance *results* from the tracking: because a photograph is produced in a way that is under the control of or directed by its object, it comes to resemble it. Even if the photograph looks more like my spouse's brother as a child than it looks like Anthony, it is still a picture of Anthony, not of his uncle.

In contrast with common interpretations of Wittgenstein's *Tractatus* as a naive fitting theory, I believe that the so-called picture theory is a two-level theory which combines elements of both fitting and tracking theories. By combining elements of both fitting and tracking theories, the early Wittgenstein offers an explanation of how it is possible for signs to point that is more sophisticated than either the fitting theories or the tracking theories so far considered. In fact, if his theory is correct, the regress of interpretations is halted in a way that yields complete determinacy and yet shows how signs can point to what is not there. The trick is to make a radical distinction between two sorts of connections that signs have to the world, fitting and tracking, and to allot different connections to different sorts of signs.

### Names and objects: Propositions and facts

The challenge Wittgenstein faces is clear: to stop the threatened regress of interpretations in a way that offers both determinacy and a solution to the problem of how signs can point to what is not there. To meet that challenge, the early Wittgenstein makes a radical distinction between Names[19] and propositions and, correspondingly, between objects and facts: Names track objects and so no Name can point to what is not there; propositions fit (or fail to fit) facts and so any proposition can point to what is not there.

According to the *Tractatus*, propositional signs are made true (or false) by facts, not by objects; moreover, propositional signs are themselves facts, not objects. Facts are determinate configurations of objects, that is, objects in a particular arrangement. Thus, both what is represented by propositions and the signs that do the representing consist of elements in a determinate configuration. The simple elements of propositions, that is, Names, correspond to the simple elements of facts, that is, objects. Names stand in for objects.

According to the *Tractatus*, propositions have sense (*Sinn*), but not reference (*Bedeutung*); Names have reference (*Bedeutung*), but not sense (*Sinn*). Since Names have only *Bedeutung* and not *Sinn*, that is, since it is only their standing in for an object in virtue of which they have any semantic content at all, no Name can fail to stand in for an object and still be a Name. Without its corresponding object, a Name would be devoid of significance, a meaningless sound or squiggle or mental event. By contrast, since propositional signs have only *Sinn* and not *Bedeutung*, that is, since their semantic content does not consist in a correspondence to something in the world, a proposition can fail to correspond to a fact and yet retain its semantic content. Without its corresponding fact, a propositional sign is not devoid of significance – it still has sense (*Sinn*).

Although Wittgenstein does not use the tracking/fitting terminology I have introduced, what he says about the relationship between Names and objects parallels to some extent what was said above about tracking theories, whereas what he says about the relationship between propositions and facts parallels to some extent what was said above about fitting theories: Names "track" their objects but they do not "fit" them; propositions "fit" (or fail to fit) the facts that make them true (or false) but they do not "track" them (false propositions occur in the absence of the facts that would make them true if they obtained).

How is error possible on this account? An example will help to convey Wittgenstein's answer. Suppose I want to model with toy cars an accident that took place with real cars. I stipulate which toy cars will stand in for which real cars and then I can place the toy cars in an arrangement that shows how the accident actually occurred. But I can misrepresent the facts by arranging the same toy cars differently. Though what the toy cars "say" in that alternative arrangement is "false," still they show how the real cars would have been arranged in the world if what they "say" were "true." My toy model shows one thing, but says another. What it says may be false, but what it shows is a genuine possibility, one among many possible arrangements of the cars both in reality and in the model. We might say that, even though a particular arrangement of the model may be false, it nevertheless makes sense. The model makes sense because toy cars have possibilities for combining with one another and with other toy cars that mirror the possibilities real cars have for combining with one another. The model has "form" (its elements have various possibilities for combining with one another and with other toy cars), not just "structure" (the particular way in which the toy cars actually are combined), and its form matches the form of the real cars even when its structure does not match the structure of the real accident. (For Wittgenstein's distinction between structure and form, see TLP, 2.15–2.151.)

The Wittgenstein of the *Tractatus* gives the same explanation for propositions: a proposition can be meaningful, but false, because the elements of propositions can be arranged in ways that present possible, but not actual, arrangements of elements in the world for which the elements of propositions go proxy; by looking at a meaningful proposition, I can see how matters would be in the world if the proposition were true without knowing how in fact they are.

> *Step 1:* A proposition (*Satz*) may be meaningful, but false, only if it is a fact, that is, a determinate configuration of

elements, such that the elements can be arranged in ways that present possible, but not actual, situations.

### What halts the regress?

Note that we made a couple of crucial assumptions in talking about arrangements of our model cars as representations of real and merely possible accidents. First is that the elements of the model (the toy cars) stand in for particular elements in reality (real cars); second, but equally important, is that the toy cars can combine with one another in the same ways that the real cars can combine with one another. If these conditions are not met, the model will not show anything about what might have occurred and it will not say (correctly or incorrectly) what did occur.

What guarantee do we have that these assumptions are met? In the case of the model cars we made the elements of the model stand in for particular elements in reality by stipulation, and we relied on the spatial similarity of toy cars to real cars to guarantee (more or less) that the ways in which the toy cars combine will match ways in which the real cars could combine (e.g., we chose three-dimensional metal or plastic toy cars rather than dots of colored paper with which to construct our model). This presupposed that we already had a system of representation, that we could, for example, say something like "Let the pink model car stand in for my 1986 Olds." In short, we made the elements of the model stand in for particular elements by translating them into another language whose elements already stand in for objects and already can be combined in ways that make sense; we "interpreted" the elements of the model by substituting other signs, signs presumed to need no interpretation.

If our goal is to explain how propositions can be meaningful, but false (or, more generally, how signs can point to what is not there), we cannot rest content with these tactics, since they presuppose what we are supposed to explain. To "interpret" the elements of our model, we appeal to other signs. We would have to raise the question of how the signs used to set up the connection between the model cars and the real cars themselves manage to point. A regress of interpretations threatens.

This is where Wittgenstein's answer to the question of how propositions can be meaningful but false diverges from our explanation of how model cars can depict an accident that did not occur. For one thing, it is not our choices, but logical form, that guarantees that our pictures/thoughts/propositions reveal what is possible for objects.[20] If logic describes the logical form of thought, language, and the world, the process of constructing pictures in accord with logically necessary rules will enable us to uncover a priori the logical form of any possible situation. It will not, however, enable us to uncover the particular structure of actual situations; that will be a matter for experience. The fact that representations have the logical form they do will guarantee that any situation we may encounter will have the same logical form. It is not our choices, but "logical form," that guarantees that the elements of a representation can combine only in ways that are possible for elements of the situation represented: the "rules" that determine how the elements of representations can combine are necessary rules of thinking. "What makes logic a priori is the *impossibility* of illogical thought" (TLP, 5.4731).

> *Step 2:* The elements of a proposition (*Satz*) can be arranged in ways that present possible, but not actual, situations only if those elements have the same possibilities of combining as do the elements for which they go proxy. Propositions must share logical form with what they represent.

But logical form is not basic on the *Tractatus* account. It rather presupposes simple objects and their powers of combination.

> The "experience" that we need in order to understand logic is not that something or other is the state of things, but that something *is:* that, however, is *not* an experience.
> Logic is *prior* to every experience – that something *is so.*
> It is prior to the question "How?", not prior to the question "What?"
> And if this were not so, how could we apply logic? We might put it in this way: if there would be a logic even if there were no world, how then could there be a logic given that there is a world? (TLP, 5.552–5.5521)

At *Tractatus* 2.025, Wittgenstein declares that simple objects are "form and content." Though one would intuitively think of them as providing the content rather than the form of our representations, Wittgenstein claims that they "constitute" logical form: "It is obvious that an imagined world, however different it may be from the real one, must have *something* – a form – in common with it. Objects are just what constitute this unalterable form" (TLP, 2.022–2.023). I suggest that Wittgenstein in the *Tractatus* takes thus a third step:

> *Step 3:* A proposition can share logical form with reality only if there are nonaccidental connections between Names and simple objects whose possibilities for combining to form facts determine/constitute logical form.

Thus, on my reading of the *Tractatus*, Wittgenstein's account of how propositions can be meaningful, but false, diverges here once again from our simple model of a car accident. Whereas we set up the connection between the elements of our model and real cars, the connection between atomic Names and simple objects is not up to us: our ability to use signs to say what we wish presupposes that connection (see TLP, 6.124). Moreover, whereas we supposed that "Let the pink toy car stand in for my 1986 Olds" was itself a representation, the connection between atomic Names and simple objects, according to Wittgenstein, cannot itself be represented in signs: that there is such a connection is something that is "shown," not "said."[21]

If this is Wittgenstein's view, it is not a pure fitting theory. Recall our simple toy car model of an accident: we might say that our model (when it is correct) "fits" the accident that makes it correct, but the "fitting" is not what makes it a model. Similarly, propositional signs "fit" the facts that make them true (when they are true), but that is not what gives them sense. Rather, they must have sense in order to be capable of fitting or failing to fit facts. They have sense, not because they fit facts, but because they share logical form with reality. This, too, is a kind of resemblance, so it may seem at first glance to be a kind of attenuated fitting theory: the possibilities Names have for combining to form propositions mirror the possibilities objects have for combining to form facts. But in my reading of the *Tractatus* this is a kind of resemblance that derives from and presupposes a connection between real Names and simple objects. The powers simple objects have of combining with one another to form facts determine the logical possibilities. And the Name/object connection, which is utterly different from and makes possible the proposition/fact connection, guarantees that atomic Names share those powers of combining.

Why should we think of the Name/object relation as a tracking relation? Recall the characterization of tracking theories above: (a) a sign's having content is a matter of its covarying in a nonaccidental or nonarbitrary way with something other than itself; (b) a sign's content is determined by that with which it covaries; (c) signs point, in the first instance, to what is there. Compare the *Tractatus* account: in the *Tractatus*, (a) a propositional sign's having content (*Sinn*) or being about something other than itself is a matter of its elements (Names) corresponding to simple objects. The Tractarian version contains a twist – propositions themselves do not covary with facts, and names, which do covary with objects, do not have full-blooded representational content.[22] But a propositional sign's having content is a matter of its elements corresponding in a nonaccidental way with objects. Moreover, in line with (c), Names have nothing more than *Bedeutung* and they cannot fail to correspond to objects: "Objects can only be *named*. Signs are their representatives. I can only speak *about* them: I cannot *put them into words*. Propositions can only say *how* things are, not *what* they are" (TLP, 3.221). Finally, (b) a propositional sign's content is determined by that with which its Names covary: "The possibility of propositions is based on the principle that objects have signs as their representatives" (TLP, 4.0312).

*No account of the mechanisms*

Of course, there are objections to thinking of the *Tractatus* as anything like a tracking theory. For one thing, we do not get any explicit account in the *Tractatus* of what mechanisms mediate the connection between Names and objects, and that may seem unsatisfying. We want to know what mechanisms connect Names and objects, language and the world. What keeps Names and objects in harmony? We would feel better if we had an answer such as: (a) God sets up a preestablished harmony between Names and objects or (b) the laws of nature connect Names and objects or (c) we set up the connection by such and such a method. Wittgenstein gives none of these explanations.

But that does not disqualify the Name/object relation as a tracking relation. It means only that Wittgenstein has no story he feels it necessary to tell about the mechanisms that mediate the connection between Names and objects. Other, more contemporary tracking theorists are almost equally adamant that the specific nature of the mediating mechanisms is irrelevant.[23]

Arguments for sophisticated fitting theory accounts of the *Tractatus* sometimes rely on the following false dilemma: Names get their *Bedeutung* in acts of ostension or "dubbing" or their *Bedeutung* is determined by the use they have within language. Since Wittgenstein does not explicitly endorse the former option, and since, for reasons considered above, acts of ostension would not succeed in establishing the connection, we should conclude that the *Bedeutung* of Names is determined by their use. In a classic article, "Use and Reference of Names," Hidé Ishiguro poses the following dilemma in the process of defending a sophisticated fitting view of Names in the *Tractatus* combined with an "antirealist" view of objects: "The interesting question, I think, is whether the meaning of a name can be secured independently of its use in propositions by some method which links it to an object, as many, including Russell, have thought, or whether the identity of the object referred to is only settled by the use of a name in a set of propositions."[24]

But this either/or ignores other possibilities. Perhaps Wittgenstein in the *Tractatus* does not think that it matters in the least what mediates the connection between Names and objects, since it is the connection that determines content, not any relations that may mediate it. Or perhaps he supposes that the Name/object connection is not something we set up in any way, either by acts of ostension or by our use of language: it is presupposed by our ability to use signs to say and to think what we wish and how things are and it is already in place in the language of thought.[25] Both alternatives are consistent with giving tracking accounts of the Name/object relation. Thus, I conclude that the objection that Wittgenstein offers no account of the mechanisms that connect Names and objects does not in any way count against interpreting the Name/object relation as a tracking relation.

### Brute vs. original intentionality

Someone may object that if the *Tractatus* gives no account of how the Name/object connection is set up, then it simply presupposes what it sets out to explain by assuming that Names do refer to objects.

Names, according to this suggestion, are taken to have *brute* rather than merely *original* intentionality, and thus their intentionality is regarded as basic and inexplicable. However, in the view proposed here Wittgenstein does not presuppose what he sets out to explain, and he does not appeal to brute "aboutness" to solve his problem. Rather, he offers an explanation of how it is possible for any sign, thought-sign or not, to make sense and yet be false. The explanation presupposes the Name/object connection, but since that connection is radically different from the propositional sign/thought/fact connection, the explanation is not circular.

If Wittgenstein had made no distinction between the relationship between propositions and facts on the one hand and the relationship between Names and objects on the other, or if he had made it merely a matter of degree, he would be open to the following objection: the account of how a proposition can be meaningful but false presupposes an account of how a Name can stand in for an object. But no such account is given. Hence, Wittgenstein presupposes what he set out to explain, just as we did in our discussion of modeling a car accident.

But Wittgenstein's radical distinction between propositions/facts on the one hand and Names/objects on the other hand enables him to evade this attack. First, Names do not point in the way that propositions do. The Name/object connection is not the same sort of connection as the proposition/fact connection. Names track objects; propositions fit facts. Names have only *Bedeutung;* propositions have only *Sinn.* In an important sense, Names, unlike propositions and arrows, do not "point" at all: "(Names are like points; propositions like arrows – they have sense)" (TLP, 3.144). So to explain one connection via the other is not to presuppose the same thing one set out to explain. Second, unlike propositions, Names cannot point to what is not there. So there is no need to explain how they *can* point to what is not there.

### Holism vs. atomism

Another objection may be raised at this point: the *Tractatus,* one might argue, is not atomistic in the way tracking theories are supposed to be. The Wittgenstein of the *Tractatus* echoes with approval Frege's famous context principle: "only in the context of a proposition has a name meaning" (TLP, 3.3, Ogden's translation). On this account, there is no possibility of separating off the Name/object relation from the relations Names bear to other Names in the language: if a Name has *Bedeutung* it is and must be able to combine with some Names and not with others. In short, the tracking and fitting elements seem to coalesce in the *Tractatus*. So it seems that the *Tractatus* is, at bottom, holistic in a way that fitting theories are and tracking theories are not.

The *Tractatus* is, however, atomistic in an important sense. Given Wittgenstein's denial of the antecedent of 2.0211, his atomism amounts to the claim that whether an (elementary) proposition has sense does not depend on whether another (elementary) proposition is true. The sense of any one (elementary) proposition is supposed to be independent of the truth-value of any other (elementary) proposition. Sense is independent of the facts, of what happens to be the case. Consequently, sense is equally independent of what I actually believe and of what pictures (correct or incorrect) I make for myself of the facts.

At the same time, the *Tractatus* is holistic in another sense: the *Sinn* of a proposition and the *Bedeutung* of a name are independent of all actual relations to other propositions and to other names, but not independent of all logically possible relations to other propositions and to other names. As Wittgenstein puts the point at *Tractatus* 2.0122: "Things are independent in so far as they can occur in all *possible* situations, but this form of independence is a form of connexion with states of affairs, a form of dependence. (It is impossible for words to appear in two different roles: by themselves, and in propositions.)" Unlike paradigmatic tracking theorists, the Wittgenstein of the *Tractatus* insists that the proposition, not the Name (or any subsentential unit), is the smallest unit to display full semantic content (and so the locus of full-fledged intentionality or "aboutness"), since only the proposition, not the Name, can "point to what is not there." Names contribute to the content of the propositions in which they occur, but they do not have content independently and on their own.

But this sort of holism is compatible with a tracking account of the Name/object relation. I have pointed out that, in order to give an account of how a proposition can be meaningful, but false (more generally, how signs can point to what is not there), the

*Tractatus* diverges from paradigmatic tracking theories by insisting on a radical distinction between Names and propositions: unlike paradigmatic tracking theories, the difference between Names and propositions is not merely one of degree, but of kind. I have also emphasized that, on the *Tractarian* account, the Name/object relation makes possible the proposition/fact relation precisely by determining, not the actual combinations of Names into true sentences, but the possible combinations of Names into meaningful sentences. Thus, it is central to the *Tractatus* account, as presented here, that the *Bedeutung* of a Name, though independent of all actual relations to other Names, is not independent of all logically possible relations to other Names. This form of holism appears to be compatible with a tracking theory account of the Name/object relation.

### Sophisticated fitting theory alternatives

Even if the text of the *Tractatus* is largely compatible with a tracking theory account of the Name/object relation, however, it may be objected that an alternative reading of the *Tractatus* as a sophisticated fitting theory is more plausible and so should be preferred. On this reading of the *Tractatus*, the reference of a Name is determined by and, indeed, constituted by, its use in propositions. As in the fitting theories described above, semantic content is fixed by the relationships among the elements of representations. But in contrast to them, if a sign has a coherent use, then it is guaranteed a reference since reference is taken to be nothing "metaphysical," nothing over and above the use of a sign in a language.

This view is defended by Hidé Ishiguro in "Use and Reference of Names."[26] Ishiguro combines a sophisticated fitting view of content with an "antirealist" reading of objects (in the sense that objects are "intensional" rather than "extensional" and "linguistic" or "dependent on language" rather than "metaphysical" or "independent of language"): "the notions of '*Bedeutung*' (reference) and '*Bedeuten*' (refer) are intensional ones in the *Tractatus* and, therefore . . . the simple objects whose existence was posited were not so much a kind of metaphysical entity conjured up to support a logical theory as something whose existence adds no extra content to the logical theory."[27]

Notice that this view promises to sidestep the central problem for fitting theories generally: if reference is guaranteed and, indeed, constituted by the coherent use of items in a language, there is no room for alternative ways of fitting signs onto that to which they point. The gap between language and world that would make such alternative mappings possible is rejected.

However, this view faces head-on the central problem we uncovered for tracking theories. Like tracking theories, it forges an intimate link between language and the world, although the link evidently differs from that posited by paradigmatic tracking theories. Whereas tracking theories insist that a name tracks its object, and so cannot be pried apart from it, this theory insists that the use of a name within propositions constitutes its object, and for that reason cannot be pried apart from it. Thus, like tracking theories, the Ishiguro view faces the problem of how signs can point to what is not there. Recall the particular form this problem takes in the *Tractatus:* Wittgenstein insists that every real proposition can be meaningful, but false. In other words, every proposition can have sense even though the situation it represents does not obtain. I do not see how theories of the sort just described can meet this demand.

Ishiguro argues, for example, that the elementary propositions by which Names are introduced cannot be false if they have sense at all. How does she arrive at this conclusion? According to her reading of the *Tractatus,* Names are linguistic elements, items that have a use in a language. Moreover, Names are the simplest linguistic elements, items that occur only in the context of elementary propositions. On the view she endorses, the semantic content of Names derives from and is constituted by their role in the language: to have a reference is simply to have the right sort of use. Names, as simple signs which cannot be defined, are supposed to refer to simple objects which cannot be described. But their so referring is nothing "metaphysical," nothing over and above their having a coherent use within elementary propositions. Names get introduced via their connections with other signs, because if reference is a matter of use within a language, that is the only way they can be introduced. But because Names are supposed to be simple, they cannot be introduced by definition or description. According to Ishiguro's reading of *Tractatus* 5.526, they are introduced through elementary propositions of the form $(\exists x)$ fx . x=a, statements that say that a basic, irreducible property is instantiated: there is a so and so which. . . . [28] Names in the *Tractatus* are like "dummy names" in elementary geometry proofs, that is, they are like names ascribed to "objects which are assumed to have no properties except those which are ascribed to them in the proofs."[29]

Similarly, Names are introduced in such a way that, if the propositions in which they occur have a coherent use, they cannot fail to refer. "Since we *introduce* the name '$A$' by saying $(\exists x)$ fx and this x is $A$, it would be quite impossible to envisage the $A$ as not having the property f. There is no other criterion for $A$ to be identified as an object. '$A$' is here what we call a dummy name." The elementary propositions by which names are introduced cannot be false if they have sense at all, since "the condition of the use of the Name '$a$' is nothing more than the conditions which enable us to say '$(\exists x)$ $\Phi x$.' " Just as "Let $a$ be the centre of the circle C" cannot be false so long as it and related propositions have a sense, so also "$(\exists x)$ fx . x=A" cannot be false so long as it and related propositions have a sense. This is not to say that every elementary proposition involving $A$ must be true: just as in the geometrical example the proposition "$a$ is on line L" may be false, so also some elementary propositions involving $A$ may be false. But some elementary propositions involving names must be true if there are names at all.[30]

The view that some elementary propositions must be true if they have sense conflicts directly with what I take to be a, perhaps *the*, central doctrine of the *Tractatus*: every genuine (nontautological) proposition can be meaningful, but false. In other words, every proposition (including elementary ones) that has sense (is not a tautology or contradiction and so says something about the world) can be false. No (nonlogical) proposition, elementary or complex, is true a priori. The basic difference between a Name and a proposition is precisely that a proposition, unlike a Name, can be meaningful but false. Wittgenstein writes in the *Tractatus*: "In order to tell whether a picture is true or false we must compare it with reality. It is impossible to tell from the picture alone whether it is true or false. There are no pictures that are true a priori" (TLP, 2.223–2.225). Ishiguro's position denies that basic thesis. On Ishiguro's view, there is no way that an elementary statement introducing a name can be false; for these elementary propositions, there is no distinction between sense and truth. On the view espoused by Ishiguro, it would seem that some elementary propositions take over the role of "Names." They become those items in the language that can't point to what is not there. I do not see how this view of Names and elementary propositions can be made compatible with the passages cited above.

By contrast, my view of the *Tractatus* solves this problem by insisting that we make a radical distinction between objects and facts, Names and propositions. According to the *Tractatus*, we must distinguish between what is necessary and what is contingent, between what can be shown and what can be said. This is the price we have to pay for having an account of how signs point that offers both complete determinacy and yet allows for error. The connection that makes error possible is not itself a connection between propositions and facts, nor is it contingent, nor can it be described or represented. Anything that can be said can be false, but the connection that makes it possible for what can be said to be false cannot itself be misrepresented (or represented) in any way at all.

### Pointing to what is not there

Traditional content theorists, because they make no radical distinction among levels, are tempted to insist that every proposition is "composed" of simpler propositions which are *true*.[31] The early Wittgenstein, on the other hand, insists that the prior level is not itself a level of representation; error is not parasitic on *truth*. Like traditional foundationalists in epistemology, content theorists are tempted to assume incorrectly that some representations must be true; they go wrong because there is nothing to guarantee that the way Names are combined in propositions will correspond to *actual* arrangements of objects, and so be *true*. *Any* proposition can be false. Pure tracking theorists insist that the distinction between signs that cannot fail to track their objects and signs that can so fail is merely one of degree. The early Wittgenstein insists that the distinction is radical and complete: only Names track objects; only propositions (determinate configurations of Names) can be true or false, correct or incorrect. According to the *Tractatus*, such a radical distinction is required to account for the possibility of error.

If, as I have suggested, the mixed theory of the *Tractatus* solves the central problems of both fitting and tracking accounts, then why does the later Wittgenstein, the Wittgenstein of the *Philosophical Investigations*, give it up? I believe that the later Wittgenstein regarded his own earlier view as the only serious alternative to his later method or way of proceeding. Whereas both fitting theories and tracking theories fail to solve the central problems, the *Tractatus* account, if correct, solves the problems left over by those theories and thus shows how representation is possible. Unfortunately, however, the Tractarian account is not correct: there are no simple objects or necessary rules of thinking, and thus the radical distinction between levels cannot be maintained.

There are no absolutely simple objects; in fact, it makes no sense to speak of absolutely simple objects. As Wittgenstein writes in the *Philosophical Investigations:* "But what are the simple constituent parts of which reality is composed? – What are the simple constituent parts of a chair? – The bits of wood of which it is made? Or the molecules, or the atoms? – 'Simple' means: not composite. And here the point is: in what sense 'composite'? It makes no sense at all to speak absolutely of the 'simple parts of a chair' " (PI, 47). Moreover, no signs are guaranteed to operate in accordance with necessary rules of logic. "F. P. Ramsey once emphasized in conversation with me that logic was a 'normative science.' I do not know exactly what he had in mind, but it was doubtless closely related to what only dawned on me later: namely, that in philosophy we often *compare* the use of words with games and calculi which have fixed rules, but cannot say that someone who is using language *must* be playing such a game" (PI, 81).

The famous rule-following passages in the *Philosophical Investigations* continue the process of undermining the Tractarian solution by pointing out that the rules according to which Names are supposed to combine are not radically different from pictures/thoughts/propositions (i.e., signs that point to or describe the world) as the *Tractatus* had supposed. It had tried to force an unbridgeably sharp distinction between what can be said and what can be shown: the connection between Names and objects and the logical rules that both must obey can be shown but not said. Whereas any fact can be described falsely, the rules that make it possible to describe the facts cannot be described in any way at all. But, according to the *Philosophical Investigations*, this is an artificial distinction. Rules can be, after all, given to us in signs. And rules are supposed to point to what we are to do if we follow the rule, in much the way that propositions are supposed to point to what the world would be like if the proposition were true. Just as any proposition may be false, so also any rule may fail to be applied correctly. Thus, the puzzles about representation recur as puzzles about rules: How can a rule direct our actions? How are mistakes in application possible?

In recent years, naturalists such as Fred Dretske and Jerry Fodor have sought to revive tracking theory accounts of representation, in an effort to escape what they perceive as the pernicious relativism of various sorts of fitting theories.[32] For them, the obvious candidates for the tracking relation are causal and/or nomological relations. To their credit, it must be said that they clearly recognize (in a way that Wittgenstein's contemporaries Ogden and Richards apparently did not) that a crude causal theory, one that says that a sign means all and only what causes it, will not stand. Contemporary tracking theorists think they can modify such crude causal theories to make them square with (most of) our pretheoretic intuitions about what we mean and to solve the problem of how signs can point to what is not there. Moreover, they insist, the trick can be turned *without* making any fundamental distinction among different levels. Whereas the *Tractatus* had admitted a level at which signs cannot point to what is not there and another, fundamentally different level at which signs can point to what is not there, contemporary tracking theorists insist that all signs (types) can point to what is not there (Dretske) or that error is always possible (Fodor). And yet, the challenge contemporary tracking theorists face (and have yet to meet) has not really changed much since Wittgenstein wrote his *Philosophical Investigations:* if there are no simple Names and simple objects to provide the fixed backdrop against which signs can point to what is not there, how can signs point to what is not there?[33]

NOTES

1 For more on the distinction between semantic theories and theories of content determination, see Barbara Von Eckardt, *What is Cognitive Science?* (Cambridge, Mass.: MIT Press, 1992).

2  It is difficult to find a pure example of a simple resemblance theory, although British Empiricists such as Berkeley and Hume are often supposed to offer theories of this type.

3  Wittgenstein's famous "picture theory of meaning" in the *Tractatus* is often supposed to be a theory of this type, although I do not believe it actually is. See the section "The *Tractatus* solution: A two-level theory" of this essay.

4  Note that the account of tracking theories given here does not require that the covariance between signs and what they "mean" results from a causal connection rather than from other sorts of connection (e.g., epistemological, nomological, or even logical). Particular tracking theories give different stories about the nature of the relation between signs and what they "mean."

5  The two differences between fitting and tracking theories just discussed are connected: fitting theories seek semantic value first and foremost in what is internal to the sign or system of signs and thus regard semantic value (e.g., "sense") as in some way independent of the world that is to be represented (e.g., "reference" or "denotation"), whereas tracking theories seek semantic value first and foremost in what is external to the sign or system of signs and thus regard semantic value (e.g., "reference" or "denotation") as dependent on the world that is to be represented. Thus, fitting theories of content determination "fit" most naturally with semantic theories that make a sharp sense/reference distinction, whereas tracking theories of content determination "fit" with semantic theories according to which the primitive expressions of the language have only reference or denotation and not sense.

6  The second and third differences between fitting and tracking theories, like the first and second, are connected: according to fitting theories, the properties that confer semantic value, since they are "internal" to the representational system, are very likely also to be epistemically accessible to the person who is doing the meaning. By contrast, according to tracking theorists, the properties that confer semantic value, since they are "external" to the representational system, are not likely to be epistemically accessible in any special way to the person who is doing the meaning. Tracking theories appeal to the world to confer meaning/content onto our signs; thus, they tend to make content depend on something that is not directly accessible to us in any special way.

7  He admits that images may be dispensed with, but insists that they have an important role to play in the learning of language: "by a telescoped process, words come in time to produce directly the effects which would have been produced by the images with which they were associated. . . . but in first learning the use of language it would seem that imagery

always plays a very important part." Bertrand Russell, *The Analysis of Mind* (London: George Allen and Unwin, 1921), pp. 206–7.

8  Russell, *The Analysis of Mind*, p. 209.

9  Ibid.

10  C. K. Ogden and I. A. Richards, *The Meaning of Meaning: A Study of the Influence of Language upon Thought and of the Science of Symbolism* (New York: Harcourt, Brace and World, Inc., 1923), p. 12. The intuition expressed in this footnote is not typical of their work as a whole, which is perhaps the clearest expression by contemporaries of Wittgenstein of a tracking theory of content determination.

11  John Haugeland makes this distinction more clearly than most, though he does not use the term "brute intentionality." John Haugeland, *Mind Design* (Montgomery, Vermont: Bradford Books, 1981), pp. 32–3; Haugeland, "The Intentionality All-Stars," *Philosophical Perspectives, 4: Action Theory and Philosophy of Mind*, ed. J. E. Tomberlin (Atascadero: Ridgeview Publishing Company, 1990), pp. 385–6, esp. n6.

12  Fitting theories that appeal to the functional role or use of a sign within the individual's cognitive system or within the individual's community face the same basic difficulty.

13  Between the time that Wittgenstein finished the *Tractatus* and before he wrote the *Investigations*, Bertrand Russell (who wrote the introduction to the *Tractatus*) flirted with and C. K. Ogden (who first translated the *Tractatus* into English) espoused a causal version of a tracking theory of content determination. Ogden and Richards, *The Meaning of Meaning;* Bertrand Russell, "Propositions: What they are and how they mean," *The Philosophy of Logical Atomism and Other Essays 1914–19*, ed. J. G. Slater (London: George Allen and Unwin, 1986).

For a useful discussion of the extent to which Wittgenstein was familiar with and critical of the writings of his contemporaries, see S. Stephen Hilmy, *The Later Wittgenstein: The Emergence of a New Philosophical Method* (Oxford: Basil Blackwell, 1987), ch. 4. Hilmy discusses the views of Russell (from this period) and Ogden and Richards, though he regards them as holding basically the same causal theories of meaning. By contrast, I believe that, though Russell flirts with a causal version of a tracking theory of content determination, the position he actually espouses during the period Hilmy discusses is much more of a fitting theory.

14  This point applies equally to versions of tracking theories according to which the connection is not causal but epistemological or nomological. So long as there is an objective relation between signs and that to which they point, what the sign is "about" will not be up to us.

15  Bertrand Russell, "The Philosophy of Logical Atomism," *The Philoso-*

*phy of Logical Atomism and Other Essays 1914–19,* ed. J. G. Slater
(London: George Allen and Unwin, 1986), p. 282.

16  I believe the point made here is independent of whether "But that is
    only . . ." is spoken by Wittgenstein in propria persona or by the inter-
    locutor. Either way, Wittgenstein seems to insist that causal connec-
    tions alone, apart from a context in which there is "a regular use of sign-
    posts, a custom," are insufficient.

        I set aside here questions about the extent to which an appeal to a
    custom or practice would help (see PI, 141). I also set aside questions
    about the extent to which the later Wittgenstein offers a positive ac-
    count of representation rather than urging us to relinquish our preoccu-
    pation with the questions that tempt us to offer such accounts.

17  As David Stern pointed out to me, no colored squares actually appear in
    any of the extant drafts of PI, 48; the squares appear in pencil, with the
    letters written inside; actual colors appear for the first time in the post-
    humously published book.

18  Russell credited Wittgenstein with convincing him that propositions
    cannot be names for facts, since they are capable of being meaningful
    even when false. Russell, "The Philosophy of Logical Atomism," p. 167.

19  "Names" is capitalized to distinguish Wittgenstein's simple Names
    from ordinary proper names.

20  Kant faced a parallel difficulty regarding what he took to be our synthetic
    a priori knowledge of geometry: what guarantee is there that our geome-
    trical constructions reveal what is possible for spatio-temporal objects?
    Wittgenstein takes a clue provided by Kant in developing an answer to his
    difficulty. Summerfield, "Wittgenstein on Logical Form and Kantian
    Geometry," *Dialogue* 29 (1990), pp. 531–50; Summerfield, "Logical Form
    and Kantian Geometry: Wittgenstein's Analogy," in R. Haller and J.
    Brandl, eds., *Wittgenstein towards a Re-Evaluation: Proceedings of the
    Fourteenth International Wittgenstein Symposium, Centenary Celebra-
    tion* (Vienna: Hölder-Pichler-Tempsky, 1990), pp. 147–50.

21  Notoriously, Wittgenstein says next to nothing in the *Tractatus* about
    what Names are. In an effort to figure out what Tractarian Names are,
    commentators sometimes pose false dilemmas. For example, it is tempt-
    ing to suppose that Names in the *Tractatus* are either (a) names in
    ordinary language or (b) merely ideal. Since names in ordinary language
    can fail to refer, can be misapplied, and admit of error, such names do not
    qualify as Tractarian Names. In fact, Wittgenstein states clearly that
    what are ordinarily called "names" are disguised descriptions, which do
    admit of error (3.24). Thus, it is tempting to conclude that Tractarian
    Names are part of an ideal language which has yet to be realized (see, for
    example, Bertrand Russell's introduction to the *Tractatus*). However,

this conclusion also conflicts with what Wittgenstein says in the *Tractatus:* "all the propositions of our colloquial language are actually, just as they are, logically completely in order" (5.5563). Though Wittgenstein's Names are not ordinary names, neither are they names merely in some "ideal" (but non-actual) language. Fortunately, there are alternatives. Elsewhere, I have argued that Names in the *Tractatus* are the simple elements of a language of thought. Summerfield, "Thought and Language in the *Tractatus,*" *The Wittgenstein Legacy*, Midwest Studies in Philosophy 17, ed. Peter A. French, Theodore E. Uehling, Jr., and Howard K. Wettstein (Notre Dame: University of Notre Dame Press, 1992), pp. 224–45.

22 For further discussion of this point, see "Brute vs. original intentionality," p. 125.

23 Jerry A. Fodor, *A Theory of Content and Other Essays* (Cambridge, Mass.: MIT Press, 1990), pp. 56, 99.

24 Hidé Ishiguro, "Use and Reference of Names," in P. Winch, ed., *Studies in the Philosophy of Wittgenstein* (London: Routledge and Kegan Paul, 1969), pp. 20–1.

25 The view that the Name/object connection is not something we set up in any way, either by acts of ostension or by our use of language, is like ostension/dubbing views in that there is a connection between Names and objects, but is unlike such views in that we do not set it up. It is like use/fitting views in that the role of Names within propositions mirrors the role of objects within states of affairs, but is unlike such views in that reference is not determined by nor constituted by use in a language.

26 Ishiguro, "Use and Reference of Names." For related views, see Brian McGuinness, "The So-called Realism of Wittgenstein's *Tractatus,*" in I. Block, ed., *Perspectives on the Philosophy of Wittgenstein* (Cambridge, Mass.: MIT Press, 1981) and McGuinness, "Language and Reality in the *Tractatus,*" *Teoria* 2 (1985), pp. 135–43; David Pears, *The False Prison*, vol. 1 (Oxford: Clarendon Press, 1987).

27 Ishiguro, "Use and Reference of Names," p. 40. She comes to this antimetaphysical conclusion largely by arguing that objects in the *Tractatus* are not particulars of which various properties can be predicated. Rather, objects are more like properties: to say that an object exists is to say that a basic and irreducible property (different from any "material" properties) is instantiated. She assumes that properties are dependent upon language and that to say that a property is instantiated is not to make a metaphysical claim. The view was popular at the time she wrote the article (due in part to the influence of the logical positivists and, following their lead, W. V. O. Quine), but it would not be accepted by contemporary tracking theorists such as Jerry Fodor and

Fred Dretske. Fodor appeals to nomic relations among repeatable properties (e.g., the property of being a cow and the property of being a cause of "cow"-tokens) to determine semantic content, but he regards these properties as real and objective rather than as in any way "dependent on language."

28 One might wonder why this doesn't count as a kind of description.

29 Ishiguro, "Use and Reference of Names," p. 45.

30 Ibid., p. 46. Ishiguro seeks to make her view consistent with Wittgenstein's strictures by denying that he requires that names exist. According to her, "Wittgenstein could not, strictly speaking, require that Names exist, but only that Names *be possible:* that we would be able to use Names" (p. 45). However, her view that Names need not exist conflicts with 4.221: "It is obvious that the analysis of propositions must bring us to elementary propositions which consist of names in immediate combination."

31 Ogden and Richards, *The Meaning of Meaning*, p. 70.

32 Fred I. Dretske, *Knowledge and the Flow of Information* (Cambridge, Mass.: MIT Press, 1981); Dretske, *Explaining Behavior: Reasons in a World of Causes* (Cambridge, Mass.: MIT Press, 1988); Jerry A. Fodor, *Psychosemantics: The Problem of Meaning in the Philosophy of Mind* (Cambridge, Mass.: MIT Press, 1987); Fodor, *Theory of Content*.

33 I am grateful to the following people for helpful comments on earlier versions of this work: Ray Elugardo, Heather Gert, Pat Manfredi, Hans Sluga, and David Stern. Thanks go also to the philosophy graduate students and faculty at the University of Iowa for their questions and comments on a version of this paper delivered as the Fall Henry and Augusta Sievert Lecture, October 1994. Finally, I would like to acknowledge support for research provided by an NEH Fellowship for University Teachers, 1992–3, and an SIUC Special Research Project Grant, 1992–4.

# 4   Philosophy as grammar

## I THE PROBLEM ABOUT PHILOSOPHY

It is one of the wonderful paradoxes of our time that the greatest and most stimulating philosopher of the century should identify his work with the stodgiest and dullest of school subjects. It is nonetheless the case that for the last twenty years of his life, the years of his greatest productivity and his profoundest work, Wittgenstein identified what he was doing, and what other philosophers really have been doing and should be doing, with grammar. This perspective is as carefully considered as it is puzzling. It emerged out of earnest and ongoing work, and its implications are felt throughout his later philosophical investigations. Although he settled into this general conception of philosophy soon after his return to Cambridge, probably in 1930, he never gave a clear and orderly account of what he meant. Nor did he succeed, in spite of the centrality of this idea from 1930 right through his last writings, in convincing all those who read his work sympathetically that he meant what he seemed to be saying; both Moore (PO, pp. 46–114) and Feyerabend,[1] for example, expressed profound skepticism about it shortly after his death.

The aim of this essay is to expound and justify Wittgenstein's idea that the stodgy school subject, or some variation on its main theme, is indeed the key to philosophy. At the same time I have considerable respect for the difficulties Moore and Feyerabend have expressed, and for others they have not. What is called for is surely not to avoid or deny the difficulties, nor even to acknowledge and then minimize them, but to portray Wittgenstein's conclusion as genuinely attractive in spite of them, and not as the lesser of evils or some other second-rate consolation. My exposition will focus on

139

five problems posed by Wittgenstein's understanding of what philosophy is. These are problems that need to be faced by anyone who approaches philosophy from any point of view. Wittgenstein's point of view, however, grew out of his personal existential or religious stance, and I will end with comments on how this conception of philosophy expresses something of his distinctive conscience and values.

The first problem is the relation of grammar to logic. Wittgenstein did not begin by identifying philosophy with grammar but with logic. Two questions naturally arise in connection with this historical fact. One is about the relation of grammar to logic, and especially whether one or the other of these two disciplines can be considered more basic. The other is what made Wittgenstein change his mind; or rather what changes in his conceptions of philosophy, logic, and grammar contributed to the change in his answer about the nature of philosophy. Both these questions prove formidable.

The second problem is the relation of Wittgenstein's grammar to linguistics. Grammar seems rather quaint in this age when every university has a department of linguistics, and when linguistics has become the general study of the forms and uses of language. One can usefully begin by comparing Saussure and Wittgenstein, as Roy Harris has done in his refreshing and enlightening book when he focuses on the centrality of games in their thought.[2] We need to note similarities in both their methods and their models, as well as their differences about which aspects of language to focus on and (decisively) about whether or not to identify and study linguistic phenomena in isolation from "the stream of life."

The third problem arises because of Wittgenstein's frequent reference to "natural history" as a kind of stopping-place for an argument or some philosophical consideration. On the face of it, natural history seems a completely different subject from grammar, and yet Wittgenstein's remarks imply a kind of identity between them.

There is next a consideration of certain metaphysical issues that arise in connection with natural history and grammar. Wittgenstein's natural history involves a commitment to the world being real independently of anyone's thought or description of it. The reality in question seems straightforward and naturalistic. Yet Wittgenstein seems equally committed to things (such as meaning and the worth of philosophy) that transcend scientific reality, and to certainty that transcends knowledge. His remark that *"Essence* is expressed by grammar" raises problems about the status of essences in this basically naturalistic framework.

At the end I shall discuss Wittgenstein's relation to Kant, Wittgenstein's conception of philosophy as grammar forming a chapter in the ongoing history of critical philosophy, and the moral message Wittgenstein saw in the discipline of critical philosophy.

## II GRAMMAR AND LOGIC

Wittgenstein's original view was that philosophy is based on logic. In his "Notes on Logic" of 1913 Wittgenstein says: "Philosophy consists of logic and metaphysics: logic is its basis" (NB, p. 106). The terms of this remark are subject to different readings. A very narrow reading (where logic is what is found in *Principia Mathematica* and metaphysics is confined to an account of the substance and necessary categories of the world) might lead us to conclude that Wittgenstein had abandoned the idea here expressed by the time he composed the *Tractatus*, while a very broad reading (in which logic includes the principles of meaning and inference and metaphysics includes our commitment to ordinary facts and objects in the world around us) might support the conclusion that this is an expression of the approach to philosophical problems through language and natural history that characterizes Wittgenstein's work to the very end. Perhaps neither extreme is reasonable. Here I assume that a relatively broad understanding of the terms in the passage gives a better understanding of Wittgenstein's conception of philosophy.[3]

He worked out the details of this conception in the *Tractatus*. The key to that work is the idea that language is a mirror of reality, and that logic is the essence of language. This does not mean that the form and substance of the world are given in advance. It does mean that reality must have the same form or structure as logic, a logical form. This idea pervades the *Tractatus* and finds particularly lyrical expression in 5.511: "How can logic – all-embracing logic, which mirrors the world – use such peculiar crotchets and contrivances? Only because they are all connected with one another in an infinitely fine network, the great mirror." It is difficult to believe that Wittgenstein had in mind the same elementary formal logic now taught to millions of university students, but that is indeed a very large part of it. Whitehead and Russell had recently published their *Principia Mathematica,* which solidified and extended the revolution in formal logic initiated by Frege. Wittgenstein shared the enthusiasm of many others for the rich promise of the new discipline, whose technical details he first mastered and then simplified. It led him to regard logic as a model or projection of reality, and therefore as providing the basis for the meaning of sentences – particularly for that of complex sentences, which he construed as truth-functions of elementary sentences, a view summarized in TLP, 5: "A proposition is a truth-function of elementary propositions." Wittgenstein probably took the main clues for the idea that logic is the key to reality from Frege and drew much more out of formal logic than students or teachers today ever conceive could possibly be there.

In his later work Wittgenstein is often thought to have totally rejected his earlier views, but this is not the whole story. He certainly did reject exclusive reliance on truth-functional form, on rigid correlation of names and objects, on hidden essences, and on there being one and only one use of language. Nonetheless he retains virtually the same view about the relation of the forms of language (whether they be grammatical or logical) to metaphysics: "*Essence* is expressed by grammar. . . . Grammar tells what kind of object anything is" (PI, 371–3). It is important not to suppose that this passage implies that there are essences independent of grammar. Just as in the *Tractatus* there are no "objects" independent of our picturing of facts,[4] so also in the later work there are no essences independent of rules of language: Wittgenstein maintained a deflationary posture toward foundationalist metaphysics. But Wittgenstein clearly also remained interested in what kinds of things there are, and he took pains to describe or determine the form or essence – though he did not call it that – of such things as pain, memory, intention, seeing, colors, numbers, and so forth. He did so on the basis of "grammar," that is, on the basis of distinctive uses of language, or language-games, with which key words are associated. Philosophy therefore seems a branch of grammar (in a broad sense), which provides the basis for description of the forms and essences of things.

In a somewhat flippant mood one might paraphrase Wittgenstein's earlier remark to formulate a motto for his later philosophy: "Philosophy consists of grammar and metaphysics: grammar is its basis."

Wittgenstein would disapprove: the motto oversimplifies complex matters and has the ring of a slogan or battle cry that might be used to rally waverers against opposing views, and neither the "grammar" nor the "metaphysics" is just what other people generally understand them to be. These are important reservations, characteristic of Wittgenstein's philosophical conscience. But it is important to remember that, for the most part, similar reservations apply to his early work as well. It is true that slogans, however useful, are always deceptively simplistic; but if one keeps the reservations in mind, the paraphrase seems little more misleading than the 1913 original.

That Wittgenstein realigned the crux of philosophy from logic to grammar is widely acknowledged. Two questions must be answered if we are to understand this change. One is what quality or character we should assign to the change: restriction to a narrower domain? or complete abandonment of the *Tractatus* view? or generalization of the insights of the *Tractatus*? This question will be much easier to deal with after we have discussed the relation of logic to grammar: whether logic provides a foundation for grammar as for all the sciences, or whether, on the other hand, it is a derivation within the larger framework of grammar. The answer to this more basic question is to be found by examining contrasts and inclusions in everyday language.

Words that form a semantic set, such as the color words, must have part of their meaning explained by reference to one another. This reference will sometimes be contrastive and sometimes be inclusive: "scarlet" and "puce" stand in semantic contrast with one another; but they both refer to shades of red, and therefore both are semantically included in the meaning of "red." It is absurd to suppose that these contrasts and inclusions are simply abstract semantic features of language in the abstract, with nothing more to be said about the matter. In fact they may well be abstract semantic markers, as Katz has argued,[5] but they reflect incompatibilities and entailments that hold between propositions. "X is puce" is incompatible with "X is scarlet," and it entails "X is red," provided it is the same X that we are talking about. It is these incompatibilities and entailments that are the basis for the structure of the lexicon of the language.

It is often thought, as for example by Whorf, Sapir, and Benveniste,[6] that these distinctly logical (truth-functional) phenomena are, or may be, peculiar aspects of the Indo-European languages with which we are most familiar. This hypothesis gains plausibility from the fact that there seem to be certain forms of sentence or phrase-structure common to these languages but absent from many other families of languages. It is much more likely, however, that they are universal. For phrase-structure is not what is at issue, and therefore it does not matter that syntax is arbitrary and varies dramatically from language to language. More to the point is that relations of inclusion and incompatibility inhere, and must inhere, in any language in which it is possible to make predications (assertions, truth-claims). Statements about things having colors are good examples of predications, but any report or factual claim of any kind would serve as well. The particular syntax or phrase-structure of the sentences makes no difference at all. What does matter is the structure of the semantic contrasts or inclusions that hold between or among sentences themselves, whatever their internal or syntactical structure. There could be no empirical or factual meaning without such contrasts, though there could be the sort of meaning that Malinowski calls "phatic communion" (salutations, farewells, reassurances, and so on),[7] or the sort involved in what Rousseau in the *Essai sur l'origine des langues* conceived as the original languages, which he supposed to convey only feelings (not thoughts or ideas). Since there is no reason to believe that there ever were such languages, and no evidence of any language into which it is impossible to translate simple factual statements, these structural phenomena involving inclusion and incompatibility are almost certainly universal. Not *necessarily* universal, but certainly so.

These semantic structures can be represented as logical relations. Semantic inclusions are logical entailments, semantic contrasts are logical incompatibilities. Suppose we are talking about a beach ball that has a single solid color and use the following letters to abbreviate sentences that might be used to report its color:

> B It is blue.
> Y It is yellow.
> G It is green.
> R It is red.
> P It is puce.
> C It is carmine.
> S It is scarlet.
> V It is vermilion.

Entailments hold between the shades of red and red itself:

$$V \rightarrow R, \; S \rightarrow R, \; C \rightarrow R, \; P \rightarrow R.$$

Incompatibilities hold among the primary colors:

$$R \rightarrow \text{not-B}, \; B \rightarrow \text{not-R}, \; R \rightarrow \text{not-G}, \; B \rightarrow \text{not-Y},$$
$$\text{or: } R/B, \qquad B/R, \qquad R/G, \qquad B/Y,$$

and so on, where "R/B" means "Not both R and B" or "R and B are not *both* true." They also hold between the secondary colors (here, the shades of red) and the other primary colors:

$$C \rightarrow \text{not-B}, \; G \rightarrow \text{not-V}, \; V \rightarrow \text{not-G},$$
$$\text{or: } C/B, \qquad G/V, \qquad V/G, \text{ and so on.}$$

It is conceivable that there could be a language with only primary colors, and hence without entailments built into the semantic net of color predicates, and also conceivable that sentences equivalent to B, Y, G, and R could be expressed without there being separate lexical items (words) for the primary colors. It is even conceivable, and indeed the case, as Berlin and Kay have shown,[8] that different languages have different systems of primary colors. But it is *inconceivable* that there *could* be a language in which there are reports about the color of things *without* there being incompatibilities of the form R/G, B/Y, R/Y, and so forth.

These ineluctable incompatibilities have a dual nature. First and foremost they are modal features of discourse, more particularly of how to proceed with discourse, or of discourse continuations. They are learned when we learn the language. When we learn the colors, we learn to make use of the incompatibilities in practice. We learn that if something is blue, it cannot have any other primary color, but it can have any shape at all; and if something is triangular, it cannot be round or square or any other shape, but it can be of any color. Without such incompatibilities descriptive words have no meaning and can have no meaning; that is, there can be no descriptive words at all. These rules and practices pertaining to discourse continuations must be implicit in any language in which truth-claims are a possible mode of discourse.

The incompatibilities, as represented by the slashes, are also abstractions. The abstractions can be iterated independently of the sentences or the discourse from which they are abstracted, thereby forming the basis for formal logic as a special discipline. Such formalization is daunting, and mastery of it is a skill separate from the very common skill of being able to make use of the incompatibilities in practice. We can learn more about our ordinary language, get more insight into its depth, through the formalization and iteration of the logical functions inherent in its discourse continuities. For this purpose, paying attention to incompatibilities is particularly rewarding.

Henry Sheffer proved that incompatibility is itself a sufficient notion for generating the propositional calculus, that is to say the complete system of truth-functional logic. Whitehead and Russell had previously proved that truth-functional logic could be derived from the logical notions of conjunction ("and") or disjunction ("or") together with negation ("not"). Sheffer showed that conjunction, disjunction, and negation can all be derived from incompatibility.[9] For example,

$$R/R = \text{not-}R$$
$$(R/G \,/\, R/G) = (R \text{ and } G) \,[\text{not-\{not both } R \text{ and } G\}]$$
$$(R/R \,/\, G/G) = (R \text{ or } G) \quad [\text{not both not-}R \text{ and not-}G].$$

Even in these simple iterations the logical functions appear daunting, and this often makes people forget that the functions themselves are already embedded in ordinary language and learned at our mothers' knees.

Logic, therefore, must not be conceived as a prior and independent discipline but as contained already within semantics. Lexicography, furthermore, necessarily involves truth-functions. Whether lexicographers consciously acknowledge this feature of the meaning of words or not, logicians can, following Sheffer's lead, extract logic from the lexicon. Truth-functional logic is an implicit feature of every natural language, already built into the simplest sorts of communication.

Given this understanding of truth-functional logic as based on iteration of abstract features of a common and almost certainly universal language-game, I can now deal quite briefly with the question about the kind of change Wittgenstein made from his earlier to his later view. It should be noted that the change was not instantaneous, and that Wittgenstein hesitated about how to express it. From 1929 to 1933 he sometimes spoke of "phenomenology" rather than (or in addition to) "grammar" as the alternative to logic.[10] Wittgenstein probably abandoned this way of speaking partly because other phi-losophers had already made "phenomenology" a specialized term, and partly because there is something irredeemably Cartesian about phenomenology, whereas grammar is a social rather than a psycho-logical or Cartesian phenomenon.

The conception of philosophy as based on grammar is a generaliza-tion of the conception of philosophy as based on logic, rather than a rejection or abandonment of it. Logic consists of rules for language-games that involve pictures of facts; it is an important part of the grammar of the language-game of predications or truth-claims. Mak-ing predications is, however, only one particular family of language-games. As Wittgenstein came to appreciate the wide range of uses of language, he came to see philosophy as concerned not only with other uses of language but also with other dimensions of predica-tions than the logical dimension. Requests, orders, and salutations are examples of the first sort of difference. The second sort of differ-ence turns on whether or not it makes sense to say "I doubt it" in continuing a discourse following an indicative sentence. Compare the appropriateness of such a retort in the following cases:

> The early bird always catches the worm.
> There are two elms growing in NN's front yard.
> Aristotle's works were written by Aristotle.
> A poet is a penguin; his wings are to swim with.
> Puce is a color.
> I have a toothache.
> I promise to call him tomorrow.

Such a comparison is what Wittgenstein would call a grammatical exercise. The last sentence is clearly not a predication at all, and the three preceding it are not knowledge-claims, as is shown by the inappropriateness of the doubting retort. Differences of these sorts cannot be symbolized in formal logic, nor can such logic illuminate the meaning of sentences used in this manner. It is not that the logic is not sharp enough, nor that the examples show that it must yield some of its rigor. Logic stays just as sharp and just as rigorous.[11] The point is that the rigor of formal logic is relevant only within certain language-games, and that the identification of those language-games and their differentiation from others is a matter of a wider discipline than logic itself.

### III  GRAMMAR AND LINGUISTICS

Roy Harris points out that Saussure and Wittgenstein both use the word "grammar" primarily in a descriptive sense.[12] This is certainly correct, and it holds for other linguists as well as for Saussure. The linguists particularly need to distinguish themselves from school teachers, who use grammar normatively rather than descriptively. Linguists aim to give an accurate description of how the language is actually used, and teachers use the description as a standard to inculcate in their pupils, by enforcing its forms and punishing deviations. Wittgenstein sides with the linguists, because he sees that there is no external fact or reality that could provide a standard for what the vocabulary or syntax of a language *ought* to be. Harris further points out[13] that both Saussure and Wittgenstein insist on the arbitrariness of language, by which is meant simply that there is no external standard for judging the appropriateness or adequacy of the vocabulary or syntax of a language. Wittgenstein puts the point this way: "Grammar is not accountable to any reality. It is grammatical rules that determine meaning (constitute it) and so they themselves are not answerable to any meaning and to that extent are arbitrary" (PG, 184).

A more subtle point is that this grammatical descriptivism does not preclude using grammar as a critical instrument, and Wittgenstein departs from Saussure (at least from Saussure's practice) in that he does not hesitate to declare, as a matter of grammar, that this or that remark is nonsense, or that it is correct or incorrect. Thus: "It is correct to say 'I know what you are thinking,' and wrong to say 'I know what I am thinking.' (A whole cloud of philosophy condensed into a drop of grammar.)" (PI, p. 222). The drop of grammar is perhaps too minuscule for Wittgenstein's meaning to be entirely clear, for he is not departing from the descriptive paradigm as much as may at first appear. However normative the words "right" and "wrong" may sound, they are used here to *report* that there is or is not a provision for such an expression in the language-game of making knowledge-claims. In this language-game it is always appropriate to ask "How do you know that?" Since this rejoinder makes no sense, except perhaps as a joke, in response to "I know what I am thinking," those words cannot express a knowledge-claim. Another way of reaching the same conclusion is by means of the general principle, constant in Wittgenstein's work from beginning to end, that a proposition makes sense if and only if its negation makes sense. Since "I don't know what I am thinking" is laughably silly when construed as a serious truth-claim (although it could be given a sense in special circumstances and is sometimes uttered just because it is laughably silly, as a self-disparaging joke), "I know what I am thinking" cannot make sense either.

The drop of grammar may still be too small. Wittgenstein considers the grammar of knowledge-claims in greater depth in *On Certainty*, where he remarks at one point,

"Knowledge" and "certainty" belong to different *categories*. They are not two "mental states" like, say "surmising" and "being sure." . . . What interests us now is not being sure but knowledge. That is, we are interested in the fact that about certain empirical propositions no doubt can exist if making judgments is to be possible at all. Or again: I am inclined to believe that not everything that has the form of an empirical proposition *is* one. (OC, 308)

If we assume that "mental states" refers to a category, there seem to be three categories referred to in this interesting passage. Being sure (elsewhere called "subjective certainty") is a mental state in the sense that I can say when I am sure, and I can be sure quite apart from any objective certainty or from anyone else being sure. Though it is a mental state rather than a sensation, being sure has all the apparent privacy of sensation. Certainty, on the other hand, seems presented in this passage as a transcendental requirement for the practice of making judgments. There are no *particular* propositions about which one must be certain, but some propositions must be certain. Since making judgments is a public practice (even though individual judgments are private), the certainty presupposed by it must be *social* rather than private, and hence must be in a different category from "mental states." "Certainty" and "knowledge" are both social rather than mental, but what is certain "lies beyond being justified or unjustified" (OC, 359), whereas a knowledge-claim is subject to doubt and confirmation. All three of these categories are identified by reference to language-games, and are distinguished by different discourse conditions (circumstances in which expressions of that category fit into the stream of life) and different discourse possibilities (appropriate discourse continuations). The categories are therefore grammatical categories, though the grammar in question has to do with discourse and with *uses* of language rather than with word-forms or phrase structures. "Right" and "wrong" are descriptive in this context. They signify being in accord or not in accord with constitutive rather than regulative rules.

If Wittgenstein and Saussure agree in using "grammar" descriptively, they disagree about three other matters. One is that Wittgenstein's grammar has to do with uses of language (discourse conditions and discourse continuation) rather than with forms and their combinations (morphology and syntax). This difference is probably what Wittgenstein had in mind when he said to Moore (PO, p. 69) that he was using the words "grammar" and "grammatical" in their ordinary sense but making them apply to things they do not ordinarily apply to.

Considering uses rather than forms is a deep rather than a superficial departure from classical linguistic methodology, and Wittgenstein seems to underestimate its significance in his rather glib response to Moore. Studying uses of language makes *context* prominent, whereas the study of forms lends itself naturally to *analysis.* There are no such things as the "structural components" of a use of language or of a language-game, whereas morphological or syntactic analysis proceeds in terms of precisely such components. Contextual setting and possibilities of discourse continuation define or differentiate uses of language in ways that are not analytic at all – certainly not in the familiar sense in which analysis requires the identification of elements and their arrangement. It is true that Wittgenstein still employs methods of contrast and difference such as are prominent in the work of Saussure and other linguists. But his rejection of analysis into elements as a way of determining the meaning of expressions makes it difficult to agree with Wittgenstein that he has simply transposed the methods of linguistics into another domain. In that sense Moore was right not to be satisfied with Wittgenstein's answer.

The second point of difference is that Wittgenstein does not aim at a systematic description of language use, but only at as much as is required for philosophical perspicuity. Moore reports that Wittgenstein stressed this point in his early lectures at Cambridge:

He ... said more than once that he did not discuss these questions because he thought that language was the subject-matter of philosophy. He did not think that it was. He discussed it only because he thought that particular philosophical errors or "troubles in our thought" were due to false analogies suggested by our actual use of expressions; and he emphasized that it was only necessary for him to discuss those points about language which, as he thought, led to these particular errors or "troubles." (PO, p. 51)

Later he repeated the point in other words: "The work of the philosopher consists in assembling reminders for a particular purpose" (PI, 127). In this disdain for the systematic, Wittgenstein's grammar stands in contrast not only to linguistics but also to the speech-act theories of Austin and Searle.[14]

The particulars referred to here are those inherent in philosophy. They have as much to do with instruction and therapy as with concepts and ideas; that is, with straightening out *people* as well as thoughts. Or perhaps better: straightening out people by straightening out their thinking. Attention to these particulars makes philosophy more personal and less scientific than it was conceived by Frege and Russell. Like the latter two, and like American pragmatists such as Dewey and Quine, Austin and Searle assimilate philosophy to science. For Wittgenstein philosophy is nothing like science. Whereas science seeks to establish generalizations (empirical ones), philosophy seeks to break down generalizations (superficial grammatical ones). Whereas science proceeds by means of hypothesis and deductive explanation, philosophy works through the perspicuous presentation of imaginary examples and intermediate cases. Conceiving philosophy as grammar means that it is sometimes like pedagogy and sometimes like therapy, never like science.

The third difference between Wittgenstein's grammar and linguistics results from his integration of language with activity and the consequent necessity for agreement in practical judgment:

> Words have meaning only in the stream of life. (LWI, 913)

> If language is to be a means of communication there must be agreement not only in definition but also (queer as this may sound) in judgments. (PI, 242)

The language Saussure deals with is always sharply isolated from the stream of life; it is *langue* rather than *parole*. Harris explains the difference well:

> For Saussure "agreement in judgments" plays no comparable role; and it would be wrong to underestimate how radically, in consequence, his position differs from Wittgenstein's. Saussurean linguistics is "segregationalist"

in the sense that it assumes the possibility of a strict segregation between linguistic and nonlinguistic phenomena within the universe of human activity. More prosaically, it assumes that human linguistic behavior can be separated out from accompanying nonlinguistic behavior, and treated independently. . . . For Wittgenstein, on the other hand, language has no segregated existence; words are always embedded in a "form of life" (PI, 19). His hypothetical language-games are inextricably integrated into purposeful human activities of some kind, as in the archetypical case of the builder and his assistant.[15]

In spite of these important differences, Wittgenstein and Saussure have in common a descriptive approach; a conception of meaning and other linguistic significance as arbitrary (not determined or required for this or that linguistic form by external reality); and a presupposition that the meaning or significance of an expression depends on its place in a system, and in particular on its contrasts with other expressions in the system. It is not unreasonable, therefore, to consider Wittgenstein as extending linguistic methods and the concept of grammar to sorts of expressions and dimensions of language normally excluded from their purview. This does not mean that there are no differences between the two disciplines, nor that linguists are good philosophers, and certainly not that philosophical problems can be best relegated to them. It does mean that there is considerable plausibility in Wittgenstein's treatment of philosophy as a variation of this old familiar language-game rather than as either a brand new game or a variation on the language-game of knowing and doubting.

## IV  THE GIVENNESS OF GRAMMAR

At the end of the *Philosophical Investigations* Wittgenstein takes note of his frequent references to very general facts of nature and fends off any overeager metaphysical use of them:

If the formation of concepts can be explained by facts of nature, should we not be interested, not in grammar, but rather in that in nature which is the basis of grammar? – Our interest certainly includes the correspondence between concepts and very general facts of nature. (Such facts as mostly do not strike us because of their generality.) But our interest does not fall back upon these possible causes of the formation of concepts; we are not doing natural science; nor yet natural history – since we can also invest fictitious natural history for our purposes. (PI, p. 230)

What Wittgenstein says here is true – especially that the focus of his interest is on grammar rather than on nature. It is the grammar rather than the natural science or the natural history that is the key to unravelling philosophical problems. His reminders about very general facts of nature, like his invention of fictitious natural history, have different purposes, for example to remind us that grammar *need* not be the way it is or that there are limits to what we call "calculating," reminders that are needed to nudge us away from certain traditionally attractive blind alleys in the quest for philosophical clarity. Nonetheless his disclaimers about inventing fictitious natural history seem a bit misleading. It is true that the builders and the woodsellers are fictitious. But it is also true that Wittgenstein is interested mainly in language–games that are *found* rather than invented, and that his treatment of metaphysical problems by reference to the grammar of actual natural language bears a resemblance to what Aristotle does in the *Categories*. Wittgenstein, that is, adopts a kind of naturalism that is more or less Aristotelian, and is certainly more Aristotelian than Quineian.[16]

Aristotle provides a classification of being by means of differentiation among "things that are said" (1a16), which in turn correspond to subjects and predicates. Most of his categories are predicables (i.e., they are said of other things), the exception being individual substance, which is neither in another thing nor said of another thing. The predicables are distinguished from one another by the possibilities of discourse continuation they support. Thus with respect to each of the categories Aristotle says whether or not it "admits of a more and a less." Qualities do, which means that it makes sense to ask whether one gentle person is more or less gentle than another. Sortal concepts do not, which means that it makes no sense to ask whether one mushroom is more or less a mushroom than another. Admitting of a more and a less is only one of a number of dimensions of possible discourse continuation to which Aristotle refers in order to distinguish the categories. Each category can usefully be thought of as a distinct bundle of discourse features along various dimensions.

Aristotle's philosophy is often thought by admirers of Wittgenstein to be hopelessly metaphysical and hopelessly systematic, but this is partly a matter of style rather than substance (difficult though it is to distinguish the two) and is in any case not true of the *Catego-*

*ries*. The first thing to say about this work is that it is an early and fragmentary version of what today we might call Wittgensteinian grammar. Like that of Wittgenstein and Saussure, his work was descriptive. He was describing actual uses of language. But he was more like Wittgenstein than like Saussure in that he did not do it analytically by means of principles of morphology and syntax but contextually in terms of possible discourse continuations. One major difference from Wittgenstein is that Aristotle focused on truth-claims, as Wittgenstein had done in the *Tractatus*, whereas in his later work (especially at the beginning of the *Investigations*, where he introduces his methods and concepts) Wittgenstein seems to go out of his way to avoid mentioning truth-claims in favor of discussing orders, jokes, stories, and so on. A second difference is that Aristotle proceeds as if the topic were a scientific one, whereas for Wittgenstein the insistence that philosophy cannot be modeled on the sciences resounds in his work from beginning to end. A third difference is that Wittgenstein's discussion of language-games early in *Philosophical Investigations* is preliminary to diagnosis and treatment of philosophical problems – laying out the medical implements, so to speak, for such later use as we see in PI, 246–55 and 304 – whereas Aristotle's *Categories* is preliminary to just the sort of scientistic metaphysics that Wittgenstein found especially in need of his therapy. But the parallels between this work of Aristotle's and Wittgenstein's introduction of language-games in the *Philosophical Investigations*, even to the point of their being put at the beginning of the corpus, are strong and significant.

Through these comments I am trying to get readers to reconsider what categories are or might be, as well as to see Wittgenstein as contributing to the tradition of Western philosophy. From this perspective the second needed comment is that Kant and Ryle seem quite wrong-headed in their criticisms of Aristotle's incomplete and inelegant set of categories. It is true that Kant produced a neat system of categories by basing them on the logical form of propositions. He began with a table of the logically possible forms of judgment, and produced his table of categories by identifying a category with each of the judgment forms; or rather by projecting a category, as a kind of a priori offspring, from each judgment form. The system is not only neat and in tabular form but is also complete. But this impressive result is achieved by completely changing the nature of the enterprise, as Ryle acerbically notes: "Kant's doctrine of categories starts from quite a different quarter from that of Aristotle, and what he lists as categories are quite other than what Aristotle puts into his index. Kant quaintly avers that his purpose is the same as Aristotle's, but in this he is, save in a very broad and vague sense, mistaken."[17] Kant's purpose could be described as an ideal language project based on analysis of propositions or judgments, rather than an empirical project based on their use.

Unfortunately Ryle proceeds in a way that has many of the same defects as Kant's way. He does not begin with a table of judgments. He begins instead with "sentence-factors" and "proposition-factors," where a factor is some part of a sentence or proposition, whether a word or a phrase. By means of this beginning Ryle avoids having a closed system. But he identifies categories with logical types, and says that a categorial sentence is one that specifies the logical type of some factor. Like Kant, therefore, he identifies categories analytically rather than contextually. Also like Kant, he does so within the framework of logic (which is just assumed) rather than within some pre-propositional domain of language, such as rhetoric, for example, or phatic communion, or contexts of purposeful activity like that of Wittgenstein's builders.

The third comment is that Wittgenstein's description of language-games and uses of language is (without, of course, intending to be) a kind of generalization of Aristotle's work on categories. Aristotle stops with noting some varieties of truth-claims – and in the *Poetics* he makes clear that there are uses of language other than truth-claims. Wittgenstein says nothing that contradicts or throws doubt on Aristotle's categories, but he initially pays more attention to uses of language that are not truth-claims (such as orders) and to truth-claims that are not knowledge-claims (such as dream reports). The attention to appropriate contexts and possible discourse continuations, by means of which he distinguishes different uses of language, is similar to Aristotle's method in the *Categories* – the principal difference is that Wittgenstein pays more attention to contexts – and provides a schema for generalizing that work.

While Wittgenstein invented language-games for particular purposes – the builders (PI, 2–8) and the woodsellers (RFM, I-148–50) are good examples – the bulk of his work focuses on language-games that are components of human life: orders, jokes, and greetings, for

example, occur in concrete contexts; reports are generally propositional, but Wittgenstein's examples are put in concrete contexts of
reporting battles, measurements, calculations, sensations, dreams, or
intentions. In the *Philosophical Grammar* (66) he says: "I am only
*describing* language, not *explaining* anything." Near the beginning of
*Zettel*, which contains several pages of remarks that bring out the
philosophical puzzles about the nature of intention, he remarks that
one could learn very many language-games without learning to report
intentions, as we do by saying "I was just about to . . . ," and notes
that there is no known language without provision for this use of
language (Z, 43). At another place there is a similarly naturalistic note
to the effect that we should just accept and not try to explain the
language-games we find:

Our mistake is to look for an explanation where we ought to look at what
happens as a "proto-phenomenon." That is, where we ought to have said:
*this language-game is played.*
The question is not one of explaining a language-game by means of our
experiences, but of noting a language-game.
What is the purpose of telling someone that a time ago I had such-and-such a
wish? – Look on the language-game as the *primary* thing. (PI, 654–6)

This remark makes evident Wittgenstein's acceptance of language-
games as *given*. They don't *have* to exist, there is no necessity
about them; but they *do* exist. They are there as features of human
life. Although we should not equate language-games with forms of
life, Wittgenstein undoubtedly has this givenness of language-
games in mind in the famous passage near the end of PI, p. xi:
"What has to be accepted, the given, is – so one could say – *forms
of life.*" Wittgenstein is a naturalist in that he takes for granted
that we have a complicated form of life whose features are accessible to observation and description but are susceptible neither to
explanation nor skepticism.[18]

There are obviously objections to the claim that rules of grammar
are among the very general facts of nature. One is that rules are not
facts. I have already dealt with the thrust of that objection in the
previous section, where I pointed out that even the words "right"
and "wrong," used in reference to linguistic practice, have a primarily descriptive meaning in Wittgenstein's work. It is a fact that many
human activities are best described in terms of the rules that consti-

tute them. The existence of such rules as components of our life, not their ultimate or metaphysical validity, Wittgenstein accepts as given. His focus on grammar and rules does not therefore compromise his naturalism.

The other obvious objection is that grammars are created by humans (linguists) as descriptions of languages or linguistic practices; they no more exist in nature than do physics texts and mathematical proofs. This objection, as Harris notes,[19] is based on the fact that Wittgenstein (like Saussure) uses both "grammar" and "rule" to refer either to descriptions of language use or to the social facts that the descriptions describe. Here is an example of grammar and rules as descriptions:

> Grammar describes the use of words in the language.
> So it has the same relation to the language as the description of the game, the rules of the game, have to the game. (PG, 60)

It is only as underlying social facts, not as descriptions, that grammar and rules are given to us.


## V  GRAMMAR AND METAPHYSICS

Wittgenstein exhibits a certain hostility to metaphysics combined with a continuing fascination with metaphysical problems, as well as with continuing contributions to descriptive metaphysics, such as his distinction of natural history from natural science[20] and his classification of different kinds of mental phenomena in *Zettel*, 488–504.[21] It was the hostility rather than the fascination that the Vienna Circle noticed and adopted, and it is easy to imagine that Wittgenstein was not unhappy to be a source for the empiricist disparagement of metaphysics, however unhappy he was with empiricist epistemology. He did not often (the quotation at the beginning of Section II from the *Notebooks* is an exception) use the word "metaphysics," as I am using it in this essay, to refer to a description of the nature or essence of things. He generally used it only to refer to one sort of traditional pursuit of this enquiry: metaphysics as the enquiry into transcendent facts. Here is an example:

> Philosophical investigations: conceptual investigations. The essential thing about metaphysics: that the difference between factual and concep-

tual investigations is not clear to it. A metaphysical question is always in appearance a factual one, although the problem is a conceptual one. (RPPI, 949; Cf. Z, 458)

In this paragraph metaphysics is presented as a confusion of two language-games – just the sort of confusion that typically results in nonsense or absurdity. There is no language-game that provides a context for such metaphysical statements, and without such a context metaphysical claims have no meaning, since: "Words have meaning only in the stream of life" (LWI, 913). Wittgenstein's grammar constitutes a powerful rebuke to speculative or scientific metaphysics. But not to descriptive metaphysics, especially not in the form of human natural history, to which Wittgenstein himself certainly does make contributions.

Wittgenstein's naturalism is the key to the relation of grammar to metaphysics in his later philosophy. Like other facts of natural history, grammar lies right in front of our eyes, in the form of instruction in regular uses of language. Although individual grammatical remarks about such uses are generally language-specific in their details, the practice of making them constitutes a universal language-game, a part of every natural language. But although universal, it could not be a primitive language-game. Unlike the famous language-games at the beginning of the *Philosophical Investigations*, it could not be learned if there were no other language-games, and could not be the whole language of a tribe. Grammar (especially as a description, rather than the structure described) presupposes the long-term existence of more ordinary uses of language as plain hard fact: "The grammar of a language isn't recorded and doesn't come into existence until the language has already been spoken by human beings for a *long* time" (PG, 62–3). There are two immediate metaphysical consequences of identifying philosophy with a natural phenomenon that cannot be a primitive language-game. One is that radical skepticism is ruled out, for many very general facts about humans and their world are presupposed, including those that Moore discussed in the famous essays which Wittgenstein examines in *On Certainty*. This leaves room for a certain moderate skepticism, since the facts of natural history "lie beyond being justified or unjustified" (OC, 359) and therefore cannot be claimed as *knowledge*; but the sort of Cartesian skepticism that supposes that life may all be a dream is left aside as nonsense. The other consequence is that metaphysics must abjure any pretension to be foundation, moral guide, or oracle. It cannot be foundationalist in a Cartesian or Russellian sense, claiming to justify first truths and to prove the existence of the external world: it can only describe and not explain, and it already presupposes truths of natural history. It cannot be moralistic, in the manner of Kant or Mill or Murdoch,[22] since the same plain facts and the same grammar hold firm no matter how morally or immorally people act; grammar only describes a range of possibilities, whereas morality restricts it.[23] Nor can metaphysics be oracular, as Plato and Heidegger would have it, explaining the difference between appearance and reality, since even the deepest of "depth grammar" is ready to hand. These two consequences are of utmost importance to Wittgenstein, and I will come back to them at the end of the essay.

In taking for granted the world and human beings using language as part of it, Wittgenstein in his later thought sticks with the main line of the *Tractatus*, which begins with the world as the totality of facts. In both the early and the later works the world and its facts are contingent. There are no rules or necessities in the natural world. In the *Tractatus* Wittgenstein expresses this in 6.37 and 6.375:

> There is no compulsion making one thing happen because another has happened. The only necessity that exists is *logical* necessity.

> Just as the only necessity that exists is *logical* necessity, so too the only impossibility that exists is *logical* impossibility.

In the *Investigations* and other later work Wittgenstein brings out the contingency of our actual ways of living by inventing crazy language-games, which he refers to in the passage cited above as "fictitious natural history." In his insistence on the contingency of the natural world Wittgenstein has often rightly been compared to Hume. After the unquestioned existence of the natural world, the radical contingency of its component facts is the most prominent feature of Wittgenstein's metaphysical commitments.

Although it is a contingent fact that there is a world and that it contains humans and their grammar (or grammars), to say this is not the end of the story. For the *human* world contains many necessities and impossibilities, and many kinds of them. Of special interest are those pertaining to essences, not *found* in the natural world: "*Essence* is expressed by grammar" (PI, 371); "Grammar tells us what kind of object anything is" (PI, 373). We might initially think of these remarks as pertaining mostly (or solely) to natural kinds and material objects. Necessities and impossibilities might then be expressed through inferences:

> Since it is a chair, you must be able to sit on it.
> Since it is wooden, it is bound to burn up in a fire.
> Since it is a fish, it cannot live long out of water.
> Since it is a garter snake, it must shed its skin.

The necessities and impossibilities expressed in these inferences, all of which (the inferences) are perfectly sound in everyday affairs, are imputed by us to the world around us by our way of classifying and labeling objects in the world. They reflect regularities pertaining to that world. But as Hume and Wittgenstein remind us, things could be different. There could be a reptile very like a garter snake in everything except that its skin stretches and is never shed. And so on.

Wittgenstein's principle, however, applies much more widely than just to natural kinds and material objects. Consider the following inferences:

> He was threatening me with a knife, so I had to shoot him.
> Saddam refused to back down, so we had no choice.
> It is the law, so you must do it.
> You cannot go there, it is private property.
> The hospital cannot admit her, she's an undocumented alien.

In each of these inferences what is at stake is the morality (the moral justifiability) of an action. The grammar involved is that of language-games that do indeed include classifications of persons and actions; but the classifications are not based on natural kinds or obvious functions, and much more than classification is involved. In particular, judgments about actions and penalties for transgressions are inseparable from these inferences. They may be defeasible or subject to qualification as the discourse proceeds, but they are there nonetheless. The grammar expresses certain essential qualities of the persons and actions – essential for purposes of the judging-game, not in an absolute sense – and expresses them as necessities and impossibilities.

Essence, necessity, and impossibility are modal features of the human experience. It is a firm and unwavering part of Wittgenstein's metaphysical posture that they belong not to the world of natural history and plain fact but rather to the world we conceive as we encounter and enter it. These modal features, in varying patterns, are tightly bound up in our various conceptions of the world. They are not in the same metaphysical category as the very general contingent facts that make up natural history, nor can they be reached by simple logical derivation from such facts. Nor, of course, can they have a transcendent or transcendental origin. Wittgenstein treats the problem of modalities (especially those connected with rules and necessities) very seriously, while at the same time insisting that they have no independent standing either in fact (agreeing with Hume) or in transcendent reality (agreeing with Kant). Wittgenstein's metaphysics includes them with grammar, no doubt in large part because grammar involves rules. Modalities are not primary, and even seem partially dependent on contingent factual reality (that is, on natural history); but they are inescapable.

Wittgenstein did not devise the structure of this metaphysics during his later period of philosophical work. Instead he modified the metaphysics of the *Tractatus*. The *Tractatus* begins with the world of contingent fact:

The world is all that is the case.
The world is the totality of facts, not of things. (TLP, 1–1.1)

Each item can be the case or not the case while everything else remains the same. (TLP, 1.21)

In this world of fact there are no necessities or impossibilities. A new factor, however, is introduced in TLP, 2.1: "We make ourselves pictures of facts" (translation altered). This picture-making turns out to be propositional, so its rules and principles are those of logic. It is because of logic, not the world of fact, that there are modalities, and that the only necessity is *logical* necessity and the only impossibility is *logical* impossibility. In his remark about grammar and essence, quoted above, as well as in his suggestion that grammar is the basis of our sense of necessity and impossibility,[24] we see a modification of his early view, in line with the generalization discussed in Section II.

## VI GRAMMAR AS A CRITICAL TOOL

Wittgenstein was first and foremost a critical philosopher. One cannot read any of his works without a powerful sense of familiar ideas being subjected to devastating scrutiny. There is regularly a constructive framework for the destructive criticism, and it usually takes the form of commitments to how things really are and what can or should be said. The picture theory and the theory of truth-functions exemplify such a framework in the *Tractatus*, as do language-games and family resemblance in the *Investigations* and the sharp distinction between knowledge and certainty in *On Certainty*. It is characteristic of these frameworks that they quickly yield critical tools. The principle (in the *Tractatus*) that all propositional complexity is truth-functional is used with great effect to criticize not only traditional philosophical views but also some very specific doctrines of Frege and Russell in the philosophy of logic. Similarly, the framework of *On Certainty* yields – and perhaps is meant to yield – criteria that are used to understand and criticize Moore. Criticism of respected and respectable views – those of Frege, Russell, and Moore are most prominent, views of Aristotle, Augustine, and Kant also come to mind – is never far from the center of Wittgenstein's concerns.

It is characteristic of Wittgenstein's critical comments that they arise from a wider perspective. His criticisms of Frege, Russell, and Moore were *principled* in that they were based solidly on his deep and comprehensive considerations about the ways of words, rather than either dialectical (turning an author's own ideas against the author's texts) or occasional (devised for a particular occasion only). The principled character of Wittgenstein's philosophical criticism is an important reason for his stature as a philosopher.[25]

One reason why Wittgenstein's critical principles and criteria emerge from a constructive framework is his conviction that such criteria must themselves be subject to criticism.[26] That is to say, they must be self-referential. The most dramatic expression of Wittgenstein's recognition of the need for self-referentiality occurs at the end of the *Tractatus*, where Wittgenstein says: "My propositions serve as elucidations in the following way: anyone who understands me eventually recognizes them as nonsensical, when he has used them – as steps – to climb up beyond them. (He must, so to speak, throw away the ladder after he has climbed up it)" (TLP, 654). The reader, that is, will understand that Wittgenstein has used the *Tractatus* to construct a criterion for philosophical criticism – or various such criteria; that the construction and articulation of that criterion (or criteria) are as subject to criticism as any philosophical idea; and that the judgment ensuing from applying the criterion to its own text is that it is nonsense. The courage of Wittgenstein's acknowledgment of self-referentiality at that point is astonishing – an exemplary instance of philosophical conscience. It escapes incoherence only by Wittgenstein's subtle shift from its being the author (the person) rather than the text that is to be understood; and some of the most distinguished commentators, such as Russell[27] and Black,[28] have refused to yield to the hard truth that Wittgenstein so succinctly states.

Recognizing that a criterion of philosophical criticism must be self-referential stems from Kant, though it is not entirely easy to see in Kant's work. The need for it is clearest in Kant's critical comments in the *Transcendental Dialectic,* particularly in the chapter on "The Antinomy of Pure Reason." The best arguments in the Antinomy are negative (reductio ad absurdum) arguments inferring the incoherence of the other philosophical view. Each of the schools, the rationalists and the empiricists (Kant gives them other names), attacks the other; and each does so dogmatically, without testing the soundness of their own critical standards. The obvious conclusion, which Kant surely drew but which he does not state explicitly, is that critical standards must themselves be tested if dogmatism is to be avoided. If they are tested by some *other* standard, that standard will require certification. This path threatens endless regress. The only alternative path seems to be for the critical standard to meet its *own* critical test. The standard cannot then provide a full justification in the strong sense, under threat of being viciously circular. So the standard must provide only certification – a kind of "nihil obstat" – and its justification or source must lie elsewhere.

The strategy of self-referential critical philosophy begins with the uncritical acceptance of some nonphilosophical facts – taking them for granted, so to speak. Kant took Euclidean geometry, Aristotelian logic, and Newtonian physics for granted in this way. When he asked how knowledge and judgment were possible, he had in mind knowledge and judgment in these fields, which seemed wholly reliable, well confirmed, and far more unshakable than they seem from our perspective today. He provided a complicated account of their success. One component, central for our interests here, is that such disciplines are made possible by a priori categories and synthetic a priori judgments, provided that concepts always apply in principle to sensations and perceptions, in accordance with the schemata, and that no constitutive use is made of regulative principles. These two provisos constitute constraints that Kant turned into critical tools. Finding synthetic a priori judgment already required by the special sciences meant that the kind of propositions needed in his philosophy were legitimate anyway, even if there were no philosophy, so that his philosophical propositions would not appear sui generis or ad hoc. His philosophy, thus devised, did not fail the critical test by means of which it undermined other philosophical views. In this way Kant's philosophy would have been successfully self-referential, if only he had been right about what he took for granted; but that was not the case.

When Wittgenstein returned to philosophy in 1929, one of the main challenges facing him was to find a criterion for philosophical criticism that is *successfully* self-referential. We can, of course, no longer take Euclid, Aristotle, and Newton for granted, because of the astonishing developments in geometry, logic, and physics over the past 150 years. Those years have further taught us that we cannot expect any complete or final science, not even in mathematics or physics. Wittgenstein therefore had to look elsewhere for his starting point. He found it in grammar, or the language-game of making grammatical remarks, where the focus of the grammar is on uses of language rather than on phonology or morphology or syntax.

What Wittgenstein takes for granted, as we have seen above, is human beings, the human form of life, and the language-games and characteristic activities that contribute to it – in short, all of what he sometimes calls "our natural history." This is a Kantian starting point, in that it assumes something nonphilosophical. It differs from Kant, however, in that it has nothing to do with knowledge, and therefore makes a more radical break than Kant did with the tradition of philosophy as epistemology which Descartes inaugurated. Descartes's radical doubt was a doubt as to whether familiar facts can be known, rather than whether they are true. Wittgenstein does not claim to *know* these facts which he assumes. Rather he points out that they *are* not doubted, and at one point he says that they "lie beyond being justified or unjustified" (OC, 359). In this connection we should no doubt take it as a rebuke to Cartesians when Wittgenstein remarks: "It is so difficult to find the *beginning*. Or better: it is difficult to begin at the beginning. And not to try to go further back" (OC, 471).

Wittgenstein's starting point has several advantages over Kant's. The most obvious is that it is not vulnerable to advances in the special sciences, since it avoids altogether commitment to any scientific or explanatory theory. That is the point of Wittgenstein's distinction between natural science and natural history. A second advantage is the perspicuity with which this starting point leads to normative criticism. Grammar is a universal language-game, in that there is no natural language in which it is not possible to instruct people in the use of the language. Such instruction involves correction and drill that aims at some (unspecified) level of competence. It is no doubt pursued more doggedly and more dogmatically in some cultures than in others, but the cultural variation casts no doubt whatever on the universality of the game. A third advantage is the relative ease with which one can appreciate the transition from what is assumed to critical philosophical criteria. Since grammar already involves describing language for normative purposes, it is a small step from doing that with words and phrases to doing it with uses of language. Though Wittgenstein introduces the term "language-game" to facilitate the transition, he needs to add little that is as technical as Kant's distinction between the regulative and the constitutive use of regulative principles. The fourth advantage is that it is both obvious and unproblematic that we teach and learn how to teach and learn language; that is, that grammar is self-referential is as unproblematic as that there is a spelling for the word "spelling."

These considerations show that Wittgenstein's conception of philosophy as grammar deserves, in historical perspective, to be credited with an outstanding achievement about which Wittgenstein himself remains mostly silent, but about which he must certainly have been aware: fulfillment of the Kantian project of a genuinely critical philosophy.

VII CONCLUSION

Wittgenstein's view of philosophy as an extension of grammar is a generalization of his earlier view of philosophy as "logic and metaphysics: logic is its basis." Logic is still inherent in truth-claims, but truth-claims are only one of countless uses of language. Wittgenstein's grammar is descriptive, and differs from linguistics by focusing on uses of language (language-games), by not being systematic, and by being self-referential. Wittgenstein's view therefore implicitly incorporates elements of naturalism, Kant, and linguistic methodology; but it forces us to rethink what these traditions mean if we are to see clearly Wittgenstein's relation to them and the use that he makes of their ideas.

It remains astonishing indeed – and no doubt helps explain the tentative and often superficial uptake of Wittgenstein's influence among thousands of the philosophers who have read him – to think of *philosophy* as *grammar*. We have been taught to think of philosophy as something grand, and of grammar as anything but grand. Wittgenstein's philosophical conscience (unlike his personality) would allow no domineering pretensions, and one might think of this view of philosophy as a more mature and more sophisticated expression of the same sort of self-denial evidenced at the end of the *Tractatus:* "My propositions serve as elucidations in the following way: anyone who understands me eventually recognizes them as nonsensical. . . ." (TLP, 6.54). Philosophy is possible only because of its limits, and philosophers become confused and fraudulent when they deliberately or even inadvertently cross over those limits. Russell treated it as a joke that Wittgenstein once answered, in response to Russell's inquiry whether he was thinking about logic or his sins, "Both!" For Wittgenstein, however, it was no joke. He wrote to Ludwig Ficker about the *Tractatus,*

The book's point is an ethical one. I once meant to include in the preface a sentence which is not in fact there now but which I will write out for you here, because it will perhaps be a key to the work for you. What I meant to write then was this: My work consists of two parts: the one presented here and all that I have *not* written. And it is precisely this second part that is the important one.[29]

Not writing down what could not be written – that is, what could only be "shown" and not "said" – respected the limits of language and preserved him from a certain corruption. Philosophical and moral clarity go hand in hand; conversely, for those who slip, there is no easy separation of intellectual from moral confusion. That is one principal reason why Wittgenstein saw philosophy as embroiled with "will" as well as "idea" (NB, 15.10.16), and hence as involving something like therapy or "treatment of an illness" (PI, 133, 255) as well as conceptual clarity and argument.

In his later renunciation of the pretensions of speculative or dogmatic metaphysics (see Section V) there is as much a moral message as there was at the time of the *Tractatus*. The message is one of humility that Wittgenstein got from Tolstoy. It is difficult to express in words, but something of it comes across in the motto for the *Philosophical Investigations:* "The special thing about progress is that it always looks greater than it really is." It is also shown in Wittgenstein's respect for the conditions and limits that make philosophical discourse possible. Good philosophizing is a humble moral achievement, and noteworthy more for its humility than for its achievement just because it cannot make much difference either to the progress of science or to the urgent practical problems of the world. As "grammarians," philosophers have no special knowledge of truth and goodness, for grammar is at best a servant of the sciences (and this role has little or none of the importance for Wittgenstein that it had for Bacon) rather than another epistemic discipline undergirding or overseeing them. Wittgenstein's philosophy does not help us to improve the world (as medicine and engineering are designed to do) or to act well in the world (as moral rules are designed to do) but only to think in a certain way about life and the world – to see things as they really are and in proper perspective. This is not easy, and Wittgenstein's life was an awesome struggle to keep trying. The various limits are features of reality, but observing them (or not) is a matter of will, in which Wittgenstein saw righteousness as well as wisdom.

NOTES

1 Paul Feyerabend, "Wittgenstein's *Philosophical Investigations*," *Philosophical Review* 64 (1955), pp. 449–83 (reprinted in J. Canfield, ed., *The Philosophy of Wittgenstein* [New York: Garland Publishing, 1986], vol. 4, pp. 231–65).

2 Roy Harris, *Language, Saussure and Wittgenstein: How to Play Games with Words* (London: Routledge, 1988).

3 See Newton Garver, *This Complicated Form of Life: Essays on Wittgenstein* (Chicago: Open Court, 1994), ch. 14, esp. pp. 217–24.

4 See TLP, 2.0121. For discussion of the controversy about the alleged real-ism of the *Tractatus* see Garver, *This Complicated Form of Life*, ch. 6.

5 See J. J. Katz, *Philosophy of Language* (New York: Harper and Row, 1966).

6 See Benjamin Lee Whorf, *Language, Thought, and Reality* (Cambridge, Mass.: MIT Press, 1956), esp. pp. 57–124; Edward Sapir, *Selected Writings*, ed. David G. Mandelbaum (Berkeley and Los Angeles: University of California Press, 1949), esp. pp. 98–103, 150–9; Emile Benveniste, *Problems in General Linguistics* (Coral Gables: University of Florida Press, 1971).

7 Bronislaw Malinowski, "The Problem of Meaning in Primitive Languages," appendix to Ogden and Richards, *The Meaning of Meaning* (London: Routledge and Kegan Paul, 1923), pp. 296–336.

8 Brent Berlin and Paul Kay, *Basic Color Terms: Their Universality and Evolution* (Berkeley and Los Angeles: University of California Press, 1969).

9 Henry M. Sheffer, "A Set of Five Independent Postulates for Boolean Algebras, with Application to Logical Constants," *Transactions of the American Mathematical Society* 14 (1913), pp. 481–8. Sheffer's work also shows that joint negation serves as well as incompatibility for this purpose. Wittgenstein made use of joint negation in his *Tractatus*, largely because it leads to more perspicuous generalization in conjunction with truth-tables and with his recursive definition of the general form of propositions. It is incompatibility rather than joint negation, however, that is conspicuously built into the semantics of everyday language, and I have therefore not followed Wittgenstein's early lead with respect to these two alternatives.

Sheffer's work had precedents in prior work of Peirce and Nicod, for details of which see H. R. Fischer, *Sprache und Lebensform: Wittgenstein über Freud und die Geisteskrankheit* (Frankfurt am Main: Athenäum, 1987), p. 295. There is no reason to think that this earlier work had any influence on Wittgenstein.

10 Herbert Spiegelberg gives an accurate and useful account of the early phase of this transitional terminology (what was printed in *Philosophical Remarks*), in "The Puzzle of Ludwig Wittgenstein's *Phänomenologie* (1929–?)," *American Philosophical Quarterly* 5 (1968), pp. 244–56 (reprinted in Canfield, ed., *The Philosophy of Wittgenstein*, vol. 15, pp. 252–64). The terminology still occurs in *Philosophical Grammar*; in addition there was a chapter entitled "Phenomenology" in the "Big Typescript" of 1933, from which *Philosophical Grammar* was prepared, but it was one of four chapters omitted from the published version. Details of the editing of the "Big Typescript" into *Philosophical Grammar* are given by Anthony Kenny, *The Legacy of Wittgenstein* (Oxford: Blackwell, 1984), ch. 3.

11 Wittgenstein's attacks on the idea of logic as sublime (PI, 89, 94), of the purest crystal (PI, 97), and as hidden in the medium of the understanding (PI, 102) are not attacks on the strictness and rigor of logic but rather on a certain philosophical picture of logical rigor. He says as much in PI, 102:

> The strict and clear rules of the logical structure of propositions appear to us as something in the background – hidden in the medium of the understanding.

The straightforward way to read this sentence is as an attack on the *appearance* of something (strict and clear rules) whose existence is not challenged. My claim is that logic is derived through the abstraction and iteration of constitutive rules of a certain language-game (or family of language-games), namely predication or making truth-claims. For details of key stages of this derivation, see Netwon Garver and Seung-Chong Lee, *Derrida and Wittgenstein* (Philadelphia: Temple University Press, 1994), pp. 154–60.

12 Harris, *Language, Saussure and Wittgenstein*, p. 62–4, 68.

13 Ibid., p. 47; see generally pp. 47–60. See also Moore's report on Wittgenstein's lecture, PO, p. 70–3.

14 John Langshaw Austin, *How to Do Things with Words* (London: Oxford University Press, 1962); John Searle, *Speech Acts: An Essay in the Philosophy of Language* (London: Oxford University Press, 1969).

15 Harris, *Language, Saussure, and Wittgenstein*, p. 113.

16 For fuller discussion of alternative forms of naturalism, see Garver, *This Complicated Form of Life*, ch. 16, and Peter Strawson, *Skepticism and Naturalism: Some Varieties* (New York: Columbia University Press, 1985). See also Garver and Lee, *Derrida and Wittgenstein*, pp. 176–87.

17 Gilbert Ryle, *Collected Papers* (London: Hutchinson, 1971), vol. 2, p. 276.

18 See Garver, *This Complicated Form of Life*, ch. 15.

19 Harris, *Language, Saussure, and Wittgenstein*, p. 69.

20 See Garver, *This Complicated Form of Life*, ch. 9.

21 See Malcolm Budd, *Wittgenstein's Philosophy of Mind* (London and New York: Routledge, 1989), pp. 10–15 and 146–65, for a useful discussion of this contribution to descriptive metaphysics. See also Joachim Schulte, *Experience and Expression: Wittgenstein's Philosophy of Psychology* (Oxford: Clarendon Press, 1993), esp. ch. 3.

22 See Iris Murdoch, *Metaphysics as a Guide to Morals* (New York: Viking Penguin, 1993), the published version of her 1982 Gifford Lectures. Wittgenstein looms as an important figure throughout this thoughtful and imposing volume, both as a defense against the pretentious excesses of existentialism and structuralism, and also as an obstacle preventing her from fully embracing the Platonic version of metaphysics as a guide to morals to which she is instinctively drawn.

23 Put in other terminology, morality requires regulative rules, since it is designed to constrain behavior which is otherwise not only thinkable but altogether too likely; whereas the rules of grammar are constitutive rather than regulative, in that without them the acts or actions in question are not even thinkable. See my article "Rules" in the *Encyclopedia of Philosophy*. While this other terminology may be useful to many readers, one should bear in mind that it is practices rather than rules that are primary for Wittgenstein.

24 There is a striking and puzzling passage conveying this suggestion which occurs at PG, 184 and then occurs again (with the initial injunction added) between the two parts of what I quoted about grammar and essence: "Consider: 'The only correlate in language to an intrinsic necessity is an arbitrary rule. It is the only thing which one can milk out of this intrinsic necessity into a proposition' " (PI, 372). This is a ringing claim, and some commentators have not been able to resist citing it as Wittgenstein's view of the matter. Perhaps. But I take the quotation marks to signify that he was unable either to embrace or to reject what is expressed here. It is too much like a slogan or a claim for him to embrace, and he cannot reject it because it contains too much of his central insight – partly critical, partly therapeutic – that the necessities and impossibilities we experience are mostly grounded in rules of language.

25 See Garver and Lee, *Derrida and Wittgenstein*, chs. 6 and 7, for a more extended account of why Wittgenstein is a philosopher and Derrida is not.

26 See Garver, *This Complicated Form of Life*, ch. 1.

27 See his introduction to the *Tractatus*.

28 Max Black, *A Companion to Wittgenstein's* Tractatus (Ithaca: Cornell University Press, 1964), pp. 376–86.

29 Paul Engelmann, *Letters from Wittgenstein, with a Memoir* (Oxford: Blackwell, 1967), pp. 143–4.

# 5   A philosophy of mathematics between two camps

The history of philosophy can partially be characterized by what Hilary Putnam has called the *recoil*[1] phenomenon: an oscillation between two extreme positions, with each camp reacting to the untenable part of the other, resulting, finally, in *two* untenable positions. The current recoil ricochets across both analytic and Continental philosophy. On one side are those who deny objectivity in all fields in all ways; there are only incommensurable narratives. On the other side are those who attempt to secure objectivity, but do so at the cost of clothing it in metaphysical mystery. The first side (justifiably) points out the illusions in the second's metaphysics, and then recoils to anarchy. The second (justifiably) shows the inherent contradictions in the anarchist position, and then recoils to building more epicycles in its metaphysical castle.

Wittgenstein argued against both sides. His ultimate achievement in the philosophy of mathematics was to stake out a defensible intermediate position between two untenable warring factions.[2] This essay will explicate Wittgenstein's position by stressing his opposition to each side, emphasizing, as well, the unity of Wittgenstein's later philosophy of mathematics with the *Philosophical Investigations*.[3]

Much of Wittgenstein's post-*Tractatus* work in the philosophy of mathematics endeavors to expose the delusions and misconceptions behind the second, metaphysical, camp. William James, a philosopher Wittgenstein admired, wrote that "the trail of the human serpent is . . . over everything."[4] Wittgenstein attempted to find the proper place for that trail in his post-*Tractatus* explorations of both mathematical and nonmathematical language. Much of the dispute among commentators concerns not the importance of such a trail, but its precise location.

171

Wittgenstein perceived his chief foe, in mathematics, as altogether denying the human serpent. His adversaries picture mathematics as transcendent: a mathematical proposition has truth and meaning regardless of human rules or use. There is an under- (or over-) lying mathematical reality which is independent of our mathematical practice and language and which adjudicates the correctness of that practice and language.[5]

Wittgenstein sometimes identified this misleading picture with the work of his friend, the Cambridge mathematician G. H. Hardy. Discussing "a false idea of the role which mathematical and logical propositions play," Wittgenstein is reported to have said "Consider Professor Hardy's article ["Mathematical Proof"] and his remark that 'to mathematical propositions there corresponds – in some sense, however sophisticated – a reality' " (LFM, p. 239). The following passage from Hardy's *A Mathematician's Apology* could very well represent the creed of the expulsion of the serpent:

I believe that mathematical reality lies outside us, that our function is to discover or *observe* it, and that the theorems which we prove, and which we describe grandiloquently as our "creations," are simply our notes of our observations.[6]

Wittgenstein never wavered from rejecting this metaphysical picture, but the form of his opposition depended on the stage of his career.

The rejection of Hardy's picture and the metaphysics of objectivity, however, does not imply that Wittgenstein was a philosopher of the first, the anarchist, camp. The instantiations of our camps vary according to the era and location, but at the beginning of Wittgenstein's career the anarchist camp would have been exemplified by a view Hardy also combatted: *psychologism*.[7] ". . . 317 is a prime," Hardy asserted, "not because we think so, or because our minds are shaped in one way rather than another, but *because it is so*, because mathematical reality is built that way."[8] Both of Wittgenstein's greatest influences, Frege and Russell, believed that identifying the laws of logic with the laws of psychology would necessarily lead to a complete loss of objectivity. Wittgenstein carried a copy of Frege's *Grundgesetze* in his World War I backpack, and that book contained a typical argument for the route from psychologism to anarchy:

If every man designated something different by the name "moon," namely one of his own ideas, much as he expresses his own pain by the cry "Ouch," then of course the psychological point of view would be justified; but an argument about the properties of the moon would be pointless. . . . If we could not grasp anything but what was within our own selves, then a conflict of opinions [based on] a mutual understanding would be impossible, because a common ground would be lacking, and no idea in the psychological sense can afford us such a ground. There would be no logic to be appointed arbiter in the conflict of opinions.[9]

Frege was accusing the psychological logicians of seeing mathematics and logic as crude emotivists see ethics: when x says abortion is wrong and y says it is permissible, they are not disagreeing, but are merely reporting different states of the pits of their stomachs. As Frege later wrote, "This means the breakdown of every bridge leading to what is objective."[10]

In *this* battle Wittgenstein and Hardy were allies; Wittgenstein never rejected his predecessors' antipsychologism, and no matter how much he objected to some characterizations of the *metaphysics* of objectivity (not objectivity itself!), he never recoiled into the anarchist camp.

### I THE TRANSITION FROM CALCULUS TO LANGUAGE-GAME

We can distinguish three relatively distinct Wittgensteinian philosophies of mathematics: early, middle ("the calculus conception"), and later ("the language-game conception").[11] The later position is the most interesting for our purposes: intertwined with and complementing the *Investigations*, it is the view that most successfully (and defensibly) steers between the recoiling camps.

Wittgenstein's first philosophy of mathematics, found in the *Notebooks, 1914–1916* and the *Tractatus*, both criticized and built on Frege's and Russell's work in the foundations of mathematics. Frege and Russell shared a project that was later called *logicism:* the attempt to prove that mathematics is reducible to logic. Much of Wittgenstein's early work involved both a rejection of logicism and a critique of the new logic its defenders developed. The early view was that "the propositions of mathematics are equations, and therefore pseudo-propositions" (TLP, 6.2). Mathematical propositions are not assertions about objects; being pseudopropositions, they are, indeed, not *about* anything at all. This claim is obviously tied in with the intricate semantics and metaphysics of the *Tractatus*, while my essay concerns the post-*Tractatus* Wittgenstein, but the theme of repudiating a transcendent mathematical reality was prominent throughout his career.

We can see this theme in Wittgenstein's next stage. "A name has meaning," he wrote in the early 1930s, "a proposition has sense in the calculus to which it belongs. The calculus is as it were autonomous. – Language must speak for itself. . . . The meaning is the role of the word in the calculus" (PG, 63). At this transitional stage Wittgenstein argued that each individual calculus is a closed, self-contained system, having no external critique. The rules (construed extremely narrowly) alone determine the meaning, and thus become the final and only court of appeal.[12] By making the rules do all the work, Wittgenstein was trying to avoid both psychologism and Hardy's overlying mathematical reality. The result in the early 1930s was a rather extreme quarantine of language: "Grammar is not accountable to any reality. It is grammatical rules that determine meaning (constitute it) and so they themselves are not answerable to any meaning and to that extent are arbitrary" (PG, 184).[13] This middle period view dominated Wittgenstein's thought from 1929 through the early 1930s.

In the middle 1930s Wittgenstein's views changed: he began to look at mathematical language as a motley[14] of language-games. There is still a complete opposition to both psychologism and Hardy's mathematical reality, but language-games, in contrast with the calculus conception, weave together language, actions, and background. One of the *Investigations*'s early characterizations of language-games (and this weaving) makes explicit reference to mathematics:

And this multiplicity [of kinds and uses of sentences] is not something fixed, given once for all; but new types of language, new language-games, as we may say, come into existence, and others become obsolete and get forgotten. (We can get a *rough picture* of this from the changes in mathematics.)

Here the term "language-*game*" is meant to bring into prominence the fact that the *speaking* of language is part of an activity, or of a form of life. (PI, 23)

Rather than seeing mathematics as a collection of self-contained calculi, the later Wittgenstein wrote:

> I want to say: it is essential to mathematics that its signs are also employed in *mufti*.
>
> It is the use outside mathematics, and so the *meaning* of the signs, that makes the sign-game into mathematics. (RFM, V-2)

We can see this change as enlarging the scope of Frege's context principle: "never to ask for the meaning of a word in isolation, but only in the context of a proposition."[15] From the *Tractatus*'s "An expression has meaning only in a proposition" (3.314), to the middle Wittgenstein's "The meaning is the role of the word in the calculus" (PG, 63), we arrive at the later Wittgenstein's "Words have meaning only in the stream of life" (LWI, 913).[16] Frege linked the context principle with his fight against psychologism,[17] as did Wittgenstein throughout his career. Wittgenstein emphasized his opposition to the Hardyan camp not because he was tempted by anarchism, but because he believed that Frege had so satisfactorily smashed the anarchist camp in its psychologistic form.

To see the dramatic difference between Wittgenstein's post-*Tractatus* conceptions, compare the following passages. "What I want to object to in this context [contradiction]," Wittgenstein wrote at the beginning of the transition, "is the view that we can define what a calculus is. One calculus is just as good as another. We can only describe a calculus, not require anything of it" (WWK, p. 202). By the end of the decade, he claimed the opposite: "If we allow contradictions in such a way that we accept that *anything* follows, then we would no longer get a calculus, or we'd get a useless thing resembling a calculus" (LFM, p. 243).[18] Although the claims are antithetical, the motivation is the same: Wittgenstein is trying to steer between anarchism and the metaphysics of objectivity. In the middle period Wittgenstein grounds meaning in the calculus itself, in the later period in the practice; in neither period does he ground meaning in the mind or in the transcendent reality.

By tracing the change in Wittgenstein's view on the concept of *number*, we can see how Wittgenstein's language-game conception of mathematics is intimately connected with the *Investigations*. "If a calculus in mathematics is altered by discoveries, can't we preserve the old calculus," the transitional Wittgenstein asked. "(That is, do we have to throw it away?). . . . . After the discovery of the North Pole we don't have two earths, one with and one without the North Pole. But after the discovery of the law of the distribution of the primes, we do have two kinds of primes" (PG, 374–5).[19] This claim is clearly a recoil from Hardy's view but at this stage the recoil goes too far, rebounding Wittgenstein into some rather strange doctrines.

We can explain this with Wittgenstein's favorite example of chess.[20] At one time the rules of chess were different from the modern ones. Pawns could only advance one square at a time – even the first time they were moved. This slowed the opening of the game considerably, as usually in the opening a player advanced a pawn once and then on the very next move advanced it again. In order to remedy this a new rule was added: the first time a pawn was moved it could be moved *either* one *or* two squares. The *en passant* rule was then added so no pawn could be promoted without the possibility of it being captured by another pawn. All this seems very reasonable, as do the following judgments: modern chess is a faster game than old chess, modern chess is a better game than old chess, modern chess without the *en passant* rule would result in some "cheap" victories. In addition, certain middle and endgame positions from old chess are the same as in modern chess, and we can compare how different players handled similar situations. Many themes present in old chess are useful for modern chess. Again, all this seems reasonable, but under Wittgenstein's calculus view the above judgments would be completely senseless.[21] There can be no such thing as the evolution of a game; a game is completely characterized by its rules alone, and if any rule is different then all that can be said is that they are different games. There can be no such thing as an improved chess; there is only chess$_1$ and chess$_2$ and chess$_3$. Since all we can appeal to is the rules, when the rules are at all different there is no more basis for saying chess$_1$ and chess$_2$ have anything in common than saying that cat and cattle have anything in common.[22]

In the language-game view the sharpness gives way to the gradual shadings of *family resemblances:* "Would it be any wonder if the technique of calculating had a family of applications?" (RFM, V-8D); and "Why should I not say that what we call mathematics is a family of activities with a family of purposes?" (RFM, V-15C). Under this view, rather than giving us a new concept, the prime distribution theory has expanded the meaning of the old one.

When Wittgenstein explains family resemblances in the *Investigations* it should not be surprising that his two chief examples are *games* and *number.* "Why do we call something a 'number,'" Wittgenstein asks. "Well, perhaps because it has a – direct – relationship with several things that have hitherto been called number; and this can be said to give it an indirect relationship to other things we call the same name. And we extend our concept of number as in spinning a thread we twist fibre on fibre" (PI, 67B). In the next remark Wittgenstein writes: "For I *can* give the concept 'number' rigid limits in this way, that is, use the word 'number' for a rigidly limited concept, but I can also use it so that the extension of the concept is *not* closed by a frontier" (PI, 68). And then he again compares the use of "number" with "game." This choice of use of a concept – rigidly limited or open-ended – is new with the language-game view.

The next paragraph of PI, 68 claims that our use of "game" is not everywhere circumscribed by rules, just as games themselves are not: "but no more are there any rules for how high one throws the ball in tennis, or how hard; yet tennis is a game for all that and his rules too." (See also PI, 84: "I said that the application of a word is not everywhere bounded by rules.") This is a radical change from the calculus notion. There rules were all we had, and once you left the boundaries of the rules there was only nonsense. Now meaning is part of the much larger concept of a language-game.

## II THE LANGUAGE-GAME CONCEPTION

It is one thing to say that "words have meaning only in the stream of life," another to cash out the slogan in a way that is helpful in understanding mathematics. It is one thing to say that mathematics is a motley of language-games, it is another to say precisely what sort of language-games they are, and how they differ from empirical ones. Since all the kinds of language are now looked at as language-games, the question arises: " 'But then what does the peculiar inexorability of mathematics consist in'?" (RFM, I-4). This question motivated much of Wittgenstein's work on the philosophy of mathematics during the late 1930s and the early 1940s.

There are two related motifs in Wittgenstein's later investigations of this problem. The first is that mathematics is a nexus of language-games with its own special role. The second is to protest against both the metaphysical and anarchist camps. When focusing on the first, Wittgenstein emphasized the inexorability and nonrevisability of mathematical statements. There he contrasted mathematical statements with empirical ones, and examined what sort of different language-game each involved. When focusing on the second (especially in the form of Hardy's picture), Wittgenstein emphasized the contingency of mathematics, and indeed of all of language, *as a whole*.

These two motifs express two different ways in which empirical considerations can bear on mathematics. (1) Within mathematics, a proposition is not revisable by experience; unlike empirical statements, mathematical ones cannot be overturned by appeals to experience. They have a special role in our language: "We deposit the picture in the archives" (LFM, p. 104), and "What I want to say is this: mathematics as such is always measure, not thing measured" (RFM, III-75). We use mathematics to judge experience, not experience to judge mathematics. (2) On the other hand, it is, after all, an empirical fact that we have the mathematics we do: "The [mathematical] proposition is grounded in a technique. And, if you like, also in the physical and psychological facts that make the technique *possible*" (RFM, VII-1).[23] This combination of views has been well described in W. W. Tait's phrase, that "necessity rides on the back of contingency."

III   THE LANGUAGE-GAME OF NONREVISABILITY

In the language-game approach there is one aspect where the meaning of mathematical and empirical language does not differ: the criterion for the classification of a proposition depends not on form, but on its *use, surroundings,* and *role.*[24] If all we have to go on is the form, then the sentence "if you add two plus two you get four" is ambiguous; it is the use, surroundings, and role that will determine whether this is a mathematical or empirical proposition.

This is analogous to Wittgenstein's discussion of pointing in the *Investigations*. When you are pointing to that object are you pointing to a *chess king* or to a *piece of wood* (PI, 35)? Utilizing the Fregean tenet that the context principle helps fight psychologism, in the surrounding sections of the *Investigations* Wittgenstein argues that the answer will depend not on mental, physiological, or occult entities, but on the specific circumstances of that pointing. (Did you ask me which piece in chess cannot be captured? I am pointing to the chess king. Are we freezing and running out of things to burn? The piece of wood.)

Frege argued that logic and psychology were sciences of an entirely different kind, and that conflating the two was fatal to mathematical objectivity. The later Wittgenstein agreed, but now, however, he examined that objectivity in terms of the kind of language-game:

> I can be as *certain* of someone else's sensations as of any fact. But this does not make the propositions "He is much depressed," "$25 \times 25 = 625$" and "I am sixty years old" into similar instruments. The explanation suggests itself that the certainty is of a different *kind.* – This seems to point to a psychological difference. But the difference is logical.
> . . . 'Mathematical certainty' is not a psychological concept.
> The kind of certainty is the kind of language-game. (PI, pp. xi, 224)[25]

What kind of language-game is mathematics? Wittgenstein considered the most important characteristic to be the *nonrevisability of mathematical statements.* There is no guarantee that our mathematics will not change (indeed it has), and certain statements that were considered nonsense will then become necessary (such as "$2 - 4 = -2$" before and after the introduction of negative numbers). *Nonrevisability* here means nonrevisable in the face of empirical fact, not in the face of mathematical considerations (such as discovering a contradiction in a system). Nonrevisability means no sensory impression or empirical fact can make a mathematical statement true or false; it does not mean we cannot revise our mathematics as our conceptions change (as indeed we have). On Wittgenstein's view mathematical statements do not describe empirical facts, but provide a framework for describing them; therefore empirical facts cannot revise mathematics. (Here there is a line of historical descent from Kant, through Frege and the *Tractatus,* to the later Wittgenstein.)

Wittgenstein sometimes expanded on these points by distinguishing three cases: (1) an experiment, (2) a prediction whether someone will successfully calculate, and (3) a mathematical statement.

(1) *The experiment.* Imagine you are given a balancing scale, a number of balls, and the following problem. (Cf. LFM, pp. 97ff.) Take 81 balls and put them in the left pan, and then 81 more balls, also putting them in the left pan. Take 162 balls and put them in the

right pan. Do the scales balance? Performing the steps in order to answer the question might be considered an *experiment*.

(2) *The prediction.* A teacher assigns a pupil the problem $81 + 81 = ?$ She makes the prediction that "if you add 81 to 81 you will get 162." This case, Wittgenstein holds, is like (1): "A calculation can be an experiment. The teacher makes the pupil do a calculation in order to see whether he can calculate; that is an experiment" (RFM, III-67E).

(3) *The mathematical statement.* Here the question is not whether the pupil will get the correct answer, but what the correct answer is. The mathematical statement is arrived at by *calculating* (which Wittgenstein sometimes conflates with *proving*) and is simply "$81 + 81 = 162$."

Wittgenstein's point is that while (2) and (3) might seem similar (after all, they can even be put in the same words: "if you add 81 to 81: then you will get 162"), they are of entirely different characters. (2) is like (1), not like (3). Both (1) and (2) are revisable by experience, whereas (3) is not. If I have performed the experiment above several times, I can use it to predict what results you will get when you perform the experiment. Similarly, I can calculate $81 + 81$ and use my result to predict what will happen when you calculate. Both cases are very different from arriving at the mathematical statement that $81 + 81 = 162$. In calculating I do not *predict* the answer. If the possibility that the prediction can go wrong is excluded, then calling it a "prediction" is merely a wheel turning idly. Thus "it will rain tomorrow" is a genuine prediction, regardless of whether it has rained for thirty-nine days and nights and is still cloudy, but "either it will rain tomorrow or it will not rain tomorrow" is no prediction.

When you get a difference of result in weighing, it is still a legitimate experiment, but if you get a different result from the calculation, then you have not legitimately calculated:

> The reason why "If you follow the rule, this is where you'll get to" is not a prediction is that this proposition simply says: "The result of this calculation is . . ." and that is a true or false mathematical proposition: The allusion to the future and to yourself is mere clothing. (RFM, VI-15)

> It must be like this, does not mean: it will be like this. On the contrary: "it will be like this" chooses between one possibility and another. "It must be like this" sees only *one* possibility. (RFM, IV-31)

The reason there is only one possibility, the reason that the allusions are mere clothing, is that unlike in an experiment, in a proof or calculation the process and result are related *internally:* " 'Suppose I do this [weigh the balls] again' – here the 'this' doesn't include this result, otherwise it is not an experiment, but a calculation – there is an internal relation. The conditions of the experiment don't include the result" (LFM, p. 97). Wittgenstein argues "there is a difference between a process having a result and being its own result" (AWL, p. 188). A difference in result between our experiments can be due to many causes: the mechanism needs oiling, dust has gotten in the scales, one of the balls has become chipped, and so forth. A difference in result in calculation can be due only to this: one of us has made a mistake. The roles an experiment and a proof play are thus entirely different. If we are certain the scales are accurate, we can use them to test the weight of the balls; if we are certain of the weight of the balls, we can use them to test the accuracy of the scale. Proofs and calculations, however, are like the standard meter bar in Paris (see PI, 50); the bar can be used to test whether a stick is a meter long, but the stick cannot be used to test whether the standard meter bar is a meter long. The propositions of mathematics have acquired a special role.[26]

If the roles of mathematical and empirical propositions were conflated, however, then mathematics would lose its peculiar inexorability *and* its objectivity, falling into the anarchist camp. "The question arises," Wittgenstein says in an extended argument, "what we take as criterion of going according to the rule" (RFM, VI-16). He then describes three failed alternatives: "Is it for example a feeling of satisfaction that accompanies the act of going according to the rule? Or an intuition (intimation) that tells me I have gone right? Or is it certain practical consequences of proceeding that determine whether I have really followed the rule?" The rejected alternatives are carefully chosen examples of different kinds of empiricism. The first is an instance of psychologism, identifying mathematical correctness with a psychological criterion.[27] The second is an example of how Wittgenstein sometimes characterized intuitionism.[28] The third exemplifies a crude kind of pragmatism (a kind that both Wittgenstein and William James have been accused of holding but which, in fact, both explicitly repudiated). Wittgenstein's argument for rejecting these alternatives is similar to Frege's arguments against psychologism. If we take any of the three alternatives as a criterion of going according to rule, then "it would be possible," Wittgenstein holds, "that 4 + 1 sometimes made 5 and sometimes something else. It would be thinkable, that is to say, that an experimental investigation would shew whether 4 + 1 always makes 5." Empiricism in mathematics leads to anarchism every bit as much as psychologism does. We could no more talk about adding than Frege's psychological logicians could discuss the properties of the moon. Denying the special and peculiar role of mathematical propositions makes mathematics arbitrary and ever-changing, subject to the shifting winds of feelings, intuitions, and practical consequences. (If I bet on a winning horse because I miscalculated the odds, does that mean I didn't really make a mistake in mathematics?)

Wittgenstein continues with his own account of the criterion of going according to the mathematical rule:

> If it is not supposed to be an empirical proposition that the rule [+1] leads from 4 to 5, then *this*, the result, must be taken as the criterion for one's having gone by the rule.
>
> Thus the truth of the proposition that 4 + 1 makes 5, is so to speak, *overdetermined.* Overdetermined by this, that the result of the operation is defined to be the criterion that this operation has been carried out.
>
> The proposition rests on one too many feet to be an empirical proposition. It will be used as a determination of the concept "applying the operation +1 to 4." For we now have a new way of judging whether someone has followed the rule. (RFM, VI-16)[29]

In the next section we will deepen our sketch of Wittgenstein's later view by contrasting it with a famous misinterpretation.

### IV DUMMETT AND "FULL-BLOODED CONVENTIONALISM"

Wittgenstein's language-game conception of mathematics attempted to account for mathematics' peculiar inexorability and objectivity while steering between the recoiling anarchist and metaphysical camps. The camps, in this case, were instantiated by psychologism and Hardy's picture. No commentator has missed Wittgenstein's rejection of the metaphysical picture; some, however, have missed the Fregean antisubjectivism in Wittgenstein's antipsychologism, and thus have concluded that he must be recoiling into the anarchist camp in another of its forms. According to this reading, rather than giving an account of mathematical objectivity, Wittgenstein has undermined it. Michael Dummett's famous article "Wittgenstein's Philosophy of Mathematics" is the ancestor to all such interpretations.[30]

Dummett labeled Wittgenstein's views as "full-blooded conventionalism."[31] According to Dummett, Wittgenstein believed that "the logical necessity of any statement is always the *direct* expression of a linguistic convention."[32] It is not that our calculations and proofs follow from an antecedent set of agreed-upon conventions, but that at *every step* a new decision is required. A whole branch of the secondary literature has grown from these seeds.

This is how the Wittgenstein-as-anarchist story usually goes. By denying the picture of an underlying mathematical reality, through his "anthropological method,"[33] by stressing the contingent factors that yield our mathematical language, and by claiming that at each step the calculation "could have been otherwise," Wittgenstein reduced any mathematical necessity to the level of the contingent and the conventional. Usually what is contingent and conventional is further specified to be community agreement. (Although in Dummett's original formulation, even though it inspired the community view, it is hard to see how an individual could agree with herself, much less a community.) It is as if Frege saved us from psychologism only to have Wittgenstein deliver us to sociologism. Here, more than anywhere, Wittgenstein has been read as being truly radical.[34]

These interpretations miss both Wittgenstein's point of the *location* of the empirical, contingent, and "anthropological" considerations and the importance he places on a natural background for conventions to make sense at all. As misguided as they are, however, such – to use an ugly word – *sociologistic* characterizations are not made up of whole cloth. Wittgenstein himself recognized that his views might be misinterpreted in the "full-blooded conventionalist" way; he saw that his objections to Hardy's misleading picture might be misconstrued as a recoil to anarchism. In LFM Wittgenstein first attacked Hardy's conception of a mathematical reality, and then, in the voice of the interlocutor, challenged himself to be clearer about the implications of his position:

You might say, "So, Wittgenstein, you seem to say there *is* no such thing as this proposition necessarily following from that." – Should we say: Because we point out that whatever rules and axioms you give, you can still apply them in ever so many ways – that this in some way undermines mathematical necessity? (LFM, p. 241)

Wittgenstein gets to the heart of the matter in RFM. "What you say," Wittgenstein writes, assuming the voice of someone who has misinterpreted what has gone before, "seems to amount to this, that logic belongs to the natural history of man. And that is not combinable with the hardness of the logical 'must' " (RFM, VI-49A).

Put this way the problem is as old as the Locke–Leibniz debate. Leibniz thought that Locke's empiricist program could not account for the necessity and universality of mathematical truths. In a sense, Leibniz was accusing Locke of committing a category mistake in arguing for the position that mathematical truths are derived from experience. Leibniz thought that Locke confused (among other things) the context of discovery with the context of justification: "for we are not concerned here with the sequence of our discoveries, which differs from one man to another, but with the connection and natural order of truths, which is always the same."[35] The propositions of natural history are empirical and contingent, the propositions of logic and mathematics are nonempirical and necessary; therefore, assimilating the second to the first loses the special character of logical and mathematical propositions. Some commentators, both sympathetic and critical, have interpreted Wittgenstein as purposely doing just that: rejecting the special character of mathematical propositions.

The full-blooded conventionalists noticed Wittgenstein's challenge to himself, but missed his answer. Unlike Locke, Wittgenstein did *not* assimilate the propositions of mathematics to the propositions of natural history; rather, he *separated* them:

But the logical "must" is a component part of the propositions of logic, and these are not propositions of human natural history. If what a proposition of logic said was: Human beings agree with one another in such and such ways (and that would be the form of the natural-historical proposition), then its contradictory would say that there is here a *lack* of agreement. Not, that there is an agreement of another kind. (RFM, VI-49)[36]

Wittgenstein repeatedly makes the same point by noting the difference between "an internal and an external negation" (RFM, V-13). An internal negation in Wittgenstein's terminology is within mathematics; and within mathematics we *do* have set criteria for determining truth. An internal negation of $25^2 = 265$ would simply mean that $25^2$ does not equal $265$, but something else. An external negation in Wittgenstein's terminology, however, would be an anthropological statement. It would state that there are no criteria, that human beings do not agree on what $25^2$ equals, or even that human beings do not have mathematics: " '$25^2 = 625$' cannot be the empirical proposition that people calculate like that, because $25^2 \neq 626$ would in that case not be the proposition that people get not this but another result; and also it could be true if people did not calculate at all" (RFM, VI-30). Wittgenstein warns us here against confusing the two different ways empirical considerations can bear on mathematics. (See "The Language-Game Conception," Section II.) It is one thing to say that we would not have our mathematics if some empirical considerations had not obtained (true to Wittgenstein), and quite another to say that the propositions of mathematics *state* these empirical considerations or can be falsified by empirical considerations (false to Wittgenstein). After all, in the same sense that our mathematics rides on the back of contingency, so does the rest of our language. If our memories were so limited that we could not remember more than two steps of a proof, then our mathematics would not be the same as it is now. But if our memories *were* so limited, we also would not have our present method of giving directions: no one could remember more than one or two landmarks. And no one should be tempted to believe that under Wittgenstein's account when someone says "turn left at the library," what the direction giver means is "human beings have adequate memories to understand directions and agree on what 'turn left' means etc."

These considerations have survived in the *Investigations:*

– Certainly, the propositions "Human beings believe that twice two is four" and "Twice two is four" do not mean the same. The latter is a mathematical proposition; the other, if it makes sense at all, may perhaps mean: human beings have *arrived* at the mathematical proposition. The two propositions have entirely different *uses.* (PI, pp. xi, 226–7)

Wittgenstein is recorded as having said earlier:

Here we see two kinds of responsibility. One may be called "mathematical responsibility": the sense in which one proposition is responsible to another. Given certain principles and laws of deduction, you can say certain things and not others. – But it is a totally different thing if we ask, "And now what's *all* this responsible to?" (LFM, p. 240)

(Note how far the sentence "*Given certain principles and laws of deduction you can say certain things and not others*" is from Dummett's interpretation; according to Dummett, at each stage you can say whatever you like.) The second sort of responsibility is Wittgenstein's concern here. This is part of his view of philosophy as nonrevisionary; he is not out to revise our mathematical practice,[37] but to understand the origin of its special character.

Stating that the set of rules as a whole are in some sense contingent does not make the individual rules within the set any less necessary. In other words, there is no inconsistency in asserting both

(1) "2 + 2 = 4" is a necessary proposition in English; and
(2) That " '2 + 2 = 4' is a necessary proposition in English" is contingent.

It is through confusing these two different things, and the corresponding two different ways in which empirical considerations bear on mathematics, that the full-blooded conventionalist interpreters have been misled.

Our next task is to examine the nature of the contingency expressed in (2).

V THE NATURE OF THE CONTINGENCY

Wittgenstein's concern here is with the underpinnings of all language, what makes language possible at all. We saw in Section I that when Wittgenstein discussed *family resemblances* in PI he chose *number* as a chief example. In the present subject, too, mathematics is the example: "Disputes do not break out (among mathematicians, say) over the question whether a rule has been obeyed or not. People don't come to blows over it, for example. That is part of the framework on which the working of our language is based (for example, in giving descriptions)" (PI, 240).[38] This

framework is the contingency or conditions on which the peculiar inexorability of mathematics rests. Indeed, Wittgenstein's view is that all language rests on such contingencies. As the very example of PI, 240 makes clear, however, the specific constitution of the contingencies might vary from practice to practice: people *do* come to blows around abortion clinics.

Wittgenstein is emphasizing that mathematical language, like the rest of our language, is part of a practice, and a practice rests on contingencies. Much of the early part of PI concentrates on this issue. The discussion culminates in PI, 197–202: "I have further indicated that a person goes by a sign-post only in so far as there exists a regular use of sign-posts, a custom" (PI, 198). The famous first sentence of PI, 202, "And hence also 'obeying a rule' is a practice," is echoed in the *Remarks*: "Only in the practice of a language can a word have meaning" (RFM, VI-41).

Although it would be too simplistic to say that this was Wittgenstein's primary motivation, analyzing language in terms of practices avoids both psychologism, on the one hand, and Augustine's and Hardy's pictures, on the other. It avoids the pictures by arguing for the necessity of the trail of the human serpent; it avoids psychologism by properly locating that trail. (The full-blooded accusation is that it avoids both by falling into sociologism.)

PI, 199 summarizes some of these themes:

It is not possible that there should have been only one occasion on which someone obeyed a rule. It is not possible that there should have been only one occasion on which a report was made, an order given or understood; and so on. – To obey a rule, to make a report, to give an order, to play a game of chess, are *customs* (uses, institutions).[39]

This goes against both the calculus conception and Dummett's interpretation. Cora Diamond reads Dummett as saying: "The argument Wittgenstein seemed to be committed to, on Dummett's view, was that the rules make the game, and different rules would not be wrong, but would just make the game a different one. Since no choice of rules is ever wrong, we are free to infer as we choose."[40] This is just the view that forbade us from comparing chess$_1$ and chess$_2$; this is just the view that Wittgenstein held in the calculus conception, and just the view the later Wittgenstein rejected.[41] The anarchist fear (or hope) in its sociologistic form is that all there is to mathematics (or indeed, any use of language) is free-floating conventions or rules; conventions that can change at any whim.

But Wittgenstein has rejected this; in the language-game conception, unlike the calculus conception, there is more than isolated conventions or rules: the rules are part of a practice embedded in an environment which blocks the spurious freedom to choose. This environment consists of both nature and human nature, it concerns the behavior of both cheese on a balance and people in pain:

> ... if things were quite different from what they actually are – if there were for instance no characteristic expression of pain, of fear, of joy; if rule became exception and exception rule; or if both became phenomena of roughly equal frequency – this would make our normal language-games lose their point. – The procedure of putting a lump of cheese on a balance and fixing the price by the turn of the scale would lose its point if it frequently happened for such lumps to suddenly grow or shrink for no obvious reason. (PI, 142)

Wittgenstein is careful here to distance himself from the full-blooded interpretation, warning us not to commit the category mistake of confusing the external contingencies of a system with the quite different internal necessity within a system. Having emphasized that we would not have our mathematics if not for some general facts of nature, Wittgenstein then asks, "Does this mean that I have to say that the proposition '12 inches = 1 foot' asserts all those things which give measuring its present point?" "No," he answers:

> The proposition *is grounded in* a technique. And, if you like, also in the physical and psychological facts that make the technique *possible*. But it doesn't follow that its sense is to express these conditions. The opposite of that proposition, "twelve inches = one foot" does not say that rulers are not rigid enough or that we don't all count and calculate in the same way. (RFM, VII-1)

One contingency that must obtain is that "the concept of calculating excludes *confusion*" (RFM, III-76). If mathematics is to be regarded as a practice, and if a practice requires, among other things, the existence of a regular use (PI, 198), then there must be enough regularity for there to be mathematics at all. Once again, Wittgenstein warned us not to use this fact to commit a category mistake:

Calculating would lose its point, if *confusion* supervened. Just as the use of the words "green" and "blue" would lose its point. And yet it seems to be nonsense to say – that a proposition of arithmetic *asserts* that there will not be confusion. – Is the solution simply that the arithmetical proposition would not be *false* but useless, if confusion supervened?

Just as the proposition that this room is 16 foot long would not become *false*, if rulers and measuring fell into confusion. Its sense, not its truth, is founded on the regular working of measurements. (RFM, III-75)

The point is not that if there were too much confusion then we would have a different mathematics; rather the point is, if there is too much confusion, then the result would be no mathematics at all.

(However, Wittgenstein carefully adds in parentheses to RFM, III-75: "But don't be dogmatic here. There are transitional cases which complicate the discussion." One complication that contributes to Wittgenstein's methodology of continually reexamining issues is that the line between sense and nonsense is both never sharp and always changing. This helps to explain why all truths [including this one] are local.)

If rulers constantly contracted and expanded, if a balance scale never showed the same object as having the same weight, if every time people multiplied 2 times 2 they got a different answer, then it would *not* be the case that the judgments, "this paper is 11 inches long," or "this book weighs 10 ounces," or "2 × 2 = 4" would be *false*. Empirical considerations will *not* overturn our mathematical judgments. Rather, these judgments would cease to be part of a practice, and thus cease to have meaning or sense: "But could I say that he calculated *wrong* this time, because the next time he did not calculate again the same way? I might say: where *this* uncertainty existed there would be no calculating" (RFM, III-73).

A practice depends on there being a regularity. If there is too much confusion then there can be no practice, and hence no sense. Confusion does not result in false mathematical propositions, but in nonsense.[42]

One special case of a lack of confusion involves *agreement*. Wittgenstein continually emphasizes that our mathematical practice requires agreement among mathematicians and agreement at different times in the same person. The temptation is to misinterpret this as meaning that the truth or falsehood of mathematical propositions is a result of some sort of mathematicians' annual convention: they vote on whether 81 + 81 equals 162 or 163, and the winning proposition goes into the archives.[43] If the vote had gone differently, our mathematics would have been different, and that is all there is to mathematical truth or necessity.

Wittgenstein, however, carefully rejects this view. The anarchists see part of what Wittgenstein is saying, but get it in the wrong context; they fail to correctly place the location of the agreement. The agreement is not over individual propositions, nor does the agreement determine the truth or falsity of our propositions; rather it provides the necessary framework in which it makes sense to attribute truth or falsity at all:

> The agreement of people in calculation is not an agreement in opinions or convictions. (RFM, VI-30C)

> It has been said: "It's a question of general consensus." There is something true in this. Only – what is it we agree to? Do we agree to the mathematical proposition, or do we agree in *getting* this result? These are entirely different.
> . . . They agree in what they do.
> Mathematical truth isn't established by their all agreeing that it's true – as if they were witnesses of it. *Because* they all agree in what they do, we lay it down as a rule, and put it in the archives. Not until we do that have we got to mathematics. One of the main reasons for adopting this as a standard, is that it's the natural way to do it, the natural way to go – for all these people. (LFM, p. 107)

> This has often been said before. And it has often been put in the form of an assertion that the truths of logic are determined by a consensus of opinions. Is this what I am saying? No. There is no *opinion* at all; it is not a question of *opinion*. They are determined by a consensus of *action*: a consensus of doing the same thing, reacting in the same way. There is a consensus but it is not a consensus of opinion. We all act the same way, walk the same way, count the same way. (LFM, pp. 183–4)

The key to avoiding the full-blooded conventionalist and sociologistic trap here is to see that it is *not* that 81 + 81 = 162 is correct means we all agree that 81 + 81 = 162, but rather that without general agreement there could be no such thing as correctness or incorrectness. Disagreement does not even make sense unless seen against the wider background of a more general agreement. Suppose we were debating whether this page has 24 or 25 *glucks*. Further suppose there were no set criteria for what a *gluck* is, or even for what "24" or "25" was. Given those conditions not only could it not be clear who was right, it would not even be clear whether we are disagreeing. There would not be enough of a common framework for us to know whether we were talking about the same thing, or even whether we were meaningfully talking, rather than just speaking in tongues.[44]

What mathematics (partly) does is to provide us with a common framework in which both agreement and disagreement become meaningful. Not only is it not Wittgenstein's belief that agreement in opinions *should* be used to explain the correctness of our calculations, he argues that such agreement *cannot* be used in this way, for "we judge identity and agreement by the results of our calculating; that is why we cannot use agreement to explain calculating" (RFM, IV-8). It is our number system that provides us with criteria for deciding whether this page is 24 or 25 *lines* long. Without such a system such questions would be outside the realm of practice, and thus of meaning.[45]

Complete agreement is not required. Historically, mathematicians have disagreed over proposed pieces of new mathematics, such as the introduction of negative numbers. The point is not that the mathematicians' ultimate agreement solved the dispute, but rather that without enough background agreement there could not even have been a dispute. Wittgenstein's target here is not our common notions of mathematical objectivity, but the misleading picture of the source of this objectivity.

Thus, in order for there to be correctness or incorrectness at all, there must be a practice; outside of the practice there is not falsehood, but nonsense. Wittgenstein's discussion of the general facts of nature, lack of confusion, and agreement are attempts to clarify what background there must be in order for there to be a practice at all. He constantly warns against confusing the *background* of the practice with the *content* of the practice.

All these themes, which were developed in Wittgenstein's philosophy of mathematics, are tied together in the *Philosophical Investigations*. Let us return to PI, 240: "Disputes do not break out (among mathematicians, say) over the question whether a rule has been obeyed or not. People don't come to blows over it, for example. That is part of the framework on which the working of our language is based (for example, in giving descriptions)." In the next remark the voice of temptation, speaking with Hardy's tone of voice, challenges Wittgenstein: " 'So you are saying that human agreement decides what is true and what is false?' " (PI, 241). The question can apply either to mathematical or nonmathematical claims. It carries the implicit charge that Wittgenstein, by repudiating the metaphysical picture of objectivity, is also denying objective truth, and claiming the psychologistic legacy in a new, sociologistic form. *So you are saying*, the accusation goes, *that human agreement decides whether there were witches and whether 2 + 2 = 4!* Wittgenstein's answer is: "It is what human beings *say* that is true and false; and they agree in the *language* they use. That is not agreement in opinions but in form of life" (PI, 241).[46] Without a natural environment of a certain constancy, without a shared humanity of similar needs and reactions; unless we spoke a shared language, unless there was enough agreement, then it would be meaningless both to deny the existence of witches and to count them. The trail of the human serpent is everywhere there is meaning, Wittgenstein is arguing, but it does not follow that truth is simply what human beings say is true.

In the end what Wittgenstein has is a view of mathematics that avoids paying Hardy's metaphysical price without recoiling into anarchy. The *Philosophical Investigations*, on the basis of Wittgenstein's philosophy of mathematics, continued to stake out this intermediate position between the recoiling camps. It is a position where both mathematical and nonmathematical statements rest on contingencies. It is a position where there is meaning and truth, but no guarantees. It is a position, therefore, which must constantly be reexplored.[47]

### NOTES

1 See Putnam's Dewey Lectures, "Sense, Nonsense, and the Senses: An Inquiry into the Powers of the Human Mind," *The Journal of Philosophy* 91, 9 (1994), pp. 445–517. On p. 446, n2, he credits John McDowell with the term.

2 Some would object to attributing *any* position to Wittgenstein, as he constantly warned against philosophical theorizing. A position, however, is not the same as a theory. (Whether this is a difference without a distinction I shall have to reserve the right to argue elsewhere.) I am offering what Burton Dreben would call a "domesticated" or "tamed" Wittgenstein. Juliet Floyd, emphasizing the critical and dialectical nature of Wittgenstein's work, has given the subtlest presentation of

those commentators on Wittgenstein's philosophy of mathematics who deny that a position can be attributed to Wittgenstein at all. See her "Wittgenstein on 2, 2, 2 ... : The Opening of *Remarks on the Foundations of Mathematics,*" *Synthese* 87 (1991), pp. 143–80; and "On Saying What You Really Want to Say: Wittgenstein, Goedel, and the Trisection of the Angle," in Jaakko Hintikka, ed., *From Dedekind to Goedel: Essays on the Development of the Foundations of Mathematics* (Dordrecht/Boston: Kluwer, 1995), pp. 373–426.

3 There is, of course, more to Wittgenstein's philosophy of mathematics; he wrote more on this field than on any other subject. Published volumes that include substantial parts on the philosophy of mathematics, with the dates of composition in brackets, are: WWK [1929–31], PR [1929–30], G. E. Moore, "Wittgenstein's Lectures in 1930–33" [1930–3] (in PO), PG [1932–4], AWL [1932–5], LFM [1939], and RFM [1937–44].

4 William James, *Pragmatism* (Cambridge, Mass.: Harvard University Press, 1975), p. 37 (Lecture 2).

5 The last two sentences are variations of two sentences in my "Wittgenstein's Philosophies of Mathematics," *Synthese* 87 (1991), pp. 125–42. Although the emphasis of that article is different, I have occasionally borrowed sentences from it for this one.

6 G. H. Hardy, *A Mathematician's Apology* (Cambridge University Press, 1967), pp. 123–4. See also Hardy's "Mathematical Proof," *Mind* 38, 149 (January 1929), p. 18; RFM, I-8 and AWL, p. 224.

7 Few contemporary exemplars of the anarchist camp would identify themselves with a science, although anthropology is a candidate.

8 Hardy, *A Mathematician's Apology,* p. 130.

9 Gottlob Frege, *The Basic Laws of Arithmetic,* trans. and ed. M. Furth (Berkeley and Los Angeles: The University of California Press, 1964), p. xix. Compare with Wittgenstein's so-called private language argument.

10 Gottlob Frege, *Posthumous Writings,* ed. H. Hermes, F. Kambartel, and F. Kaulbach, trans. P. Long and R. White (Chicago: University of Chicago Press, 1979), p. 144. See also Frege, *The Foundations of Arithmetic,* trans. J. L. Austin (Oxford: Basil Blackwell, 1953), p. vii: "But this account makes everything subjective, and if we follow it through to the end does away with truth."

11 Scholars' recognition of a distinct middle period in Wittgenstein's philosophy is a relatively recent phenomenon. Some would add a fourth period: the post-*Investigations,* where philosophical psychology dominated Wittgenstein's work. See, however, David Stern's proper cautions about too cleanly dividing Wittgenstein's career in "The 'Middle Wittgenstein': From Logical Atomism to Practical Holism," *Synthese* 87 (1991), pp. 203–26. In line with this, the changes in Wittgenstein's views

of mathematics did not occur at the same rate; his views on contradiction, for example, changed more slowly than the rest.

Partly (but only partly) due to the failure to distinguish the different stages (thus saddling Wittgenstein with views he later rejected), the early secondary literature was not kind to Wittgenstein's philosophy of mathematics. Two early reviews of RFM set the negative tenor: Alan Ross Anderson, "Mathematics and the 'Language-game,' " *Review of Metaphysics* 11 (1957–8), pp. 446–58, and G. Kreisel, "Wittgenstein's Remarks on the Foundations of Mathematics," *British Journal for the Philosophy of Science* 9 (1958–9), pp. 135–58. The last sentence of Anderson's review is: "But it is very doubtful whether this application of his method to questions in the foundations of mathematics will contribute substantially to his reputation as a philosopher" (p. 458). Kreisel's closing clause is: "now it seems to me to be a surprisingly insignificant product of a sparkling mind" (p. 158). By far the most influential commentary is Michael Dummett's "Wittgenstein's Philosophy of Mathematics," *The Philosophical Review* 68 (1959), pp. 324–48 (reprinted in George Pitcher, ed., *Wittgenstein: The Philosophical Investigations* [Notre Dame: University of Notre Dame Press, 1968]; page references will be to Pitcher). An early and also influential attempt to refute Dummett's interpretation is Barry Stroud, "Wittgenstein and Logical Necessity," *The Philosophical Review* 74 (1965), pp. 504–18. V. H. Klenk, a student of Alan Anderson's, gives a sympathetic interpretation of Wittgenstein in *Wittgenstein's Philosophy of Mathematics*. Two more recent books also interpret Wittgenstein sympathetically: Crispin Wright, *Wittgenstein on the Foundations of Mathematics* (Cambridge, Mass.: Harvard University Press, 1980), and S. G. Shanker, *Wittgenstein and the Turning-Point in the Philosophy of Mathematics* (Albany: State University of New York Press, 1987). Cora Diamond's *The Realistic Spirit* (Cambridge, Mass.: MIT Press, 1991) contains sympathetic and excellent discussions of Wittgenstein's philosophy of mathematics.

12  I have borrowed the last two sentences from S. Gerrard, "Wittgenstein's Philosophies of Mathematics," *Synthese* 87 (1991), pp. 125–42. See Stern, "The 'Middle Wittgenstein,' " for a compatible but broader view, and S. Stephen Hilmy, *The Later Wittgenstein* (Oxford: Basil Blackwell, 1987), for another view that pays careful attention to Wittgenstein's use of calculi and language-games, but comes to very different conclusions than Stern and I do.

13  See also PG, 143: "It is *in language* that it's all done." The view of language here, as of rules above, is extremely restricted.

14  See RFM, III-46A: "I should like to say: mathematics is a Motley [*Buntes Gemisch*] of techniques of proof. – And upon this is based its manifold

applicability and its importance," and RFM, III-48: "I want to give an account of the motley [*Buntheit*] of mathematics."

15 Frege, *Foundations of Arithmetic*, p. x.

16 See also Norman Malcolm, *Ludwig Wittgenstein: A Memoir* (Oxford: Oxford University Press, 1978), p. 93; and Z, 173. Compare David Stern's summary in Stern "The 'Middle Wittgenstein,'" p. 216.

17 See, for example, Frege, *Foundations of Arithmetic*, p. x. Frege gives an example of violating the context principle leading to psychologism in section 60, p. 71.

18 Wittgenstein's views on contradiction are as complicated as they are notorious. This was a major theme of Gerrard's "Wittgenstein's Philosophies of Mathematics."

19 Wittgenstein is partly objecting here to modeling mathematics on a natural science, as he did throughout his career. He wrote of the misleading way in which mathematics is treated like mineralogy (RFM, IV-11), zoology (AWL, p. 225), or even pomology (AWL, pp. 101–2). His most common example was physics, and here Wittgenstein identified this view with Hardy: "Professor Hardy is comparing mathematical propositions to propositions of physics. This comparison is extremely misleading" (LFM, p. 240).

20 I have stolen the rest of this paragraph from Gerrard's "Wittgenstein's Philosophies of Mathematics."

21 See WWK, pp. 35–6 and PR, 178: "The system of rules determining a calculus thereby determines the 'meaning' of its signs too. Put more strictly: The form and the rules of syntax are equivalent. So if I change the rules – seemingly supplement them, say – then I change the form, the meaning."

22 In AWL, p. 71 Wittgenstein explicitly compares chess with mathematics.

23 Wittgenstein's next sentence is: "But it doesn't follow that its sense is to express these conditions." Wittgenstein is being very careful here to distinguish the sense of mathematical propositions from the sense of propositions of natural history.

24 See LFM, p. 111 and RFM, VII-18F.24.

25 See also RFM, IV-5.

26 See AWL, pp. 159–61 (Lecture XV); LFM, pp. 287 and 292; RFM, III-75; and PI, p. 218:

Meaning is not a process which accompanies a word. For no *process* could have the consequences of meaning.

(Similarly, I think, it could be said: a calculation is not an experiment, for no experiment could have the peculiar consequences of a multiplication.)

27  For another example of a rejected psychologistic formulation, see RFM, VI-22A.

28  See, for instance, LFM, p. 237.

29  See also RFM, IV-7: "A mathematical proposition stands on four feet, not three; it is over-determined," and RFM, VI-22: "It is as if we had hardened the empirical proposition into a rule. And now we have, not an hypothesis that gets tested by experience, but a paradigm with which experience is compared and judged. And so a new kind of judgment."

30  M. Dummett, "Wittgenstein's Philosophy of Mathematics," p. 445, writes, for instance, of "Wittgenstein's main reason for denying the objectivity of mathematical truth."

31  Ibid., p. 425.

32  Ibid.

33  See RFM, VII-33; D. Bloor, *Wittgenstein: A Social Theory of Knowledge* (New York: Columbia University Press, 1983), p. 83, and Dummett "Wittgenstein's Philosophy of Mathematics," p. 442 where Dummett says Hao Wang has called Wittgenstein's views "anthropologism."

34  Dummett himself agrees. After pointing out that "Frank Ramsey (who was so enormously influenced by Wittgenstein's earlier work, the *Tractatus*) accused the intuitionists, Brouwer and Weyl, of introducing Bolshevism into mathematics," Dummett writes "if Brouwer and Weyl were Bolsheviks, then Wittgenstein, in his later phase, was an anarchist" ("Reckonings: Wittgenstein on Mathematics," *Encounter* 50, 3 [March 1978], p. 64).

35  G. W. Leibniz, *New Essays on Human Understanding*, ed. and trans. P. Remnant and J. Bennett (Cambridge University Press, 1981), p. 412. Frege, *Foundations of Arithmetic*, p. 23, writes: "for we are concerned here not with the way in which [the laws of number] are discovered but with the kind of ground on which their proof rests; or in LEIBNIZ'S words," and then gives the same quotation.

36  See also Wittgenstein's response in LFM, p. 241 to his own challenge given above: "We must distinguish between a necessity in the system and a necessity of the whole system."

37  This clearly separates Wittgenstein from the intuitionists. See also *Brouwer's Cambridge Lectures on Intuitionism*, ed. D. van Dalen (Cambridge University Press, 1981), p. 4: "FIRST ACT OF INTUITIONISM Completely separating mathematics from mathematical language . . . recognizing that intuitionist mathematics is an essentially languageless activity of the mind. . . ." At no stage of his career would Wittgenstein have agreed with this. It is a striking character of his philosophy of mathematics that he investigated mathematics by concentrating on mathematical language.

38  See also RFM, VI-21.

39  See also RFM, VI-21A.

40  Diamond, *The Realistic Spirit*, p. 253.

41  Our pair of quotations on contradiction (WWK, p. 202 and LFM, p. 243) in Section I shows precisely this change. (Strangely enough, Dummett's interpretation *would* almost hold true for Wittgenstein's calculus period, but not only did Wittgenstein reject that conception, none of Dummett's references are to those texts.)

42  See also AWL, p. 152: "The terms 'sense' and 'nonsense,' rather than the terms 'true' and 'false' bring out the relation of mathematical to nonmathematical propositions."

43  M. Dummett, "Reckonings: Wittgenstein on Mathematics," *Encounter* 50, 3 (March 1978), p. 67, interprets Wittgenstein this way: "What makes a [. . . mathematical] answer correct is that we are able to agree in acknowledging it as correct."

44  See G. P. Baker and P. M. S. Hacker, *Wittgenstein: Rules, Grammar and Necessity* (Oxford: Basil Blackwell, 1985), vol. 2, p. 250.

45  Putnam's summary is that "ways of 'going on' that are natural to us, given the 'forms of life' that we have inherited, are prior to and presupposed by everything that could be called 'convention' " ("Convention: A Theme in Philosophy," in *Realism and Reason* [Cambridge University Press, 1983], p. 174).

46  See also RFM, VI-49: "The agreement of humans that is a presupposition of logic is not an agreement in opinions on questions of logic."

47  I am grateful to Jenny Gerrard, Lydia Goehr, and Amelie Rorty for heroically helping to reduce a much larger draft.

# 6 Necessity and normativity

Logical necessity is one of the perennial problems of philosophy. Statements like "g = 9.81 m/sec$^2$" or "Radioactivity causes cancer" may be *physically* necessary, but they are contingent: they could be false, and be refuted by new experience. By contrast, it seems that statements like "$\neg(p \,\&\, \neg p)$," "$2 + 2 = 4$," and "All material objects are located in space" are *logically* necessary. They do not just happen to be true, since their being false is not merely extremely improbable, but inconceivable. By the same token, disciplines like logic, mathematics, and metaphysics, which seek to discover such truths, seem to be a priori, completely independent of experience.

At the turn of the century there were three accounts of this special type of truth.[1] According to psychologistic logicians like Boole, the laws of logic describe how human beings (by and large) think, their basic mental operations, and are determined by the nature of the human mind. Against this Platonists like Frege protested that logical truths are strictly necessary and objective, and that this objectivity can only be secured by assuming that their subject matter – thoughts and their structures – are not private ideas in the minds of individuals, but abstract entities inhabiting a "third realm" beyond space and time. Finally, according to Russell, logical propositions are completely general truths about the most pervasive traits of reality, a view which is in some ways reminiscent of Mill's claim that mathematical propositions are well-corroborated empirical generalizations.

The nature of logical necessity preoccupied Wittgenstein from the beginning of his career, partly because he followed Russell in holding that philosophical problems are logical in nature (TLP, 4.003–4.0031). The early Wittgenstein took over elements of Frege's and Russell's logical systems. But his "philosophy of logic," his understanding of the character of logic, and hence of philosophy, departed radically from his predecessors (TLP, 4.1121, 4.126). All of the positions mentioned so far assume that logic is a science which makes statements about entities of some kind, just as empirical sciences make statements about physical objects. The "fundamental thought" of the *Tractatus* is that this assumption is false. In the first instance, Wittgenstein attacks Frege's and Russell's idea that the "logical constants" are *names* of entities (functions inhabiting a Platonic realm in the former case, "logical objects" with which we are acquainted through "logical experience" in the latter). The role of propositional connectives and quantifiers is not to name objects of any kind, but to express truth-functional operations (TLP, 4.0312, 5.4, 4.441).

Wittgenstein's general target, however, is the resulting view that necessary propositions are *statements* about entities. The only genuine propositions are pictures of possible states of affairs. These are bipolar – capable of being true but also capable of being false – and hence cannot be necessarily true (TLP, 2.225, 3.04–3.05). In contrast, necessary propositions are not statements at all. They do not represent a special kind of object but reflect the "rules of logical syntax" which determine whether a combination of signs is meaningful (TLP, 6.126). For example, the Law of Noncontradiction is neither a statement about the way people actually think, as psychologism maintained, nor about the most pervasive features of reality, as Russell had it, nor about abstract objects in a Platonist hinterworld. It reflects a linguistic rule which excludes a combination like "p & ¬p" as nonsensical. The special status of necessary propositions is not due to the peculiar character of what they represent, but to the fact that they are linked to rules which provide the pre-empirical framework of representation.

The nature of this link varies with the type of necessary proposition. Mathematical equations are pseudopropositions. They do not say anything about the world, but equate signs which are equivalent by virtue of rules governing reiterable operations (TLP, 6.2–6.241). Metaphysical propositions are nonsensical. They either covertly violate logical syntax, as in the case of traditional metaphysics, or, like the pronouncements of the *Tractatus*, try to express what can only be shown, namely the essential structure of reality, which must be mirrored by the linguistic rules for depicting reality, but cannot itself be depicted (TLP, 3.324, 4.003, 4.12–4.1212, 6.53–7). Logical propositions are tautologies and hence senseless in a quantitative way. They say nothing about the world – have zero sense – because their constituent propositions are so combined (according to the rules governing propositional connectives) that all factual information cancels out. Being vacuous, tautologies cannot themselves be rules. But *that*, for example, "p & (p → q) → q" is a tautology shows that q follows from p and p → q, and thus provides a form of proof – modus ponens (NB, pp. 108–109; TLP, 6.1201, 6.1264).

There is an important analogy with Kantianism. Kant holds that synthetic judgments a priori are possible insofar as they express necessary preconditions for experiencing objects. Wittgenstein holds that the special status of necessary propositions is due to the fact that they reflect the necessary preconditions for depicting reality. Both draw a sharp contrast between science, which represents the world, and philosophy, which reflects on the preconditions of this representation. In contrast to Kant, these preconditions no longer reside in a mental machinery: it is logic which comprises the preconditions of symbolic representation, not transcendental psychology. Moreover, the principle of bipolarity stipulates that only empirical propositions are meaningful, and thereby excludes the synthetic a priori. The only expressible necessity is logical necessity, which is tautologous and hence analytic (TLP, 6.1–6.113, 6.3211).

This last claim stimulated the logical positivists. Their goal was to develop a form of empiricism that could account for logical necessity without reducing it to empirical generality, lapsing into Platonism or admitting synthetic a priori truth. Necessary propositions, the positivists argued, are a priori, but do not amount to knowledge about the world. For, with the help of the *Tractatus*, it seemed that all necessary propositions could be seen as analytic, that is, true solely in virtue of the meanings of their constituent words. *Logical* truths are tautologies which are true in virtue of the meaning of the logical constants alone, and *analytical* truths can be reduced to tautologies by substituting synonyms for synonyms – thus "All bachelors are unmarried" is transformed into "All unmarried men are unmarried," a tautology of the form "$\forall x \, (Fx \, \& \, Gx \rightarrow Gx)$." Necessary propositions, far from mirroring the superempirical essence of reality, are true by virtue of the conventions governing our use of words.

This deceptively simple picture differs in many respects from its inspiration. For example, the logical positivists ignored Wittgenstein's distinction between the tautologies of logic, which are vacuous but not nonsensical, and the equations of mathematics, which are pseudopropositions. More importantly, the analytical character of necessity notwithstanding, Wittgenstein's early conception is *not* conventionalist. The rules of logical syntax, though linguistic, are not arbitrary. Rather, they are essential elements of any symbolism, any sign-system capable of representing reality. Hence they must be present – if only under the surface – in any intelligible language. The preconditions of linguistic representation are determined by the essential structural features which language (thought) and reality must have in common in order for the former to depict the latter. There is only one "all-embracing logic which mirrors the world" (TLP, 5.511; see also 3.34–3.3442, 6.124).

The later Wittgenstein preserves the idea that logical necessity is to be explained by reference to linguistic rules, but abandons the idea that these rules are grounded in reality (in this respect he moved in the direction of logical positivism, but there are considerable differences discussed below). As in the *Tractatus*, he resists the reduction of necessary propositions to empirical generalizations (TLP, 6.1222–6.1233, 6.3–6.31; PR, 64; LWL, pp. 9, 57, 79–80). Indeed, the contrast between them is even greater than traditionally assumed. Empirical propositions can be said to describe possible states of affairs, but necessary propositions cannot be said to describe necessary states of affairs. For their role is not descriptive at all. The key to understanding the status of necessary propositions is the concept of a grammatical rule. Grammatical rules are standards for the correct use of a word which "determine" its meaning (PO, p. 51; OC, 61–2). Unlike their predecessors (rules of logical syntax), grammatical rules are said to be "conventions" (*Übereinkunft, Konvention*). Although they are not subject to individual decisions, their *function*, if not their history, is that of conventions (PI, 355; AWL, pp. 89–90, 169–70; PG, pp. 68, 190).

The traditional picture of logic, mathematics, and metaphysics goes wrong, not in denying that these disciplines are empirical, but in treating them as a kind of "ultra-physics" or "physics of the abstract" which differs from the physical sciences merely by virtue of describing a more abstract kind of reality. Like the *Tractatus*, and unlike the Vienna Circle, the later Wittgenstein emphasizes the differences between various kinds of necessary propositions. He holds on to his earlier account of logical propositions as tautologies (AWL, pp. 137–40; LFM, pp. 277–81). But he no longer simply condemns other necessary truths as nonsensical pseudopropositions. Arithmetical equations, geometrical propositions, and analytic propositions are grammatical rules (see respectively WWK, p. 156; PG, p. 347; RFM, VII-6; WWK, pp. 38, 61–3; LWL, pp. 8, 55; PI, 251). Metaphysical propositions *mask* grammatical rules (BLBK, pp. 35, 55; AWL, pp. 65, 69; Z, 458). Their linguistic appearance is that of statements of fact, but their actual role is that of grammatical propositions, that is, of expressions which are typically used as grammatical rules. (However, this is not to rehabilitate metaphysics as a discipline, since a characteristic feature of the latter is held to be the assimilation of grammatical and factual propositions.)

The role of necessary propositions is normative, not descriptive. They function as or are linked to "norms of description" or of "representation" (see PI, 122, 50, 104, 158; AWL, p. 16; OC, 167, 321). These norms lay down what counts as intelligible description of reality, establish internal relations between concepts ("bachelor" and "unmarried"), and license transformations of empirical propositions (from "Wittgenstein was a bachelor" to "Wittgenstein was unmarried"). It is this special, nonrepresentational role and not the abstract nature of their alleged referents which accounts for their nonempirical character. As norms of representation, grammatical rules "antecede" experience in an innocuous sense (RFM, I-156; cf. PR, 143; LWL, p. 12; AWL, p. 90). They can neither be confirmed nor confuted by experience. A grammatical proposition like "All bachelors are unmarried" cannot be overthrown by the putative statement "This bachelor is married," since the latter incorporates a nonsensical combination of signs. This antecedence to experience renders intelligible the apparently mysterious "hardness" of necessary propositions and conceptual relations (PI, 437; RFM, I-121). It is logically impossible for bachelors to be unmarried, simply because we would not *call* anybody both "married" and "bachelor." Given our linguistic rules, it makes no sense to apply both terms to one and the same person. Thus Wittgenstein explains logical necessity by reference to the distinction between sense and nonsense which we draw by means of our norms of representation.

Wittgenstein's account of the difference between the necessary and the contingent is both radical and ingenious.[2] The best way of

assessing its merits is through contrasting it with an equally ingenious alternative, namely Quine's radical empiricism. Many commentators have detected striking similarities between Quine and
the later Wittgenstein, while others have noticed sharp contrasts.[3]
This is not as surprising as it may seem. For, as will be shown,
similarities between Wittgenstein and Quine in matters of detail are
usually the result of positions which are fundamentally at odds with
each other. The situation seems akin to the arrangement of seats in
the French Parliament, where the extreme left and the extreme right
come spatially close to one another, in spite of representing diametrically opposed points of view.

Their accounts of logical necessity provide the most important
case of this similarity-in-difference. Both react negatively to the "linguistic" doctrine of necessary truths provided by the logical positivists. They both reject the idea that necessary propositions are truths
of a special, analytic kind. But whereas Wittgenstein denies that
necessary propositions are *truths* in the first place, Quine denies
that they are *qualitatively distinct* from empirical truths. On occasion he comes close to simply holding that necessary propositions
are empirical generalizations which describe the most pervasive
traits of reality. This view, which Wittgenstein had already criticized
in the *Tractatus*, implies that the negation of a necessary proposition could be true, with the absurd consequence that we might discover, for example, that on some distant planet, exceptionally, white
is darker than black.[4] However, unlike Mill or Russell, Quine backs
his position by a skeptical line of argument which questions the
very sense of the traditional distinctions – "analytic/synthetic,"
"necessary/contingent," "a priori/a posteriori." This strategy operates on three increasingly fundamental levels. On the first, he challenges anyone who wishes to endorse the notion of analyticity to
explain it in a way which meets certain standards (Section I). On the
second, he advances a view of theory formation which is supposed to
rule out the idea of a priori statements (Section II). On the third, he is
no longer concerned with the positivists' notion of analyticity, but
rejects the notion of necessity on the basis of a reductionist picture
of language which denies the normative aspects of language (Section
III). Although this attack is initially directed against the logical positivists, Wittgenstein is also in the target area. My aim is to show
that Wittgenstein's distinction between grammatical and empirical

propositions does not fall prey to Quine's attacks, but helps to undermine the latter's position.

## I THE ATTACK ON "TRUTH BY VIRTUE OF MEANING"

Quine's first line of attack on the analytic/synthetic distinction provisionally accepts the notion of logical truths (tautologies). But he challenges the proponents of the analytic/synthetic distinction to provide a clear explanation of "analyticity." He shows that this notion belongs to a cluster of intensional concepts including "synonymy," "self-contradiction," "necessity," "definition," and "semantical rule." These concepts can only be explained by using other members of this family. As we have seen, analytical truths are propositions which can be reduced to tautologies by substituting synonymous expressions (definitions) for certain constituents. But none of these concepts can be explained in purely extensional terms, for example, by means of words like "truth" or "reference." Quine thinks that this amounts to a *vicious circularity*. He concludes that these intensional concepts cannot be adequately explained and that the corresponding dichotomies (analytic/synthetic, necessary/contingent) are ill-founded.[5]

This conclusion is unwarranted.[6] There is no reason to suppose that analyticity can be reduced to extensional notions. Indeed, one cannot explain that notion without using those concepts to which, as Quine himself has shown, it is *synonymous* or *conceptually* related, that is, the notions he prohibits. Consequently Quine's circularity charge comes down to the absurd complaint that "analytic" can only be explained via synonyms or notions it is conceptually related to and not via notions with which it is conceptually unrelated. It is clear, therefore, that the circle of intensional notions need not be avoided since it is not vicious in the least and does not set "analytic" apart from any other concepts. It remains possible to claim that explaining analyticity by way of other intensional notions is a case of *obscurum per obscurius*. But this requires independent arguments to the effect that "analytic" and its intensional relatives are obscure in the first place.

Quine's demand for a clear explanation is itself a smoke screen. Behind it lies an urge, not to clarify intensional notions, but to remove them from "canonical notation," Quine's version of an ideal language. This is part of his "flight from intensions," his attempt to avoid ontological commitment to abstract entities like propositions or attributes which are assigned to sentences or predicates as their *meanings*. Quine maintains that "intensions" must be rejected because they lack clear criteria of identity – principles for individuating entities of that kind. This is a charge that Wittgenstein, at any rate, could not dismiss as irrelevant, since he himself uses it in his private language argument, and in his claim that thoughts can be ascribed only to creatures which are capable of expressing them, since something must count as thinking that p rather than thinking that q (see PI, 353, 376–82; p. i). But Quine grants that criteria of identity for intensions could be provided if we could appeal to notions like analyticity, necessity, or synonymity. (Two predicates mean the same attribute, for example, if they are synonymous, i.e., necessarily apply to the same objects.) He rejects that solution precisely because he repudiates these notions as unclear.[7] This means, however, that in his attempt to show that the notion of analyticity is obscure he cannot appeal to his misgivings about intensions without circularity – a truly vicious one this time.

Consequently, Quine's circularity charge does not show that intensional notions like analyticity or meaning are dubious. However, he has a second argument to this effect. It is based on a certain picture of belief formation, the so-called Duhem–Quine hypothesis: our statements do not admit of confirmation or disconfirmation individually, but face the tribunal of experience only as a whole. For specific predictions are never deduced from a single hypothesis, but from the whole of science, namely under the assumption of other propositions of various kinds. This holism conceives of our knowledge as an all-inclusive network or fabric. In principle, beliefs on any topic may become relevant to the determination of beliefs on any other topic. Only the periphery of this web of beliefs, consisting of observation sentences concerning sensory stimulations, confronts experience directly. By the same token, even the center, consisting of the allegedly a priori sciences of logic and mathematics, is indirectly linked to experience. If a scientific prediction is refuted, we could in principle react by abandoning the mathematical and logical propositions used in deriving the prediction from the theory in question.[8]

Quine uses this epistemic holism to attack the logical positivists' conception of both analyticity and the a priori. In spelling out the implications of holism for analyticity, he comes closest to Wittgenstein. According to Quine, the analytic/synthetic distinction is based on the idea that each individual truth involves a "linguistic" component and a "factual" component, and that the latter is zero in the case of analytical truths. Holism shows, however, that it is impossible to distinguish between these components at the level of individual statements, since only clusters of statements are confronted with experience. It also removes the need for such a distinction by showing how even logic and mathematics are meaningful in virtue of being connected to experience, namely by contributing to the derivation of predictions from scientific theories.

Quine explains what it would be for truths to have components of this sort as follows:

(1) Brutus killed Caesar

would be false either if any of its constituent expressions meant something different or if the facts were different. In contrast

(2) Brutus killed Caesar or Brutus did not kill Caesar

seems to owe its truth purely to the fact that we use certain words ("or" and "not") as we do. What Quine rejects is what the "linguistic doctrine of logical truth" makes of the difference between (1) and (2). It holds that analytical truths are true *solely* in virtue of the meaning of their constituents – the logical constants in the case of logical truths – independently of the nature of the world and ultimately by convention. This suggests that there is something about an individual proposition like (2) – its linguistic form or structure, the meaning of its constituents or a semantical rule – which forces us to hold on to it come what may. But according to holism, the treatment of individual propositions is sensitive to the integrity of the system as a whole. Moreover, the idea that "meanings" – abstract or mental entities – force us to use signs in a certain way is the "myth of a museum."[9]

Insofar as Quine's reservations about analyticity are directed against the logical positivists, they are on target. Not only can we "holistically" abandon analytical propositions, the idea that their logical form or meaning might prevent us from doing so is mysterious. However, this verdict does not separate Quine and Wittgen-

stein. For Wittgenstein's distinction between grammatical and empirical propositions deviates from the positivists' analytic/synthetic
dichotomy in several respects.[10] Two of these are relevant to the
confrontation with Quine.

(A) The analytic/synthetic distinction is set up in terms of the
forms and constituents of type-sentences. But whether a sentence
expresses a grammatical proposition, i.e., is used to express a linguistic rule, depends on its role on an occasion of utterance, on whether
in the particular case it is used as a standard of correctness. For
example, the sentence "War is war" is not typically used to express
the law of identity (PI, p. xi).

(B) Even if the distinction could be adapted to token sentences, it
would involve the idea that the truth of necessary propositions is a
consequence of the meaning of their constituents. But according to
Wittgenstein necessary (grammatical) propositions *determine* rather
than *follow from* the meaning of words.

The analytic conception of logical truths suggests that there is
something outside and independent of our linguistic activities from
which flow the truth or necessity of certain propositions, their logical relations, and the proper use of expressions. Quine rejects this as
the "myth of a museum"; Wittgenstein on the grounds that it appeals to "meaning-bodies." Indeed Wittgenstein goes beyond Quine
in locating the root of the mistake. Necessary propositions, he argues, do not *follow* from the meanings of signs or from linguistic
conventions, they partly *constitute* them, being themselves norms
of representation. For to abandon a necessary proposition is to
change the meanings of at least some of its constituent signs (PG, p.
184; RFM, Appendix I-5–6). Rules of inference, for example, determine the meaning of the logical constants, rather than proceeding
from them (AWL, p. 4; PG, pp. 243–6). Whether a specific transformation of symbols is licensed or not is one aspect of the correct use and
hence of the meaning of the terms involved. For example, that we
use "$p = \neg\neg p$" as a rule of inference contributes to the meaning of
"$\neg$." If the rule were changed, the meaning of "$\neg$" would change
correspondingly.

However, even if the myth of meaning-entities is abandoned, there
remains the idea that certain properties of type-sentences – e.g., their
logical structure or their relation to linguistic rules – render them
true in a special way. By explaining the status of necessary truths by

reference to normative rather than descriptive uses of language, Wittgenstein not only rejects the claim that the source of logical truth is meaning or convention instead of experience, but also the very idea that necessary propositions are a special kind of truths.

It is noteworthy that Quine has no qualms about distinguishing a linguistic and a factual component of truth, as long as this is done for the whole of science, not individual sentences. He also accepts that certain kinds of conventions – "legislative postulates" or "definitions" – are capable of creating truths. Adopting propositions on the basis of "deliberate choices" which are justified only "in terms of elegance and convenience" renders those propositions true by convention.[11]

Wittgenstein breaks more radically with logical positivism. He rejects entirely the notion of truth by convention, and consequently the idea of linguistic and factual components of truth, whether these are thought of as components of individual sentences or of sets of sentences. In my view, he is right to do so. For what could it mean for a convention to *create* a truth? Of course we can choose to *assume* that a certain proposition is true, in the course of constructing hypotheses or for the sake of argument. But this does not *render* that proposition true. In the sense in which, for example, the fact that the cat is on the mat might be said to render true the statement that the cat is on the mat, conventions cannot be said to render anything true. The only truths conventions could "create" are truths such as "In 1795 France adopted the metric system," which are precisely not true by convention. What conventions can do, however, is to establish rules. Thus we can remove a sentence from the scope of empirical refutation by using it normatively rather than descriptively. But in that case we have not created a *truth* but *adopted a norm* of representation.

This general qualm about "truth by convention" is reinforced by specific problems concerning logical and analytical truths respectively. If tautologies are degenerate propositions which *do not say anything* – a point the logical positivists accepted – in what sense could they be true? And although an analytical proposition like "All bachelors are unmarried" may be said to be true, its role is not to make a true statement of fact about bachelors but to partially explain the meaning of "bachelor." We do not verify it by investigating the marital status of people who have been identified as bachelors, and its denial displays not factual ignorance but a linguistic misunderstanding.

Finally, the most fundamental insight which separates Wittgenstein from the logical positivists is that logical necessity is a property an expression can have because of its distinctive employment. Even if we disregard their claim that necessary propositions are truths, the positivists go wrong in explaining the necessary (normative) status of a sentence by reference to its inherent properties like linguistic structure or form. Whether a sentence is a rule or an empirical proposition does not depend on its form but on how it is used on the occasion of its utterance (WWK, pp. 153–4; PR, 59; AWL, pp. 64–5; BT, p. 241). We confer normative or empirical status on certain expressions by using them in a particular way on a given occasion. Wittgenstein emphasizes this point in terms of his distinction between "criteria" and "symptoms" (BLBK, pp. 24–5, 51–7; AWL, pp. 17–20, 28–31). We can treat certain evidence either as symptomatic (inductive evidence) or as criterial, that is, due to the grammar of the terms involved. For example, we can treat benevolence either as a criterion or a mere symptom of love, by accepting or ruling out the legitimacy of calling "love" an emotion unaccompanied by benevolence (AWL, p. 90). What concept of love we employ depends on whether we use the sentence "If A loves B she will treat her kindly" as an empirical prediction or as a grammatical proposition which partially explains what we mean by "love."

The upshot is that Wittgenstein shares Quine's justified qualms about the positivists' notion of analyticity. But his criticism is more fundamental. He does not complain that "truth by virtue of meaning/convention" cannot be explained at the level of individual statements, but questions the very notion itself.

## II THE WEB OF BELIEFS AND THE FLUCTUATION BETWEEN CRITERIA AND SYMPTOMS

This verdict might be cast in doubt by Quine's second line of attack.[12] This onslaught also invokes holism. However, it does not question the *intelligibility* of the concept of *analytical* truth (truth in virtue of meanings) but straightforwardly *denies* that there are a priori truths, statements which are unassailable by experience and hence confirmed come what may.

According to epistemic holism, when we revise a theory of the form "∀xFx" in the face of new experiences, we make choices. We may choose to reject one of the theories involved in deducing the prediction, such as "∀xFx ⊢ Fa," or even to discard a refuting observation like "¬Fa" on the grounds that it is based on erroneous measurement. That there is a choice in dealing with "recalcitrant experience" means two things: first, *any* statement can be held true, come what may, by making appropriate readjustments elsewhere; second, *no* statement is immune from revision, since it can be abandoned for the sake of upholding others. This universal fallibilism implies that there are no a priori statements in the traditional sense. Being absolutely unfalsifiable is not a special property that some propositions possess. The impossibility of abandoning mathematical or logical propositions is merely psychological or pragmatic. It ultimately derives from the fact that revising such centrally located beliefs violates the "maxim of minimum mutilation" according to which the overall system is to be disturbed as little as possible. In fact, even such radical changes have on occasion been proposed in the light of new experiences, as is shown by constructivist mathematics and intuitionist or quantum logic.

It seems that even if Wittgenstein's distinction between rules and descriptions avoids the shortcomings of the analytic/synthetic distinction, it is ruled out by this powerful fallibilism which casts doubt on the idea that certain sentences could have a logically distinct role of anteceding experience. It would be surprising, however, if Wittgenstein's distinction fell prey to fallibilism. For this idea can be traced back to Wittgenstein's own transition period, during which he claimed that "hypotheses," that is, all statements going beyond what is immediately given to the senses, cannot be conclusively verified or falsified, because recalcitrant evidence can be accommodated by auxiliary hypotheses (WWK, p. 225; PR, 228–32; note, however, that Wittgenstein did not apply this model to logical and grammatical propositions).

Unlike Quine, Wittgenstein later dropped the empiricist myth of the given, the idea that unconceptualized sense experiences provide the foundation, albeit a fallible one, of human knowledge. But the fallibilist lesson survives in his functional conception of grammatical rules, according to which an expression is a rule, irrespective of its linguistic form, if it is *employed* as a standard of correct use. This implies that the logical status of sentences can change according to our way of using them. As a matter of fact such changes are commonplace in science and everyday discourse. Empirical propositions are "hardened" into rules (RFM, VI-23; cf. III-65, VII-36), while rules lose their privileged status and are abandoned. For example the sentence "An acid is a substance which, in solution, turns litmus paper red" lost its normative status – acids now being defined as proton donors – and turned into an empirical statement which holds true of most, but not all acids. Conversely the statement "Gold has 79 protons" was originally an empirical discovery, but is now partly constitutive of what scientists mean by "gold."

Changes of the conceptual framework can themselves be caused and motivated by theoretical considerations ranging from new experiences to simplicity, fruitfulness, or sheer beauty. But they themselves are distinct from theoretical changes, like the falsification of a theory. There is no such a thing as the falsification of a grammatical rule. For the normative status of the latter is constitutive of the meaning of its constituent expressions. For example,

(3) Nobody under the age of ten can be an adult

is a grammatical proposition which partly determines what we call an adult. If we were to allow a statement like

(4) Jane's three-year-old daughter is an adult

for example, because she has amazing intellectual capacities, we would not have falsified (3). For allowing (4) amounts to a new way of using "adult," and this introduces a new concept. Consequently (3) and (4) would not contradict each other, since "adult" means something different in each case. A grammatical proposition cannot be contradicted by an empirical proposition.

This means that, although grammatical rules can be *abandoned*, they cannot be *falsified* in the sense in which empirical propositions can. A difference in status between rules and statements is preserved, since the empirically motivated abandonment of a grammatical proposition differs from empirical discoveries or theoretical changes. It is conceptual in the sense of involving a *change in the meaning* of the expressions in question (BLBK, pp. 23, 56; AWL, p. 40). What is abandoned or revised is not a truth about the world, but a rule for the use of an expression. After such a revision, it makes sense to use words in ways which were previously excluded as nonsensical.

Quineans have objected that the distinction between conceptual and theoretical change is just as problematic as the original analytic/ synthetic dichotomy, since there are no clear criteria for distinguishing between conceptual and theoretical change.[13] In reply it should be conceded that the distinction between conceptual and theoretical change is not a sharp one. But the fact that there are borderline cases does not show that the distinction is not clear. Indeed, we can provide a clear criterion: a change involves the meanings of certain expressions – our norms of representation as Wittgenstein would say – if and only if these expressions either can now be used meaningfully in ways that used to be excluded as senseless, or can no longer be used meaningfully in ways that previously made sense.

Putnam has directed a more searching set of objections against the claim that every case in which it appeared as if an analytical/ grammatical proposition is falsified amounts to a change in the meaning of the terms involved. He maintains, first, that many such changes cannot be characterized as changes of meaning, and second, that if they all could, then scientific progress would be reduced to triviality.

Putnam denies that there is a distinction between conceptual and theoretical change, between cases in which a term is redefined and those in which we discover new facts about the thing denoted by the original concept. He backs this claim by examples like the following. In Newtonian physics *momentum* was defined as "mass times velocity." It soon turned out, moreover, that momentum is conserved in elastic collision. But with the acceptance of Einstein's Special Theory of Relativity a problem emerged. If momentum was to remain a conserved quantity, it could not be exactly equal to rest-mass times velocity. Consequently it was not only possible but rational for Einstein to revise the statement that momentum is equal to mass times velocity, in spite of the fact that this statement was originally a definition. The view that this is a case where scientists decided to change the meaning of the term is mistaken. For it implies that we are now talking about a different physical magnitude. "But no, we are still talking about the same good old momentum – *the magnitude that is conserved in elastic collisions.*"[14]

However, as this quotation shows, Putnam's argument trades on the possibility of *oscillating* between two different definitions of momentum. What we are still talking about is momentum in one of the two senses that the term previously had, namely "whatever quantity is preserved in elastic collision," while giving up the other of "mass times velocity."

The plausibility of his story turns on the fact that before Einstein both could equally be regarded as constitutive of the meaning of "momentum." Since the two seemed to coincide invariably, there was no need to decide which one of them should have normative status and which one should be regarded as empirical. This changed when it was discovered that mass times velocity is not strictly preserved in elastic collision. What Einstein did in reaction to this discovery was to accord normative status exclusively to "preserved in elastic collision," which amounts to altering the rules for the use of the term "momentum." Scientific revolutions of this kind show that

- (a) norms of representations change;
- (b) scientific concepts are typically held in place by more than one connection, more than one explanation;
- (c) in certain cases there is no answer to the question "Which one is the definition and which one is an empirical statement?"

This last point may seem to support Putnam, but actually illustrates an important lesson of Wittgenstein's account: "The fluctuation in grammar between criteria and symptoms makes it look as if there were nothing at all but symptoms" (PI, 354; cf. 79). In cases where several phenomena (fever, presence of virus) are found together in association with, for example, a particular disease, the only way to distinguish those phenomena which accompany the disease as a matter of definition (criteria), from those which accompany it as a matter of empirical fact (symptoms), may be an arbitrary decision (BLBK, p. 25). The status of sentences does not just change diachronically. Even when the use of a term is relatively stable, a type-sentence can be used either normatively by one and the same person in different contexts. And it may be indeterminate whether a token-sentence expresses criterial or empirical relations. For there may not have been a need to decide (AWL, p. 90), as in the case of momentum before Einstein.

The possibility of leaving open the precise status of certain statements and connections, of treating them either as criterial or symptomatic, may even be a precondition for the fruitful development of science. *Pace* Quine and Putnam, however, there is nevertheless a distinction between the normative and the factual, between conceptual and empirical connections. For once the question of logical status arises, it is possible to distinguish between those connections which are then adopted as norms of representation (conservation) and those which are abandoned (mass times velocity). And with respect to specific scientific experiments or lines of reasoning, it is often possible to decide whether or not particular statements are used normatively or empirically (although there need not *always* be an answer).

The fact that there may be a fluctuation between normative and descriptive uses, and even an indeterminacy of status, does not obliterate the difference between the two roles. To deny this would be to deny that one can distinguish, with respect to a particular measurement, between the *role* of the ruler and the role of the object measured. Of course, in another context the ruler may itself be the object of measurement, for example, by a laser beam. But again we can and must hold apart the normative role of the laser beam from the role of what is now no more than a rod. For inasmuch as it is used to measure other objects, a measuring rod is not what is being measured (PI, 50).

Ultimately the idea that revisability rules out a distinction between normative and empirical role amounts to a fallacy. The fact that a Prime Minister can be relegated to an ordinary Member of Parliament does not entail that there is no difference in political status between the Prime Minister and a Member of Parliament. By the same token, the fact that we can deprive certain sentences of their normative status does not mean that they never really had this special logical status in advance of the conceptual change.

Putnam's second argument runs as follows. The distinction between conceptual and theoretical change implies that scientific changes which involve abandoning "analytical" propositions never provide better answers to a given question ("What is momentum?") but rather attach old labels ("momentum") to new things (the quantity preserved in elastic collision). This does not just trivialize scientific revolutions, but actually presents them as based on a fallacy of equivocation.

However, at least in Wittgenstein's case this suspicion is unfounded. He would not deny that scientific revolutions involve factual discoveries, in our case that mass times velocity is not preserved in elastic collision. To be sure, he would claim that such discoveries may lead to changes of the grammar of scientific terms. But grammar in his *functional* sense comprises much more than school-grammatical or syntactical rules. It determines the network of connections between our concepts and thus constitutes our form of representation, our way of seeing things. Those fundamental aspects of scientific theories which Kuhn has called "paradigms" can be seen as systems of norms of representations.[15] Wittgenstein's anticipation of Kuhnian ideas is most obvious in his claim that Newton's first law of motion is not an empirical statement, but a norm of representation. If a body does not rest or move at constant motion along a straight line we postulate that some mass acts upon it. And if there are no visible masses, we postulate "invisible masses," as did Hertz (AWL, pp. 16, 39–40, 70, 90). Such paradigms or norms of representation determine the meaning of key scientific expressions. But they do more than simply label things. They provide a way of making sense of experience, of making predictions and of dealing with recalcitrant experiences, and thus they inform complex scientific practices. This means that changes to our norms of representation may be far from trivial as concerns both their grounds and their results. The result of conceptual change is not mere renaming, but a new way of speaking and theorizing about the world. Obviously these observations do not establish that Wittgenstein's proto-Kuhnian conception of science is correct. But they suggest that to distinguish between theoretical and conceptual change is not necessarily to trivialize scientific revolutions.

It emerges that fallibilistic holism is compatible with ascribing a special logical role to norms of representation which distinguishes them from empirical propositions. Nevertheless the rejection of this distinction is an essential feature of Quine's position. For him there is only a difference of degree between the beliefs in the center and those at the periphery: while the latter are directly responsible to experience the former are more "firmly accepted," which means that we are more reluctant to abandon them.

Unfortunately, this assimilation of the a priori to the empirical sits uneasily with Quine's own holistic picture of a web of beliefs.[16]

Unless certain relations had a special status as logical or internal, there would be no web of beliefs adapting to experience. For observation sentences at the periphery would not be logically linked to theories closer to the center and hence could not confirm or refute them. It would be unclear whether the general statement "∀xFx" is incompatible with an observation sentence like "¬Fa," or one like "Fa," or "¬Ga." Consequently there could be no rational procedure for deciding what changes should be made in the face of recalcitrant experiences.

Quine's mistake is to assume that the logical and mathematical statements at the center of the web are "simply further statements of the system, certain further elements of the field."[17] But a collection of beliefs can only be woven into a web if certain propositions are not merely abandoned with greater reluctance, but a play a different *role*, namely that of establishing logical connections between different beliefs. Wittgenstein's norms of representation do just that. They have a normative, prescriptive function, as opposed to a descriptive function, and guide our transactions with the periphery. (Wittgenstein's insight into the need for propositions with such a role is a more radical and general version of Lewis Carroll's insight into the need to distinguish between the axioms and the rules of inference of a formal system.)

Even the question of revisability is more complex than Quine suggests. Like Quine, Wittgenstein acknowledges that there are *pragmatic* limits to the possibility of abandoning necessary truths. Norms of representation cannot be metaphysically correct or incorrect. But given certain facts about us and the world around us, they can be "impractical," or even *inapplicable* (AWL, p. 70; RFM, I-200; RPPII, 347–9). People who employed alternative ways of calculating or measuring for purposes similar to ours would have to make tedious, and perhaps unworkable, adjustments. Unlike Quine, Wittgenstein also considers the possibility of conceptual limits to revisability. We have to distinguish between different cases. First there are sentences which, as things are, *have* both a normative and an empirical use, such as "This is red" – either a color-statement or an ostensive definition – and sentences which are subject to the fluctuation between criteria and symptoms. Next there are sentences which as a matter of fact have *only* a normative use. But they do not have this use because of some independent authority, and it is possible to think of an empirical use for them. This group contains those cases which Wittgenstein occasionally refered to as synthetic a priori because they *can* be (not *are*) used either normatively or empirically. Finally, there are cases which are conceptually linked with notions like "reasoning," "thinking," "inferring," et cetera, such as modus ponens. Of course it is conceivable that these norms of representation might be abandoned. But they are indispensable in the sense that the resulting behavior would not be what we call "reasoning," "following a rule," or "speaking a language" (RFM, I-116, 132–4).[18]

### III THE DEEP NEED FOR THE CONVENTION

Thus it turns out that a qualitative distinction between the necessary and the empirical is essential to the holism behind Quine's fallibilism. Yet Quine's refusal to distinguish between the necessary and the empirical goes deeper than his holism. He has rejected attempts to explain the difference as unclear, and he has defended his standards of clarity as asking for no more than "a rough characterization in terms of dispositions to verbal behaviour."

What he demands, however, is an account of our linguistic practice in terms of a reductive behaviorism. Neither the explanation of the analytic/synthetic dichotomy provided by Grice and Strawson, nor the account given here of the difference between conceptual and theoretical change in terms of what it does and does not make sense to say, appeals to arcane mental entities. These explanations refer to perfectly accessible forms of linguistic behavior. But they do so in normative terms which Quine rejects. According to Quine, human beings must be seen as black boxes whose behavioral dispositions are triggered by external stimuli – "physical irritations of the subject's surface." Verbal behavior is not described in terms of meaning or rules, or as correct or incorrect, meaningful or nonsensical, but only in terms of statistical regularities obtaining between movements, sounds, and the environment.[19] Quine demands a description of linguistic practices in a language cleansed of the normative concepts which regulate those practices.

Ultimately Quine's rejection of any distinction between the necessary and the empirical (the conceptual and the factual) is based on a reductionism which refuses to acknowledge the phenomenon of normative behavior. As usual, however, he does not just reject a certain phenomenon, but offers an intriguing line of argument.

The first step in this argument is the claim that there is only one difference actually displayed in linguistic behavior, upon which a legitimate notion of analyticity could be founded, namely the merely quantitative one between more or less firmly entrenched beliefs. On that basis one can define "stimulus-analytical" truths as those which are accepted under any circumstances (and by all speakers). But this will not distinguish between beliefs which are constitutive of the meaning of our words and very well confirmed "collateral information." For "There have been black dogs" and "Lions roar" are stimulus-analytical but not constitutive of the meaning of the terms involved.

Quine also considers a second notion of analyticity: analytical beliefs are those which are learned together with language in such a way that their nonacceptance signifies that a person has failed to learn the meaning of these expressions. We react with disbelief to an utterance like "Jane's three-year-old daughter understands Russell's theory of types"; but we fail to understand and demand an explanation when we encounter "Jane's three-year-old daughter is an adult."

Nevertheless, Quine denies that this kind of account has any "explanatory value," and gives two reasons for this claim.[20] The first is that this element of normativity concerns only the acceptance or genesis of the beliefs in question and hence it is not an "enduring trait" of the truths thus "created." The antigeneticism which underlies this objection is shared by Wittgenstein, who explicitly condoned the logical possibility of being born with the ability to follow rules (PG, p. 188; BLBK, pp. 12–14), and is arguably correct. Nevertheless, the objection itself is unconvincing. For the difference between conventional rules and propositions, as we have seen, is a matter of their roles within our linguistic behavior, not a genetic matter at all. *How* or *why* norms are adopted is irrelevant. What counts is *what we subsequently do or say:* whether we use certain sentences as norms of representation or as empirical propositions, whether we accept a certain combination of signs as meaningful and regard certain transformations of propositions as legitimate. And if this is insufficient to ensure the kind of endurance Quine seeks, his point seems to boil down to his fallibilism, which, as we have seen, does not preclude a distinction between rules and propositions.

Quine's second argument (which has subsequently been taken over by Davidson) is more powerful. The distinction between learning conventions and coming to accept statements has no explanatory value because the conventions which underlie necessary propositions would have to be implicit. According to conventionalism the necessary truths of logic and mathematics are consequences of general conventions (the definitions of the logical constants). Quine points out that this derivation would involve a "self-presupposition" of basic concepts. The difficulty is that in order to communicate these general conventions we already have to use the "logical idiom" (e.g., "if . . . then") in accordance with the relevant definitions. More generally, we could only communicate explicit conventions by using words in accordance with their definitions, that is, once these conventions are already in place.[21]

Quine recognizes that there is a possible reaction to this difficulty. Why not say that we first observe conventions in our behavior, without announcing them in words, and formulate them only subsequently? He thinks, however, that by dropping the requirement that conventions be explicitly and deliberately adopted, the very idea of a convention loses its point. For we cannot distinguish behavior which involves such *implicit* conventions and behavior which involves *no* conventions at all. Once again we are left with the quantitative difference between more or less firmly accepted statements.

The idea of implicit conventions which Quine rejects is compatible with Wittgenstein's functional conception of rules. For that conception budgets not just for metalinguistic propositions which mention linguistic signs, such as school-grammatical or syntactical rules. It also covers explanations of meaning, including, for example, definitions by exemplification, ostensive definitions, and color charts: standards by which we explain, criticize, and justify our use of words. Some of these explanations are institutionalized, in school-grammars and dictionaries for example. But most of them play an essential normative role within a host of pedagogic and critical activities (the teaching of language, the explanation of particular words, the correction of mistakes) without being explicit conventions in Quine's sense, that is, without being the result of a deliberate decision to adopt a convention.

The fundamental point of contention between Wittgenstein and Quine is therefore this: is a distinction between well-entrenched beliefs and linguistic conventions in this functional sense necessary for making sense of our linguistic practices? Unless it can be demonstrated that language is inconceivable in the absence of linguistic rules, Quine's position will not be refuted.

What would a form of linguistic behavior look like which lacked any normative structure? It is striking that Wittgenstein actually anticipated such a radical challenge to his normativist conception of language – presumably because he saw it as the inevitable consequence of Russell's and Ramsey's empiricist conception of mathematics. Thus he writes:

> But what if someone now says: I am not aware of these two processes, I am only aware of the empirical not of formation and transformation of concepts which is independent of it; everything seems to me to be in the service of the empirical. (RFM, IV-29)

In this context Wright[22] has drawn attention to the following passage:

> I say, however: if you talk about *essence* – , you are merely noting a convention. But there one would like to retort: there is no greater difference than that between a proposition about the depth of the essence and one about – a mere convention. But what if I reply: to the *depth* that we see in the essence there corresponds the *deep* need for the convention. (RFM, I-74)

According to Wright, this remark claims that the indispensability of linguistic conventions is the intelligible core of the venerable idea that things must have essential as well as accidental properties. This interpretation is supported by the following passage (not mentioned by Wright):

> I should like to say, if there were only an external connection no connection could be described at all, since we only describe the external connection by means of an internal one. If this is lacking we lose the footing we need for describing anything at all – just as we can't shift anything with our hands unless our feet are planted firmly. (PR, 26)

Alas, this only provides the sketch of an argument. It remains to be shown in what sense the empirical use of language presupposes its normative use. Part of the answer has already been provided: without some sentences having a distinct, normative role, there could be no logical connections between beliefs (Section II). But what of a radical reductionist who is prepared to abandon the holistic picture of a web of beliefs? Here we must ask: if we surrender all linguistic conventions, what will remain of language itself?

Consider first the case of a single term like "bachelor." If all of the internal connections set up by grammatical rules were transformed into external ones this would mean that, for example, all of the following sentences could be rejected.

(5) Bachelors are unmarried men.
(6) Bachelors are human beings.
(7) Bachelors are made of flesh and blood.

Under these circumstances anything at all could be called "bachelor," since there would be no reason to deny that anything falls under the concept. Consequently the use of this term would have become totally *arbitrary*. But this would simply mean that the expression had lost all meaning. It would have become senseless.

Correspondingly, if we surrendered the grammatical rules governing the use of all our words, these words would lose all meaning. Of course our habit of uttering words might continue: a communal phonetic babbling without rules is a conceivable form of behavior. However, it is doubtful whether it should be called "language" (PI, 207, 528). At any rate, it would resemble speaking in tongues more than meaningful discourse involving empirical propositions. If anything can be said, nothing can be *meaningfully* said.

Quine might protest that he recognizes that statements like (5)–(7) are more firmly entrenched than others. And why should language not simply be based on regularities in linguistic behavior which give rise to expectations on the part of the participants? One could strengthen this suggestion by pointing out that we can conceive of a linguistic practice that proceeds without explanations of meaning or any other linguistic instructions. It is logically possible that we should all have been born with the ability to speak English, without the benefit of training and teaching. This does not yet fit the bill of a norm-free language, since it might still incorporate normative elements like correction or justification. But why should there be any inconsistency in supposing that a practice could proceed not just without instruction, but also without correction or justification, namely, if everything runs smoothly?

Here the first question is what "running smoothly" amounts to. It might mean what it would mean with respect to our linguistic practices, namely, that no one commits any mistakes. But in that case a normative element remains. Normative behavior – explanation, criticism, justification – remains possible, although it happens to be rare. Although there may be no need for it, it makes sense to demand and provide explanations, to criticize misuses and to justify one's employment of words by reference to certain standards. And that this possibility remains is essential to the practice at issue, which means that this kind of "smooth" practice does not vindicate Quine's reductionism.

On the other hand, "running smoothly" might simply mean that the exchange of noises and gestures continues uninterrupted. But in that case we could once more employ words any way we please, and the difference between correct and incorrect uses would vanish. The connection between applying "bachelor" and "unmarried" would be one of mere regularity, although it would rarely be severed. In response to your utterance "I just met a married bachelor" I might be *surprised*, but I could not reject it as *unintelligible* or demand an *explanation*. Under such circumstances one could form expectations concerning the future behavior of individuals or use words with the intention to cause a certain result. But linguistic utterances would merely be *empirical indicators* of other phenomena, just as clouds indicate rain. They would have indicative value (natural significance), but could not be understood as having linguistic meaning.

The point of my argument is not that we have to retain a certain *number* of beliefs – a point Quine accepts – but that some uses of sentences must be *normative* rather than descriptive. There must be standards of correctness which exclude certain combinations of words as nonsensical. A predicate like "bachelor" is meaningful only insofar as its application is *incompatible* with that of certain other predicates, for example, "married." Quine's "norm-free" view of language reduces itself to absurdity. The activity of advancing empirical propositions, which preoccupies him, makes sense only if there are internal relations, and a qualitatively distinct normative use of language. The point is not that linguistic behavior cannot be causally explained or seen as a natural phenomenon. But in order to understand it as meaningful we have to react to it as subject to a distinction between correct and incorrect, meaningful and nonsensical.

In one respect, there is an important parallel between Wittgen-

stein and Quine. Traditionally, logical truths have been characterized in terms of their form or structure. By contrast, both Quine and
Wittgenstein explain logical truths ultimately by reference to linguistic behavior. At the same time, their account of that behavior
differs radically. Quine views human beings as black boxes producing a "torrential output" of noise as result of physical irritations of
their surfaces.[23] Wittgenstein views them as creatures that are,
among other things, capable of following linguistic rules, and of
characterizing their behavior in normative terms. It is this normativist, anti-Cartesian and antireductionist, perspective on linguistic
behavior which allows him to make sense of, rather than to reject,
the notion of logical necessity.

Ironically, some followers of Wittgenstein have maintained that
he did not subscribe to this normativist conception of language,
and that it is, in any case, incorrect.[24] According to them, his comparison of language to rule-following activities should be seen as a
dispensable, if not misleading, heuristic device, which perhaps beto-
kens a schoolmasterly attitude. This view is correct insofar as Wittgenstein became suspicious of his own idea of logical syntax as
hidden below the surface of natural languages. However, his reaction was not to abandon the notion of a linguistic rule, but to
clarify it. This is precisely the role of the celebrated discussion of
rule-following, which rejects the idea that rules are inexorable or
independent of human activities, while retaining the idea that human practice is in many respects rule-governed. In particular, Wittgenstein changed his conception of linguistic rules by comparing
language no longer to a calculus of hidden and rigid rules, but to a
game. *That* comparison, however, is not just a dispensable heuristic
device. Wittgenstein continued to insist that linguistic understanding involves mastery of techniques concerning the *application of
rules* (PI, 199), and to stress the link between grammatical rules
and meaning (LWL, p. 36; OC, 61–2). Finally, he maintained that
"following according to the rule is FUNDAMENTAL to our language-game" (RFM, VI-28).

My discussion suggests that Wittgenstein not only stressed the
normative aspects of language, but showed, against empiricist reductionism, that they are crucial to the very possibility of meaningful
discourse. As a result, Wittgenstein, not Quine, holds out the promise of an account of logical necessity which avoids the pitfalls of

logical positivism without lapsing into traditional positions like Platonism or psychologism.[25]

NOTES

1  For a more detailed account of Wittgenstein's early position, see P. M. S. Hacker, *Insight and Illusion* (Oxford: Oxford University Press, 1986), ch. 2; G. P. Baker, *Wittgenstein, Frege and the Vienna Circle* (Oxford: Blackwell, 1988), chs. 6–7; H.-J. Glock, "Cambridge, Jena or Vienna— The Roots of the *Tractatus*," *Ratio* 5 (1992), pp. 1–23. For both early and later positions see H.-J. Glock, *A Wittgenstein Dictionary* (Oxford: Blackwell, 1996), 'Form of Representation,' 'Logic,' 'Mathematical Proof,' 'Mathematics.'

2  The same holds for the other part of his treatment of logical necessity, his account of what one might call "pure" logic and mathematics, which concerns not the role logical and mathematical propositions have vis-à-vis experience (what one might call their "application") but the way in which they are proven within mathematical and logical *calculae.* This part of Wittgenstein's work cannot be discussed here and is in my view more problematic. The most impressive defense is provided by G. P. Baker and P. M. S. Hacker, *Rules, Grammar and Necessity* (Oxford: Blackwell, 1985), ch. 6. For a historical account see S. G. Shanker, *Wittgenstein and the Turning-Point in the Philosophy of Mathematics* (Albany: State University of New York Press, 1987).

3  Contrast R. Rorty, *Consequences of Pragmatism* (Sussex: Harvester, 1982), ch. 2; C. Hookway, *Quine* (Cambridge, Mass.: Polity Press, 1988), p. 47 and G. D. Romanos, *Quine and Analytical Philosophy* (Cambridge, Mass.: MIT Press, 1983), ch. 3; I. Dilman, *Quine on Ontology, Necessity and Experience* (London: Macmillan, 1984).

4  Baker and Hacker, *Rules, Grammar and Necessity*, p. 286. See B. Russell, "The Limits of Empiricism," *Proceedings of the Aristotelian Society* 36 (1935–6), pp. 140, 148–9; W. V. Quine, *Ways of Paradox* (Cambridge, Mass.: Harvard University Press, 1976), p. 113; "Replies to Critics," in L. E. Hahn and P. A. Schilpp, eds., *The Philosophy of W. V. Quine* (La Salle: Open Court, 1986), p. 206.

5  *From a Logical Point of View* (Cambridge, Mass.: Harvard University Press, 1980), pp. 37, 46, 56–7.

6  This was first pointed out by P. Grice and P. F. Strawson, "In Defense of a Dogma," *Philosophical Review* 65 (1956), pp. 147–8.

7  See Quine, *Logical Point of View*, p. 152; *Ontological Relativity* (New York: Columbia University Press, 1969), pp. 19–23; *Philosophy of Logic* (Cambridge, Mass.: Harvard University Press, 1970), pp. 1–2, 67–8.

8  Quine, *Logical Point of View*, pp. 41–2; *Philosophy of Logic*, pp. 99–102; *Word and Object* (Cambridge, Mass.: MIT Press, 1960), pp. 275–6.

9  Quine, *Ways of Paradox*, ch. 12; *Philosophy of Logic*, ch. 7; *Ontological Relativity*, p. 27.

10  See Baker and Hacker, *Rules, Grammar and Necessity*, pp. 267–8; Dilman, *Quine on Ontology*, ch. 5.

11  Quine, *Logical Point of View*, p. 42; *Ways of Paradox*, pp. 117–20.

12  Quine, *Logical Point of View*, pp. 42–4; *Philosophy of Logic*, p. 100, ch. 6.

13  Hookway, *Quine*, pp. 37–8.

14  *Representation and Reality* (Cambridge, Mass.: MIT Press, 1988), p. 11.

15  T. Kuhn, *The Structure of Scientific Revolutions* (Chicago: University of Chicago Press, 1962).

16  This point is made by A. Quinton, *The Nature of Things* (London: Routledge and Kegan Paul, 1973), pp. 216–17; M. Dummett, *Frege: Philosophy of Language* (London: Duckworth, 1973), pp. 596–601; C. Wright, *Wittgenstein on the Foundations of Mathematics* (London: Duckworth, 1980), pp. 329–30.

17  Quine, *Logical Point of View*, p. 42; *Ways of Paradox*, p. 102.

18  There are interesting parallels and differences between this line of thought and Davidson's celebrated argument against the possibility of alternative conceptual schemes. I discuss them in my "On Safari with Wittgenstein, Quine and Davidson," in R. L. Arrington and H.-J. Glock, eds., *Wittgenstein and Quine* (Routledge: London, 1996), pp. 144–72.

19  *Word and Object*, pp. 235, 207, ch. 1.

20  *Ways of Paradox*, pp. 112–13, 119–20, 128; "Replies to Critics," pp. 93–5, 138, 206–7.

21  Quine, *Ways of Paradox*, pp. 104–6; similarly D. Davidson, *Inquiries into Truth and Interpretation* (Oxford: Oxford University Press, 1984), p. 280.

22  Wright, *Wittgenstein on the Foundations of Mathematics*, pp. 94–113, 415–19.

23  Quine, *Ontological Relativity*, p. 83; see *Word and Object*, p. 26.

24  O. Hanfling, *Wittgenstein's Later Philosophy* (London: Macmillan, 1989), 146–51; B. Rundle, *Wittgenstein and Contemporary Philosophy of Language* (Oxford: Blackwell, 1990), pp. 5–8, 33–4, 64–9. The first "unruly" interpretation is in S. Cavell's "The Availability of Wittgenstein's Later Philosophy," *Philosophical Review* 71 (1962), pp. 67–93.

25  I am grateful for comments by Bob Arrington, Peter Hacker, John Hyman, and Hans Sluga, as well as to audiences at Oxford, Bielefeld, and Berkeley.

# 7    Wittgenstein, mathematics, and ethics: Resisting the attractions of realism

> A main source of our failure to understand is that we do not
> *command a clear view* of the use of our words. – Our grammar
> is lacking in this sort of perspicuity. (PI, 122)

How does Wittgenstein's later thought bear on moral philosophy? Wittgenstein himself having said so little about this, philosophers have been free to take his ideas and methods to have the most various implications for ethics.[1] I shall in this essay be concerned with Wittgenstein's ideas about mathematics and some possible ways of seeing their suggestiveness for ethics. I shall bring those ideas into critical contact with a rich and thoughtful treatment of ethics, that of Sabina Lovibond in *Realism and Imagination in Ethics*.[2] She defends a form of moral realism which she takes to be derived from Wittgenstein (RIE, p. 25); and her work is thus of great interest if we are concerned not only with questions about how Wittgenstein's work bears on ethics but also with questions about the relation between his thought and debates about realism. Wittgenstein is misread, I think, when taken either as a philosophical realist or as an antirealist. Elsewhere I have argued against antirealist readings.[3] One aim of this present essay is to trace to its sources a realist reading of Wittgenstein – its sources in the difficulty of looking at, and taking in, the use of our words.

## I

At the heart of Sabina Lovibond's account of ethics is a contrast between two philosophical approaches to language. Here is a sum-

226

mary of the approach she rejects, which she refers to as the empiricist view.[4] Language, on that view, is an *"instrument* for the communication of thought," thought being logically prior (RIE, p. 17); the language used in description is conceived of as like a calculus, and descriptive propositions are thought of as "readable" from the facts via determinate rules (RIE, pp. 18–19, 21). The meaning of descriptive terms (and thus the truth-conditions of propositions capable of truth and falsity) is tied to sense experience (RIE, p. 19). Reality is the reality described by the natural sciences; only entities admitted by science are real entities (RIE, p. 20). The "empiricist" view allows for two sorts of judgment, judgments of fact and judgments of value, corresponding to activities of recognition of facts (on the basis ultimately of sense experience) and affective responses to facts. There is thus also, on this view, a distinction between two sorts of meaning: descriptive or cognitive meaning and evaluative or emotive meaning (RIE, p. 21).

A central feature of the contrasting position on language, which Lovibond associates with Wittgenstein's later philosophy, is that it takes language to be "metaphysically homogeneous":[5] there are different regions of assertoric discourse, concerned with different ranges or kinds of features of reality, different subject matter, but the relation between language and reality is the same in all regions.

> What Wittgenstein offers us . . . is a homogeneous or 'seamless' conception of language. It is a conception free from invidious comparisons between different regions of discourse. . . . Just as the early Wittgenstein considers all *propositions* to be of equal value . . . , so the later Wittgenstein – who has, however, abandoned his previous normative notion of what counts as a proposition – regards all *language-games* as being of 'equal value' in the transcendental sense of the *Tractatus*. On this view, the only legitimate role for the idea of 'reality' is that in which it is coordinated with . . . the metaphysically neutral idea of 'talking about something.'. . . It follows that 'reference to an objective reality' cannot intelligibly be set up as a target which some propositions – or rather, some utterances couched in the indicative mood – may hit, while others fall short. If something has the grammatical form of a proposition, then it *is* a proposition: philosophical considerations cannot discredit the way in which we classify linguistic entities for other, non-philosophical, purposes . . .
>
> The only way, then, in which an indicative statement can fail to describe reality is by *not being true* – i.e. by virtue of reality not being as the statement declares it to be . . .

Thus Wittgenstein's view of language confirms us – provisionally, at least – in the pre-reflective habit of treating as 'descriptive,' or fact-stating, all sentences which qualify by grammatical standards as propositions. Instead of confining the descriptive function to those parts of language that deal with a natural-scientific subject-matter, it allows that function to pervade all regions of discourse irrespective of content. (RIE, pp. 25–7)

The quotations bring out that, as Lovibond sees Wittgenstein's later thought, it is incompatible with the idea that there is a philosophical task of investigating whether an indicative sentence which appears to be a description is *misleadingly* of that appearance. She puts the matter as if any denial that such a sentence functioned as a description had to imply that it *fell short of a target* (or that the language-game to which it belonged was of lesser value than others), but there she is making a slide. To deny (as I shall) that this – "the descriptive function pervades all regions of discourse" – is Wittgenstein's view is not to ascribe to him any belief in a kind of ranking, of sentences or of language-games, or any idea that indicative sentences which do not function as descriptions fall short of a target.

In quoting Lovibond I omitted her footnotes, but one of them is relevant to my argument. In that footnote she refers to a later section of her book (§17), in which she emphasizes that Wittgenstein, as she reads him, does not deny that language-games differ from each other in the "reach" assigned to intellectual authority. The greater the role of intellectual authority, the less scope there is for individual response. The activity of *counting* comes from one end of a spectrum of cases: at this end of the spectrum there is no scope for individual response. We are all trained to count in the same way: we expect and get consensus on *how many* chairs were in the room or houses in the street. Talk of what *fun* something was (or was not) illustrates the other extreme, the other end of the spectrum: each of us has the last word on what we call fun (RIE, pp. 66–7). Against this background, Lovibond can make a contrast between a sort of fact–value *continuum*, allowed for on her view, and the traditional fact–value *distinction*. On the traditional view, the fact–value distinction rests on a metaphysical account of the relation between language and reality, which she has rejected. This is the account that holds that descriptive sentences have genuine truth-conditions and are answerable to reality, and that there is no reality to which evaluative sentences are answerable; they are not genuinely true or false.

Her recognition of a fact–value "continuum" is based simply on there being a greater or lesser role for intellectual authority in various language-games. She then places moral discourse somewhere between the two extremes exemplified by counting (and scientific discourse) and talk of what is fun: in moral discourse the acceptance of authority has a "far from negligible" role, but reaches less far than in scientific discourse (RIE, p. 67; see also the discussion of historical change in §21).

There is an assumption Lovibond is making, the assumption that there are just two alternatives: if we do not make a metaphysically-based distinction between sentences which genuinely describe reality (and are made true or false by the facts) and sentences which do not do so, then we shall accept an account in which all indicative sentences are treated equally as descriptions of reality, as "about" the things they grammatically appear to be about. The language-games involving such sentences are allowed, on her view, to differ in the pressures toward consensus, in the scope allowed to authority, but not in "descriptiveness." Here is a remark of hers which suggests that she is making that assumption, and that it guides her reading of Wittgenstein: "Wittgenstein's view of language implicitly denies any metaphysical role to the idea of 'reality'; it denies that we can draw any intelligible distinction between those parts of assertoric discourse which do, and those which do not, genuinely *describe* reality" (RIE, p. 36).

Attention to Wittgenstein's later writings on mathematics shows that for him there are not just the two alternatives recognized by Lovibond. By making clear that those are not the only possibilities, he provides a point of view from which we can question what Lovibond takes to be the implications of his views for ethics. Indicative sentences may have *various* functions: indicativeness itself indicates neither the kind of use a sentence has, nor whether it has any use.

What looks like a proposition may be quite useless; what we say may fail to make sense, and we may be unaware of that failure. The quotation from Lovibond raises some questions about Wittgenstein's view of such failures. I cannot discuss these in detail but shall simply note them in Section II, before turning in Section III to remarks of Wittgenstein's suggesting a view of descriptive language quite different from that ascribed to him by Lovibond.

II

Wittgenstein held, Lovibond says, that what has the grammatical form of a proposition *is* a proposition. But Wittgenstein calls this into question; see PI, 520: "It is not every sentence-like formation that we know how to do something with, not every technique has an application in our life; and when we are tempted in philosophy to count some quite useless thing as a proposition, that is often because we have not considered its application sufficiently."

Lovibond writes that Wittgenstein abandoned his earlier normative notion of what a proposition is. It is not entirely clear what a normative notion of propositions is. But consider the case of saying to someone (quite outside of philosophy) "What you've said makes no sense." We criticize what was said by standards that are internal to *saying something*. (By offering such criticism, we show that we take the context to be one in which the standards are appropriate: the other person is not, for example, playing with language.) Does the availability of such standards show that we have a normative notion of saying something, of propositionhood? That we can, by talking nonsense, fail to say anything is part of the "grammar" of "say"; it is not a view that Wittgenstein held in the *Tractatus* and abandoned later. In both earlier and later periods he was concerned to show how we can in philosophy be *unaware* of the bearing on our thought of modes of criticism involving notions of sense and nonsense; we can be unaware of the relevance of standards or norms that we use easily and unproblematically in *other* contexts. This is explicit in his characterization of his aim in PI, 464: "What I want to teach you is to pass from a piece of disguised nonsense to something that is patent nonsense." Wittgenstein's point there connects directly with his idea that the grammatical appearance of a sentence is no guide to whether it *has* a role in language or is a mere useless thing that, in philosophy, we are tempted to count as a proposition.

An underlying problem with Lovibond's reading may be the idea that, if a philosopher criticizes our taking something to be a senseful sentence, he must be imposing some special philosophical conception of what a sentence *should be*. What Wittgenstein in fact tried to do (early and late) was to enable us to see our own sentences differently, but not by holding them up against new or specially philosophical norms. The philosopher is regarded by Wittgenstein as someone who does not know his way about with his old norms, who can talk nonsense through a kind of disorientation.[6]

Wittgenstein held neither that everything that looks like a proposition is one, nor that every proposition that looks as if its function is descriptive has that function. It is the latter issue that I shall be concerned with in the rest of this essay.

### III

In the lectures he gave in 1939 on the foundations of mathematics, Wittgenstein argued that the relation of mathematical propositions to reality was entirely different from that of experiential propositions. He further tried to show how we could be seriously misled by the similarities of grammatical appearance between mathematical and experiential propositions: those similarities hide from us their contrasting kinds of relation to reality (LFM, Lectures XXV and XXVI).

Wittgenstein was responding to remarks of the mathematician G. H. Hardy, whom he quotes as having said that "to mathematical propositions there corresponds – in some sense, however sophisticated – a reality."[7] Hardy, Wittgenstein went on, was comparing mathematics with physics. The idea is that, just as physics is about physical features of reality, so mathematics is about mathematical features of reality. Hardy's picture is of two "regions of discourse" (to use Lovibond's expression), differing in subject matter, but within which language itself functions in parallel ways: its function in both "regions" is the description of the relevant subject matter. It was precisely that idea of parallelism of function that Wittgenstein questioned.

To illustrate the points he wanted to make about mathematical (and logical) propositions he used an analogy with another case in which we may misjudge how a sentence is being used:

Suppose you had to say to what reality this – "There is no reddish-green" – is responsible. Where is the reality corresponding to the proposition "There is no reddish-green?" (This is entirely parallel to Hardy's "reality.") – It makes it look the same as "In this room there is nothing yellowish-green." This is of practically the same appearance – but its use is as different as hell.

If we say there's a reality corresponding to "There is no reddish-green," this immediately suggests the kind of reality corresponding to the other proposition. Which reality would you say corresponds to that? We have in mind that it must be a reality roughly of the sort: the absence of anything which has this colour (though that is queer, because, in saying that, we are saying just the same thing over again). It is superhuman not to think of the reality as being something similar in the case of "There is no reddish-green."

Now there *is* a reality corresponding to this, but it is of an *entirely* different sort. One reality is that if I had arranged for myself to call something reddish-green, other people would not know what to say . . .

If you were to say what reality corresponds to "There is no reddish-green" – I'd say: You may say a reality corresponds, only (1) it is of an entirely different kind from what you assume; (2) [what you have is a *rule*,] namely the [rule] that this expression can't be applied to anything. The correspondence is between this rule and such facts as that we do not normally make a black by mixing a red and a green; that if you mix red and green you get a colour which is "dirty" and dirty colours are difficult to remember. All sorts of facts, psychological and otherwise. (LFM, pp. 243–5)

Sabina Lovibond ascribed to Wittgenstein a "homogeneous or 'seamless' conception of language," meaning that all assertoric discourse has the same relation to reality. But it is precisely such homogeneity that Wittgenstein rejects in the lecture I have quoted: similarlooking propositions can differ in use, can differ in what it is for them to be "responsible to reality." In the following lecture, Wittgenstein introduced a new comparison to make clearer what he meant by there being two entirely different ways in which reality could be said to correspond to a proposition.

If one talks about a reality corresponding to mathematical propositions and examines what that might mean, one can distinguish two very different things.

(1) If we talk of an experiential proposition, we may say a reality corresponds to it, if it is true and we can assert it.

(2) We may say that a reality corresponds to a *word*, say the word "rain" – but then we mean something quite different. This word is used in "it rains," which may be true or false; and also in "it doesn't rain." And in this latter case if we say "some phenomenon corresponds to it," this is queer. But you might still say something corresponds to it; only then you have to distinguish the sense of "corresponds." (LFM, p. 247)

Wittgenstein went on in the lecture to develop the idea of an "enormous difference" between reality corresponding to an experiential proposition and reality corresponding to a *word*. He then argued that the source of much philosophical confusion about mathematical and logical propositions is that we imagine them to have a kind of correspondence to reality like that of experiential propositions, whereas, if we look at their use, we can see that correspondence to reality in their case is like the correspondence to reality of a word.

What then does he mean by the correspondence to reality of a word? He does not think that we already have some clear idea what this means. There are words ("sofa" and "green" are his examples) such that, if we were asked what the reality is that corresponds to them, we should all point to the same thing, but with other words (like "perhaps," "and," "plus") we should not know what to say. What he does here is *introduce* a way of talking about reality corresponding to a word, a way of talking intended to be helpful in dealing with particular philosophical problems. He invites us to say of a word that the reality corresponding to it is our having a use for it (LFM, pp. 248–9). And this ties directly back to his remarks in the previous lecture about what it is for reality to correspond to a *rule:* a rule is made important by and justified by all sorts of facts, about the world and about us; and we can speak of the rule as corresponding to reality in that there are such facts, making it a rule we shall want (LFM, p. 246).

For there to be a reality corresponding to a word is then for there to be things (about us, about the world) which make it useful to have the word as part of our means of description. Wittgenstein emphasizes the difference between activities in which we develop our means of description and linguistic activities in which we are using, in experiential propositions, the means of description we have developed. Mathematical propositions look as if, in them, we were using a language of mathematical description to describe mathematical reality; but Wittgenstein tries to get us to see mathematics as like other activities in which we develop the means of description used in experiential propositions. If I say to someone who does not know the meaning of "chair," "This is a *chair*," the use of that sentence is as a "preparation" for descriptions like "The chairs are all terribly uncomfortable." Analogously, "20 + 20 = 40" is a preparation for description: "In mathematics the signs do not yet have a meaning; they are *given* a meaning. '300' is given its meaning by the calculus – that meaning which it has in the sentence 'There are 300 men in this college' " (LFM, pp. 249–50).[8]

Wittgenstein's idea that in mathematics we are developing our means of description should be seen with his view that there are many different kinds of description, in which a variety of techniques are used. One technique of description, for example, is the formulation of some kind of "ideal case," which enables us to describe actual cases as *departures* of one or another sort from the ideal. Wittgenstein thinks of kinematics, for example, as providing such a means of description. The ideally rigid rod of kinematics is a standard used in description of ordinary rods. There need be no confusion in thinking of kinematics as "about" ideally rigid rods; but it would be entirely possible for philosophical confusion to arise from that idea of what kinematics is about. We might, for example, be puzzled how we can have epistemic contact with the ideally rigid rods that are its subject matter. Much of the usefulness of mathematics in description lies in its role in the construction of such "ideal" cases. In language-games involving description, there will be methods of arriving at descriptions, and standards for carrying out those methods properly. Mathematics is integrated into the body of standards for carrying out methods of arriving at descriptive propositions, for locating miscounts (for example), or mistakes or inaccuracies of measurement. The *application* of mathematics, the modes of integration of mathematics into other language-games, will be extremely various. And Wittgenstein emphasizes the need for philosophers to attend to the application of mathematics in order to see the kind of meaning mathematical propositions have.

Wittgenstein's contrast between giving descriptions and developing the means of description is connected with his views about the significance of consistency in mathematics and about the question what would go wrong if we did mathematics or logic in some different way. Whether a certain means of description will be useful or not depends on all sorts of facts. You might say that you can see by a proof:

1 2 3
. . .
4 5 6
. . .
7 8 9
. . .

that "3 × 3 = 9" *has* to work. But whether, when you actually try to apply "3 × 3 = 9," you will get into trouble is a different matter.[9] Wittgenstein struggled for years to put the issues here with lucidity. Here is a remark about the *series of natural numbers*, one great and significant part of a large number of different language-games of description.

> We copy the numerals from 1 to 100, say, and this is the way we *infer, think*.
>
> I might put it this way: If I copy the numerals from 1 to 100 – how do I know that I shall get a series of numerals that is right when I count them? And here *what* is a check on *what*? Or how am I to describe the important empirical fact here? Am I to say experience teaches that I always count the same way? Or that none of the numerals gets lost in copying? Or that the numerals remain on the paper as they are, even when I don't watch them? Or *all* these facts? Or am I to say that we simply don't get into difficulties? Or that almost always everything seems all right to us? . . . (Z, 309)

The series of natural numbers, and the mathematical proposition "3 × 3 = 9," are then among the means of description which are useful and important, which have a place in our lives, because of numerous facts of the sort Wittgenstein draws to our attention in the passages I have quoted.

In connection with these ideas about mathematics, Wittgenstein says that in a sense mathematical propositions do not *treat of* numbers (this is because they give the symbols for numbers their meaning), and that we should say instead that what does "treat of" numbers are such sentences as "There are three windows in this room" (LFM, p. 250).

Sabina Lovibond claimed that, on Wittgenstein's later view, there is only one legitimate role for the idea of reality, the role in which it is coordinated with a "metaphysically neutral" idea of "talking about something." But, just as Wittgenstein asks us to note two "entirely different" roles for the idea of correspondence to reality, he also asks us to note two entirely different uses for the word "about," two different ways of speaking of what a proposition is *about*. It is because we are likely to muddle those two uses that Wittgenstein recommends that we not say that "2 + 2 = 4" is *about* 2.

There need be nothing misleading in saying of a mathematical proposition that it is about *circles*, for example, or in saying that mathematical propositions are *about numbers*. (Those ways of speaking are not wrong, as anti-Platonists might suggest.) But what is likely to mislead us in philosophy is the idea that mathematical propositions are about numbers in the same sort of way as "Prince has blue trousers" is about Prince's trousers. The heart of Wittgenstein's recommendation is the pointing out of the difference: "As soon as you talk about the reality corresponding to mathematics, there is an enormous confusion if you do not see that 'being about' means two entirely different things" (LFM p. 251). If you *are* clear that "30 × 30 = 900" is not about 30 in the way that "Prince has blue trousers" is about Prince's trousers, if you see that it is "about 30" in the sense that it helps prepare the number-sign "30" for its applications, then you will not imagine the reality corresponding to the mathematical proposition as some sort of realm of numbers. The realm with which we are concerned, when we work out mathematical propositions, is found by considering their application. (Wittgenstein went on to emphasize the particular importance of these points in connection with transfinite arithmetic, and the temptation to think of that branch of mathematics as dealing with, as about, a particularly exotic realm of numbers.)

## IV

In an earlier lecture in 1939, Wittgenstein asked whether the sentence "20 apples plus 30 apples is 50 apples" is *about apples*. He replied to his own question that it might be: the sentence might mean that apples do not join up. But the sentence could be used differently, could be used to make a mathematical statement.

> Might we not put all our arithmetical statements in this form – statements in which the word "apple" appears? And if you were asked what an apple was, you would show the ordinary thing we call an apple . . .
> . . . when we prove that 20 apples + 30 apples = 50 apples, we may have thereby proved also that 20 chairs + 30 chairs = 50 chairs or we may not. – What is the difference between proving it for apples alone and proving it for chairs, tables, etc? Does it lie in what I write down? Obviously not – nor in what I think as I write it. But in the use I make of it.
> "20 apples + 30 apples = 50 apples" may not be a proposition about apples. Whether it is depends on its use. It *may* be a proposition of arithmetic – and in this case we could call it a proposition about numbers.
> (LFM, p. 113)

Mathematical propositions are instruments of the language, and in this respect might be compared with proverbs. What makes a sentence a proverb is its use. It is brought into contact with, expected to shed light on, or change our way of seeing, particular situations: that is its application. A sentence like "A soft answer turneth away wrath" becomes (in a way ordinary sentences do not) part of the English language. It remains in the language as one of its instruments, an instrument whose use is in some respects more like that of a word than of an ordinary sentence. Learning the use of proverbs is learning the activity of bringing them usefully or interestingly or wittily or . . . to bear on different situations. Making up proverbs is itself a language-game. When someone makes up a proverb, it may or may not be taken up into the language. Its being taken up into the language as a proverb depends on any number of things including its usefulness and its wit.

How does all this bear on ethics? We have seen Wittgenstein's view that a particular sentence might belong to pomology or might belong to mathematics, and *which* it belongs to depends not on what it is apparently about but on its use. Why not consider the question, then, whether a sentence's belonging to ethics is a classification by use rather than by subject matter? Why should not something like what Wittgenstein says about mathematics be true of ethics? He believed that failure to see that mathematical sentences are not mathematical in virtue of what they are about (in the way the sentences of botany are about plants) creates a kind of philosophical confusion, in which we think of mathematics as the exploration of mathematical reality. His treatment of metaphysical confusion about mathematics involves getting us to recognize that mathematical propositions are not "responsible to reality" in the same sort of way ordinary experiential propositions are; can anything similar be said about ethical propositions?

Putting this now in relation to Sabina Lovibond: she thinks that once we have rejected a metaphysical view of the relation between language and reality, we shall accept a Wittgensteinian view of language, in which the "descriptive function" has no metaphysical underpinnings, and in which indicative sentences are all equally descriptions of reality. (They are all, also, on her view, "expressive" or "emotive," but I am not here concerned with what she says about the expressive function of language.) Our language-games with indicative sentences differ in subject matter and in the role they give to authority and consensus, but not in the kind of relation to reality the sentences have. Applied to ethics, this view of language will (Lovibond thinks) enable us to see "moral facts" in a metaphysically unexciting way, as facts which we become aware of in perception and report in moral discourse. I have shown that there might be a philosophical approach to ethics entirely consistent with Wittgenstein's understanding of language, but quite different from Lovibond's moral realism. She had argued that, once we had got rid of the empiricist view of language and had arrived at a sound view, in essence Wittgenstein's, we should see that all indicative sentences are "about reality" in the same way. So, calling that general argument into question calls into question the main argument for her view of ethics.

My argument so far leaves entirely open what philosophical account of ethics we should give. But, if Wittgenstein is right that consideration of use shows the possible misleadingness, in philosophy, of taking mathematical propositions to be statements of mathematical facts, how could we tell without looking at moral thought and talk whether it is equally misleading to take moral discourse to be the stating of moral facts?

There is an underlying source of the trouble in Lovibond's argument. It comes out in her moving from a general account of language to an account of ethics. In the sense in which she puts forward a general account of language, Wittgenstein himself does not have an alternative general account, but none. That is, what can be said, on his view, about mathematical propositions (for example) *waits for* an examination of *them:* of the practices through which we arrive at them, the practices in which they are taught, and those in which they are applied. And even *such* an examination does not yield a general account; mathematics itself is a "motley." Although Wittgenstein does refer to "descriptive propositions," he does not think that there is a single way in which they all function. "What we call 'descriptions' are instruments for particular uses" (PI, 291); and only by looking at those various uses can we see what is getting called "description" in any particular case.

But what about Wittgenstein's arguments in *On Certainty?* Does he not there show us something about what all activities in which there is assertion must be like? Are there not generalizations reached in *On Certainty* which apply across the board to the natural sciences, ordinary talk about chairs and tables, the study of history, mathematics and logic, ethics, esthetics, religion, and so on?[10] I should rather suggest that Wittgenstein's remarks show us a possible way of looking at mathematics (for example): we can ask how far the remarks he makes about certainty in *On Certainty*, in relation to science and history (say), apply to mathematics. His remarks in *On Certainty* have a particular context; they are directed to particular philosophical confusions. He wants to turn our attention to various linguistic activities of which we have (he thinks) a false and oversimple picture; we think they have to be like this or like that. His remarks are not meant to be substitutes for such attention. We can indeed ask whether what Wittgenstein says about the possible kinds of room for doubt in science, or the role in it of acceptance of authority, is interestingly applicable to ethics. But Wittgenstein's method does not provide shortcuts. In the *Tractatus*, he wrote that everyday language is a part of the human organism and is no less complicated than it (TLP, 4.002). That thought is still present in his later writings: our language-games are more complicated than we think, and in unforeseeable ways.

Lovibond's reading of Wittgenstein depends in part on her way of taking his remarks "Philosophy may in no way interfere with the actual use of language" (PI, 124) and "Grammar tells what kind of object anything is" (PI, 373). She sees that his remarks imply that "philosophical considerations cannot discredit the way in which we classify linguistic entities for other, non-philosophical purposes" (RIE, p. 26). She is entirely right that Wittgenstein rejects any appeal to any metaphysical understanding of "description" (say), which would provide a standard which what we think of as descriptions might meet or fail to meet, so our ordinary classifications could be discredited. The point for Wittgenstein is not the rightness or wrongness of ordinary classifications. In philosophy, we are properly interested in differences in use which can cut across other classifications. The kinds of similarities which underlie classification for nonphilosophical purposes may lead us, in philosophy, to suppose similarities in use, and may therefore stop us *looking at* use. It is only by looking at use that we can make clear what Wittgenstein referred to as the "grammatical kind" to which something belongs. Two sections prior to the section in which Wittgenstein says that philosophy may not interfere with use, he says that a main source of failure of under-standing, in philosophy, is that the use is not open to view: our grammar, he says, lacks that sort of openness to view. But it is exactly such openness to view that Lovibond seems to assume, when she moves from sentences sharing indicativeness to their all functioning in the same way as descriptions. Wittgenstein's discus-sion of mathematics provides an excellent example of how, without seeking to discredit any ordinary ways of categorizing linguistic en-tities, he brings out differences in function ("the use is as different as hell"), differences the overlooking of which in philosophy can cause great confusion. We cannot ascribe to Wittgenstein the idea that sentences which resemble each other in being indicative can thus be known not to have enormous differences in function.

(Lovibond's reading of Wittgenstein also appeals to his remark "Not empiricism and yet realism in philosophy, this is the hardest thing." I discuss this remark in the Appendix.)

## V

There is another possible response to my argument in Sections III and IV. Wittgenstein's view of mathematics, as I have sketched it, depends on a distinction between two kinds of linguistic activity: describing, and developing means of description. It might be claimed in support of Sabina Lovibond's view that that distinction is a hang-over from Wittgenstein's earlier philosophy and that it is decisively repudiated in *On Certainty*. Or it might be argued that the distinc-tion is undermined by Wittgenstein's discussion of rules, which (so the argument would go) does not allow for a significant distinction between our adhering to existing practices of description and our developing our means of description. I shall discuss only the first version of the argument.

Wittgenstein did indeed say that the contrast between rules of description and descriptive propositions "shades off in all direc-tions," but he added that that did not imply that the contrast was not "of the greatest importance" (RFM, p. 363). In *On Certainty* we see him investigating the distinction itself. It is important not only that there is no sharp boundary between propositions of logic (in a broad sense) and empirical propositions, but also that a proposi-tion's function may change: what was an empirical proposition (i.e., what had that use) may become a "norm of description" (OC, 318–21). If a proposition may thus change in function, it follows that we cannot tell what the function is from an examination of the proposition itself. The *look* of a sentence (its being an indicative sentence, say) does not make clear what its use is. Such passages, in *On Certainty* and other late writings, far from showing that Wittgenstein gave up the distinction between description and rule or norm of description, show him continuing to explore the distinction and its ramifications.[11]

Mathematics *is* discussed in *On Certainty*, but only briefly; and Wittgenstein is not concerned with what had been the central topics of his writings and lectures on the foundations of mathematics. Thus, for example, in formulating an argument in §654 he refers to the fact that "$12 \times 12 = 144$" is a mathematical proposition, and he looks at some implications of the difference between mathematical and nonmathematical propositions. He is not here asking (what had been a central question) what is involved in "$12 \times 12 = 144$" *being* a mathematical proposition. That a proposition is a mathematical proposition in virtue of its use, a use which is very different from that of ordinary experiential propositions, is not something which *On Certainty* calls into question.

Nor does *On Certainty* call into question a further point: that propositions may be brought together in some classification not by subject matter but by use. "Proverbs" is a categorization of sentences by use; "mathematical propositions" was certainly taken by Wittgenstein to be a categorization by use (in the sense in which categorization by use can be contrasted with categorization by subject matter). So the question I asked in Section IV remains askable: might some of what Wittgenstein held about mathematical propositions be true of ethical propositions? On Sabina Lovibond's view, there are moral features of the world, as there are botanical features of the world; the propositions of botany are about the latter and the propositions of ethics about the former. If one said that there are "mathematical features of the world," which mathematical propositions are about, Wittgenstein might have replied that, however innocuous that way of speaking may be in some contexts, it can make it extremely difficult for us to see *how* different mathematics is from botany: "An unsuitable means of expression is a sure means of remaining in a state of confusion" (PI, 339). Is the description of ethical propositions as about moral features of the world a good or useful description of them?

## VI

In this section, I investigate whether *moral discourse* is identifiable by its subject matter. Again, I develop a view by contrast with Sabina Lovibond's. Her conception of moral discourse emphasizes the significance of moral predicates:

> We saw . . . that, according to Wittgenstein, "it is our *acting* which lies at the bottom of the language-game." The categories employed in natural languages, then, articulate distinctions which are of interest to us in deciding how to act. The presence in our language of any given predicate displays the fact that, on some occasions, we see fit to distinguish between cases – to *treat cases differently* – in a way reflecting the distribution of the property denoted by that predicate. And the degree of ease, or difficulty, with which we can imagine a language lacking the relevant predicate mirrors our capacity, or incapacity, to imagine what it would be like not to care about the distribution of the corresponding property . . .
>
> Now the idea that our linguistic categories articulate our practical concerns applies, *a fortiori* to *moral* categories. These can be seen as registering distinctions which are of *unconditional* practical interest to us in virtue of our concern to live a life deserving of praise and not of contempt. (RIE, pp. 51–2)

(Later in the same section, Lovibond adds [RIE, p. 53] that Wittgenstein's view of language "allows us to recognize the existence of *propositions* which record the incidence of properties possessing an unconditional practical interest for us.")

Lovibond's account is meant to be Wittgensteinian in tying the use of expressions in our language-games to human interests and ways of acting. What I find problematic is the argument that goes from a general account of what is reflected by our having a given predicate in our language to an account of moral predicates as reflecting an interest in a particular group of properties. What we should learn from Wittgenstein is that there is no *a fortiori*. We need to look: what would it be like to have a language in which moral predicates had no, or virtually no, use? Would people not care about the things we care about? *How much* of our moral thought is actually dependent on such predicates?[12]

Let me start with a striking fact: that some talk and writing that one might very well take to be the expression of moral thought involves no specifically moral words at all, or involves relatively few such words, which bear relatively little weight. Here are some examples. (The point of having several is that they are very different among themselves.)[13]

(1) Chapters 25 to 29 of Laura Ingalls Wilder's *The Long Winter*[14] tell a story about human actions in the face of danger and desperate need. Moral predicates *could* be used of many of the actions and motives in the story, but Mrs. Wilder eschews such language. The absence of explicitly moral language is particularly evident in the case of the great bravery shown by two of the characters and their moral facing down of another character: Mrs. Wilder presents the actions with no moral commentary. The story, though, expresses Mrs. Wilder's moral sensibility; further, it could clearly form part of a child's moral education. No doubt an adult, reading the book to a child, might comment "Weren't they brave!" but the relevance of the book to moral education does not depend on such comments. A child reading the book might be fully aware of its moral force without needing moral predicates any more than Mrs. Wilder needs them.

There are in those chapters ideas of Mrs. Wilder's about human virtue and about the relation between the good life for human beings and the character of their communities. But what it *is* for ideas about such things to be in something said or written is not at all obvious. That is, "thoughts about life" are not in a piece of discourse in anything like the way that "thoughts about ferns" might be said to be in a piece of botanical discourse.

(2) The young men described in *The Long Winter* do something very fine. The book is a book for children; I want to consider in contrast writing for adults descriptive of great evils. I have in mind books and essays that do not, like *The Long Winter*, form part of moral upbringing but are written because the author takes *telling* the things he or she tells of to be of great importance. Two good examples are Primo Levi's *If This Is a Man* and John Prebble's *The Highland Clearances*.[15] Although moral predicates do appear in these books, they have no very considerable role. In the first chapter of Prebble's book, the word "betrayal" does appear; in the first chap-

ter of Levi's, the words "without pity" appear. But the moral force of the writing is independent of their use. If it is "about good and evil" it is not because words for good or evil play a role in it; moral outrage is carried in such things as the tension of the prose.[16]

(3) "A shell exploded. Twenty or thirty young men were blown up in France, among them Andrew Ramsay, whose death, mercifully, was instantaneous." Shuli Barzilai has written about the use that that pair of sentences is given in To the Lighthouse.[17] Mr. Ramsay, in To the Lighthouse, repeatedly quotes Tennyson's "Charge of the Light Brigade"; and Barzilai argues for the moral expressiveness of the contrast between the pair of sentences about Andrew Ramsay's death and the quotations earlier in the novel from "Charge of the Light Brigade." "By way of subversive and complete contrast to Tennyson's resounding refrain, [Woolf's] reference to 'twenty or thirty . . . among them Andrew Ramsay' serves to underscore (because, and not in spite, of the inexact number) the importance of one particular life for one mother, one wife, or one friend."

This example is meant to bring out the resemblance between the point Wittgenstein makes about what it is for a sentence to be a sentence about mathematics and a point one might make about ethics. "20 apples + 30 apples = 50 apples" might be experiential, might be mathematical – which, depends on its use. "A shell exploded. Twenty or thirty men were blown up . . ." might be merely a record of what happened, might express moral thought – which, depends on its use.

(4) G. E. M. Anscombe discusses Tolstoy in her exposition of the ideas of the Tractatus. Wittgenstein probably had him especially in mind, she suggests, when he noted the inability of people to whom the meaning of life had become clear to state what they wished to state. What Tolstoy wanted to say about life "comes through," she says, in Hadji Murad, whereas the explanations he gives in his explicitly ethical writings are "miserable failures."[18] Wittgenstein himself, writing to Norman Malcolm in 1945, recommends Hadji Murad and criticizes Resurrection; Tolstoy's moral thought, he says, is impressively present, not when he addresses the reader, but when it is left "latent in the story."[19]

I wanted to set these examples over against Sabina Lovibond's idea that it is primarily the use of moral predicates in a language that reflects human moral interests. The presence of moral thought (I have been arguing) may be reflected in language, not in the use of moral predicates, tied to our interest in moral properties, but in some of the ways we use language about all sorts of not specifically moral things, like death in war, for example, or pulling horses out of deep snow. The idea that moral discourse is tied to moral predicates shows, I think, a false conception of what it is for our thought to be *about* something moral. Being about good and evil is a matter of use, not subject matter.

The examples which I have taken to suggest the lack of parallel between talk being about good and evil and talk being about plants (say) might be taken not to suggest that. It might thus be argued that the reader of *The Long Winter* is meant to recognize the moral property of bravery in the acts described. The absence of explicit moral terms in the story (so the argument would go) is entirely consistent with the idea that the recognition of moral properties is central in moral thought.

We can impose that idea on our understanding of the cases I have cited; we can see moral thought that way. But let me try to make it less attractive to do so. Imagine people among whom moral education is *simply* the telling of stories. Perhaps children's admiration for some characters in the stories is encouraged ("Wouldn't you like to be like Almanzo?" Almanzo being one of the characters in *The Long Winter*) and perhaps contempt for others. But they do not in this society have words for moral properties. If asked why they admire someone, they tell a story about the person in reply. They are certainly interested in ethics – that interest comes out in the role the stories have. But is there any reason for insisting on describing this as an interest in moral properties? The insistence on *moral properties* expresses the wish to draw analogies between moral discourse and what we agree to be branches of factual discourse. But that very insistence leads us away from recognition of the varieties of forms which moral discourse itself can have.

Suppose it is said that "like Almanzo" is, in fact, a term that these people use for the property for which we have the word "brave." I am not denying that "like Almanzo" might be used that way; but that is not the only possible use. I shall in Section VII explain how our idea of a person and what he or she is like may have a kind of use in moral thought different from the use of "brave" as a predicate.

Lovibond says "It is our use of moral concepts to describe our own, and one another's, behaviour which endows that behaviour with moral meaning" (RIE, p. 63); there must be publicly acknowledged moral categories. But, in the case of the people whose moral talk is a matter of telling stories, not of applying moral predicates, it would be implausible to suggest that either their behaviour has no moral meaning, or they must have terms like "brave," "just," and so on, the rules for the use of which shape moral thought within the community.

There is a stronger objection to my argument. *Manners*, it might be said, is certainly a subject of some discourse, just as plants are the subject of botany. And yet thought about manners need not make use of "rude," "polite," "discourteous," "snub," and so on. Think of some Proustian description of people not acknowledging acquaintance with each other, as an example of thought about manners which might entirely lack manners-predicates. So (this objection to my argument goes) a type of discourse may include *indirectness of description* (description of its subject without any use of predicates characteristic of that subject matter) without there being any suggestion that it is not *about* its subject matter in the same way botany is about plants.

A discussion of that argument would lead, I think, not to abandonment of what I have suggested about ethics but to refinement of it, and to greater clarity about the role of *indirection* in thought. But there is not here space for the kind of discussion that the objection requires.

## VII

In Section VI, I gave examples of moral thought, intended to suggest that Wittgenstein's point about pomology and mathematics might have some application to ethics – that is, that a sentence might belong to ethics rather than (say) military history (or, might belong to ethics as well as to military history) because of its use. But the question how far what Wittgenstein says about mathematics might hold of ethics requires us to look also at how resources of language may be applied in our thought about the particular situations in which we find ourselves. Here again I shall need to consider a range of cases.

Sometimes we decide how to act by bringing a moral rule or princi-ple into contact with our situation. We think of the situation in terms which perhaps invite an application of the rule. But consider a quite different form of moral thinking. Simone Weil suggests that one meditate on *chance,* chance that led to the meeting of one's father and mother, chance that led to one's being born.[20] Suppose one is thinking what to do, and brings to that deliberation the thought "It is only through chance that I was born"; and suppose that one acts in the light that that thought casts. It may put what one values in a different perspective, helping one to recognize what is precious, and to accept its and one's own vulnerability to chance, its and one's own ephemeral existence; such recognition and accep-tance may then inform one's action.[21] What is brought into contact with the situation here is not a moral rule but a thought, a sentence, "I was born only through the chance meeting of two people." This case is indeed quite different from applying a rule, but it is not the less a form of moral thought. One may indeed look to rules for guidance; but this does not in any way suggest that what guides one might not be such a sentence as Simone Weil's.

I mentioned earlier that proverbs may be applied in all sorts of ways, obvious and unobvious. This case is like the Simone Weil case. What was there brought into contact with the situation is a sentence about chance in human life. But "sentence," in its old meaning, is itself a word for proverb. A proverb, a sentence, may be something we keep by us, as it were, for use when appropriate; it is *given* connections with what we need to do, or may do, or cannot do, with how we see life, or good and evil, on this occasion or that. Proverbs may guide us, may be central in someone's moral thought, or in the moral thought of a whole tradition; and again this is differ-ent from guidance by rules or principles. My treatment of "guid-ance" here is not based on any specific passage in Wittgenstein, but is meant to be an application of Wittgenstein's methods. What we can make sense of as *guidance* has no general form, needs to be looked at.

Suppose that what is brought into contact with a situation is the story in *The Long Winter* of the two men struggling through the snow. The person making this connection acts in the light the story casts. To understand the sense that the person's action has is to see in it its relation to the story, not to see it as tied to some principle or rule. The use of stories as a way of shaping moral attention in a particular situation, or of guiding future thought, is characteristic of such traditions as the Sufi and the Hasidic; stories are here resources, told and retold, applied and understood in different ways on different occasions.

A *word* may be brought into contact with a situation; one may act in the light of a word, or understand the situation in its light: the word "chance" for Simone Weil (say), or "abundance," "overflow" for Blake. I do not want to deny that virtue-words, or words like "duty," might have this role, but my examples are intended to bring out that moral thought, concerned with how to act in particular situations, or with how to understand those situations, may not be tied to the words we think of as specifically moral, and to bring out that the use even of a moral word need not be as a predicate, but rather as a sort of organizing concept. Because words can have that role, it matters *what* words are available for such a use, what words have not been cheapened. The poet Zbigniew Herbert tells us to "repeat great words repeat them stubbornly." He means words like "truth" and "justice": he tells us to repeat such words after telling us to "repeat old incantations of humanity fables and legends."[22] The "great words" and the legends may have similar kinds of significance for our understanding.[23] And if a moralist reflects on how we may reshape our understanding of a situation by bringing this or that particular word into contact with it, he is likely to note the possibility of words darkening thought, as Blake, for example, thought words like "prudence," "shame," or "futurity" would.

Whole sentences, stories, images, the idea we have of a person, words, rules: anything made of the resources of ordinary language may be brought into such a relation to our lives and actions and understanding of the world that we might speak of the thinking involved in that connection as "moral." There is no limit to be set. We cannot, that is, say that *these* are the words, moral words for moral subject matter, that can have this character. If a sentence or image or word has this character, it arises not through its content but from its use on particular occasions.

We should here see a connection to the *Tractatus*, to Wittgenstein's description of the book's intention as ethical.[24] The idea that the book has an ethical intent is often taken to mean that it has some sort of ethical *content*, which (supposedly) cannot be expressed in what count officially on the *Tractatus* view as propositions. Sections VI and VII of this essay are compatible with an entirely different view of what it might mean for the book to have an ethical intent. In the book Wittgenstein leads us toward a specification, through a variable, of *all* propositions. That specification can be brought into a kind of contact with our lives, a liberation from taking the problems of life as questions needing to be answered. In our then going ahead with the tasks that confront us (digging a hole, for example, if that is what needs to be done), we might be *applying* the book in the way it is meant to be applied. On this reading of its intention, the book belongs to what I have referred to as "instruments of the language." It is in certain respects then meant to be like a proverb, a sentence available for repeated applications, meant to be brought into contact with a variety of situations not givable in advance. Only in its ethical use (and in the intention or hope that it have such use) is there anything ethical about it.[25]

My argument so far has established a partial parallel between what Wittgenstein says about mathematics and what can be said about ethics. I have not suggested that ethics is tied to *preparation for description* in the way Wittgenstein held mathematics to be. The suggestive analogy is rather this: for a sentence to be mathematical, or to be ethical, is for it to belong to the resources of the language in something like the way a word does. It follows that to see what the mathematicalness or ethicalness of a sentence is, you have to look at its application: there you see what kind of "linguistic instrument" it is. It is possible to speak of "responsibility to reality" in the case of linguistic resources, but what is meant by such responsibility is different from what it is in the case of ordinary experiential propositions: do the world, and our nature, make the resource in question one that we shall want or need? Another important part of the parallel is that, in ethics as in mathematics, the fact that our linguistic resources include *indicative sentences* can lead us into philosophical misunderstandings, because the sentences are understood on the model of experiential propositions.

## VIII

Sabina Lovibond's arguments for moral realism draw on Wittgenstein's arguments in several ways; I have considered only her principal argument. In this section I consider another argument of hers, used in support of a kind of moral intuitionism (and bearing thus on the question whether moral thought involves "description of reality"). She argues for a parallel between Wittgenstein's idea that we can *see* a person's grief or joy (and may not need to *infer* it from behavior) and the idea that we see moral properties of a situation – see, that is, with our eyes. The parallel makes it possible to have a kind of moral intuitionism that does not invoke supernatural moral entities knowable via some nonphysical sense. Being able to give a moral description of reality will then be nothing but being able to use one's ordinary senses together with mastery of moral concepts, just as the capacity to describe the feelings of those whom we see and hear may involve nothing beyond our eyes and ears, and our mastery of the relevant linguistic skills (see RIE, pp. 47–50). Wittgenstein claimed (Z, 223) that it was only philosophical prejudice that stops us recognizing that we see the glance of the eye; and Lovibond takes that remark to imply that it would correspondingly be only prejudice that led to a denial that we could see moral properties of situations.

There are cases in which we do use our eyes in applying moral concepts in roughly the way Lovibond suggests. Courage in a person's walk can literally be seen; and if you were not there to see it, you would not be in as good a position to judge as someone who was there (and similarly if you were there but your eyes were not as good as your neighbor's). That is, the sort of thing that can be said about seeing the glance of someone's eye can be said about seeing courage in someone's walk. But the courage of acting in a certain way (for example, of going back to Rome, knowing that one will be executed) is not the object of sight. You would not be better placed to judge the courage of such an act if you saw it; people who did not see it, and took it to be courageous, would not be making a sort of guess at what might be seen had they been present. Similarly with justice: to say that it would be unjust to do so-and-so is not to say what it will look like, and eyewitnesses are not usually the best judges of justice and injustice (as they are of whether someone's eyes flashed with anger). (Think of the games: if I say "His eyes flashed with anger," you may reply, "How do you know, you weren't even there!" But such a reply is not open to you if I say that the seizing of someone's land was a terrible injustice.) What is the matter with Lovibond's account is that it is appropriate only for a "narrowly circumscribed region" and not for the whole of what she was claiming to describe (see PI, 3). Here again what is necessary is to look at a range of different cases, to take into account the unforeseeable complicatedness of the language-game.

## IX

In the *Tractatus*, Wittgenstein rejected any realist or cognitivist view of ethics. Was the conception of language in the rest of the *Tractatus* the basis for rejecting such views? The answer *Yes* may reflect a general picture something like this. Some form of moral realism is what we would all accept, or take for granted, *unless* we were led away from it by some philosophical confusion capable of leading us to find fault with the indicative *form* of moral judgments (see RIE, p. 26) – confusion which would thus underlie a noncognitivist or antirealist theory of ethics. The *Tractatus* may then be understood in terms of that general picture: its rejection of realism about ethics rests on the philosophical confusion in its conception of language. The idea that Wittgenstein's later writings help to liberate us from such confusion may then seem to imply that those writings support a form of moral realism.

By appealing to Wittgenstein's writings on mathematics, I have tried to show that the question whether an indicative sentence is being used to describe what it is ostensibly about is, he thinks, something to be investigated in particular cases; the answer may be *No*. He is not "finding fault" with the indicative form of such sentences but pointing out that *indicative form* reveals nothing about the use of a sentence.[26] And so I am trying to undercut any idea that the *Tractatus* view of ethics is the mere result of philosophical confusion.

Sabina Lovibond mentions that realists and antirealists in ethics may be inclined to consider different portions of our moral vocabulary (RIE, pp. 14–15), but the differences that she has in mind are the differences between the use of terms like "courageous" (relatively "thick" moral concepts)[27] and that of terms like "wrong" and "duty"; the antirealist and the realist alike, as she describes them, focus on judgments expressed in indicative sentences with predicates that it is natural to think of as "moral." The very idea of "the moral vocabulary" is the idea of a particular group of nouns and adjectives; it expresses the hold on our minds, when we think philosophically about ethics, of bits of language having the form of *judgments*.[28] Wittgenstein asks what it would be like if people did arithmetic, but did not teach it in the form of *little sentences* (RFM, p. 93). We should ask similar questions about ethics. We do use little sentences with moral words in moral teaching, and big and little sentences with moral words in our moral thought; but the existence of these indicative sentences has had too great a fascination for us in moral philosophy. If we want to see what moral thinking is, we need to be able to look away from the case of "moral propositions," and to free ourselves from the idea that goes easily with exclusive focus on that case, of sentences as about moral subject matter through the presence in them of moral words.

I mean this to sound *not terribly far* from the *Tractatus* view of ethics. The *Tractatus* approach to ethics differs greatly from that of philosophical ethics: its starting point is the idea that "ethics" is not a term for a subject matter alongside other subjects, any more than "logic" is. The *Tractatus* argues that there is no need for logical propositions (TLP, 6.122). *Inference* has a place in our lives and thought simply through our being thinking beings, having a world; and the justification for our inferring as we do cannot be tied to laws of logic, taken to be specific judgments (sentences in which "*we* express what we wish with the help of signs," TLP, 6.124). We might say that *the* logical sign is the variable that gives the general form of all propositions, all thought (TLP, 5.47–5.472). Ethics comes from our having a world and a will;[29] and the sign that is, in a sense, "for" one's having a world, namely, the general form of proposition, of thought, can be taken to be the sign "for" the ethical. This brings out that ethics, like logic, is not a sphere in which we mean some kind of fact by using signs with this or that specific meaning. The comparison Wittgenstein makes between logic and ethics, in speaking of both as "transcendental" (TLP, 6.13, 6.421) has at its heart a contrast: between propositions with a specific subject matter, and logic/ethics, "symbolized," as it were, by the variable for *every* particular thing we might say, a variable none of whose values is a proposition with logical or ethical subject matter.[30] There is not, on this view, a "moral vocabulary," a vocabulary through which we mean moral things. If one wanted to give sense to "moral vocabulary" one might mean: vocabulary we use in saying things that might have application in moral life, but that excludes no words. Since the *Tractatus* might have such use (and was intended to), "variable," "Frege," and "Theory of Types" belong, in this sense, to "moral vocabulary."

Sabina Lovibond's conception of ethics puts in the center the learning of language-games in which we use specifically moral words, learning which begins by getting us to do with those words what in the game counts as correct. What we learn is a technique of classification using evaluative categories (see, e.g., RIE, p. 160). She allows that we, or some of us, may become alienated from the use of some of the moral words; the words may thus come to have a mere "inverted commas" use. Ethicalness is (on this picture) originally tied to the descriptive use of specific terms, but the ethicalness is not present in the derivative, alienated use. If we were to begin with the *Tractatus* conception of ethics, and try to remove from it what comes from *Tractatus* ideas about logical generality, we should get something very different. Ethicalness might be well exemplified by cases like the Simone Weil use of "I would not have been born, had my parents not happened to meet." Language-games in which we describe actions or institutions or people, using words like "just" or "unjust" (and so on) might *also* be thought of as belonging to what ethics is for us, but those language-games would not have the kind of central place in ethics that they have for Lovibond. And we should be able to imagine language-games, forms of ethical thinking, quite different from those important for us.

It would be a matter that needs investigating how exactly the *Tractatus* insight about ethics, that it is like logic or mathematics (or philosophy) in not being a subject alongside others, gets shaped by specifically *Tractatus* conceptions, for example, the conception of that through which a group of different symbols can all express the same sense or same kind of sense. That conception excludes any genuine variety within ethical thought. That is, if proposition 6 of the *Tractatus*, which gives the general form of proposition, can be central in the "ethicalness" of the *Tractatus* itself, although it uses no specifically moral terms, then the ethicalness of *no* proposition can depend on its use of specifically moral terms. The *Tractatus* conception of generality precludes our giving any account of ethics as a "family," in the sense of *Philosophical Investigations*, 67, any account of ethics as a "motley," in the sense of *Remarks on the Foundations of Mathematics* (p. 182).

The trouble with the *Tractatus* view of ethics is not that it treats the indicative form of ostensibly ethical sentences as misleading. The *Tractatus* looks for a general characterization of the ethical; it does not look at the real variety of cases. The *Tractatus* approach to ethics is shaped by a general conception of language; in that respect it resembles Sabina Lovibond's. She is closer to the *Tractatus* than she recognizes. The moral, if there is a moral, is that what we need to learn from Wittgenstein's later philosophy is not "the right view of language" but rather: how hard it is to look.[31]

### APPENDIX

In support of her reading of Wittgenstein as a kind of philosophical realist, Sabina Lovibond appeals to his remark, "Not empiricism and yet realism in philosophy, that is the hardest thing."[32] Any interpretation of that remark must explain in what sense Wittgenstein took empiricism to be a form of (or attempt at) realism, must explain why he says "Not empiricism and *yet* realism." Lovibond recognizes the need for such an explanation, and ascribes to Wittgenstein an understanding of empiricism as involving an "absolutist" foundational epistemology, serving as a basis for what he thought of as a form of philosophical realism, a form which he himself rejected (see RIE, p. 45). But there are problems with the idea that he conceived empiricism or realism in the way she suggests. To think of them that way requires an extension of the philosophical meaning of "realism" so that it can include some forms of empiricist reductionism, an extension invented and argued for by Michael Dummett. Dummett's interest was in distinguishing between two different issues: "whether statements of one kind could in any sense be reduced to statements of another kind, and whether statements of the one kind could be held to be determinately either true or false";[33] he did not think it was important whether "realism" was used for one side of the first issue or one side of the second, but subsequent philosophical discussion, including Lovibond's, has tended to accept his use of the term in formulating the second issue, thus making it possible to describe some forms of reductionism as also forms of realism.

The possibility of an interpretation like Lovibond's of Wittgenstein's remark about empiricism and realism depends on taking Wittgenstein to have been using the word "realism" in something like Dummett's way. Dummett himself, in recommending the shift in usage which allows some forms of reductionism to count as philosophical realism, is clearly aware of it as an innovation, and explains in detail how his usage is related to traditional philosophical uses of "realism." His thought about how the philosophical issues could best be classified took years to develop. A version of his innovative reclassification is presented in "Realism" in 1963, but that version does not actually go so far as to allow the treatment of forms of reductionism as cases of realism; we find that further development in 1969.[34] The classification of any reductionism as a form of philosophical realism would have appeared very odd or even unintelligible prior to Dummett's discussions. It requires some argument, then, to show of *any* philosopher prior to 1960 that he should be taken to have used the word "realism" in such a way that reductionism could count as a form of philosophical realism.

To return to Wittgenstein and "Not empiricism and yet realism." "Empiricism" here means the kind of empiricist reductionism with which Wittgenstein was particularly concerned (e.g., the interpretation of arithmetical propositions as about experiments, the interpretation of sensation-language as reducible to behavior); and such reductionism, far from being seen by Wittgenstein as a kind of philosophical realism, is frequently contrasted with it in his later writings. He does not anticipate a Dummettian use of "realism"; when he speaks of realism, he does not construe it, as Lovibond takes him to, in terms of *language describing reality* (as opposed to merely appearing to do so), in terms of there being a robust conception of truth for sentences of some philosophically disputed subject matter. Rather, philosophical realism is taken by Wittgenstein to be tied to the idea that our language reaches to things *beyond what is given in experience* (so it contrasts with forms of empiricism including empiricist idealism and solipsism); and Wittgenstein repeatedly asserts, of both philosophical realism and the rejections of it by idealists and solipsists, that they share underlying philosophical confusions about the nature of the issue between them. Both sides take there to be a question whether our ways of speaking are or are not metaphysically in order, one side attacking the ways of speaking, and the other side defending them "as if they were stating facts recognized by every reasonable human being" (PI, 402). Lovibond's use of "realism" in the philosophical sense, which follows Dummett in freeing the term from its ties to the issue of reduction to what is "in experience," and which allows empiricist reductionism to count as a form of philosophical realism, is anachronistic when read into Wittgenstein. But unless it is read into Wittgenstein, Lovibond's appeal to "Not empiricism and yet realism" in support of her reading of Wittgenstein as a kind of philosophical realist opposing an empiricist type of philosophical realism collapses.

A question then remains how Wittgenstein's remark *can* be understood. The only way to do so, I think, is to see it as not about realism in any of its specifically philosophical senses. I have argued (in "Realism and the Realistic Spirit") that it belongs to a group of remarks (in RFM, VI and RFM, III) criticizing the idea that, in order to be realistic in philosophy, in order to avoid "obscurantism," "moonshine," about mathematics (or about sensations, physical objects, etc.), we must go in for a reduction of the problematic subject matter to the empirical. Wittgenstein is suggesting that what is difficult in philosophy is to be realistic without going in for such reduction.[35] Lovibond ignores the important clue to the meaning of Wittgenstein's remark provided by the two words following it: "(Against Ramsey)." Wittgenstein rejected Ramsey's understanding of how the *usefulness* of logic could be explained. For Ramsey such usefulness indicated that logical rules were *experiential* in character;[36] and Ramsey's account thus links empiricism with the need for "a human logic," a logic that, without losing its normative character, attends to human practices and modes of investigation – the need for what might be called "realism" about logic. Wittgenstein's point is that empiricism does not meet that real need.

NOTES

1 See Cora Diamond, "Ludwig Wittgenstein" (*Encyclopedia of Ethics*, ed. Lawrence C. Becker [New York: Garland Publishing, 1992], pp. 1319–22) for a brief account of ethics in Wittgenstein's writings, and Cora Diamond, "Wittgensteinian Ethics" (ibid., pp. 1322–4), for a discussion of how moral philosophers have drawn on Wittgenstein.

2  *Realism and Imagination in Ethics* (Oxford: Blackwell, 1983). I refer to
the book as RIE.

3  See *Realism and the Realistic Spirit* (Cambridge, Mass.: Bradford Books,
MIT Press, 1991), Introduction II ("Wittgenstein and Metaphysics"), esp.
pp. 14–22, "Wright's Wittgenstein," esp. pp. 209–14, and "The Face of
Necessity," pp. 243–66; also Cora Diamond, "¿Qué tan viejos son estos
huesos? Putnam, Wittgenstein y la verificación," in *Diánoia* 38 (1992),
pp. 115–42. On these issues see also Hilary Putnam, *Realism with a
Human Face* (Cambridge, Mass.: Harvard University Press, 1990), p. 20.

4  Her use of the term "empiricist" is meant to be "loose." *How* loose is
not clear. That is, Lovibond explicitly ascribes to the Wittgenstein of the
*Tractatus* one of the main features of the "empiricist" view, and she may
mean to imply that it has at least some of the other features. She does
not explicitly discuss how far the contrast she is centrally concerned
with, between the "empiricist" view and an "expressivist" view exemplified by Wittgenstein's later thought, can be identified with the contrast between Wittgenstein's own earlier and later views. At p. 30, she
identifies the view of language criticized in the opening sections of *Philosophical Investigations* as a version of the empiricist view.

5  RIE, analytical table of contents, unnumbered page.

6  See Edward Minar, "Feeling at Home in Language (What Makes Reading *Philosophical Investigations* Possible?)," *Synthese* 102 (1995), pp.
413–52.

7  LFM, p. 239; see Hardy, "Mathematical Proof," *Mind* 38 (1929), p. 18.

8  There is another important discussion of the difference between developing means of description, on the one hand, and, on the other, describing
(using the means of description which we have) in Lecture VI (LFM, pp.
58–61). "He did the calculation in the same way I did the earlier one"
may describe what he did, if what counts as *doing it the same way* is
settled. But, if you say to a pupil, with both calculations, yours and his,
in front of him, "*This* is not doing the calculation in the same way as
*this*," you are not describing the calculation but showing him a part of
the use of the expression "the same way." An insistence that moral
propositions *describe* can lead to our ignoring comparable differences in
their use.

9  See E. J. Craig, "The Problem of Necessary Truth," in S. Blackburn, ed.,
*Meaning, Reference and Necessity* (Cambridge University Press, 1975),
pp. 1–31, for a criticism of this view, and Crispin Wright, *Wittgenstein
on the Foundations of Mathematics* (London: Duckworth, 1980), ch. 22,
for a full discussion of what Craig's argument shows.

10  See, for example, Lovibond's appeal to *On Certainty*, RIE, p. 59.

11  That §§318–21 of *On Certainty* in fact go against Lovibond's reading of

Wittgenstein (by making clear his view that we cannot tell the function of a sentence from the sentence itself) was pointed out to me by James Conant. He has also noted that the un-Quinean character of *On Certainty* goes against Lovibond's attempts to see parallels between Quine and Wittgenstein, but that raises issues which I cannot go into.

12  There is in any case an unclarity in Lovibond's argument. When she speaks of our having or lacking a predicate of some type, does she mean by there being a predicate there being a single word? In English we can certainly predicate of a person that he or she enjoys embarrassing people about their deformities (for example), but there is no single word (or fixed phrase) for that property (call it $p$). It is not clear whether the connection she asserts between not having a predicate and not caring about the distribution of a property is supposed to have as its first term not having a word for the property, or lacking the capacity to express the property. The capacity to express property $p$ using words of our language reflects our interest in psychological description, but we might have that capacity despite not caring about $p$; and the incapacity to express $p$ by a single word does not show a lack of interest in its distribution.

13  For a further example, different again from any I discuss here, see Cora Diamond, "Martha Nussbaum and the Need for Novels," *Philosophical Investigations* 16 (1993), pp. 128–53. Part 5 of that essay is about the linguistic means through which our sense of particularity – the particularity of this person, or of this animal – gets expressed.

14  *The Long Winter* (New York and London: Harper and Brothers, 1940).

15  Primo Levi, *"If This Is a Man" and "The Truce"* (Harmondsworth: Penguin, 1979); John Prebble, *The Highland Clearances* (Harmondsworth: Penguin, 1969).

16  Another example that stays in my mind is Kathy Wilkes's account of the Serbian attack on Dubrovnik, "Lead upon Gold," in *Oxford Today* 5, 1 (Michaelmas 1992), pp. 23–5, reprinted from *Oxford Magazine*, Second Week, Trinity Term 1992. Writing could hardly be informed by greater moral urgency, yet there is virtually no use of specifically moral words.

17  "The Politics of Quotation in *To the Lighthouse*: Mrs. Woolf Resites Mr. Tennyson and Mr. Cowper," *Literature and Psychology* 31 (1995), pp. 22–43.

18  G. E. M. Anscombe, *An Introduction to Wittgenstein's Tractatus* (London: Hutchinson, 1963), p. 170.

19  Norman Malcolm, *Ludwig Wittgenstein: A Memoir* (Oxford: Oxford University Press, 1984), pp. 95–9. I am grateful to James Conant for the reference to the letters to Malcolm, and for pointing out the continuity in Wittgenstein's views about *Hadji Murad*. Wittgenstein's admiration for *Hadji Murad* can be seen as early as 1912, in a letter to Russell

(Wittgenstein, *Letters to Russell, Keynes and Moore*, ed. G. H. von Wright [Oxford: Blackwell, 1974], p. 16).

20 "Chance," in *Simone Weil: An Anthology*, ed. S. Miles (New York: Weidenfeld and Nicolson, 1986), pp. 277–8.

21 Weil also mentions meditation on death as something that can be salutary in the same way as meditation on chance, i.e., as something that can penetrate one's conception of oneself in relation to other people and the world, and can thus be tied to love. The implicit moral psychology has parallels to that of Dickens in (e.g.) *A Christmas Carol*.

22 "The Envoy of Mr. Cogito," in Z. Herbert, *Selected Poems* (Oxford, London, New York: Oxford University Press, 1977), pp. 79–80.

23 See Iris Murdoch on the uses of stories and "sustaining concepts," "Vision and Choice in Morality," in *Proceedings of the Aristotelian Society*, supp. vol. 30 (1956), pp. 32–58, at pp. 50–1.

24 See, e.g., Wittgenstein's letter (some time during autumn 1919) to Ludwig von Ficker: "the point of the book is ethical" ("der Sinn des Buches ist ein Ethischer"); the letter is reproduced in G. H. von Wright, "Historical Introduction," in Ludwig Wittgenstein, *Prototractatus*, ed. B. F. McGuinness et al. (London: Routledge and Kegan Paul, 1971), pp. 15–16.

25 Similarly, the book takes itself to be philosophical not in virtue of its content but in virtue of the use that is made of it. When Wittgenstein says (TLP, 4.112) that a "philosophical work" consists essentially of elucidations, the range of meanings in "work" (in "*Werk*") is important: philosophical activity, work, consists of the use of propositions as a means to logical clarification; a philosophical work – a work, a book, considered as philosophical – consists of propositions conceived as instruments for the work, the undertaking, the performance, of philosophy. On the sense in which the *Tractatus* is a work with an ethical point, and its relation to the issue of ethics as a subject matter, see James Conant, "Throwing Away the Top of the Ladder," *Yale Review* 79 (1990), pp. 328–64, esp. p. 352.

26 Compare his remark, "To say that a sentence which has the form of information has a use, is not yet to say anything about the *kind* of use it has" (LWII, p. 78). For an interesting connection with the problems raised by Saul Kripke's discussion of Wittgenstein, see Norton Batkin, "On Wittgenstein and Kripke: Mastering Language in Wittgenstein's *Philosophical Investigations*," in Ted Cohen, Paul Guyer, and Hilary Putnam, eds., *Pursuits of Reason: Essays in Honor of Stanley Cavell* (Lubbock: Texas Tech University Press, 1993), pp. 241–62, esp. pp. 251–2.

27 See Bernard Williams, *Ethics and the Limits of Morality* (Cambridge, Mass.: Harvard University Press, 1985), p. 129.

28 But cf. RIE, p. 22, where Lovibond describes noncognitivist theories in a

different way: as not emphasizing any specific vocabulary. The focus, however, is still on judgments. In any case, most noncognitivist theories do attach special significance to "moral vocabulary"; see, for example, R. M. Hare, *Moral Thinking* (Oxford: Clarendon Press, 1981), pp. 3–4, and Hare, *The Language of Morals* (Oxford: Clarendon Press, 1961), pp. v, 1–3, as well as the title itself. See Cora Diamond, "Moral Differences and Distances: Some Questions," in Lilli Alanen, Sara Heinämaa, and Thomas Wallgren, eds., *Commonality and Particularity in Ethics* (Basingstoke, Hampshire: Macmillan, 1997) for further discussion of how the exclusive focus, within moral philosophy, on judgments leads to the omission of some important kinds of moral thought.

29 There is a problem in my formulation. The capacity to will this or that particular thing is not the source of ethics; "will" in the sense in which it is relevant to ethics is the capacity to respond ethically to the world and life. So it is not an explanation of any sort to say that ethics arises from the fact that we are beings who have a world and a will. It is equally uninformative to say, as I did, that inference has a place in our lives through our being thinking beings, having a world.

30 I have discussed the use of "transcendental" in the *Tractatus* in "Ethics, Imagination and the Method of Wittgenstein's *Tractatus*," in *Bilder der Philosophie*, ed. R. Heinrich and H. Vetter, *Wiener Reihe* 5 (1991), pp. 55–90, at pp. 84–5.

31 James Conant and A. D. Woozley gave me extremely helpful comments on earlier versions of this essay. I want also to thank Garry Dobbins, David Stern, and Hans Sluga for their suggestions.

32 Wittgenstein, RFM, VI-23, discussed in RIE, §11, also pp. 148, 207.

33 *Truth and Other Enigmas* (Cambridge, Mass.: Harvard University Press, 1978), pp. xxxi–xxxii; cf. also pp. 359–60.

34 "Realism" (1963), in *Truth and Other Enigmas*, pp. 145–65; "The Reality of the Past" (1969), in *Truth and Other Enigmas*, pp. 358–74.

35 See Diamond, *The Realistic Spirit*, pp. 39–72.

36 "Truth and Probability," in F. P. Ramsey, *The Foundations of Mathematics and Other Logical Essays* (Totowa, N.J.: Littlefield, Adams, 1965), pp. 190–8.

# 8 Notes and afterthoughts on the opening of Wittgenstein's *Investigations*[1]

The notes to follow formed the basis of the first weeks of a lecture course on *Philosophical Investigations* initially given at Berkeley in 1960, then irregularly at Harvard and progressively amplified some half dozen times through the 1960s and 1970s. The last of such lectures, offered in 1984, was radically altered since by then my *Claim of Reason* had appeared. I would not have thought to present these notes without entering into a sort of uneven, late conversation with them, preceding, interrupting, and succeeding them with certain afterthoughts a decade after they were used in a classroom. Why this presentation was made in 1991, and to what purpose, will emerge. The lecture notes appear in italic type, the afterthoughts in upright. Of course – it is more or less the point of the enterprise – I begin with afterthoughts.

The clearest unchanging feature of the course over the decades was the opening question: How does the *Investigations* begin? Against even the brief, varying introductory remarks I would provide – all omitted here – concerning Wittgenstein's life and his place in twentieth-century philosophy, in which I emphasized the remarkable look and sound of Wittgenstein's text and related this to issues of modernism in the major arts, the opening question was meant to invoke the question: How does philosophy begin? And how does the *Investigations* account for its beginning (hence philosophy's) as it does? And since this is supposed to be a work of philosophy (but how do we tell this?), how does it (and must it? but can it?) account for its look and sound?

A number of reasons move me to make the notes public.

(1) There is still, I believe, no canonical way of teaching the *Investigations* (unless beginning with the *Tractatus* and contrasting the *Investigations* with it counts as such a way), and young teachers have expressed to me their greatest dissatisfaction with their own teaching of it precisely over the opening weeks; typically, it seems to me, because they are unsure that when they step back from Wittgenstein's text they are doing justice to their sense of the particularity of that text. (To give some account of what has been called its "fervor," sensed as something like its moral drive, is among the motives of my "Declining Decline," in *This New Yet Unapproachable America*.) Some who attended my lectures, and others who know of them, have suggested that their publication might accordingly be of pedagogical help.

(2) I had thought that these lectures would provide a beginning for what became *The Claim of Reason*, but I did not manage in preparing a final version of that manuscript to get them to motivate its present opening – with its focus on criteria, leading straight to the issue of the role of skepticism in the *Investigations* – well enough to justify their significant lengthening of an already lengthy book. I think I may be able to do better this time around. What's left of these opening lectures in *The Claim of Reason*, or epitomized there, is its paragraph-length opening sentence.

(3) Because these lectures began as I was publishing my first two papers (the first two of what became *Must We Mean What We Say?*); and, as will emerge here, because the subject of beginnings is immediately on my mind as I have turned to work on certain autobiographical materials; and because the precipitating stimulus for making these notes presentable was to distribute them to the members of the seminar I offered at the School of Criticism and Theory at Dartmouth in the summer of 1991, where the members varied in culture, in field, and in age, so that the common thread through the range of work I asked them to think about was the fact of its running through the work I do; I allowed myself, as these notes proceeded, to locate various crossroads as they come in view in the intellectual geography implied by texts I had published, or was preparing to publish, sometimes quoting bits of them when they seemed to me both clarifying and to exist in a fuller, or stranger, or more familiar, context that one or another reader might one or another day wish to explore.

(4) There is an independent reason for wanting a readable statement of this material. Whatever its shortcomings in placing the opening of *The Claim of Reason*, it will help me place a recent turn in my thinking about the state of the child "learning" language, as presented in Augustine's portrait of (that is, his literary–philosophical remembering of himself as) such a child, which Wittgenstein uses to open his own book (his "album," he calls it) of literary–philosophical reminders. This recent turn, which was a significant feature of the greatly modified 1984 lectures, is sketched at the end of my consideration (in chapter 2 of *Conditions Handsome and Unhandsome*) of Kripke's *Wittgenstein on Rules and Private Language*. This will come up in good time, when its possible value can be more readily assessed.

Since preserving the individual strata of the versions from 1960 to 1979 is of no interest to me here, and since the process of revision was a normal part of preparing successive versions, I mostly assume that the later are the better ones and mostly just give those. I have made a conscious effort to leave the wording of the notes (except for filling in their telegraphese) as it is. When I was moved to intervene in the moment of transcription (mostly the spring of 1991), this is indicated, if the fact is not sufficiently obvious from the context, by reverting from italic to regular type.

I

*How does* Philosophical Investigations *begin? There are many answers, or directions of answer.*

*One might say, uncontroversially: It begins with some words of someone else. But why say this? Perhaps to suggest that Wittgenstein (but what or who Wittgenstein is is, of course, not determined), is not led to philosophical reflection from his own voice (or what might be recognized, right off, as his own voice), but from, as it were, being* accosted. *The accosting is by someone Wittgenstein cares about and has to take seriously; in particular, it is by such a one speaking about his childhood, so in words of memory, and more particularly, about his first memory of words, say of first acquiring them.*

*Let's have a translation of Augustine's words before us:*

When they (my elders) named some object, and accordingly moved towards something, I saw this and I grasped that the thing was called by the sound they uttered when they meant to point it out. Their intention was shown by their bodily movements, as it were the natural language of all people: the expression of the face, the play of the eyes, the movement of other parts of the body, and the tone of voice which expresses our state of mind in seeking, having, rejecting, or avoiding something. Thus, as I heard words repeatedly used in their proper places in various sentences, I gradually learnt to understand what objects they signified; and after I had trained my mouth to form these signs, I used them to express my own desires.

*The assertions of Augustine's memories are not, rhetorically, accosting, or insisting, as, say, Socrates's interlocutors are in stopping him on the street with their accostive certainties. On the contrary, we need not see at once anything to stop or to puzzle a philosopher, anything he might be finding remarkable about Augustine's words. I note that I had read Augustine's* Confessions *before reading* Philosophical Investigations, *and I remember wondering, philosophically as it were, over his passages concerning time, but not over his passages concerning the acquisition of language. So if there is something disturbing or remarkable about those words, then I am prepared to find that that is itself a remarkable fact about them. As if to suggest: one does not know, in advance, where philosophy might begin, when one's mind may be stopped, to think.*

*Put otherwise: To open this book philosophically is to feel that a mind has paused* here – *which no doubt already suggests a certain kind of mind, or a mind in certain straits. Wittgenstein has* come back *here. Why? If we are stopped to philosophize by* these *words, then what words are immune to philosophical question?*

*Suppose you are not struck by the sheer (unremarkably) remarkable fact that Wittgenstein has set down Augustine's passage to begin with – in order, so to speak, to begin by not asserting anything. I have later come to speak of this theme – sometimes I think of it as the theme of philosophical silence, anyway of philosophical unassertiveness, or powerlessness – by saying that the first virtue of philosophy, or its peculiar virtue, is that of responsiveness, awake when all the others have fallen asleep. You might in that case find that the book begins with any one of several remarkable things Wittgenstein says about Augustine's passage.*

*He says, for example, that the passage "gives a particular picture of the essence of human language." This doesn't seem obviously true. How does Wittgenstein know this? And if it does give such a picture, what is wrong with that? Is the picture wrong? Is giving a picture a wrong thing to do? Is picturing an essence wrong? Or wrong in picturing language? Or is it the wrong essence?*

*Again, Wittgenstein will speak of Augustine's description as containing a "philosophical concept of meaning" (PI, 2). Yet Augustine's words seem ordinary enough. They are arch and over-precise maybe, even pedantic. Why does Wittgenstein say "philosophical"?*

*Wittgenstein records other responses he has to Augustine's words, but what interests me already is what Wittgenstein does* not *say about that passage, having singled it out as philosophically remarkable. He does not say, for example, that it is false, or that there is insufficient evidence for it, or that it contradicts something else Augustine says elsewhere, or that it is unclear, or that it contains an invalid argument. These are familiar terms of criticism in philosophy; and they are strong ones. If any of them does fit a statement, then that statement has been severely and importantly chastised.* This paragraph is specifically dated by its having been taken up, marked especially by its idea of "terms of criticism," as footnote 13 of "The Availability of Wittgenstein's Later Philosophy," first published in 1962, and collected as the second essay of *Must We Mean What We Say?*

*One of Wittgenstein's first responses to Augustine's passage had been to say, "If you describe the learning of language in this way you are, I believe, thinking primarily of nouns like 'table,' 'chair,' 'bread,' and of people's names, and only secondarily of the names of certain actions and properties; and of the remaining kinds of word as something that will take care of itself" (PI, 1). So one might think that Wittgenstein will criticize the passage as (i.e., that he will use such terms of criticism as) (1) incomplete, though all right as far as it goes, or (2) a faulty generalization. He does not, and it is important that he does not. The avoidance of the obvious here suggests that it is not philosophically clear beforehand what is wrong with Augustine's assertions and that Wittgenstein will not falsify his sense of finding words astray by resorting to an anxiously impatient explanation. To see the intellectual danger, or say emptiness, in imposing a judgment of error (as if the human forms of fallacy, or fallibility, have been well noticed and logged), let's see what is astray in using here either of the expected terms of criticism (i.e., either "incomplete," or "faulty generalization").*

*About (1). Augustine's description, it emerges, is not "all right as far as it goes," even about nouns and proper names. It contains assumptions or pictures about teaching, learning, pointing, naming – say these are modes of establishing a "connection" between language and the world – which prove to be empty, that is, which give us the illusion of providing explanations. Moreover, to the extent that we lack a good idea of what a "complete description" of the learning of a language would be, to the extent we lack a good idea of what we are saying if we criticize a description as "incomplete." Wittgenstein goes on, in PI, 2, to ask us to "conceive" a set of four spoken words as "a complete primitive language." We will come back to this request, to what it may mean to enter it.*

*About (2). What does "faulty generalization" say? Where does it fit? Take these cases:*

   *a) Having drawn five red marbles from a bag of marbles you say, "The marbles in this bag are red."*
   *b) "Courses in physics are harder than courses in philosophy."*
   *c) "I like European films better than Hollywood films."*

*About a) Suppose the next marble is green. Then it may be said to you: "See. One is green. You're wrong." You might defend yourself by saying: "I thought, could have sworn, that the marbles were all the same color. They were the same in the other bags I opened." That could just be the end of the matter. You accept it as clear that you are wrong, and clear what you are wrong about. And, if you offer an explanation, it is to make clear why you are wrong, even how you could have been wrong about something you were so confident of. Or you might take a different line, and in instead of admitting wrong and giving an excuse or explanation, defend your original claim, or something close to it: "Well, one or two might not be red. It's still right to call this a bag of red marbles, and to sell it as such." Again this could be the end of the matter.*

*About b) Suppose someone objects: "Physics 3 is certainly not harder than Philosophy 287." You may reply: "That's not what I mean. Those courses aren't comparable. I had in mind characteristic courses like Physics 106, which is harder than most middle group philosophy courses." Which amounts to saying something like: "Of course, but on the whole they're harder." Here you are accounting for your "wrongness" as a lack of explicitness. Your statement was abbreviated. Perhaps you should have been more explicit. But what you* meant *was right.*

About c) *Someone objects: "But you hated* My Hitler *and I know you love* Citizen Kane." *To which an acceptable (accommodating) defense might be: "True. But I wasn't thinking of such cases; they are exceptions. As a rule I do enjoy European films more."*

*If these are characteristic examples of accusations against general- izations, and of certain excuses or defenses against the accusations, then if Augustine is guilty of faulty generalization, these accusations and defenses should apply to his remarks. Do they? Could Augustine accommodate Wittgenstein's worries by, as it were, saying:*

> *a' [as in the case of the marbles]: "I thought, could have sworn, that all words were uniformly taught."*
>
> *or b' [as in the case of the courses]: "I didn't mean what I said to apply to each and every word. Words like "today," "but," "perhaps," aren't comparable to words like "table," "bread," and so on. On the whole, however, what I said was true."*
>
> *or c' [as in the case of the movies]: "I wasn't thinking of such words. They are exceptional. As a rule, however, . . . "*

*These defenses don't seem so satisfying now. They do not bring the matter to a close. "Bring to a close" means: With straightfor- ward (empirical) generalizations, the defenses explain how the mis- take or the odd case is to be accommodated, explained. But, ap- plied to the case of Augustine's statements, these defenses either make no obvious sense and strike us as false or faked ("I thought all words were taught uniformly" – granted that you had ever given a thought to the matter of how all words are taught, it is hard to imagine that you had ever thought that); or they make claims which we wouldn't know how to substantiate ("aren't comparable" – how are they not comparable?); or we don't know what weight to attach to them (are the other words "excep- tional"?). So: if Augustine is in error, has erred, if something he says has wandered off the mark, is inappropriate, we don't know how he can be, how it can have, what might explain it.*

*This is a more important matter than may at once appear. It* suggests that we may at any time – nothing seems special about the matter of false generalization, saying more than you quite know – be speaking without knowing what our words mean, what their meaning anything depends upon, speaking, as it were, in emptiness. For me an intellectual abyss gives a glimpse of itself here, causes an opening before which the philosophical conscience should draw back, stop.

Different philosophers have given different lines of explanation for falsehood or error or intellectual grief, depending on what they have taken philosophical assertions and errors or griefs to be. For example, Bacon's Idols find the mind variously faced with prejudices and fanaticisms. Locke was less interested in mapping the specific, local, shortcomings of the human intellect than in humbling it, speaking of clearing it of rubbish. Kant seems to have been the first to make the diagnosis of reason's failures an internal feature of tracking reason's powers, developing terms of criticism of intellectual arrogance that show reason to be subject to "dialectical illusion." (Each of these theories of intellectual grief bear comparison with Plato's account of the human subjection to illusion by his construction of the Myth of the Cave.) Wittgenstein is radically Kantian in this regard, but his terms of criticism are, as they must be, specific to his mode of philosophizing.

Look for a moment at his first response to Augustine's passage, that it gives us "a particular picture" of the essence of human language. We shall return to this term of criticism many times. Here its implication is: What Augustine says (or is remembering about his learning to speak) is not just inappropriate; it is also appropriate, but to something else (something more limited, or more specific) than Augustine realized. In PI, 3 Wittgenstein puts a response this way: "Augustine, we might say, does describe a system of communication, but not everything we call language is this system." That is not a very clear remark, but it is clear enough to show that it would not even seem to be a comprehensible explanation of the faultiness of a faulty empirical generalization: Suppose for the case of the red marbles we had said: "What you say, in saying the bag is of red marbles, is true of the red marbles in it, for example, true of the five red marbles you have taken from it; but it is not true of the marbles in the bag that are not what we call red; and there are some." This form of explanation, in this context, is, if serious, empty; but if, as *likelier, it is parodistic, it rudely implies that what the other has said is empty.*

*Why is it illuminating, if it is, to say to what it is that Augustine's descriptions are appropriate? Well, obviously, to know the source of appropriateness would be to know how we can have passed it by; how, we might say, its remarkableness, its motivatedness, has been disguised. (This is the role, in other modes of thinking, that a theory of "ideology" is to play. It is a feature of the importance of Freud's discovery of phantasy.) Wittgenstein portrays the disguised remarkableness by noting the presence in Augustine's passage of (1) what Wittgenstein calls a particular way of conceiving language; and, moreover, (2) a way which it is natural or tempting to conceive of it when we are philosophizing about it (writing our Confessions? remembering something? – is it necessary to suppose Augustine is writing about events in his life that he is actually remembering?).*

Before going on to comment on each of these points in Wittgenstein's diagnosis, I pause to mark one feature of our progress so far. We began the discussion of the opening of the *Investigations* by asking why Wittgenstein had quoted – brought himself to stop before – certain words of a certain saint. And we were asking how it was that we (he, before the day he stopped) could have passed over those words.

This pair of questions, or rather this double question, has marked my insistence, since the versions of this material in the early 1970s, on the existence of two principal and conflicting ways Wittgenstein shows of taking Augustine's words: either as – as I said earlier – remarkable or as unremarkable. Wittgenstein characteristically says: as philosophical (or metaphysical) or as ordinary. Hume, in the concluding section of Part I of his *Treatise of Human Nature,* speaks of the philosophical (or "refined reasoning") as the *"intense* view of [the] manifold contradictions and imperfections in human reason," and contrasts the intense view with what we may, on his behalf, call the natural or sociable view. These views differ, among other ways, as malady and melancholy differ from cure and merriment. The radical differences between Hume and Wittgenstein on this point are, first, that Hume does not, apparently, find that the philosophical view requires, or allows, a philosophical account; and (or because), second, Hume does not doubt that the intense view is not inferior (intellectually, if not morally) to the natural or sociable view. While both Hume and Wittgenstein see philosophy as an unsociable activity (like most – mostly male? – philosophers; Austin is an exception important to me), Wittgenstein is essentially more distrustful of *this* way of being unsociable. I imagine this is in part a function of the differences between writing half a century before the French Revolution and writing a century and a half after it, when "everyone and no one" as Nietzsche puts it, or "all and sundry" as Emerson had put it, arrogate to themselves the cloak of philosophy – Presidents and Secretaries and Professors of This and That. No wonder professors of philosophy are happier with themselves when they can rely in philosophizing on their technical accomplishments. Part of the discomfort, as well as part of the elation (both are to be distrusted), in reading Wittgenstein is his refusal of, even apparent contempt for, this intellectual reliance, technical or institutional. (This is surely related to Emerson's preaching of Self-Reliance, also part of the discomfort and elation in reading him. Both responses are to be distrusted in his case as well. Both writers, in their relation to, let's say, the systematic, have had good effects and bad. This is, so far, hardly unusual.) It is, I believe, sometimes inferred from philosophy's unsociability that philosophy is inherently, if not quite inveterately, undemocratic. It is a way of putting the motivation of my *Conditions Handsome and Unhandsome* to say that it is meant to make that inference unattractive.

To anticipate further than these notes will reach: Wittgenstein's *Investigations* is designed to show that (what I call) the voices of melancholy and merriment, or of metaphysics and the ordinary (or, as in my "Availability of Wittgenstein's Later Philosophy," the voices of temptation and correctness), are caused by one another, and form an argument that is not to be decided but is to be dismantled. These various characterizations of the voices paired in philosophical argument are not to be dismissed as "merely literary" variations, amounting intellectually or philosophically to the same thing. They are meant to cite the need for an investigation of the voices, even to mark the beginnings of such an investigation.

In my lecture on Kripke's *Wittgenstein on Rules and Private Language* (chapter 2 of my *Conditions Handsome and Unhandsome*), I say of such paired or locked voices that they are engaged in the argument of the ordinary. To bring this juncture of my thinking about up to date (or to 1988), and to indicate where I have (I trust) taken the matter further, and ask that it be taken further still, I quote a pertinent passage from that chapter:

The altercation over two ways [of taking the Augustine passage] may sound as follows: One observes, "What could be less remarkable than Augustine's remark about his elders moving around and uttering sounds?" Another retorts [intensely, let us now add], "Less remarkable – when we are in a maze of unanswered questions about what *naming* is, what it *is* to call a thing or a person, what constitutes an *object*, *how* we (with certainty) grasp one idea or image or concept rather than another, what makes a pointer *point*, a talker *mean!*" Nothing is wrong; everything is wrong. It is the philosophical moment. (*Conditions Handsome and Unhandsome*, p. 98)

I will want to come back to this passage.

*Go back to what I presented as Wittgenstein's double way of accounting for the disguised remarkableness in Augustine's passage – that it (1) contains a particular idea of language which (2) seems natural in the act of philosophizing.*

*About (1). "A particular idea of something" is, in Wittgenstein's way of speaking, as much as to say, a particular "picture" of the thing. A point of speaking this way is that it makes me recognize that the idea or picture is* mine, *a responsibility of mine to be responsive to, a piece of my life that is, whether natural or violent, not inevitable, a contingency of having something as constraining (a freighted term of Kant's) as a human life, a life constrained to make itself intelligible (to itself), to find itself in words.* The excited prose of the preceding sentence indicates, I think, the mounting sense of the number of paths leading off from the topics I'm touching upon, here in particular the idea of the human as a life form among others, as described in an essay of mine ("Declining Decline," mentioned earlier) on Wittgenstein as a philosopher of culture. I might say: In noticing distortion in my language I feel thrown back upon myself – except that I am simultaneously thrown forward upon the particular objects I am thinking about, and the particular words in which I found myself thinking about them.

*About (2). Philosophy, on such a view of the process as Wittgenstein's, has no facts of its own. Its medium – along with detecting the emptiness of assertion – lies in demonstrating, or say showing, the obvious. This bears comparison, at some stage, with Heidegger's characterization, scrupulous to the point of the comic, of "phenome-*

nology" early in Being and Time *(p. 58)*: *"to let that which shows itself be seen from itself in the very way in which it shows itself from itself."* Then the question is unavoidable: How can the obvious not be obvious? What is the hardness of seeing the obvious? This must bear on what the hardness of philosophizing is – a hardness itself made obvious in the Investigations' shunning of the technical, one way of stating Wittgenstein's demand upon the ordinary. Whereas other philosophers, on the contrary, find that the technical is indispensable precisely for arriving at the obvious. Is this a conflict about what "obvious" means? (Mathematicians favor the word "obvious." Wittgenstein's rather competing term is "perspicuous." This is an aside for those who are way ahead of us here.) It is, in any case, a philosophical conflict, not to be settled by taking sides. (Thereby hangs another tale, starts another path. For the moment I ask what causes the sensory privileging in the idea of the philosophically hard as "seeing the obvious." When Thoreau is minded to note our philosophical falling off, he sometimes calls us hard of hearing. This fits moments in Wittgenstein at least as accurately as the idea of a difficulty in seeing does. Why don't we say – why do we have no concept of – being hard of seeing?)

All this will come back. Let's for now go on to ask how Wittgenstein concretely constructs the picture whose presence in Augustine's passage he finds to account for our passing it by as natural, unremarkable. This task begins explicitly in PI, 2:

Let us imagine a language for which the description given by Augustine is right. The language meant to serve for communication between a builder A and an assistant B. A is building with building-stones: there are blocks, pillars, slabs and beams. B has to pass the stones, and that in the order in which A needs them. For this purpose they use a language consisting of the words "block," "pillar," "slab," "beam." A calls them out; – B brings the stone which he has learnt to bring at such-and-such a call. – Conceive this as a complete primitive language.

Wittgenstein will later, in PI, 48, refer to a related task as "applying the method of PI, 2." It is the twin of the task he describes as "providing the language game," as called for summarily in PI, 116: "When philosophers use a word – 'knowledge,' 'being,' 'object,' 'I,' 'proposition,' 'name' – and try to grasp the *essence* of the thing, one must always ask oneself: is the word ever actually used in this way in the language game which is its original home?" Beginning as I have, wishing to make explicit in one or two strokes issues that Wittgenstein allows to develop in steps through scores of examples, this critical example of the builders is not ideal for my purpose of illustrating unobvious obviousness, since it is not obvious that we *can* follow Wittgenstein's order to "Conceive this as a complete primitive language." That will itself prove to be a fruitful uncertainty, but it is at the moment in the way. I will return to it after first interpolating a set of examples that use the "method of PI, 2," or rather of the twin "providing the language game," and that, in principle, at each use of it arrives at a moment of our acceptance that seems, or soon enough will seem (unless the game is provided ineptly) an instance of the obvious. (In PI, 48 Wittgenstein describes the method as "consider[ing] a language game for which [an] account is really valid.") For this purpose, and again for purposes of locating a region in which to consult further explorations of an issue, I reproduce herewith some stretches of pages 73–5 of *The Claim of Reason*. (It is important to me that the pages concern examples precisely of pointing to something, which is one of the significant features of Augustine's passage.) As follows:

The concept of "pointing to" can be used in conjunction with the concepts of such "objects" as colors, meanings, . . . places, cities, continents, . . . indeed, it would seem you can point to anything you can name; . . . . But, of course, each of these different "objects" will (= can) be pointed to only in definite kinds of contexts. If one thinks one or more of these kinds of objects *cannot* be pointed to, that is because one has a set idea ("picture") of what pointing to something must be (consist in), and that perhaps means taking *one* kind of context as inevitable (or one kind of object as inevitable) [or one kind of language game as inevitable]. For example, if you are walking through Times Square with a child and she looks up to you, puzzled, and asks "Where is Manhattan?," you may feel you ought to be able to *point* to something, and yet at the same time feel there is nothing to point to; and so fling out your arms and look around vaguely and say "All of this is Manhattan," and sense that your answer hasn't been a very satisfactory one. Is, then, Manhattan *hard* to point to? [What are language games for pointing to a city?]. . . . If you were approaching La Guardia Airport on a night flight from Boston, then just as the plane banked for its approach, you could poke your finger against the window and, your interest focused on the dense scattering of lights, say "There's Manhattan"; so could you point to Manhattan on a map. Are such instances not really instances of pointing to *Manhat-*

*tan?* Are they hard to accomplish? Perhaps we could say: It feels hard to do (it is, then and there, impossible to do) when the *concept* of the thing pointed to is in doubt, or unpossessed, or repressed.

Take Wittgenstein's example of "pointing to the color of an object." In philosophizing one may compare this with "pointing to the object" and find that it is either difficult to do (feeling perhaps that a color is a peculiar kind of physical object, a *very* thin and scattered one?) or that it cannot literally be done at all: to point to the color of an object just *is* to point to the object (with a special effort of attention on its color? or saying under your breath "I mean the color"?) [What is the tip-off here that this is in the grip of the *intense* view? I introduced this example with the words "In philosophizing." How do you know when you are philosophizing? For Wittgenstein this is an urgent, definitive question; for others not. When is this a significant difference?] But why? Wittgenstein's explanation is, we know, that "we are misled by grammar," that "we lay down rules, a technique, for a game, and . . . then when we follow the rules, things do not turn out as we had assumed . . . we are therefore as it were entangled in our own rules" (PI, 125). I wish I were confident that I understood this explanation fully; but what he is getting at is, I think, clearly enough illustrated in the present case. The "rule," the "technique," we have laid down for "pointing to the object," is the trivially simple one of pointing to an object whose identity we have agreed upon or can agree upon with the act of pointing [to that object]. Then we suppose that we follow *this* technique in pointing to that object's color, and when we point to the color according to that rule it seems a *difficult* thing to do (in trying it, I find myself squinting, the upper part of my body tense and still, and I feel as though I wanted to dig my finger into the object, as it were, just under its skin). But one *needn't* become entangled. If we look at the way "Point to the color of your car" is actually used [give its language game; apply the method of PI, 2; scientists used to call some such things thought experiments; lawyers refer to something of the sort as hypotheticals], we will realize that the context will normally be one in which we do not point to *that* object, but to something else which has that color, and whose color thereby serves as a *sample* of the original. And as soon as we put the request in its normal context [give its language game], we find that nothing could be easier (e.g., the shape of the hand in pointing will be different, more relaxed). And it won't seem so tempting to regard pointing to something, or meaning it, as requiring a particular inner effort – nor to regard a color as a peculiar material object – once we see that, and see how, the difficulty was of our own making. Someone may feel: "Doesn't this show that pointing to a color is, after all, pointing to an object which has that color?" I might reply: It shows that not all cases of "pointing to an object" are cases of "pointing to an object which has a color."

[Does this imply that some objects have no color? And does this mean that some are colorless?] Using the method of PI, 2, let us imagine a case for which "pointing to an object which has a color" is right. ["Is right" translates "stimmt" in PI, 2; in PI, 48 the German for the analogous "is really valid" is "gilt." *Stimmen* and *gelten* are fateful ideas for this fateful point of Wittgenstein's methods, the former invoking voice and conscience and mood, the latter invoking currency and recognition and the worth of questioning – matters broached in *The Claim of Reason* under the rubrics of "the aesthetics of speech," and "the economics of speech," pp. 94–5.]

. . . The case might be the one in which we are shown a group of variously shaped and differently painted blocks and then [when this group is covered or removed] shown a homologous group of unpainted blocks, each of which corresponds in shape to one block in the former group. . . . We are then given a sample color and told "Point to the object which has this color." [I don't say you couldn't poignantly search, as it were, for an absent or invisible (painted) block to point to; in the meantime there is a perfect candidate among the present and visible (unpainted) blocks to point to.] (It may be significant that in the two passages [in the *Investigations*] in which the examples of "pointing to an object" and "pointing to its color" occur, Wittgenstein does not actually provide language games for *pointing* at all, but moves quickly to remarks about *concentrating one's attention*; and at PI, 33 he goes on to give varying contexts [using the method of PI, 2] for *that*).

*Now let's go back to Wittgenstein's instruction in PI, 2 to "Imagine a language for which the description given by Augustine is right." Unlike providing language games for pointing, "imagining a language for which" (and moreover, one which the last sentence of PI, 2 directs us to "conceive as a complete primitive language") is not something it is clear we know how to do. Evidently we are to describe a language. Is a language described in PI, 2? And, moreover, a complete one?*

One might say that there is no *standing* language game for imagining what Wittgenstein asks. Wittgenstein is then to be understood as *proposing* his game in PI, 2 as one which manifests this imagining; it is his invention, one may say his fiction. That is perhaps the differentiating feature of "the method of PI, 2." (Austin, the other candidate I take as definitive of ordinary language philosophy, does not go in for such invention. Yet another hanging tale.) That we can, as speakers, invent language, or let me say, propose inventions of language, is radically important in Wittgenstein's "vision of language" (an unguarded phrase I use in the title of chapter VII of *The Claim of Reason*). But this is as language-dependent as any other act of speech, say of speaking ironically, or in tongues. Wittgenstein's inventiveness may be part of the reason why so many of his readers get the idea that philosophy, in Wittgenstein's practice, is a particular language game. I set it down here as provocation – since it is too early even to begin being sensible or orderly in exploring the idea – that philosophy, in Wittgenstein [and in Austin], is the quintessential activity that has no language games of its own; which perhaps will amount to saying that it has no subject of its own (call this metaphysics).

This is not to say that in the history of the West philosophy has developed no language (or discourse) of its own, that it has not proposed concepts of its own. The origin and status of this language has been the incessant question of philosophy since, I guess, Plato, until by now it can seem philosophy's only question. Since it is reasonably apparent that both Wittgenstein and Heidegger incessantly philosophize by putting the language of philosophy under fire (from which it follows that one cannot rest assured that what they are doing is philosophizing, but that that is an incessant question for each of them), and equally apparent that these fires are not the same (both are progeny of Kant's, but not both are progeny of Hegel's), the question is bound to arise (if, that is, one regards these figures as principal voices of the present of philosophy) whether both or neither of the fires will survive when they are turned upon one another. Since I do not believe that the question has yet been fully engaged, I philosophize, to the extent I do, within the sense of a split in the spirit of philosophy, of two live, perhaps dying, traditions that are to an unmeasured extent blank to one another. (And what does literary studies mean by "philosophy"? I do not assume that it means just one thing, nor that it should, nor that it is an "it.")

The endless importance (to me) of thinking within the split mind of philosophy, is something that would be mentioned in the introductory remarks I alluded to at the beginning of these notes. It shouldn't go unsaid. But what then is said? (How does philosophy begin?) I think I understand what it may mean to say that philosophy is a leaking boat that must be repaired while at sea. But what if the edifices of philosophy are in flames, like sections of cities? Shall we hope it is true after all that philosophy begins in water? And what is it that Wittgenstein's builders are building?

*What is described in PI, 2 seems to be not so much a language as the learning of a language. But then isn't that what Augustine's passage is describing? And Wittgenstein's point in picturing the language for which Augustine's account is right is then to suggest the thought that our idea of what language is is bound up with our ideas of what acquiring language is (and what using language is). (We don't, I believe, say that we* learn *our first language, our mother tongue. We say of a child who cannot talk yet that he or she cannot talk yet, not that he hasn't learned his native language.* If not (quite) as a feat of learning, how do we conceive of our coming into language, or "acquiring" it? I will have a late suggestion about this. *Specifically, the implication is: If language were acquired and used as Augustine's description suggests, then language would be something other than we think it or know it to be – communication, meaning, words, speech, would be different. It would, for example, look like what is going on in PI, 2.*

*Wittgenstein says of the language there that it is "meant to serve for communication." Evidently he wishes to avoid saying that the builder* is speaking *to his or her assistant. I think one senses why. To "conceive this as a complete language" we have, presumably, to conceive that these people only use their words when they are in* this *situation, doing* this *work. They cannot then, for example, use the words to "discuss" their work or "reminisce" about past work –* not, at any rate, without inventing (or, as I proposed earlier, proposing) an expression. Perhaps one of them gives the other a look, or nod, in the direction of a certain one or pair of the building-stones, at dawn or dusk, sitting together before or after work. (Wittgenstein is imagining something comparable, I believe, when at PI, 42 he imagines something he calls "a sort of joke" between the builders; it is a joke, so to speak, about a theory of language as the correspondence of name and thing. As though to suggest: as primitive as having words is having a theory of words and being anxious in the theory.) In speaking of inventing forms of expression, turns of thought, I am, remember, speaking of inventing *currency*, something that *stimmts* or *gilts*. Inventing language is not counterfeiting it.

*If this is the way I am to conceive what is happening, then how* can I not be in doubt whether these people can speak at all? Those four so-called words, of which their language is said to consist, then may seem like more or less articulate grunts. Wittgenstein refers to them as calls (Rufe, as in PI, 2 and PI, 6). Would it be less prejudicial, or less theoretically dangerous, to speak of these things as "signs"; or would it be more prejudicial? We will want eventually to consider Wittgenstein's associating an idea of the sign with an idea of death, as at PI, 432. How does the association come about? Not, I think, in Wittgenstein, through a philosophical (metaphysical) interpretation of writing. Are we reluctant to call this a language because its vocabulary is so small? What is our measure here? I feel that the builders' responses (or I picture them so that they) are "too mechanical" for them to be using language, even using one word (and is my picture arbitrary?). Does this mean that I am not able to conceive that they are understanding their words, and therefore not speaking? I can imagine robots, or men hypnotized, doing the things the builders do at the same four calls. What is missing?

Wittgenstein at PI, 5 remarks that "A child uses such primitive forms of language when it learns to talk." And it does seem easy to imagine a child with only four words. (Baby Books list the number of words a child can say. One may ask why keeping such a list stops so soon.) And is there a question about whether the child "understands" the words? I think we do not feel that we have to answer this, because, as Wittgenstein says, the child is "learning to talk" – that is, we do not have to imagine that the child is (yet, exactly) speaking a language, has, as it were, entered the language. The child's language has a future. But when I try to imagine adults having just these words – e.g., the builder and his assistant – I find that I imagine them moving sluggishly, as if dull-witted, or uncomprehending, like cave men.

Try it out. Make yourself call out one of your only four words, making one of your only four choices (except for the choice not to work, if that is a choice in these circumstances). I confess to shuffling slowly down the sides of classrooms moaning out my four "words." I want this experience in this room to bring itself, in contrast, to the way a child "says" its four words – with what charming curiosity, expectation, excitement, repetitions. . . . The child has a future with its language, the builders have, without luck, or the genius of invention, none – only their repetitions. We *must imagine Sisyphus happy, Camus reports. But isn't that possibility a function of our knowledge that Sisyphus is being punished, hence that he has possibilities* denied *him? (The suggestion of the builders as constituting a scene, or allegory, of political denial comes up later, pp. 290–3).*

*Wittgenstein lets the question of understanding present itself at PI, 6 – or rather Wittgenstein backs into the question and then backs out right away: "Don't you understand the call 'Slab!' if you act upon it in such-and-such a way?" It is one of Wittgenstein's signature nonrhetorical rhetorical questions designed, among other causes, to elicit conflicting responses within a group, and within an individual, as if to display the farce, and desperateness, of the philosopher's drive to take a side, intensely. Let's give the two conflicting responses.*

*1 One side says: "Acting on the call correctly is understanding the call. What more do you want, or imagine that there is to want?" This seems like something happening near the end of PI, 1, where Wittgenstein says about an implied question of a hearer's understanding: "Well, I assume that he acts as I have described. Explanations come to an end somewhere." This coming to an end (of philosophy, endlessly), is a great theme of* Philosophical Investigations. The theme of ending has struck me as perhaps containing the most telling contrast between this way of philosophizing the overcoming of metaphysics, and other ways, in particular deconstruction's Heideggerean way. I am going to take this up at the end. *But here, in the beginning section of the book, Wittgenstein's remark about coming to an end is comic; no doubt for some it is infuriating. I assume the effect is deliberate. What is the deliberation? This way of taking the question about understanding takes on the familiar reading of Wittgenstein as a behaviorist.* Perhaps this is less common a way of deciding about him than when the lectures represented in these notes were first being given; but it is surely not over. *Wittgenstein allows himself to be questioned about this many times. For example, "Are you not really a behaviorist in disguise?" (PI, 307). In the present case, however, if he is a behaviorist he is quite without disguise, without clothes altogether. That he* can *be read without apparent difficulty – sometimes almost irresistibly – as a behaviorist (think of this for now as denying the (independent) reality of our inner lives) is an important fact about his teaching, perhaps something essential to it (as he suggests at PI, 308). Some of Wittgenstein's followers, as much as some of his enemies, take him so, take him to be asserting (as a thesis, let me say, to mark another path untaken that we must go back to) that "Acting on the order is understanding it." (I assume here that Wittgenstein's (non-)rhetorical question about understanding is not assuming a definition of "acting on" which assures that that is not to be taken in a behaviorist way. The untaken path about "theses" is more visibly, if not more clearly, marked at pp. 33–4 of The Claim of Reason.)*

2 *Other readers, furious at this way of taking or deciding the question, decide the opposite way:* "What more do I want? I want understanding, *something going on upstairs, in the mind?"* Thirty years ago, when this beginning was still beginning for me, I would call such readers "traditional philosophers"; there are vestiges of this habit in the first three parts of The Claim of Reason. Traditional philosophy was marked out for me by its blindness or deafness – so I took it – to the modern in letters and in the arts, most particularly to the questioning of the tradition raised precisely in Wittgenstein, and also in Austin. As I came to recognize that I did not know what a tradition is, nor what it takes to overcome tradition, I stopped speaking so, anyway so lightly. What I used to think of as traditional philosophical reading overlaps, I believe, with what today is called "humanism." The mark of this side of things is perhaps expressed – in the present "opposite" (or oppositional) way of making Wittgenstein's question into (or leaving it as) a thesis – by an obsessional searching for mind, innerness, understanding that seems suspiciously close to searching for substance. This search, or temptation, is part of what is under scrutiny in Wittgenstein's interlocutors. "Interlocutor" is the name by which certain quoted voices in the *Investigations* are conventionally identified by Wittgenstein's readers. Characteristically, I believe, there is in that convention the assumption that there is really one voice, held by an "interlocutor," together with a picture that that figure is someone other than Wittgenstein, which is in a sense true, but in a sense not.

*If I were forced to pick between these alternative decisions – the behaviorist and the antibehaviorist – I would pick the antibehaviorist, without a doubt. (The general reason, I think, is that the behaviorist seems to be denying something. Denial generally* strikes me as more harmful, more fixated, than enthusiasm.) But not without a qualm.

*The behaviorist reading gives me a sinking feeling, or a feeling of isolation – as though I am thinking that just possibly it is true that there is no depth to human kind. Wittgenstein can give me the feeling more starkly than behaviorist psychology ever did. I could always dismiss the psychology as mere theory, or what used to be called "methodology." But Wittgenstein carries the suggestion that the option of behaviorism may, as it were,* become *true, that human kind can no longer afford its historical depth, or what it counts to itself as depth.* But can we wait for it to figure itself out here, re-count itself? For me this becomes the question whether philosophy is to give way to politics, to give up its patience in favor of the urgency of polemics, of taking sides. As if giving up on the idea that the conditions of philosophy can be achieved through philosophy – which is how I see the "paradox" Plato expressed by the idea of the Philosopher–King. The issue of the intolerability of the price of philosophy, its powerlessness, is the subject of my "Emerson's Constitutional Amending."

*The antibehaviorist reading leaves me cold. What would I get if I decided that way, beyond the idea that understanding isn't* just *behavior, or* merely *or* simply *behavior, or behavior* alone, *or itself? And now instead of there being no depth, or say no soul, the body and the soul are too far apart. The soul is ineffective, a mere hypothesis, which many will conclude that they have no need for, as in the case of God (when God became a hypothesis).*

*Let us try to see a little past the edges of the antibehaviorist fantasy. Let us grant that there* is *something inside the builders, something we might call "understanding." What might we imagine a candidate for such an object, a meant, a referent, a significate, to be?*

*A Let's suppose it is some mechanism of the brain that establishes a much-needed "connection" between the call and the object it calls for. Of course I know of no such mechanism, nor what any such "connection" might be. It must have something to do with the electrical/chemical linkages of nerves; but some connection of this kind between calls and objects is patently already in place in the case of the builders; it is what causes my problem with their life.*

*The connection is – what shall I say? – too direct, too hard; it lacks mediation. (Does this equally invite me to imagine something specific going on in the nerves? Something perhaps more devious?)*

*When would saying "There's a mechanism inside" be informative? (What is a language game for this? What is "the role of these words in our language" (PI, 182).) Take a case: You bring a human-size doll into the room, stand it up, and say to it "Slab!" and "Pillar!" etc., and at each command the doll goes off to the corner of the room and "fetches" back the object named in the call. I am impressed. I ask you how it works and you reply: "There's a mechanism inside." Does this* explain *how it works? It could mean: "You wouldn't understand." It could mean: "It's not a trick" (which might mean that you're not working with a confederate in the basement who holds a magnet under the place the doll is standing and walks the doll, via the magnet, to the correct places). "Try to figure out where a mechanism might be that runs this apparently transparent object" (a toy car, a real clock) is hardly an explanation of its working. In any case, the mechanism of connection is here not* supplying *understanding.*

*B What else might we feel is missing when we feel that understanding is missing in acting on a call? Wittgenstein's interlocutors sometimes like to introduce the idea of having an image into such perplexities. Would it help in attributing the concept of understanding to the builders if we conceived them to have images of the respective building-blocks on saying or hearing their names? (Wittgenstein raises the question of images so-caused in PI, 6.)*

*Let's give the builder an image, so that instead of, or as supplement to, saying "Slab!" he holds up a painting of a slab. Why not, indeed, supply him with a real slab and with one of each of the other building-stones, and so enable him to hold up an instance of what he wants? This might strike you as better or as worse, from the point of view of establishing communication, or establishing connection. As better: Now a connection is* insured, *he cannot fail to know what I want (that is, can't mistake which one). Or as worse: It makes it seem even harder to establish connection; if there is doubt about the establishing of connection, the doubt deepens or sharpens. Because the doubt is now clearly not whether he knows which one but whether he knows* that *I* want *the thing I want, and that I want him to respond in such a way as to extinguish my desire. Suppose he stands and admires the picture I present of the object, or else thinks (if I hold up an instance of the object) that I am telling him that I* already have *one, have what I want. How do we imagine that having an image can establish a connection between my words and the desire that my saying them expresses? Might the character of the image enter in? Suppose the builder holds up his instance of the object he wants, e.g., a slab, and exaggeratedly (that is, for the benefit of the assistant) hugs and kisses it. You can see that this is subject to interpretation, and that it might or might not be interpreted to mean that he wants* another *object just like the one he is embracing. Would it help if the image comes up inside the assistant's head? Would greater intimacy of association be established?*

*One is not encouraged, from the fate of these examples, to go on searching for a something – if not a mechanism, or an image, then a meaning, a signified, a interpretant – that explains how calls reach what they call, how the connection is made; searching as it were for a new function for a new pineal gland. The philosophical interest in a philosophical search for a connection between language and mind, and between the mind and world, so far as I recognize an intellectual enterprise not taking its bearings from the current institutions of science, is to determine what keeps such a search going (without, as it were, moving). Wittgenstein's answer, as I read it, has something to do with what I understand as skepticism, and what I might call skeptical attempts to defeat skepticism.* Heidegger's answer has something to do with Nietzsche's nihilism, with the metaphysics of the subject, and with the interpretation of thinking as representation. Derrida's answer has something to do with Heidegger's interpretation of western metaphysics as a metaphysics of presence. I might say that, so far as I have seen, the question "Why does philosophy persist in the search for substances in which understanding, intention, reference, etc. consist?" cannot be satisfied by the answer "Because of the metaphysics of presence." That answer seems to repeat, or reformulate, the question. Say that Wittgenstein shows us that we maintain unsatisfiable pictures of how things must happen. The idea of presence is one of these pictures, no doubt a convincing one. But the question seems to be why we are, who we are that we are, possessed of this picture.

*At some such stage (we must ask what this stage is), Wittgenstein will remind us that there are ordinary circumstances in which (language games in which) we say such things as "B acted as he did (made the connection) because he understood the order, or the hint; he didn't just do it out of luck or entrancement." A case may be of a teacher observing his or her chess student in a difficult game of chess. The student glances at the teacher, the teacher returns the glance and glances away sharply at the student's remaining knight. The student evinces no understanding, looks over the board another instant and smoothly reaches out and makes the move the teacher wanted made. Did the student understand the hint? Didn't he, since he acted on it correctly? But did he act that way because he understood? Suppose as he passes the teacher on the way out he says, almost under his breath, "Thanks." Is there any doubt that he understood? Do I wonder whether something was going on, or is, in his mind, upstairs? I suppose not; which is not to say that I suppose that nothing was going on, or is. If there is a doubt now, looking inside the student will not reach it.*

We have along the way of these remarks distinguished, among ordinary language procedures, what Wittgenstein calls giving a language game for which an account is right, which resembles what Austin calls "reminding ourselves of what we say when" (something that requires that there be standing, recurrent when's, as in using a present object to point to the color of an absent object), from Wittgensteinian language games that extend to mythological cases (as when we gave the builder's assistant an image in his head, which failed to produce a case of "establishing a connection" amounting to understanding), and both from what I called proposals of scenes which may or may not be satisfying realizations of some form of words (as in the case of the builders taken as illustrating a complete language). It may even now be worth noting that Wittgenstein's idea of a criterion has only with my latest example, that of taking a hint, come well within view, and still quite unthematically or unceremoniously. The example takes the idea that our concept of understanding (our ordinary understanding of understanding) is grammatically related to, or manifested in, the concept of taking a hint, and the scene in question produces a criterion of giving a hint, here a gesture of the eyes in a particular circumstance of obscurity. This production of an instance of our criteria fits Wittgenstein's description of his procedures as producing "reminders" since this chess story could do its work only if we already know what giving and taking hints consist in. We might summarize what we learned from the example in the following form: It is part of the grammar (as described in *The Claim of Reason* at, for example, pp. 7off.) of following a gesture that *this* is something we call "taking a hint"; which is to say that following the gesture is a criterion of taking or understanding the hint.

We might now find ourselves at the beginning of *The Claim of Reason* – not quite, no doubt, just as it stands – since that beginning rather assumes the importance of criteria for Wittgenstein's understanding of philosophical investigations as matters of grammar. Then this transcription of early lecture notes would have accomplished one of its conscious purposes, to rebegin, or reopen, that material. Unless, however, it turns out that what we have come close to here is, on the contrary, Wittgenstein's understanding of grammar as showing the importance of producing criteria; that is, as showing that what we produce when we consult ourselves (in a certain way) as to what we call something, are precisely criteria, grammatically decisive crossroads. To understand that decisiveness is hardly something for a beginning project, since that issue can be taken as the burden of the whole of Part One of *The Claim of Reason*.

Preparing these pages for the press, in late 1993, I report a new tack begun in a lecture course mostly on the *Investigations* that I offered jointly with Hilary Putnam in the spring of 1993, in which these "Notes and Afterthoughts" were distributed for a week's discussion about halfway through the course. The question whether they actually do represent a reopening of *The Claim of Reason* rather lost its appeal when a representative group of students in the class found the transcription harder to relate to than that book's actual opening. I think I might have found helpful ways to contest that judgment, but in the course of looking for them I came upon the new tack just mentioned. I had not taken it in before that the work of what Wittgenstein calls criteria – for all the importance many of us attach to that development – is (is precisely, I would now like to say) delayed in its entry into the *Investigations*, precisely absent from its opening. Its first appearance, I believe, is at PI 51, and it doesn't really get going until some hundred sections later; it may not reach its height until PI, 580 and following. The significance of this opening or "delayed" absence seems bound up with Wittgenstein's impulse to begin and maintain his thoughts in the region of the "primitive," with a child before the life of language, with work-ers before their culture's possession (or permitting them possession) of a shared, undoubted language. Imagining, following Wittgen-stein's instructions, the primitiveness of the builders – questioning their capacity to understand their words and actions; which is to say, questioning their possession of *words* – is imagining them without the possibility and necessity of exercising judgment, which is a philo-sophical way of saying: without the possession of (shared) criteria. Their humanity is the stake of the game. Ideas associated with the primitiveness of civilization will take on more life as my transcrip-tion proceeds.

My sense of Wittgensteinian criteria, as articulating what in *The Claim of Reason* I come to call our (whose?) agreement or at-tunement in ordinary words, depends as decisively on appreciating their triviality as much as their importance, their weakness as much as their strength. One could say that their weakness is the source of their methodological strength, small stakes with large shadows. (It may help certain readers of these notes to suggest comparing what "articulating criteria of ordinary words" will prove to mean with what Kant calls providing the "schematism of our concepts.") And since now, a dozen years after the publication of *The Claim of Rea-son*, and getting somewhat more familiar with the onslaught of French thought over the past quarter of a century, timed in my life from my finishing in the late 1960s the essays in *Must We Mean What We Say?*, I am increasingly aware of a new phase in philoso-phy's chronic distrust of the ordinary. There is, notably in that strain of radical thought called deconstruction, but widespread beyond that in modern radical sensibilities of other sorts (a point of compari-son with certain conservative sensibilities, of whom perhaps Witt-genstein seems one) something I think of as a horror of the common, expressed as a flight from the banal, typically from banal pleasures. It stretches from a horror of the human, to a disgust with bourgeois life, to a certain condescension toward the popular. It is of high importance to me to determine to which of these, or from which, Emerson's aversion to conformity begins. It is with respect to their apparently opposite attitudes toward the ordinary that I have some-times distinguished the philosophizing of Heidegger and that of Witt-genstein, the former seeking distinction from the ordinary con-ceived as "averageness," the latter practicing transformation into it.

But back to my transcription.

*I was saying that we should mark the philosophical "stage" at which we had to remind ourselves of our orientation in the ordinariness of language. I might have described this as remarking our subjection to our language. The stage was one in which the philosophical search for some explanatory substance in the subject (some inner mechanism, image, etc.) came to grief. We might say philosophy had come to a halt, or say that we have had to stop to think. This bears comparison with the stopping or halting we noted as remarkable in Wittgenstein's taking up of Augustine's unremarkable passage. It will help to recognize that Wittgenstein, for all his repudiation of philosophical "theory," intermittently if not continually provides rigorous descriptions of his own practice, which you might call his (or his text's) theory of itself (presumably not of itself alone).*

*Among these self-descriptions of his practice is the following, in a region of the* Investigations *full of such descriptions: "A philosophical problem has the form: 'I don't know my way about' " (PI, 123). I understand this as a theorization of the search for the beginning of philosophy which produced the beginning of these lectures. It conceives philosophy's beginning for me as one of recognizing that I have lost my way, and in that way am stopped.* This way of putting things is meant, as in *This New Yet Unapproachable America*, pp. 36f., to associate the project or quest of enlightenment, or coming to oneself, in the *Investigations*, fairly immediately with projects portrayed in *The Divine Comedy*, in Emerson's "Experience," and in Nietzsche's *Genealogy of Morals. Given this beginning, the end that matches it I take to be given in the preceding section: "The concept of a perspicuous presentation is of fundamental significance for us. It earmarks the form of presentation we give, the way we look at things" (PI, 122). The progress between beginning and ending is, accordingly, what Wittgenstein means by grammatical investigation, which, since we begin lost, may be thought of as a progress in finding ourselves. (When it comes time to make this less crude, or less abstract, I will be sure not to seem to deny that "perspicuous presentation" might be taken to apply to the whole of Wittgenstein's practice, not solely, even if preeminently, to its (local, momentary – but how does one know that these restrictions contrast with anything?) end.)*

*Go back to Wittgenstein's saying that he wants to begin with primitive "kinds of application" of words. (The primitive is in principle a far more important theme to work out for the* Investigations *than we have brought out, or will bring out here. It would require accurately characterizing one's sense of the ethnological perspective Wittgenstein characteristically takes toward human kind as such.) He says that beginning with the primitive will "disperse the fog" surrounding the "working of language" produced by "this general notion of the meaning of a word" (PI, 5) – namely the notion, or the "particular picture of the essence of human language," in which, he goes on to say, "we find the roots of the following idea: Every word has a meaning. This meaning is correlated with the word. It is the object for which the word stands" (PI, 1). An obvious motive for his description of his motives is to insinuate the idea that there is a "fog" coming in with the general notion of the meaning of a word. And this allows him to sketch a place for the philosophical goal of this motive, namely, to "command a clear view of the aim and functioning of [the] words" (that is, I take it, to arrive at perspicuous presentation).*

*But another motive for stressing the primitive is to prepare the idea of our words as* lived, *of our language as containing what Wittgenstein will shortly call, in one of his most familiar turns of thought, "forms of life": "To imagine a language means to imagine a form of life" (PI, 19). As my earlier description of the builders in PI, 2 was meant to bring out, the clear view we are supposedly initially given is one in which not "merely" the language is primitive, but in which the corresponding life of its speakers is clearly expressed in the language.* We might wish to say that not the language but each word is primitive; the words don't go anywhere. This intuition might come into play when, in discussion, we consider Derrida's idea of the sign as alienated from itself, already elsewhere. This seems to mean something in contrast with Wittgenstein's idea of the primitive.

*Wittgenstein's phrase "form of life" has become a runaway phrase among certain of his readers.* I have since tried to bring a little structure into the discussion of the phrase by distinguishing the ethnological and the biological directions or perspectives encoded in the phrase (in "Declining Decline," pp. 40f.). The ethnological, or horizontal direction (I believe the favored, virtually exclusive, reading) emphasizes differences between cultures, for example, in whether they count or measure or sympathize as we do. The biological, or vertical, direction emphasizes differences between, we might rather say, life forms, for example, as between lower and higher, perhaps expressed in the presence or absence of the hand.

*Let us go back over a way I imagined the lives of the builders in PI, 2 – as moving laboriously, sluggishly, as if vacantly. This seemed interpretable as their dull-wittedness, as their lacking as a matter of fact (but as a matter of nature, or a matter of history?) a certain power of understanding. I was, it seems, responding to the fact that they only spoke in single "words" or "calls," as if they were* incapable of *speaking in complete sentences, as if incapacitated or handicapped with respect to a certain kind of performance, of rising to an occasion; as though their words, hence their lives, were forever somehow truncated, stunted, confined, contracted. But there are contexts in which it is perfectly natural for there to be one-word commands or orders. "It is easy to imagine a language consisting only of orders and reports in battle" (PI, 19). I think of "Forward march," "Enemy at 10 o'clock," "Battle stations." Athletic contests provide another context: "On your marks; get set; go!" There is, I suppose, no reason to think that the builders of PI, 2 are using "formulas" of this kind.*

*We also know of contexts in which commands or orders are (conventionally?) given in one word where there are no special formulas: e.g., (1) the context, beloved in old movies, of "scalpel," "suture," "wipe"; (2) the context in which builders are doing their jobs in a noisy work area, the context more familiar to us nonprimitives, an area surrounded by traffic, spectators, featuring heavy machinery. If in that noisy environment I imagine the calls "Slab," "Pillar," etc., I do not imagine them said sluggishly and vacantly (unless I were to imagine one of the workers ill or drunk), but vigorously, in shouts, perhaps with hands cupped around the mouth. Wittgenstein does not say that his builders are not in such an area. I imagined them alone, and in an otherwise deserted landscape. As though they were building the first building. Was this arbitrary?*

*And why have I not been interested in what they were building, or even that they were building a particular building – for the fact that they are building something in particular would influence the order and repetition and conclusion of the series of "four calls." If I could think of the task as dictating the (order of the) calls, hence of the builder as* ready *for the next item, I might have imagined him or her differently. Or is it to be supposed that we might merely see (what we perceive as) a "heap" of items mounting at A's location? I gather that I cannot exactly make my perplexity comprehensible to these workers. And can I make myself comprehensible to myself when at the end of the working day the builder and the assistant find a way to climb in carefully among the heap of building-stones and go to sleep? Nor does the heap look like what we think of as a result of* preparing *to build, where stacks of materials are neatly laid. (How do things look at B's location?) For me to imagine their lives, they have to make sense to me. And this seems to me to mean: I have to imagine them making sense to themselves, which is presumably not a gloss I would add were I trying to understand the behavior of bees or beavers.*

*In the cases of the operating room, or the real (noisy) environment, there are obvious reasons why the orders are one-word, or say stylized: to save time, or gain maximum speed and efficiency, to conserve energy. Try it out. Imagine that the workers are on a populous construction site. Now take away the spectators, and traffic, and turn off for the moment the heavy machinery. They may still be doing things essential to the job at hand, but don't we feel that there is no reason for them to shorten or stylize their sentences, anyway none beyond the effect of the repetitiveness of the familiar routines themselves? To raise the voice, stylize the sentence, is as inappropriate there, without some practical purpose, as it would be at a concert. That the voice is understood as responsive to its circumstances, but that there is no certainly unambiguous level at which to pitch the voice or fix the distance over which to project it, creates anxiety expressed in our laugh, familiar at talkies, when one character continues to yell for a few words after a persistent noise suddenly ends, or the distance is closed, that had made the yelling necessary.*

*But it is not accurate, or not enough, to say about Wittgenstein's builders that there is no reason for them to truncate or stylize their sentences. I would like to say that they just do* speak, *or behave in the way described. But that is our problem. We might express it by saying: They* cannot *behave anyway else, they have no alternative. Earlier we imagined that they do not speak apart from working;*

*now we may imagine that they do not speak differently in noisy than in peaceful environments. They are not* free. *Maybe this is the sense of their behaving "mechanically" that I expressed earlier; and maybe this lack of alternative is the way to describe what was missing for me when I agreed that I missed a sense of understanding in them. But what is the connection between understanding and having or seeing an alternative? There is a connection between interpretation and seeing an alternative, since interpretation is a matter of taking something one way rather than another. Perhaps the connection with the case of understanding is that the alternative to carrying out an order is* refusing *to carry it out, disobedience to it. Disobedience has been taken (in Eden, to divine command; in Kant's moral philosophy, to inclination) as a criterion of freedom. But which comes first? Earlier I felt that without endowing the builders with understanding I was not fully prepared to say that they were speaking, and hence not prepared to see them as fully human. But now what emerges is that I did not see them as human because they did not seem to me to have freedom.* And now I feel I want to go beyond the thought that freedom is shown in the capacity to say no, to the thought that it is shown in saying no in one's own voice (responsive to different circumstances, capable of distinguishing consent from duress) – perhaps related to the cause of Emerson's and Nietzsche's search for a ground on which to say yes, the yes they took as the sign of a human existence, that thinkers before them, whom they were going beyond, not repudiating, had taken as the sign of a political existence.

In somewhat intensifying the linking of understanding with freedom, and in the explicit emergence of the connection of having a voice with having a political existence (a connection stressed, but not systematically pursued, early in *The Claim of Reason*, pp. 22–8), I am prompted to interpolate here parts of a long paragraph from the Wittgenstein lecture in *This New Yet Unapproachable America;* the passage (pp. 62–4) is the most recent in which I have put into print thoughts about the builders:

One may well sometimes feel that it is not language at all under description [in the *Investigations* section 2] since the words of the language . . . seem not to convey understanding, not to be *words*. . . . But while this feeling is surely conveyed by the scene, . . . we need not take it as final, or unchallenged, for at least three lines of reason: (1) [There follows a lightning rehearsal of the figures of the primitive or "early human," of the sense of truncation in the calls in different environments, of the child with four words, ending:] Instead of the feeling that the builders lack understanding, I find I feel that they lack imagination, or rather lack freedom, or perhaps that they are on the threshold of these together. (2) Something *is* understood by the builders, that desire is expressed, *that* this object is called for. . . . Therewith an essential of speech is present, a condition of it, and not something that can, as new words are taught, be taught. ("Therewith"? There I am taking the builders also as illustrating Augustine's scene as of an advent of language (challenging a picture of the accumulative "learning" of language), something that comes "with" an advent of the realm of desire, say of fantasy, "beyond" the realm of (biological) need. I have been instructed, here particularly concerning Freud's concept of *Trieb*, spanning the "relation" between biological and psychological drive, by the exceptional study of Freudian concepts in Jean Laplanche's *Life and Death in Psychoanalysis*.)

[The instruction I speak of, as it enters, for example, into the scare quotes I have set in the previous sentences around "with" and "relation," etc., calls particular attention to Augustine's description of the use to which he puts the names he has lined up with the objects his elders line them up with, the description that ends the Augustine passage: "After I had trained my mouth to form these signs, I used them to express my own desires." The part of the picture of language here, forming other "roots" of the idea or philosophical concept of meaning Wittgenstein divines in Augustine (and evidently not there alone), is something like this: The preparation for my acquiring language is my possession of a structure of desires and a nameable world; when I have acquired my set of signs, I may then use them to insert those desires into that world. Then again I may not. What determines whether I invest in the world, say yes to my existence? When (historically) did this become an issue? (My little book on Thoreau's writing, *The Sense of Walden*, is, perhaps above all, about this investment, something I call (roughly in Thoreau's name) taking an interest in the world; this is not so much a cure of skepticism as it is a sign of its mortality. In *In Quest of the Ordinary*, I comparably take up in this relation to skepticism Wordsworth's declaration of his wish "to make the incidents of common life interesting" (pp. 6–7). The figure of the child, under the shadow of such questions, returns yet again at the end of these notes.)]. . . . (3) A further, noncompeting interpretation of the builders is as an allegory of the ways many people, in more developed surroundings, in fact speak, forced as it were by circumstances to speak in more or less primitive, unvaried expressions of more or less incompletely educated desires – here the generalized equipment of noise and the routines of generalized others, are perhaps no longer specifiable in simple descriptions, having become invisible through internalization. (Is it theory that is wanted, more than fuller description?] [If there is a theory it must, I suppose, be understandable as one that demonstrates the modes whereby, in Foucault's words, power "reaches into the very grain of individuals, touches their bodies and inserts itself into their actions and attitudes, their discourses, learning processes and everyday lives."] This allegory may be seen as a kind of political parody of the repetition (or say the grammar) without which there is no language. (I take the workers as political allegory in terms that allude to Heidegger's description of the everyday ("generalized equipment," "noise") in order to indicate a possible site of meeting, or passing, of Wittgenstein and Heidegger on the topos of the everyday – a place from which it can be seen both why Heidegger finds authenticity to demand departure and why Wittgenstein finds sense or sanity to demand return.)]

*From a certain point of view, especially in certain moods of philosophizing, it would hardly occur to us to think that radical conceptual differences – for example, between calling something a language or not, or between calling a creature human or not – could turn on whether these creatures speak differently (for example, use different tones of voice) in noisy and in quiet environments. It would seem that when we "took away" the familiar, or everyday, or "natural" context in which the builders would speak in single words, we were taking away only something inessential, trivial, quite external – the builders are surely the same, surely they are doing the same thing, their behavior is the same, whatever their tone of voice! And yet the lack we felt in trying to attribute understanding to the builders, which we sought to compensate for by imagining some inner mechanism or image, was filled up precisely, i.e., it quite vanished, as we (re)supplied "outer" surroundings.*

*The mutual regulation of inner and outer is a great theme of the* Philosophical Investigations, *specifically forming the background against which criteria function – against which they do the little, the indispensable little, they do to keep body and soul, or world and mind together.* Since a version of this theme motivates the opening – the direct discussion of criteria – of The Claim of Reason, we are again at a goal of this transcription of these lecture notes. That discussion of criteria in The Claim of Reason reaches a plateau at the conclusion of chapter 4; it starts up afresh, in the form of an extended discussion of privacy, as the beginning of Part Four.

*The sense of the builder's lack of freedom is confirmed, as suggested earlier, by Wittgenstein's description (in PI, 6) of this lan-*

*guage as the* whole *language of a tribe. He says there that "the children are brought up to perform these actions, to use these words as they do so, and to react in this way to the words of others." Surely it is easy to feel here: This group would have to exert great efforts to* suppress *certain natural responses of the children.* It suggests itself that a perception housed in this feeling gives on to an idea that the concept of the natural at some point becomes linked (dialectically or not) with the concept of transgression. Suppose this link is expressed in the Kantian picture of discovering the limits of knowledge, to transgress which is to enter one of several systematically related forms of madness (dialectical illusions). (As if it is nature itself (herself?) which has become the thing-in-itself.) And suppose we give a sexualized reading (roughly what Laplanche calls a perverse reading, in his interpretation of Freud's mapping of the human creation of, i.e., the creation of human "drives") of the violence exercised in the course (or curriculum) of "being brought up to perform, use, react" in prefigured ways certain actions, words, and reactions. Then we perhaps have a way, in what I sometimes speak of as "our" part of the forest, of coming to see what Foucault means (and he seems to be speaking out of a thriving culture in his part of the forest – what is the conviction that these are parts of the same expanse of thought?) in speaking of Sade's placement, in the discovery of sexuality, of "that firmament of indefinite unreality . . . , the discovery of those systematic forms of prohibition which we now know imprison it, the discovery of the universal nature of transgression," (I've been reading Foucault's "Preface to Transgression," in *language, counter-memory, practice,* ed. Bouchard.)

*So that the training of children is a process of stupefying them into the state in which we encounter the grown-up builders. I do not, in these phantasms, wish to appear extreme. We need not imagine the grown-ups, the representative men and women (presumably there are women) of the builder's culture, taking brutal measures in moulding their charges. If the charges are recalcitrant, that is to say, fail the test of serious participation in performing, speaking, reacting, as the elders require, the consequences may be merely that the elders will not speak to them, or pay them full attention, or else that they perpetually express disappointment in the children, and tell them they are bad. As our kind mostly does.*

## II

With that last paragraph (whose rhetoric I recognize as going with the sketches of children in the ending paragraphs of Part One, chapter 5 of *The Claim of Reason*, hence as dating from 1970–1, when that material was being revised into its present form), I come to the end of the notes I had chosen to transcribe. The notes for the lectures that continue from there take up various specific topics of the *Investigations*, versions of many of which found their way into the early chapters of *The Claim of Reason*, others of which became the general sketch of Wittgenstein's "vision of language" that forms chapter 7, and still others constitute the opening couple of dozen pages of Part Four. What follows here may be thought of as an epilogue to the transcription, unless indeed it is better thought of as an introduction to the interventions that intersperse the transcription, interventions without which I would not have been able to provide it, i.e., to deliver the lectures from where I now find myself.

NOTES

1 This contribution is a reprint of part I of an essay that originally appeared in Cavell, *Philosophical Passages: Wittgenstein, Emerson, Austin* (Cambridge, Mass.: Blackwell, 1995). The text, reproduced here with permission of the author and the publisher, conforms to the original except for the correction of an erroneous reference to "the Augustine passage" to the intended "PI, 2," in the passage quoted on p. 291.

# 9 Mind, meaning, and practice

In one of his harshest judgments on philosophy Wittgenstein observes at PI, 194: "When we do philosophy we are like savages, primitive people, who hear the expressions of civilized men, put a false interpretation on them, and then draw the queerest conclusions from it." He does not document the extent to which this actually goes on in philosophy, or where it goes on, if it does. When he makes the remark he has been discussing possibility. In that case perhaps he has a point. It might well apply as well to much of what is said in philosophy about thought, meaning, and understanding – in short, about the mind. When we reflect philosophically on those "mental" or "intentional" ways of speaking in which we describe so much of what we do it is easy to start down a path, no one step of which is exactly "savage" or "uncivilized," but which ends up with something "queer" in the sense of being completely and irretrievably mysterious.

I want to look at one – but only one – way in which Wittgenstein thinks this happens, and what he does, or suggests, to counteract it. It can start with puzzlement over the meanings of words. Not with wondering what some particular word means, but with wonder at the very phenomenon of meaning. Words as we encounter them are sounds or marks, but obviously not all sounds or marks are meaningful. Leaves make sounds in the wind, and a snail makes marks in the sand. It is not even their being produced by human beings that makes sounds or marks meaningful. Humans also produce sounds and marks which have no meaning, and often do so intentionally. As Wittgenstein puts it, mere sounds or marks on their own seem "dead" (BLBK, p. 3). Those that are meaningful are uttered or produced with meaning. They are meant in a certain way, while other sounds and marks are not. Meaningful sounds and marks are responded to in certain particular ways, with understanding. They have a kind of "life" which is not shared even by sounds or marks that happen to be signs or indications of something else, as the marks on the trunk of a tree are signs of its age, or the faint sound of a train is an indication of its distance from the hearer.

So far it seems undeniable and unproblematic that many sounds and marks are meaningful and are responded to with understanding and many are not. It is when we take the next, apparently natural, step that trouble looms. We ask "How do the marks made on paper as a person writes differ from the marks made by a snail as it crosses the sand?" and it seems natural to take that as the question "What has to be added to otherwise 'dead' marks or sounds to give them 'life' and so to make them meaningful?" The thought is that meaningful sounds or marks differ from others in being *accompanied* by something. They either produce something, or are produced by something, that is not present among the causes or effects of merely "dead" signs. That added something is what is thought to give the signs their "life," and we come to think of it as something that can occur only "in the mind."

It seems that there are *certain definite* mental processes bound up with the working of language, processes through which alone language can function. I mean the processes of understanding and meaning. The signs of our language seem dead without these mental processes; and it might seem that the only function of the signs is to induce such processes, and that these are the things we ought really to be interested in. . . . We are tempted to think that the action of language consists of two parts; an inorganic part, the handling of signs, and an organic part, which we may call understanding these signs, meaning them, interpreting them, thinking. (BLBK, p. 3)

Once we have the idea of these two distinct parts of the "action of language" it is almost inevitable that we will focus on the "mental" or "organic" part. That will seem to be what "we ought really to be interested in" because "inorganic" or "dead" signs alone, or the mere addition of "inorganic" signs to "dead" signs that are already there, could never give signs "life" or meaning. Something completely different, it seems, must be added. "And the conclusion which one draws from this is that what must be added to the dead signs in order to make a live proposition is something immaterial, with properties different from all mere signs" (BLBK, p. 4). "Mental" goings-on such as understanding, meaning, interpreting, and thinking are the sorts of things that have to be added. And because they belong to the "live" or "organic" part of language, and cannot be understood as involving only material and so "dead" signs, it seems that they "take place in a queer kind of medium, the mind; and the mechanism of the mind, the nature of which, it seems, we don't quite understand, can bring about effects which no material mechanism could" (BLBK, p. 3).

The effects are special in all the ways that thought and meaning are special or unique in the world. A thought, which is something mental, can "agree or disagree with reality" (BLBK, p. 4). Nothing merely material or "inorganic" can do that. You can think of someone, or "mean" him when you say something, even if he is thousands of miles away, or dead, or doesn't and never did exist. You can believe what is not so, and fear something that could not even possibly be so. " 'What a queer mechanism,' one might say, 'the mechanism of wishing must be if I can wish that which will never happen' " (BLBK, p. 4).

To understand these familiar phenomena as special activities or operations performed by or occurring in "the mind" would be to draw what Wittgenstein calls the "queerest conclusions" from a false interpretation imposed on the expressions civilized persons use to talk about thought, meaning, understanding, and other "mental" goings-on. It is what leads us to think of something called "the mind" as the repository or locus of such activities, and so to think of it as an agent, or a thing, or at least as kind of place, and to think of it as hidden or "inner" in some way, despite our having no idea of its even approximate dimensions or location.

We know where the brain is, and it is inner in the straightforward sense of being inside the skull. No doubt we could not think, mean, or understand anything if the brain were not there or did not function more or less as it does. We have the language of chemical reactions, electrical impulses, protoplasm, and so on with which to describe the operations of brains, but for what is said to go on "in the mind," or what "the mind" does, we need "mental" or "intentional" or psychological ways of speaking. Events that go on literally inside skulls remain as devoid of meaning, or as "dead" in Wittgenstein's sense, as most events that occur outside skulls. If thought, intention, or understanding are needed to give otherwise "dead" objects or events "life" or meaning of the relevant "mental" kind, then because they possess special features apparently not shared by any "inorganic" or "dead" material mechanism, those activities or operations will have to be seen as taking place in a special, and so a mysterious or occult, medium.

The general strategy of Wittgenstein's resistance to this apparently natural line of thought is to show that the puzzlement which we wrongly interpret to be about the nature of a medium is really a puzzlement "caused by the mystifying use of our language" (BLBK, p. 6). The mystification is due to our thinking of thought, meaning, and understanding as something that *accompanies* the handling of sounds, marks, or other objects. Wittgenstein tries to expose that disastrous assumption by showing that *whatever* might be thought to accompany the use of a sound or mark would be nothing better than another "dead" mark or object or event. He does this by first inviting us to replace whatever "mental" thing is thought to accompany the handling of physical signs with something which is itself overt and accessible. If the presence "in the mind" of an image of a red flower is what is thought to be essential to a person's meaning or understanding the English words "a red flower," think instead of the person holding a picture of a red flower in his hand. If an inner act of interpretation or understanding is thought to take place in his mind when he hears and understands the phrase, think instead of the "outer" act of his drawing his finger from left to right across a chart with the words "a red flower" on the left and a picture of a red flower (or even a real red flower) on the right. Wittgenstein says that "we could perfectly well, for our purposes," replace every allegedly "inner" or "mental" object or process with some such "outer" object or act (BLBK, p. 4). "Our purposes" here refers to his aim of exposing the futility of appealing to a mysterious or occult "inner" medium. It is futile because an external chart or picture or other object would be in itself no help in giving meaning to a written sign.

... why should the written sign plus the painted image be alive if the written sign alone was dead? – In fact, as soon as you think of replacing the mental image by, say, a painted one, and as soon as the image thereby loses its occult character, it ceases to seem to impart any life to the sentence at all. (It was in fact just the occult character of the mental process which you needed for your purposes.) (BLBK, p. 5)

"Your purposes" here are those of expressing the apparently natural puzzlement about thought, meaning, and understanding.

Much more would need to be said to identify and to explain the force of each of the steps that are thought to lead to these deep and compelling misconceptions. My goal here is to understand Wittgenstein's opposition to them, and what he suggests should take their place. It is summed up in his now-famous remarks:

> But if we had to name anything which is the life of the sign, we should have to say it was its *use*. (BLBK, p. 4)

> The sign (the sentence) gets its significance from the system of signs, from the language to which it belongs. Roughly: understanding a sentence means understanding a language. (BLBK, p. 5)

> For a *large* class of cases – though not for all – in which we employ the word "meaning," it can be explained thus: the meaning of a word is its use in the language. (PI, 43)

It should be clear from the target against which these slogans are directed that the use of an expression, or the system of expressions within which it has a use, are not to be thought of as something merely accompanying the expression and thereby somehow endowing it with meaning or "life." Nor should we think that Wittgenstein is here trying to identify something that can be called "the meaning" of a particular word. He is not pressing the question "What is the meaning of a word?" in the sense of "What is that thing that is a word's meaning?" Rather he is here summing up a response to the concern with the general meaningfulness of words with which we began – with what distinguishes meaningful sounds or marks from those which are "dead" or mean nothing. The answer does not appeal to anything going on in "the mind"; those sounds or marks are meaningful which have a distinctive role or use in a system of signs like a human language.

This is only a summary or capsule answer. There is no suggestion that the use of an expression is something that is easy to describe or explain. In fact, it can be felt that for certain philosophical purposes it cannot be fully or satisfactorily explained at all. I will come back to that idea.

The slogan "the meaning is the use" has been understood and appropriated in a number of different ways, not all of them helpful in understanding Wittgenstein. An expression's having a use has sometimes been explained as there being conditions under which the expression can be correctly or justifiably or appropriately applied – "criteria of application." Someone who knows the meaning of an expression would therefore know how and when to apply it to something, and when not. As an explanation of the notion this does not take us very far. For one thing, only certain words are properly said to be applied to something; for example, the word "peacock" when I say of something directly before me "That is a peacock." Even in that remark the words "That" and "is" are not in the same way applied to anything, but they too contribute distinctively to what is said. And when I say "A peacock roaming my garden would certainly enliven the scene" not even the word "peacock" is applied to something in the same way as before; there is nothing of which it is then being asserted that it is a peacock. Nor are the other words in that remark applied to anything, but they too are meaningful, so they too must have uses in Wittgenstein's sense.

The "use" or "application" of whole sentences has similarly been thought of as the conditions under which they can be truly or justifiably or appropriately asserted or used assertively. This view suffers from comparable difficulties and limitations. Many sentences we utter and understand are never used to make assertions. Of those that sometimes or often are so used, they also appear unasserted and still have a meaning and so a use. Uttering a sentence with meaning, or understanding a sentence, is something much richer than simply being able to assert or acknowledge the truth of what a sentence says. If the notion of "application" is widened to include not only assertion but all other fully sentential speech acts, and to include among words not only predicates but all other expressions needed to form whole sentences, we are left only with the unhelpful observation that an expression's having a use is a matter of there being conditions under which it can be correctly or justifiably or appropriately used in communication.

It is closer to Wittgenstein's conception of the use of an expression to think of it as the distinctive role of the expression in all those human activities in which it is or might be employed. This can be seen as a generalization of the idea, present in Frege and the *Tractatus*, that the meaning of an expression is displayed in the contribution it makes to the truth or falsity of all the sentences in which it can appear. The new direction of thought in which Wittgenstein was moving on his return to philosophy in 1929 goes beyond truth-conditions and purely linguistic items like sentences to encompass an utterance's contribution to whatever human beings manage to do in uttering or responding to it.

The meanings of the expressions "Slab," "Pillar," "Block," and "Beam" of the "complete primitive language" described in PI, 2 can be seen in that way. Their whole use lies open to view; we can see exactly what role the utterance of each of them plays in the lives of those people. Even if we think of the expressions as sentences, there is no need to think of them as being used to make assertions, or even to predicate something of certain objects. They nonetheless have "life" or meaning in a way that no other sounds or marks do in that community. Of course, the difference that the utterance of a particular sound or mark makes in everything people do cannot always be so easily described, or perhaps even described at all in reasonably complete terms, especially in the kinds of languages and lives that we are all familiar with. The point so far is only the very general fact of a difference between a sound or mark's having a use or role in human activities and its having no such role. The sounds of the leaves in the wind and the snail's marks in the sand are "dead" and without a use in that sense.

It is in this light that we are to understand Wittgenstein's observation that a sentence or expression has "life" "as part of the system of language" (BLBK, p. 5), and that understanding a sentence means understanding a language. Understanding a language, in turn, "means to be master of a technique" (PI, 199). The "technique" involved is the technique of acting and responding linguistically in appropriate ways, of being a human language speaker, and so being capable of the sorts of activities and reactions that language makes possible. The builder in the language-game in PI, 2 knows how to get the building-stones he needs; the assistant understands him and brings the right stones. In that case, being master of a language means being master of only one or two very simple "techniques" – perhaps too few for it to qualify as a language at all. Real life as we know it involves many more. The kinds of things that human beings can do in and with language are virtually limitless.

Whatever the actions or activities or responses involving language might be, in order for someone to have mastery of certain techniques there must be such a thing as carrying out those techniques, or doing the things in question correctly. In order for the builder to have mastered the technique of ordering the kind of building-stone he needs, there must be a way of ordering a certain kind of building-stone. There must be something he has mastered. This is nothing more than the platitude that there must be some difference between performing an action of a certain kind and not performing it, between engaging in a certain activity and not engaging in it. If not, there would be nothing to master. Someone who calls out "Slab!" or "Pillar!" randomly from time to time has not mastered the "technique" that the experienced builder follows in the community Wittgenstein describes. A would-be assistant who simply jumps up and down in distinctive ways on hearing a builder's utterances has not understood those utterances correctly. He has not mastered the technique of passing stones to the builder as he needs them and orders them.

This shows that there must be such a thing as the correct way of using or responding to a sound or mark that has meaning or a use. Exhibiting mastery of a technique involves doing the thing correctly. This could be put by saying that one who utters or responds to an utterance correctly is following the rule for the use of that utterance. That is not to imply that the person consults some rule book or set of instructions. It means only that the person utters or responds to the expression in the right way. Wittgenstein does not object to talk of rule-following. It is his exploration of the only ways in which this undeniable condition of mastery can be satisfied that is meant to lead away from any appeal to a mysterious inner realm or medium as essential to understanding thought, meaning, and understanding.

For someone's performance to be the correct way to do something there must be some standard or pattern to which it conforms. For the use of linguistic expressions, those standards can be provided ultimately only by the ways in which the expressions are in fact used. Nothing else could give a particular, distinctive significance to an expression; meaning is not something a sound or mark carries with it in itself, independently of how it is used. Of course, an expression can be endowed with meaning, or its meaning can be explained, by the use of other expressions, but those expressions in turn must have a use and be used correctly if the explanation is to succeed. That requires that there be some way in which those expressions are used, some regularities or general practices to which an individual speaker's performance can conform or fail to conform.

It is not possible that there should have been only one occasion on which someone obeyed a rule. It is not possible that there should have been only one occasion on which a report was made, an order given or understood; and so on. – To obey a rule, to make a report, to give an order, to play a game of chess, are *customs* (uses, institutions). (PI, 199)

Someone who stands near a partly built building and shouts out "Slab!" is not thereby giving an order if there has been no practice of sounds' having been uttered and responded to for certain purposes in certain regular ways in the past. Someone who carries a stone to a building site shortly after hearing such a shout has not thereby understood it to have a particular meaning if there is no general practice of responding to it or to other sounds in that way. The sound "Slab!" would simply have no "life" or use in those circumstances, or at any rate it would not have the use and so the meaning it has in the language-game in PI, 2.

From Wittgenstein's description of what he calls that "complete primitive language" we can see what those expressions mean in that community, what those who use them correctly mean by them, and what those who understand them understand them to mean. In thinking of that situation in the ways we do, we do not need to add to the description any supposition to the effect that some objects or acts appear in mysterious "inner" regions called the "minds" of those people. We know what they are doing, and we can see from the description of their practice alone how their use of those sounds contributes to it. They build, and the particular ways in which they build involve communication between a builder and his assistant. In PI, 6 Wittgenstein explains how children of that community might be brought up to perform those actions, to use those words as they do so, and to react in the right ways to the words of others. Even if that training involves "ostensive teaching" of the expressions in the presence of the different kinds of stones, it would be no help to think that that "ostensive teaching" succeeds by producing a connection between the sound and some act or item "in the mind" of the pupil. The teaching is successful if the pupil learns to carry the right kinds of stones to a builder, or to order the stones he needs if he is a builder. That is the only "connection" the teaching has to establish, since whoever receives the teaching and uses and responds to those sounds in the right ways understands them and knows what they mean. Even if the "ostensive teaching" did always produce some object or act "in the mind," no such thing would be sufficient for meaning or understanding, since the very same "ostensive teaching," and so the production of the very same thing "in the mind," could have brought about a quite different understanding of those sounds. For example, if pupils were trained not to carry a slab to the building but rather to break another kind of stone into pieces when they hear the sound "Slab!," that sound would then have a different meaning in those circumstances – it would not be an order for a slab. But what happened in the "ostensive teaching," and what object was produced "in the mind" as a result of that teaching, might have been just as they are in the case Wittgenstein describes. It is in people's capacities or abilities to use and respond to sounds and marks in the right way that their meaning and understanding them resides.

It is perhaps easy to feel that the "primitive" situation described in PI, 2 and 6 and even 8 is not rich or complex enough to be a case of a full-fledged human language. The range of behavior involving those sounds is so limited it might seem that automata could be trained to engage in it without thinking, meaning, or understanding anything. But even if that is so, the lessons illustrated schematically in that simple case might be carried over to more realistically complex linguistic behavior.[1] Anyone in our society who systematically responds to questions of the form "What is $x$ plus $y$?" by giving the sum of $x$ and $y$ shows that he understands the word "plus" to mean *plus*. That is in fact how the word is used in English. Someone who knows what it means and understands it has mastered the "technique" of using that word – the "technique" of asking for, giving, and in other ways talking about the sum or the addition function in English.

Saul Kripke, in a provocative and influential book,[2] has elaborated a "skeptical" view according to which there is no such fact as a person's meaning *plus* by "plus," or understanding that word as used on particular occasions to mean *plus*. On that view, given all the applications of the word that a person has made or responded to in the past, and everything there is or could be "in his mind," it is still not determined what he means by the word "plus"; it is compatible with all those facts that he means and understands by it something different from *plus*. This view represents a challenge to the very idea of "the rule for the use of an expression." It applies just as much to general practices or customs as it does to individual applications of a "rule."

Many different "rules" are all said to be compatible with everything that has actually happened in the community and every item that has ever been in anyone's mind up to any given point, yet many of those "rules" differ from one another in what they imply would be the correct move the next time. That *this* rather than *that* is the correct move at a particular point is therefore held not to be fixed by any past or present fact. There is therefore no such fact as a person's (or everyone's) following *this* particular rule rather than some other; there is no such unique thing as *the* rule by which a person (or everyone) proceeds. This has the unsettling consequence that there is no such fact as an expression's meaning one thing rather than another, or a person's understanding it one way rather than another. "It seems that the entire idea of meaning vanishes into thin air" (K, p. 22). Kripke finds this "skeptical" view in Wittgenstein; or at least the problem to which it seems such a discouraging answer he finds to be "perhaps the central problem of *Philosophical Investigations*" (K, p. 7).

One thing that casts doubt on the attribution of this "skeptical" view to Wittgenstein is that it involves something that Wittgenstein forcefully and repeatedly rejects. Kripke describes the problem as that of finding a fact that constitutes a person's meaning or understanding an expression in one particular way rather than another, and he holds that any such fact must somehow "contain" within it some "directions" or "instructions" to the person to say or do things in a certain way in virtue of meaning or understanding the expression in the way he does (K, p. 11). That is because, for Kripke, there must be something that "justifies" a person in doing what he does when, for example, he says "125" in answer to the question "What is 68 plus 57?"; he cannot just be proceeding "blindly." The right answer to give is "125" if "plus" means *plus*, but the problem is to say what fact it is that shows him, or shows anyone, that that is what that expression means on this occasion, as opposed, say, to Kripke's *quus*.[3] If there is such a thing as his meaning or understanding "plus" to mean *plus* on that occasion, or his following the rule according to which the correct answer to give to such questions is always the sum, what is it that determines that that is the meaning he understands it to have, or that that is the rule he is following? The "skeptical" answer is: nothing does or could determine that. So there is no such thing as meaning or understanding an expression in one particular way rather than another.

Wittgenstein would certainly endorse the idea that there could be no item in the person's "mind," or anywhere else for that matter, that instructs the person, or tells him what to do, in the sense that its presence there guarantees that the person understands the expression "plus" to mean *plus*. That is just the point brought out by the "ostensive teaching" of builders and their assistants in PI, 6. With a different training in using and responding to the expression, the very same "ostensions" and the very same item produced by them in the speaker's "mind" would bring about a quite different understanding of the expression. What an expression means is to be found in its use, not in any fact or item which is supposed to give it or specify its meaning. Disconnected from any particular ways in which it would be correct to use or to respond to it, any such fact or object on its own would be at best only one more "dead" sign. That is the key to recognizing the futility of appealing to an object or item in the mind or anywhere else. The "skeptical" view concludes from the failure of any such appeal that there is no such thing as an expression's meaning or being understood to mean one thing rather than another. Wittgenstein on the contrary brings out how and why it cannot be a condition of an expression's meaning what it does, or of its being correctly understood in one way rather than another, that there be some object or item or fact that instructs its users or determines what they are to do and so in that way justifies their responses. Nor is that a condition of there being such a thing as the rule by which they proceed, or a "technique" or practice of which they are masters.

We make sense of what happens in the community described in the language-game in PI, 2 by understanding them to be following the rule, or engaging in the practice: when a builder calls out "Slab!" he is ordering a certain kind of building-stone – let us call it in English a slab – and assistants who understand that expression correctly carry a slab to the builder when they hear that sound. A builder who orders a slab in that way on a particular occasion, and an assistant who carries him a slab when he hears that order, conform to the general rule or practice for that expression. They are using and responding to "Slab!" correctly. That there is that practice in that community is what the fact that "Slab!" means what it does there amounts to. Similarly, that English speakers follow the rule that when asked "What is $x$ plus $y$?" it is correct to give the sum, is part of what the fact that "plus" means *plus* amounts to. Someone who speaks English and conforms to that general practice on a particular occasion understands that word to mean *plus*.

The "skeptical" view holds that there are no facts of meaning or understanding an expression in a particular way – that there is no difference in what happens or what is so in the world between a person's or a community's meaning one thing by a certain expression and their meaning something different by it. Nothing in anyone's "mental history" or "mental history of past behavior" establishes that by "plus" someone means *plus* rather than *quus*, for example (K, p. 21). On the "skeptical" view there is no fact anywhere which is the fact that "Slab!" is an order for a slab in the language-game in PI, 2, or that "plus" means *plus* in an English-speaking community. "There can be no such thing as meaning anything by any word" (K, p. 55).

Now it must be admitted that there are a great many facts about the past behavior of a community or an individual in connection with a particular expression which do not together imply – and so cannot be taken to be equivalent to – the fact that that expression means what it does or that the community or the individual understands it in one particular way rather than another. The introduction of concepts like Kripke's *quus* helps to bring that out. There are many facts of what has actually gone on in the community described in the language-game in PI, 2 that are perfectly compatible with assistants' now doing something different on hearing "Slab!" and builders' accepting what they do with approval or without objection. Perhaps from now on when they hear "Slab!" they will break into pieces whatever stone lies next to a slab in the stone pile, or they will carry to a builder what we call a block, not a slab, and builders will make appropriate use of what is brought. This could be so if the community simply started using "Slab!" in a different way, and so changed its meaning. But, more importantly, it could be so even if "Slab!" continues to mean the same as it has meant before. If the rule those speakers have been following is something like: when a builder calls out "Slab!" he is ordering a slab if it is before time $t$ but otherwise he is ordering a block, then our original understanding of them would be wrong. It would be wrong even though every correct response in the past has involved carrying a slab to a builder. On the alternative rule or practice, it would not be correct, after the time in question, for an assistant to carry a slab to a builder on hearing "Slab!"

The same is true of the English word "plus." Even if every particular answer every English speaker has ever given to questions of the form "What is x plus y?" has been the sum of x and y, it does not follow that those who understand the expression correctly will give the sum tomorrow, even if "plus" continues to mean the same as it has meant in the past. Nor does it follow that the sum will be the right answer to give. If "plus" meant *quus*, and tomorrow we were asked a question of the form "What is x plus y?" about numbers beyond those which have actually been computed so far, it would not be correct to give the sum as the answer even though every right answer to such questions in the past has been the sum. In that sense it is possible for something other than the sum to be the right answer, given all those facts of past behavior.

To say that it is possible for a slab to have been delivered, or for the sum to have been given, every time in the past, and yet it not be correct tomorrow to deliver a slab, or to give the sum, even though the meanings of "Slab!" and "plus" have not changed, is to say that it is possible for those facts of past behavior to have been as they are and for those speakers not to be following the rule that "Slab!" is an order for a slab, or that "plus" means *plus*. What is not possible is for those to be the rules they are following and it not be correct to deliver a slab, or to give the sum. Whether a community or an individual is following a particular set of rules or not is a contingent matter of fact. It is possible for us to be wrong about what rules they are following. But in identifying the rules or practices they are following we thereby specify, if only implicitly, what a correct response or a proper understanding of the expressions in question would be.

The fact that there are many descriptions of what has been so or has gone on in the past which do not together imply, and hence are not equivalent to, intentional or semantical statements like " 'Slab!' is an order for a slab" or " 'Plus' means *plus*" does not show that there is something more to an expression's meaning what it does, or a response to an expression's being correct, than the expression's being used in a certain way in the community. It is a matter of how that "use" or rule or practice is to be described. What an expression or a speaker means, or what rule for an expression an individual or a group of speakers is following, or what is a correct application of or response to an expression, are not equivalent or reducible to facts which are not themselves specified in similarly intentional or semantical or normative terms. The "use" of an expression as it is relevant to meaning is the distinctive role the expression plays in the activities in which human beings utter it and respond to it as they do. Those actions and responses can help identify that meaning only if they are seen and understood as intentional; to ascribe them to those agents is to ascribe attitudes with intentional contents. A description in nonintentional terms of what happens whenever certain sounds are uttered or certain marks are made would not say what human beings are doing with those sounds or marks. It would leave the sounds and marks "dead" or without "life" or meaning. Facts of what human agents are intentionally doing are not equivalent or reducible to facts merely of physical or physiological happenings specified in nonintentional terms.

This intentional character of thought and action and language is indispensable to our understanding of them in the ways we do. An order, for example, is something with particular content; fulfilling the order requires that what was ordered be done. That is what gives the order its particular identity. An order for a slab is fulfilled by bringing a slab. That gives the standard of correctness of response for those who understand the utterance. We certify the correctness of that response in saying that those who make the utterance are ordering a slab.

"An order orders its own execution." So it knows its execution, then, even before it is there? – But that was a grammatical proposition and it means: If an order runs "Do such-and-such" then executing the order is called "doing such-and-such." (PI, 458)

An order to do such-and-such orders no more than what is specified in its content. Even if every slab ever brought in response to orders in the language-game in PI, 2 has in fact been grey and has weighed less than ten pounds, it does not follow that what was ordered on all those occasions were grey slabs weighing less than ten pounds, or that it would not be in accord with such an order to deliver a black slab that weighs more. Similarly, it is not simply the fact that every correct answer to "What is $x$ plus $y$?" in the past has been the sum that determines the correctness of giving the sum in answer to such a question this time. Every correct answer might in fact have been the sum even though the sum was not what the question asked for. As things are, it is correct to give the sum because "plus" means *plus*; asking in English "What is $x$ plus $y$?" is asking for the sum of $x$ and $y$.

The "skeptical" view represents the challenge: if those alleged facts of meaning, correctness, or accord with a rule cannot be identified with or shown to be equivalent to anything that actually happens or is so in the world, what could they possibly amount to? But to put the objection in that way is to expose the assumption or prejudice that lies behind it. It assumes that it never happens or is never so in the world that, for instance, a builder orders a slab and an assistant obeys the order, or that someone asks for the sum of two numbers and someone else gives the right answer. What can be said in support of that assumption?

The possibility of "quus"-like interpretations of sounds or marks or other items does succeed in refuting any view of meaning or understanding which requires that there be some item in a speaker's or hearer's "mind" which tells him what to do in using or responding to an expression. No such item could determine the speaker's or hearer's response, or its correctness. If the item that was present when a speaker hears "What is $x$ plus $y$?" meant *plus* it would "tell" him to give the sum, but if that same item was present and meant *quus* it could "tell" him to give the answer "5." Introduction of further items to try to settle the matter would lead to a regress.

But if the requirement of "instruction" or "guidance" has been dropped from an account of meaning or understanding, as for Wittgenstein it must be, what support remains for the "skeptical" view? The possibility that "plus" might mean *quus* shows only that facts of meaning or understanding or correctness of response do not follow from and so are not reducible to any nonintentionally described goings-on, no matter how complex or long-standing. All the nonsemantical or nonintentional facts of what has happened or what has been so in the world up to any given point are compatible with different and conflicting intentional or semantical or normative statements. Given all those past facts, an utterance of "Slab!" in the language-game in PI, 2 could be an order for a slab or it could be an order for a slab if it is before time $t$ and otherwise for a block; uttering "What is $x$ plus $y$?" could be asking what is $x$ plus $y$ or it could be asking what is $x$ quus $y$. But that does not directly imply that there simply are no such semantical or intentional facts of meaning or understanding or of responses' being correct. Nor does it show that "Slab!"'s being an order for a slab is not something that ever happens or is so in the world, or that nothing that could be so in the world is incompatible with its being an order for a slab if it is before time *t* and otherwise for a block. We take it to be true of the community described in the language-game in PI, 2 that "Slab!" is an order for a slab. If that is so, then what is so in that community is incompatible with "Slab!"'s being an order for a slab if it is before time *t* and otherwise for a block. If it is true that "plus" means *plus,* that rules out its meaning *quus.* Those incompatibilities are essential to the very point of an appeal to "quus"-like terms; at most one of the conflicting intentional or semantical statements can be true. But that does not imply that *none* of them is true. So it gives no support to the "skeptical" view that there are no facts at all of what speakers or expressions mean, or of how or whether they are correctly understood.[4]

That conclusion could perhaps be reached on the further assumption that nonintentionally specified facts are somehow the only facts there are, or that they are privileged in some way. But to make that assumption with no further support would seem to be nothing but prejudice. If statements of one kind are not equivalent or reducible to statements of another kind, it does not in general follow that the irreducible statements say nothing and are neither true nor false. Mathematical truths, for example, are not reducible to nonmathematical truths, but that is no reason to conclude that there are no mathematical truths. It shows only that they are different from nonmathematical truths in ways that presumably can be described and understood. Similarly, statements about what expressions mean, or how they are understood, or about the correctness of certain responses to them, are not equivalent or reducible to nonsemantical or nonintentional descriptions of what goes on when certain sounds or marks are made. It shows only that they differ from nonsemantical or nonnormative statements in ways that presumably can be described and understood.

Intentional or semantical remarks like " 'Slab!' is an order for a slab" or " 'Plus' means *plus*" are things we say and mean and understand every day. To explain what they mean and how they differ from other statements would be to understand and describe their use; that is what determines that they have the meanings they do. Saying " 'Slab!' is an order for a slab" serves to identify what "Slab!" means in the community in the language-game in PI, 2, and so to distinguish its use or meaning from that of "Pillar!," "Block!," and "Beam!," which each have different uses in that language." " 'Plus' means *plus*" says what a certain English expression means, and so distinguishes its use or meaning from that of other expressions like "minus" or "times." We make similarly intentional remarks about what an individual speaker means or understands on a particular occasion. A builder who calls out "Slab!" means it as an order for a slab, an assistant who hears him and delivers a slab understands that order correctly. A pupil who answers "125" when asked "What is 68 plus 57?" has correctly understood "plus" to mean *plus* (and has also got the sum right). It seems that we would be unable to make the right kind of sense of the familiar phenomena of speaking and meaning and understanding without thinking of them in these ways. We would be restricted to describing a series of sounds and marks and movements without seeing them as having any particular "life" or meaning.

The "skeptical" view must somehow account for these familiar remarks about the meanings of expressions or speakers' understanding of them while nonetheless holding that they do not say what they seem to say and are neither true nor false. Kripke suggests that on Wittgenstein's conception of "use" there is a way of doing that. It is a matter of describing the conditions under which such things are "legitimately assertable," and showing that "the game of asserting them under such conditions has a role in our lives" (K, p. 78). Our social interaction with others depends on our trusting and relying on them in many ways, so it is not surprising that "the 'game' of attributing to others the mastery of certain concepts or rules" is important to social life (K, p. 93). This is especially clear in child-rearing, education, and training, for example. Someone who has performed successfully in a sufficient number and variety of tests is deemed to have mastered the concept of addition and is accordingly "admitted into the community as an adder; an individual who passes such tests in enough other cases is admitted as a normal speaker of the language and member of the community" (K, p. 92). Those who are incorrigibly deviant in certain respects are to that extent excluded. In extreme cases they cannot participate in the community or in communication at all. The "game" of ascribing concepts and understanding to speakers is to be understood as a complex activity of social "admittance" and "exclusion."

It is certainly in accord with Wittgenstein's conception of meaning as use to include in the description of the use of expressions an account of what human beings are doing in using them as they do and what point or role those activities have in the lives of those people. But what has been said so far along the lines Kripke suggests falls short of a full and adequate description of the familiar use of those expressions. For one thing, it does not explain what is being done or said in remarks about a general practice in a community and not about an individual speaker's performance. To say " 'Slab!' is an order for a slab in the language-game in PI, 2" is not to "admit" some speakers into one's linguistic community, or to encourage or approve of anyone's behavior in any way. To say " 'Plus' means *plus*" is not to "admit" anyone into the English-speaking community either. Such remarks appear to be descriptions of what goes on in a certain community; what those who use and understand the expressions correctly are doing and saying.

Even though to say of a particular person "He understands 'plus' to mean *plus*" can be a way of "admitting" that person into the community, that is not enough to identify what the speaker is thereby saying about the person, or in what way or in what respect he is "admitting" him into the community. We might say of a person who has passed certain other tests "He understands 'minus' to mean *minus*," and thereby "admit" him into the community in a certain respect. But "He understands 'plus' to mean *plus*" does not mean the same as "He understands 'minus' to mean *minus*." Those two remarks do not have the same use. In uttering one of them a speaker is not doing in every respect the very same thing as he is doing in uttering the other. What is missing so far from the description of their uses is any indication of the difference between the two remarks.

Conformity to the general practice in the community is what determines the correctness of a person's employment of or response to expressions. But to say of someone who is deemed to have shown himself master of the concept of addition "He understands 'plus' to mean *plus*" is not simply to say of him that his employment of "plus" conforms to that of the community. It might also be said of him "He understands 'minus' to mean *minus*" on the grounds that his employment of that expression conforms to that of the community as well. To say that he uses and responds to an expression as others do is not in itself to say what particular meaning he or they understand that expression to have. Nor do I specify that meaning if I say of him only that he uses the expression in the same way as I do. A remark like "He understands 'plus' to mean *plus*" does specify that meaning. Saying only that he uses and responds to "plus" as I or as others do in the community does not. To say that we "admit" him because he conforms to community practices in his use of both "plus" and "minus" therefore does not explain how his use of one of those expressions differs from his use of the other. It does not say what my or the community practices in question actually are. We can of course go on to say that in that community, or as I use them, "plus" means *plus* and "minus" means *minus*. That then does serve to specify how he uses and understands them, if he conforms to those practices. But that is a statement about the meaning of certain expressions, or how they are understood. It says more than simply that there is a consensus in the community, or with me, in the use of those expressions.

In trying to describe the "game" or practice of "admitting" certain people into the community – which on the "skeptical" view is all that anyone is doing in saying things like "He understands 'plus' to mean *plus*" – Kripke says the person "is admitted into the community as an adder," as someone who "has grasped the concept of addition" (K, p. 92), or as giving the right answers to "addition problems" (K, p. 96). That does serve to specify a particular respect in which the pupil is "admitted" into the community. But it does so only by attributing to those who thereby "admit" the pupil a recognition or acknowledgment that, not only does the pupil's use conform to that of the community, but also in the community "plus" means *plus*. The "skeptical" view cannot allow for any such specific recognition or acknowledgment, since it would be recognition of something which on that view has no truth-conditions and so is neither true nor false. The "skeptical" view denies that there are any such facts. But without some such particular specification of a pupil's understanding there can be no adequate explanation of the differences in use and so in meaning between remarks like "He understands 'plus' to mean *plus*" and "He understands 'minus' to mean *minus*." The "skeptical" view gives no satisfactory account of such remarks.

Wittgenstein's reminders of the way in which the meanings of expressions are determined by their use in the community, and the correctness of an individual's understanding is determined by his conformity to that practice, stand opposed to any appeal to an "inner" or "mental" object or item as essential to understanding the facts of meaning, understanding, and thinking. Even if there is no good reason to accept the "skeptical" view that there are no such facts to be understood or accounted for, consideration of the challenge represented by that paradoxical view nonetheless brings out a very important point. It is that how someone means or understands certain expressions, or what those expressions mean in the sense of what are the rules or practices for their correct employment in a community, are facts which in general cannot be adequately specified except by using the very concepts that the speakers in question are thereby said to be masters of. Because we know what an order is, and can pick out a certain type of stone we call a slab, we can say that builders in the language-game in PI, 2 who utter "Slab!" are ordering a slab. Equipped as we are with the concept of addition, we can say what a pupil who responds to certain utterances in distinctive ways has mastered; he has got the concept of addition, he understands and gives the right answers to addition problems, he understands "plus" to mean *plus*. If we were restricted to saying without interpretation only what utterances a speaker responds to, what distinctive movements of his body are caused by those utterances, and what utterances he himself is thereby disposed to make in different circumstances, we could not make the right kind of sense of what he is doing in responding and uttering as he does. No description which falls short of identifying *what* speakers mean and understand by the expressions they utter and hear, and *what* they are doing and saying and understanding when they utter and respond in those ways, will succeed in fully specifying the meanings of those expressions or the thought those speakers have in using them as they do. We have access to facts of meaning and understanding that the "skeptical" view denies only because we already possess concepts and thoughts that are embodied or expressed in those very facts.

This is important, if correct, because it suggests that the paradoxical "skeptical" view derives much of its appeal from a recognizable sense of philosophical dissatisfaction or disappointment it is possible to feel in the face of a more robust, non-"skeptical" view of meaning and thought. Wittgenstein's writings reveal an intimate familiarity with that dissatisfaction.

When we see the richness, complexity, and intricate interrelations among the rules, techniques, and practices that determine the meanings of even some of the apparently simplest things we say and understand, there seems little or no hope of our gaining a single commanding view and describing those rules or practices perspicuously once and for all. There is no difficulty for us in using the expressions and following the rules as we do. The difficulty is in stating clearly and fully what those uses or practices are. That is one of the apparent dissatisfactions of the appeal to nothing more than "use" as an explanation of meaning. It is not just a matter of complexity. It is that in giving descriptions of the practices we and others engage in we must employ and rely on the very concepts and practices and capacities that we are trying to describe and understand. One reason it is difficult to describe them correctly is that we see right through them, as it were; they are too close to us to be seen for what they are. This inability to command a clear view of our concepts, and the apparently natural tendency in philosophical reflection to wrongly assimilate the use of one kind of expression to that of another, is for Wittgenstein a continuous source of philosophical problems.

The conclusion can be philosophically dissatisfying or disappointing in another, and deeper, way. If facts of what expressions mean, of the correctness of certain ways of understanding them, or of the rules by which speakers and hearers proceed, can in general be expressed only in semantical or intentional statements which make use of the very concepts that they attribute to those they describe, then they would seem not to be the kinds of facts that could ever explain how language or meaning in general is possible, or what facts or rules human beings rely on, as it were, to get into language in the first place, from outside it. That can seem to leave the phenomena of meaning, understanding, and thinking as philosophically mysterious as they would be on the hypothesis of an occult mental medium. No explanation of thought or meaning in nonsemantical or nonintentional terms would be available. That can be felt as deeply dissatisfying.

Much of Wittgenstein's later philosophy deals in one way or another with the aspiration or demand for a different and potentially more illuminating kind of explanation of meaning. There is rich material for philosophical "treatment." His investigations bring out in as many ways as possible how nothing does or could "instruct" or "guide" us in speaking or in understanding the speech of others. Nothing could "tell" us how to speak, or how to understand what others are saying. Meaning or rules can be told or explained only to those who know how to speak and understand what is said. We get into language at all, not by following instructions or explanations of how to do it, but only because we share enough natural responses, interests, and inclinations with those who already speak. Nothing "deeper" or intellectually more satisfying is available, or would help. We recognize what builders in the language-game in PI, 2 are doing, and understand them to be ordering a slab. We understand what those who respond to addition problems in certain ways are doing, and see that they understand "plus" to mean *plus*. "The common behavior of mankind is the system of reference" by means of which we understand each other (PI, 206). Mankind is a talking species. Such essentially linguistic practices as "commanding, questioning, recounting, chatting, are as much part of our natural history as walking, eating, drinking, playing" (PI, 25).

NOTES

1 "Our clear and simple language-games are not preparatory studies for a future regularization of language – as it were first approximations, ignoring friction and air-resistance. The language-games are rather set up as *objects of comparison* which are meant to throw light on the facts of our language by way not only of similarities, but also of dissimilarities" (PI, 130).

2 Saul A. Kripke, *Wittgenstein on Rules and Private Language* (Cambridge, Mass.: Harvard University Press, 1982). Further references will be made in the text by "K" and page number.

3 "x quus y" denotes the sum of x and y if x and y are both less than the highest numbers for which the function has actually been computed; if not, it denotes 5. It is imagined for purposes of the example that for "68 plus 57" on this occasion only the second condition is fulfilled.

4 The blanket introduction of "quus-like terms without further restriction would have devastating effects on our efforts to understand or learn anything, not just about meaning and understanding. If the possibility that someone means *quus* rather than *plus* by "plus" shows that there is

no such fact as his meaning anything at all by it, then there would also be no such fact as our having confirmed an empirical generalization or having any more reason to believe one thing rather than its opposite, as Nelson Goodman showed (*Fact, Fiction, and Forecast* [Indianapolis: Bobbs-Merrill Co., 1965], 2nd ed.). By parallel reasoning it could be shown that there is no such fact as a person's performing an action of some determinate kind (e.g., walking, rather than walking-if-observed-before-time-$t$-and-otherwise-flying), and even no determinate facts at all (e.g., there is a tree in the meadow, rather than there is a tree-if-observed-before-time-$t$-and-otherwise-a-hippopotamus in the meadow).

# 10 "Whose house is that?"
# Wittgenstein on the self

## I

"Think of a picture of a landscape, an imaginary landscape with a house in it. – Someone asks 'whose house is that?' – The answer, by the way, might be 'It belongs to the farmer who is sitting on the bench in front of it.' But then he cannot for example enter his house" (PI, 398). Wittgenstein tells this mild joke in the midst of a discussion on the self, the I, or better: on the ways we use the word "I." The gist of his discussion appears to be that there is no self to which the "I" might refer. But how does the jocular story fit in? Does it suggest that it is not I who imagines the landscape, house, and farmer? Does the farmer stand for the self even though there is no such thing? What does it mean that he can own but not enter the imagined house? What does the story tell us about the I and/or the "I"? There is a roundabout answer to all this.

## II

Wittgenstein reflected on questions concerning the mind, mental states, processes, and acts throughout his life and in that context he came regularly back to the I, self, soul, or subject as he called it more or less indiscriminately. The first time he talks about the mind – in the middle of a difficult passage on the things that make up the world – he announces unexpectedly: "There really is only one world soul, which I for preference call *my* soul . . . " (NB, p. 49) and a few weeks before his death, thirty-six years later, he writes in another notebook: "But it is still false to say: . . . I is a different person from L.W" (LWII, p. 88). No wonder that somewhere on that

320

road he came to think that "The I, the I is what is deeply mysterious" (NB, p. 80).

The scope and complexity of his writings on the mind establish that these were not by-products of other, more immediate concerns – such as an interest in language. Wittgenstein said in the 1930s that philosophy needed to deal only "with those points about language which have led, or are likely to lead, to definite philosophical puzzles or errors." Everything else he considered "not the philosopher's business."[1] This does not mean that he had no genuine interest in language, but that it was always motivated by philosophical considerations. Philosophical questions concerning language he saw, in turn, linked to questions concerning the mind. To trace Wittgenstein's discussion of the self means, therefore, to trace the complex web of connections between questions of mind and language.

## III

As one reads Wittgenstein, one must keep an eye on the changing landscape of this thought. But it is just as important to be alert to the continuities in his thinking and such continuities are particularly visible in what he says about the mind. One unifying theme in this area is his enduring hostility to the idea of an individuated, substantive self. Insofar as the belief in such a self is most easily associated with Descartes, we can call Wittgenstein's position an anti-Cartesianism.[2] This attitude is already evident in the *Tractatus* where he asserts that "there is no such thing as the subject that thinks or entertains ideas" (TLP, 5.631). That he intended this to be an anti-Cartesian remark is made clear in the *Blue Book* where he writes, first, that our language creates the illusion that the word "I" refers to "something bodiless, which, however, has its seat in our body," and then concludes: "In fact *this* seems to be the real ego, the one of which it was said, 'Cogito, ergo sum' " (BLBK, p. 69). He returns to the theme once again in the *Philosophical Investigations* where he writes:

"I" is not the name of a person, nor "here" of a place, and "this" is not a name. But they are connected with names. Names are explained by means of them. It is also true that it is characteristic of physics not to use these words. (PI, 410)

322 THE CAMBRIDGE COMPANION TO WITTGENSTEIN

IV

In order to appreciate how deeply anti-Cartesianism infuses Wittgenstein's thinking about the mind, we must look at a notoriously obscure passage in the *Tractatus* where this idea is first vented (TLP, 5.54–5.55), a passage that begins with the claim that "propositions occur in other propositions only as bases of truth-operations" (TLP, 5.54) and proceeds from there at hazardous speed to the conclusion that "there is no such thing as the soul" (TLP, 5.5422). The argument is so dense, that it requires some spelling out to make it transparent.

The first requirement for that is to pay close attention to the truth-functionality thesis with which the passage starts. The thesis says that the relations between a complex proposition made up out of simpler ones and those simpler propositions themselves are inevitably truth-functional in character. But the claim appears to run into immediate counterexamples. Are there not contexts in which the truth and falsity of the complex proposition is independent of the truth or falsity of the component ones? Are modal propositions like "It is possible that p" or "it is necessary that either p or q" not such counterexamples? Wittgenstein sees himself forced to admit that "at first sight it looks as if it were also possible for one proposition to occur in another in a different way" (TLP, 5.541). He points to what he calls "certain forms of proposition in psychology," that is, propositions of the form "A believes that *p*" and of the form "A has the thought *p*" where "A" is taken to stand for some subject or self and "p" for a proposition believed or entertained by *A*. By focusing on these propositions he has forged a link between his discussion of the logical structure of complex propositions and the question how we are to understand the relation between a judging, believing subject and the contents of his judgments or beliefs. It remains to be seen whether that linkage is accidental.

Wittgenstein's counterexamples are, clearly, open to three different responses. The most straightforward one would be to abandon or to restrict the scope of the truth-functionality thesis. A second response would be to maintain that the apparent counterexamples are not bona fide propositions at all. A third, and perhaps the most problematic response, would be to argue that the apparent counterexamples do not, in fact, conflict with the truth-functionality thesis. That would amount to saying that they do not really have the logical form which they seem to possess. It is this third response which Wittgenstein makes his own, as he indicates right from the start when he writes that "at first sight it looks as if" the apparent counterexamples were exceptions to the truth-functionality thesis.

His response requires, first of all, an appeal to the distinction between the apparent and the real form of the proposition which Wittgenstein had made earlier in the *Tractatus* when he had written: "Language disguises thought. So much so, that from the outward form of the clothing it is impossible to infer the form of the thought beneath it" (TLP, 4.002). In discussing his apparent counterexamples to the truth-functionality thesis he contrasts accordingly what they look like "if they are superficially considered" with their supposedly real form (TLP, 5.541 and 5.542). Superficially considered it looks in both cases "as if the proposition *p* stood in some kind of relation to an object *A*" (TLP, 5.541). That relation would not be truth-functional in character and, hence, on the superficial account these propositions would indeed be counterexamples to the truth-functionality thesis.

At this point Wittgenstein introduces a new thought. It is that "modern theory of knowledge" actually takes the superficial appearance of these propositions to display their real logical form (TLP, 5.541). Modern theory of knowledge is thus tainted by a pervasive philosophical flaw since "most of the propositions and questions of philosophers arise from our failure to understand the logic of our language" (TLP, 4.003). In case we are in any doubt, Wittgenstein goes on to mention "Russell, Moore, etc." as representatives of the modern theory of knowledge he is attacking. It may surprise us to find him accusing Russell here of a failure to distinguish between the superficial appearance of a proposition and its real logical form, since elsewhere in the *Tractatus* he credits him with having introduced that distinction into philosophy. "It was Russell who performed the service of showing that the apparent logical form of a proposition need not be its real one" (TLP, 4.0031). It has long been understood, however, that Wittgenstein's criticism at 5.541 is directed against a specific Russellian text, a book on the theory of knowledge which Russell was writing while Wittgenstein was in Cambridge and which he never completed as a result of Wittgenstein's criticisms.[3]

In that text Russell had argued for a broadly Cartesian conception of the self as a necessary presupposition for a coherent theory of meaning.[4] He had reached that conclusion in the context of a question that had long preoccupied him, the question of the unity of the proposition. Already in the *Principles of Mathematics* of 1903 he had pointed out that there is surely a difference between a proposition and a list of its components. The first, he had said, exhibited a peculiar kind of unity which was absent from the second. But how was this unity to be explained? Russell's initial response had been to adopt an essentially Fregean solution and to argue that within every proposition there occurs one component which ties the elements of the proposition together. But by 1903 he had already convinced himself that the conception of propositions as real unities was problematic, since it seemed to lead to a type of logical antinomy. By 1911 he had, therefore, come around to thinking that the solution lay in the assuming that the apparent unity of a proposition was in each case due to a thinking subject holding the elements of the proposition together in its thinking. Every proposition "p" was thus really of the form "A judges/thinks that p." The unity of the proposition was grounded in the unity of the thinking subject which stood in a relation of thinking or believing to the proposition. A broadly Cartesian conception of the mind, thus, appeared to be a prerequisite for a satisfactory theory of meaning.

It was precisely this theory which Wittgenstein attacked in sections 5.54ff. of the *Tractatus*. Once we are aware of this, we can see that his choice of the apparent counterexamples to the truth-functionality thesis was motivated by the idea that he would, thus, be able to defeat, at one stroke, both a certain theory of meaning and an associated theory of the mind. His argument can therefore be understood to be illustrating the claim (made in the preface of the *Tractatus*) that misunderstandings of the logic of our language give rise to philosophical problems and as a result generate philosophical theories. In the passage beginning with 5.54, Wittgenstein is clearly showing how Russell's misconceived account of the unity of the proposition generates the need for this misguided conception of the self.

Against Russell, Wittgenstein declares at this point simply that "it is clear, however, that 'A believes that p' and 'A says p' are of the form ' "p" says $p$' " (TLP, 5.542). The remark must remain mysterious until we are clear about the form of the proposition " 'p' says $p$." It evidently speaks of a relation between the proposition "p" and the situation $p$; but what kind of relation is here under discussion? Wittgenstein characterizes it elsewhere in the *Tractatus* in the words: "This proposition represents such and such a situation" (TLP, 4.031). He also says that in order for the proposition "p" to succeed in this task of representation, it must have some structure to it. "It is only in so far as a proposition is logically articulated that it is a picture of a situation" (TLP, 4.032). In fact, the proposition and the situation must, in some way, be equivalent to each other. "In a proposition there must be exactly as many distinguishable parts as in the situation that it represents. The two must possess the same logical (mathematical) multiplicity" (TLP, 4.04).

These words contain an implicit critique of the Russellian view of propositions. They say that a proposition has a unity in itself which does not depend on a thinking or judging subject. A proposition is essentially articulate and as such is "not a blend of words" (TLP, 3.141). In the proposition there exists, rather, a "nexus" between the signs. "Only in the nexus of a proposition does a name have meaning" (TLP, 3.3). The articulated proposition is for that reason itself a fact – i.e., something in which the elements hang together like links in a chain (TLP, 3.14). We can see then that the sentence " 'p' says p" expresses for Wittgenstein a relation between a fact (i.e., the proposition) and a situation that has the same logical multiplicity. As he says in the passage under discussion, the sentence "does not involve a correlation of a fact with an object, but rather the correlation of facts by means of the correlation of their objects" (TLP, 5.542).

When Wittgenstein says that "A believes that p" and "A says p" are really of the form " 'p' says $p$" he is, in effect, telling us that believing and saying (as well as thinking, to which his earlier example referred) are or involve representation relations. In order for $A$ to believe that p or to say p, A must be able to represent the content of the proposition "p" to itself. But this means that A or something in A (that which does the representing) must have the same logical multiplicity as p; A or something in A must, as a result, be itself a fact. It cannot be a simple object. The idea that a Cartesian self can represent situations for itself must, therefore, be abandoned as logically incoherent.

Two things are apparent as far as Wittgenstein is concerned. The first is that the unity of the proposition cannot be sought in the Cartesian subject that Russell had postulated. The Russellian account can, in fact, not explain why only certain combinations of words form propositions. "A correct explanation of the form of the proposition 'A makes the judgment p', must show that it is impossible for a judgment to be a piece of nonsense. (Russell's theory does not satisfy that requirement)" (TLP, 5.5421). Since for Russell the unity of the proposition is brought about by a subject holding its components together in consciousness, the elements "drinks," "eats," "merry," should under appropriate conditions form the content of a meaningful judgment, which they clearly do not.

Wittgenstein applies this account immediately to the phenomenon of Gestalt perception. With respect to the well-known Necker cube he asserts that "there are two possible ways of seeing the figure" because "we really see two different facts" (TLP, 5.5423). I take the remark to mean that the shifting perception is not to be explained by saying that the subject perceives the cube in two different ways; the explanation is rather that there are two "ways of seeing," two perceptual representations, verbally expressed as

(1) the *a* points of the cube are in front of the *b* points and
(2) the *b* points are in front of the *a* points.

These different representations picture two different facts, two different positions of the cube in space, and they stand to these facts in the relation of a logical isomorphism. The perceiving subject, thus, drops out of the account of Gestalt perception.

The second thing that becomes apparent to Wittgenstein at this point is that the subject cannot be conceived of in Cartesian terms as both simple and representing (i.e., thinking, believing, judging, etc.). These two characteristics, which the classical modern tradition from Descartes through Leibniz to Russell has taken to be compatible, are, in fact, not so. And with this observation he cuts through the Gordian knot of the modern conception of the subject. The idea that a simple self could also be a representing self is, indeed, absurd. That conclusion might lead one to postulate, instead, a complex representing subject. But Wittgenstein is certain that this is an equally unviable notion. Laconically he writes: "A composite soul would no longer be a soul" (TLP, 5.5421). While he does not tell us from where he takes the force of this conviction, its radical consequences within the structure of the *Tractatus* are obvious. For Wittgenstein sees himself now justified to conclude "that there is no such thing as the soul."

This can hardly be called a proof, since the premise that the soul cannot be composite is not argued for. And it is, in fact, not clear that Wittgenstein means to be giving a proof. When he says: "This shows too that there is no such thing as the soul" we need not take the word "shows" to mean "proves"; we might take the sentence instead to be saying that this makes once again evident that there is no such thing as the soul. Such a reading fits the fact that he ascribes belief in a soul to "the superficial psychology of the present day." And this "psychology" – which we might want to interpret literally here as a theory of the psyche, that is, of the soul or the subject – had already been dismissed earlier as "no more closely related to philosophy than any other natural science" (TLP, 4.1121), that is, as irrelevant to philosophy.[5]

### V

By the time Wittgenstein was writing the *Tractatus* anti-Cartesianism was, of course, a well-rehearsed idea and objections to the Cartesian conception of the mind were familiar. Hume and Kant, Schopenhauer and Nietzsche, as well as Mach and Freud come to mind as exponents of one or another form of anti-Cartesianism. In *Beyond Good and Evil*, for instance, Nietzsche argues against what he calls "soul atomism," a view he characterizes as "the belief which regards the soul as something indestructible, eternal, indivisible, as a monad, as an *atomon*," adding, "this belief ought to be expelled from science."[6] Shortly after, Mach writes: "The primary fact is not the ego, but the elements (sensations). . . . The elements constitute the I. . . . The ego must be given up."[7] By 1918 Wittgenstein must have been aware of these ideas. He was certainly familiar with Schopenhauer by then; he had also studied parts of Kant's *Critique of Pure Reason*, knew some of Nietzsche's writings, and was acquainted with Mach's *Analysis of Sensations* from which the quoted sentences are taken.

But anti-Cartesianism is only one component in Wittgenstein's thinking about the mind and not the most original at that. What makes his position unusual is rather the view that underlies his anti-Cartesian stand. We may call it, for short, Wittgenstein's anti-objectivism. In his *Notebooks* he writes, for instance, in accordance with his anti-Cartesian position that "the thinking subject is surely mere illusion," but he adds to this what I call the antiobjectivist claim that "the I is not an object" (NB, p. 80). I take this to mean that the I cannot be a constituent of the world at all, that the word "I" can neither be a name for a simple object nor a description of a complex.[8]

A superficial reading of these remarks might convince one that Wittgenstein commits himself here to a simple-minded eliminative reductionism according to which all there is, in any possible sense of the word, is the physical world describable by natural science and which concludes that within this world there occurs no subject. One might, in other words, conceive of Wittgenstein's position in the *Tractatus* as a radical objectivism of a behaviorist, materialist, or (more generally speaking) physicalist kind. But this would be to misunderstand his views altogether. While he took the physicalist picture of empirical reality for granted, he also thought that physicalism was philosophically insufficient because it could not provide an understanding of human subjectivity. The observation that the I is not an object means for him that objectivism proves unworkable with respect to the self. Wittgenstein holds that the I cannot be conceived as any kind of object: it can be neither a mental, Cartesian substance, nor a material thing; but the subject is thereby not abolished. This is made explicit in his further observation that "I objectively confronts every object. But not the I." And, if this was not sufficiently clear as an expression of antiobjectivism, he adds: "So there really is a way in which we can and must acknowledge the I *in a non-psychological sense* in philosophy" (NB, p. 80).[9]

To acknowledge the I here in a nonpsychological sense means to consider it as something which is not subject to scientific theorizing and which is not objectively given as part of the world. The I has not been reduced to nothing, but it also does not have the status of an object in the world, of a something. We are reminded here of Wittgenstein's analogous later point that the sensation of pain is "not a *something*, but not a *nothing* either" (PI, 304). In parallel we might say here that according to the *Tractatus* the I is not a something, but not a nothing either.

To this we must add another idea. For the antiobjectivism of the *Tractatus* is linked to a view which we may label "referentialism" for short. The referentialist view assumes that every meaningful expression which is not a sentence or a logical symbol has meaning by either naming a simple object or describing a complex. Since Wittgenstein has concluded, in accordance with his antiobjectivism, that the I is neither a simple object nor a complex, it follows that any word we might want to use to speak about the subject must, according to the assumptions of referentialism, be meaningless. In the *Notebooks* and in the *Tractatus* the peculiar status of the self is explained by the observation that "The I makes its appearance in philosophy through the world's being *my* world" (NB, p. 80 and TLP, 5.641). While there is no such thing as a worldly subject or self for Wittgenstein, there still remains for him the phenomenon of subjectivity. That is made visible in the fact that a complete description of the world will not (and need not) mention the I, but the world so described is still called "The World as *I* found it." In other words: the objective world has to be conceived as a world given to a subjectivity and it is in this that the subject makes its appearance.[10]

On the Tractarian account there can, in any case, be no objective account, no science of the subject at all, since science deals only with objects in the world and their relations. Psychology as a science of the soul is therefore impossible. But the meaning of nonobjectivism is for Wittgenstein not exhausted in this negative observation, as we have seen. Nonobjectivism means for him, rather, that the I is given in a nonobjective way and not as an object in the world. As Wittgenstein writes: "The philosophical self is not the human being, not the human body, or the human soul, with which psychology deals, but rather the metaphysical subject, the limit of the world – not a part of it" (TLP, 5.641). And it is useful to remind ourselves here that "the limits of my language signify the limits of my world" (TLP, 5.6). Hence, that which is conceived as the limit of the world must also be conceived as being at the limit of language.

While we can give an exhaustive objective, scientific description of the world, according to Wittgenstein, that description cannot touch on the (transcendental) fact that the world is after all my world. This fundamental feature of subjectivity cannot be accounted for by postulating an objectively available subject (or objectively available subjects) within the world. The mental is not a sphere within the world nor is it an object outside the world; "the metaphysical subject" is, rather, the nonobjective condition of the possibility of the objective world. On this account the self is neither a Humean or Machian logical construct, nor a Kantian subject that is somehow both an empirical and transcendental consciousness, nor a causal construct as Nietzsche and Freud would have it. All these philosophers remain caught within the framework of objectivism. For Kant the empirical self is an *object* within empirical reality and thus has its own causal efficacy; Nietzsche and Freud see themselves as psychologists, as investigators of an *objectively* constituted ego; even Hume and Mach who speak of the self as a fictional object treat it thereby as an *object*.

Wittgenstein seeks to set himself off from all of them. But that attempt carries a heavy price. The relation of Wittgenstein's philosophical self to the everyday self of which we commonly speak remains unspecified. Unlike the Cartesian self, the philosophical self is unindividuated and Wittgenstein describes it accordingly also in his *Notebooks* as a "world soul."[11] When we conceive it in this way, it becomes impossible to speak about a plurality of subjects. Wittgenstein's view thus appears to force him into a transcendental solipsism for which "there is really only one world soul, which I for preference call *my* soul" (NB, p. 49).[12]

## VI

It took Wittgenstein great effort to overcome this transcendental solipsism, which initially seemed to him both problematic and unavoidable. His later reflections on the mind can be read as one long argument designed to show that one can hold on to the insights of anti-Cartesianism and antiobjectivism without falling into such a solipsism. However, in order to reach that conclusion, he first had to change three assumptions about language and meaning.

(1) In the *Tractatus* Wittgenstein had assumed that language constitutes a formal unity. While he had allowed that "man possesses the ability to construct languages" (TLP, 4.002), he had also argued that insofar as these languages are intertranslatable, "they are all constructed according to a common logical pattern. . . . They are all in a certain sense one" (TLP, 4.014). By the early 1930s Wittgenstein came to think that language is made up of a number of distinct language-games. In illustration of this point he wrote at the time: "The picture we have of the language of the grown-ups is that of a nebulous mass of language, his mother tongue, surrounded by dis-

crete and more or less clear-cut language-games, the technical languages" (BRBK, p. 81). And still later he wrote more generally: "We see that what we call 'sentence' and 'language' has not the formal unity that I imagined, but is the family of structures more or less related to one another" (PI, 108).

(2) This new openness went hand in hand with the rejection of the idea that our sentences are meant to mirror the logical structure of the world. We cannot justify the choice of a system of notation by reference to the structure of the world. Wittgenstein is therefore ready to accept now the legitimacy of the solipsist's preferred way of speaking.

There is, as we have said, no objection to adopting a symbolism in which a certain person always or temporarily holds an exceptional place. . . . What, however, is wrong, is to think that I can *justify* this notation. . . . There is nothing wrong in suggesting that the others should give me an exceptional place in their notation; but the justification which I wish to give for it: that this body is now the seat of that which really lives – is senseless. (BLBK, p. 66)

This principle of tolerance is made possible, because Wittgenstein no longer holds that language serves a single function, that of depicting reality. In the *Tractatus* he had written: "A proposition is a model of reality as we imagine it" (TLP, 4.01). And: "The totality of propositions is language" (TLP, 4.001). But now he argued that language may serve very different needs. "Thus we sometimes wish for a notation which stresses a difference more strongly, makes it more obvious, than ordinary language does, or one which in a particular case uses more closely similar forms of expression than ordinary language. Our mental cramp is loosened when we are shown notations which fulfil these needs. These needs can be of the greatest variety" (BLBK, p. 59). The crucial point for him was now that language is primarily a "system of communication" rather than one of representation (BRBK, p. 81).

(3) And this recognition of different functions of language went together with the rejection of Wittgenstein's earlier referentialism. He called referentialism now "one of the great sources of philosophical bewilderment" (BLBK, p. 1). The mistake, he said, was "that we are looking for the use of a sign, but we look for it as though it were an object *co-existing* with the sign" (BLBK, p. 5). This had the consequence that, whenever we look for such an object and cannot find it,

we may start looking for it in an "ethereal" sphere. We appeal to the gaseous and ethereal in philosophy "when we perceive that a substantive is not used as what in general we should call the name of an object, and when therefore we can't help saying to ourselves that it is the name of an ethereal object" (BLBK, p. 47). The assumptions of an invisible Platonic realm, of an inaccessible transcendent reality, of a transcendental perspective, and of Cartesian mentalism are all dismissed as a subterfuge "when we are embarrassed about the grammar of certain words, and when all we know is that they are not used as names for material objects" (BLBK, p. 47).

## VII

These changes in Wittgenstein's thinking about language and meaning were based on a variety of grounds. The *Blue Book* shows that they are also intimately linked to his concerns with the nature of the mind. His remarks about the ethereal as a subterfuge in that text are characteristically followed by the assertion: "This is a hint as to how the problem of the two materials, *mind* and *matter*, is going to dissolve" (BLBK, p. 47). The *Blue Book* gives us, in fact, reasons to think that the shifts in Wittgenstein's thinking about language are intimately connected with his worries about the nature of the mind.

In considering how that work tackles this issue we must pay attention to the fact that Wittgenstein dictated it to his students at Cambridge over a period of two terms and that the text therefore divides into two natural parts of roughly equal size. The first deals with various problems surrounding the concept of meaning while the second deals almost exclusively with questions in the philosophy of mind, and specifically with the problem of solipsism.

The general point of the discussions in the first half of the book is summed up at the end of that section when Wittgenstein says that the investigation of how we use words like "thinking," "meaning," "wishing," and so forth "rids us of the temptation to look for a peculiar act of thinking, independent of the act of expressing our thoughts, and stowed away in some peculiar medium" (BLBK, p. 43). The conclusion, he also says, is that "the experience of thinking *may* be just the experiencing of saying" (BLBK, p. 43). One might call this an antimentalistic conclusion and this reading is confirmed by the details of Wittgenstein's exposition. He writes for instance:

We are tempted to think that the action of language consists of two parts; an inorganic part, the handling of signs, and an organic part, which we may call understanding these signs, meaning them, interpreting them, thinking. These latter activities seem to take place in a queer medium, the mind; and the mechanism of the mind, the nature of which, it seems, we don't quite understand, can bring about effects which no material mechanism could. (BLBK, p. 3)

Wittgenstein rejects this view by insisting that what we might call "the life of the sign" is really its use. "And when we are worried about the nature of thinking, the puzzlement which we wrongly interpret to be one about the nature of a medium is a puzzlement caused by the mystifying use of our language" (BLBK, p. 6). When we think of "the meaning" of a sign as something necessarily located in the medium of "the mind" we are making the same logical mistake twice over, that is, the mistake of "looking for a 'thing corresponding to a substantive' " (BLBK, p. 5).

Wittgenstein seems to be saying that there is no such thing as the mind and no such thing as the meaning of a sign, that there are only uses of language. Insofar as using language is a behavior we might classify this view as a form of behaviorism. While this appears to be the conclusion of part one of the *Blue Book*, it is not, however, the conclusion of the book as a whole. Part two of the *Blue Book* begins, rather, with the warning that once we start to consider the nature of personal experience "all we have said about signs and the various objects we mentioned in our examples may have to go into the melting-pot" (BLBK, p. 44). There follows a lengthy metaphor according to which handling philosophical problems is like arranging the books in a library. As we proceed we may have to move books again and again to new shelves. The point is that "no philosophical problem can be solved until all philosophical problems are solved; which means that as long as they aren't all solved every new difficulty renders all previous results questionable" (BLBK, p. 44).

Wittgenstein draws our attention next to the different kinds of proposition in our language. "There are propositions of which we may say that they describe facts in the material world (external world). . . . There are on the other hand propositions describing personal experiences, as when the subject in a psychological experiment describes his sense-experiences" (BLBK, pp. 46–7). This acknowledgment removes, in one stroke, his earlier claim in the *Tractatus* that all meaningful propositions will have to be propositions of natural science describing facts of external reality. His principle of tolerance allows him now to acknowledge the existence of meaningful descriptions of personal experience.

Wittgenstein goes on to say that the existence of these two types of proposition has encouraged a number of different interpretations. "At first sight it may appear . . . that here we have two kinds of worlds, worlds built of different materials; a mental world and a physical world" (BLBK, p. 47). Another interpretation holds that "the mental phenomena, sense experience, volition, etc., emerge when a type of animal body of a certain complexity has been evolved" (BLBK, p. 47). A third view maintains that "personal experience, far from being the *product* of physical processes, seems to be the very *basis* of all that we say with any sense about such processes" (BLBK, p. 48). Finally, there is the view that "the whole world, mental and physical, is made of one material only" (BLBK, p. 48). What Wittgenstein describes here are the positions of Cartesian dualism, materialist emergentism, idealism, and neutral monism.

It is, however, clear that he wants to adopt none of these – and, hence, presumably also not the materialist behaviorism that seems to be suggested in the first part of the *Blue Book*. He insists, rather, that the common-sense man, with whom he identifies here, "is as far from realism as from idealism" (BLBK, p. 48). The remark reminds us of his earlier assertion that metaphysics "leads the philosopher into complete darkness" (BLBK, p. 18) and is in accord with the disparaging later comment in the *Philosophical Investigations* that disputes between idealists, solipsists, and realists are merely disagreements about forms of expression and not about "facts recognized by every reasonable human being" (PI, 402). Or, as he puts it in the *Blue Book:* "We are up against trouble caused by our way of expression" (BLBK, p. 48). The difference between propositions describing the external world and propositions describing sense-experience is then not to be explained metaphysically.

Antiobjectivism remains an integral component of Wittgenstein's reflections on the mind in the *Blue Book*. But in the light of his modified views about language and meaning it now takes on a new form. Where the distinction between the objective and the nonobjective had previously been thought to coincide with the distinction between that which is sayable and that which is not sayable, it is now taken to coincide with a distinction between two different ways of speaking that serve different human needs. This insight is now put to the service of rethinking the whole area of the philosophy of mind. Wittgenstein is now ready to admit that the word "I" can serve a meaningful function in language. He assumes it to have, in fact, two distinct functions. There is, as he puts it, its "use as object" and its "use as subject" (BLBK, p. 66). His examples make clear that he means to say that we use "I" (or "my") to refer to an object when we use it to speak of a human body and its physical characteristics. Hence, we have "My arm is broken," "I have grown six inches," "I have a bump on my forehead," and "The wind blows my hair about." The word "I" is used as subject, on the other hand, when we speak of mental states, mental processes, and sensations such as seeing, hearing, trying, thinking, feeling pain. Wittgenstein's examples are: "I see so-and-so," "I hear so-and-so," "I try to lift my arm," "I think it will rain," "I have toothache" (BLBK, pp. 66–7).

But what are the different functions of the term in these two uses? What different needs are being served by them? In the first kind of sentence, Wittgenstein says, an object is identified and something is said about it. In the second no object is referred to. It follows that "to say, 'I have pain' is no more a statement *about* a particular person than moaning is" (BLBK, p. 67). By uttering "I have pain" I am not trying to state a fact; instead I am trying to "attract attention" to myself. By means of a number of thought experiments Wittgenstein seeks to show that in such utterances the word "I" does not serve as a description of a body. It has, in fact, no referential function at all. We fail to recognize this only because we are inclined to take every meaningful noun to be standing for an object. "We are up against one of the great sources of philosophical bewilderment: a substantive makes us look for a thing that corresponds to it" (BLBK, p. 1). Referentialism in conjunction with the correct observation that the word "I" does not denote a physical body in certain contexts, is then seen as the source of the Cartesian conception of the self. The last sentence of the *Blue Book* says accordingly: "The kernel of the proposition that that which has pains or sees or thinks is of a mental nature is only, that the word 'I' in 'I have pains' does not denote a particular body" (BLBK, p. 74). We might say that referentialism in conjunction with the observation that the word "I" does not denote a body drives us into Cartesianism. In order to escape from this metaphysical quandary we must, first of all, abandon referentialism and that, in turn, will allow us to abandon objectivism. This is, in effect, the message of the crucial statement from the *Blue Book* with which I initially substantiated his anti-Cartesianism. For Wittgenstein says here that "we feel that in the case in which 'I' is used as subject, we don't use it because we recognize a particular person by his bodily characteristics; and this creates the illusion that we use this word to refer to something bodiless, which, however, has its seat in our body" (BLBK, p. 69).

The argumentative strategy of the *Blue Book* seems clear. Having convinced ourselves in the first half that the mind is not a "queer medium" and that thinking is just an operating with signs, we are made to see in the second half that materialism and behaviorism cannot explain propositions like "I am in pain." The word "I" cannot be taken to refer to something material and the predicate "being in pain" cannot be taken to refer to some physical state or physical behavior of such a material thing. Given the assumption that either materialist behaviorism or a Cartesian mentalism must be true, the insoluble difficulties of the former seem to drive us into the latter – a conclusion that is in flat conflict with the results of part 1 of the *Blue Book*. We can resolve the dilemma only when we come to see that the alternative "either materialist behaviorism or Cartesian mentalism" rests on the assumption that objectivism is true: *If* objectivism is true, then either materialist behaviorism or Cartesian mentalism. Since part 1 of the *Blue Book* has produced compelling arguments against mentalism and part 2 equally compelling arguments against behaviorism, we must conclude that objectivism is false.

There remain two serious problems with the *Blue Book* account. The first is that Wittgenstein admits the existence of connections between statements like "My arm is broken" and "I am in pain" but fails to account for these connections. As a result he comes close to a "conceptual dualism" according to which the two utterances belong to two different language games and are, thus, logically and conceptually independent of each other. The shortcomings in the argument are taken up in the *Philosophical Investigations* where Wittgenstein offers a more detailed and more satisfactory treatment of this difficulty.

The second problem left unresolved in the *Blue Book* concerns the positive content of Wittgenstein's nonobjectivist understanding of the mind. In the *Blue Book* he says very little about this matter. In the passage from which I have just quoted he answers the question whether on his conception there is then no mind by saying: "The word 'mind' has meaning, i.e., it has a use in our language; but saying this doesn't yet say what kind of use we make of it" (BLBK, pp. 69–70). That response might strike one as evasive, since he does not go on to say what meaning the word "mind" has for him. And this evasion, if that is the right word, continues in Wittgenstein's later writings. Neither the *Philosophical Investigations* nor the subsequent notes overcome it, though these writings give evidence of his lasting preoccupation with these matters.

### VIII

In the *Philosophical Investigations* Wittgenstein continued to affirm that the physical and the mental belong to different language games, but also now acknowledged the need to explain their relations in detail. Accordingly he wrote: "Here we have two different language-games and a complicated relation between them. – If you try to reduce their relations to a *simple* formula you go wrong" (PI, p. 180). The crucial insight that takes him beyond the position reached in the *Blue Book* is expressed in the formula that "an 'inner process' stands in need of outward criteria" (PI, 580). It assures us of a linkage between utterances of the form "His arm is broken" and "He is in pain" as well as between "My arm is broken" and "I am in pain." Wittgenstein illustrates the point as follows:

This is how I think of it: Believing is a state of mind. It has duration; and that independently of the duration of its expression in a sentence, for example. So it is a kind of disposition of the believing person. This is shown me in the case of someone else by his behavior; and by his words. And under this head, by the expression "I believe . . . " as well as by the simple assertion. (PI, pp. 191–2)

The behavior, Wittgenstein says, serves here as my criterion for ascribing an enduring belief. Without such external criteria we would not be in a position to ascribe inner states. It follows that "only of a human being and what resembles (behaves like) a living human being can one say: it has sensations; it sees; hears; is deaf; is conscious or unconscious" (PI, 281). For this reason, too, we can imagine pain in the wriggling fly but not in the dead rock, unless we imagine a living being embedded in it.

Such considerations might make it appear that Wittgenstein has now, after all, slipped into the materialist behaviorism that he had tried to resist in the *Blue Book*. He is well aware of the possibility of this misunderstanding and, therefore, repeatedly and vehemently rejects the charge of behaviorism. He writes in five successive remarks:

304. "But you will surely admit that there is a difference between pain-behavior accompanied by pain and pain-behavior without any pain?" – Admit it? What greater difference could there be? . . .

305. "But you surely cannot deny that, for example, in remembering, an inner process takes place?" – What gives the impression that we want to deny anything . . .

306. Why should I deny that there is a mental process? . . .

307. "Are you not really a behaviorist in disguise? Aren't you at bottom really saying that everything except human behavior is a fiction?" – If I speak of a fiction, then it is of a *grammatical* fiction.

308. . . . And now it looks as if we had denied mental processes. And naturally we don't want to deny them.

### IX

To understand the tenor of these remarks, it is useful to focus on the aphorism that immediately follows them: "What is your aim in philosophy? – To show the fly the way out of the fly-bottle" (PI, 309). Fly-bottles, we must know, are devices for catching flies. Attracted by a sweet liquid in the bottle, the fly enters it from an opening at the bottom and when it has stilled its hunger tries to leave by flying upward toward the light. But the bottle is sealed at the top and so all attempts to escape by that route must fail. Since it never occurs to the fly to retrace its path into the bottle, it will eventually perish inside. The aphorism is thus evidently meant to alert us to two sentences in the preceding remark where Wittgenstein has said of the philosophical problems surrounding mental processes, mental states, and behaviorism that "the first step is the one that altogether escapes notice" and that, as a result, "the decisive movement in the conjuring trick has been made, and it was the very one that we thought quite innocent" (PI, 308).

The aphorism tells us then that behaviorism is a dead end; it is the fly-bottle from which Wittgenstein is trying to extract us. More generally speaking, he is trying to help us escape from our philosophical problems concerning the nature of the mental, but he is aware that the way we pursue them is driving us into behaviorism. So behaviorism, far from being the position Wittgenstein advocates, is what he wants to liberate us from, and this attempted liberation takes the form of retracing the steps by which we had got into our behaviorism.

But what is the decisive first step in our thinking about the mind that takes us in the end all the way to behaviorism? Wittgenstein's answer is short and decisive: "We talk of processes and states and leave their nature undecided. . . . But that is just what commits us to a particular way of looking at the matter. . . . For we have a definite concept of what it means to learn to know a process better" (PI, 308). He goes on to speak of an analogy which falls apart at this point. And the result of the failed analogy is that "we have to deny the yet uncomprehended process in the yet unexplored medium." Since the analogy was meant to explain the nature of our thoughts, it now looks as if we had denied mental processes.

The misleading analogy seems to be this. In physics we may have an idea of certain processes going on inside elementary particles, but we may also think that we understand neither these processes nor the particles well enough, and so we see ourselves as struggling with yet uncomprehended processes in a yet unexplored medium. Now we turn to mental phenomena and start talking about them, as if they, too, were yet uncomprehended processes in a yet unexplored medium. We think of these processes as going on "in the mind" and then add that the mind is something ethereal and difficult to understand. But, Wittgenstein suggests, the assumed analogy between the problems of physics and our questions about the mind is false and quickly falls apart. He does not tell us immediately how the analogy fails, but he is sure that it is mistaken and that it is only this mistaken analogy that drives us into our usual views about the mind.

In order to understand how talk about physical particles differs from talk about the mind and its states and processes, we must look more closely at how statements about the human body are connected to psychological utterances. Here we must distinguish two cases: the case where we are speaking about a third person ("He is in pain") and the case where we are speaking in the first person ("I am in pain"). He tells us, accordingly, that "My own relation to my words is wholly different from other people's" (PI, p. 192). When I say of someone else that he is in pain, I depend directly on the availability of outer criteria for my assertion. I say that he is in pain because I see his pain-behavior. Wittgenstein writes:

"I noticed that he was out of humor." Is this a report about his behavior or his state of mind? . . . Both; not side-by-side, however, but about the one *via* the other. A doctor asks: "How is he feeling?" The nurse says: "He is groaning." A report on his behavior. (PI, p. 179)

Though outer behavior serves here as a criterion for the ascription of a psychological state, the latter is not just a statement about the behavior. There are a number of reasons for this. One is that the criterial relation connecting behavior and pain is not absolutely tight. It is possible that someone may feel pain and yet not show it and it is equally possible for someone to simulate pain, that is, to exhibit pain behavior without feeling actual pain. On the other hand, it is also obvious that our practice of ascribing pain to others would not get off the ground, if there were no general and natural relation between pain and pain-behavior.

But there is still another and more powerful reason for denying that an ascription of pain is a *statement* about a behavior and for that we must look at first-person utterances. When I say that I am in pain, I do not do so on the basis of observing my own behavior. In this case, "words are connected with the primitive, the natural, expressions of the sensation and used in their place . . . the verbal expression of pain replaces crying and does not describe it" (PI, 244). For this practice to get going, for children to learn to say "I am in pain" as a replacement for crying demands, of course, a linkage between nonlinguistic behavior and the utterance. For children are taught to say "I am in pain" by adults who speak the language and they will teach the child to use the utterance when they see the child's pain behavior. "A child has hurt himself and he cries; and then adults talk to him and teach him exclamations and, later, sentences. They teach the child new pain-behavior" (PI, 244).

The first-person case makes the difference between a description of a behavior and a pain utterance clear. When I say "I am in pain" I am not describing anything, I am rather *expressing* pain. My utterance has a different function from a description. That holds true even in the third-person case. When I say of someone "I believe that he is suffering," I am not describing his behavior, though my ascription is surely based on his behavior; I am rather expressing an attitude toward him, "my attitude towards him is an attitude towards a soul" (PI, p. 178).

The problem with behaviorism is that it has correctly diagnosed the existence of connections between pain and the expression of pain (pain behavior), but it has misinterpreted this fact by arguing that pain utterances are descriptions of behavior. To overcome behaviorism means to "make a radical break with the idea that language always functions in one way, always serves the same purpose: to convey thoughts – which may be about houses, pains, good and evil, or anything else you please" (PI, 304). And this questionable assumption behaviorism shares, in fact, with Cartesian mentalism, its apparent opposite. For that, too, operates on the assumptions of referentialism and objectivism. It, too, assumes that words always have meaning by standing for something. Both behaviorism and mentalism are thus driven into paradoxes, because both of them are forms of objectivism.

These considerations are at the heart of what is known as Wittgenstein's private-language argument. For if we construe the grammar of the expression of sensation on the model of "object and designation," we are left with the idea that there are inner objects designated by our sensation language. In his private-language argument Wittgenstein seeks to show that the inner objects that are here presupposed can play no role in our language. "The thing in the box has no place in the language-game at all; not even as a *something*; for the box might even be empty" (PI, 293). The conclusion is that if we follow the objectivist and construe meaning on the model of "object and designation," then "the object drops out of consideration as irrelevant" (PI, 293).

The private-language argument can, thus, be read as directed against the objectivism embedded in the Cartesian conception of the mind. The private language that Wittgenstein means is evidently the kind of language a Cartesian subject would speak. In Wittgenstein's account: "The individual words of his language are to refer to what can only be known to the person speaking. . . . So another person cannot understand the language" (PI, 243). A private language, as here characterized, is *essentially* private in the sense that what it talks about is in principle accessible only to the speaking subject. Since the language which the subject of the first two Cartesian Meditations speaks cannot be an external language – for it is accepted that we may be confused and deceived about everything external – it must be an internal language which only the speaking subject can use. But the conception of such a language is incoherent.[13]

It is easy to misread these anti-Cartesian arguments as supporting behaviorist conclusions. We are likely to succumb to such a misreading when we fail to notice that Wittgenstein's argument is really directed against assumptions that the mentalist and the behaviorist share, that is, the assumptions that the subject must be conceived as an object and that any meaningful noun or pronoun in our language must be a name or description of an object.

## X

The question whether and in what sense one can speak of a self – what plausibility there attaches to the idea that there exist individual selves or that there is only one world soul of which individual selves are aspects or manifestations or that the self is some sort of construct or even just an illusion – was for Wittgenstein connected with profound moral and personal concerns. That is evident already in the *Tractatus* where he speaks of a link between the way we see ourselves and the problem of the meaning of life. Having argued that there is no such thing as the soul in the world and that the metaphysical subject must be conceived as the limit of the world, not as part of it, he insists that "the solution of the problem of life in space and time lies *outside* space and time" (TLP, 6.4312). Against first impressions he is not hankering here for a solution in some transcendental or transcendent sphere. The point of the remark is rather that the problem of life does not have the kind of solution which problems concerning things in space and time have, that is, it has no scientific or theoretical solution. Hence, Wittgenstein's conclusion that "the solution of the problem of life is seen in the vanishing of the problem" (TLP, 6.521). The compelling thought is that anyone beset by that problem (even to the extent of advancing a theoretical solution to it) shows thereby that he has not yet solved it. We have solved the problem only when it no longer concerns us and when our attention is turned to the process of living itself. Wittgenstein expresses, thus, an unwavering conviction that our deepest human problems call for practical resolution not for a theoretical answer.

This antitheoretical attitude forms the ultimate underpinning to both the antiobjectivism of the *Tractatus* and the antireferentialism of the later writings. The problem of the nature of the self is not resolved by advancing a theory. The I is not an object and the word "I" is not a name or description of anything. Just like the problem of life, the problem of the nature of the self finds its solution in the disappearance of the problem. It is resolved only when we no longer concern ourselves with the I and have learned to face the world without being bothered over the question of its nature.

Wittgenstein offers us, for that reason, no positive account of the nature of the self. Readers who have searched for such an account have found no more than a few sparse and unsystematic remarks that might with an effort be taken for such. One is struck by this most forcefully when one compares Wittgenstein's discussion of the mental with the rich theoretical accounts advanced by Freud and his followers. The difference is not simply that Wittgenstein has a less fully developed picture, but that the aim of his discussion is utterly different and that he is deeply suspicious of any attempt to offer a positive account of the mental.[14]

It is, in fact, unrewarding to try to characterize his thinking about the mental in positive terms. His key insights are unfailingly expressed in negative terms: "There is no such thing as the self," "the word 'I' is not the name of a person," "there is no such thing as a private language," and so forth. His position is best described in the way I have done here, as antagonistic to certain common philosophical viewpoints. Thus, we can say that he is anti-Cartesian, anti-Russellian, anti-Freudian, antiobjectivist, and antibehaviorist in his thinking about the mind, without being able to identify anything positive from which these negative conclusions might be thought to derive.

This approach is ultimately grounded in the moral temper of Wittgenstein's thinking. When he insists in the *Tractatus* that the subject cannot be a thing in the world, we must surely link this to the book's austere moral outlook which treats the world as "a matter of complete indifference for what is higher" (TLP, 6.432), which insists that "the sense of the world must lie outside the world" and that "all that happens and is the case is accidental" (TLP, 6.41), which inclines, moreover, to the belief that "not wanting is the only good" (NB, p. 77), and sees salvation in a life of knowledge: "How can man be happy at all, since he cannot ward off the misery of this world? Through the life of knowledge" (NB, p. 81). His later views avoid the solipsistic tone of these early remarks, but he still ties moral insights to the discovery that the I is not an object and that to speak of the subject is not to refer to a thing. In the *Philosophical Investigations* he links his remarks about the relations between the feeling of pain and its expression to the observation that my attitude toward another human being can be "an attitude towards a soul" (PI, p. 178). "How am I filled with pity for this man?" he asks (PI, 287), and supplies an answer in a preceding remark: "Look at a stone and imagine it having sensations. . . . And now look at a wriggling fly and at once these difficulties vanish and pain seems able to get a foothold here" (PI, 284).

The thought that conceptions of the self are linked to differing moral ideals is not new. Interpreters have frequently pointed out how the Cartesian conception of the self historically accompanied the emergence of an ethics of individual self-fulfillment. In opposition to this moral view, later thinkers like Schopenhauer and Mach held that an ethics of compassion and unselfishness required the abandonment of the belief in individual minds. In *The World as Will and Representation* Schopenhauer wrote:

If that veil of Maya, the *principium individuations*, is lifted from the eyes of a man to such an extent that he no longer makes the egoistical distinction between himself and the person of others, but takes as much interest in the suffering of other individuals as in his own, and thus is not only benevolent and charitable in the highest degree, but even ready to sacrifice his individuality whenever several others can be saved thereby, then it follows automatically that such a man, recognizing in all beings his own true and innermost self, must also regard the endless sufferings of all lives as his own, and thus take upon himself the pain of the whole world.[15]

Mach argued similarly that to abandon the assumption of a substantive ego would have positive moral consequences. In *The Analysis of Sensations* he wrote: "In this way we shall arrive at a freer and more enlightened view of life, which will preclude the disregard of other egos and the overestimation of our own" (p. 25).

Wittgenstein held that neither Cartesianism nor behaviorism can give us an adequate account of the subject since both are committed to the assumptions of objectivism. The moral implications of his own view derive from this antiobjectivism, the recognition that we can think neither of ourselves nor of others in fully objective terms. Practical and moral attitudes are, rather, inherent in the way we understand ourselves and others.

## XI

Appealing as this may be, it presents us with questions Wittgenstein has done little to answer. Does a phenomenology of experience not suggest that there are forms of consciousness in which we objectify other human beings and even ourselves, that is, in which we look at them or ourselves as objects in a detached, disinterested, objectifying manner? If another person's behavior can alert us to his suffering and can engender in us a sense of pity, there is also that other possibility: that his suffering fails to ignite our pity or that we see his behavior and refuse to recognize his suffering, that we dehumanize the other and close ourselves off from him. As far as the relation to ourselves is concerned, we may also discover in ourselves the possibility of a detachment from our own feelings and of looking at ourselves, as if we were looking at another person or even at something inanimate. Wittgenstein is not unaware of such possibilities. In passing he notes: "If I listened to the words of my mouth, I might say that someone else was speaking out of my mouth" (PI, p. 192). Do we not at times look at ourselves in such a detached fashion, for example, when we consider the past or future or when we think about our own fixed character?[16]

We can put the matter in terms familiar from Wittgenstein's writings. Consider, then, the following types of utterance:

(1) "My arm is broken" and "I have blue eyes";
(2) "I am in pain" and "I am seeing the table";
(3) "I am not a genius, I am only a talent" (something Wittgenstein once said of himself, CV, p. 18) and "Knowing myself as I do, I will now act this way" (an example he once considered, LWII, p. 8); and finally
(4) "I am L.W."

Let us tentatively agree with Wittgenstein that in utterances of type (1) the word "I" refers and that it refers to something that has bodily characteristics as Wittgenstein writes in the *Blue Book*. Let us also tentatively agree that in type (2) utterances the word "I" does not refer and that such utterances function as expressions of pain or perception. But how are we supposed to treat utterances of type (3)? Here we are certainly not talking of bodily characteristics as in type (1) utterances. Should we assimilate them to utterances of the second type? Should we treat them as expressions of feeling? When Wittgenstein wrote in his diary: "I am not a genius, I am only a talent," he may, indeed, have been giving voice to a feeling of inner turmoil or a sense of despair. But even so the remark seems to be more than an expression of feeling; it seems to be saying something true or false about Wittgenstein's mind. And when someone says that "Knowing myself as I do, I will now act this way" or "These days I am inclined to say . . . "(LWII, p. 9), he may be giving us simply a cool assessment of his own mental resources. Such utterances appear to be therefore more similar to type (1) than to type (2) utterances. When we utter them we seem to be saying something factual about ourselves; but we seem to be speaking of the mind rather than of the body. How is that possible without assuming that there is, after all, a mind or self to which we can attribute objective characteristics? Do utterances of type (3) commit us to the assumption that in them the word "I" refers to a something that has definite, objective, fixed characteristics?

Before deciding on this issue, it may be useful to consider the last type of utterance. Wittgenstein says with a view to such utterances:

The word "I" does not mean the same as "L.W." even if I am L.W. nor does it mean the same as the expression "the person who is now speaking." But that doesn't mean: that "L.W." and "I" mean different things. All it means is that these words are different instruments in the language. (BLBK, p. 67)

It should be obvious that "I" and "L.W." cannot mean the same thing, for otherwise the sentences "I am L.W." and "L.W. is L.W." would mean the same thing; but the second is a tautology whereas the first can be a very informative (true or false) assertion. It should also be clear that "I" cannot mean the same as "the person who is now speaking," even though that is widely held to be the correct explication of the meaning of "I." But when we are sitting in an auditorium listening to a lecture and I whisper into your ear "The person who is now speaking is L.W.," I don't mean to be saying that I am Ludwig Wittgenstein and you are not likely to be in doubt about that. The phrase "the person who is now speaking" can occasionally mean the same as "I" – though we might then chide the speaker for being prolix – but it generally does not.

So far it is easy to follow Wittgenstein's reasoning in the quoted remark; but what about his conclusion that "I" and "L.W." do not "mean different things," that they are, rather, "different instruments"? The first part of this claim implies, presumably, that while "L.W." refers to something, the word "I" does not; it contains what I have called Wittgenstein's antiobjectivism. But his terse remark that "I" and "L.W." are different linguistic instruments appears uncomfortably elliptical. What kind of instrument is each one of them? What functions does it serve?

We can clarify the point by considering that on Wittgenstein's account the sentence "I am L.W." cannot be taken to be an identity-statement. An identity-statement says that such and such an object is the same as such and such another object ("The morning star is the evening star"). But if "I" is not a referring term, then "I am L.W." cannot be an identity-statement. What then are we to say about it? We must look back here at a remark we have quoted early on to the effect that the word "I" is not a name but that it is connected with names and that names are explained by means of it. In illustration of this we might observe that when someone reads out a list of names and asks in a crowded room "which of you is L.W.?" the answer "I am L.W." may serve as an explanation of the meaning of the name the questioner has found on the list. By saying "I am L.W." Wittgenstein is making it clear which of a number of people has that name. But is that the distinctive function of the utterance "I am L.W."? The explanation of who L.W. is, may also be given by someone else saying "He is L.W." (pointing to Wittgenstein) or "The person sitting in the corner is L.W." and so the utterance "I am L.W." is not essential for such an explanatory task. But there is another and more distinctive function which the utterance performs. When Wittgenstein says "I am L.W." he is, we might put it, *identifying* himself.

The observation suggests an answer to the question how we should understand utterances of the form "I am not a genius, I am only a talent." Perhaps we should consider them, too, as identifying statements, that is, as statements in which the speaker makes certain observable and objectively determinable characteristics his own, in which he "recognizes" himself as a mere talent rather than a genius, as having such and such fixed characteristics. And having taken this step, we may want to go further and say that even in utterances of type (1) we are not simply using the word "I" as a name for a body – as the *Blue Book* has it – but here, too, the word "I" indicates that the utterance serves the purpose of identification. Finally, we may extend this account even to utterances of the second type involving sentences like "I am in pain." Wittgenstein's own account of these types of utterance as verbal expressions replacing natural expressions of sensations fails to tell us why they have the specific syntactic structure they possess. Is it not possible that they actually serve a double function: as expressions of feelings *and* as statements of identification in which we declare those feelings to be our own?

But this seems to lead us back to the question what it is we are speaking of in such utterances. Is there an I, a something we identify in such statements of identification? Our account commits us to neither a Cartesian nor a behaviorist analysis of the self. We are saying rather that the utterances under consideration have a dual function and that only one of them is described by Wittgenstein. To say "I am in pain" is certainly also to express pain. In other "I"-utterances we are likewise giving vent to a subjectivity that cannot be conceived as some object in the world. But our utterances have, in addition, a second function. By speaking again and again of an "I" these utterances define a self with a location in space and time, a self that has a fixed character, that has desires, purposes, goals, and hopes. It is this self that is identified in statements of identification. But this self is not a real thing, it is rather a conception and image we construct, in terms of which we make sense of ourselves, of our states, experiences, and thoughts and in terms of which we project a coherent future for ourselves. We are, thus, forced to modify Wittgenstein's account of the self by adducing a notion of self-image or self-conception as being inherently appealed to in our "I"-utterances. Formally speaking, such a self-conception or self-image is, of course, an object just like the fictional land of Cockaigne; but it is not a real object existing with causal powers and in this sense Wittgenstein was surely right when he said that the self is not an object. But

Wittgenstein said almost nothing about this notion of self-conception, though it is surely of crucial significance when we think about ourselves historically backward-looking or forward-looking as moral agents.

## XII

We can contrast his thought here with that of Michel Foucault. He, too, started his reflections on the self with a denial of Cartesian mentalism, but eventually he came around to seeing that such negative conclusions had to be supplemented with an analysis of "the practices by which individuals were led to focus their attention on themselves, to decipher, recognize, and acknowledge themselves as subjects of desire, bringing into play between themselves and themselves a certain relationship that allows them to discover, in desire, the truth of their being, be it natural or fallen." For Foucault "it seemed appropriate to look for the forms and modalities of the relation to the self by which the individual constitutes and recognizes himself *qua* subject." Holding that "all moral action involves a relationship with the self," he argued: "The latter is not simply 'self-awareness' but self-formation as an 'ethical subject,' a process in which the individual delimits that part of himself that will form the object of his moral practice, defines his position relative to the precept he will follow, and decides on a certain mode of being that will serve as his moral goal."[17] In his last books, *The Use of Pleasure* and *The Care of the Self*, and in a series of important late interviews Foucault has shown what wealth of philosophical insight can be gained from an exploration of these themes.

But these are not Wittgenstein's issues. He stays, on the whole, with the negative conclusions that the word "I" either refers to a body or does not refer at all. The moral conclusions he reaches are those that follow from the negative discovery that the self is not an object. Hence, he never gets to the positive ideal of an "esthetics of existence" that Foucault envisaged. Wittgenstein's moral attitudes, as he expressed them in his own life and in his remarks to friends, tend rather toward a life of ascetic denial. In this respect he remains close to Schopenhauer's ethics whereas Foucault's affirmation of a positive self-constitution links him to Nietzsche. The critique of Wittgenstein's views suggested in these observations is, in effect, that which Nietzsche directed against what he called Schopenhauer's nihilism. What is certain is that Wittgenstein saw his task as demolishing objectivist accounts of the self and that he did not address the philosophical issues arising from the process of self-formation. In this we can surely see a limitation in his thinking about the self; it is a limitation, moreover, which restricted the scope of Wittgenstein's reflections on moral issues.

## XIII

Only once did Wittgenstein touch on these issues and then only in a passing remark which did not bear on the moral significance of the notion of self-conception. I am referring here to the passage from which we started and which for that reason has a unique importance in Wittgenstein's work. The remark alerts us to a lacuna in Wittgenstein's thinking and to the fact that he was vaguely aware of its presence. In maintaining in section 398 that the house in the imaginary landscape "might be" said to belong to the farmer in the picture, Wittgenstein is, first of all, reaffirming his commitment to the idea that there is no such thing as the self. I may, of course, say that *I* imagine the landscape, the house, and the farmer, but I cannot take this to imply that there is a real self that owns these things. If I want to speak of someone owning the imaginary house or anything else in the imaginary landscape, I can only talk of an imaginary object, the farmer sitting in front of the imagined house. But in this case I am really only adding an item to the contents of my imagination, an item I invest with a symbolic relation of ownership of the others. This imaginary self is not a real object; it is rather a self-conception, the kind of thing that Foucault has in mind when he speaks of the care of the self. Because it is merely imaginary, this self has no causal powers. That is suggested by Wittgenstein's observation that the imaginary farmer cannot enter his imaginary house. We can *imagine* him doing such things, but he cannot do them in reality. As such the remark is one more nail in the coffin of objectivism. For Wittgenstein is trying to show us here that the belief in a real self results from confusing this self-conception with an objectively real thing.

NOTES

1 G. E. Moore, "Wittgenstein's Lectures in 1930–33," *Philosophical Papers* (London: Allen and Unwin, 1959), p. 324. The same attitude is reflected in the *Tractatus*, where Wittgenstein writes that he is concerned with "the problems of philosophy" and that language is of interest to him because these problems arise out of a misunderstanding of "the logic of our language" (TLP, p. 3). In the *Philosophical Investigations* he writes in a similar vein that "the work of the philosopher consists in assembling reminders for a particular purpose" (PI, 127). The philosopher, we might spell this out, assembles reminders about how language is used for the philosophical purpose of uncovering "plain nonsense" and "bumps that the understanding has got by running its head up against the limits of language" (PI, 119). Again, it is the philosophical puzzle that motivates the concern with language.

2 How much did Wittgenstein actually know about Descartes? How much had he read? There are no reliable estimates concerning either question. He did discuss Descartes in connection with the "Cogito," but insisted that it was unnecessary to reconstruct his thinking, instead "one must do this for oneself." I take the "this" here to refer to a reflection on the Cogito that will determine what made Descartes's view plausible to him though not necessarily to us (O. K. Bouwsma, *Conversations 1949–1951* [Indianapolis: Hackett, 1986], pp. 12–14).

3 David Pears, "The Relation between Wittgenstein's Picture Theory of Propositions and Russell's Theories of Judgment," in C. G. Luckhardt, *Wittgenstein: Sources and Perspectives* (Ithaca: Cornell University Press, 1979), pp. 190–212.

4 I call Russell's conception "broadly Cartesian" since I do not want to imply that he adopted Descartes's complete picture of the self. Russell did hold that (1) there is a real self which is (2) capable of thought and perception, and (3) logically simple.

5 The context makes clear that Wittgenstein associates "the superficial psychology of the present day" with Russell's theory of knowledge. Theory of knowledge as a whole is dismissed as "the philosophy of psychology" (TLP, 4.1121).

6 Friedrich Nietzsche, *Beyond Good and Evil*, §12.

7 Ernst Mach, *The Analysis of Sensations* (New York: Dover Publications, 1939), pp. 23–4; originally published 1897, trans. C. M. Williams.

8 My interpretation of the statement "The I is not an object" assumes that Wittgenstein is not using the word "object" to refer exclusively to the simple objects of the *Tractatus*. My assumption is, rather, that his terminology corresponds here to that of other parts of the *Notebooks* where he

speaks of complex as well as of simple objects (NB, pp. 50, 59, 60, etc.). Understood in this sense, the assertion can be taken to mean that the I is not a constituent of the world at all and that a full description of the world, that is, a description which lists all simples and all complexes, would not mention the I. That view is, indeed, made explicit both in the *Notebooks* and in the *Tractatus*. In both places Wittgenstein insists that a complete description of the world, "a book called *The World as I found it*," would not mention the I, the subject (NB, p. 50 and TLP, 5.631).

9 The sentence and its counterpart in the *Tractatus* (TLP, 5.641) have proved difficult for the translators. Wittgenstein writes in German that "vom Ich die Rede sein kann und muss." Since "Rede" commonly means "speech," Anscombe translates the sentence in the *Notebooks* as saying that "there can and must be mention of the I"; Pears and McGuinness render it in the *Tractatus* as "philosophy can talk about the self." Both translations make Wittgenstein's view self-contradictory. For if we can meaningfully speak only of items in the world, as he asserts over and over again, then a self we can talk about must be part of the world and then we can also talk about it objectively and scientifically. The translators have failed to notice that the German "Rede" derives from Latin "ratio" and that the original meaning is preserved in the phrase "davon kann die Rede sein," which says roughly "such and such is reasonable."

10 For an earlier discussion of these ideas see my essay "Subjectivity in the Tractatus," *Synthese* 56 (1983), pp. 123–39.

11 Wittgenstein may have taken this notion from one of a number of different sources. A plausible one is William James, *The Principles of Psychology* (New York: Henry Holt, 1890), vol. 1, p. 346.

12 The road to this conclusion and its difficulties are spelled out in my "Subjectivity in the Tractatus."

13 According to O. K. Bouwsma, Wittgenstein said in conversation: "Now a scrupulously honest Descartes will not say: 'There goes my horse. A bird singing up in the tree, etc. There's a woman holding an umbrella.' . . . So Descartes can present nothing. One can say that he might say: 'Ah!' or 'This!' or 'Awareness!' But if he now said anything of this sort, his words would have no meaning. There would be nothing to provide a contrast. 'I think' is or would be like: 'Ah!' " (O. K. Bouwsma, *Conversations*, pp. 13–14).

14 Rush Rhees reports that during the 1940s Wittgenstein spoke of himself as a "disciple" and "follower" of Freud; but throughout this period he remained hostile to Freud's theoretical claims. What appealed to him was the psychoanalytic practice not the theory that was meant to justify and support that practice. When he spoke of his own enterprise as thera-

peutic he was, no doubt, thinking of similarities to the kind of therapy promised in psychoanalysis. But he never bought into Freud's belief that the self was a causal construct whose characteristics and principles of constructions could be the subject matter for a new kind of science.

15 Arthur Schopenhauer, *The World as Will and Representation*, trans. E. F. J. Payne (New York: 1969), vol 1, §68, pp. 378f. There can be little doubt of the affinity between Schopenhauer's thought at this point and Wittgenstein's remarks in the *Notebooks* that "the world and life are one" (p. 77, repeated in TLP, 5.621), that "the spirit of the snake, of the lion is *your* spirit" (p. 85), and that "my will is the world-will" (ibid.).

16 Cf. Jean Paul Sartre's *Being and Nothingness*. Wittgenstein never thinks about the self in temporal terms. It may well turn out to be the case that we cannot clearly distinguish between a self and its state when we focus only on current states of consciousness, as both Hume and Lichtenberg had, in fact, observed long before Wittgenstein, but it may still be true that such a distinction becomes plausible to us when we think about ourselves over time, about changing states of consciousness which are nevertheless all experienced as being mine.

17 Michel Foucault, *The Use of Pleasure*, trans. R. Hurley (New York: Vintage Books, 1986), pp. 5, 6, and 28.

DAVID BLOOR

# 11   The question of linguistic idealism revisited

The notion of "family resemblance" concepts seems to have particularly impressed itself on Wittgenstein in connection with historical and cultural categories.[1] In describing, say, religions or ideologies, we find we cannot delineate them by giving clear, necessary, and sufficient conditions. The same applies to schools of thought such as "materialism" or "idealism" or "naturalism." These labels are family resemblance concepts: we use them to refer to something that is many-faceted and historically evolving. When we try to locate Wittgenstein within existing philosophical traditions we need to remember this exercise, too, will involve our using just such a variety of crisscrossing similarities, some general and some specific (PI, 66). We must not assume a similarity in one respect will be accompanied by similarities in others, or that any inconsistency or defect in the comparison is necessarily indicated by this. The value of these comparisons is to be assessed pragmatically, by their power to illuminate the structural features of his difficult arguments.

## I   THE IDEALIST READING

A particularly interesting example of such a cultural classification is involved in the thesis, argued and opposed in different ways by a number of writers, that Wittgenstein was an "idealist" (in the philosophical sense or senses of the word). For example, attempts have been made by Williams and by Lear, among others, to assimilate the later Wittgenstein to the Kantian tradition of transcendental idealism.[2] They claim Wittgenstein's central concern was to exclude the possibility of skepticism. His aim, it is said, was to legitimate our basic understanding of the world by leaving us with no alternative to

354

our own conceptual scheme. To call our rationality into question, or to challenge it by posing alternatives, results in our speaking overt or covert nonsense. Incoherence is the only alternative to our basic categories of thought, hence Wittgenstein's concern that philosophers leave everything as it is, constructing no theories, and engaging in no revisionary activity.

Others have seen quite different projects in his work, classifying him as naturalistic and relativistic. Strawson sees Wittgenstein as subscribing to a form of "social naturalism,"[3] while Malcolm draws attention to the references to real or imagined cultural diversity in Wittgenstein's writings and offers this as evidence against the transcendental reading.[4] Meredith Williams emphasizes the differences between Wittgenstein's contextualism, that is, his grounding of meaning in use and social practices, and Kant's transcendental arguments.[5] Likewise Stroud has challenged the transcendentalists to justify their identification by citing chapter and verse,[6] and Bolton has sought to oppose them by demonstrating elements of *Lebensphilosophie* in the *Investigations*.[7] Doesn't the emphasis there on life and activity exclude the otherworldly, absolutist orientation associated with idealism? Malcolm sums up the rejection of the Kantian, transcendental reading by declaring that there was "no tendency towards any form of idealism . . . in Wittgenstein's later philosophy."[8]

I think Malcolm is right to reject the attempts to assimilate Wittgenstein's project to Kant's, but I don't think it is true to say there were *no* idealist elements in Wittgenstein. The family resemblance character of the idealist tradition would, in any case, make Malcolm's claim a hazardous one. Specifically, I shall argue that, with an appropriate understanding of "idealism," there *are* such elements, and very important ones, though they are consistent with also seeing Wittgenstein as a naturalistic thinker. To justify this I want to re-examine a paper by G. E. M. Anscombe called "The Question of Linguistic Idealism."[9] She argues that some of the central themes of the *Investigations* are expressions of varying strengths of what she calls "linguistic idealism." I think this is correct and fastens on deep and revealing issues. In particular it sheds light on the conventional elements in language-games. I will sketch the argument and then offer my own development of these themes, showing how Anscombe's account can be carried further. I will explain how the phenomenon she calls "linguistic idealism" is the upshot of a particular and identifiable social mechanism. The so-called idealist strands in Wittgenstein, it will transpire, are really the sociological strands in his thinking under another name.[10]

## II  LINGUISTIC IDEALISM

Linguistic idealism is the claim that some truths or realities are created by our linguistic practices. The contrast is with cases where language transmits or reflects an independent reality. "Linguistic idealism" is a label applying wherever, and so far as, language creates what it refers to. Thus Anscombe proposes the following "test": "If we want to know whether Wittgenstein is a 'linguistic idealist' . . . ask the question: Does this existence, or this truth, depend upon human linguistic practice?" (p.116). Recall Wittgenstein used the phrase, "*Essence* is expressed by grammar" (PI, 371). As Anscombe explains, linguistic idealism implies that some "essences" can be created in the course of being expressed. This sounds suspiciously circular: what is it that is being expressed, if it is the expression which does the creating? We shall see there is indeed an element of circularity involved in the notion of linguistic idealism but that, properly understood, it is of a nonvicious kind. For the moment the claim is simply that there are cases where the grammar of our language does not mould itself to a set of independent "essences": rather, these are constituted in and by the grammar. In this context "grammar" is used in the Wittgensteinian sense, referring to the taken-for-granted routines of some linguistic practice: the rules that govern its symbols. It is also important to realize that for Anscombe, as for Wittgenstein, "linguistic practices" are not just a matter of using words (p.117). They always include the patterns of activity into which those words are woven (cf. PI, 23). This nonverbal matrix of action is at least as important as the words themselves.

Applying her test for linguistic idealism, Anscombe reaches two conclusions. First, human *concepts* call for an "idealist" analysis and are given such an analysis by Wittgenstein (p.118). Concepts are created through our linguistic practices. She is at pains to add that typically the *objects* which fall under concepts cannot be analyzed idealistically. In these cases the objects exist independently of talk about them or references to them, and hence call for a "realist" account (p. 121). Her point is that the concept of, say, "horse" is an instrument we use to group or classify bits of an independent reality. The mere encounter with a horse does not furnish us with the concept "horse," because it does not by itself determine how the label is to be applied or withheld on future occasions: it doesn't determine how we will group things. Usage can't just be "read off" an object. Nor can it be explained just by the perceived similarity of the things we refer to. As Wittgenstein noted, we don't have a concept everywhere we see similarity (Z, 380). Nor do we always see similarity between objects that fall under the same concept. There must, therefore, be an active, creative element in concept formation. To grasp this we must appeal to something over and above the object being referred to. We must attend to the linguistic practice associated with the word, and its point and purpose for its users. Anscombe calls this position (which she attributes to Wittgenstein) a "partial idealism" (p. 118) – the qualification "partial" reminding us that what applies to the concept itself does not necessarily apply to its object.

Anscombe's second conclusion is that, elsewhere, a full and not just a partial idealism is called for. Wittgenstein, she tells us, endorsed or provided the grounds for an idealist account of rules, rights, promises, games, rituals, etiquette, and ceremonial proceedings (p. 119). These are realities whose characteristic features are wholly created by human linguistic practices. Thus we have rights because, collectively, these rights are accorded to us, and they are created by being so accorded. Some of the rights might involve objects, for example, the right to use a piece of land; but the right itself is wholly the creature of our belief in, and reference to, something called a "right." Similarly we are under an obligation to keep promises because we collectively sustain the institution of promising. The acts of reference to the obligation actually constitute the reality of the obligation that is being referred to – along with the rest of the activities (such as sanctioning) making up the linguistic practice. The same can be said of games, rituals, etiquette, and ceremonies. The proper way to perform in such a context is not derived from something independent of that context; it is not answerable to something outside itself, but only to itself. A game is something people create by playing it; there is no reality to the game other than the playing of it – a "move" is a move *in* the game. Given the prominence of the metaphor of "game" in Wittgenstein's philosophy, that is, in his talk of "language-games," the "idealist" character of games assumes a striking significance.

Rule following provides an especially important feature of language-games. We often say a rule compels us to do things in a certain way. A procedure has been specified and it "has" to be carried out thus and so, but the compulsion is not a constraint existing independently of the practice of following the rule. It isn't like the law of gravity, imposing itself on our activities regardless of our attitude to it or knowledge of it. We *can't* levitate at will; but we *can* choose to break the rules of a game. There is, moreover, usually no way of responding to such an infraction, for example, by justifying the rule, that does not ultimately refer back to the rule itself. Whatever our myths about rules, and whatever our feelings may tell us to the contrary, the compulsion has no existence outside the sanctions and constraints we collectively, as rule-followers, and in the name of the rule, impose on ourselves. Here again, then, our linguistic practices do not reflect or express an independent reality so much as create a new reality. As Anscombe says, "if there is such a thing as idealism about rules and about the necessity of doing *this* if you are to be in conformity with *this* rule, then here Wittgenstein was a linguistic idealist" (p. 122).

Clearly the idealism imputed to Wittgenstein is not a subjective or Berkeleyan idealism. This is not a spiritualist ontology. There is no question of the desk in the study, or the tree in the quad, disappearing if no one is looking at them. Things and people, and what they see and say, will be taken for granted by a linguistic idealist. Nor need a linguistic idealist say that what is created by our linguistic practices is unique, historically unchanging, or in any way transcends the natural order. What, then, *is* the link with the idealist tradition? It comes, surely, from breaking down the distinction between the subject and the object of knowledge. The resonance is with those aspects of the idealist tradition associated with Hegel, not Berkeley. The attention is not on the individual psyche, but on history, traditions, cultures, and states. Discourse, and the object of discourse, we might say, here merge into one another. We refer to our "rights," but ultimately our rights *are*, or *reside in* those very acts of reference – and so also with the other items amenable to this analysis. Had Anscombe been looking for further examples she could have pointed to any instance of social status or a social institution. We have here a thesis of broad scope about the basis and mode of being of social kinds, but it isn't meant to dissolve away the physical nature of the people and things having these statuses or performing a role in these institutions. For example, a coin is currency, ultimately, because it is accepted and known as currency, but that doesn't destroy its reality as a metal disc existing independently of our belief in it.

## III WITTGENSTEIN AND HUME

An intriguing feature of Anscombe's account of linguistic idealism is the connection she makes between Wittgenstein and Hume, two philosophers from very different intellectual traditions.[11] The Wittgensteinian account of rules – glossed as a species of idealism – is juxtaposed with and likened to the famous Humean account of the "artificial" virtues – that is, promise keeping, respect for property, obedience to the magistrate, loyalty to the monarch, and the rules of modesty and chastity. For Hume these are grounded neither in the supernatural nor wholly in our individual, psychological dispositions. They are the result of complex social interactions he called "conventions." We are not moved in these cases by, say, an innate sense of duty, or by a moral insight into where our duty lies. When we sense our duty we are responding, ultimately, to a pattern of shared expectations and sanctions. This is sustained by countless tiny, individual calculations of self-interest. Each calculation consists in the individual trying to work out what other individuals will do, given that they too are engaged in a similar, but reciprocal calculation. Hume brought out the central role played by the agents' orientation to one another. Individually this takes the form of decisions to do and say certain things if, and because, other people do and say them. Collectively, where everyone is making conditional decisions of this form, the discourse of the group can be seen as wholly self-referring. Everyone is referring to everyone else's referring, not to anything outside that practice of referring itself. If the situation achieves stability, and becomes not merely self-referring but self-reinforcing, the behavior which is the outcome of these calculations may become habitual, and then a convention becomes a custom. Confronting and participating in this new moral reality will, of course, engender its own characteristic feelings and, indeed, its own illusions. From the perspective of each individual it will come to seem external, natural, and morally compelling.[12]

The main Humean conclusion – and this is the point of Anscombe's comparison – is that the special necessity involved in (say) promise-keeping is simply part and parcel of the institution, where the institution itself consists of people who are all actually or potentially oriented to one another's actions. The obligation which is created, the sense in which we "must" or "have to" do certain things, is created by and within the practice itself. It neither pre-exists and finds expression in the practice, nor does it magically spring into existence as something independent but caused by the practice. It just *is* part of the practice. Wittgenstein did not reach his conclusion about rules and their necessity in the same way Hume reached his, namely by appeal to the picture of reciprocal calculations. (Wittgenstein's "convention" or "rule" is more akin to Hume's "custom," a taken-for-granted regularity in the way we coordinate ourselves.) Nevertheless, both were describing a species of necessity where the reality expressed by references to this necessity consists in precisely the practices of invoking the necessity. For every individual the appeal is to an independent reality, but that reality is, ultimately, just other people's readiness to make a similar appeal and act accordingly. The sense of circularity mentioned earlier derives from the interconnections of this self-referential activity. Taken collectively, the whole process is indeed a circulation of self-referring acts, but this is not a logical defect: it is just a property of the system. It might be compared with the circulation of water in the hydrological cycle, with its story of evaporation from rivers and oceans, followed by condensation and cloud formation, and then by precipitation that replenishes the rivers and oceans. This is not a logically defective story, though we may feel the need for a further account, standing outside the cycle, explaining how the process begins. The same applies to obligations, promises, and rules. How did they begin? Hume tried to provide such an account in his appeal to self-interest; Wittgenstein didn't. All we have are references to the "spontaneous" emergence of language-games (cf. PI, pp. xl, 224; RFM, IV-23). Wittgenstein, we might say, is Hume without the origin myth. Nevertheless, Anscombe is right to see a profound similarity in their final positions.

The category of linguistic idealism thus provides a somewhat surprising link between two bodies of work that have for too long been kept apart. Despite this impressive piece of bridge building, there are difficulties with these conclusions and with Anscombe's way of reaching them. I shall identity three such difficulties. First, the link with Wittgenstein's text is sometimes tenuous. The attribution of a "partial idealism" stands in need of a more secure grounding in Wittgenstein's own words. Second, the connection between this "partial idealism" and the full idealism of the rule-following doctrines calls for clarification. How are insights gained in cases where our words have no extralinguistic correlates to be applied to cases where they do have such correlates? Third, the significance of these "idealist" strands in providing a general overview of the later philosophy, and in suggesting lines of further development, is likewise left implicit. Having discovered Wittgenstein was a species of idealist, what can we do with this knowledge?

Of these difficulties it is the second – concerning the link between partial and full idealism – which is the most profound. The substantial task is to show how the special features of rules that justify the epithet "linguistic idealism" are also at work in the "partial" case. On a purely verbal level there is no problem: Anscombe calls Wittgenstein's account of rules "idealist," so the idealist component of, let us say, natural-kind terms like "horse," is nothing but the rules for their use. "Partial idealism" just means concepts with an empirical reference also have rules of use. As far as it goes this is correct, but we must exhibit and not merely imply the operation of self-referential processes in these cases. Let us start, however, with the first of the three problems, that of locating the idealist elements in Wittgenstein's text.

## IV  IDEALISM OR MATERIALISM?

Anscombe quotes the following passage from Part II of the *Investigations*:

If anyone believes that certain concepts are absolutely the correct ones, and that having different ones would mean not realizing something that we realize – then let him imagine certain very general facts of nature to be different from what we are used to, and the formation of concepts different from the usual ones will become intelligible to him. (PI, pp. xii, 230)

She comments:

This is one of the passages from Wittgenstein arousing – in my mind at least – the question: have we in his last philosophical thought what might be called a linguistic idealism? (p. 112)

Why should this passage arouse this thought? The passage is about the absolute rightness of our concepts, and it recommends a method for throwing doubt on any claim that they have this virtue. The dichotomy in the passage is between absolute and relative, not between the ideal and the real. So where does the theme of linguistic idealism come in? These worries are reinforced if we ask *how* a change in the facts of nature might intelligibly lead to the formation of concepts different from ours. Wittgenstein generally professed not to be interested in causal and explanatory links – and made such a profession in close proximity to the quoted passage. Nevertheless, if changes in nature prompt changes in our thinking about it, this suggests a causal link. It suggests a dependence of our concepts on the reality to which they refer. (Perhaps they have become "adapted" to it, and honed into shape by some cognitive analogue of natural selection.) Plausible though they are, doctrines of this kind surely deserve to be called linguistic "materialism," not linguistic "idealism."

We are therefore confronted by a problem: Anscombe launches her argument by a quotation from Wittgenstein apparently pointing in the opposite direction to the idealistic conclusion she draws. Fortunately, some detective work in the text of the *Investigations* allows us to construct an acceptable connection. The passage Anscombe cited picks up themes that occurred earlier. Thus, at §142 we were told:

It is only in normal cases that the use of a word is clearly prescribed; we know, are in no doubt, what to say in this or that case. The more abnormal the case, the more doubtful it becomes what we are to say. And if things were quite different from what they actually are – if there were for instance no characteristic expression of pain, of fear, of joy; if rule became exception and exception rule; or if both became phenomena of roughly equal frequency – this would make our normal language-games lose their point – the procedure of putting a lump of cheese on a balance and fixing the price by the turn of the scale would lose its point if it frequently happened for such lumps to suddenly grow or shrink for no obvious reason. (PI, 142)

Notice Wittgenstein didn't just say: imagine objects mysteriously get bigger or smaller. He focused on a particular procedure playing a part in an important social institution, namely, putting an object on a pair of scales and fixing its price, as a commodity, in the course of buying and selling. His concern was not just the physical properties of things, but the way these objects are treated and regarded in the course of our relating to, and interacting with, one another. It is the disruption of an institution, as well as the disruption of a law of nature, that is being paraded before us. This is why it is also an affirmation of those themes in his work that Anscombe calls "idealist" because, as we have seen, linguistic idealism is an account of the ontology of social institutions. This dimension of the example needs to be stressed because it did not appear casually or inadvertently. It is central to the vision that Wittgenstein was trying to convey as he developed the argument of the *Investigations*. Let us look at how that vision was given expression.

## V THE STRATEGY OF THE *INVESTIGATIONS*

Throughout the *Investigations* Wittgenstein was concerned to reinstate the neglected social and interactional dimensions of meaning. These were passed over in his own earlier writing, and by the psychological and individualistic assumptions of prominent contemporaries such as Russell. (In many quarters they are still neglected today.) His aim was not to deny the possible connections between words and an independent reality, but to enrich our picture so that the other, equally vital, components were not left out. This explains Wittgenstein's strategy in the opening sections of the *Investigations* where he introduced his idea of "language-games." The striking quotation from Augustine with which he began was used as an example of the approach to language he rejected, that is, one focusing abstractly on the correlation of words and things. The meaning of a symbol is assumed to be the thing it stands for. Any further properties of language are then explained by psychological assumptions about our further capacity to form intentions and to read the intentions of others from their demeanor, expressions, and gestures. Wittgenstein saw this as a picture of language sustained by our concentrating on a hopelessly narrow range of examples. As he put it: we must be thinking of how we learn words like "table," "chair," "bread," and people's names. It is not an adequate account even here, but it is an intelligible response to such cases. In general, however, we need to broaden our view, embrace a wider range of examples, and let this richer material evoke other pictures in our minds.

Suppose we utilize a diagram of the kind shown below:

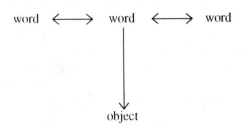

We may call the connection between words and independent objects, "vertical" links; and the connection between words and other words, "horizontal" links. "Word," here, is doing duty for the broad notion of linguistic practice. In these terms, Augustine was presented in the *Investigations* as having a model of language founded on the "vertical" links, while Wittgenstein wanted to enrich the picture by doing justice to the "horizontal" ones. His strategy was to begin with the "vertical" connections, and then progressively undermine or remove or complicate them in order to throw the "horizontal" dimension into relief.[13]

In his first examples of very simple language-games, he considered the verbal exchanges that might take place between a builder and his assistant. The builder calls "block!" or "slab!" or "pillar!" or – in later examples – the name of some tool. The assistant then fetches what is needed. The correlation of words and object is prominent and taken for granted, though even at this stage the "name" of the object operates in connection with its role in a shared enterprise. Wittgenstein then introduced carefully contrived complexities into the story. For example, indexical words like "this" come into the picture, that is, words that "stand for" different things on different occasions (PI, 8). Then come words that function as numerals which seem to "refer to" deeply problematic objects, namely, numbers (PI, 8–10). Then we are asked to point to an object, but point to its color, not its shape (PI, 33); or point to a chess piece, but point to it as a *piece*, not as a bit of wood (PI, 35). He also supposed that the builder orders his assistant to fetch a previously named tool, when the item in question is broken and no longer exists (PI, 41). Then he dealt with a case where there has *never* been a connection between the symbol and a thing, rather than a connection that once existed but has now been severed (PI, 42). This technique was carried yet further as the discussion progressed. The "vertical" link might be disturbed by mistakes (PI, 51). Or the bizarre behavior of the designated object might lead us to reconsider previous applications (PI, 80). Again, there are cases where the subtlety and variety of the link with reality is brought to light, for example, with perfectly serviceable but highly inexact orders such as "stand roughly there" (PI, 88). It would be pedantry to object to such a command on the grounds that it lacked precision, but the point is that where a reasonable demand for exactitude ends and pedantry begins is a matter of context. There is then the celebrated discussion of pains and sensations where, he argued, the link with reality need not be one of reporting or designating at all: words can act as *replacements* for a natural expression of the pain or sensation (PI, 244). Finally, there is the invitation: "Compare a concept with a style of painting" (PI, pp. xii, 230). A drawing of the human figure may represent it in various styles (Wittgenstein cites "The Egyptian, for instance"). There need be no calling into question of the representational significance of the painting; it is meant to stand for something, but that aim can be realized in many ways. The way it is realized, the style in which the representation is made, is underdetermined by the object. It is mediated by the conventions of the style.

Addressing an imaginary critic, for whom the word–object scheme says all that needs to be said about meaning, Wittgenstein retorted: "You say: the point isn't the word, but its meaning, and you think of the meaning as a thing of the same kind as the word, though also different from the word. Here the word, there the meaning. The money, and the cow that you can buy with it. (But contrast: money, and its use)" (PI, 120). The comparison is abrupt and disconcerting: here the word, there the meaning – the money, and the cow you can buy with it. Was Wittgenstein telling us the relation of a word and its referent *is* like that between money and a commodity, or that it isn't like this? I take it Wittgenstein was accepting the comparison, but only if the financial link is properly understood. The parenthetical remark gives us the clue. The words, "But contrast: money, and its use," mean: in contrast to the "vertical" connection the critic wants to emphasize, we are to notice how the monetary comparison highlights the importance of "horizontal" links, that is, the role played by the surrounding interactions. Without an enveloping system of commercial practices we can't even think of "buying." If the use of money were not taken for granted, "the money, and the cow that you can buy" wouldn't stand in *any* determinate connection at all. But the use of money is a clear case of an institution requiring analysis as a collective, self-referring practice. The concepts which mediate the practice don't simply mirror an independent reality. "Price," for example, doesn't reflect the scarcity of something, only scarcity relative to demand within some market. "Price" only makes sense within such a market. The suggestion in the passage is that for something to be the object of a concept is akin to a thing becoming a commodity. This is not because there is no world outside language – that would be like saying there were no cows outside the practice of buying and selling them. The point, rather, is that without the surrounding linguistic practice there would be no "correspondence" between words and the world of the kind we encounter in ordinary uses of language (cf. PI, 6; PI, 30; PI, 51).[14]

This reading is supported by a later passage also making reference to money. Wittgenstein asked:

Why can't my right hand give my left hand money? – My right hand can put it into my left hand. My right hand can write a deed of gift and my left hand a receipt. – But the further practical consequences would not be those of a gift. When the left hand has taken the money from the right, etc., we shall ask: "Well, and what of it?" And the same could be asked if a person had given himself a private definition of a word; I mean, if he has said the word to himself and at the same time has directed his attention to a sensation. (PI, 268)

The mere passing of an object from hand to hand, whether inter- or intrapersonally, does not capture the essence of gift giving. Gifts are not gifts in virtue of their trajectory through space (nor their size, shape, color, density, or temperature). To be a gift is to have a characteristic over and above those dealt with by physicists or chemists: it is to have a moral property which derives from how the given object is regarded and treated in the course of a social encounter. A gift must be given *as* a gift, that is, as something understood to express regard or esteem, something meant to create a bond or symbolize a relationship. Something can't be a gift without the giver and receiver sharing the concept of gift, and they can't have that without the institution of gift giving.[15]

Wittgenstein was constructing example after example designed to show how the connection between words and things is mediated by patterns of interaction. He called into play a whole variety of analogies to convey his point: styles of painting, economic relations, the institution of the gift; even his famous suggestion "Think of the tools in a tool-box" (PI, 11) can be read in this way. It transpires that the "vertical" link in our diagram has no existence independent of the "horizontal" links. Of the various shortcomings in what he called the "object and designation model," the most dramatic is its inability to deal with the case where the "object" has no existence at all outside the talk about it and the references to it. It breaks down entirely where our talk is about other talk, and the linguistic practice has a wholly self-referring character. This is where the label "idealism" has its most plausible and revealing application. It is this self-referring, self-sustaining, and self-justifying feature of discourse Anscombe emphasizes when drawing the comparison between Wittgenstein's account of rule and Hume's account of artificial virtues.

Perhaps the simplest cases of self-referring and self-justifying talk are the so-called performative utterances. When I say, "I greet you" then, irony and jest apart, I do indeed greet you and thereby make what I have just said true. The same applies to "I curse you," "I beg you," "I bless you."[16] Performative utterances are perfect, miniature cases of linguistic idealism in action, that is, a truth and a reality created and constituted by a linguistic practice. Wittgenstein did not discuss such utterances in detail,[17] but he did cite larger-scale examples. For example he asked: "What sort of certainty is it that is based on the fact that in general there *won't* actually be a run on the banks by all their customers; though they would break if it did happen?!" (RFM, VII-35). This is a request to analyze our confidence in the "soundness" of a bank. Clearly it consists in part, but crucially, in the beliefs of its depositors. These beliefs are beliefs about other people's beliefs, and in particular about their beliefs in the bank's soundness. No matter how "fundamentally" sound we think the bank is, if nobody else believes in its soundness we had better get our savings out quickly. Others' beliefs in the bank's unsoundness make it *true* that it isn't sound. The soundness or otherwise of the bank is ultimately *constituted* by beliefs about its soundness or unsoundness. The very beliefs are the substance of what they are themselves about. The *content* of the beliefs, that the bank is unsound, and the *object* of the beliefs, the unsoundness itself, are one and the same. This is a case tailor-made for the linguistic idealist. When we invoke linguistic idealism, examples such as this help us see we are talking about "performatives" existing on the collective scale.

## VI  HOW GENERAL IS THE THESIS?

Can we make good the claim that all and any linguistic practices have such an "idealist" or "performative" component? While some thought and talk is almost wholly self-referring, can we assert that *all* thought and talk is to some extent of this character, and *none* of it is wholly devoid of a self-referential or performative component that is vital to its operation? It is one thing to identify such a component in examples like gifts, or money, or the soundness of the banks, or moral obligations, and other quasi-moral necessities, but what about ordinary empirical knowledge? An object might count as a gift because of how people regard it, rather than how it is in itself; but what about (say) an object's being an oxide of mercury, or being colored red? Here, surely, we are responsive to properties belonging to the thing itself, not to other people's treatment of it or response to it. Clearly language-users make an active contribution to the use of all empirical terms, but there is still a gap between this acknowledgment and the analysis of rules and conventions and statuses. The gap will be closed when we can specify precisely the performative, self-referential, and self-justifying aspects of our empirical talk about substances, properties, and natural kinds.

To sharpen the issue let us take the property of color, and see if we can locate the self-referential and performative aspects of calling something "red." Wittgenstein insisted that we don't possess concepts like "red" just because we look at and see red things. "Do not believe that you have the concept of color within you because you look at a colored object – however you look" (Z, 332; cf. Z, 333).[18] Genuine concept possession involves more than this. It involves coordinating our use of the word "red" by means of what he called "paradigms." These are samples which play a central role in the teaching of the word and which remain constantly available to sustain the shared language-game that is transmitted in such teaching. Wittgenstein provided the following gloss on the use of such samples in the process of ostensive learning: "This sample is an instrument of the language used in ascriptions of colour. In this language-game it is not something that is represented, but is a means of representation. . . . It is a paradigm in our language-game; something with which comparison is made" (PI, 50). In the normal language-game of color ascription we refer to the color itself, not the color sample. Nevertheless, the reference is achieved by exposure to the sample during training. In the course of training we are learning how to convey information about color, rather than actually conveying it. In order to learn we must be receptive to information on two channels at once. Ostensive learning requires us to learn about objects and properties *and* about the people who have commerce with them and, through that, commerce with one another. The information which is transmitted to us by the use of such samples or paradigms is social information. Ostensive learning by paradigms is enculturation or socialization into the local practices of reference.

Wittgenstein was indicating something fundamental to all talk about natural kinds. From the simplest to the most sophisticated, from our everyday talk to scientific theorizing, all such talk needs "paradigms." Of course, paradigms themselves vary in complexity. At their simplest they can be objects of comparison, like color samples, which can be laid by the side of the thing to be classified. More complicated forms might involve sophisticated tests or experimental procedures and lines of theoretical analysis acting as models for further research. This would be the case, for instance, in the paradigms involved in identifying something as an "oxide."[19] An object's having the role of "paradigm," however – and this is the vital point – does not reduce to its possessing this or that intrinsic nature. It has and requires such a nature, but it also has something else: a role that is accorded to it by virtue of how people regard it and treat it. This is a moral or social status, rather than something inherent in it. Nothing can be a paradigm "in itself," but only because a group uses it in that way. Its paradigmatic status derives from its being used *as* a paradigm, for example, in teaching and transmitting part of the local culture or in guiding routine usage. It facilitates interaction because it is available, and known to be available, as a reference point for coordinating our talking and doing.

Something's being a paradigm, or a sample, or an instrument of language, is therefore significantly similar to something's being a gift, or money, or a commodity, or somebody's property, or a chess piece. Something is truly a paradigm because we deem it to be so. The performative and self-referential elements in the situation should now be clear. The ultimate authority for what our paradigms shall be is our own shared practice, so the self-justifying element is present too. The formal correctness of applying Anscombe's label "linguistic idealism" to such uses is therefore borne out. These, then, are some of the features that allow us to exhibit the self-creating character of our linguistic practices, including our practices of referring to independent objects. As the passage from Wittgenstein makes clear, none of this compromises the material reality of the object being used as a paradigm, nor the reality of the properties (such as color) referred to in the language-game. Quite the contrary. It is *because* of the ascribed status of the paradigm that it becomes a possible vehicle for coordinating and defining our shared responses to the external characters of things.

Once given a shared paradigm, much of our linguistic usage becomes routine. After due initiation into the linguistic practices of a group, most new members automatically and without collusion use words in ways that allow subsequent interactions to go smoothly. In practice we are not always looking over our shoulder and monitoring other people. But even here the performative element hasn't vanished: when order has been established, it still has to be sustained. In a passage from Wittgenstein quoted above, reference was made to "normal" cases where the application of a word is routine. When routines break down, then collective decisions and choices must be made to reestablish them under the new conditions. Authority may be needed to maintain the cohesion of usage, and to cope with any divergent tendencies. These tendencies may emerge at any time as a result of divergent goals and interests, and may be provoked or brought into view by novelty and anomaly. Occasionally in such circumstances it may even be deemed necessary to reestablish consensus by a change of paradigms. In these cases experts may be consulted and authorities must pronounce. But from where does authority derive? And who decides where expertise resides? There is no higher court of appeal than the community itself. Whatever its division of labor, or internal structure and hierarchy, ultimately the community will consult its own traditions, its own achievements, and its own goals as it reflexively evaluates them. There is nothing else it can consult. We can't say "consult the world" – as if that were a separate option – because the very point at issue is how such consultations are to be managed. With what paradigm do we approach the world? We are back with performative acts of self-reference and self-justification of a collective kind. This is testimony to the *ultimate* character of our accepted social and cultural forms. As Wittgenstein put it: "What has to be accepted, the given, is – so one could say – *forms of life* (PI, pp. xi, 226).[20]

## VII NORMATIVITY

Appeal to the history of science might lead us to accept that the usage of terms such as, say, "oxygen" varies as their theoretical analysis alters along with our changing understanding. We might accept that biological and botanical classification change and with them the meaning of the labels employed. We know that even the physicists' concept of simultaneity has had to be revised.[21] But as we stare intently at samples of red it is easy for us to ignore the collective work that goes into policing our response. The difficulty is that our eyes and brains seem to furnish us with the concepts automatically, without the need to introduce any element of social interaction such as Wittgenstein supposed. It seems as if our brains contain a special-purpose device, or "module," whose autonomous operation yields up the relevant concepts. Isn't this why we can directly apprehend colors and remember them if we need to? So this must be what possessing the concept of "red" amounts to.[22] All that we have to learn is the local name that is allocated to the concept. Once the label is attached, then that concept governs its subsequent application and use. The only conventional component, on this account, is that of choosing the label, and there seems to be nothing deep about this. What is more, anthropological studies suggest that every culture has a word for red, everybody's usage clusters around the same focal wavelengths of the spectrum; and everybody identifies the same color samples as central cases of redness.[23] Red, it seems, is a cultural universal, and is sustained by a universal feature of our psychology. A psychological model gives us all the understanding we need, so there is no room here for "linguistic idealism."

Tempting though this psychological model is, it cannot be the whole truth. To see this we must ask a number of questions. We will find the cumulative significance of the answers reinstates the Wittgensteinian emphasis on social interaction and convention, and hence "idealist," self-referential, and performative processes. Let us grant that Nature has, so to speak, issued us at birth with devices – "modules" – whose function can be said to be that of discriminating red things. Now we need to ask: by what right do we treat these numerically different devices, my module and your module, as detecting the same thing or property, for example, the property we both call "red"? What decides whether my device is working properly (e.g., that it is really detecting red and only red)? What happens if the deliverances of my device (e.g., my judgment that something is red) clash with the deliverances of yours (e.g., your judgment that something is red)? What will happen when our individual judgments are operating at some distance from the central cases, for example, when we hesitate or vacillate about calling something red? If our thresholds are different, as they might well be, whose is right? What happens if our detecting device is sensitive to the idiosyncratic history of its use, that is, to past experience? Or if its thresholds are modified by the goals and interests that inform our use of it?

These considerations show the psychological model to be incomplete and unrealistic. It presents a false estimation of the problems typically caused by individual variability, by malfunctions, disputes, and divergent judgments, not to mention random fluctuations or large-scale systematic causal influences. Indeed, what legitimate sense is there, on the psychological model, for notions like "malfunction," "error," or even "dispute"? These presuppose a notion of getting a right answer and, as yet, no provision has been made for such an idea. So far, what seems right to every red-detector is right – which, as Wittgenstein insisted, means in effect that there we can't really talk about right (PI, 258). The entire dimension of normativity, which is central to something's being a "concept," is as yet unaccounted for. It is no help to say that the notions of right and wrong are built into the idea that the red-detector has a certain "function," for example, that it is failing to work "properly" when it doesn't do what it is "meant" or "supposed" or "designed" to do by evolution. Function talk does indeed carry such implications, but these considerations could only solve the present problem under rather special conditions, namely, that such talk and such theories are taken up and employed to this effect by a group of actors themselves. They must become the actors' own categories and operate as the currency of their own self-understanding. Functions that are not acknowledged, understood, or conceded by the owners and users of the red-detectors are powerless to provide these agents with genuine standards. And if such ideas ever do play this role, they do so by virtue of their being an aspect of a shared culture, that is, by themselves becoming institutions. They must become sociological, not merely biological, phenomena.[24]

A plausible, naturalistic account of normativity can be got by setting the individual possessors of the "red-detectors" the task of coordinating themselves, of achieving common goals, of facing shared tasks, of distributing effort, communicating with one another, and maintaining a consensus. To do this they must create the machinery for handling breakdown in coordination, and for discounting or adjusting disruptive deliverances by their respective detecting devices. In short the individuals will have to behave like members of a community. They will have had to create a "common good" in the form of a shared standard. They will be sustaining a convention or making the category of "red" into an institution. Now we can make proper sense of there being "correct" and "incorrect" judgments. There will be a genuine role for such evaluations in sustaining their interactions. The idea of good and bad judges of red, of right or wrong parties to a dispute over red, will have something on which to gain a purchase, though none of this implies that "red" *means* "what other people call 'red.'" By imagining social interaction we have provided the conditions for the word-users to create something more recognizable as a "concept" of red than was present in their individual performances. Social interaction, however, is action taken with reference to others, who are in their turn acting relative to us. This strategic character of interaction, and the patterns it creates, therefore reintroduces the elements of self-reference and self-creativity into the story, that is, it reintroduces precisely those things to which the linguistic idealist is drawing our attention.

The argument that has just been developed in terms of norms, conventions, institutions, standards, and common "goods," can be summarized very simply. We could say the use of the word "red" must be part of a language-game. The difficulties of disruptive and divergent testimony all amount to this: how are the "players" of the language-game to keep the game going in the face of such endemic problems? Managing this task must be a constitutive part of the game itself, depending on the tacit knowledge of how to be a competent player, and how to use the codes of cognitive decorum implicit in the game.[25]

We have now located within Wittgenstein's text the two connected dimensions along which self-referential and performative processes operate: in the choice of paradigms and the sustaining of a shared language-game. If there is any difficulty in making these identifications and seeing these interconnections it will derive from our impoverished response to Wittgenstein's basic metaphor: that of language as a "game." It is all too easy to treat references to "language-games" as little more than a terminological idiosyncrasy on Wittgenstein's part. The metaphor then falls dead on the page. Some commentators have, accordingly, felt able to dismiss it as a shallow and unconvincing comparison.[26] A pedantic listing of what games and languages have, or have not, got in common will certainly reinforce such a conclusion – unless we realize that the crucial point of contact derives from the performative and self-referential character of games. Anscombe's alternative metaphor "idealism" can thus reactivate for us the full significance of Wittgenstein's original insight. It can make us realize just what is involved in calling something, metaphorically, a "game."

### VIII    CONVENTIONS AND INSTITUTIONS

I have now repaired two of the three difficulties identified in Anscombe's treatment. First, I have gone some way further in anchoring her identification of Wittgenstein's "idealism" in the text of the *Investigations*, showing how it runs through many of the themes that are characteristic of the later philosophy. The category of "linguistic idealism" helps bring out connections between different parts of that philosophy, such as the account of ostensive definitions, the appeal to "paradigms," the discussion of rules, the rejection of the object and designation model, and the subtle but progressive development and complication of the idea of language-games. By bringing these under the rubric of idealism we can articulate linkages in ways that might otherwise be seen but remain unstated. Second, and most importantly, by exposing the performative elements that can be found even in empirical discourse – and by seeing how these become particularly visible in connection with the role of paradigms – we have located the missing link between the "partial" idealism of natural-kind concept and the fuller, more uncompromising idealism of rules and conventions.

In the course of this discussion, however, we have also discovered something else: an alternative and arguably better idiom for capturing the same insights. For what is Anscombe's "linguistic idealism" other than a way of acknowledging the operation of convention? Social processes have taken over the role played by mental and spiritual processes in the older, obscurantist forms of idealism.[27] The truths and realities created by "linguistic practices" are clearly social institutions. Self-reference is the only mechanism by which something can be *created* in our linguistic practices. It is only here that our saying and believing something to be so can, nonmysteriously, make it so, that is, by accomplishing something like a collective and self-fulfilling "performative utterance." Partial idealism is the acknowledgment that we cognize nature, not in spite of or instead of, but through and with our conventions.[28] This is not to say there is anything technically wrong with Anscombe's choice of idealist terminology – though there might be dangers arising from its inappropriately antinaturalistic overtones.[29] It would be unfortunate if this terminology and these overtones distracted us from the true character of Wittgenstein's central categories. His concern throughout the *Investigations* was with the workings of conventions, customs, norms, institutions, and the background conditions that help sustain our social interactions.[30]

Identifying the sociological thrust of the *Investigations* suggests ways in which Wittgenstein's work might be developed, thereby repairing the third and last of the difficulties I set out to address. As I have indicated in the notes, Wittgenstein's project makes contact – in varying degrees – with a number of long-standing themes and classic works in the sociological tradition: with Simmel on money, with Mauss on gifts, with Durkheim on spiritual powers as the transfigured experience of the social, and with Kuhn on the scientific community's routine dependence on, and exploitation of, exemplary scientific achievements, or "paradigms." Recent scholarship, represented by Shapin's work on the language-game of early modern experimental science, shows these connections being carried forward and deepened. Each of these points of contact indicates ways in which Wittgenstein's insights can be tested against historical and empirical material. We can ask: have Wittgenstein's ideas any power to illuminate the historical record? Conversely, have the demands of historical description shown up weaknesses and omissions? What aspects of Wittgenstein's philosophy stand out as maximally useful? Is it specific metaphors like "language-game," or "paradigm," or diffuse orientations like the priority of the concrete over the abstract and the particular over the general, or middle-range positions like his debunking of Platonist myths about meaning and rules? Different commentators will certainly offer different answers to these questions.[31] There is also no reason to assume that all of Wittgenstein's ideas should stand or fall together. We can expect no easy or quick consensus on such difficult issues, but they are the right questions to ask.

Anscombe's own link with Hume carries the same message. Though Anscombe doesn't express herself this way, it suggests that, for Wittgenstein, rule following is an artificial virtue. Such a formulation immediately suggests the question: what, then, in Wittgenstein's philosophy, are the equivalents of Hume's *natural* virtues?[32] What are Wittgenstein's assumptions about the capacities, dispositions, and propositional attitudes that individuals bring to their social interactions? This amounts to taxing him with one of the standard problems of sociological theory: the problem of specifying the relation between the individual and society. That this should come out of a comparison with Hume should occasion no surprise, for Hume too was a sociologist. His declared intention on the title pages of the *Treatise* was to bring the experimental method into moral subjects. He wanted to follow Boyle and Newton and be factual, inductive, naturalistic, and explanatory. He therefore took care to connect his insights to the data of political, legal, and economic history. Unfortunately Wittgenstein, personally, showed little inclination in this direction, and seemed to have eschewed it in some of his pronouncements about his aims and goals (cf. PI, 109, 126). Unlike Hume he did not want his work to be treated as explanatory. The symbolic figure lurking behind his text is not Newton but Goethe, the critic of Newtonian experimental methods.[33] There is, however, no compelling reason to follow him in this regard, since this self-denying and negative stance is logically independent of the rest of his philosophy. It merely seems to have been the part of the antiscientific, and anticausal,

Spenglerian milieu in which he wrote and to which he was personally attracted.[34] We should be suspicious of those who fasten upon such pronouncements and inflate their significance, as if not accepting them were tantamount to not understanding Wittgenstein. On the contrary, the more we understand him, the less significant and more subjective does such self-commentary become. What are philosophical problems, for Wittgenstein, other than entanglements in the misleading forms of self-commentary that we are prone to give on our own practices? The *Investigations* is a veritable monument to the fallibility of our self-awareness. Once we see that Anscombe's "idealist" Wittgenstein is really the sociological Wittgenstein, we should feel free to draw the obvious conclusion as to where and how his substantial insights can best be tested and developed.[35]

NOTES

1 "Spengler could be better understood if he said: I am *comparing* different cultural epochs with the lives of families; within a family there is a family resemblance, though you will also find a resemblance between members of different families. . . . " *Culture and Value* (Oxford: Blackwell, 1980), p. 14.

Spengler, by contrast, sought to identify the *soul* of a culture, i.e., its spiritual principle of unity. He did, however, also say that the realm of the cultural historian was "the art of portraiture transferred to the spiritual domain." O. Spengler, *The Decline of the West* (New York: Knopf, 1939), p. 101.

2 B. Williams, "Wittgenstein and Idealism," in G. Vesey, ed., *Understanding Wittgenstein*, Royal Institute of Philosophy Lectures, vol. 7, 1972–3, (London: Macmillan, 1974), pp. 76–95. Jonathan Lear, "Leaving the World Alone," *The Journal of Philosophy* 79 (1982), pp. 382–403. Jonathan Lear, "The Disappearing 'We,'" *Proceedings of the Aristotelian Society*, supp. vol. 57 (1984), pp. 219–42. The link with idealism is also a theme running through P. Hacker, *Insight and Illusion* (Oxford: Clarendon Press, 1972); see also D. Pears, *The False Prison*, vol. 2 (Oxford: Clarendon Press, 1988). Pears takes issue with Lear, but concedes "an element of idealism," p. 626.

3 P. F. Strawson, *Skepticism and Naturalism* (London: Methuen, 1985), p. 24.

4 Norman Malcolm, "Wittgenstein and Idealism," in G. Vesey, ed., *Idealism Past and Present*, Royal Institute of Philosophy Lectures, vol. 13 (Cambridge University Press, 1982), pp. 249–67.

5 M. Williams, "Wittgenstein, Kant, and the 'Metaphysics of Experience,' " *Kant Studien* 81 (1990), pp. 69–88.

6 Barry Stroud, "The Allure of Idealism: The Disappearing 'We,' " *Proceedings of Aristotelian Society*, supp. vol. 58 (1984), pp. 243–58, esp. pp.
253–4.

7 Derek Bolton, "Life-Form and Idealism," in G. Vesey, ed., *Idealism Past
and Present*, pp. 269–84.

8 Malcolm, "Wittgenstein and Idealism," p. 249.

9 G. E. M. Anscombe, "The Question of Linguistic Idealism," *Acta Philosophica Fennica* 28 (1976), pp. 188–215. The paper is reprinted in
Anscombe's *From Parmenides to Wittgenstein*, vol. 1 of *Collected Philosophical Papers* (Oxford: Blackwell, 1981), pp. 112–33. Page numbers are
from the collected papers.

Similar suggestions have been advanced by E. K. Specht in his *Foundations of Wittgenstein's Late Philosophy*, trans. D. E. Walford (Manchester: Manchester University Press, 1969), ch. 6. Interestingly, Specht's
argument has recently been dismissed as an "egregious" example of
"wild speculation." See the editorial introduction to R. L. Arrington and
H.-J. Glock, eds., *Wittgenstein's 'Philosophical Investigations': Text
and Context* (London: Routledge, 1991), pp. 1, 2. Presumably the same
dismissal would be applied to Anscombe. I take the opposite view and
think neither Specht nor Anscombe is bold enough in stating their case.
An earlier formulation which can be read as anticipating some of
Anscombe's themes is P. Winch's *The Idea of a Social Science* (London:
Routledge, 1958).

10 I have benefited enormously from studying B. Barnes, "Social Life as
Bootstrapped Induction," *Sociology* 17 (1983), pp. 524–45. Barnes's important paper covers much of the same ground as Anscombe's, but his independent treatment is both more concrete and more systematic. No one
interested in the issues discussed by Anscombe should be ignorant of it.

11 Links between Hume's philosophy and Wittgenstein's are central to
Kripke's important study: S. Kripke, *Wittgenstein on Rules and Private
Language* (Oxford: Blackwell, 1982). The difference is that whereas
Kripke makes the link with Book I of the *Treatise*, Anscombe makes it
with Book III. I believe the link goes further than that so far indicated by
Anscombe and, indeed, can be used to shed light on the controversy
surrounding Kripke's reading. I have developed these claims in a forth-
coming book, provisionally entitled *Rules and Institutions: An Essay on
Wittgenstein and Hume* (forthcoming).

12 D. Hume, *A Treatise of Human Nature*, ed. L. A. Selby-Bigge (Oxford:
Clarendon Press, 1960), Book II, part ii, section 5.

13 The same strategy is to be found in the opening pages of the *Blue Book*.

14 An important sociological analysis of the concept of money is to be found in G. Simmel, *The Philosophy of Money* (London: Routledge, 1978). Simmel's book, first published in 1900, may be called a study of the forms of life of the money economy. In the light of Wittgenstein's analogy between words and tools (PI, 11) it is interesting to see Simmel calling money "the purest example of the tool" (Simmel, p. 210).

15 Compare the sociological account of gifts and giving in M. Mauss, *The Gift: Forms and Functions of Exchange in Archaic Societies*, trans. I. Cunnison (London: Cohen and West, 1966; first published in 1925).

16 J. L. Austin, "Performative Utterances," in J. Urmson and G. Warnock, eds., *Philosophical Papers* (Oxford: Clarendon Press, 1961), ch. 10.

17 But see PI, 682.

18 Strictly speaking, Z, 332 is about "color" rather than "red," but the context makes it clear that the point is meant as a general one.

19 A justly celebrated extension of the Wittgensteinian approach into the history of empirical science, and one that brings out the above themes with great clarity, is T. S. Kuhn, *The Structure of Scientific Revolutions* (Chicago: University of Chicago Press, 1962).

20 There are a number of readings of "forms of life," ranging from the biological to the social. At one extreme it means something like organic "life-form"; at the other it means "culture," or a way of life. The biological reading fits some cases in which Wittgenstein used "Lebensformen," but not all of them. Here I adopt a sociological reading. For some interesting textual support for a pluralistic, social reading, see E. von Savigny, "Common behavior of many a kind, *Philosophical Investigations, 206*," in Arrington and Glock, eds., *Wittgenstein's 'Philosophical Investigations,'* ch. 5. For a sense of the range of options, see J. F. M. Hunter, "Forms of Life in Wittgenstein's *Philosophical Investigations*," *American Philosophical Quarterly* 5, 4 (1968), pp. 233–43.

21 The most thorough discussion of these issues from the present standpoint that I know of is M. Hesse, *The Structure of Scientific Inference* (London: Macmillan, 1974), chs. 1, 2.

22 Cf. J. Fodor, *The Modularity of Mind* (Cambridge, Mass: MIT Press, 1983).

23 B. Berlin and P. Kay, *Basic Colour Terms: Their Universality and Evolution* (Berkeley and Los Angeles: University of California Press, 1969).

24 A vigorous and influential case for the importance of the biological idea of "function" has been made by R. G. Millikan in her *Language, Thought and Other Biological Categories* (Cambridge, Mass: MIT Press, 1984). I believe that all such biological approaches are vulnerable to the sociological argument indicated above.

25 Decorum and etiquette are, of course, phenomena that call out for an

"idealist" analysis. I have taken the idea of cognitive or epistemological decorum from S. Shapin, *A Social History of Truth, Gentility, Credibility and Scientific Knowledge in Seventeenth-Century England* (Chicago: University of Chicago Press, 1994). This work deals with the emergence of the language-game developed by Boyle and his contemporaries for handling problematic experimental reports, e.g., conflicting reports by astronomers about the location of comets; conflicting reports by divers about underwater pressure; anomalous accounts by travelers about icebergs; and, of course, the controversies about what observers were seeing in the evacuated chamber of Boyle's air-pump. The orientation throughout this work is clearly informed by Wittgensteinian ideas about language-games and forms of life.

26 See for example Max Black, "Wittgenstein's Language Games," *Dialectica* 33 (1979), 337–53; reprinted in Stuart Shanker, ed., *Ludwig Wittgenstein: Critical Assessments* (London: Croom Helm, 1986), vol. 2, ch. 29. Others, however, take the "game" metaphor more seriously, e.g., J. Hintikka, "Language-Games," *Dialectica* 31 (1977), pp. 226–45 (reprinted in Shanker, op. cit., vol. 2, ch. 30).

27 One of the classic attempts to reinterpret and demystify idealism by giving "spirit" a sociological reading is in E. Durkheim, *The Elementary Forms of the Religious Life*, trans. J. W. Swain (New York: Collier Books, 1961; first published 1912).

28 Anscombe expresses this by saying, somewhat darkly, "The essence is not what I mean or am speaking of: it is rather that through which I understand or think of (mean) etc." "The Question of Linguistic Idealism," in Anscombe, *From Parmenides to Wittgenstein* (Oxford: Blackwell, 1981) p. 115. Combining this with Wittgenstein's claim: "If you talk about essence – you are merely noting a convention" (RFM, I-14) – i.e., substituting "convention" for "essence" in Anscombe's claim, we get the version I offer.

29 Could this be why Anscombe adopts this label? She certainly draws attention to, and endorses, Hume's description of the obligation to keep promises as being naturally unintelligible (p. 196). Elsewhere, in a similar treatment, this is strengthened into their being *naturalistically* unintelligible: cf. "Rules, Rights and Promises." "I shall be arguing that *no* naturalistic account of a rule, as of a promise, will work" (Anscombe, *Ethics, Religion and Politics*, vol. 3 of *Collected Philosophical Papers* [Oxford: Blackwell, 1981], ch. 10, p. 97). This, of course, is not Hume's view, as he makes clear. His contrast of the natural and the artificial is a contrast of the psychological with the social, i.e., a contrast *within* naturalism. In a broader sense of "natural," conventions are perfectly natural, cf. *Treatise*, Bk. III, pt. ii, §1, p. 484.

30 Recent commentary on the self-referential and performative aspects of rule-following – that is, on those aspects that Anscombe calls "idealistic" – has indirectly acknowledged them by calling them "internal relations." See, for example, G. Baker and P. Hacker, *Scepticism, Rules and Language* (Oxford: Blackwell, 1984). Unfortunately the appeal to these "internal relations" has been used as an argument *against* a sociological reading of Wittgenstein's account of rules. In the light of what has been said above, deriving from Anscombe and Barnes, it is clear that the opposite is the case, and it speaks *for* a sociological reading; cf. D. Bloor, "Wittgenstein on Rule-following: The Old and the New Individualism," *The Polish Sociological Bulletin*, nos. 3–4 (1989), pp. 27–33.

31 For example, Gellner argues that the data of history and anthropology are fatal to Wittgenstein's later philosophy. (Gellner's main target is Winch: see note 7.) See E. Gellner, "The New Idealism – Cause and Meaning in the Social Sciences," in I. Lakatos and A. Musgrove, eds., *Problems in the Philosophy of Science* (Amsterdam: North Holland, 1968), pp. 377–406. On the other hand, if we think of the Wittgensteinian tradition flowing into the history of science through T. S. Kuhn's *Structure of Scientific Revolutions*, we get a different answer.

32 Hume spoke of our "confined generosity" and contrasted it with the unconfined, that is, universal requirements of moral obligation. Similarly, Wittgenstein clearly believed in a certain degree of natural or "confined" cognition. Thus he spoke of the primitive curiosity of an animal (RPPII, 345), and suggested that a dog might be afraid that his master would beat him, but could not be afraid that he would beat him tomorrow (PI, 650). So curiosity and fear can exist in a limited "confined" form on a purely natural basis.

Hume, like Wittgenstein, also used the technique of imagining the general facts of nature to be different in order to reflect on how this might change our concepts – hence his appeal to the philosophical fiction of the state of nature and the poets' Golden Age. If the rivers flowed with wine and milk, and cordial affection were the only sentiment, the convention of *mine* and *thine* would not exist. Justice and injustice alike would be unknown. There would be no concept of property; cf. *Treatise*, Bk. III, pt. ii, §2, pp. 493–5. We might even sense a family resemblance between Hume's social fictions and the faintly arcadian quality of Wittgenstein's simple language-games. Certainly his conclusions converged with Hume's. "If agreement were universal," said Wittgenstein, echoing Hume on property, "we should be quite unacquainted with the concept of it" (Z, 430).

33 In 1931 Wittgenstein wrote: "Does Goethe's contempt for laboratory

experiment and his exhortation to go out and learn from untrammelled nature have anything to do with the idea that a hypothesis (interpreted in the wrong way) already falsifies the truth? And is it connected with the way I am now thinking of starting my book – with a description of nature?" *Culture and Value* (Oxford: Blackwell, 1980), p. 10. Perhaps the closest connection with Goethe comes out in Wittgenstein's remarks on color. See J. Westphal, *Colour: Some Philosophical problems from Wittgenstein* (Oxford: Blackwell, 1987).

34  See D. Bloor, *Wittgenstein: A Social Theory of Knowledge* (London: Macmillan, 1983), ch. 8.

35  I should like to thank Barry Barnes, Celia Bloor, Martin Kusch, Peter Lewis, and the editors, Hans Sluga and David Stern, for their valuable criticisms of earlier drafts of this paper. They are not responsible for, or necessarily in agreement with, the final version of the argument.

# 12 Forms of life: Mapping the rough ground

Recognizing what we say, in the way that is relevant in philosophizing, is like recognizing our present commitments and their implications; to one person a sense of freedom will demand an escape from them, to another it will require their more total acceptance. Is it obvious that one of these positions must, in a given case, be right?[1]

## I "NEITHER SUPER-IDEALIZED GUIDANCE NOR CAPRICE"

We have got onto slippery ice where there is no friction and so in a certain sense the conditions are ideal, but also, just because of that, we are unable to walk. We want to walk: so we need friction. Back to the rough ground! (PI, 107)

Terry Eagleton, in his script for Derek Jarman's film, *Wittgenstein*, takes up Wittgenstein's image of the "crystalline purity of logic" in contrast to the "rough ground" of what we actually say and do.[2] A young man, we are told, dreams of "reducing the world to pure logic," a dream he succeeds in realizing in a world "purged of imperfection and indeterminacy, like countless acres of gleaming ice." That world, perfect as it is, is uninhabitable: "he had forgotten about *friction*." As an older man, he "came to understand that roughness and ambiguity and indeterminacy aren't imperfections – they're what make things work." He dug up the ice to uncover the rough ground, but, "homesick for the ice, where everything was radiant and absolute," he was unable to live on the rough ground, and he ended up "marooned between earth and ice, at home in neither."

383

The image of the ice as, precisely, home is Eagleton's and Jarman's, not Wittgenstein's, but, as I will argue, there is something oddly right about it, and, taking it seriously, we can ask: Why does the place of perfection and purity seem like home, rather than like an alluring, exotic locale? Why would an inability to stay on the rough ground manifest itself as an inability to feel at home there, rather than as, say, esthetic dissatisfaction? What is Wittgenstein urging himself and us to return to when he urges us back to the rough ground, back to what we say and do, and why might such a return fail to still the urges that sent us off in search of the perfection of ice? Why does it seem to us, as it continues to seem to Wittgenstein, that in turning away from the ice he "means to deny something" (PI, 305)?

One important thing Wittgenstein can seem to be denying us is, precisely, ground to stand on, if among our concerns is the possibility of casting a critical eye on the world we inhabit. When he writes that "what has to be accepted, the given is – so one could say – forms of life" (PI, 226), what – so one could ask – is the force of this "has to"? If, as Wittgenstein wants to lead us to see, it is only against a background of shared practices and shared judgments that doubt can be intelligible, (how) can we register, let alone argue for, disapprobation of a form of life, whether it be one in which we are enmeshed (making our attempted critique self-refuting) or one to which we are alien (making our critique, referentially, off the mark)? In either case, it would seem, we fail to say anything that is both about the form of life in question and critical of it.

Conundrums such as this have a place not only in Wittgensteinian exegesis. The question of where one can stand to obtain a perspective on a set of practices that is simultaneously informed and critical is a deep and central question for political theory, and it arises with special urgency in the context of current disputes about "multiculturalism." Is there some privileged point, available perhaps through the resources of reason, from which diverse practices can be neutrally surveyed? Or are all perspectives necessarily partial, in both senses of that word, and all judgments colored by the lenses through which they are made?

It has been argued, most pointedly by J. C. Nyiri, that Wittgenstein provides a way of responding to these puzzles, not by providing such critical ground, but by persuading us to do without it. On this reading

Wittgenstein is at once theoretically pluralist and practically conservative.[3] We are, on this account, tragically misled if we attempt to step outside of the practices in which we are engaged in order to provide a justification of them or, worse, to argue for their reform. It is certainly true that Wittgenstein was deeply distrustful of the employment of practice-transcendent reason ("a medicine invented by an individual," RFM, II-23) in the attempt to shape changes in forms of life. One can, to go further, connect this distrust with his remarks, in relation to purely philosophical theorizing, about taking language on a holiday, detaching it from its everyday employment in the futile hope that, detached from quotidian dross, essential truths will be revealed. Time and again, he draws us back to the dross: there, where everything looks at once too mundane and too multifarious, is what, if we could only recognize it as such, would be what we seek.

Yet time and again, the interlocutor voices his – and our – sense that that cannot be all there is:

Here we come up against a remarkable and characteristic phenomenon in philosophical investigation: the difficulty – I might say – is not that of finding the solution but rather that of recognizing as the solution something that looks as if it were only a preliminary to it. "We have already said everything. – Not anything that follows from this, no, *this* itself is the solution!" . . . The difficulty here is: to stop. (Z, 314)

One might say that our difficulty is our inability to recognize home when we are in it: we are in the grip of a picture akin to the fantasy of having been left as a foundling on the doorstep of our putative parents, banished for mysterious reasons from our true, incomparably grander, home and birthright.

But it is not only a philosopher's taste for the crystalline purity of ice that might lead one to think that home was another sort of place than here. The rough ground, that which lies beneath our feet, may be problematic for quite other reasons. It is one thing to speak of bringing our words home from the (non)places to which philosophers had tried to drag them when what we do, what we are inclined to say, the practices that shape the senses of our words, are relatively uniform and unproblematic – as they are, for example, in the sorts of cases Wittgenstein uses in his discussions of rule-following, counting, and the like. Our resistance to accepting that we do what we do,

our temptations toward the ice, seem different, however, less specifically philosophical in the sense Wittgenstein wants to problematize,
when the temptation to seek other homes for our words is prompted
by a sense that our relation to what we do is somehow troubled: in
the name of *what*, if not what's *really* the case, can we mount a
critique of what we say? " 'So you are saying [Wittgenstein's interlocutor accuses him] that human agreement decides what is true and
what is false?' It is what human beings say [he replies] that is true
and false; and they agree in the language they use. That is not agreement in opinions but in forms of life" (PI, 242).

Wittgenstein's emphasis on agreement is important, since he aims
to break us of the conviction that no amount of concordance in
human practices could effect reference or truth, that such things
cannot be a matter of what we do, that it must always be a possibility that we, all of us, do it wrong, that our words and sentences
misfire in their attempts to hit the target of reality. But the emphasis
on agreement can mislead us into thinking of Wittgensteinian forms
of life as internally homogeneous, leading to what Stanley Cavell
has dubbed the "Manichean" reading of Wittgenstein on rules (similar, he points out, to Carnap's distinction between "internal" and
"external" questions).[4] On such a reading, one is either inside or
outside of a language game, the contours of which are arbitrary, and,
if inside, one just does what "we" do; if outside, one is clueless – not
a participant, certainly not an intelligible critic.

But it is not just clumsy readings of Wittgenstein that can lead
to this impasse. There is the temptation, centrally a concern of
Wittgenstein's, voiced as frequently as any by his interlocutor, to
think that our options are, in David Pears's words "either super-
idealized guidance or caprice."[5] That is, the "Manichean" reader of
Wittgenstein is importing into his or her reading of Wittgenstein
exactly the philosophical move it was his aim to cure us of the
felt need for, the move, that is, away from taking our practices as
either adequate to our demands of them or, if inadequate, then
immanently and empirically revisable, in favor of a search for
"super-idealized guidance," thought by such a reader to reside in
those practices themselves, sublimed and transcendentalized.

Wittgenstein writes that "the real discovery is the one that makes
me capable of stopping doing philosophy when I want to. – The one
that gives philosophy peace, so that it is no longer tormented by

questions which bring *itself* in question" (PI, 133). It might seem that what would allow one to stop would have to be a sense of quiet (peace), a sense that one's questions had been either answered or dissolved. But there's no need to take Wittgenstein in this way – it could just as well be that what stops, what is given peace, is, specifically, philosophizing, not because quiet takes its place, but because what has seemed a philosophical problem becomes something else.[6] We can come to identify our sense of dis-ease with what we do as calling not for a repudiation of human practice in favor of something independent of it, but for a change in that practice, a change that begins with a politically conscious placing of ourselves within, but somewhere on the margins of, a form of life.

The Manichean reading will keep resurfacing (as it does for Wittgenstein himself) so long as such a shift, from the philosophical to the political, does not or cannot occur – so long, for example, as one remains closeted. The closet works rather like children's attempting invisibility by placing their hands over their eyes: the hope is that I will not be seen as who I am if I refuse to acknowledge, perhaps even to myself, that I see the world from the location of that identity. So long as I give my reports on how things seem ventriloquistically, from the imagined vantage point of a more authoritative, because more generic, subject, my actual location may go undetected. In this sense, anyone can be closeted, even, or especially, the privileged, since no one actually occupies the position of the wholly generic subject.

What Quine refers to as "the pull toward objectivity"[7] is precisely this sort of ventriloquizing, and for him (as for Sabina Lovibond in her discussion of what she argues is Wittgenstein's realism)[8] it is of the essence of our talk about the objectively real world that we do this. In one sense I agree, but it will be the burden of this paper to argue that a fully robust realism requires us not to ventriloquise prematurely, but, rather, to recognize when more is to be learned from a careful account of how things look from *over there,* when the fictive point that serves as the locus of the objective gaze encodes not what we all have in common but the interests of privilege that have come spuriously to be accepted as universal.

I want to argue, that is, that the epistemic resources of variously marginal subject positions provide the ground for a critique of "what we do" that rejects both the possibility of transcending human practice and the fatalism of being determined by it, but that those resources are not available to someone who is unwilling or unable to stand on that ground.

For complex reasons that it is far beyond the scope of this paper to explore, Wittgenstein himself was so unwilling or unable. He was, by chance or choice, intellectually and socially marginal. He was not trained as a philosopher, and he resisted both the professional normalization of his own life and work and the possibility (since actualized) of such normalization on the part of those who would follow him. He lived most of his life outside of his native Austria and never gave up the idea that there might be somewhere he could feel at home, although he was certain it could not be in Cambridge, which was where he mostly lived and worked. He was also, in some sense of the words, Jewish and homosexual, but neither was an identity he could straightforwardly claim: insofar as either could have provided him with a vantage point marginal to forms of life of the Europe of his day, with which he was profoundly disaffected, such possibilities were wholly unacknowledged.[9]

An explicitly political reading of Wittgenstein, one that starts from somewhere on the margins with an articulation of estrangement from a form of life, although alien to his personal sensibilities is, I want to argue, both responsible to his later work and illuminating of it. Such a reading can, furthermore, provide us with a map out of the thicket of the seemingly endless disputes between various forms of objectivism and relativism – disputes that stem from the idea that justification is either absolutely grounded in bedrock or wholly capricious.

When we think we are faced with a forced choice between the extremes of objectivism or relativism, it is because we are in the thrall of a picture whose hold on us Wittgenstein aims to break with his calls to attend to what we do. What he expects us to find is that justification is a practice we engage in with particular other people for particular reasons, to lay to rest particular worries – and that sometimes it works. If we have reason to believe that it "worked" prematurely or suspiciously, we can reopen it, raise new worries, and lay them to rest – or not. But there is no response to the claim that new worries can always be raised, and that there is no a priori assurance that they can be laid to rest – except to say "yes, and just what did you have in mind? What have we ignored; whose voices have not been heard; what further, specific objections can you raise?" This process is neither absolutely grounded nor capricious: it can be engaged in conscientiously or dishonestly, democratically or autocratically; we do or do not have reason to trust it – but in any case there are things to say, ways to proceed, objections to raise and answers to give.

To say that at this point we are on the terrain not of reason but of politics is to invoke a distinction that does no work: if a particular discussion seems not to respect the facts or the formal relationships between the facts, that's something to say, something to argue; and if those arguments seem to be going nowhere, that may be reason to change the rules of the discussion. The point is that these are all things we do, things we know how to do, things we argue about the doing of; and there is nothing outside of what we do to determine whether or not we are doing it right, which is not to say that we cannot meaningfully be said to be doing it wrong, only that such a claim cannot rest on hand-waving. Anything we think might ground our practices – whether it be Reality or Reason – is just one more thing to argue about.

## II  PRIVILEGED MARGINALITY

As much as I am inclined to believe that the last couple of paragraphs are an appropriate response to the worries about grounding,[10] there is a problem with this response, signaled by my unmarked use of "we."

Feminists and others have urged caution about the uses of "we," as about the allegedly generic masculine or the reference to (generic) women.[11] Who is inclined, and who excluded, when, in particular, the relatively privileged use terms meant to include others in their scope? When I query the "we" of those paragraphs, it seems most centrally to refer to those who, marginal to the discussions in question, nonetheless have the standing to intervene in them, to make their voices heard, to articulate a critique simultaneously intelligible to those who "own" the discussion and adequate to the expression of dissatisfaction with it. The counsel of those paragraphs is likely to seem a cruel joke to those who stand little chance of being heard or who have to choose between saying what they mean and saying what those in power can understand.[12] From such a location what seems to make sense is, rather, either Scylla or Charybdis – either a deeply held conviction in the absolute wrongness of one's oppression and the faith that that conviction is warranted from some objective standpoint (for example, God's), or a determination to acquire the power to overthrow the structures of one's subordination, to acquire the might to make right.

The social location of the "we" of those paragraphs can, I think, best be understood as one of "privileged marginality." Privilege and marginality are central concepts in recent feminist and other liberatory theorizing, in which they are generally taken to be opposed to each other: privilege resides at the center of whatever system is being analyzed, and marginality is the condition of being removed from that center, having an identity peripheral to the structures of privilege, being "different." But there are certain social locations that are at once privileged and marginal, complex amalgams that are of particular relevance for an understanding of the nature of philosophy and of theorizing.[13]

In particular, in societies such as ours, the position of the academic, and of the philosopher within the academy, are positions of privileged marginality. In each case – in society as a whole or in the academy – to the extent that power is centered anywhere, it is centered elsewhere than with the (non–technology- or policy-oriented[14]) academic or the philosopher, both of whom have identities regarded by most people as, literally, eccentric: philosophers are seen within the academy much as most academics are seen outside of it – as amusingly out of touch with what is regarded as the "real world." But in both cases a certain form of privilege attends the marginality, both the privilege of class that attaches to academic employment, along with the more specific privileges of tenure and academic freedom, and, again most strikingly in the case of philosophers, the privilege of being intellectually deferred to, even if not concerning anything regarded as of practical importance. The privilege and the marginality are not just two features of this social location; they are inextricably bound together. Philosophers and academics are privileged *as marginal:* their social location on the margin is itself a location of privilege.

Privileged marginality is a location from which the felt need for the generic standpoint is peculiarly both poignant and problematic, a combination present throughout Wittgenstein's writings and enacted especially in the interchanges with the interlocutor in the

*Investigations* and other later work. It is, consequently, a social location from which a radical break from epistemology can be called for, even as it is the location from which epistemology emerges and is pursued. (This doubleness is connected to Wittgenstein's characterization of philosophy as both the disease and the cure, as well as to the ways that for him the ills of philosophy both are and are not contained in our ordinary uses of language, as though the virus of being led astray both by and from those uses were one that infected everyone but made only some actually ill.)

It is, however, only the explicit politicizing of that location, along with the explicit politicizing of epistemology generally, that can take us beyond the diagnosis of the pull toward the generic – the pull, that is, away from diversity – to a clearer sense of how more responsibly to live in the forms of life we – variously – inhabit. Such a perspective provides a gloss on Wittgenstein's remark that "Not empiricism and yet realism in philosophy, that is the hardest thing" (RFM, VI-23).[15] Empiricism is an epistemology of parsimony: the problem for knowledge is taken to be the problem of partiality in the sense of bias: what we need is to strip away the influence of everything that might lead to doxastic idiosyncrasy. The hallmark of reality, however, is that it looks different to those differently placed in it; consequently realism requires an epistemology of largesse: the problem for knowledge is the problem of partiality not in the sense of bias but in the sense of incompleteness.

Not only do we have to learn from diversely located subjects, but we have to recognize when our own locations are distinctively limiting, when what we say is especially problematically partial. Central to this contention is the idea that, while it cannot be the task of philosophy to change the homes to which words need to be brought back, such changes are, in many areas of our lives, urgently called for, and that Wittgenstein is best read as recognizing that fact, however unsuited he took himself to be to engage in the – nonphilosophical – work that it entails.

III  "GRIEF DESCRIBES A PATTERN . . . IN THE
WEAVE OF OUR LIFE"

There is a scene in the film of Harvey Fierstein's *Torch Song Trilogy* (1988) in which Arnold, the gay protagonist, and his mother are at the cemetery where Arnold's father and his lover are both buried. His mother comes over from her husband's grave to Arnold at his lover's, furious at what she (correctly) perceives as his sense of commonality in their losses. It is obscene to her that he might take himself to feel anything like the grief she feels, to be deeply mourning his lover's death, to have shared with Alan love in the same sense as the love between husband and wife. Significantly, the commonality in their actions is called into question along with the commonality of emotion. Arnold's mother demands to know what he thinks he's doing (he has taken a slip of paper from his pocket and is reading from it the Jewish prayer for the dead); when he replies that he's doing the same thing she's doing, she insists he's not: "I'm reciting Kaddish for my husband; you're blaspheming your religion."

What would it be to settle the dispute between them: is Arnold feeling what his mother is feeling, or is he not? One way of going about it would be to say that there is an objective fact of the matter, that our words "grief," "love," and the like refer to particular states that people can be in, states that we are not yet in a position to specify with any clarity, but when science has sufficiently progressed and we can do that, we will know the answer, and until then we can gather evidence that would point in one direction or the other.

Wittgenstein's remark that " 'grief' describes a pattern which recurs, with different variations, in the weave of our life" (PI, p. 174), is telling here. On a Wittgensteinian account the answer to the question of whether or not Arnold and his mother are feeling the same thing is not to be found above or below the details of what they say and do, but in those details and, importantly, in what those details mean in the contexts of their lives. Arnold and his mother disagree on whether or not the pattern of his feelings, in the context of his life with Alan, was a variation on the same pattern of feelings she felt, in the context of her life with her husband. The "facts" (both those we have and any we might acquire) tell us that there are similarities in their situations and that there are differences. The question is what those similarities and differences mean, how to weigh them, and we can answer that question only against the background of our beliefs and attitudes about, for example, homosexuality.

It is the background, the history, the context – and what we make of them – that make whatever is currently in Arnold's mind or heart (or head or molecules) *grief*, just as it is the background, the history, the context, that make the speaking of certain words reciting Kaddish. We need, that is, to see in Arnold's life and in his world a pattern that we will take as relevantly similar to the pattern in his mother's life and world. We need not only to know more about Arnold, but to situate what we know in what Jonathan Lear refers to as the "perceptions of salience, routes of interest, feelings of naturalness in following a rule that constitute being part of a form of life."[16]

Thinking about this scene, and about the film itself, especially about its ambitions with respect to the beliefs and attitudes of heterosexual audiences, can lead us to ask about diversity in locations within and relationships to a form of life. This is a slightly but crucially different way of framing such a question than the more usual one, the one Lear discusses, namely what to make of diversity – actual or imagined – *among* forms of life.[17] The question arises for Lear, as it does for most readers of Wittgenstein, as a way of placing Wittgenstein on the terrain of realism and idealism and, relatedly, of objectivism and relativism. For Lear, Wittgenstein's position in the *Philosophical Investigations* is a form of transcendental idealism, where empirical realism is secured by the "we are so-minded," which, on Lear's interpretation, accompanies all our judgments, as "I think" accompanies them for Kant, and by the lack of any empirical contrast to the "we." If we entertain the concrete empirical possibility of being differently minded, Lear argues, if we "make the 'we' vivid, then Wittgenstein's philosophy collapses into philosophical sociology, studying how one tribe among others goes on."[18]

In some important sense, that is, the "we" disappears. But Lear is also concerned to allow that there is a place, although an odd and problematic one, on Wittgenstein's view for what Lear calls "reflective understanding." Although we are in need of "therapy" to treat the "neurosis" of "philosophical perplexity," the neurosis is neither silly nor peculiar to philosophers, and, crucially, "post-neurotic consciousness is fundamentally more complex than a healthy consciousness that has never suffered disease or cure."[19] It is also possible to become aware of the fact "that our form of life is not some fixed, frozen entity existing totally independently of us."[20] Lear notes the spatially metaphorical nature of his attempt to give an account of our reflective relationship to our form of life – we cannot, for example, "look down upon" it; we can be aware of it only "from the inside." But he does not consider the nature of the space within, of the epistemic resources of its internal differentiations, of its having, for example, margins.[21]

The issue is related to Barry Stroud's critique of Lear's paper. Stroud finds reason to resist Lear's Kantian reading of Wittgenstein in part because of what he takes to be the necessity, on such a reading, of taking another, highly problematic, step, one that would take us from the *necessity* of "we are so-minded" to its *objective validity*, a step corresponding to Kant's arguments for the categories as securing empirical realism.[22] For Stroud, we ought rather to resist the urge to start down that, or any other, metaphysical road in our reading of the *Investigations*. While Lear downplays the importance to Wittgenstein's (or Kant's) aims of providing an answer to the skeptic, Stroud sees answering the skeptic's challenge as central – but he doesn't think that the answer is in the form of an argument that demonstrates, for example, that the skeptic is self-refuting.

The answer is not so much an argument to the conclusion that what the skeptic wants us to think might be so could not in fact be (coherently thought to be) so as it is an invitation to actually try to carry through the demands that the skeptic makes, with the aim of showing that what are taken to be impediments to an immediate, unquestionable epistemic relationship to reality, or at best mere pieces of stage-setting, are in fact crucial to anything we can mean by the questions we ask or by anything we would take as an answer. What we take to be either part of the problem or an irrelevant distraction is where we need to look, not for an answer to the questions we'd posed – there are no answers to the questions we'd posed; there is no "refuting" the skeptic – but for a less vexed relation to what we do, an attentive respect for the resources in our language and practices.

What I want to suggest is that part of what we can learn is that internal diversity in forms of life – the fact that we do not all stand in the same relationship to what "we" say and do – is part of what gives what we say and do a claim to legitimacy. If we take Wittgenstein as Lear does, then there being empirical, criticizable content to a form of life becomes a problem for anything that would count as realism; we seem to need, that is, to transcendentalize the idealism by disappearing the "we." But we needn't start down that path. The sort of awareness from within that Lear says we can in fact have of our form of life is frequently not nearly as evanescent and empirically contentless as he makes it out to be: it can be as concrete and as critical as what Arnold brings his mother – and the film aims to bring its heterosexual audience – to see about the forms of life they share but in which they occupy very different places.

Pattern perception – what is involved in deciding whether or not what Arnold feels is, like what his mother feels, grief – is sensitive to perceivers' locations, both as a matter of what can be seen and what is occluded, and as a matter of how what is seen is interpreted. We also have standards, sometimes explicitly moral standards, about what gets to count as the same. People who have lost pets, for example, often find others reluctant to take their feelings of loss as real grief. We are not all similarly minded about such things: we find, depending on our individual and cultural histories, different degrees of similarity and difference in the feelings some people have toward animals and the feelings people (are supposed to) have toward other people. Sometimes we just "agree to disagree," recognizing the limits to our shared practices (hence, to the objectivity of our judgments).[23] But there are occasions on which it can be important not to accept that we differ, but to argue about which set of attitudes is in some way better or more appropriate.[24]

With Arnold and his mother in the cemetery, the film clearly intends us to see the similarities as more salient than the differences. The burden of the film in relation to a heterosexual audience is to bring that audience to a recognition of shared humanity, of shared emotions, needs, and desires, with gay men, including those who, like Arnold, who works as a female impersonator, are not attempting to be in all respects but one indistinguishable from those who are normatively straight.

For Arnold's mother the form of life in which love and grief and the reciting of Kaddish have their home is the world of heterosexual marriage and family, a world in which Arnold is the "outsider within."[25] He knows that form of life, but he knows it from the margins – not from some disjoint elsewhere, but not simply from within. He wants marriage and family, and he knows what's needed to live them, but, unlike his mother, he doesn't see there being one man and one woman as a necessary part of the picture. As with love, grief, and the reciting of Kaddish, he parses the patterns of marriage and family differently, and, in so doing, sees the same.

The politics of the film are, I suspect, dated. It wants on the one hand to insist on Arnold's difference – gayness is his life, not, as his mother wishes he would keep it, simply a matter of what he does in the bedroom. At the same time it stresses a fundamental commitment to humanism: underneath our differences we are basically all the same. For many reasons, the AIDS crisis among them, the simultaneous foregrounding of similarity and difference has become less possible. The frightening rise in respectable homophobia has led many, in pressing for civil rights, to minimize the difference that homosexuality makes, to argue that in all the ways that society has any reason to care about, gay men and lesbians are just like straight people. Others, through the politics of queerness, have responded to the pandemics of AIDS and hatred with a principled refusal of the implicit bargain of conformity for compassion, refusing, in particular, to acknowledge the authority of what has been named "heteronormativity." Rather than simply asserting and celebrating queer difference, the politics of queerness challenges straight "sameness": "We are not like *you*, but *you* are a lot more like *us* than you like to think."[26] In this fracturing of responses to a politics of hate, into an attempt, on the one hand, to broaden the norms of sameness and, on the other, to reject their authority, we seem to have lost the space in which *Torch Song Trilogy* takes place, a space that does not require the minimizing of difference as the price for the recognition of commonality.

It is arguable that such a space was always only an illusion, that some differences (similar arguments have been made concerning, especially, race and gender) have always had to be denied or downplayed if those who are defined by them are to be enfranchised in liberal terms. Various separatisms and nationalisms are grounded precisely in the rejection of the terms of this liberal demand. Part of why *Torch Song Trilogy* works, I think, is that it can eloquently evoke nostalgia even in those for whom its politics were always an illusion and a trap. In the space of the film, liberal humanism provides a home to which words like "grief" and "love" could be brought. There was, the film is telling us, something we meant by those words, along with a hopeful, generous sense of who "we" were, something the homophobe, that is, could be brought to see – and it is this that we seem to have lost (as we seem, nostalgically, once to have had it, or at least the hope of it).

In the terms of the film, disputes such as those between Arnold and his mother about what we should say can be settled, but clearly not by noting what we do say. That is, contra many readers of Wittgenstein, the correctness of our judgments is not simply a matter of community agreement, which is surely in any event an odd way of thinking about the practices of creatures whose forms of life are so many of them characterized by fractiousness and, in particular, fractiousness that makes sense only on the supposition that there is something to be arguing about, that one's antagonists are *wrong*. Arnold doesn't just want his mother to see things some other way – nor does the film want that of its audience: she and we are asked to get beyond prejudices that keep us from seeing the *truth* – that Arnold deeply loved Alan and is grieving his death.

But the matter is not so simple. Unlike the position of those like Arnold's mother, who would say that what Arnold claims is just *false*, those espousing a queer politics are more likely to recognize the element of choice that can, with the proper contextualization, be seen to underlie all our ascriptions. What they urge is not that the liberal invitation be shown to be somehow mistaken (sent, as it were, to the wrong address), but that it be *declined*. If one takes this response to be intelligible (whether or not one takes it to be politically advisable), a natural conclusion to draw is that it shows that all along, even when things seemed as they do in the movie, it really was (just) a matter of choice. Not only was there no fact of the matter above or below what Arnold and his mother said and felt and did in the contexts they were in, but there was no fact of the matter at all: it's just a (philosophical) mistake to talk about right or wrong, true or false.

Such a conclusion, I want to argue, is not one Wittgenstein would have us draw,[27] nor is it one forced on us once we recognize the possibility that what holds our judgments in place, makes some claims true and others false, can be put into question (as, for example, by queer theory and politics). We are not, that is, forced into an uncritical relativism. To the extent that one believes in the possibility of objective knowledge about some range of phenomena (say, human emotions), one will be hopeful about the possibilities of reaching a sufficiently complex account of them to be adequate to the fullest possible range of diverse perspectives on them. One way of putting this point is that one will be a realist about those phenomena, meaning that one takes them to be the sort of things one can view from a range of different perspectives, learning different things about them in the process. Importantly, what goes on is not simply additive: different perspectives exist in critical relation to each other; we argue with as much as we supplement each other's views, and none of our perspectives would be rendered more reliable for being stripped of the interests and values that make it distinctive.[28]

Our not all going on in the same way about many things we all care about is part of the background against which our judgments get to be true or false about the world. The agreement in judgments Wittgenstein refers to (PI, 242) does the work it does in part because we cannot take it for granted: we find it in some places and not in others. That is, in those cases where we can't quite imagine not finding it (the examples of counting and such), it's not that we *can't* question how we go on (as though someone or something were *stopping* us): rather, we can't quite make sense of the question; we don't feel the need to ask it. All that would be needed to make the question intelligible – and to give us a way of going about answering it – would be the real need to ask it. The questions that seem to lack answers are just the ones we have no need to ask.

Often, however, we do not find agreement where it seems important to us that we do, where consensus, at least among some group to which we (do or want to) belong, seems important and is lacking. In such cases, we have lots of resources to turn to (in any case, they might or might not be adequate) – resources that range from logical argument to an appeal to agreed-on facts to well-chosen images or metaphors to novels, poems, plays, movies.[29]

It is, on the other hand, also part of what "we" do to find ourselves needing to disrupt what others take to be settled consensus, to re-open what is taken to be closed.[30] Very often the "we" who do this are marginal to the practices in which consensus was reached; our voices hadn't been attended to; perhaps we had not yet found them. Justification is no less real for the continuing possibility that still others will someday find *their* voices: on the contrary, it is precisely this possibility that gives our collective attempts at knowledge a claim to objectivity.[31]

As rich and diverse as are our ways of resolving disagreements, and as important as it is to note that those resources do frequently accomplish that aim and that when they do we are in the best position we can coherently want to be in to say that our claims are really true, nonetheless, it doesn't always work. And sometimes, speaking from the margins, what we want to do is not to make it work, not, that is, to accept the apparatus and shift the angle of vision. Rather than arguing, or showing, that as our words are used there is just no good reason (only, for example, reasons that spring from what we would call prejudice) not to go on with them as we would urge (not to include Arnold's experiences as ones of grief), we want to argue, or show, that the whole apparatus *is* an apparatus, and that it's one we do not have to accept, although the cost of rejecting it may well be unintelligibility, even, perhaps, to ourselves. We want to disrupt the prevailing sense that there is something we would all say about some situation not in favor of another, slightly or significantly different one, but to unsettle the sense that there *is* a "we," that we do share a form of life, that there is a home to which our words can be brought.[32] How can we make intelligible that depth and extent of dissatisfaction with the rough ground of our forms of life without invoking transcendent standards?

### IV   TOWARD A DIASPORIC CONCEPTION OF HOME

Wittgenstein was concerned, throughout his work, with questions of where and how the self stands in relation to the world. Are we, as Descartes would have it, essentially separate from (the rest of) the world, though somehow in a position reliably to know it; or is the world, as Kant would have it, in some deep sense our world, one we constitute by our placement in it? Wittgenstein's response in the *Tractatus* is clearly on the Kantian side of this divide. His later work appears so as well, but, more deeply, it challenges the idea that one can, as both Kant and the earlier Wittgenstein would have us believe, prove the Cartesian skeptic wrong, using philosophy to demonstrate that the world is ours.[33]

In the *Tractatus* Wittgenstein provided, as had Kant, a "minimal metaphysics" to establish the mutually defining relation of the self to the knowable world, thereby delimiting the scope of properly philosophical inquiry. The very move that guaranteed to the self the knowability of the world made any more substantive metaphysical inquiry nonsensical precisely by putting such inquiry outside the bounds of the knowable (or sayable). To argue that the phenomenal world is constituted in part by the categories of the understanding, or that the limits of language are the limits of the world, simultaneously guarantees both the possibility of science and the impossibility of metaphysics: there is no place to stand from which we can meaningfully query, let alone describe, our relationship to the world we know.

Wittgenstein's later work, notably the private language argument in the *Investigations*, is in many ways still Kantian in spirit. The private language argument can be read on one level as a restatement of Kant's Refutation of Idealism. Both arguments have the form of rendering incoherent the purported stance of a knowing subject agnostic about the existence of anything outside the self, and they both do so by demonstrating the dependence of such a self's internal coherence – the possibility of an autobiography, however fragmentary – on the structures that ground the possibility of knowledge of an external world. Thus, for Kant, the self cannot be an object of experience, nor, as the empiricists would have it, store up impressions from which to infer the existence of an external world – without always already placing itself in a world of real external objects. For Wittgenstein, on this reading, the meaningful attribution to oneself of experiences, such as the having of sensations, is impossible without the criteria in terms of which such experiences can be ascribed to others or by others to oneself. As idealism is impossible for the Kantian self, solipsism is impossible for the later Wittgensteinian self.

But on this reading the unquestionable link of self to world that led to the embracing of an indescribable solipsism in the *Tractatus* remains, only now the "self" has been broadened to include all the others who with me make up the indescribable "we." Just as the earlier solipsism is indistinguishable from realism (since "my" or "from here" drop out: there is nothing they can mean, no contrast they can mark, no world that is "yours" or "hers" or "from there"), so the "we" of Lear's "we are so-minded" contrastlessly marks the limits of *our* world. The agreement in judgments that constitutes a "we" is what makes any language at all possible: what is incoherent is the picture, inherited in modern terms most explicitly from Locke, but implicit in even most twentieth-century theorizing about reference, that language rests at bottom on an immediate connection, in each individual speaker's mind or brain, between word and idea.

We cannot, however, take as *given* the conditions of agreement in judgments, of attunement in forms of life, that would shut the skeptic out of intelligibility. (I take it that something like this idea is central to Cavell's reading of the *Investigations* and of the private language argument in particular.)[34] To say that the loss of my knowing my way around a world I share with others carries with it the loss of my knowing my way around myself, is not to say that I cannot be so lost, nor that the threat or fear that I might become so – or might even be so now, unknowingly – is an unreal one.

The philosophical demand for proof that the world is my world, that it makes sense to me, that I make sense in it, that I inhabit it with others who are intelligible to me and to whom I am intelligible leads words away from our uses of them not capriciously, but because those uses are seen as misleading, as not giving what we think we need of our words, be that definiteness of sense or assurance of reference. The illusion of philosophy is that we can get such definiteness, such assurance, by bringing words to what we take to be their true homes, whether that be in direct unmediated relation to ideas in each of our minds, in a Platonically ordered realm of concepts, or at the ends of scientifically respectable causal chains. Philosophy of language, on such views, becomes in part a matter of tracing how it can be that, getting their significance from their placement in such a realm, words can manage to work in the humdrum hodgepodge of our varied uses of them.

My characterization of the philosophers' move as one of bringing words to what (they take to be) their true homes is, of course, a deliberate echo of Wittgenstein's so describing his own task, where the homes to which he would bring our words are precisely the messy places from which the philosophers thought they needed to be extricated. Stanley Cavell writes in this context about the exile of words, and about the need to bring them home, "shepherding" them.[35] He goes on to say that it is not just our words, but our "lives themselves [that] have to return," that they and we are lost, that the ordinariness of our words in the forms of our ordinary lives is neither immediately evident nor easily returned to.

I have in the past frequently responded to Cavell's writing out of an uneasy discrepancy I felt between the subject position in which the text placed me as a philosopher and my sense of myself as a woman. In the present instance I was struck by what seemed to me the same sort of discrepancy, but the identity in terms of which I felt it was that of a

Diasporic Jew.[36] Cavell links his writing about Wittgenstein on exile and home to Kierkegaard on faith, to the idea of being lost as perdition: "Spiritually and religiously understood, perdition consists in journeying into a foreign land, in being 'out' [i.e., 'never at home']."[37] What left me uneasy is the idea that to be where one ought to be, to be in the place in which one's words and one's actions are intelligible,[38] responsible, is to be at home, since I take it to be the task of Diasporic Jews, as it is of others who live diasporically, to find oneself properly in the world precisely *not* "at home."

I want to suggest that we can think about our words as diasporically linked to home, building on a view of diasporic identity brilliantly articulated by Daniel and Jonathan Boyarin,[39] in which home is neither any presently existing location nor some place of transcendence. Rather, it presents itself to us as an ethical and political imperative to create forms of life that would place our words and us in right relation. To succeed in thus bringing our words home (or even to be sufficiently hopefully engaged in the struggle) would not demonstrate the falseness or unintelligibility of the skeptic's challenges, but would make us less desperately susceptible to them. On such a view it would be a mistake to bring our words prematurely home, to claim that the set of practices we now have for them are all right as they are. There are no other homes for our words than the ones we create in and through our practices, nor any predetermined ways of specifying what it is to have gotten those practices right, but that does not mean that there is no sense to the idea that we might not be going on as we should be.

### V  CONCLUSION

At the end of *The Wizard of Oz* Dorothy and the others appear before the Wizard to ask for what they take themselves to lack: a heart, a brain, courage, and the way home. Were the wizard a real one, he would grant those wishes. Being not a wizard but a balloonist from the Midwest, he cannot grant their wishes as expressed, but he can lead them to see that what they really wanted was not some magically granted "something," but rather qualities of character that they in fact already possessed, and that home, like heart, brain, and courage, was there for the asking, that the fearful journey away from it had been launched by a yearning for some place both obscurely grander and more in keeping with a dimly perceived sense of a "true self" inexpressible in Kansas, and that the journey could be reversed by a simple acknowledgment of the desire to return. All very well and good, but what about those of us who cannot quite bring ourselves to click our ruby slippers and intone "there's no place like home"? We may see through the illusions of Oz, give up on wizards, and still not be able to return to Kansas.

One way of making sense of the appeal of objectivist epistemologies and realist metaphysics to those who are oppressed is that such epistemologies and metaphysics are likely to seem the only alternative to an unacceptable acceptance of the status quo. I have been arguing that we can find in Wittgenstein's later writing a way of rejecting that choice, by attending to those aspects of our practices that are critical and transformative, that are, as much as the unreflective following of a rule, part of what "we do." We can find, in our practices, many alternatives to simply staying in Kansas, accepting it as it is, and taking off for Oz. Objectivity becomes, on such a view, as Lovibond argues, less an epistemic than a social and political achievement.[40]

I mean the link between diasporic identity and a diasporic view of words as more than metaphorical. If we are to reject both the idea that words have true, Platonic, homes and the idea that the homes afforded by current practice are in order just as they are, we need to confront the question of how such critiques can be made intelligible – by whom and to whom. Those who are wholly strangers to the form of life in which our words now find themselves may regard such forms of life as abhorrent, but are unlikely to bring to their abhorrence sufficient insight to give it any standing. Those who are wholly native to those practices are, on the other hand, unlikely to find them anything other than unquestionably natural: "we do what we do."

But there are others, people who are neither stranger nor native, who for the widest range of reasons, within and beyond their own choosing, live somewhere other than at the centers of the forms of life they inhabit. And the views from all those various "there"s can tell us a great deal about those forms of life and provide critical perspectives on them. The alternatives, that is, are not only two: the transcendentalizing of our lives or the claim to be viewing them from some mythical outside that is nowhere at all. It is, I would argue, an important part of the health at least of large, modern societies, that they have within them members who are not truly at home there, who see with the eyes of the "outsider within," and that such members are in positions to be listened to and to be intelligible.

Diasporic identity is one form the outsider within can take, and it is crucial to it that it's not a matter of just passing through, not having any real connection to the place where one finds oneself, caring deeply and responsibly only for home, wherever and when- ever that may be. Rather, those who live diasporically can and often do bring resources of moral intelligence, conviction, and courage to the places in which they sojourn. On the rabbinical view articulated in Boyarin and Boyarin, one reason for this is clear – it's only by engaging in and ultimately succeeding at the work of world repair that we'll ever be able to go home. In Lovibond's account, one moti- vation is the overcoming of alienation, the creation of a world in which one will be able to speak one's words nonironically, without the inverted commas that mark an unwillingness to accept the com- mitments that would make one's words meaningful *en pleine voix*.[41]

Rather than struggling concretely with and against this alienation, we can succumb to philosophy's promises of transcendence by, as Cora Diamond puts it, the "laying down of requirements."[42] What we happen to do cannot, we think, possibly be the sort of thing that could tell us what we ought to do, what it would be right to do. But if what we ought to do is something quite different from what we do do, the question arises of how we can be persuaded that it is the right thing to do, whether morally or epistemically: Where do these re- quirements come from? (The problem has been most discussed un- der the heading of moral motivation, but the issues are the same in epistemology.) Probably the most common and compelling answer to that question within the philosophical tradition has been some variant of "they come from *us*, from our truest natures." We only find them alien, so the story goes, because we have been in some way led astray.

Again we have the image of home, but like the Platonic picture of the true, unearthly home for our words, this home is not anywhere that anyone actually lives. Those who would be at home in such places are not any actual ones of us, but the idea that those are our true homes feeds the sort of scapegoating that projects onto some the features of human existence that are taken to be the cause and the symptoms of our being led astray. The litany is a familiar one: all the messy business of being born and dying, along with the various dependencies that afflict us along the way, the vicissitudes of attachment and desire, and the need for physical labor to keep body and soul together.[43]

To finally resist those temptations would be to come to terms with the unseemly contingencies of being human, not to accept everything as we find it, but to give up on the fantasy of being saved from the human condition or of being, in our truest natures, not really defined by it. If we ask what makes our words refer, our sentences true or false, our moral injunctions truly binding, the answer is that nothing does, because nothing could. Only we can do such things for ourselves, and, if, as many of us think about many of our words, sentences, and injunctions, we have not yet succeeded at these tasks, it falls to us to do better, to create homes to which our words can be brought, words that would, as Sabina Lovibond puts it, "represent deeds I can perform without shame."[44,45]

### NOTES

1 "The Availability of Wittgenstein's Later Philosophy," in Stanley Cavell, *Must We Mean What We Say?* (New York: Scribner's, 1969), p. 57.

2 Terry Eagleton, *Wittgenstein: The Terry Eagleton Script/The Derek Jarman Film* (London: British Film Institute, 1993), p. 55.

3 J. C. Nyiri, "Wittgenstein's Later Work in Relation to Conservatism," in Brian McGuinness, ed., *Wittgenstein and His Times* (Oxford: Basil Blackwell, 1982); and J. C. Nyiri, "Wittgenstein 1929–31: The Turning Back," in S.G. Shanker, ed., *Ludwig Wittgenstein: Critical Assessments*, vol. 4, *From Theology to Sociology: Wittgenstein's Impact on Contemporary Thought* (London: Croom Helm, 1986).

4 "The Availability of Wittgenstein's Later Philosophy," in Cavell, *Must We Mean What We Say?* p. 47.

5 David Pears, *The False Prison: A Study of the Development of Wittgenstein's Philosophy* (Oxford: Oxford University Press, 1988), vol. 2, p. 488.

6 See Joachim Schulte, "Wittgenstein and Conservatism," in S. G. Shanker, ed., *Ludwig Wittgenstein: Critical Assessments*, 5 vols. (Wolfeboro, N. H.: Croom Helm, 1986), vol. 4, p. 62.

7 W. V. Quine, *Word and Object* (Cambridge: MIT Press, 1960), pp. 5–8.

8 Sabina Lovibond, *Realism and Imagination in Ethics* (Minneapolis: University of Minnesota Press, 1983), pp. 58–62.

9 For a discussion of Wittgenstein's (problematic) Jewishness and homosexuality, as well as for an excellent general discussion of the relation of

his life to his work, see Ray Monk, *Ludwig Wittgenstein: The Duty of Genius* (New York: The Free Press, 1990).

10 They are analogous to the response Helen Longino gives to questions about objectivity in *Science as Social Knowledge: Values and Objectivity in Scientific Inquiry* (Princeton: Princeton University Press, 1990), and she is concerned to address the analogous sorts of concerns with it.

11 For a very illuminating summary and critical discussion of these concerns, see Elizabeth V. Spelman, *Inessential Woman: Problems of Exclusion in Feminist Thought* (Boston: Beacon Press, 1988).

12 See June Jordan, "Nobody Mean More to Me Than You and the Future Life of Willie Jordan," in *On Call: Political Essays* (Boston: South End Press, 1985) for a discussion of this question in relation to Black English.

13 Some of the most useful attempts to complicate the margins are in the work of Patricia Hill Collins, bell hooks, and Patricia Williams, all of whom write from the complex social location of Black women in the academy. See, especially, Patricia Hill Collins, *Black Feminist Thought: Knowledge, Consciousness, and the Politics of Empowerment* (Boston: Unwin Hyman, 1990); bell hooks, *Yearnings: Race, Gender, and Cultural Politics* (Boston: South End Press, 1990); and Patricia Williams, *The Alchemy of Race and Rights: Diary of a Law Professor* (Cambridge, Mass.: Harvard University Press, 1991).

14 Thanks to Sandra Harding for pointing out to me that the picture I had of academics was fed by a limited diet of examples, and ignored the burgeoning ranks of professors quite central to the exercise of political and economic power.

15 See Cora Diamond's discussion in "Realism and the Realistic Spirit," in *The Realistic Spirit: Wittgenstein, Philosophy, and the Mind* (Cambridge, Mass.: MIT Press, 1991), to which I am, however quixotically, indebted.

16 Jonathan Lear, "The Disappearing 'We,'" *Proceedings of the Aristotelian Society*, supp. vol. 58 (1984), p. 229.

17 The possibility of such diversity is significantly much more obvious in a strikingly similar quote from Cavell: "That on the whole we do [make and understand the same projections] is a matter of our sharing routes of interest and feeling, modes of response, senses of humor and of significance and of fulfillment, of what is outrageous, of what is similar to what else, what a rebuke, what forgiveness, of when an utterance is an assertion, when an appeal, when an explanation – all the whirl of organism Wittgenstein calls 'forms of life'" ("The Availability of Wittgenstein's Later Philosophy," 1969, p. 52). Both the nature of Cavell's list and his use of the plural (*"forms* of life") make it less likely that we will feel the temptation to transcendentalize that Lear's formulation produces.

18 Lear, The Disappearing 'We,' " p. 238.

19 Ibid., p. 240.

20 Ibid., p. 242.

21 Lear acknowledges (in Jonathan Lear, "Leaving the World Alone," *Journal of Philosophy* 79 [1982], pp. 383–403) both the changeableness of our forms of life and philosophy's role in bringing us to see that change is possible, but he locates Wittgenstein's lessons to us mainly at the point at which we run out of justifying things to say. I'm interested in giving a Wittgensteinian account of what goes on when we do have things to say, things that do not fit the usual accounts of what justification is. Cf. "Introduction II: Wittgenstein and Metaphysics" and "Anything But Argument?" in Diamond, *The Realistic Spirit.*

22 In addition to his reply to Lear (Barry Stroud, "The Allure of Idealism," *Proceedings of the Aristotelian Society,* supp. vol. 58 [1984], pp. 243–58), see Barry Stroud, "Wittgenstein's 'Treatment' of the Quest for 'A Language which Describes My Inner Experience and which only I Myself Can Understand,' " in Paul Weingartner and Johannes Czermak, eds., *Epistemology and Philosophy of Science: Proceedings of the Seventh Annual Wittgenstein Symposium* (Vienna: Hölder-Pichler-Tempsky, 1983).

23 Cf. the discussion of "fun" in Lovibond, *Realism and Imagination in Ethics,* p. 66.

24 Cf. the discussion of attitudes toward animals in "Eating Meat and Eating People" and "Experimenting on Animals: A Problem in Ethics," in Diamond, *The Realistic Spirit.* See also feminist discussions about the relevance of similarities and differences among rape, pornography, and "normal" heterosexual activity. The classic statements of the view that salience lies in the similarities, that neither in representation nor in practice can the sexual be separated from the paradigms of dominance/ subordination, can be found in the writing of Catharine MacKinnon and Andrea Dworkin. (Dworkin more than MacKinnon seems to think that the difference marked by lesbianism is capable of creating an alternative range of meanings; MacKinnon takes dominance/subordination to characterize the sexual *tout court.*) See, in particular, Catharine A. MacKinnon, *Feminism Unmodified: Discourses on Life and Law* (Cambridge, Mass.: Harvard University Press, 1987); and Andrea Dworkin, *Intercourse* (New York: The Free Press, 1987).

25 I owe the term to Patricia Hill Collins. See, esp., "Learning from the Outsider Within: The Sociological Significance of Black Feminist Thought," in Mary Margaret Fonow and Judith A. Cook, eds., *Beyond Methodology: Feminist Scholarship as Lived Research* (Bloomington: Indiana University Press, 1991); reprinted from *Social Problems* 33 (1986), pp. 14–32.

26 See Michael Warner, ed., *Fear of a Queer Planet: Queer Politics and Social Theory* (Minneapolis: University of Minnesota Press, 1993), esp. the Introduction.

27 See Diamond, *The Realistic Spirit* and Lovibond, *Realism and Imagination in Ethics*. Both authors read Wittgenstein, as I do, in ways deeply influenced by Stanley Cavell.

28 See Donna Haraway, "Situated Knowledges: The Science Question in Feminism and the Privilege of Partial Perspective," in *Simians, Cyborgs, and Women: The Reinvention of Nature* (New York: Routledge, 1991).

29 On the prejudice involved in stigmatizing these latter sorts of things as not arguments and, hence, of no or lesser value when it comes to persuading those who are rational, see "Anything But Argument?" in Diamond, *The Realistic Spirit*.

30 An emphasis on practices such as these as shaping an interpretation of Wittgenstein as a moral realist is at the heart of the argument in Lovibond, *Realism and Imagination in Ethics*.

31 Such a view of objectivity in science is worked out in Longino, *Science as Social Knowledge*.

32 For an understanding of queerness in this way – as naming not a given identity but a shifting positionality in resistance to heteronormativity – see David Halperin, "The Queer Politics of Michel Foucault," in *Saint Foucault: Two Essays in Gay Hagiography* (New York: Oxford University Press, 1995).

33 The (neo)Kantian character of Wittgenstein's work has, of course, been remarked, and much debated. See, in particular, P. M. S. Hacker, *Insight and Illusion: Wittgenstein on Philosophy and the Metaphysics of Experience* (Oxford: Oxford University Press, 1972), along with the extensive rethinking of the relationship between Kant and Wittgenstein in the (much revised) second edition, *Insight and Illusion: Themes in the Philosophy of Wittgenstein* (Oxford: Oxford University Press, 1986); and Lear, "The Disappearing 'We.' " Intriguingly, Kant – in particular, the *Critique of Judgment* – has been used by some authors to ends similar to those to which I am using Wittgenstein, namely the articulation of the moral and political significance of attending to diverse perspectives in a way that promotes, rather than undercuts, the achievement of rational consensus. See, for example, Onora O'Neill, "The Power of Example," *Philosophy* 61 (1986), pp. 5–29; and Lisa J. Disch, "More Truth than Fact: Storytelling as Critical Understanding in the Writings of Hannah Arendt," *Political Theory* 21 (1993), pp. 665–94.

The point about the relationship of Wittgenstein's later work to skepticism is one I have learned from Stanley Cavell. See, in particular, *The Claim of Reason: Wittgenstein, Skepticism, Morality, and Tragedy* (Oxford: Oxford University Press, 1979); and "The Argument of the Ordinary: Scenes of Instruction in Wittgenstein and in Kripke," in *Conditions Handsome and Unhandsome: The Constitution of Emersonian Perfectionism* (Chicago: University of Chicago Press, 1990).

34 See, for example, Cavell, *The Claim of Reason*, part four, "Skepticism and the Problem of Others." See also Lovibond, *Realism and Imagination in Ethics*, pp. 109–10.

35 Stanley Cavell, *This New Yet Unapproachable America: Lectures after Emerson after Wittgenstein* (Albuquerque: Living Batch Press, 1989), p. 35.

36 Cavell has himself explored the relevance of this identity, which is, of course, his as it is mine, in *A Pitch of Philosophy: Autobiographical Exercises* (Cambridge Mass.: Harvard University Press, 1994).

37 Cavell, *This New Yet Unapproachable America*, p. 39. Cavell is quoting Kierkegaard's *The Book of Adler, or A Cycle of Ethico-Religious Essays*.

38 I am indebted in how I think about intelligibility to Sarah Lucia Hoagland, *Lesbian Ethics: Toward New Value* (Palo Alto, Calif.: Institute of Lesbian Studies, 1988), and to an unpublished paper by Janet Binder, as well as to Lovibond, *Realism and Imagination in Ethics*.

39 Daniel Boyarin and Jonathan Boyarin, "Diaspora: Generation and the Ground of Jewish Identity," *Critical Inquiry* 19 (1993), pp. 693–725.

40 Lovibond, *Realism and Imagination in Ethics*, pp. 210–19.

41 Ibid., pp. 159–65. Richard Eldridge has suggested to me that I miss the depth, and the persuasiveness, of Wittgenstein's distrust of political solutions to the fantasy of the true home. His concern, which I think is right, is that we need not lose the tension between this distrust and a serious political conviction that the world and the practices that shape it can and should be significantly better than they are. He is also right to note in my writing a tendency toward the political utopian and toward dismissing Wittgenstein's distrust as *simply* a matter of his own inability to acknowledge his politicized identities. My hope is that a view of diaspora that places home always beyond a receding horizon goes some way toward keeping that tension alive. For an interesting discussion of a similar tension, between commitment and irony, see Sabina Lovibond, "The End of Morality?" in Kathleen Lennon and Margaret Whitford, eds., *Knowing the Difference: Feminist Perspectives in Epistemology* (New York: Routledge, 1994).

42 "Introduction II: Wittgenstein and Metaphysics," in Diamond, *The Realistic Spirit*.

43 Lovibond argues that for Wittgenstein "the sickness which philosophy sets out to treat . . . has its origins . . . in the incomplete acceptance of

our embodied condition" (Lovibond, *Realism and Imagination in Ethics*, p. 206).

44  Lovibond, *Realism and Imagination in Ethics*, p. 123.
45  I read earlier versions of this paper at the University of South Florida, Cornell, and New York University, and I appreciate the comments I received, especially from Linda McAlister and Richard Boyd, as well as from the lesbian and gay faculty study group at NYU and from Michael Root. The Cornell Society for the Humanities has been a wonderful place in which to write, and I'm very grateful for the critical comments of my fellow fellows, especially David Halperin, Lauren Berlant, and Michael Warner, who helped me understand queer theory and its relevance to this project, and the friendly assistance of the staff, especially of Linda Allen, who rescued me when, in the final stages, my software crashed. My greatest thanks go to David Stern, who helped me to situate my essay in the context of Wittgenstein scholarship, and to him and Hans Sluga for extensive comments on earlier drafts.

# 13 Certainties of a world-picture: The epistemological investigations of *On Certainty*

In his philosophical writings Wittgenstein was mainly concerned with questions concerning language and its various uses. But he was also always aware of the fact that any account concerning the limits of meaningful applications of language has an impact on the limits and/or the foundations of what can be known (compare, for instance, TLP, 5.5561, 5.6, 6.51, 6.53 with OC, 80, 114, 369–70, 514, 528). As he never questioned the possibility of knowledge, his critical attitude toward traditional philosophical theories and problems included a skeptical attitude toward skepticism as well. This became obvious in particular in his notes of 1949–51 which have been compiled and published under the title *On Certainty*.

Due to an unhappily written preface by the editors of that text, many readers have come to believe that Wittgenstein admired G. E. Moore's *Defense of Common Sense* and *Proof of an External World* and that he was commenting in his notes on these two papers with the intention of showing Moore to have been right in his philosophical attitude, but wrong in the way he argued for it. This is, however, not the case. Norman Malcolm reports[1] that while Wittgenstein liked Moore as a decent man and felt stimulated by "Moore's Paradox" (cf. PI, pp. 190–92), he was not at all impressed by Moore's attempts to refute or reject idealism and/or skepticism. It is true that the two discussed these subjects after Wittgenstein's return to Cambridge in 1929,[2] but these issues were scarcely mentioned, even less scrutinized in Wittgenstein's writings.[3] He hardly ever read the works of other philosophers carefully (Russell and W. James may have been the only exceptions),[4] and this certainly was the case with Moore's papers. While Wittgenstein was visiting Malcolm in Ithaca, New York, in 1949, the two were discussing portions of Malcolm's recently completed paper *Defending Common Sense*,[5] and it was these discussions which caused Wittgenstein to think about skepticism and the foundations of knowledge again. It can be shown[6] that examples in *On Certainty* which are not invented by Wittgenstein himself were all taken from Malcolm's paper rather than directly from Moore's essays. In criticism of Moore, for example, Wittgenstein emphatically points out that it is not only Moore who knows that the earth has existed for millions of years, but that we all know it (cf. OC, 84, 93, 100, 116, 137, 389, 440, 462); while Moore made this one of his main theses,[7] that is not mentioned anywhere in Malcolm's paper. It is, of course, true that especially the beginning of *On Certainty* echoes Malcolm's account of Moore and skepticism; however, Wittgenstein's remark "Anyone who is unable to imagine a case in which one might say 'I know that this is my hand' (and such cases are certainly rare) might say that these words were nonsense," which undoubtedly aims at Malcolm's way of arguing, criticizes this kind of approach very well.

Many interpreters believe that Wittgenstein actually dissolves skepticism in *On Certainty* along lines he had adumbrated in the *Tractatus* and in the *Philosophical Investigations*. Whether or not that is correct depends on what kind of skepticism one has in mind, but with regard to a "strong" version of skepticism that is simply wrong. It seems to me, indeed, hopeless to try to refute a "strong" skepticism by means of Wittgenstein's philosophy. I want to show here that the main outcome of *On Certainty* is not a dissolution of skepticism, but *a philosophically illuminating picture of the epistemic structure of language-games and their epistemically relevant settings.*

I will proceed as follows: After indicating which aspects of knowledge and certainty concerned Wittgenstein and combining several epistemologically relevant concepts into one systematic account (Section I), I will try to elucidate Wittgenstein's notion of "world-picture" and show that it is a label for all the kinds of knowledge a community may share (Section II). Wittgenstein's approach to the acquisition of knowledge, which is supposed to explain why we hold fast to our certainties and knowledge claims, will then be laid out (Section III). After that, I will try to show that what is taken to be certain has normative force, insofar as it sets up truth- and rationality-standards (Section IV), and I will then outline Wittgenstein's conception of truth and its idealistic consequences (Section V). The problems of understanding alien cultures and how a world-picture can change will then be discussed (Section VI), and I will close with an assessment of Wittgenstein's fully developed epistemological account in the face of skepticism (Section VII).

## I KNOWLEDGE AND CERTAINTY, BELONGING TO DIFFERENT CATEGORIES

The verb "to know" can be used in many ways: it may indicate competence, acquaintance, assurance, conviction, consent, responsibility, etc., and – of course – knowledge. These uses however do not have to be distinct from each other; rather they may overlap. For example, the utterance "I know that Jim cannot be the murderer, since we were together in lecture when the crime was committed" expresses knowledge, conviction, assurance, and taking upon oneself responsibility for the correctness of the information (RPPII, 736; OC, 8, 18, 176, 181, 243, 424, 591, 620, et passim). Undoubtedly, the use of "I know" in particular may sometimes indicate my own psychological states of being certain, of being convinced, and the like (OC, 42, 91, 230), but in what follows only those aspects of using the expressions "to know" and "to be certain" will be considered which can be explicated in terms of public criteria and practices, that is, uses which concern actions expressing knowledge claims for which reasons can be given, or which indicate certainties whose truths are taken for granted. For psychological states or feelings are merely accompanying aspects of what we call "knowledge" or "certainty," since the criterion of whether or not one is actually knowing something must be shown in one's actions, for example, in answering questions correctly or being able to justify one's assertions (cf. PI, 150; OC, 535; Z, 71–2, 75–83; LWII, p. 79):

The accompanying feeling is of course a matter of indifference to us, and equally we have no need to bother about the words "I am certain that" either. – What is important is whether they go with a difference in the *practice* of the language. (OC, 524, Paul's and Anscombe's translation modified)

Don't think of being certain as a mental state, a kind of feeling, or such thing. The important thing about certainty is the way one behaves . . . (LWII, p. 21; cf. PI, p. 225; LWI, 891; OC, 38, 308)[8]

Wittgenstein sometimes calls the psychological aspects of knowledge and certainty "subjective" and the epistemically relevant, or publicly testable aspects "objective" (OC, 194, 563; PI, 265; PI, p. 225).[9] The same distinction can be applied to doubting or giving reasons as well: Doubting can be seen as a psychological state (RPPI, 836; cf. OC, 21), but the most important expression of doubt is the way one behaves (cf. LWII, p. 21), that is, to be able to give reasons for one's assuming an error concerning a proposed claim (cf. OC, 4, 154, 231, 255, 333–4). This understanding of doubt also discriminates doubt from mere hesitation of belief.

Giving reasons is of course a kind of action, and it is carried out within public practices or language-games of a community.[10] Justification is therefore seen as an activity which has to meet the rules and norms appropriate to the practice in question, and the way of justifying a claim has to meet the demands of the respective language-game. Justification may vary from practice to practice: it may be offered for claims in mathematics, in physics, in history, or in medicine; for advice regarding everyday behavior or in legal matters; for beliefs in moral and/or religious matters. Justifications in all these cases will accord with the standards, that is, rules or norms, of each language-game. Indeed, there may be different standards within a game. Moreover, these rules and norms are not fixed and may indeed change over time, that is, within the history of the respective community, as the practices themselves evolve and change.

Explicit knowledge claims or implicitly presupposed equivalents (epistemic implicatures, one may say) can be detected within many kinds of language games – e.g., the command "Shut the door!" rests under normal circumstances on the presupposed knowledge that the door is open – but for the remainder it will be assumed that only discursive or epistemic language-games will be investigated, that is, language-games which primarily consist in making claims, asserting, arguing, doubting, giving reasons, trying to persuade, et cetera. The description or conceptual understanding of (the structure of) discursive language-games is the task of the following considerations.

To begin with, I am presenting well-known phenomena by means of an invented example: John, a native speaker of English, and just graduating from a college, is proud of his knowledge. He knows German as a foreign language, and he is able to show this competence by rendering German sentences like "Feuerwehrautos sind rot" into "Fire engines are red." Being challenged by "How do you know?," John may justify this claim in various ways, for example, by looking into grammars and dictionaries, asking professional translators or Germans speaking English – that is: he may appeal to something independent of his convictions (cf. PI, 265), that is, to some public fact or object to verify his claim. But if someone were to challenge him by asking "How do you know the meaning of 'red'?" John would look puzzled: he cannot conceive of being wrong in this respect (OC, 630), and "English is my mother tongue" might be his way out (PI, 381). Competence with regard to the basics of one's mother tongue, in which one cannot properly make an error under normal circumstances or concerning which no place for a mistake is prepared in the game (OC, 649), cannot genuinely be called "knowledge" (OC, 526–31, in contrast to knowing a foreign language, cf. OC, 565, 649). John has also studied geography and, if asked to justify his geographical claims, he may refer to textbooks, maps, photos, his teachers, or he assures you he has visited the places. However, if he is asked to justify a claim like the earth is round (this may not even be claimed by him, rather it may merely belong to the unmentioned presuppositions of his remarks), he shrugs his shoulders: "Well – that is out of the question." He does not assume the possibility of an error in this respect while doing somehow geography on the one hand, and he does not know to justify it by more obvious matters on the other (cf. OC, 206).[11] "Giving grounds . . . comes to an end; – but the end is not certain propositions' striking us immediately true, i.e. it is not a kind of *seeing* on our part; it is our *acting*, which lies at the bottom of the language-game" (OC, 204). We should feel ourselves intellectually very distant from someone belonging to our community and taking the earth to be flat (cf. OC, 108).

These surely familiar phenomena regarding knowledge and the limits of justification and doubt within an actual practice can be expressed by the following diagram, which tries to develop a more precise terminology as Wittgenstein has set out to do, and in which what lies at the bottom of a language-game or practice is called "a certainty" (it can be shown by our acting, but can nevertheless be expressed by means of sentences):

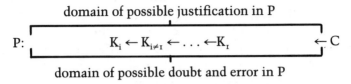

domain of possible justification in P

$$P: \qquad K_i \leftarrow K_{i\neq 1} \leftarrow \ldots \leftarrow K_1 \qquad \leftarrow C$$

domain of possible doubt and error in P

Within a (discursive) practice P of a community, a knowledge claim $K_i$ should be or might indeed be justified by another knowledge claim $K_{i-1}$ (OC, 243, 438), which again might be justifiable by another knowledge claim $K_{i-2}$, et cetera. Practices have internal ways or standards of justification: "What people accept as a justification – is shewn by how they think and live" (PI, 325), for example, the claim of competence in repairing something can be 'justified' by actually repairing it. Justifications are given either if someone has indeed doubted a claim, that is, someone has suspected an error concerning $K_i$, or if such a need for justification is expected. It is assumed that reasons can be given for the doubt or that it can be argued for the assumption of an error. However within P, "the chain of reasons comes to an end" at a certainty C (BRBK, p. 143; Z, 301; PI, 326; OC, 110, 192, 204, 563): "A *reason* can only be given *within* a game. The chain of reasons comes to an end, and that is at the boundary of the game" (PG, 97, Kenny's translation modified). Examples of this specific end or boundary of the game are, "This is a hand" (OC, 448) or, "The earth is round" (OC, 291). What is considered to be a certainty is not a proposition or assertion "as such" but the role such a sentence plays, that is, indicating and belonging to the boundaries – or more precisely: to the constitutive foundations – of a language-game or practice (this will be clarified in what follows): "Knowing interests us only within the game" (PO, p. 393; cf. OC, 105). It is therefore not necessary that such certainties – in contrast to things known – be known explicitly or be potentially enumerated, for certainties can also be mastered unconsciously (LWI, 892; OC, 360, 414, 446) by all members of a community: " 'Knowledge' and 'certainty' belong to different *categories*" (OC, 308).

Certainties of a practice P[12] cannot be justified within P, since their truth is there taken for granted. In P, it is impossible that an error is involved in C (OC, 155), so that it is senseless to doubt C within P:

"The reasonable man does *not have* certain doubts" (OC, 220). "What we call 'a mistake' plays a quite special part in our language-games" (OC, 196); "Doubting has an end" (PI, p. 180); "The game of doubting itself presupposes certainty" (OC, 115; cf. OC, 56, 232). If a sentence expressing a certainty of a practice P – like "This is red" or "This is a hand" under appropriate circumstances concerning an English speaking community, or "The earth is round" in a geography class at a twentieth-century Western university – is doubted, there must be extraordinary circumstances, in which this sentence is playing the role not of a certainty, but of a knowledge claim $K_i$* in another practice P*. For discursive language-games may crisscross, overlap, and support each other within a world-picture. It should be added that justifications do not have to form a linear chain, that is, the diagram above, which is supposed to represent the slogan that "the chain of reasons comes to an end," shows merely a highly simplified model: knowledge claims are rather part of a more complicated network (cf. OC, 105, 225, 432), and a language-game usually rests on more than on just one certainty.

The main concern of the present investigation is to understand what "a certainty of a practice" is. What is considered to be a certainty of a practice depends on the way the practice is described or reconstructed.

## II LIFE FORMS AND THEIR WORLD-PICTURE

Certainties of practices are certainties of a community or a form of life whose members are engaged in these practices: "I am certain, by reason of what has been said to me, of what I have read, and of my experience. To have doubts about it would seem to be madness – of course, this is also in agreement with other people; but *I* agree with them" (OC, 281, Paul's and Anscombe's translation modified). What is a form of life? Let me begin with the fact that Wittgenstein refrained from defining one of his key notions: language-game. In accordance with his view on language acquisition (see below, Section III), he merely gives some characteristics ("the whole process of using words" or "the whole, consisting of language and the actions into which it is woven," both PI, 7). He describes a few language-games in some detail (cf. PI, 2, 8, or 258), or mentions some actual (PI, 23, 249, 363) or some fictious ones (PI, 2, 258, 282, 409). In addition, Wittgenstein suggests that the notion of a language-game exhibits a family resemblance (PI, 65–7). This finally means: we need no definition of "language-game" or "practice," listing essential features.

But at least one aspect of language-games is very important: "the term 'language-game' is meant to bring into prominence the fact that the *speaking* of language is part of an activity, or of a form of life" (PI, 23; cf. PI, 19; Z, 173). Forms of life consist of a plurality of language-games, "a complicated network of similarities overlapping and criss-crossing: sometimes overall similarities, sometimes similarities in detail" (PI, 66). I take this to mean that a form of life does not need to be a kind of system exhibiting a certain structure. Rather, it resembles a medley-like[13] mixture or garland of practices somehow supporting or complementing one another. Forms of life are not related to individual performers, but require a community sharing practices, customs, uses, institutions (PI, 199; RFM, VI-32, 43). It is certainly not required that any one member be competent in all language-games performed by a community. Taking academic disciplines as an example, no one today is required to be more than superficially competent in more than just a few of the following: physics, psychology, mathematics, history, medicine, economics, meteorology, art, and theology.

Yet, the notion of a form of life alone does not explain anything. Rather, it describes, or labels, the setting in which (e.g., discursive) language-games are practiced. That is to say: the concept of a practice or a language-game has to be linked with the concept of a community.[14]

Similar things can be said of Wittgenstein's term "world-picture," which is characterized by him as a kind of myth (cf. OC, 95).[15] A myth exhibits the views and the convictions of a cultural community or form of life. It may contain traditions, tales, or legends concerning the origin of the world, the world's shape and processes (the seasons, the weather, the behavior of plants and animals, the sexes, reproduction of the species, etc.) as well as political structures, instructions of medical and/or psychological treatment, and religious beliefs – in brief, all those matters which may be of interest in a community's life (cf. PO, pp. 125–9). Though it is often so, these views do not need to be presented verbally as legends, et cetera, but can be also exhibited in customs, usages, rituals (for example, a certain location may be highly taboo and therefore never gets mentioned in any public speeches, and this is indicated by the behavior of the members of a community who are very careful to avoid coming close to it or talking about it).

A myth or a world-picture is not necessarily a theory of the world,[16] although it guides the behavior of those holding fast to it. To fulfill this task, not everything contained need be true, and performing some rituals may simply have the function of showing the community a decision (e.g., that one has married or adopted a child; PO, p. 125). Hence some attempts to detect errors in it may turn out to be pointless (cf. PO, pp. 125, 129, 137). A world-picture serves as a basis, a foundation ("Grundlage," OC, 167), or a "point of departure" (OC, 105) of a community's looking at the world, though it contains both certainties and knowledge claims resting on them (perhaps in form of theories, but not necessarily so): "Above all it is the substratum of all my enquiring and asserting. The propositions describing it are not all equally subject to testing" (OC, 162; cf. OC, 234, 281–2, 327, 621). A world-picture also resembles a medley-like mixture or garland of different practices or discursive language-games (OC, 274). It does not have to be a consistent system,[17] and it does not need to be worked out or well reasoned (OC, 167, 236). The notion of a world-picture merely describes a familiar cultural or anthropological phenomenon: the intuitive, practical (OC, 103, 167; cf. PI, 129) rather than discursive sharing of views exhibited in customs or institutions somehow overlapping, supporting, or supplementing each other (OC, 102, 275, 281, 298).[18] For instance, hardly any of us has really scrutinized the truth of "The earth is round," but it is embedded in several of our practices: our accepting pictures of the earth from satellites, using globes, looking for flight paths, detecting the form of the earth's shadow during a lunar eclipse, listening to tales from trans-world travelers, reading the history of Europeans conquering many parts of the "remaining" world, et cetera. That is to say: our picture of the earth being round also serves as the basis of some of our actions (OC, 411) or to make the other issues understandable for ourselves (OC, 146): "The picture of the earth as a ball is a *good* picture, it proves itself everywhere, it is also a simple picture – in short, we work with it without doubting it" (OC, 147). A world-picture is a view of things particular to a location, held by a particular group of individuals at a certain period of time; it does not need to be a sophisticated, philosophical or scientific system aiming at being once and for all true. But the notion of a world-picture itself does not have any explanatory power, it rather labels a setting.

A world-picture, being somehow a "body of knowledge" (OC, 288), may nevertheless contain theories. There is no contradiction between world-pictures and/or myths on the one hand and a scientific world-view on the other. As a matter of fact, science is an important part or component of at least our world-picture, that is, the world-picture which is shared by the Western communities of the twentieth century. Perhaps one can say that science, philosophy, and theology belong to a community's attempt to systematize its world-picture, for whatever reasons. That world-pictures can change will be treated in Section VI.

### III THE ACQUISITION OF KNOWLEDGE AND CERTAINTY VIA TRAINING AND EDUCATION

Why do we obey or acknowledge rules and certainties belonging to our form of life or world-picture, although a short reflection shows us their not being grounded or – whatever that means – "completely" justified?[19] Wittgenstein insists on considering problems concerning knowledge and justification side by side with considerations on language use (PI, 381; OC, 114, 306, 472, 560). Hence he reacts to this question by attending to how we learn to speak and understand a language, that is, he descriptively outlines the process through which we become a competent actor in our community's language-games or discourses: "I cannot describe how (in general) to employ rules, except by *teaching* you, *training* you to employ rules" (Z, 318). "I want to regard man here as an animal; as a primitive being to which one grants instinct but not ratiocination. As a creature in a primitive state. . . . Language did not emerge from some kind of ratiocination" (OC, 475). Wittgenstein here simply presumes man's primitive, that is, "pre-linguistic" (Z, 541) innate abilities ("instinct"; cf. Z, 545; RPPII, 689) to recognize regularities in the world and in the (especially linguistic) behavior of human beings. Going along with this is the children's natural eagerness to copy the behavior and/or the practices of their family members and other persons of their environment.[20] From the beginning infants live in a social setting (Z, 587), their behavior – crawling, gestures, babbling, et cetera – is guided (approved or punished) by others, so that they are brought to act as other normal, competent members of their community do. That is: children are brought to act in agreement with the remainder of their community, except cranks and the like: " 'Learning it' will mean: being made able to do" (PI, 385). "The basic form of the game must be one in which we act" (PO, p. 397)." . . . I have been trained to react to this sign in a particular way, and now I do so react to it . . . , insofar as there exists a regular use . . . , a custom" (PI, 198). As there is, especially in the beginning, no place for any justification – infants not having developed a language yet are obviously unable to understand or ask for justifications – Wittgenstein hesitates to call the process of conditioning "learning" (OC, 279) and prefers "training" (PI, 5, 6, 189, 206, 441; PI, p. 187, et passim): giving justifications to the infant why *this* is called "hand" and *that* "red" are out of place – children simply have to absorb it, if they are raised within an English speaking community, and they indeed do. "For how can a child immediately doubt what is taught? That could mean only that he was incapable of learning certain language-games" (OC, 283). "*The basic form* of our game must be one in which there is no such thing as doubt" (PO, p. 377). "The origin and the primitive form of the language-game is a reaction; only from this can more complicated forms grow. Language – I want to say – is a refinement. 'In the beginning was the deed' " (PO, p. 395). Wittgenstein's term "training" should not remind one of animal training,[21] as if children were merely trained by energetically repeated commands or advice like "*This* is a chair" or "*That* is a book," combined with ostensive gestures. Rather they learn to sit in chairs and learn how to bring books (OC, 476), and thereby children somehow get the point and follow the rules of the respective practices little by little, just as the others do. To be sure, there is no defect on the part of the family members or the child: children being still unable to speak are incapable of doubting or understanding or even of asking for justifications. They do not have competence in justification procedures yet, and they therefore simply have to trust the adults (trust is here conceived to be a natural propensity). "The child learns by believing the adult. Doubt comes *after* belief" (OC, 160). "Must I not begin to trust somewhere? That is to say: somewhere I must begin with not-doubting; and that is not, so to speak, hasty but excusable: it is part of judging" (OC, 150). " 'Anyone who doesn't doubt is simply overlooking the possibility that things might be otherwise!' – Not the least – if this possibility doesn't exist in his language" (PO, p. 387). "The primitive form of the language-game is certainty, not uncertainty. For uncertainty could never lead to action" (PO, p. 397). "A child learns there are reliable and unreliable informants much later than it learns facts which are told it" (OC, 143).

Further instructions may involve any of a number of things possibly far from being evident: That the earth is round has been said by a teacher at school perhaps. Again, there is probably no justification offered (which may involve knowledge or acceptance of other hardly evident theories or convictions), rather the children are brought to accept it blankly. Only at relatively advanced levels of education are theoretical justifications given or possible doubts raised. Again, children and pupils simply have to believe in their teachers, and they indeed trust them (OC, 538). "And the game which includes doubt is simply a more complicated one than a game which does not" (PO, p. 381; cf. OC, 317); "a language-game does not have its origin in *reflection*. Reflection is part of a [more complicated] language-game" (Z, 391, Anscombe's translation improved). There is no rational choice concerning the language the children acquire or the world-picture they adopt (OC, 317). Children are born into a community and simply acquire the community's language and the community's world-picture, that is, children do not learn single sentences or issues, but a whole language or a whole world-picture (cf. OC, 140–2). And the certainties of the acquired language-games are for the time being "certain beyond all reasonable doubt" (OC, 416; cf. OC, 380, 607). Of course, considerations on very advanced levels – for example, within academic research – may later cause us to revise some of our certainties (think of Einstein changing our views of space and time, mass and energy): "the *reasons* for doubting are now reasons for leaving a familiar track" (PO, p. 379, Rhees's translation modified).

In order to cope with the intuition that certainties like "This is a hand" are different from certainties like "The earth is round," since the latter one can surely be justified in some, though perhaps highly sophisticated way, a distinction between primitive and elaborated language-games has still to be introduced. Unfortunately, this distinction can hardly be detected within Wittgenstein's writings.[22] "Primitive" is here understood in at least two ways: It may mean something like "fundamental," "original," "unfounded," perhaps even "not justifiable" (cf. OC, 475; LWI, 789, 828, 899; PI, 244), and it may also mean "simple," "common," or "everyday" (LWI, 299), that is, something familiar to every sane member of a community. Language-games based on certainties like "This is a hand" or "This is red" can be regarded as primitive language-games – "primitive" here involving both aspects (cf. RPPII, 453).

Whereas certainties of primitive language-games can probably be seen as obvious and therefore need no justification (cf. OC, 204), this is certainly not always the case with certainties of "more complicated" (PO, p. 381) or elaborate language-games, that is, language-games being extended and more developed out of primitive ones. Examples might be academic disciplines. I call them "elaborate," since not mere training, but an extended, reflected education is necessary in order to become competent in them. Therefore, its certainties, for example, "The earth is round" or "There are electrons," might be far from being evident. Nevertheless they are constitutive for their respective disciplines, geography or nuclear physics, and held in common by every competent participant of these practices. The justification of certainties of elaborated practices within other discourses may be possible, but these discourses are probably as elaborated as the one which is called in question. For example, trying to justify the roundness of the earth by pointing to the earth's round shadow during a lunar eclipse requires the acceptance of hardly obvious astronomical theories. There is no strict distinction between primitive and elaborated language-games (PG, 62), since the more complicated ones gradually grow from the primitive ones (cf. BLBK, p. 17; PO, p. 395; OC, 673). Still, the presence of doubt- and justification-procedures may indicate that a more elaborate language-game is practiced.

Although "The earth is round" is not obvious or evident, almost every adult of our community would assent to it. Children belonging to an English speaking community of the twentieth century and unable to learn "This is a hand" or "The earth is round" would probably be considered mentally disturbed (cf. OC, 155, 314–15). The ability to understand these sentences becomes therefore a rationality standard of individuals belonging to the community. Natives living in Amazonia do not have to accept the roundness of the earth; pupils getting raised today in Western societies however have to.

In summary, a criterion of successful education is agreement in acting and acceptance of the relevant rules and certainties of the very community in which the children were raised (cf. PI, 385). " 'We are quite sure of it' does not mean just that every single person is certain of it, but that we belong to a community which is bound together by science and education" (OC, 298; cf. OC, 279, 288, 600). Only on the basis of such an adopted world-picture, which includes practices of proper doubt and justification, can some certainties be called in question.

## IV CERTAINTIES AS NORMS

The status or role of a certainty in a practice still needs to be characterized more carefully, and especially the troubling effect of sentences like "This is a hand," being a true or false empirical proposition on the one hand and something else – a certainty or rationality standard – on the other, demands elucidation.

The application of the game analogy proves to be useful here. Games are played according to rules which limit possible and meaningful moves. Whether or not a move makes sense depends on the tactical, regulative, and constitutive rules of the game. Constitutive rules of a game G define the game G, and they can hardly be changed without changing the very game G. One has to follow these rules in order to participate in that game. However, someone not obeying the constitutive rules of G does not need to play the game G falsely: he may play it incorrectly, but if he insists on his deviation, he may simply be playing another game G* (cf. Z, 320). Of course, such a person might nevertheless be excluded from the game G. Whereas it might be part of a game G to discuss tactical rules or strategies, it is impossible to discuss, justify, or call in question constitutive rules of a game G within the very game G they constitute – they cannot be justified within G. Of course, constitutive rules of a game G can be changed or even dropped, but this is a move or an action not belonging to the game G itself. For example, the rulebook of chess or soccer may be rewritten by an established committee or board.

My suggestion is that certainties are like the rules of games and belong to the constitutive rules of a (discursive) language-game. Certainties are neither true nor false, rather they define truth with regards to the epistemological aspects of a language-game (OC, 497):

"If the true is what is grounded, then the ground is not *true*, nor yet false" (OC, 205).

Under appropriate circumstances, *"This* is a hand" or *"This* is red" define how one has to talk about the world in English (the italics indicating a kind of ostension). Someone not obeying these certainties is not speaking English (to say the least) and will be excluded from the respective practices. "The earth is round" is a certainty of many practices in geography, from which the chairman of a "flat earth society" or a native looking at the "earth" somehow differently are excluded. Certainties cannot be justified within the practices they constitute, just as constitutive rules cannot be justified within the game they constitute. Rather certainties get applied to justify knowledge claims within the discourses, and that is why " 'knowledge' and 'certainty' belong to different *categories*" (OC, 308).

Constitutive rules of games may tell us what we have to do in particular situations of a game, and they do restrict the range of possible moves – they are normative or prescriptive.[23] In Indo-European languages, prescription is often indicated in rule formulations by the imperative mode or by means of deontic auxiliary verbs like "ought" or "must not," but the attempt to reformulate certainties this way – "Let this be a hand!" or "This ought to be a hand" – yields ridiculous results. I therefore prefer to look at certainties not as constitutive rules, but as constitutive norms (cf. OC, 473).

"It is clear that our empirical propositions do not all have the same status, since one can lay down such a proposition and turn it from an empirical proposition into a norm of description" (OC, 167; cf. OC, 321). " 'I can't be making a mistake; and if the worst comes to the worst [i.e., I do not know how to justify it] I shall make my proposition into a norm' " (OC, 634). "To accept a proposition as unshakably certain – I want to say – means to use it as a grammatical rule: this removes uncertainty from it" (RFM, III-39).

Wittgenstein indeed had first written "rule" in OC, 167 and later added "norm" as a variant into his manuscript.[24] I prefer "norm" to "rule" because of its systematic ambiguity, since from this noun both the adjectives "normal" and "normative" can be derived. The word "normal" admits of a descriptive use, since it is applied in sentences stating what is normally the case – e.g., the normal human being is healthy, an ill one is not normal. The word "normative," however, is used in a prescriptive sense and indicates what should be the case. Certainties, being constitutive norms, show both these characteristics, since, for example, the sentence "This is a hand" can be used both descriptively in one language-game – and then the sentence is true or false – and normatively in another language-game – and then it determines or prescribes the true or correct descriptive uses of the word "hand" (i.e., the word "hand" has to refer to something like *this*). This is not to deny the familiar distinction between "is" and "ought," rather it is an allusion to the fact that one and the same sentence can be looked upon in two different ways.

Examples may be helpful: an architect's plan of a house is not normative or descriptive "as such." It is normative before the building of the house is taken up, and it may be descriptive after the building has been finished. It is the role or the use of the plan which has changed. Similarly, the standard meter in Paris can be looked at as a mere stick – especially if one does not know that this is the stick which is the standard meter (cf. RFM, III-36) – so that its length can be determined descriptively to be one meter long. But one may also say that it is the standard meter which defines or determines prescriptively what it means to be one meter long: the stick now plays another "role" and becomes "a means of description" (PI, 50, Anscombe's translation modified). No doubt there may be circumstances in which the sentence "This is a hand" can be used descriptively (cf. OC, 355, 460–1), but the same sentence can also be used in a language class in order to teach the meaning of the word "hand," and this is a normative use of that sentence, since the teacher aims at causing his students to use the word correctly (cf. OC, 530). It may even be the case that the sentence "This is a hand" in a descriptive use is part of a play performed by the teacher in order to introduce the new word "hand" normatively. That is to say: it is not the sentence as such, its words or its word order alone, which determine its descriptive or normative use.

"To say that a sentence which has the form of information has a use, is not yet to say anything about the *kind* of use it has" (RC, III-336). "Sentences are often used on the borderline between logic and the empirical, so that their meaning changes back and forth and they count now as expressions of norms, now as expressions of experience" (RC, I-32; cf. OC, 319). "The same proposition may get treated at one time as something to test by experience, at another as a rule of testing" (OC, 98). "I want to say: propositions of the form of empirical propositions, and not only propositions of logic, form the foundation of all our operating with thoughts (with language)." (OC, 401; cf. OC, 308)

A philosophical muddle may consist in failing to see these possibilities (cf. OC, 467). Weak philosophers only look at sentences "as such" or have only one use of them in mind; they unfortunately do not look at other possible uses of them (OC, 347, 350, 406–7, 463–5, et passim).

As long as you are not a Platonist, you will claim neither that logical rules are descriptive, since they do not describe how humans normally think, nor prescriptive, since they do not aim at making people think or calculate in the same way as laws of a state aim at making people always behave in a certain way. Logical rules are rather standards which you should obey only if you want to think, calculate, or argue correctly, that is, according to the standards of certain practices.[25] Similarly, certainties express how words or sentences are used under normal circumstances, but do not describe how they are always used. They do not compel you to follow them unconditionally. Rather, certainties induce you to follow them, if you want to participate in certain practices of one community or another, that is, they determine your acting only if you want to communicate with others. Certainties like "This is a hand" conceptualize the world. They are epistemic norms of their respective practices and neither true nor false "as such" (cf. OC, 205). They however determine how one has to talk about the world within these practices: a certainty is "a norm of description" (OC, 167, 321)[26] and determines truth. Therefore, certainties cannot be doubted. For it does not make any sense to doubt the truth of sentences which themselves are determining truth (OC, 54, 454).

## V TRUTH AND IDEALISM

As is usual within the philosophical tradition, Wittgenstein neglects uses of the word "true" occurring in phrases like "true blue," "true love," or "a true friend" and confines himself to investigating propositional truth, that is, questions of truth having somehow something to do with sentences and their uses. He distinguishes between truth and truthfulness, the latter being something psychological, that is, an attitude (cf. OC, 404) depending on subjective criteria (LWI, 897–8), though even the truth of sentences expressing truthfulness asks for objective, that is, behavioral criteria (LWI, 956).

Wittgenstein rejects a plain consensus theory of truth (LFM, pp.

183–4; RFM, VI-30; PI, 241), since we discriminate between " . . . is true" and " . . . is taken to be true" (PI, p. 226; cf. OC, 179; Z, 417). He accepts the idea of the redundancy theory, since " . . . is true" is indeed sometimes used in order to express a strong conviction (OC, 424; RPPI, 1127), but this is not the whole story. The equation " 'p' is true = p" (PI, 136) also means that " 'p' is true" can only be asserted in a situation or in a language-game, if it would make sense to assert merely "p": " . . . to say that $p$ is true is simply to assert $p$ . . . It is a question of whether we assert $p$" (LFM p. 188). That is to say: a sentence is not "as such" true or false. Rather, it depends on the use in a language-game whether or not it is true or false (RFM, I-Appendix III, 6; OC, 83; cf. RPPI, 290–1). Hence the truth conditions of a sentence depend on, or are even part of, its utterance conditions within a certain game (cf. OC, 191). This amounts to a rejection of the correspondence theory of truth:[27]

. . . "to say that $p$ is true means that it corresponds with reality, or that it is in accordance with reality."
    Saying this need not be futile at all. – "What is a good photograph?" "One which resembles a man." We explain the words "good photograph" by means of "resemble," etc. This is all right if we know what "resemble" means. But if the technique of comparing the picture with reality hasn't been laid down, if the use of "resembles" isn't clear, then saying this is no use. For there may be many kinds of resemblance. (LFM, pp. 68–9)

Accordingly, it depends on the rules, norms, or certainties of a language-game whether or not a sentence can be said to be true (PG, 88), or whether or not we can apply the calculus of truth functions to it (PI, 136): "It is what human beings *say* that is true and false; and they agree in the *language* they use. That is not agreement in opinions but in form of life" (PI, 241). I take this to mean that it is not primarily the consensus of a form of life or community which is seen as the criterion of truth or falsehood. It is rather the language-games practiced by a community, in which the determination of truth and falsehood is carried out. But such a language-game itself is not true or false, not correct or adequate or in accordance with reality. Language-games are not true or false; language-games are played or not. However, (discursive) language-games will only be played if their participants very often agree on the truth value of proposed sentences, that is, they also have to agree without any doubt in most cases under normal circumstances in their judgments (PI, 242; OC, 27, 150). A community is therefore able to change its consensus, for example, new information may induce a community not to conceive the earth to be flat, but round (the community then may or may not have changed its doubting or justification standards).

Hence, the constitution of a language-game or practice, to which the certainties as truth standards belong, is the frame of reference of judging particular sentences or theories to be true or false (OC, 83). "There seem to be propositions that have the character of empirical propositions, but whose truth is for me unassailable. That is to say, if I assume that they are false, I must mistrust all my judgments" (RC, III-348, McAlister's and Schättle's translation modified; cf. OC, 82, 401–3). The justification of judgments or knowledge claims therefore comes to an end at the constitutive norms of a language-game. These certainties, which are perhaps not consciously known but are exhibited in practice within the language-game (OC, 204), determine whether or not judgments are true.

In my view, the move to make truth conditions depend on utterance conditions given in the rules and norms of a practice amounts to a kind of idealism.[28] I do not say that Wittgenstein is developing and claiming a particular ontological theory – he actually refrains from doing this (cf. PI, 402; OC, 10, 19, 37, 59). But his approach can be characterized as a kind of idealism, to which I want to give the horrible label "collective-external idealism." Collective, because Wittgenstein's descriptive philosophy takes the practices of a community as its starting points. External, because norms or certainties like "This is a hand" or "The earth is round" refer to something language-external (OC, 509) – and if the world would change drastically, for example, "if the cattle in the fields stood on their heads and laughed and spoke comprehensible words" (OC, 513), our language and our world-picture may collapse (OC, 558, 616–19). It is nevertheless idealistic, because the world alone does not completely determine the norms and rules of a language-game (OC, 139). For many practices associated with different forms of life may somehow fit to the same Facts or fragments of Reality (this is of course a hopelessly metaphysical use of language), and no sort of argumentation can be offered outside a given practice (OC, 105):

I am not saying: if such-and-such facts of nature were different people would have different concepts (in the sense of a hypothesis). But: if anyone believes that certain concepts are the absolutely correct ones, and that having different ones would mean not realizing something we realize – then let him imagine certain very general facts of nature to be different from what we are used to, and the formation of concepts different from the usual ones will become intelligible to him. (PI, p. 230)

## VI UNDERSTANDING OTHER CULTURES AND THE POSSIBLE CHANGE OF WORLD-PICTURES

It is a well-known fact that other cultures have world-pictures of their own, differing from ours, and that even within the history of our own culture the world-picture has changed in so many aspects – we then talk about different epochs – that it might be difficult to say whether it is still the same culture.[29] This raises at least three questions: (i) How – if at all – is it possible to understand other cultures? (ii) Is it possible to judge one world-picture to be better than another? (iii) How is it possible that a world-picture changes? Wittgenstein does not develop a precise account of these questions in *On Certainty* or elsewhere, but at least some of his remarks allude to a certain picture.

I usually understand activities of other members of my community – for example, buying or selling apples on the marketplace – since I am also able to play these roles in these practices. For, due to my education, I am a competent player of the language-games in question and, implicitly or explicitly, know the rules and norms one should or has to obey. To understand an activity here means to know the rules or norms to be obeyed. But some members of my own community sometimes perform activities in which I do not participate – for example, they play whist – and which I am not capable of performing, since I have not learnt them. Yet, I know what they are doing, that is, I have some understanding, since I am a competent player of other card games and know about different sides competing with each other, discussing possible tactics, being happy about winning, smiling about a successful move, talking about the course of the game, etc. Understanding an activity in this somewhat restricted sense means being able to draw analogies to activities one is already competent in or is acquainted with. This enables me to look at whist as a card game and not as a mystical or religious custom, like tarot. I am able to express my understanding explicitly by saying "It is as if . . . " or "It looks like . . . " or "This seems to amount to. . . . " It requires a descriptive, somewhat flexible vocabulary, that is, the concepts I then use are not fixed and can be modified.

My interpretation of activities in which I do not participate requires a partial understanding of some of the actions involved in them (PI, 206), but I do not need to project myself into the minds of the others (PI, 655). Such a partial acquaintance of rules and norms of a practice is probably the normal case, as a game analogy suggests: on the one hand, there might be some very simple games consisting of a few rules only, or in which you will always win if you know a certain tactic. On the other hand, an absolutely complete knowledge of games like chess has never been gained by any master player yet and is presumably an unattainable ideal anyway.

It should be obvious that the partial understanding of the activities of members of other cultures is what we aim at if we try to understand them. For there is no need to share their religious customs, their medical treatment, or their convictions concerning the earth's shape.[30] Wittgenstein's remark that "The common behaviour of mankind is the system of reference by means of which we interpret an unknown language" (PI, 206) does not imply the belief that such a particular system must subsist or can even be identified once and for all. It would be senseless to take, for example, the practice of giving and obeying orders as a point of reference if the respective alien community does not know such a practice. I take the quoted remark to mean rather that understanding other cultures requires only some accidental commonalities, so that we can understand at least these kinds of activities, which can then be used as points of reference on which to model the understanding of other practices (that they are indeed like our practices has to be guessed in the beginning; cf. PI, 32). Ethnologists may decide whether or not there are kinds of behavior which can be observed in every human community. As philosophers, we may say only that it would not be surprising to discover that human beings indeed have some innate dispositions and therefore exhibit some universal forms of behavior, perhaps in connection with organizing their food intake (cf. OC, 284; PI, 249); or perhaps each kind of behavior is modified so extensively in the course of education and acculturation that no universals are detectable (even shouting with pain might be formed into the peculiar utterance "I am in pain"; PI, 244). Neither the thesis that there must be culturally invariant ways of behavior nor the counterthesis that these cannot be determined is justifiable, either philosophically (see below) or empirically (cf. PI, 207; PI, p. 230).

There may be practices which baffle all our attempts at understanding. This is easy to grasp, if it is a nonhuman practice ("If a lion could talk, we would not understand him"; PI, p. 223; cf. OC, 540). For such behavior does not belong to the common behavior of mankind (PI, 206), and we will never participate as competent members in such a form of life, being unable to play their roles (we merely project our understanding of human activities onto the possible behavior of animals or, say, Martians). Understanding certain human practices may turn out to be equally unattainable, if we are unable to detect any regularities (PI, 207; Z, 390; RFM, VI-45; LWII, p. 72). Hence, even the observable actions of one particular person may never become transparent to us (PI, p. 223): "Here one can only *describe* and say: this is what human life is like" (PO, p. 121). In my view, Wittgenstein neither maintains that understanding other cultures must be possible (cf. PI, 200), nor does he maintain that such an understanding is ever impossible (PI, 243; cf. RC, III-281–5). Perhaps one may say: Wittgenstein does not develop a philosophical thesis concerning the limits and possibilities of understanding practices in which one does not participate. Rather he describes the practice of, for example, ethnologists (cf. PI, 109).

The second problem, whether or not it is possible to judge one form of life and its world-picture to be better than another, will now be discussed. To begin with, it should be noted that the question at hand – "Better – in which respect?" – is begging the philosophically most interesting question. Of course, only if you adopt Western physics will you be able to fly to the moon. But an Indian may ask what sense it makes to do that, and the discussion of senses and values is connected with many other issues of a world-picture. The claim that $x$ is better than $y$ in respect of $z$ obviously rests on certain assumptions or convictions – not to say: certainties – concerning the importance of $z$ and is therefore anchored in or dependent on a form of life and its world-picture. The philosophically interesting problem consists rather in the question of whether or not there are absolutely neutral standards against which world-pictures can be measured. However, all kinds of standards seem to belong to what is going to be measured. The discussion therefore does not treat world-pictures as dividable into several smaller parts, but looks at them holistically.

It is of course impossible to judge a world-picture without an understanding of the majority of its features, and according to the preceding discussion, Wittgenstein would not deny such a possibility (cf. Z, 387–8; PI, p. 230). Accordingly, he could not exclude the possibility of cultural relativism, for example, the thesis that different world-pictures as a whole cannot be compared competitively, so that actually developed world-pictures should be respected and treated on a par. But this line of reasoning is only valid if, in fact, no common practice capable of serving as a point of reference has been found yet within an actual study. Ethnologists, as far as I know, never encountered such a situation. Anyway, to say that no such common practice has been discovered yet, does not exclude the possibility that such a situation may be detected tomorrow – there is no way to prove that no common practice can be found.

Rationalists do not deny that many concepts make sense only within the practices of particular cultures, but they also believe that at least some concepts which are involved in comparing two world-pictures can be culturally neutral, since they are developed by human reason (*ratio*, therefore rationalism) or belong somehow to the uniform and culturally independent biological human organism. For that reason, this counterthesis against relativism consists in the assumption that comparing different world-pictures will always be possible, and consequently that it will also be possible to judge one better than the other. That Wittgenstein assumes the possibility of comparing different cultures has been shown above (cf. PI, 206), and he even assumes the possibility of claiming a superiority of one world-picture in certain respects (OC, 286). But rationalists believe that world-pictures can be compared and judged *tout court*, due to methods of justification being valid "as such" and not relativized to certain practices of a form of life. Rationalists accordingly assume that at least some rules, norms, or certainties belong to mankind and its rationality "as such" and are therefore culturally invariant. However, self-critical rationalists would presumably grant that they do not justifiably know any rules, norms, or certainties of this sort – perhaps we are not even acquainted with them yet. This shows that their conviction rests on the metaphysical idea of an absolutely objective truth, whose existence may be assured dogmatically, but for which there is no generally accepted argument.

If one accepts Wittgenstein's descriptive conception of knowledge as always belonging to a certain practice of a certain form of life involving a certain world-picture, the dispute between relativists and rationalists turns out to be unresolved.[31] For any question as regards the truth of a sentence or a theory is embedded within a certain practice. Within a world-picture practices overlap and crisscross, some of them supplementing or supporting others. But whether or not a world-picture as a whole is true or correct cannot be determined. For this would require a point of reference which would be world-picture–external and –neutral. But we do not know by argument whether or not such a point of view is possible, since all the words or concepts we use may only be words or concepts of our form of life, and we do not know of any criterion showing us one of them being world-picture neutral. As both the relativistic and the rationalistic account would need such a criterion in order to substantiate their own point of view, the question of which view is correct is not decidable.[32] Truth can only be determined within a practice.

These considerations are relevant if one is confronted with views of others one would regard as wrong, senseless, or irrational: "Men have judged that a king can make rain; *we* say this contradicts all experience" (OC, 132; cf. OC, 106, 239, 264, 667, 671). "But is there no objective character here? *Very* intelligent and well-educated people believe in the story of creation in the Bible, while others hold it as proven false, and the grounds of the latter are well known to the former" (OC, 336). "And others have concepts that cut across ours" (Z, 379; see Z, 380–3, 388). It may then be the case either that their world-picture (at least at this point) is indeed wrong, or that our attempts to understand them are still inadequate and the process of interpreting their activities has not yet come to a proper end: "I might therefore interrogate someone who said that the earth did not exist before his birth, in order to find out which of my convictions he was at odds with. And then it *might* be that he was contradicting my fundamental attitudes, and if that were how it was, I should have to put up with it" (OC, 238). That is to say: There might be cases in which one simply has to accept other views as well. One's conviction may tempt one to combat the alien's beliefs (OC, 608–11), but "at the end of reasons comes *persuasion*" (OC, 612; cf. OC, 92, 262).

This leads us to our third question: If earlier epochs of our own culture shared world-pictures differing from ours in many respects, how is it possible that changes of world-pictures happen? "At certain periods men find reasonable what at other periods they found unreasonable. And vice versa" (OC, 336); "new language-games . . . come into existence, and others become obsolete and get forgotten" (PI, 23); " . . . a language-game does change with time" (OC, 256). Wittgenstein also recognizes this possibility with regard to his notion of a world-picture, and he makes clear that no issue, for example, even no certainty, should be excluded from the possibility of alteration (OC, 95–9, 300). In *On Certainty* Wittgenstein's investigation is confined to describing changes of scientific practices only. As it is a discursive language-game within a world-picture which gets changed, the components of the game have to be considered: the theoretical concepts, the methodological principles, meta-scientific considerations (the range of a theory, or looking for its simplicity or symmetry; cf. OC, 92), paradigm cases, accepted problems, et cetera. Changes may happen with regard to any of these components (cf. Z, 352, 438; OC, 65, 87), and they may take place gradually (OC, 63) or dramatically (cf. OC, 96–7; PO, pp. 373–5; Z, 608–10). But it is rarely a whole practice and certainly not a whole world-picture which gets changed suddenly and at once in all its components. Some parts stay hardened (OC, 96) for some time and can be used as a common frame of reference, as a starting point of understanding one practice from the point of view of another. A world-picture therefore changes only partially. Some practices will stay longer than other ones, and the medley-like mixture of discursive language-games constituting a world-picture is a product of a heterogenous historical development: Our world-picture "can be seen as an ancient city: a maze of little streets and squares, of old and new houses, and of houses with additions from various periods; and this surrounded by a multitude of new boroughs with straight regular streets and uniform houses" (PI, 18). Hence it does not cause any difficulty (cf. OC, 111) that Wittgenstein's own example of a certainty – that no human being can ever reach the moon (OC, 108, 661–7) – was out of place twenty years later.

Certainly, if the world were to change abruptly, many of our practices would collapse (OC, 517, 616–19). Yet, the world does not completely determine our discursive language-games (OC, 130), since according to Wittgenstein's collective-external idealism the world and our practices are rather loosely connected: "Our rules leave loopholes open, and the practice has to speak for itself" (OC, 139). Practices also depend on the aims of a community, "what matters to them and what doesn't" (RC, III-293). Norms and rules of elaborated practices especially may be understood and obeyed slightly differently from generation to generation (cf. RFM, I-113), and such a change may even pass unnoticed.

## VII   SKEPTICISM

Before the conversations with Norman Malcolm in 1949 in Ithaca, Wittgenstein's critical attitude toward skepticism can fairly be outlined by a remark occurring already in the *Tractatus*: "Skepticism is *not* irrefutable, but palpably senseless, if it would doubt where a question cannot be asked. For doubt can only exist where there is a question; a question where there is an answer, and this only where something *can* be *said*" (TLP, 6.51). The dissolution of skepticism accordingly consists in showing it to be senseless or pointless (cf. PI, 84, 87, 109, 119, 133, et passim; RPPI, 117; RPPII, 737). For example, someone denying the existence of his hands by stressing the possibility of permanent illusions as regards his sense perceptions can be relieved from this kind of skepticism by pointing out to him that he is deviating from his own ordinary practices, since he is then doubting what he usually takes for granted. Something similar can be said if someone believes himself to be always dreaming. One may regard such an all-encompassing doubt as senseless, since in the case of permanent illusions alleged perceptions can neither be unmasked as illusory (i.e., there is no problem or question) nor definitely established as veridical (i.e., there would not be an answer). Such a skeptic would have misused the word "illusion," for such a word requires criteria which dictate its reasonable and its unreasonable uses: "Here it strikes me as if this doubt were hollow" (OC, 312). To be sure, this ad hominem attack – which is detectable in *On Certainty* in so many remarks – can only be said to be a dissolution of skepticism, if the skeptic indeed accepts it as a criticism of his procedure.

However, a more trenchant and philosophically significant skeptic presents his doubt differently. He does not assert anything, for example, he does not deny the existence of an external world or will not claim that *this* is not a hand. He would merely ask a question: "Granted that you are now in circumstances which are from an epistemic point of view the most favorable ones in which we can actually be, how do you know that you are not dreaming?" As this use of the word "dreaming" does not accord completely with its ordinary use, it detaches the skeptic from his ordinary practices and their presuppositions. His skeptical question therefore belongs to a purely theoretical undertaking and does not involve concerns about any practical needs.[33] Although this astonishing situation still is in need of a philosophical investigation, no argument has been developed yet showing why such a use of "dreaming" is a misuse of language.[34] It seems rather to be a fact that we all understand very well the question and its skeptical threat, for example, we all take this extraordinary doubt to be grounded in reasonable considerations.

On the one hand, Wittgenstein's descriptive account via certainties of a practice P drilled into members of a form of life and sharing a world-picture explains

(i) why certainties of P can neither be justified nor doubted in P (OC, 110, 125, 243, 282, 307, 372, 563),

(ii) why it is senseless in P to suspect an error concerning its certainties (OC, 25, 32, 138, 155, 558, 574, 633),

(iii) why propositions formulating certainties can be regarded as empirical propositions or as logical ones stating a norm (OC, 308, 321, 494, 634),

(iv) why all those participating competently in P know these certainties or take them to be natural or evident (they are drilled into them; OC, 170, 240, 298),

(v) why it may be pointless to assert them as if one is giving a piece of information (all participants of P already have to master them somehow; OC, 237, 347–50, 409, 461, 468),

(vi) why members of cultures practicing P as a practice belonging to the core of their form of life and not following the certainties of P may be considered strange or even mentally deranged (OC, 155, 222–3, 231, 257, 315–17), whereas members of other cultures, for example, cultures in which P is not practiced, need not believe certainties of P (OC, 92, 264, 671).[35]

On the other hand, such a reconstructive account – describing practices of a form of life, for hermeneutic reasons, "from within" – cannot dissolve a detached skepticism. For such a skepticism sets up the possibility of a gap between the World or Reality and our talk about it, and this gap cannot be bridged by means of a collective-linguistic idealism, just as it cannot be met by any other kind of idealism (or nonrealism). For idealisms by definition do allow such gaps between a descriptive use of language and the World, insofar as they concede that the World perhaps is not mirrored in language, but merely interpreted in some way or another. Distortions have to be taken into account, names of nonexisting entities may be contained in the language, whereas existing ones might be overlooked. To make us realize this possibility, however, is what skepticism is aiming at.[36]

NOTES

1  N. Malcolm, "Moore and Wittgenstein on the Sense of 'I know,' " in N. Malcolm, *Thought and Knowledge* (Ithaca: Cornell University Press, 1977), p. 172, n9.

2  I have seen one typed transcription of notes Norman Malcolm has made during one of these discussions in Moore's garden (which probably caused the "That is a tree" kind of example occurring in Malcolm's papers and in *On Certainty*).

3  In Wittgenstein's published writings, they appear only in RPPI, 117 and RPPII, 737 (cf. PI, p. 221 and Z, 405–6).

4  This impression of mine was confirmed by G. H. von Wright in conversation (in March 1990).

5  N. Malcolm, "Defending Common Sense," *Philosophical Review* 58 (1949), pp. 201–22. This paper shows just one out of several attempts over the decades in which Malcolm is trying again and again to reconstruct Moore's refutation of skepticism right in a way which Malcolm believed (not entirely without right) to be Wittgensteinian.

6  Cf. M. Kober, *Gewissheit als Norm: Wittgensteins erkenntnistheoretische Untersuchungen in "Über Gewissheit"* (Berlin, New York: de Gruyter, 1993), pp. 19–24.

7  It is thesis (2) in G. E. Moore, "A Defense of Common Sense," in G. E. Moore, *Philosophical Papers* (London: George Allen and Unwin, 1959), p. 34.

8  Wittgenstein also puts it this way: he is not interested in the psychological aspects of knowledge, but in the logical ones (OC, 447). "Logic" is a

term in Wittgenstein's latest notes (LWI, LWII, RC, and OC) which plays the same role as "grammar" in the preceding ones (PG and after), for example, it concerns a description of a language-game by noting some of its rules (LWI, 845; OC, 51, 56, 82, 628). A more thoroughgoing discussion of "grammar" and "logic" can be found in Kober, *Gewissheit als Norm*, pp. 50–67.

9 Occasionally, Wittgenstein also compares objective knowledge with subjective certainty or sureness (OC, 30, 174, 179, 245, 415). Of course, he does not aim at introducing a philosophically systematic terminology in opposition to ordinary language (PI, 130; OC, 406). As long as one keeps the possible distinctions in mind, the vagueness and ambiguity of ordinary language should not trouble us.

10 I will use "language-game" and "practice" interchangeably, without any intended differences. I do not argue for Wittgenstein's theses (1) that disputes have to be settled by public criteria (cf. PI, 138–55, 258, 293) and (2) that language-games have to be considered conceptually as being related to a community (cf. PI, 198–9, 202, 240–2).

11 Another example Wittgenstein mentions is history and its unfounded assumptions; cf. OC, 163, 185.

12 I am aware of the fact that the phrase "a certainty of a practice P" is awkward English. But I am indeed using it as a somewhat artificial or technical expression whose meaning should become clear in the Sections I, III, and IV.

13 I owe the medley analogy to Hans Sluga, who had Anscombe's use of "motley" in RFM III-46, in mind.

14 I do not enter into Wittgenstein's discussion of the so-called private language argument showing that speaking a language with respect to being involved in a language-game conceptually implies the reference to a community (cf. PI, 202, 243, 256–8). A detailed, though critical exposition of this thesis can be found in Kober, *Gewissheit als Norm*, pp. 70–5.

15 Wittgenstein says in OC, 95 that propositions describing a world-picture may belong to a mythology, and I take that to imply that what a mythology describes, that is, a world-picture, is a (kind of) myth.

16 In his so-called "Remarks on Frazer's 'Golden Bough,' " Wittgenstein accuses the famous anthropologist of looking at myths only as if they were like scientific theories, which can be regarded as true or false (PO, 119–25, in contrast to OC, 162).

17 Unfortunately, Wittgenstein sometimes uses the word "system" (OC, 102, 105), but I read it as a system or theory of a restricted practice only, for example, as "our whole system of physics" (OC, 108; cf. OC, 134, 142). In OC, 410–11, I would prefer my expression "medley-like mixture" or his own "body of knowledge" (OC, 288) instead of "system."

18 Wittgenstein's expression "mein Weltbild" in OC, 93–4 ("my world-picture," Paul's and Anscombe's translation modified) should therefore be understood as "the world-picture of the community in which I live"; cf. "unser Weltbild" in OC, 262 ("our world-picture," translation again modified).

19 Many ideas of this chapter are due to N. Malcolm, "Wittgenstein: The Relation of Language to Instinctive Behavior," *Philosophical Investigations* 5 (1985), pp. 3–22, and to L. Hertzberg, "On the Attitude of Trust," *Inquiry* 31 (1988), pp. 307–22.

20 Traditional epistemology was concerned with the question of how we do this: exhibit regularities. Wittgenstein's descriptive or (in this respect) naturalistic approach however ignores this question and simply states the fact that we can do it. The naturalist Quine adds that psychology or neurophysiology may perhaps find out some day how we can do it, but perhaps they will not. Anyway, this shift in perspective on this phenomenon is not regarded as a philosophical problem any more (W. V. Quine, *Ontological Relativity and Other Essays* [New York: Columbia University Press, 1969], pp. 78–9, 82–3). Cf. Wittgenstein: "By this I naturally do not want to say that men *should* behave like this, but only that they do behave like this" (OC, 284).

21 Still in the *Blue and Brown Books* Wittgenstein considered language acquisition "strictly analogous to" animal training (BRBK, p. 77; cf. BLBK, p. 12), but already in his own revision of the *Brown Book* into a German version – the so-called *Eine Philosophische Betrachtung* (Werkausgabe, Band 5, Frankfurt am Main: Suhrkamp, 1984), p. 117 – this feature disappeared. "Training" merely means causing someone to follow some rules without giving any reasons for these rules.

22 J. Hintikka and M. B. Hintikka, *Investigating Wittgenstein* (Oxford: Blackwell, 1986), ch. 11, and J. Schulte, *Erlebnis und Ausdruck* (München: Philosophia, 1987), pp. 27, 31, make similar suggestions.

23 Many considerations concerning rules and norms have been adopted from G. H. von Wright, *Norm and Action* (London: Routledge and Kegan Paul, 1963), pp. 6, 93, 96.

24 See MS 174, p. 36 (according to the so-called von Wright catalog, PO, 480–510).

25 Cf. von Wright, *Norm and Action*, pp. 3–6.

26 In OC, 321 Wittgenstein is suspicious of the claim that every empirical proposition can be transformed into a norm or certainty. As regards the "every" in this formulation, he might be right: presumably not every sentence can be used as a certainty.

27 Wittgenstein does not discuss the coherence theory of truth. But looking at a form of life which is thought of playing language-games showing a

family resemblance, or at a world-picture as a medley of discursive practices amounts in my view to a rejection of a coherence theory of truth.
For a world-picture may contain contradictions between different practices (this seems to be a correct account of our world-picture, for example, think of the plausibility of pure mentalism, mind–body dualism,
and mere materialism, which are incompatible with each other).

28 This way of looking at Wittgenstein's later philosophy was elicited by
G. E. M. Anscombe, "The Question of Linguistic Idealism," in J.
Hintikka, ed., *Essays on Wittgenstein in Honour of G. H. von Wright,
Acta Philosophica Fennica* 28, nos. 1–3 (Amsterdam: North Holland
Publishing Co., 1976), pp. 188–215; cf. D. Bloor, "The Question of
Linguistic Idealism Revisited," Chapter 12, in the present *Companion*.

29 Unfortunately, the central concepts "culture" and "world-picture" are
vague and demand an intuitive understanding. It should be difficult to
develop identification criteria for a culture or a world-picture detached
from any particular context of investigation.

30 Without changing my view of the earth as round I understand the Ro-
mans looking at the earth as flat, if I realize that they meant by "earth"
the territory around the Mediterranean Sea.

31 The following argumentation fits nicely into Wittgenstein's account,
though I was unable to detect it in his writings. It has been adopted
from Donald Davidson, "On the Very Idea of a Conceptual Scheme," in
Davidson, *Inquiries into Truth and Interpretation* (Oxford: Clarendon
Press, 1984), pp. 183–98.

32 The argument has been made prominent by Davidson, "Radical Interpretation," in Davidson, *Inquiries into Truth and Interpretation*, pp. 125–39.

33 As even Descartes explicitly acknowledges; R. Descartes, *Oeuvres de
Descartes,* ed. C. Adam and P. Tannery (Paris: L. Cerf, 1897–1913), vol.
7, pp. 350–1.

34 Cf. B. Stroud, *The Significance of Philosophical Scepticism* (Oxford:
Oxford University Press, 1984), which includes a critique of Moore and
Malcolm. How these discussions can be related to Wittgenstein's *On
Certainty* is shown in detail in Kober, *Gewissheit als Norm*, pp. 352–77.

35 I am inclined to say that Wittgenstein has indeed developed a philosophical assessment of Moore's approach. That is: he shows why Moore was
right in insisting on the fact that "Here is a hand" in the context of
Moore's lecture or that the earth has existed for many years past is
undoubtedly true for us. Unfortunately, this line of reasoning does not
dissolve "strong" skepticism.

36 I am grateful to John Holbo who attempted to convert my English written text into written English.

# 14 The availability of Wittgenstein's philosophy

I ought to be no more than a mirror, in which my reader can see his own thinking with all its deformities so that, helped in this way, he can put it right.

(CV, pp. 17–18. Source: MS 112, p. 225. 1931)

Nearly all of my writings are private conversations with myself. Things that I say to myself *tête-à-tête*.

(CV, p. 77. Source: MS 137, p. 134. 26 December, 1948)

Whatever the reader can do too, leave to the reader.

(CV, p. 77. Source: MS 137, p. 134. 27 December, 1948)

Although Wittgenstein is widely regarded as one of the most important and influential philosophers of this century, there is very little agreement about the nature of his contribution. In fact, one of the most striking characteristics of the secondary literature on Wittgenstein is the overwhelming lack of agreement about what he believed and why. Over forty years after his death, despite the publication of over a dozen books from his *Nachlass* (the usual term for his unpublished papers), hundreds of books on his work, and thousands of scholarly articles, his philosophy remains unavailable to many of his readers. In part, that is because Wittgenstein's writing asks for a change in sensibility that many of his readers are unwilling or unable to accept. The continuing unavailability of Wittgenstein's philosophy is also due, in large part, to the expectations of those interpreters who disregard his way of writing, looking for an underlying theory they can attribute to him. Philosophers in search of Wittgenstein's theory of language or experience or practice focus on a relatively small number of

442

much-discussed remarks in which he appears to summarize his real reasons for accepting (or rejecting) a specific view, looking for "evidence" of his "underlying commitments" without giving sufficient consideration to the context from which those quotations are taken.[1] For such readers, Wittgenstein's writing is a mirror which reflects "their own thinking" so completely that his challenge to the "deformities" of systematic philosophy is regarded as incidental. Much of what passes for interpretation of Wittgenstein is really a discussion of other interpreters' readings, so that a forbidding and intricate secondary literature has taken on a life of its own.[2]

Stanley Cavell's "The Availability of Wittgenstein's Later Philosophy," a critical study of one of the first books on Wittgenstein's later philosophy, first published in 1962, is still one of the best discussions of how, and why, Wittgenstein has so frequently been misread by his philosophical expositors. In it, Cavell criticized David Pole, the author of *Wittgenstein's Later Philosophy*, for his failure to take Wittgenstein's characteristic and highly personal style seriously.[3] Pole took for granted, and assumed Wittgenstein took for granted, that philosophy is the systematic study of a determinate and rule-bound structure, the structure of our language. Treating Wittgenstein's unsystematic and unconventional way of writing as nothing more than an idiosyncrasy, Pole construed some of the conflicting voices in Wittgenstein's writing as a partial exposition of a systematic and quite conventional set of philosophical views. Thus he took it to be unproblematically obvious that Wittgenstein believed that the rules of ordinary language can authoritatively resolve philosophical problems, and that language is always governed by a fully determinate set of rules. Most of Cavell's critical study consists of a careful critique of Pole's assumptions, in which Cavell shows that they are among the very views that are subjected to relentless criticism in Wittgenstein's later work. In the concluding pages, Cavell emphasizes the importance of Wittgenstein's style, pointing out the affinities of *Philosophical Investigations* to the genres of confession and dialogue. Cavell characterizes Wittgenstein's writing as a dialogue between "the voice of temptation," the voice that tempts the reader to theorize, and "the voice of correctness" which aims to return the reader to ordinary life. In PI, 107, Wittgenstein describes the "intolerable conflict" between philosophical theorizing and ordinary life in the following terms: "We have got on to slippery ice where there is no friction and so in a certain sense the conditions are ideal, but also, just because of that, we are unable to walk: so we need *friction*. Back to the rough ground!" On Cavell's reading, neither the voice that tempts us onto the ice, nor the voice that returns us to the rough ground, sets out Wittgenstein's real views. Instead, he construes them as two opposing voices, opposing trains of argument, which form part of a larger dialogue in which they ultimately cancel each other out. On this reading, the aim of Wittgenstein's dialogues is not to lead his reader to any philosophical view, neither an idealized, frictionless, theory of language, nor a pragmatic theory of ordinary language, but rather to help us see through such ways of speaking and looking. While Wittgenstein's writing, just as Cavell's, contains arguments, ultimately it asks for a new sensibility, a change in the way one sees things:

There are questions, jokes, parables, and propositions so striking (the way lines are in poetry) that they stun mere belief. (Are we asked to believe that "if a lion could talk we could not understand him"? [PI, p. xi]) Belief is not enough. Either the suggestion penetrates past assessment and becomes part of the sensibility from which assessment proceeds, or it is philosophically useless.[4]

At the end of his review, Cavell recognized that such a style runs the risks of either uncritical acceptance ("the suggestion penetrates past assessment") or uncritical rejection ("it is philosophically useless"). While Wittgenstein certainly has attracted both the disciples and debunkers that Cavell predicted, most of the secondary literature on the *Tractatus* and *Philosophical Investigations* consists of exegetical and critical discussion of the theories of language, mind, and culture that are supposedly found in those books. Most of his philosophical expositors find his "real views" in a small number of crucial passages which, taken out of context, can easily be made to provide support for almost any view one looks for. One reason for this state of affairs is the widespread conviction that the real interest in Wittgenstein's work lies in the particular arguments or ideas that he offered, rather than in his style of writing or conception of philosophy. This often leads to interpretations that provide their authors with an opportunity to find their own preconceptions at work in Wittgenstein's philosophy.

One way of countering such reductive readings is to stress the connections between Wittgenstein's arguments and his style, as Cavell does. Another is to emphasize the dangers of extracting any particular passage of Wittgenstein's writing from its context, without considering its role in the work from which it is taken. As we shall see, in view of the tangled history of the Wittgenstein papers, identifying the context of a given remark is more problematic than one might expect. However, despite the importance of the Wittgenstein *Nachlass* as a whole for an understanding of his work, the *Tractatus* and *Philosophical Investigations*, the pieces of writing that came closest to satisfying him, deserve a central place in any interpretation of his work, and cannot be treated on a par with the later posthumous publications. Interpreters have frequently defended their partial readings of particular passages from the *Tractatus* and *Philosophical Investigations* by selective citation of appropriate passages from the other publications. Cavell has gone to unusual lengths in opposing this approach; in a recent interview, he discussed how he avoided reading the remark in *On Certainty* about how knowledge is based on acknowledgement, a central theme in his own reading of the *Investigations*, until it was placed in front of him by a friend.[5] After telling his interviewer that he was suspicious of those who preferred *On Certainty* to the *Investigations*, he explained his stance in the following terms: "The text of Wittgenstein's that I have mostly responded to – felt I could understand in its responses to itself – has been the *Investigations*. How it relates to other texts of Wittgenstein is for me as open a question as how it relates to the texts of other writers."[6] Cavell is certainly right to stress the importance of the *Investigations*, a book that contains the most finished products of Wittgenstein's work from 1929 to 1949, especially when compared to a first-draft manuscript that never received the same attention and elaboration. But Cavell is wrong, I believe, to take the notion of a work of Wittgenstein's at face value, as he does in treating the *Investigations* and *On Certainty* as autonomous texts, sufficiently separate from the rest of his writing that it is an open question how they are related to it. Neither the *Investigations* nor *On Certainty* can best be understood in this way, for each is internally related to other Wittgenstein texts. Wittgenstein's "private conversations with himself" are often much clearer if one looks at his writing as a whole. In insisting on the need to see the posthumously published works of Wittgenstein's as parts of a larger network of texts, I do not mean to suggest that either the books published after the *Investigations,* or the unpublished papers, contain the esoteric key to understanding his philosophy, or that much of his best work remains unpublished. But I do believe that both the *Investigations* and *On Certainty,* like Wittgenstein's other posthumously published works, are much more accessible if one approaches them as selections from a larger body of work. Looking at this larger body of work makes it easier to grasp the problems that occupied his attention.

One of the principal reasons for the continuing unavailability of Wittgenstein's philosophy, despite all the attention it has received, is the conventional understanding of the posthumously published books as a number of separate texts, "works of Wittgenstein's," rather than as selections from the *Nachlass.* Although Wittgenstein devoted a great deal of time and effort to the editing and rearrangement of his work, and most of the posthumous books are based on fair copies that were given a more or less finished form, none of the material in the *Nachlass* has the finished form a publisher would expect. Because of the way he continually revised and rearranged what he had written, never reaching a final decision about the state of the text, nearly every book that has been published under Wittgenstein's name has called for extensive and far-reaching decisions about how to select and arrange the source material in order to produce a conventional text, decisions that were either left entirely unstated, or described in the broadest terms in a brief preface. Except for *Prototractatus,* an edition of an early version of the *Tractatus* that includes a facsimile of the source manuscript, and the forthcoming Vienna edition of Wittgenstein's writing from the 1929–33 period, none of the books published from the Wittgenstein *Nachlass* aims to provide a critical edition of the source texts.[7] The editors' self-effacing methods have led most readers to take the notion of a "work," or "text," of Wittgenstein's at face value, unaware of the intricate relationship between the published books and the *Nachlass.* His editors' decisions about the presentation of his work, which apart from the *Tractatus* and a very short paper on logical form, he never saw to the press, have shaped our perceptions of his writing to an extent that is hard to appreciate until one looks at his alternative drafts and other arrangements of the published material.[8]

Both *Philosophical Investigations* and *On Certainty* are good examples of this. *On Certainty*, first published in 1969, is a selection of remarks from manuscripts Wittgenstein wrote during 1949–51, none of which reached the typescript stage. After learning he would die of prostate cancer in November 1948, he did very little further work on the *Investigations* or the other writing he had worked on previously, so there is a sense in which the 1949–51 manuscripts form a relatively self-contained epilogue to the Wittgenstein papers. The series of manuscripts on which *On Certainty* is based also includes extensive discussion of topics such as vision, color, mind and body, thought and expression, topics closely connected with the concerns of *On Certainty*. Nearly all of the remaining material has since been published in *Remarks on Colour* (1977), *Last Writings on the Philosophy of Psychology, Part II* (1992), and the last pages of *Culture and Value* (1977/1980/1994). While it is true, as the editors note, that the material that has been put in different books is separated by occasional lines across the page in the notebooks, there is no indication that Wittgenstein conceived of it as separate pieces of work, nor was he responsible for the titles of the separate works we now have. The published text of *On Certainty* is, therefore, not a work of Wittgenstein's, as the term is ordinarily understood: the title, the numbering of the sections, and the decision to print this material apart from the other writing in the source notebooks, were all editorial decisions. There is a good case for reprinting all the material from these manuscripts, in a single volume, arranged in the order in which it was written. While the other publications from this period have attracted a substantial literature, few readers of *On Certainty* have paid much attention to the connections between Wittgenstein's final writings. Nor have they seen that many of the leading themes in *On Certainty* were already anticipated in material Wittgenstein had written in 1937, shortly after he had assembled the first 188 sections of the *Investigations* ("Cause and Effect," PO, pp. 368 ff.). Instead, *On Certainty* has generally been read as a set of suggestive but inconclusive first drafts, or as a response to discussions of skepticism and G. E. Moore with Norman Malcolm.

The case of the *Investigations* is considerably more complex. In reading Wittgenstein, it is essential to keep in mind that his characteristic unit of writing was not the essay or the book, but the "remark" (*Bemerkung*). A remark is a unit of text that can be as short as a single sentence or as long as a sequence of paragraphs covering a page or two. The beginning and end of a remark in his own writing – and in most of the published texts – is usually indicated by an extra blank line between paragraphs. The numbering of the remarks in Part I of *Investigations* is Wittgenstein's; however, in most of the other published texts, the numbering is the editors'. Throughout his life, his writing took the form of a large number of these relatively small units which he repeatedly revised and rearranged. In the preface to the *Investigations*, Wittgenstein describes his writing as composed of "*remarks*, short paragraphs, of which there is sometimes a fairly long chain about the same subject, while I sometimes make a sudden change, jumping from one topic to another." During the 1930s Wittgenstein experimented with a number of ways of organizing the material into a single coherent piece of writing, "in which the thoughts should proceed from one subject to another in a natural order and without breaks" (PI, p. vii), none of which entirely satisfied him. Eventually, he realized that he would never succeed, that "the best I could write would never be more than philosophical remarks" (PI, p. vii). The way of writing and thinking that Wittgenstein describes in his preface led him to continually rewrite and rearrange his work, with the result that it can be extremely difficult to separate one piece of writing from another.

In an editorial note to the *Investigations*, Anscombe and Rhees said that if "Wittgenstein had published his work himself, he would have suppressed a good deal of what is in the last thirty pages or so of Part I [PI, 525–693] and worked what is in Part II, with further material, into its place" (PI, p. vi). Von Wright has suggested that Wittgenstein may have planned to use the remarks published as *Zettel* as a way of " 'bridging the gap' between the present Part I and Part II of the *Investigations*."[9] Wittgenstein's final preface, dated January 1945, was, in any case, written before Part II was even drafted, and nothing he wrote provides any support for the view that he regarded what we know as "Part II" as the second part of the *Investigations*. Unfortunately, the typescripts used to print the *Investigations* were lost shortly afterward, and there is no surviving typescript of Part II. There are, however, two surviving typescripts of the preface and what we now know as Part I, both of which Wittgenstein had revised extensively. Although neither corresponds precisely to the published text, the book almost always follows one typescript or the other; the published text is apparently the result of collating the revisions from the two type-scripts. However, there is no indication, either in Wittgenstein's hand or anyone else's, that the main text, which begins on the same page as the preface ends, is to be printed as "Part I."[10] While the editors' inclusion of Part II is presumably based on Wittgenstein's oral request, the fact remains that it is only the last of a number of arrangements that he had settled on for the time being. But because he never carried out the revisions that he envisaged, "Part II" is a collection of material he might have used in revising Part I, not a sequel. Recently, Oliver Scholz has argued that Part II is best approached as a collection of material that Wittgenstein had typed up to show Norman Malcolm on his visit to Cornell in 1949, and that it had a much more provisional character than the first part of the book.[11]

The source texts for the *Philosophical Investigations* span a twenty-year period and are, in large part, still unpublished. In addition to the published text, we have a number of earlier arrangements of the book, the source manuscripts and typescripts that were used in producing those drafts, other arrangements of that source material, much of it extensively and repeatedly revised and rewritten, and even a translation of the first half of an early version of the *Investigations* by Rhees with corrections in Wittgenstein's hand (TS, 226).[12] Wittgenstein's insistence in the preface to the *Investigations* that he was unable to write a book as a seamless whole, proceeding in an orderly way from topic to topic, has rarely been heeded. Considered as an isolated text, it can seem self-contained. But the published *Investigations* is only one of a number of possible arrangements Wittgenstein proposed, many of which extend, amplify, or cast light on the remarks in the published book. The *Nachlass* contains multiple drafts of previous versions of most of the remarks in the *Investigations* and includes several other attempts to put those remarks, and related ones, into a publishable format.

The dialogues that animate Wittgenstein's writing are often much clearer when one looks at his multiple and varying drafts, the different contexts in which he placed his remarks, and the words he later left out, than the compressed and polished formulations in the published work. Consider, for example, *Tractatus*, 5.6 ff. and PI, 398–410, which provide extremely compressed summaries of the results of Wittgenstein's work on solipsism and the self, a topic which received extensive attention in the pre-*Tractatus* and pre-*Investigations* notebooks. The changes and continuities in Wittgenstein's conception of solipsism are a central thread in the development of his philosophy. In both the *Tractatus* and *Investigations*, he dismisses solipsism, the view that only I exist, as nonsense. However, in his earlier work, he was drawn toward the idea of the solipsist as attempting to express an inexpressible insight, while by the time he assembled Part I of the *Investigations*, he had concluded that the only insight solipsism provides is insight into the nature of philosophical misunderstanding. Wittgenstein's later approach to solipsism emerged out of his critique of his transitional writings from the early 1930s. Most aspects of this critique can already be found, together with much more expository detail, in the second half of the *Blue Book*, which dates from 1934. However, it is easier to see the connections between the *Tractatus*, the *Blue Book*, and the *Investigations* on solipsism if one also looks at the extensive unpublished discussion of these issues in his manuscript volumes from the 1930s and the preparatory typescripts, culled from the manuscript volumes, that were the source material for PI, 398–410.[13]

The discussion of solipsism is a particularly clear example of a case of Wittgenstein's extended "conversations with himself" that lead up to a very compressed statement of his position in his principal writings. However, Wittgenstein's overall aim of getting the reader to use his work as mirror that would enable the reader to "see his own thinking with all its deformities so that, helped in this way, he can put it right" often made him leave out the track he had followed in arriving at his own views, so that the manuscript source material is more specific about what views Wittgenstein had once entertained and subsequently responded to.[14] As he put it at one point, what was of value in his work were the "remedies" he had developed, not a diary of the particular problems he had suffered from.[15]

This attempt to separate the results of his work from the path he had taken has led to much controversy over the relationship between the "early Wittgenstein" and the "late Wittgenstein," the authors of the *Tractatus* and *Investigations*, very little of it based on acquaintance with the *Nachlass*. It is often taken for granted that early and late Wittgenstein held diametrically opposed philosophical positions, and much exegesis works on the principle of establishing a series of oppositions between their supposed views.

While the continuities and discontinuities between his earlier and his later work are complex, the broad outline of that relationship can be summarized as follows. On his return to full-time philosophical work in early 1929, Wittgenstein soon came to see that the logical atomism of the *Tractatus*, according to which ordinary language could be analyzed into logically independent "atomic propositions," had been a dogmatic requirement, one that could not be satisfied in practice, not even for his own examples in the *Tractatus*, such as the analysis of color discourse. The logical atomism of the *Tractatus* gave way, therefore, to a transitional "logical holism" on which each significant statement belonged to a specific whole – a whole he at first compared to a formal calculus, or a system of Cartesian coordinates, governed by formalizable rules. Analysis would lead to logically interrelated propositional systems and their grammar, not the atoms he had once postulated. The principal areas that occupied Wittgenstein's attention at that time had to do with various aspects of the grammar of visual experience and mathematics.[16] For most of 1929, Wittgenstein conceived of a "phenomenological" language for immediate experience as "primary," as contrasted with "secondary" language, which included both ordinary language and scientific language. However, in October, he gave up the goal of such a "primary" language, maintaining that we must start with ordinary language. Despite his rejection of not only the logical atomism of the *Tractatus*, but the very idea of analyzing ordinary language into some other, supposedly primary language, he still thought of language as made up of a number of autonomous systems, each with its own grammar, and the task of philosophy as elucidating grammar. During this transitional period, he somewhat modified the *Tractatus* conception of a proposition as a picture of reality. Because the comparison of a proposition to a picture did not do justice to the role of the grammatical links between propositions, he now compared saying something to making a measurement with a measuring stick, which can give any one of a range of possible lengths. By the mid-1930s, he gave up the calculus model, and the measuring stick analogy, and came to think of language as a fluid and open-ended activity, more like a game than a calculus, and more like play than a game with precisely defined rules.[17] In his later philosophy, Wittgenstein continually made use of what he called language-games, descriptions of imagined or actual linguistic activities. The German *"Spiel,"* usually translated as "game," also covers those more open-ended activities that would usually be thought of as "play" in English, and Wittgenstein did not restrict his use of the term to activities with clearly defined rules. His language-games, which are usually quite specific types of linguistic activity, an activity which includes not only the use of words but also the relevant context, serve a variety of different purposes: as illustrations, unexpected alternatives, and provocative points of departure for subsequent discussion. In PI, 130, Wittgenstein warned against taking them as intimations of a grand design: "Our clear and simple language-games are not preparatory studies for a future regularization of language – as it were first approximations, ignoring friction and air-resistance. The language-games are rather set up as *objects of comparison* which are meant to throw light on the facts of our language by way not only of similarities, but also of dissimilarities."

From 1929 to 1951 Wittgenstein wrote and rewrote, repeatedly rearranging and revising his remarks: his literary legacy is an intricate network of multiple rearrangements and revisions. The great majority of the unpublished manuscript writing takes the form of a series of bound volumes, and notebooks that were sources for the manuscript volumes. These "manuscript volumes" were substantial ruled ledgers of the kind a small business might use to keep its accounts. They contain a diary of Wittgenstein's work in progress, including both a regular record of the first draft material that he would consider using in subsequent revisions, and extensive revision and rearrangement of remarks in earlier manuscript volumes. The sheer size and scale of these volumes, and the way the material was written up on a regular basis, strongly suggest that Wittgenstein used them to write up and revise earlier drafts, contained in pocket notebooks he might have carried around.[18] The thirty or so manuscript volumes, containing 8,000 pages of writing dating from 1929 to the late 1940s, can be regarded as a sequential record of his first drafts and his thoughts about how to revise them. Wittgenstein would often write on a number of different topics at once, sometimes dropping a topic for weeks, months, or even years, before returning to it. At times, Wittgenstein would select remarks from the manuscript volumes that he would dictate to a typist, producing several carbon copies of remarks that he would then revise and rearrange again.

Most of the manuscripts and typescripts contain extensive revisions or rewriting. Every manuscript contains variant wordings, alternatives that Wittgenstein was unwilling or unable to choose between, and these are often carried over verbatim into the subsequent typescripts. There are also a large number of deletions and additions, both above the line of the text and in the margin. As a result, there is a great deal of duplication and repetition in the *Nachlass*. Over forty typescripts record the repeated revisions and rearrangements that led from the manuscript volumes to his most polished work. Entries in the manuscript volumes show us Wittgenstein at work, raising questions, rejecting old ideas and developing new ones; the revisions and the typescripts show which parts he accepted and the uses he made of them. The manuscript volumes are a record of the inner dialogue that was the driving force in the development of his philosophical work; they contain lengthy exchanges that are the starting point for a protracted struggle between conflicting intuitions, in which the final result is a telegraphic recapitulation of his earlier train of thought. The Wittgenstein *Nachlass* is not a haphazard pile of working papers that happened to survive his death, nor is it a collection of works that only awaited publication. While it is both a carefully selected and highly structured record of his life's work, a collection of material that he deliberately assembled and left to posterity, it is also the record of a writer continually in flux, never entirely satisfied with anything he had written. As a result, although he devoted enormous attention to revising and refining his words, every publication from his *Nachlass* has required substantial editorial work.

During his lifetime, Wittgenstein published only one philosophical book, *Tractatus Logico-Philosophicus*, written while he was a soldier in the First World War and published shortly afterward. After publishing a short conference contribution in 1929, which he had repudiated by the time he was due to read it, none of his subsequent work satisfied him enough that he was willing to give it to the printer. In his will, he left his *Nachlass* – approximately twelve thousand pages of manuscript and eight thousand pages of typescript – to G. E. M. Anscombe, Rush Rhees, and G. H. von Wright.[19] That will was entered in the District Probate Registry of the High Court of Justice at Camarthen on July 10, 1951. It consists of six numbered parts, preceded by an introduction that states that it disposes "of all my estate except any money or other property situate or being in Austria which I own or to which I am entitled." The first part revokes all prior wills, and the second appoints Rhees as his executor. The third part reads as follows:[20]

3. *I GIVE* to Mr. R. Rhees Miss G. E. M. Anscombe, and Professor G. H. von Wright of Trinity College Cambridge All the copyright in all my unpublished writings and also the manuscripts and typescripts thereof to dispose of as they think best but subject to any claim by anybody else to the custody of the manuscripts and typescripts

I intend and desire that Mr. Rhees Miss Anscombe and Professor von Wright shall publish as many of my unpublished writings as they think fit but I do not wish them to incur expenses in publication which they do not expect to recoup out of royalties or other profits

All royalties or other profits resulting from the publication after my death of my writings are to be shared equally between Mr. Rhees Miss Anscombe and Professor von Wright

If any of the three persons named in this clause shall die in my lifetime his or her share of the copyright and royalties and profits is to belong to the survivors or survivor

Until the discovery of a chest containing a large number of Wittgenstein's papers some time after his death, his literary heirs were unaware of the sheer quantity of material with which they had been entrusted. Additional typescripts and manuscripts have continued to turn up from time to time.[21]

Shortly after Wittgenstein's death, Anscombe and Rhees edited, and Anscombe translated, *Philosophical Investigations*, the book Wittgenstein had worked on from 1929 to 1949. Over the course of the next forty years, all three of Wittgenstein's original literary trustees edited for publication a number of substantial selections from his other writings, either accompanied or followed by an English translation. From his enormous literary legacy, they edited many of the most polished and carefully revised pieces of work in the *Nachlass*, mostly typescripts that were based on multiple previous drafts and rearrangements of earlier typescripts and manuscripts, but also some selections from his manuscripts. These texts include many of Wittgenstein's most thoroughly revised pieces of writing, but also include selections from work at every stage of revision.

The books that resulted from the editorial work of Wittgenstein's literary trustees can, for the most part, be arranged in a tidy sequence, based on the order in which they were written. Taken together, the published material provides a chronological record of the principal stages in the development of Wittgenstein's philosophical work. Two books provide much of the background to the composition of the *Tractatus: the Notebooks 1914–1916*, which contains selections from three of Wittgenstein's wartime notebooks, sources for the composition of the *Tractatus*, as well as notes dictated to Russell and Moore before the war; and *Prototractatus*, an early version of the *Tractatus*.[22] Apart from personal correspondence, virtually nothing survives from the ten year period between the completion of the *Tractatus* in 1919 and his return to Cambridge in 1929. Three books date from the first half of the 1930s: *Philosophical Remarks*, a selection of remarks from 1929–30, the first year of Wittgenstein's post-*Tractatus* return to philosophical writing; *Philosophical Grammar*, a reconstruction of some of Wittgenstein's plans for revising the beginning of the Big Typescript, a book draft he put together during 1932–3, accompanied by some unrevised chapters from the end of the Big Typescript, on the philosophy of mathematics; *The Blue and Brown Books*, notes dictated (in English) to students in the 1933–4 and 1934–5 academic years.

Late in 1936, Wittgenstein drafted an early version of the first 188 sections of the *Philosophical Investigations*; he did very little work on the book after the end of 1948. In addition to the *Investigations* itself, five books have been published from this period of his work. *Remarks on the Foundations of Mathematics* begins with Wittgenstein's most polished later writing on mathematics, a typescript written in 1937–8, that was intended as a sequel to the first part of the *Investigations*. Parts II to VII contain substantial excerpts from manuscripts on mathematics dating from the late 1930s and early 1940s. *Remarks on the Philosophy of Psychology, Volumes I and II* and *Last Writings on the Philosophy of Psychology, Volume I* are based on source material from the second half of the 1940s that was used in writing Part II of the *Investigations*. *Zettel* is a collection of cuttings from Wittgenstein's typescripts, spanning the years from 1931 to 1948, but mostly from the 1945–8 period.

Three books contain most of what Wittgenstein wrote during the last two years of his life, rearranged by the editors into three topical groupings: *On Certainty*, *Remarks on Colour*, and *Last Writings on the Philosophy of Psychology, Volume II*. Three other books span the entire range of Wittgenstein's writing: *A Wittgenstein Reader*, a selection of readings from the published work, which begins with an abridgment of the *Tractatus* and follows the chronological development of Wittgenstein's philosophical interests; *Culture and Value*, a selection of short "nonphilosophical" remarks culled from the entire *Nachlass*; and *Philosophical Occasions, 1912–1951*, an anthology that includes some minor pieces that Wittgenstein published during his lifetime, all of the previously published shorter excerpts from the *Nachlass*, and some new material.[23]

The principal texts in the published corpus have been reprinted in the eight volume Suhrkamp edition of Wittgenstein's work, which includes indexes and editor's notes, and incorporates extensive corrections to the previous editions.[24] The published corpus contains approximately a million words of Wittgenstein's writing; the *Tractatus* and *Investigations* account for roughly an eighth of the total. Most of these texts are now also available in an electronic edition, in which each text is supplied in the language in which it was originally written.[25] The electronic edition makes it easy to trace connections between remarks, and facilitates different paths through Wittgenstein's writing. In view of the interrelated character of Wittgenstein's remarks and his elaboration of central terms in a wide variety of different contexts, often in a variety of different drafts, electronic searching is particularly valuable, as it makes it possible to compare and contrast Wittgenstein's use of key terms.

The sheer scale of the literary corpus created by the Wittgenstein trustees, the product of over thirty years of shared labor, has fostered the widespread impression that ample material has already been made available for a critical appraisal of Wittgenstein's philosophy. This view is endorsed by von Wright in the most recent version of his catalog of the Wittgenstein papers, where he states that the result of the trustees' work has been to "make the full body of Wittgenstein's philosophy accessible to the public" and that "all the works of major interest have, in my view, now been published (save for the Big Typescript, perhaps)" (PO, p. 504). But what is "the full body of Wittgenstein's philosophy" or a "work of major interest"? What are the appropriate editorial criteria for identifying a "work" of Wittgenstein's? What reasons are there for thinking that Wittgenstein's unpublished drafts of the *Investigations*, or the manuscript volumes that set out the journey that led from his early to his late work, are not works of major interest? What should be included and what should be left out? The question of the extent of the Wittgenstein *oeuvre*, the question of what counts as a work of Wittgenstein's, or as Wittgenstein's philosophical writing, is rarely discussed at any length in the literature on Wittgenstein's work. In practice, few of Wittgenstein's interpreters make much use of the unpublished material, or discuss its significance. Most of what has been written about the Wittgenstein *Nachlass* has been written by experts for experts, and may actually have served to reinforce the expectation that the unpublished material is only of marginal interest.

Joachim Schulte, one of the participants in the first attempt to edit the *Nachlass*, and the editor of the current German edition of the Wittgenstein publications, has recently proposed that in order to count as "a finished work of Wittgenstein's," a piece of his writing should satisfy the following conditions:

(1) the assessment by Wittgenstein himself that the text in question is an independent creation with a form suitable to its content; (2) a line of argument apparent to the reader, with theses, arguments, objections, underlying considerations, and examples, etc.; and (3) the formal stylistic polishing and formulation of the text which make it possible to call it "finished" and "complete."[26]

Applying these standards to Wittgenstein's writings, Schulte eliminates all first draft writing, both in the notebooks and manuscript volumes, and selections from them that eliminate unwanted passages without rearranging the material into some more comprehensive order. However, Schulte acknowledges that "this clearly graduated picture is clouded somewhat by the fact that Wittgenstein was never quite satisfied with what he wrote"[27] and this leads him to propose that one regard Wittgenstein's writings as "experiments" rather than something "finished and complete." Schulte, unlike von Wright, explicitly states and defends his criteria; but they both take for granted that one must draw a line between the "finished" and the "unfinished," and that only the "finished" material is worthy of serious attention. While the result of the application of Schulte's criteria to the published Wittgenstein texts is certainly debatable, there can be no doubt that all those based on the editors' selections from the *Nachlass* would fail this test, as the texts are not independent creations of Wittgenstein's. (It is not so clear that the manuscript volumes do fail Schulte's test, provided one follows Wittgenstein's discussion of a particular topic, rather than reading every remark in sequence.) Although Schulte does not actually say so, the unpublished early versions of the *Investigations*, and the alternate arrangement of much of the material in PI, 188–693 known as *Bemerkungen* II (TS, 230), which are in many ways as "finished" as the final version, surely qualify as "works" under his criteria.

In the opening pages of *The Archaeology of Knowledge*, Michel Foucault argues that the traditional notion of "the author," the person responsible for a writer's work, and the correlative notion of "the work," or *oeuvre*, the collection of texts that the author put in a finished form, are fictions. Ordinarily, we conceive of the author as expressing him- or herself in the work, the work as giving us access to the author, and so turn the mass of records that a writer left behind into a coherent collection of finished texts on the one hand, and preparatory work, fragments, and notes, on the other. In defense of his claim, Foucault points out that what counts as a "work" by an author varies greatly from case to case: what might appear to be a simple distinction, turns out, on closer inspection, to vary in practice. Usually, one counts as an author's work those texts that the author had published, removing publications which do not count as "works," and adding works that were finished but remained unpublished. When one identifies an author's *oeuvre* in this way one imposes on it a unifying principle, according to Foucault, a principle concerning the variety of written records associated with a particular writer. In so doing, one tells a story that provides a rationale as to which pieces of writing are to count as the author's work: which pieces of writing are not sufficiently finished to count as works, which apparently insignificant pieces of writing should be included among the works. Foucault's remarks are particularly apposite when considering the work of a dead writer. Significantly, two of his examples are philosophers who left a substantial *Nachlass*: Nietzsche and Wittgenstein.[28] Both of them left a mass of writing that included plans for unpublished books, and notebooks that could not easily be separated into philosophical and nonphilosophical texts. However, in the case of the Nietzsche *Nachlass*, one can at least begin from the substantial number of texts that he did publish, while Wittgenstein published very little.

Apart from the *Tractatus*, Wittgenstein's works are the product of his trustees' decisions. Despite their differences, the author that Wittgenstein's editors have given us and the author that Schulte envisages, is one who attempted to write a series of works. Left out are not only the first drafts in the manuscript volumes but the process of rethinking and rewriting that links the published and unpublished texts. The published work is no substitute for a full publication of the Wittgenstein *Nachlass* as a whole, and has actually served, in certain respects, to obscure the nature of Wittgenstein's philosophical legacy. The assumption that Wittgenstein's principal works consist of his most polished writing, principally found in his typescripts, has led his trustees to adopt very different approaches to editing his typescripts and his manuscripts. While most of the posthumous publications that are based on typescripts make use of the entire source typescript, almost every publication from the manuscript sources has been heavily edited, often with little or no indication of the extent of the editorial intervention. Consider the example of the *Philosophical Grammar*, which is based on both typescript and manuscript sources. Part I of that book, an unfinished work on philosophy of language dating from the years 1930 to 1934, consists of Rhees's reconstruction of the first two of three sets of manuscript revisions that Wittgenstein made to the opening chapters of the Big Typescript. Although the text of Part I of the *Grammar* is a reconstruction that zigzags between a patchwork quilt of sources extracted from a group of source texts, the preface says next to nothing about how that trail was reconstructed.[29] Nor does the preface mention that several of the later chapters of the Big Typescript, on phenomenology, idealism, and philosophical method, were left out of the published book, even though the unrevised chapters on mathematics were published as Part II of the *Grammar*.[30] Rather than setting out his editorial decisions, so that a reader could see how the published text had been produced, Rhees took an almost authorial role in the production of the text, publishing his own synoptic table of contents to Part I alongside Wittgenstein's own table of contents for the chapters included in Part II. Although he appears to have followed Wittgenstein's plans for the production of Part I with great fidelity, there is no comparable basis for the choice of material included in Part II.[31]

While the books based on Wittgenstein's typescripts usually provide the entire source text, save only for information about variant readings, corrections, deletions, that one would only expect to find in a critical edition, a number of the publications that are based on manuscript sources have been much more heavily edited, usually without specifying the location or extent of the breaks in the text. In the case of Parts II–VII of the *Remarks on the Foundations of Mathematics*, and Rhees's edition of the "Notes for Lectures on 'Sense Data' and 'Private Experience,' " the editors judged that although the manuscript contained material of great interest, it was too long to publish in full. The prefaces to the published texts do state that cuts were made, but give no indication of their location, and so make it impossible to follow Wittgenstein's train of thought. The cuts are not a matter of dropping a few poorly chosen phrases, or of leaving out passages that are irrelevant to the main line of discussion, but rather involve extensive elimination of supposedly inferior writing, yielding a patchwork composed of a large number of relatively short selections from the source text. For instance, Part II, §§1–40 of the *Remarks on the Foundations of Mathematics*, was assembled from pages 9–17, 21–9, 31–3, 42–3, 52–7, 59–67, 71–88, 90–7, 99–118, 121–3, 128–9, 131, 135–40, 143–7 and 149–50 of MS 122. After I became aware of the extent to which the "Notes for Lectures" had been edited, I produced a new edition of that text in which the missing passages were restored; that edition has recently been published, together with an appendix that specifies the principal differences between the two editions, as part of *Philosophical Occasions*. Readers who wish to study the sources of the *Remarks on the Foundations of Mathematics* or the *Philosophical Grammar* will find that Alois Pichler's source catalog of the published texts provides an extremely valuable guide to the manuscript and typescript sources of each publication based on the Wittgenstein *Nachlass*.[32] Even those who have no intention of actually looking at those sources would be well advised to take a look at the catalog, which provides an excellent overview of the *Nachlass* and its complex relationship to Wittgenstein's posthumous works. Some indication of the complexity of the relationship between sources and published texts is provided by the fact that the tables which summarize the sources of the *Philosophical Grammar* and the *Remarks on the Foundations of Mathematics* occupy ten pages each.

The editors of *Notebooks 1914–1916* gave no indication that the book only reproduces part of the source manuscripts. The omitted material, which consists of diary entries and personal reflections, was for the most part written in a simple letter-substitution code, presumably designed to conceal their contents from a casual reader. This became public knowledge when the missing passages were published by Willhelm Baum in a Spanish journal in 1985, without the permission of the trustees; the decoded German text is now available in book form, under the title *Geheime Tagebücher* (secret diaries).[33] These omissions, coupled with the fact that the coded material was covered up in the 1967 Cornell microfilm edition of the papers, have led to farfetched speculation about the motivations for these decisions. Wittgenstein's literary heirs were students and friends of his who discovered that they had inherited the unexpected responsibility of deciding how to make his work available; it would be entirely inappropriate to judge them by the standards of a definitive scholarly edition. It is understandable that they should have chosen to keep his more personal writing, which included references to people who were still alive, out of the public domain in the years immediately following his death. Fortunately, they have decided that the coded material, much of which is of considerable interest, both biographically and philosophically, will be included in the forthcoming Bergen and Vienna editions of the *Nachlass*. Substantial selections from it have already been included in *Culture and Value*, and the Monk and McGuinness biographies.

Another striking example of a published text that involves a substantial editorial contribution is Wittgenstein's *Zettel*, Peter Geach's arrangement of a collection of remarks that Wittgenstein had cut out of a number of typescripts and placed in a box file. The collection of cuttings is apparently connected with Wittgenstein's work on what we now know as Part II of the *Investigations*. Most of the remarks are taken from the source typescripts for Part II, but a substantial minority have sources dating from 1929 to 1945, and belong to the group of remarks that Wittgenstein had considered using in the final arrangement of Part I. Although the published book gives no indication of where one cutting starts and another stops, and no sources for the cuttings, the preface does explain that the arrangement was Geach's responsibility. While the collection clearly fails Schulte's criteria, and is disappointing if one reads it looking for the kind of arrangement one finds in the *Investigations*, it is much more valuable if one looks at it as a collection of cuttings that Wittgenstein had considered using in his book. Thanks to the work of André Maury, who has published a full list of the manuscript and typescript sources of each of the remarks in both *Zettel* and the *Investigations*, one can reconstruct Wittgenstein's cuttings from Geach's continuous text.[34] The third edition of *Culture and Value* includes a similar list of sources for each passage included in that collection.[35] Those with access to a copy of the *Nachlass* can read these lists as pointers to the contexts from which those remarks are taken, a starting point for exploring the typescript and manuscript sources of Wittgenstein's work on the *Investigations*.

On the approach to Wittgenstein's writing advocated here, all of Wittgenstein's *Nachlass* should be included in his *oeuvre*. In other words, we should consider his surviving papers as a family of works, connected by the constant process of reworking and rewriting that links the notebooks, manuscript volumes, manuscript rearrangements, typed selections from the manuscripts, and the subsequent typescripts. This is not simply because of the vast number of revisions, deletions, alternative wordings and the like, to be found on most pages of the *Nachlass*, but also because so many passages have a complex genealogy, having been copied and revised from one text to another. The Wittgenstein *Nachlass* is in certain respects poorly served by the linear arrangement of remarks of a traditional printed text. The intertextual links between his remarks are either left out altogether, or provided in the form of a lengthy list of correlations that would take days or weeks of research to follow. Because the Wittgenstein *Nachlass* is the result of such an extensive act of rewriting, it is less a collection of texts than a hypertext, an interconnected network of remarks. The forthcoming electronic edition of the Wittgenstein papers, currently in preparation by the Wittgenstein Archives at the University of Bergen, could make the paths through the unpublished papers that are described here as accessible as the published works. But before looking at what can be expected from the projected edition of the *Nachlass*, we need to consider its history and the resources that already exist for reading the *Nachlass*.

In May 1969, Wittgenstein's literary heirs signed a deed of trust with Trinity College, Cambridge, giving the Wittgenstein papers in their possession to Trinity's Wren Library; a few exceptions, which were not part of the legacy, are now kept in the Austrian National

Library, Vienna; the Brenner Archive, Innsbruck; the Bodleian Library, Oxford; and the Bertrand Russell Archive, Hamilton, Ontario. Under the terms of the agreement with Trinity, the heirs would continue to receive royalties and copyright on publications from the *Nachlass*, which would pass to Trinity when the last one died. The deed of trust instituted two committees: a board of trustees, which administered the copyright, and a board of editors. Until Rhees died in 1989, both committees were composed of the three heirs; shortly afterward, Anscombe and von Wright invited Anthony Kenny and Peter Winch to join both committees. Around the time the papers were given to Trinity, von Wright published the first catalog of the Wittgenstein *Nachlass*, which has become established as the point of departure for work on the unpublished papers. It has been updated as further texts have come to light and presently lists eighty-two manuscript items, forty-five typescript items, and eleven dictations (PO, pp. 480–506). The catalog provides a reference system which allows one to refer unambiguously to any given item in the collection. Each physical entity, whether it is a notebook, a sequence of typed pages, or a bound volume, is assigned to one of the three categories mentioned above; within each category, the items are assigned to a numbered series, arranged in the order in which they were composed. Sometimes several items that are closely related are grouped under the same number and are distinguished by an additional letter. In addition to this comprehensive list of the contents of the *Nachlass*, the catalog also provides a classification and description of the papers as a whole, and includes considerable information about such matters as the title of the item, its chronology, and its relationship to other items.

Most of the material in the *Nachlass* is available in the form of a microfilm edition, produced at Cornell in 1967. Copies, either on microfilm or in the form of dozens of bound volumes, have been sold to researchers and university libraries. In principle, this has made most of Wittgenstein's surviving writing accessible to scholars, if not to the general public, but in practice there have been major limitations. Even the best facsimile cannot be a substitute for an edition of the text, and these facsimiles had serious shortcomings. The quality of the photography was poor, some pages were illegible or omitted, and some manuscripts were left out altogether. The microfilm of the typescripts is, for the most part, quite legible, but the extensive handwritten revisions to many of the typescripts, and the manuscripts themselves, often written with a blunt pencil, are less easy to follow. While it is possible to become familiar with Wittgenstein's handwriting, the overall limitations of the format, coupled with the lack of an index, make it almost impossible to use the Cornell edition to track the development of Wittgenstein's thought from one text to another.[36]

In October 1974, the Wittgenstein trustees signed an agreement establishing the *Wittgenstein-Archiv Tübingen*, a research team at the University of Tübingen that aimed to edit a complete edition of Wittgenstein's writings, led by Mr. Michael Nedo and Professor H. J. Heringer. Much of the funding was provided by the Fritz Thyssen Foundation. Over the next five or six years, more than half of the *Nachlass* was transcribed into a computer database, a search program was developed, and the question of how best to edit a published complete works was discussed. However, the team members quarreled, and work on the project came to an end around 1980–1; none of the transcriptions have ever been published. In the final report, Professor Heringer stated that Mr. Nedo was "incapable of directing such a project in an organizationally serious or personally responsible manner" and that "there arose with all the collaborators considerable doubts concerning Mr. Nedo's scholarly competence."[37]

While the Tübingen project was running into trouble, much of the groundwork for tracing the relations between Wittgenstein's drafts and revisions was being done by von Wright and two of his colleagues at the University of Helsinki, Heikki Nyman and André Maury. After he published the catalog of the Wittgenstein papers in 1969, von Wright continued his research into the process of revision that led to the production of the *Tractatus* and *Investigations*. The results of this research are summarized in his highly informative studies of the origins of those books, reprinted in his *Wittgenstein*.[38] The meticulously edited "Helsinki edition" of the principal sources of the *Philosophical Investigations* reconstructs five successive stages in the construction of the *Philosophical Investigations*, showing not just the result of Wittgenstein's revisions to the typescript, but also where revisions were inserted, variant readings, deletions and the like and every significant difference between their text and the printed "final" text. This research on the origins of the *Philosophical Investigations* led to the production of thousands of pages of carefully edited typescripts of the surviving drafts of the book. Although the Helsinki edition, completed fifteen years ago, offers an invaluable overview of some of the principal stages in the composition of the *Investigations*, it remains unpublished. Copies are, however, available in Helsinki, Bergen, Oxford, Cambridge, and Cornell.[39] The early, intermediate, and final versions of the *Investigations*, as von Wright calls them, were constructed circa 1936–9, 1942–4, and 1945–9, respectively. The early version is divided into two parts: the first, which was composed in late 1936, is closely related to §§1–188 of the final version, although it contains a number of remarks that were either substantially changed or dropped from later versions of the book. Part II of the early version of the *Investigations* is the basis for the published Part I of the *Remarks on the Foundations of Mathematics*. The intermediate version consists of a slight revision and rearrangement of the material in the first part of the early version, followed by roughly half of the material in PI, 189–425. Part I of the late version was constructed circa 1945, primarily by adding remarks from *Bemerkungen* I (TS, 228), a typescript containing a large number of remarks selected from his previous work; Part II was composed in 1946–8 and probably reached its final form in 1949. Von Wright and Nyman also edited manuscript volume XII (MS 116), a collection of remarks from earlier work, written up in 1937 and 1945, many of which were incorporated into the final version of Part I. The edited typescripts consist of a main text accompanied by an editorial apparatus which gives variant readings and the closest typescript and manuscript sources of the remarks. This apparatus, together with a copy of the relevant parts of the *Nachlass*, makes it possible to explore some of the successive formulations and rearrangements of Wittgenstein's remarks in the *Investigations*, although it does not attempt to trace the full genealogy of each remark.

In October 1981, the Wittgenstein trustees applied to the principal Austrian national research foundation, the *Fonds zur Förderung der wissenschaftlich Forschung*, for support for a new editing project, under Nedo's direction. The project was to aim at the complete transcription of Wittgenstein's posthumous writings into a database and the development of appropriate computer programs; the aim was to produce a complete edition of Wittgenstein's works by 1989. The proposal did not mention the previous project or the fact that Nedo had been denied access to those transcriptions, so that much of the work would repeat what had already been done. In September 1982 the *Fonds* agreed to support a one year pilot project, and IBM offered to donate computer time. According to Hintikka, the only person who has so far published an account of these events, "the subsequent history of the project is not easy to chronicle, one reason being Mr. Nedo's failure to keep his own sponsors apprised of what he had done and what he had not."[40] Apparently, Nedo's reports were approved by Professor Anscombe on behalf of the other trustees, and as a result the funding was renewed for the next few years. However, the project did not proceed according to plan. Nedo had promised to produce a transcript of the first four manuscript volumes that Wittgenstein had written in 1929–30 and the first typescript that was based on it, by October 1984. In September 1987, Professor Anscombe once again approved another renewal application on behalf of the trustees. However, in November of that year Professor von Wright wrote to the *Fonds* to say that he still had not seen the promised material, and that he was therefore withdrawing his support, with the result that the application was not approved. Early in 1988, Nedo produced a transcript of the first two manuscripts, but they were still not in publishable form. In 1990, a year after the projected completion date, the situation remained essentially unchanged. Shortly after joining the trustees, Kenny inspected Nedo's office in Trinity College, Cambridge, and saw 10,000 or more pages of computer printout. However, Kenny reports that he "was unable to obtain from him a satisfactory account of the reasons for delay. So far as I could ascertain, he had spent his time designing software for formatting the pages to be published according to his own taste."[41] As a result, the trustees established two further deadlines, in May and December 1991, for the production of material ready for publication. After these ultimata produced no results, the trustees severed all connections with Nedo as editor of the Wittgenstein papers, and decided to move ahead with an electronic edition in collaboration with the Wittgenstein Archives at the University of Bergen. However, in December 1992, Nedo produces six volumes ready for the printer. "This placed the Trustees in a difficult position. In the light of past experience, they did not wish to co-operate further with Nedo in the production of a *Gesamtausgabe*; on the other hand, it seemed to them harsh to forbid the publication of the result of such long periods of work. In the event, they decided that while they would take no initiative in publishing these texts, they would not stand in the way of their publication. Nedo was given permission to make arrangements of his own with a publisher, but not as part of an authorised edition of the collected works. In summer 1993 the trustees authorised a contract . . . for the manuscripts and typescripts from 1929 . . . to 1933. Rights of electronic publication were explicitly excluded."[42]

Despite this long and troubled history, the Wittgenstein papers should soon be available in several different formats. While the Nedo edition will only cover a small fraction of the *Nachlass*, the entire *Nachlass* should soon be available in a CD-ROM edition, produced by the Wittgenstein Archives at the University of Bergen, in the form of photographic images of each page of the papers and an extraordinarily thorough transcription of the text. The first edition, due to be published in the spring of 1997, will contain a complete set of photographs, and a transcription of a little less than half the total; the remainder should be available not long afterward.[43] The electronic edition of the Wittgenstein papers will contain both black and white and color photographs of each page of the papers and a comprehensive transcription of the text. The black and white images will offer rapid reference to any part of the *Nachlass*, while the more detailed color images will facilitate close examination when needed. The transcript has been recorded in a specially developed language, which will allow the accompanying software to display the text in a number of formats, each representing a different set of editorial choices. For instance, when studying a heavily revised typescript, one could move between editions which would show the unrevised typescript, the text as finally revised, and a fully comprehensive "diplomatically" edited text which shows every semantically significant mark on the page, including all revisions, deletions, and variant wordings. While the electronic edition will not include a printed edition of the text, it will be possible to produce a printout of particular pages in whatever format one prefers.

The electronic edition of the Wittgenstein papers will make it possible to look at his writing as an interconnected whole, rather than as a discrete number of self-contained texts. The solid physical boundaries of a printed volume that separate one text from another in the traditional library become just one way of organizing information within the fluid world of hypertext. In hypertext, each paragraph or screenful of text can be multiply interlinked with many other paragraphs of text, connected not only by the numerical sequence of published pages in a particular edition, but also with different editions of the same text, variant drafts and footnotes inserted by the author on a number of occasions, editorial information, previous drafts of the sentences in question, a translation into another language, relevant passages in other parts of the corpus, glossaries, dictionaries, a concordance for every term in the text, references to the collection of the most relevant secondary literature, pictures of illustrations or problematic passages in the original manuscript draft, and so forth. While the links that animate hypertext are familiar, and can, at least in principle, already be followed by a sufficiently skilled reader, in practice, it promises to change our understanding both of Wittgenstein's way of writing and his philosophy. Readers of the electronic edition will be able to compare different stages of Wittgenstein's revisions, systematically review his use of key terms, or search customized concordances. Questions that could not have been answered before will be answered in less time than it takes to ask them. Readers will approach Wittgenstein's writing in new ways, exploring connections and relationships that have received little attention in the past.

Perhaps one of the most important morals that the later Wittgenstein drew from his critique of his own earlier work is that there is a great danger in philosophy of taking a particular way of seeing things as though it were the only way of looking at them. In this chapter, I have argued that there is a comparable danger in treating Wittgenstein's posthumously published works at face value, as though they correspond to the books that he would have published. One reason for the overview I have provided of Wittgenstein's literary remains, and of his editors' decisions as to how to publish them, is to indicate some of the main connections between the published works and his *Nachlass*, connections that provide strong reasons for not taking his published works at face value, and for expecting that in the future readings of his work will increasingly be informed by a reading of the *Nachlass* as a whole. However, for most readers of this essay, there will be no need to consult the unpublished parts of the *Nachlass*. For those who are beginning to read Wittgenstein, or who wish to concentrate on the writing that comes closest to satisfying Schulte's criteria for being a "finished work of Wittgenstein's," the essential texts – the *Tractatus*, Part I of the *Investigations*, and Part I of the *Remarks on the Foundations of Mathematics* – have long been in print. For those who are interested in reading those works in the context of Wittgenstein's other writing, the published corpus of his writing already includes a substantial fraction of his surviving writings, including not only much of his most polished writing, but also texts from every stage of revision. It is these readers, for whom the published Wittgenstein is Wittgenstein enough, who are most in need of an outline of the relationship between Wittgenstein's published and unpublished writings, and it is for them that this chapter was written.

NOTES

1  Leading examples include PI, 43, 199, 242, 258.
2  For some further elaboration of these claims, see Stern, "Recent Work on Wittgenstein," *Synthese* 98 (1990), pp. 415–58.
3  Stanley Cavell, "The Availability of Wittgenstein's Later Philosophy," in *Wittgenstein: The Philosophical Investigations*, ed. G. Pitcher (New York: Doubleday, 1966).
4  Cavell, "The Availability of Wittgenstein's Later Philosophy," p. 184.
5  Stanley Cavell, *Philosophical Passages: Wittgenstein, Emerson, Austin, Derrida* (Oxford: Blackwell, 1995), p. 96.
6  Ibid., p. 96.
7  Only the introduction to the Vienna edition, dated 1993, had reached me when this was written. Although the third volume had just been printed when this book went to press in September 1995, and I had an opportunity to look at the first three volumes at a book display this summer, they had not reached the Berkeley library. The "Plan of the Edition" states that "Between two and five volumes will appear annually.... Fifteen volumes of edited text are initially envisaged, containing the writings from 1929 to 1933. These will be thoroughly indexed by an accompanying series of concordance volumes. An extension of the edition is intended" (M. Nedo, ed., *Vienna Edition. Introduction* [Vienna: Springer, 1993], p. 127). Volumes 1–5 will contain the ten manuscript volumes from this period (MSS, 105–14). According to the Introduction, volumes 6–13 will consist of the Big Typescript and the typescripts that led up to it (TSS, 208, 210–18). Finally, a set of manuscript notebooks dating from 1931–2, which contain rough drafts for MSS 110–14, will be published in volumes 14–15. However, the prospectus for the edition circulated by Springer in 1995 divides the same texts into eleven volumes, and promises six additional concordance volumes, which will be

updated every two years or so as the edition progresses. While the Vienna edition will find a home in a number of research libraries, this
small selection from the *Nachlass* will cost far more than the entire
electronic edition, cannot easily be revised to ensure editorial consistency or to correct mistakes as they are discovered, and will contain far
less information.

8  Those who have challenged the editors' decision have for the most
part questioned particular inclusions or exclusions, rather than the
construction of the *oeuvre* as a whole, and there has been little recognition of the extent to which their decisions have shaped the recep-
tion of Wittgenstein's philosophy. What discussion there has been of
the problems in editing the *Nachlass* has, for the most part, occurred
either in the popular press or relatively obscure scholarly journals, and
has had little impact on most of his readers.

9  G. H. von Wright, *Wittgenstein* (Oxford: Blackwell, 1982), p. 136.

10 For further discussion of the publication history of the *Investigations*
see G. H. von Wright, "The Troubled History of Part II of the *Investiga-*
*tions,*" *Grazer Philosophische Studien* 42 (1992), pp. 181–92, O.
Scholz, "Zum Status von Teil II der *Philosophische Untersuchungen,*"
in E. von Savigny and O. Scholz, eds., *Wittgenstein über die Seele*
(Frankfurt am Main: Suhrkamp, 1995), pp. 24–40; and Stern, "New
Evidence Concerning the Construction // the Troubled History // of
Part I of the *Investigations,*" *Papers of the Eighteenth International*
*Wittgenstein Symposium* (Kirchberg, Austria: The Austrian Ludwig
Wittgenstein Society, 1995), pp. 789–95.

While there are relatively few discrepancies between the published
text of Part I of the *Investigations* and the two surviving typescripts, the
typescripts should provide the basis for a thoroughly revised critical
edition of the text of Part I. A comparison of the two typescripts and the
published text which I carried out in the summer of 1993 made it clear
that the published text contains some errors which should be corrected.
For instance, in §85, line 3, the published text reads "Also kann ich
sagen, der Wegweiser lässt doch keinen Zweifel offen" (therefore I can
say, the signpost leaves no doubt open), which does correspond to the
typed text of the source typescript. On checking the source typescripts,
one finds that in both typescripts, Wittgenstein changed "keinen" (no)
to "einen" (a), a much more readily intelligible reading, but the editors
later decided to keep the original wording. (This passage was brought to
my attention by Eike von Savigny.)

Another significant divergence between the typescripts and the published text concerns the so-called *Randbemerkungen* or marginal remarks. These slips contained additional remarks that were attached to

particular places in the typescript; most of them include instructions as to where they should be inserted in the main text. In most cases, those instructions were not followed, and the material in question was published at the bottom of the page, separated from the main text by a line. For instance, both copies of the *Randbemerkungen* that are printed on pp. 11 and 14 explicitly state that they should be inserted at the end of PI, 22 and 28 respectively. Other *Randbemerkungen* may have been footnotes: in the second copy of typescript 227, the *Randbemerkung* on page 33 of the published text has a "1" next to the words "On page 60," and one finds a corresponding "1," in the same hand, at the end of PI, 70, on page 60 of the typescript. In both copies of the typescript, the end of the penultimate sentence in PI, 142 has a superscripted "1" connecting it with the *Randbemerkung* printed at the bottom of that page. Several *Randbemerkung* are attached to PI, 138; one is printed at the bottom of that page, two more on the next page, and two others on page 147; there is no evidence in either typescript to explain why this decision was made. It is likely that these discrepancies were the result of last-minute misunderstandings between the editors and publisher.

11 Scholz, "Zum Status von Teil II der *Philosophische Untersuchungen.*"

12 Those who read the *Investigations* in the English translation should be warned that the present translation is not entirely reliable and was apparently constructed without consulting Wittgenstein's comments on Rhees's translation. While Wittgenstein's writing is extremely difficult to translate well, a more accurate and faithful translation is certainly possible. Although the translation was substantially improved in the second edition of the book, it still contains a number of egregious errors, such as the omission of an entire clause in the translation of PI, 412, and the translation of *Sprache*, language, in PI, 116 as language-game. The English translation of §116 has seemed to many readers to provide strong textual grounds for conflating language-games, Wittgenstein's term for quite specific uses of language (see his introduction of the term in PI, 23), with language as a whole. More generally, the use of a variety of English words for important German expressions makes it impossible for the English reader to see connections which are manifest in the German text. For instance, *übersichtlich* and *übersehen*, which are adjectival and verb forms of the same root, are translated as "perspicuous" and "to command a clear view" respectively in PI, 122, where the central importance of this expression is emphasized; elsewhere "surveyable" and "to survey" are also used. The translation of a family of related German terms by a single English word has been equally misleading. For instance, the translation of *Gebrauch* (custom), *Verpflogenheit* (an institu-

tionalized practice), *Verwendung* (use), and *Anwendung* (application) by the English word "use" has helped to create the mistaken impression that Wittgenstein accepted what has become known as a "use theory of meaning." There is further discussion of specific problems with the translation of the *Investigations* in Baker and Hacker's commentary on the *Investigations.*

The Ogden translation of the *Tractatus* was reviewed by Wittgenstein, who made a number of suggestions for changes, and can be regarded as having received his considered approval. The correspondence is documented in *Letters to Ogden,* which includes facsimiles of Wittgenstein's comments written on the proofs. While the Pears and McGuinness translation is somewhat more colloquial and accessible than the Ogden version, it sometimes sacrifices consistency in the interest of a fluid translation. For instance *sich zeigen,* which literally means "to show itself," is closely related to *zeigen,* "to show," yet Pears and McGuinness depart from the Ogden translation, instead using the expression "makes itself manifest."

13 For further discussion of the development of Wittgenstein's treatment of solipsism, see: Stern, *Wittgenstein on Mind and Language* (New York: Oxford University Press, 1995); Hacker, *Insight and Illusion* (Oxford: Clarendon, 1986); Pears, *The False Prison* (Oxford: Clarendon, 1987, 1988). Hallett's *A Companion to Wittgenstein's Philosophical Investigations* (Ithaca: Cornell University Press, 1977), p. 439 ff. provides a large number of cross- references to passages in both the published and unpublished writings, and includes a number of quotations from the *Nachlass.*

14 The preparatory work for the *Investigations* contains many more references to the authors Wittgenstein had read than the published texts. In some cases, this even takes the form of an explicit reference to the author Wittgenstein had in mind in a particular remark (e.g., early versions of PI, 122 contain a parenthetical reference to Spengler in connection with the use of the term *Weltanschauung*). There are numerous references, both explicit and implicit, to Köhler's *Gestalt Psychology* and William James's *Principles of Psychology* in the *Remarks on the Philosophy of Psychology* and Part II of the *Investigations.* Although Wittgenstein liked to give the impression that he had read very little, this was far from the truth. In a remark in *Culture and Value,* written in 1931, he even described himself as a "reproductive thinker," someone who had never discovered a train of thought but had only made use of others' for his "work of clarification," which involved the discovery of "new similes." He initially listed "Frege, Russell, Spengler, Sraffa" as his influences, but later expanded the list so that it read "Boltzmann Hertz Schopenhauer Frege, Russell, Kraus, Loos Weininger

Spengler, Sraffa." In view of Wittgenstein's biography, and the care he took over the order, it is very likely that the authors are arranged in chronological sequence. While Hallett's appendix to his *Companion to Wittgenstein's Philosophical Investigations*, an extensive list of authors and books that Wittgenstein read, has some gaps, in it is a valuable indication of the range and character of Wittgenstein's literary tastes.

15 Wittgenstein, quoted by Rhees, in "Correspondence and Comment," *The Human World* 15–16 (1974), p. 153. Rhees does not give a precise reference, simply stating that the quotation is taken from a manuscript written in 1948. The passage is cited in full in Stern, *Wittgenstein on Mind and Language*, pp. 6, 193.

16 There is a programmatic outline of this transitional metaphysics of experience in "Some Remarks on Logical Form" (PO, pp. 28–35) and parts of it, despite his change of mind in October 1929, can be found in the *Philosophical Remarks*, assembled in the spring of 1930. But the best record of this phase of Wittgenstein's work is to be found in Wittgenstein's manuscript volumes from 1929, which are now available in the first two volumes of the Vienna edition of his work.

17 For further discussion, see Stern, *Wittgenstein on Mind and Language*, pp. 98–104, 125–7, 186–92.

18 There is also some anecdotal evidence that he intentionally destroyed other papers. In an interview in the *Daily Telegraph*, Mrs. David Ennals described her friendship with Wittgenstein and told the reporter that "when the philosopher died, she took three rucksacks of his papers and, alone, burnt them in Wales, Austria and Norway as he had wished."

19 The number of pages in the Wittgenstein *Nachlass* has recently become a matter of some controversy. If one follows the convention that von Wright adopts in his catalog, of counting each side of a sheet of paper with writing or type on it as a "page," one arrives at a result of approximately 20,000 pages, roughly 12,000 manuscript pages and 8,000 typed pages (many with manuscript revisions), the figure cited by the Wittgenstein Archives at the University of Bergen. Nedo's figure of 30,000 manuscript pages is hard to understand, and no reasons are given (Vienna edition *Introduction*, pp. 51, 52.)

Huitfeldt and Rossvaer, the editors of *The Norwegian Wittgenstein Project Report 1988* (Bergen: Norwegian Computing Center for the Humanities, 1989), estimated that their electronic complete works would occupy about 40 megabytes, or well over 5 million words. While a substantial fraction of this would consist of drafts of published remarks and the coding needed to represent every variant draft, erasure, and rearrangement, there is at least as much material that does not fall into these categories.

20  Parts 4–6 give away the remainder of his estate. Part 4 contains the following gifts:

> To Dr. Benedict Richards my French Travelling Clock my Fur Coat my complete edition of Grimm's Fairy Tales and my book "Hernach" by W. Busch
>
> To Dr. Ludwig Hänsel in Austria my volume of Lessing's Religious Writings
>
> To Mr. R. Rhees the rest of my books and what I call my Collection of Nonsense which will be found in a file
>
> To Miss Anscombe all my furniture

21  A lost typescript of the first part of the *Investigations* and two manuscript notebooks were rediscovered in 1993 and given to the Wren Library. In the same year, a number of Wittgenstein's papers, including the missing "Gmunden" typescript of the *Tractatus* and the manuscript of the early version of the *Investigations*, together with a previously unknown notebook from the 1930s, were found in the *Nachlass* of Rudolf and Elisabeth Koder and given to the Brenner Archive in Innsbruck. The notebook, which contains extremely interesting diary entries and personal reflections, dating from 1930–2 and 1936–7, has already been edited and will be published as *Ludwig Wittgenstein. Tagebuch 1930–1937*, ed. Ilse Somavilla. (Innsbruck: Hayman Verlag, 1996.)

22  The best printed index to all three books is to be found in the one-volume Suhrkamp edition; the *Tractatus* and *Notebooks 1914–1916* are included in the *The Published Works of Ludwig Wittgenstein* (Clayton, Ga: Intelex, 1993), but not *Prototractatus*.

23  In addition to these books, all based on the Wittgenstein *Nachlass*, much of his correspondence, and notes of his lectures and conversations, have also been published; these are included in the list of primary sources in the bibliography.

24  Wittgenstein, *Werkausgabe*, 8 vols., ed. Joachim Schulte (Frankfurt: Suhrkamp, 1984).

25  *The Published Work of Ludwig Wittgenstein.*

26  J. Schulte, *Wittgenstein: An Introduction* (Albany: SUNY Press, 1992), p. 34.

27  Ibid.

28  Foucault uses the expression "the author of the *Tractatus* (Wittgenstein)" to remind us of the peculiarly problematic status of posthumous authorship. Cf. H. Sluga, "Thinking as Writing," *Grazer Philosophische Studien* 33/34 (1989), pp. 115–141, and Derrida on Nietzsche's "I have forgotten my umbrella" in *Spurs: Nietzsche's Styles* (Chicago: University of Chicago Press, 1978), pp. 122–43.

29  For instance, the first nineteen sections of the *Philosophical Grammar*

are based on the following sources: pp. 1–4, 12, 4–5, 25–6, 25, 5–13, 14, 13, and 14 of MS 140; pp. 28–32, 31, 32–3, 93, 52, 33–7, 179 of MS 114, part II; p. 26 of the Big Typescript.

30 The "Philosophy" chapter, which includes versions of many of the most well-known remarks on philosophical method in the *Investigations*, was published as a journal article in 1989, and can be found in *Philosophical Occasions*. The chapters on "Phenomenology" and "Idealism, etc." remain unpublished.

31 Kenny, the translator of the *Philosophical Grammar*, wrote a judicious and extremely informative discussion of how that book was edited, under the title "From the Big Typescript to the *Philosophical Grammar*," reprinted in his *The Legacy of Wittgenstein* (Oxford: Blackwell, 1984).

32 A. Pichler, "A Source Catalog of the Published Texts," in M. Biggs and A. Pichler, eds., *Wittgenstein: Two Source Catalogues and a Bibliography* (Bergen: Working Papers from the Wittgenstein Archives at the University of Bergen, no. 7, 1993). The book, like all the publications of the Wittgenstein Archives at Bergen, can be obtained from the Archives by writing to them at Harald Hårfagres gt 31, N-5007 Bergen, Norway, or by E-mail at wab@hd.uib.no.

33 Wittgenstein, *Geheime Tagebücher*, ed. W. Baum (Vienna: Turia and Kant, 1991).

34 A. Maury, "Sources of the Remarks in Wittgenstein's *Zettel*," *Philosophical Investigations* 4 (1981), pp. 57–74 and "Sources of the Remarks in Wittgenstein's *Philosophical Investigations*," *Synthese* 90 (1994), pp. 349–78.

35 *Vermischte Bemerkungen*, 3rd ed. (Frankfurt am Main: Suhrkamp, 1994). A new edition of the English translation, *Culture and Value*, is currently being prepared by Peter Winch.

36 For a brief review of the work that has been done on the *Nachlass*, see Stern, "Recent Work on Wittgenstein," Part III.

37 J. Hintikka, "An Impatient Man and His Papers," *Synthese* 87 (1991), p. 192.

38 Von Wright, "The Wittgenstein Papers," PO, p. 504, n19. The footnote refers the reader to von Wright, *Wittgenstein*, pp. 7–10 and pp. 111–36 (the introduction and the essay on the origin and composition of the *Investigations*).

39 This work on a number of carefully edited typescripts of successive versions of the *Philosophical Investigations* is outlined in the preface to von Wright's *Wittgenstein* (1982, pp. 6–10). The sources include TSS 220, 221, 225, 227, 239, all of which are drafts for Part I, together with a similarly edited typescript of MS 144, the only surviving draft of the

published Part II (the typescript on which the published book was based is lost).

40  Hintikka, "An Impatient Man and His Papers," pp. 193–4.

41  A. Kenny, "Wittgenstein's Troubled Legacy," *Times Higher Education Supplement*, August 26, 1994.

42  Ibid.

43  The Wittgenstein Archives at the University of Bergen, *The Collected Manuscripts of Ludwig Wittgenstein on Facsimile CD-ROM* (New York: Oxford University Press, 1997).

The Norwegian Wittgenstein Project aimed at a complete electronic version of the Wittgenstein papers, but was discontinued in 1987; it is described in more detail in Huitfeldt and Rossvaer, *The Norwegian Wittgenstein Project Report 1988*. The work is being continued by the Wittgenstein Archives at Bergen, which was restarted in 1990 with the approval of the Wittgenstein trustees. Further discussion of the work of the Wittgenstein Archives at Bergen can be found in Claus Huitfeldt, "Computerizing Wittgenstein. The Wittgenstein Archives at the University of Bergen," in K. Johannessen et al., eds., *Wittgenstein and Norway* (Oslo: Solum Forlag, 1994), pp. 275–94, and "Multi-Dimensional Texts in a One-Dimensional Medium," in P. Henry and A. Utaker, eds., *Wittgenstein and Contemporary Theories of Language* (Bergen: Working Papers from the Wittgenstein Archives at the University of Bergen, no. 5, 1992), pp. 142–61.

# BIBLIOGRAPHY

## FURTHER READING

The literature on Wittgenstein's life and work is extensive. The bibliography by Shanker and Shanker, which is already ten years out of date, contains over 6000 items; a more selective bibliography, by Frongia and McGuinness, which includes short summaries of many of the principal entries, still lists well over 1000 items. Our bibliography makes no claim to comprehensiveness, but does offer a representative selection of work on Wittgenstein, and especially recent material that will not be found in the standard reference works. Readers who would like easy access to a wide range of secondary literature on Wittgenstein's philosophy might like to consult the five-volume anthology edited by Shanker, or the fifteen-volume anthology edited by Canfield. The anthology edited by Pitcher contains a number of papers which have had a considerable influence on the secondary literature.

The best general introductions to Wittgenstein's philosophy are Kenny's *Wittgenstein*, which stresses the chronological development and continuities in his thought, Pears's *Ludwig Wittgenstein*, which outlines some of the central problems that preoccupied him, Fogelin's *Wittgenstein*, which concentrates on the argument of the *Investigations*, and Schulte's *Wittgenstein: An Introduction*. Kripke's *Wittgenstein on Rules and Private Language* provides a clear and provocative interpretation of Wittgenstein's conception of rule-following which has generated an enormous amount of critical discussion. Hacker's *Insight and Illusion*, Hintikka and Hintikka's *Investigating Wittgenstein*, Pears's *The False Prison*, and Stern's *Wittgenstein on Mind and Language* offer conflicting but complementary accounts of the development of Wittgenstein's philosophy. Those engaging in a close study of the *Philosophical Investigations* will want to consult the commentaries by Baker and Hacker, Hallett, and von Savigny, each of which provides a very different style of commentary and interpretation of the text. Books that contain information about the primary literature and its relationship to the Wittgenstein

*Nachlass* are discussed in the chapter of this book on "The Availability of Wittgenstein's Philosophy."

Monk's biography of Wittgenstein provides the best overview of his life, but there is much valuable information in the first volume of McGuinness's biography. The biographies contain references to most of the other literature on Wittgenstein's life, but the best memoirs of Wittgenstein by those who knew him are to be found in Malcolm's *Ludwig Wittgenstein: A Memoir* and Rhees's *Recollections of Wittgenstein*, which includes an insightful piece by Fania Pascal, Wittgenstein's Russian teacher, and informative notes by Maurice Drury, an old friend of Wittgenstein's.

PRIMARY TEXTS

*The Blue and Brown Books*. Oxford: Blackwell, 1958; 2nd ed., 1960.
*The Collected Manuscripts of Ludwig Wittgenstein on Facsimile CD-ROM.* Ed. by the Wittgenstein Archives at the University of Bergen. Oxford: Oxford University Press, 1997.
*Culture and Value*. Ed. G. H. von Wright, trans. P. Winch. 2nd ed. Oxford: Blackwell, 1980; Chicago: University of Chicago Press, 1980.
*Geheime Tagebücher 1914–1916*. Ed. W. Baum. Wien: Turia and Kant, 1991.
*Last Writings on the Philosophy of Psychology*. Vol. 1: *Preliminary Studies for Part II of the "Philosophical Investigations."* Eds. G. H. von Wright and H. Nyman, trans. C. G. Luckhardt and M. A. E. Aue. Chicago: University of Chicago Press, 1982.
*Last Writings on the Philosophy of Psychology*. Vol. 2: *The Inner and the Outer, 1949–1951*. Eds. G. H. von Wright and H. Nyman, trans. C. G. Luckhardt and M. A. E. Aue. Oxford: Blackwell, 1992.
*Logisch-philosophische Abhandlung: Kritische Edition*. Eds. B. McGuinness and J. Schulte. Contains text of *Tractatus*, *Prototractatus*, and *Notebooks*; shows correspondences between *Tractatus* and Wittgenstein's previous writings. Frankfurt am Main: Suhrkamp, 1989.
*Notebooks, 1914–1916*. Eds. G. H. von Wright and G. E. M. Anscombe, trans. G. E. M. Anscombe. Oxford: Blackwell, 1961; 2nd ed., 1979.
*On Certainty*. Eds. G. E. M. Anscombe and G. H. von Wright, trans. G. E. M. Anscombe and D. Paul. Oxford: Basil Blackwell, 1969.
*Philosophical Grammar*. Ed. R. Rhees, trans. A. Kenny. Oxford: Blackwell, 1974.
*Philosophical Investigations*. Eds. G. E. M. Anscombe and R. Rhees, trans. G. E. M. Anscombe. Oxford: Blackwell, 1953; 2nd ed., 1953; 3rd ed., 1973.
*Philosophical Occasions, 1912–1951*. Eds. J. Klagge and A. Nordmann. Indianapolis: Hackett, 1993.

*Philosophical Remarks.* Ed. R. Rhees, trans. R. Hargreaves and R. White. Oxford: Blackwell, 1964; 2nd ed., 1975.

*Prototractatus.* Eds. B. F. McGuinness, T. Nyberg, and G. H. von Wright, trans. D. F. Pears and B. F. McGuinness. Ithaca: Cornell University Press, 1971.

*The Published Works of Ludwig Wittgenstein.* Clayton, Ga.: Intelex, 1993. Part of the Past Masters electronic text database series.

*Remarks on Colour.* Ed. G. E. M. Anscombe, trans. L. McAlister and M. Schättle. Oxford: Blackwell, 1977.

*Remarks on the Foundations of Mathematics.* Eds. G. H. von Wright, R. Rhees, and G. E. M. Anscombe, trans. G. E. M. Anscombe. Oxford: Blackwell, 1956; 2nd ed., 1967; 3rd ed., 1978.

*Remarks on the Philosophy of Psychology.* Vol. 1. Eds. G. E. M. Anscombe and G. H. von Wright, trans. G. E. M. Anscombe. Chicago: University of Chicago Press, 1980.

*Remarks on the Philosophy of Psychology.* Vol. 2. Eds. G. H. von Wright and H. Nyman, trans. C. G. Luckhardt and M. A. E. Aue. Chicago: University of Chicago Press, 1980.

*Tractatus Logico-Philosophicus.* Trans. C. K. Ogden. London: Routledge, 1922. Trans. D. F. Pears and B. McGuinness. London: Routledge, 1961.

*Vermischte Bemerkungen, Eine Auswahl aus dem Nachlass.* Ed. G. H. von Wright, assisted by Heikki Nyman. Revision by Alois Pichler. Frankfurt am Main: Suhrkamp, 1994.

*Vienna Edition, Introduction* and vols. 1–3. Ed. Michael Nedo. Vienna: Springer Verlag, 1993–5.

*Wörterbuch für Volksschulen.* Eds. W. Leinfelner, E. Leinfelner, and A. Hübner. Vienna: Hölder-Pichler-Temsky, 1977.

*Zettel.* Eds. G. E. M. Anscombe and G. H. von Wright, trans. by G. E. M. Anscombe. Oxford: Blackwell, 1967; 2nd ed., 1981.

LECTURES, CONVERSATIONS, AND CORRESPONDENCE

*Lectures and Conversations on Aesthetics, Psychology and Religious Belief.* Ed. C. Barrett. Oxford: Blackwell, 1978.

*Letters from Ludwig Wittgenstein, with a Memoir.* Ed. P. Engelmann. Oxford: Blackwell, 1967; New York: Horizon, 1968.

*Letters to C. K. Ogden with Comments on the English Translation of the Tractatus Logico-Philosophicus.* Ed. G. H. von Wright. Oxford, London: Blackwell, Routledge, 1973.

*Letters to Russell, Keynes and Moore.* Eds. G. H. von Wright and B. F. McGuinness. Oxford: Blackwell, 1974.

*Ludwig Hänsel – Ludwig Wittgenstein. Eine Freundschaft.* Ed. I. Somavilla.

Innsbruck: Brenner Studien vol. 14, 1994. Contains Wittgenstein's correspondence with Hänsel.

*Ludwig Wittgenstein: A Memoir.* N. Malcolm, with biographical sketch by G. H. von Wright. Oxford: Oxford University Press, 1986; 2nd ed. includes Wittgenstein's letters to Malcolm.

*Ludwig Wittgenstein and the Vienna Circle: Conversations Recorded by Friedrich Waismann.* Ed. B. F. McGuinness. Oxford: Blackwell, 1979.

*Wittgenstein: Conversations, 1949–1951.* O. K. Bouwsma; eds. J. L. Craft and R. E. Hustwit. Indianapolis: Hackett, 1986.

*Wittgenstein's Lectures, Cambridge 1930–1932.* Ed. D. Lee. Oxford: Blackwell, 1980; Totowa, N.J.: Rowman and Littlefield, 1982.

*Wittgenstein's Lectures, Cambridge 1932–1935.* Ed. A. Ambrose. Totowa, N.J.: Littlefield and Adams, 1979.

*Wittgenstein's Lectures on Philosophical Psychology 1946–47.* Ed. P. T. Geach. London: Harvester, 1988.

*Wittgenstein's Lectures on the Foundations of Mathematics, Cambridge 1933.* Ed. C. Diamond. Ithaca: Cornell University Press, 1976; Chicago: University of Chicago Press, 1989.


SECONDARY LITERATURE

Ackermann, R. *Wittgenstein's City.* Amherst: University of Massachusetts Press, 1988.

Albritton, R. "On Wittgenstein's Use of the Term 'Criterion.' " *Journal of Philosophy* 56 (1959), pp. 845–57. Reprinted in Pitcher, ed., *Wittgenstein: The Philosophical Investigations,* pp. 231–51.

Anderson, A. R. "Mathematics and the 'Language-Game.' " *Review of Metaphysics* 11 (1957–8), pp. 446–58.

Anscombe, G. E. M. *Introduction to Wittgenstein's Tractatus.* New York: Harper and Row, 1959.

"On the form of Wittgenstein's Writing." In R. Klibansky, ed., *Contemporary Philosophy: A Survey,* vol. 3, pp. 373–8. Florence: La Nuova Italia, 1969.

"The Question of Linguistic Idealism." In Anscombe, *From Parmenides to Wittgenstein.* Oxford: Blackwell, 1981, pp. 112–33.

"The Reality of the Past." In Anscombe, *Metaphysics and Philosophy of Mind.* Oxford: Blackwell, 1981, pp. 103–19.

"A Theory of Language?" In Block, ed., *Perspectives on the Philosophy of Wittgenstein,* pp. 148–59.

"Wittgenstein: Whose Philosopher?" In Griffiths, ed., *Wittgenstein Centenary Essays,* pp. 1–10.

Arrington, R. L., and H.-J. Glock, eds. *Wittgenstein's Philosophical Investigations: Text and Context*. London: Routledge, 1991.

Ayer, A. J. *Wittgenstein*. New York: Random, 1985.

Baker, G. *Wittgenstein, Frege and the Vienna Circle*. Oxford: Blackwell, 1988.

Baker G., and P. M. S. Hacker. *Scepticism, Rules and Language*. Oxford: Blackwell, 1984.

*Wittgenstein: Rules, Grammar and Necessity. An Analytical Commentary on the Philosophical Investigations*. Vol. 2. Oxford: Blackwell, 1985.

*Wittgenstein: Understanding and Meaning. An Analytical Commentary on the Philosophical Investigations*. Vol. 1. Chicago: University Chicago Press, 1980.

Bambrough, R. "Universals and Family Resemblances." *Proceedings of the Aristotelian Society* 61 (1960–1), pp. 207–2.

Bartley, W. W. *Wittgenstein*. Philadelphia and New York: Lippencott, 1973; revised 2nd ed., with response to critics, LaSalle, Ill.: Open Court, 1985.

Bates, S. "Scepticism and the Interpretation of Wittgenstein." In T. Cohen, P. Guyer, and H. Putnam, eds., *Pursuits of Reason*. Lubbock: Texas Tech Press, 1993, pp. 225–40.

Batkin, N. "On Wittgenstein and Kripke: Mastering Language in Wittgenstein's *Philosophical Investigations*." In T. Cohen, P. Guyer, and H. Putnam, eds., *Pursuits of Reason*. Lubbock: Texas Tech Press, 1993, pp. 241–62.

Black, M. *A Companion to Wittgenstein's Tractatus*. Ithaca: Cornell University Press, 1964.

"Wittgenstein's Language Games." *Dialectica* 33 (1979), pp. 337–53. Reprinted in Shanker, ed., *Ludwig Wittgenstein*, vol. 2.

Blackburn, S. "The Individual Strikes Back." In Wright, ed., *Essays on Wittgenstein's Later Philosophy*.

*Spreading the Word*. Oxford: Clarendon, 1984.

Block, I., ed. *Perspectives on the Philosophy of Wittgenstein*. Cambridge, Mass.: MIT Press, 1981.

Bloor, D. *Wittgenstein: A Social Theory of Knowledge*. London: Macmillan, 1983.

"Wittgenstein on Rule Following: The Old and New Individualism." *The Polish Sociology Bulletin* 3–4 (1989), pp. 27–33.

*Wittgenstein: Rules and Institutions* (forthcoming).

Bogen, J. *Wittgenstein's Philosophy of Language*. London: Routledge, 1972.

Boghossian, P. "The Rule-Following Considerations." *Mind* 98 (1989), pp. 507–49.

Bolton, D. "Life-Form and Idealism." In G. Vesey, ed., *Idealism Past and Present*. Cambridge University Press, 1982, pp. 269–84.

Bouveresse, J. *Wittgenstein Reads Freud: The Myth of the Unconscious*. Trans. Carol Cosman. Princeton: Princeton University Press, 1995.

Bouwsma, O. K. "The Blue Book." In Fann, ed., *Wittgenstein's Conception of Philosophy*, pp. 149–70.

Brill, S. *Wittgenstein and Critical Theory: Beyond Postmodernism and Towards Descriptive Investigations*. Athens: Ohio University Press, 1994.

Broad, C. D. "Wittgenstein and the Vienna Circle." *Mind* 71 (1962), p. 251.

Brockhaus, R. *Pulling Up the Ladder*. LaSalle: Open Court, 1991.

Budd, M. *Wittgenstein's Philosophy of Psychology*. London: Routledge, 1989.

Butler, R. J. "A Wittgensteinian on 'The Reality of the Past.' " *Philosophical Quarterly* 6 (1956), pp. 203–18.

Canfield, J. *Wittgenstein: Language and World*. Amherst: University of Massachusetts Press, 1981.

   ed. *The Philosophy of Wittgenstein*. 15 vols. New York: Garland Publishing, 1986.

Cavell, S. "The Availability of Wittgenstein's Later Philosophy." In Cavell, *Must We Mean What We Say?* and Pitcher, ed., *Wittgenstein: The Philosophical Investigations*, pp. 151–86.

*The Claim of Reason, Wittgenstein, Skepticism, Morality, and Tragedy*. Oxford: Oxford University Press, 1979.

*Conditions Handsome and Unhandsome: The Constitution of Emersonian Perfectionism*. Chicago: University of Chicago Press, 1990.

"Existentialism and Analytical Philosophy." In Cavell, *Themes Out of School*. San Francisco: North Point Press, 1984, pp. 195–234.

*Must We Mean What We Say?* Cambridge University Press, 1976.

*Philosophical Passages: Wittgenstein, Emerson, Austin, Derrida*. Oxford: Blackwell, 1995.

"Postscript (1989): To Whom It May Concern." *Critical Inquiry* 16 (1990), pp. 248–90.

*This New Yet Unapproachable America: Lectures after Emerson after Wittgenstein*. Albuquerque: Living Batch Press, 1989.

Cerbone, D. "Don't Look But Think: Imaginary Scenarios in Wittgenstein's Later Philosophy." *Inquiry* 37 (1994), pp. 159–83.

Cioffi, F. "Wittgenstein and the Fire Festivals." In Block, ed., *Perspectives on the Philosophy of Wittgenstein*, pp. 212–37.

Conant, J. "Kierkegaard, Wittgenstein and Nonsense." In T. Cohen, P. Guyer, and H. Putnam, eds., *Pursuits of Reason*. Lubbock: Texas Tech Press, 1993, pp. 195–224.

"Must We Show What We Cannot Say?" In R. Fleming and M. Payne, eds., *The Senses of Stanley Cavell*. Lewisburg, Pa.: Bucknell University Press, 1989, pp. 242–83.

"Putting 2 and 2 Together: Wittgenstein, Kierkegaard and the Point of View for Their Work as Authors." In D. Z. Phillips, ed., *The Grammar of Religious Belief*. London: MacMillan, 1994.

"The Search for Logically Alien Thought: Descartes, Kant, Frege, and the Tractatus." *Philosophical Topics* 20 (1991), pp. 115–80.

Conway, G. D. *Wittgenstein on Foundations*. Atlantic Highlands, N.J.: Humanities Press, 1989.

Cook, J. "Solipsism and Language." In A. Ambrose and M. Lazerowitz, eds., *Ludwig Wittgenstein: Philosophy and Language*. London: Allen and Unwin, 1972, pp. 37–72.

"Wittgenstein on Privacy." *The Philosophical Review* 74 (1965), pp. 281–314, and in Pitcher, ed., *Wittgenstein: The Philosophical Investigations*, pp. 286–323.

"Human Beings." In Winch, ed., *Studies in the Philosophy of Wittgenstein*, pp. 117–51.

*Wittgenstein's Metaphysics*. Cambridge University Press, 1994.

Coope, Christopher, et al. *A Wittgenstein Workbook*. Oxford: Blackwell, 1970.

Copi, I. M., and R. W. Beard, eds. *Essays on Wittgenstein's Tractatus*. New York: Macmillan; London: Routledge, 1966.

Dasenbrock, R. W., ed. *Redrawing the Lines: Analytic Philosophy, Deconstruction, and Literary Theory*. Minneapolis: University of Minnesota Press, 1989.

Diamond, C. "Ethics, Imagination and the Method of Wittgenstein's *Tractatus*." In R. Heinrich and H. Vetter, eds., *Bilder der Philosophie, Wiener Reihe* 5 (1991), pp. 55–90.

"Ludwig Wittgenstein," and "Wittgensteinian Ethics." In L. Becker, ed., *Encyclopedia of Ethics*. New York: Garland, 1992, pp. 1319–22 and pp. 1322–4.

"¿Qué tan viejos son estos huesos? Putnam, Wittgenstein y la verificación." *Diánoia* 38 (1992), pp. 115–42.

*The Realistic Spirit: Wittgenstein, Philosophy and the Mind*. Cambridge, Mass.: MIT Press, 1991.

"Rules: Looking in the Right Place." In Phillips and Winch, eds., *Wittgenstein: Attention to Particulars*, pp. 12–34.

Dilham, Ilham. "Universals: Bambrough on Wittgenstein." *Proceedings of the Aristotelian Society* 79 (1978–9), pp. 35–58.

Dreben, B., and J. Floyd. "Tautology: How Not to Use a Word." *Synthese* 87 (1991), pp. 23–49.

Dummett, M. "Reckonings: Wittgenstein on Mathematics." *Encounter* 50, 3 (March 1978).

"Wittgenstein on Necessity: Some Reflections." In B. Hale and P. Clark eds., *Reading Putnam*. Oxford: Blackwell, 1994, pp. 49–65; also in Dummett, *The Seas of Language*. Oxford: Oxford University Press, 1993, pp. 446–61.

"Wittgenstein's Philosophy of Mathematics." *Philosophical Review* 68 (1959), pp. 324–48; reprinted in Dummett, *Truth and Other Enigmas* (London, 1978), and Pitcher, ed., *Wittgenstein: The Philosophical Investigations*, pp. 420–48.

Edwards, J. *Ethics without Philosophy: Wittgenstein and the Moral Life*. Gainesville: University of Southern Florida Press, 1982.

Eagleton, T. *Wittgenstein: The Terry Eagleton Script/The Derek Jarman Film*. London: British Film Institute, 1993.

Eldridge, R. "The Normal and the Normative: Wittgenstein's Legacy, Kripke, and Cavell." *Philosophy and Phenomenological Research* 46, 4 (June 1986).

Fann, K. T. *Wittgenstein's Conception of Philosophy*. Berkeley and Los Angeles: University of California Press, 1971.

ed. *Wittgenstein: The Man and His Philosophy*. New York: Dell, 1967.

Feyerabend, P. "Wittgenstein's *Philosophical Investigations*." In Fann, ed., *Wittgenstein: The Man and His Philosophy*, pp. 214–51, and Pitcher, ed., *Wittgenstein: The Philosophical Investigations*, pp. 104–51.

Findlay, J. N. *Wittgenstein: A Critique*. London: Routledge, 1984.

Floyd, J. "On Saying What You Really Want to Say: Wittgenstein, Gödel, and the Trisection of the Angle." In J. Hintikka, ed., *Essays in the Development of the Foundations of Mathematics*. Dordrecht: Kluwer, 1996, pp. 373–425.

"Wittgenstein on 2, 2, 2 . . . : The Opening of *Remarks on the Foundations of Mathematics*." *Synthese* 87 (1991), pp. 143–80.

Fogelin, R. "Negative Elementary Propositions." *Philosophical Studies* 25 (1974), pp. 189–97.

"Wittgenstein and Classical Skepticism." *International Philosophical Quarterly* 21 (1981), pp. 3–15.

*Wittgenstein*. London: Routledge, 1976; revised 2nd ed., 1987.

"Wittgenstein and Intuitionism." *American Philosophical Quarterly* 5 (1968), pp. 267–74.

"Wittgenstein on Identity." *Synthese* 56 (1983), pp. 141–53.

"Wittgenstein's Operator N." *Analysis* 41 (1982), pp. 124–7.

Frongia, G., and B. McGuinness. *Wittgenstein: A Bibliographical Guide*. Cambridge: Blackwell, 1990.

Gabel, G. *Ludwig Wittgenstein: A Comprehensive Bibliography of International Theses and Dissertations.* Köln: Edition Gemini, 1988.

Galison, P. "Aufbau/Bauhaus: Logical positivism and architectural modernism." *Critical Inquiry* 16 (1990), pp. 709–52.

Garver, N. *This Complicated Form of Life: Essays on Wittgenstein.* LaSalle and Chicago: Open Court, 1994.

"Wittgenstein and the Critical Tradition." *History of Philosophy Quarterly* 7 (1990), pp. 227–40.

"Wittgenstein on Private Language." In Klemke, ed., *Essays on Wittgenstein*, pp. 187–96.

Garver, N., and S. Lee. *Derrida and Wittgenstein.* Philadelphia: Temple University Press, 1994.

Geach, P. T. "Saying and Showing in Frege and Wittgenstein." In Hintikka, ed., *Essays on Wittgenstein in Honor of G. H. von Wright*, pp. 54–70.

Gebauer, G. et al., *Wien, Kundmangasse 19. Bauplanerische, morphologische und philosophische Aspekte des Wittgenstein-Hauses.* München: Fink, 1982.

Gerrard, S. "Is Wittgenstein a Relativist?" In Haller and Brandl, eds., *Wittgenstein – Towards a Reevaluation.*

"Two Ways of Grounding Meaning." *Philosophical Investigations* 14 (1991).

"Wittgenstein's Philosophies of Mathematics." *Synthese* 87 (1991), pp. 125–42.

Gert, B. "Wittgenstein's Private Language Arguments." *Synthese* 68 (1986), pp. 409–39.

Gier, N. F. *Wittgenstein and Phenomenology, A Comparative Study of the Later Wittgenstein, Husserl, Heidegger, and Merleau-Ponty.* Albany: State University of New York Press, 1981.

Glock, H.-J. "Abusing Use." forthcoming in *Dialectica.*

"Cambridge, Jena, or Vienna? – The Roots of the *Tractatus*." *Ratio* 5 (1992), pp. 1–23.

"Eine ganze Wolke von Philosophie kondensiert zu einem Tröpfschen Sprachlehre." In v. Savigny and Scholze, eds., *Wittgenstein über die Seele*, pp. 233–52.

"*Philosophical Investigations* §128." In Arrington and Glock, eds., *Wittgenstein's Philosophical Investigations.*

*A Wittgenstein Dictionary.* Oxford: Blackwell, 1995.

"Wittgenstein vs. Quine on Logical Necessity." In S. Teghrarian, ed., *Wittgenstein and Contemporary Philosophy.* Bristol: Thoemmes Press, 1994, pp. 185–222.

Glock, H.-J. and J. Preston "Externalism and First Person Authority." *The Monist* (October 1995).

Goldberg, B. "The Correspondence Hypothesis." *Philosophical Review* 77 (1968), pp. 438–55.

Goldfarb, W. "I want you to bring me a slab. Remarks on the opening sections of the 'Philosophical Investigations.' " *Synthese* 56 (1983), pp. 265–82.

"Kripke on Wittgenstein on Rules." *Journal of Philosophy* 82 (1985), pp. 471–88.

"Wittgenstein, Mind, and Scientism." *Journal of Philosophy* 86 (1989), pp. 635–42.

"Wittgenstein on Fixity of Meaning." In W. W. Tait, ed., *Early Analytic Philosophy: Essays in Honor of Leonard Linsky.* LaSalle, Ill: Open Court, forthcoming.

"Wittgenstein on Understanding." In P. French, et al., eds., *Midwest Studies in Philosophy XVII: The Wittgenstein Legacy.* Notre Dame: Notre Dame University Press, 1992, pp. 109–22.

Griffin, James. *Wittgenstein's Logical Atomism.* Oxford: Clarendon, 1964.

Griffiths, A. P., ed. *Wittgenstein Centenary Essays.* Royal Institute of Philosophy Series, 28, supplement to *Philosophy.* Cambridge University Press, 1990.

Hacker, P. M. S. *Insight and Illusion: Themes in the Philosophy of Wittgenstein.* Oxford: Clarendon, 1972; revised 2nd ed., 1986.

"Semantic Holism: Frege and Wittgenstein." In Luckhardt, ed., *Wittgenstein,* pp. 213–43.

*Wittgenstein: Meaning and Mind. An Analytical Commentary on the Philosophical Investigations.* Vol. 3. Oxford: Blackwell, 1990.

*Wittgenstein: Mind and Will. An Analytical Commentary on the Philosophical Investigations.* Vol. 4. Oxford: Blackwell, 1996.

Haller, R. *Questions on Wittgenstein.* London: Routledge, 1988.

Haller, R., and J. Brandl, eds. *Wittgenstein – Towards a Reevaluation: Proceedings of the Fourteenth International Wittgenstein Symposium, Centenary Celebration.* Vienna: Verlag Holder-Pichler-Tempsky, 1990.

Hallett, G. *A Companion to Wittgenstein's "Philosophical Investigations."* Ithaca: Cornell University Press, 1977.

Hanfling, O. *Wittgenstein's Later Philosophy.* London: MacMillan, 1989.

Hark, M. T. *Beyond the Inner and the Outer: Wittgenstein's Philosophy of Psychology.* Dordrecht: Kluwer, 1990.

Henry, P., and A. Utaker, eds. *Wittgenstein and Contemporary Theories of Language.* Working Papers from the Wittgenstein Archives at the University of Bergen, no. 5, 1992.

Hertzberg, L. "Acting as Representation." In K. S. Johannessen and T. Nordenstam, eds., *Wittgenstein – Aesthetics and Transcendental Philosophy.* Vienna: Hölder-Pichler-Temsky, 1981, pp. 136–51.

*The Limits of Experience. Acta Philosophica Fennica* 56. Helsinki, 1994.

Hilmy, S. *The Later Wittgenstein: The Emergence of a New Philosophical Method.* Oxford: Blackwell, 1987.

Hintikka, J. "An Impatient Man and his Papers." *Synthese* 87 (1991), pp. 183–202.

"Language-Games." *Dialectica* 31 (1977), pp. 226–45. Reprinted in Shanker, ed., *Ludwig Wittgenstein,* vol. 2.

"Rules, Games, and Experiences: Wittgenstein's Discussion of Rule-following in the Light of His Development." In Meyer, ed., *Revue Internationale de Philosophie.*

ed. *Essays on Wittgenstein in Honor of G. H. von Wright. Acta Philosophical Fennica* 28. Amsterdam, 1976.

ed. *Ludwig Wittgenstein.* Proceedings of a conference sponsored by the Austrian Institute. *Synthese* 562–3 (1983), pp. 119–388.

Hintikka, M. B., and J. Hintikka. *Investigating Wittgenstein.* Oxford: Blackwell, 1986.

Holtzmann, S. H., and C. M. Leich, eds. *Wittgenstein: To Follow a Rule.* London, 1981.

Huitfeldt, C. "Computerizing Wittgenstein. The Wittgenstein Archives at the University of Bergen." In Johannessen and Åmås, eds., *Wittgenstein in Norway,* pp. 251–73.

"Multi-Dimensional Texts in a One-Dimensional Medium." In Henry and Utaker, eds., *Wittgenstein and Contemporary Theories of Language.*

"Das Wittgenstein-Archiv der Universität Bergen. Hintergrund und erster Arbeitsbericht" with appendix: "Wittgenstein-Nachlaß: Nothing is hidden." *Mitteilungen aus dem Brenner-Archiv* 10 (1991) pp. 93–106.

Huitfeldt, C., and V. Rossvaer. *The Norwegian Wittgenstein Project Report 1988.* The Norwegian Computing Center for the Humanities.

Hunter, J. F. M. "Forms of Life in Wittgenstein's *Philosophical Investigations.*" *American Philosophical Quarterly* 5 (1968), pp. 233–43.

*Understanding Wittgenstein.* Edinburgh: Edinburgh University Press, 1985.

Ishiguro, H. "Use and Reference of Names." In Winch, ed., *Studies in the Philosophy of Wittgenstein.*

"Wittgenstein and the Theory of Types." In Block, ed., *Perspectives on the Philosophy of Wittgenstein,* pp. 43–59.

Janik, A. *Essays on Wittgenstein and Weininger.* Amsterdam: Rodolpi, 1985.

"Wittgenstein, Ficker, and *Der Brenner.*" In Luckhardt, ed., *Wittgenstein: Sources and Perspectives,* pp. 161–90.

Janik, A., and S. Toulmin, *Wittgenstein's Vienna.* New York: Simon and Schuster, 1973.

Johannessen, K., R. Larsen, and K. O. Åmås, eds. *Wittgenstein in Norway.* Oslo: Solum Forlag, 1994.

Johannessen, K., and P. Nordenstrom, eds. *Culture and Value. Philosophy and the Cultural Sciences.* Kirchberg: Austrian Ludwig Wittgenstein Society, 1995.

Johnston, P. *Wittgenstein and Moral Philosophy.* London: Routledge, 1989.

*Wittgenstein: Rethinking the Inner.* New York: Routledge, 1993.

Kaal, H., and A. McKinnon. *Concordance to Wittgenstein's Philosophische Untersuchungen.* Leiden: E. J. Brill, 1975.

Kenny, A. "From the Big Typescript to the *Philosophical Grammar.*" *Acta Philosophica Fennica* 28 (1976), pp. 41–53; reprinted in Kenny, *The Legacy of Wittgenstein,* pp. 24–38.

*The Legacy of Wittgenstein.* Oxford: Blackwell, 1984.

*Wittgenstein.* Cambridge, Mass.: Harvard University Press, 1973.

"Wittgenstein on the Nature of Philosophy." In McGuinness, ed., *Wittgenstein and His Times;* and Kenny, *The Legacy of Wittgenstein.*

"Wittgenstein's Troubled Legacy." In "Times Higher Education Supplement," August 26, 1994.

Kerr, F. *Theology after Wittgenstein.* Oxford: Blackwell, 1986.

Klagge, J. "Wittgenstein and Neuroscience." *Synthese* 78 (1989), pp. 319–43.

Klemke, E. D., ed. *Essays on Wittgenstein.* Urbana: University of Illinois University Press, 1971.

Klenk, V. H. *Wittgenstein's Philosophy of Mathematics.* Martinus Nijhoff, 1976.

Kober, M. *Gewißheit als Norm. Wittgensteins erkenntnistheoretische Untersuchungen in "Über Gewißheit."* Berlin, New York: de Gruyter, 1993.

"Wittgenstein and Forms of Scepticism." In G. Meggle and U. Wessels, eds., *Analyomen 1, Proceedings of the 1st Conference, "Perspective in Analytic Philosophy."* Berlin, New York: de Gruyter, 1994, pp. 187–97.

Kreisel, G. "Wittgenstein's Remarks on the Foundations of Mathematics." *British Journal for the Philosophy of Science* 9 (1958–9), pp. 135–58.

Kripke, S. *Wittgenstein on Rules and Private Language.* Cambridge, Mass: Harvard University Press, 1982.

Lapointe, F. *Ludwig Wittgenstein: A Comprehensive Bibliography.* Westport: Greenwood Press, 1980.

Lear, J. "The Disappearing 'We.'" *Proceedings of the Aristotelian Society* supp. vol. 58 (1984), pp. 219–42.

"Leaving the World Alone." *Journal of Philosophy* 79 (1982), pp. 382–403.

"Transcendental Anthropology." In P. Pettit and J. McDowell, eds., *Subject, Thought and Content*. Oxford: Clarendon, 1986, pp. 267–99.

Lovibond, S. *Realism and Imagination in Ethics*. Minneapolis: University of Minnesota Press, 1983.

Luckhardt, C. G. "Philosophy in the "Big Typescript": Philosophy as Trivial." *Synthese* 87 (1991), pp. 255–72.

ed. *Wittgenstein: Sources and Perspectives*. Ithaca: Cornell University Press, 1979.

Malcolm, N. "Language Game (2)." In Phillips and Winch, eds., *Wittgenstein: Attention to Particulars*, pp. 35–44.

"Moore and Wittgenstein on the Sense of 'I Know.'" In Malcolm, *Thought and Knowledge*. Ithaca: Cornell University Press, 1977, pp. 170–98.

*Nothing Is Hidden: Wittgenstein's Criticism of His Early Thought*. Oxford: Blackwell, 1986.

*Wittgenstein: A Religious Point of View?* With postscript by P. Winch, "A Discussion of Malcolm's Essay." Ithaca: Cornell University Press, 1994.

"Wittgenstein and Idealism." In G. Vesey, ed., *Idealism Past and Present*. Cambridge University Press, 1982, pp. 249–67.

"Wittgenstein's *Philosophical Investigations*." In Pitcher, ed., *Wittgenstein: The Philosophical Investigations*, pp. 65–104.

Maury, A. "Sources of the Remarks in Wittgenstein's *Philosophical Investigations*." *Synthese* 90 (1994), pp. 349–78.

"Sources of the Remarks in Wittgenstein's *Zettel*." *Philosophical Investigations* 4 (1981), pp. 57–74.

"Wittgenstein and the Limits of Language." *Acta Philosophica Fennica* 31 (1981), pp. 149–67.

McDonough, R. "Toward a Non-Mechanistic Theory of Meaning." *Mind* 98 (1989), pp. 1–21.

McDowell, J. *Classical Philosophy, Moral Philosophy, Wittgenstein*. Vol. 1 of McDowell, *Selected Papers*. Cambridge, Mass.: Harvard University Press, 1996.

"Meaning and Intentionality in Wittgenstein's Later Philosophy." *Midwest Studies in Philosophy* 17 (1992).

"Non-Cognitivism and Rule-Following." In Holzman and Leich, eds., *Wittgenstein: To Follow a Rule*, pp. 141–62.

"One Strand in the Private Language Argument." In McGuinness and Haller, eds., *Wittgenstein in Focus*, pp. 285–305.

McGinn, C. *Wittgenstein on Meaning*. Oxford: Blackwell, 1984.

McGinn, M. *Sense and Certainty*. Oxford: Blackwell, 1989.

McGuinness, B. F. "The So-Called Realism of Wittgenstein's *Tractatus*." In Block, ed., *Perspectives on the Philosophy of Wittgenstein*, pp. 60–74.

*Wittgenstein: A Life. Young Ludwig: 1889–1921*. London: Duckworth, 1988.

ed. *Wittgenstein and His Times*. Oxford: Blackwell, 1982.

McGuinness, B. F., and R. Haller, eds. *Wittgenstein in Focus. Grazer Philosophische Studien* 33/34 (1989).

McGuinness, B. F., and G. H. von Wright. "Unpublished correspondence between Russell and Wittgenstein." *Russell* 10 (1990–1), pp. 101–24.

Meløe, J. and V. Rossvaer. *Proceedings of the Tromsø Wittgenstein Seminar. Inquiry* 31 (1988), pp. 251–406.

Meyer, M., ed. *Revue Internationale de Philosophie* 43 (1989), pp. 171–310. Wittgenstein centennial issue.

Minar, E. "Feeling at Home in Language (What Makes Reading *Philosophical Investigations* Possible?)." *Synthese*, forthcoming.

"Paradox and Privacy: On §§201–202 of Wittgenstein's *Philosophical Investigations*." *Philosophy and Phenomenological Research* 54 (1994), pp. 43–74.

"*Philosophical Investigations* §§185–202: Wittgenstein's Treatment of Following a Rule. New York: Garland, 1990.

Monk, R. *Ludwig Wittgenstein: The Duty of Genius*. New York: Free Press, 1990.

Moore, A. W. "On Saying and Showing." *Philosophy* 62 (1987), pp. 473–97.

Mounce, H. O. *Wittgenstein's Tractatus: An Introduction*. Chicago: University of Chicago Press, 1981.

Mulhall, S. *On Being in the World: Wittgenstein and Heidegger on Seeing Aspects*. London: Routledge, 1990.

"Reviews." *Philosophical Investigations* 17 (1994), pp. 444–56.

Nedo, M., and M. Ranchetti, eds. *Ludwig Wittgenstein: Sein Leben in Bildern und Texten*. With an introduction by B. McGuinness. Frankfurt am Main: Suhrkamp, 1983.

Nevo, I. "Religious Belief and Jewish Identity in Wittgenstein's Philosophy." *Philosophy Research Archives* 13 (1987–8), pp. 225–43.

Nyiri, J. C. "Ludwig Wittgenstein as a Conservative Philosopher." *Continuity: A Journal of History* 8 (1984), pp. 1–23. Reprinted in Shanker, ed., *Ludwig Wittgenstein*, vol. 4, pp. 29–59 as "Wittgenstein 1929–31: The Turning Back."

*Tradition and Individuality*. Dordrecht, Boston: Kluwer, 1992.

"Wittgenstein's Later Work in Relation to Conservatism." In McGuinness, ed., *Wittgenstein and His Times*, pp. 44–68.

Palmer, A. *Concept and Object*. London: Routledge, 1988.

Pears, D. F. *The False Prison*. Vol. 1. Oxford: Clarendon, 1987.

*The False Prison*. Vol. 2. Oxford: Clarendon, 1988.

*Ludwig Wittgenstein*. 2nd ed., with a new preface by the author. Cambridge: Harvard University Press, 1986.

"The Relation between Wittgenstein's Picture Theory of Propositions and Russell's Theories of Judgment." In Luckhardt, ed., *Wittgenstein*, pp. 213–43.

"The Structure of the Private Language Argument." In Meyer, ed., *Revue Internationale de Philosophie* 43 (1989), pp. 264–78.

Phillips, D. Z., and P. Winch. *Wittgenstein: Attention to Particulars. Essays in honour of Rush Rhees*. London: Macmillan, 1989.

Pichler, A. *Untersuchungen zu Wittgensteins Nachlass*. Working Papers from the Wittgenstein Archives at the University of Bergen, no. 8, 1994.

Pinsent, D. H. *A Portrait of Wittgenstein as a Young Man*. Ed. G. H. von Wright. Oxford: Blackwell, 1990.

Pitcher, G. *The Philosophy of Wittgenstein*. Englewood Cliffs, N.J.: Prentice Hall, 1964.

"Wittgenstein, Nonsense, and Lewis Carroll." In Fann, ed., *Wittgenstein: The Man and His Philosophy*, pp. 315–36.

ed. *Wittgenstein: The Philosophical Investigations*. New York: Doubleday, 1966.

Pitkin, H. *Wittgenstein and Justice*. Berkeley and Los Angeles: University of California Press, 1972.

Putnam, H. "Analyticity and a Prioricity: Beyond Wittgenstein and Quine." In Putnam, *Realism and Reason*. Vol. 3 of *Philosophical Papers*. Cambridge University Press, 1983, pp. 115–38.

"Essays after Wittgenstein." Part 4 of H. Putnam, *Words and Life*. Cambridge: Harvard University Press, 1994.

*Renewing Philosophy*. Cambridge: Harvard University Press, 1993.

"Reply to Conant." *Philosophical Topics* 20 (1991), pp. 374–7.

Ramsey, F. P., "Critical Notice of L. Wittgenstein's *Tractatus Logico-Philosophicus*." *Mind* 32 (1923), pp. 465–78; reprinted in *Foundations of Mathematics*. London: Routledge, 1931, pp. 270–86.

Redpath, T. *Ludwig Wittgenstein: A Student's Memoir*. London: Duckworth, 1990.

Rhees, R. "Critical notice of Bartley." *The Human World*, February 1974.

*Discussions of Wittgenstein*. London, 1970.

"The Language of Sense Data and Private Experience." Parts I and II, *Philosophical Investigations* 7 (1984), pp. 1–45, 101–40.

*Without Answers*. London: Routledge, 1969.

ed. *Recollections of Wittgenstein.* New York: Oxford University Press, 1984.

Ricketts, T. G. "Frege, The *Tractatus*, and the Logocentric Predicament." *Nous* 15 (1985), pp. 3–15.

Rorty, R. *Essays on Heidegger and Others.* Cambridge University Press, 1991.

*Consequences of Pragmatism.* Minneapolis: Minneapolis University Press, 1982.

Rubinstein, D. *Marx and Wittgenstein: Social Praxis and Social Explanation.* London: Routledge, 1981.

Rundle, B. *Wittgenstein and Contemporary Philosophy of Language.* Oxford: Blackwell, 1990.

Sass, L. *The Paradoxes of Delusion: Wittgenstein, Schreber, and the Schizophrenic Mind.* Ithaca: Cornell University Press, 1994.

von Savigny, E. "Common Behaviour of Many a Kind, *Philosophical Investigations,* §206." In Arrington and Glock, eds., *Wittgenstein's Philosophical Investigations,* ch. 5.

*Wittgenstein's "Philosophical Untersuchungen," Ein Kommentar für Leser.* Frankfurt am Main: Klostermann, Band 1 1988, 2. Überarbeitete und vermehrte Auflage 1994, Band 2, 1989.

von Savigny, E., and O. Scholz. *Wittgenstein über die Seele.* Frankfurt am Main: Suhrkamp, 1995.

Scheman, N. "From Hamlet to Maggie Verver: The History and Politics of the Knowing Subject." *Poetics* 18 (1989): pp. 449–69.

"Individualism and the Objects of Psychology." In S. Harding and M. P. Hintikka, eds., *Discovering Reality: Feminist Perspectives on Metaphysics, Epistemology, Methodology, and Philosophy of Science.* Reidel, 1983.

Schulte, J. *Experience and Expression: Wittgenstein's Philosophy of Psychology.* New York: Oxford University Press, 1993.

*Wittgenstein: An Introduction.* Albany: SUNY Press, 1992.

"Wittgenstein and Conservatism." *Ratio* 25 (1983), pp. 69–80. Reprinted in Shanker, ed., *Ludwig Wittgenstein,* vol. 4, pp. 60–9.

Schwyzer, H. "Essences without Universals." *Canadian Journal of Philosophy* 4 (1974), pp. 69–78.

Shanker, S. G., ed. *Ludwig Wittgenstein: Critical Assessments.* Vols. 1–5. Wolfeboro, N.H.: Croom Helm, 1986.

*Wittgenstein and the Turning-Point in the Philosophy of Mathematics.* New York: State University of New York Press, 1987.

Shields, P. *Logic and Sin in the Writings of Ludwig Wittgenstein.* Chicago: University of Chicago Press, 1993.

Sluga, H. "Das Ich Muß Aufgegeben Werden." In D. Heinrich and R.

Horstmann, eds., *Zur Metaphysik in der Analytischen Philosophie.* Klett-Cotta, 1988.

"Wittgenstein's Blauer Buch." *The Tasks of Contemporary Philosophy.* Proceedings of the 10th Wittgenstein Symposium, ed. W. Winfelluer and F. Wuketits. Vienna: Hölder-Pichler-Tempsky, 1986, p. 411–19.

"Zwischen Modernisms and Postmoderne. Wittgenstein und die Architektur." In J. Nautz and R. Vahrenkamp, eds., *Die Wiener! Winolestwenole.* Cologne, Graz: Böhlen, 1993, pp. 241–56.

"Subjectivity in the *Tractatus.*" *Synthese* 56 (1983), pp. 123–39.

Specht, E. C. *The Foundations of Wittgenstein's Late Philosophy.* Trans. D. E. Walford. Manchester: Manchester University Press, 1969.

Staten, H. *Wittgenstein and Derrida: Philosophy, Language and Deconstruction.* Oxford: Blackwell, 1984.

Stern, D. G. "The 'Middle Wittgenstein': From Logical Atomism to Practical Holism." *Synthese* 87 (1991), pp. 203–26.

"Heraclitus' and Wittgenstein's River Images: Stepping Twice into the Same River." *The Monist* 74 (1991), pp. 579–604.

"A new exposition of the 'private language argument': Wittgenstein's notes for the 'Philosophical Lecture.' " *Philosophical Investigations* 17 (1994), pp. 552–65.

"New Evidence Concerning the Construction //the Troubled History// of Part I of the Investigations." In K. Johannessen and P. Nordenstram, eds., *Papers of the 18th International Wittgenstein Symposium.* Kirchberg, Austria: The Austrian Ludwig Wittgenstein Society, 1995, pp. 789–95.

"Models of Memory: Wittgenstein and Cognitive Science." *Philosophical Psychology* 4 (1991), pp. 137–52.

Review of *The Published Works of Ludwig Wittgenstein. Canadian Philosophical Reviews* 14 (1994), pp. 147–51.

"Recent Work on Wittgenstein, 1980–1990." *Synthese* 98 (1994), pp. 415–58.

"The Wittgenstein Papers as Text and Hypertext: Cambridge, Bergen, and Beyond." In Johannessen, Larson, and Åmås, eds., *Wittgenstein in Norway,* pp. 251–74.

Strawson, P. F. "Critical Notice: L. Wittgenstein, *Philosophical Investigation.*" *Mind* 63 (1954), pp. 70–99. Reprinted in Strawson, *Freedom and Resentment and Other Essays.* London and New York, 1974, pp. 133–68. Also, in Pitcher, ed., *Wittgenstein: The Philosophical Investigations,* and Canfield, ed., *The Philosophy of Wittgenstein.*

Stone, M. "Focusing the Law: What Legal Interpretation Is Not." In Andrei Marmor, ed., *Law and Interpretation: Essays in Legal Philosophy.* Oxford: Oxford University Press, 1994.

Stroll, Avrum, *Moore and Wittgenstein on Certainty*. Oxford, New York: Oxford University Press, 1994.

Stroud, B. "The Allure of Idealism: The Disappearing 'We.' " *Proceedings of the Aristotelian Society* supp. vol. 58 (1984), pp. 243–58.

"Wittgenstein and Logical Necessity." *The Philosophical Review* 74 (1965), pp. 504–18. Reprinted in Pitcher, ed., *Wittgenstein: The Philosophical Investigations*, pp. 477–97.

"Wittgenstein on Meaning, Understanding, and Community." In Haller and Brandl, eds., *Wittgenstein: Towards a Reevaluation*.

"Wittgenstein's Philosophy of Mind." In G. Flöistad, ed., *Contemporary Philosophy: A New Survey*. Vol. 4. The Hague: Nijhoff, 1983. Reprinted in Canfield, ed., *The Philosophy of Wittgenstein*, vol. 9.

"Wittgenstein's 'Treatment' of the Quest for 'A language Which Describes My Inner Experiences and Which Only I Myself Can Understand.' " In P. Weingartner and J. Czermak, eds., *Epistemology and Philosophy of Science*. Proceedings of the 7th International Wittgenstein Symposium. Vienna: Hölder-Pichler-Tempsky, 1983, pp. 438–45.

Summerfield, D. M. "Logical Form and Kantian Geometry: Wittgenstein's Analogy." In Haller and Brandl, eds., *Wittgenstein: Towards a Reevaluation*, pp. 147–50.

"On Taking the Rabbit of Rule-Following out of the Hat of Representation: Response to 'the Reality of Rule-Following." *Mind* 99 (1990), pp. 425–32.

"*Philosophical Investigations* 201: A Wittgensteinian Reply to Kripke." *Journal of the History of Philosophy* 28 (1990), pp. 417–38.

"Thought and Language in the *Tractatus*." *Midwest Studies in Philosophy* 17 (1992), pp. 224–45.

"Wittgenstein on Logical Form and Kantian Geometry." *Dialogue* (1990), pp. 531–50.

Suter, R. *Interpreting Wittgenstein: A Cloud of Philosophy, A Drop of Grammar*. Philadelphia: Temple University Press, 1989.

Tait, W. "Wittgenstein and the 'Skeptical Paradoxes.' " *Journal of Philosophy* 9 (1986), pp. 475–88.

Tilghman, B. R. *Wittgenstein, Ethics, and Aesthetics*. Albany: SUNY Press, 1991.

Unterkircher, A. Review of Wittgenstein's *Geheime Tagebücher* in *Mitteilungen aus dem Brenner-Archiv* 10 (1991), pp. 114–21.

Vesey, G., ed., *Understanding Wittgenstein*. Royal Institute of Philosophy Lectures, vol. 7. London, 1974.

Westphal, J. *Colour: Some Philosophical Problems from Wittgenstein*. Oxford: Blackwell, 1987.

Weiner, D. *Genius and Talent: Schopenhauer's Influence on Wittgenstein's*

*Early Philosophy*. London and Toronto: Associated University Presses, 1992.

Williams, B. "Wittgenstein and Idealism." In Vesey, ed., *Understanding Wittgenstein*, vol. 7; reprinted in Williams, *Moral Luck*. Cambridge, 1981, pp. 144–63.

Williams, M. "Wittgenstein, Kant, and 'the Metaphysics of Experience.' " *Kant-Studien* 81 (1990), pp. 69–88.

Winch, P. "Critical Study of Kripke (1982)." *Philosophical Quarterly* 33 (1983), pp. 398–404.

"A Discussion of Malcolm's Essay," Postscript to Malcolm, *Wittgenstein. Ethics and Action*. London: Routledge, 1972.

"Persuasion." In P. French, et al., eds., *Midwest Studies in Philosophy XVII: The Wittgenstein Legacy*. Notre Dame: Indiana University Press, 1992, pp. 123–37.

*Trying to Make Sense*. Oxford: Blackwell, 1987.

ed. *Studies in the Philosophy of Wittgenstein*. London, 1969.

Wright, C. *Wittgenstein on the Foundations of Mathematics*. London, 1980.

ed. *Essays on Wittgenstein's Later philosophy. Synthese* 58, 3 (1984).

von Wright, G. H. "The Troubled History of Part II of the *Investigations*." *Grazer Philosophische Studien* 42 (1992), pp. 181–92.

*Wittgenstein*. Oxford: Blackwell, 1982.

"Wittgenstein in Relation to His Times." In McGuinness, ed., *Wittgenstein and His Times*, and von Wright, *Wittgenstein*.

Wünsche, K. *Der Volksschullehrer Ludwig Wittgenstein, mit neuen Dokumenten und Briefen aus den Jahren 1919–1926*. Frankfurt: Suhrkamp, 1985.

# INDEX